LIBERATORS

By the same author

LIBERATORS

Latin America's Struggle for Independence
1810–1830

ROBERT HARVEY

THE OVERLOOK PRESS
WOODSTOCK & NEW YORK

For Jane and Oliver

First published in the United States in 2000 by
The Overlook Press, Peter Mayer Publishers, Inc.
Lewis Hollow Road
Woodstock, New York 12498
www.overlookpress.com

Library of Congress Cataloging-in-Publication Data

Harvey, Robert.
Liberators : Latin America's struggle for independence / Robert Harvey.
p. cm.
Includes bibliographical references (p.) and index.
1. Latin America—History—Wars of Independence, 1806-1830—Biography.
2. Latin America—History—To 1830. 3. Self-determination, National—
Latin America—History. 4. Latin America—Biography. I. Title
F1412 .H417 2000   980—dc21   00-055753

Manufactured in the United States of America
First Edition
1 3 5 7 9 8 6 4 2
ISBN 1-58567-072-3

Contents

Illustrations

The author and publishers wish to thank the following for permission
to reproduce illustrations: Plates 1, 4 and 15, Canning House; 2, 10 and
20, Archivo Iconografico, S.A./CORBIS; 3, 7, 11, 19, 30 and 32, AKG
London; 5, 26, 29, 36, 37 and 38, Hulton Getty; 6 and 27, National
Portrait Gallery; 8, Michael Nicholson/CORBIS; 9, Mary Evans Picture
Library; 13, Tony Morrison/South American Pictures; 14, Bettman/
CORBIS; 16 and 23, North Wind Picture Archives, 17, 24, 31 and 33,
Peter Newark's American Pictures; 18, CORBIS; 21, Peter Newark's
Pictures; 22, Carlos Reyes-Manzo/Andes Press Agency; 25 and 34, South
American Pictures; 35, Billie Love Historical Collection.

Acknowledgements

The idea for this book resulted from a visit in 1990 to Ciudad Bolívar, where in its previous incarnation as Angostura, after many disappointments and false starts, Simón Bolívar's great adventure to liberate South America began. The highest navigable point on the mighty Orinoco for sea-going ships, suggestively sited on a bend on the river towards the eastern end of Venezuela's huge but sparsely-inhabited interior, Ciudad Bolívar still boasts a fine colonial centre, including Bolívar's old government palace and the cathedral square in which he had his bitter rival, Manuel Piar, shot.

The veneration in which Bolívar and his fellow Liberators are held by people from all social backgrounds always astonishes visitors to Latin America. As most of the countries of the continent at last appear to be attaining the political and social stability for which the Liberators fought so hard, this admiration for the founders of their nations can only increase. I have tried to approach the subject with admiration and respect, but also, I hope, with critical objectivity towards these often nearly superhuman, and sometimes deeply flawed, personalities.

The more I researched the subject over a period of five years, the more astonishing – and indeed hardly believable – the stories of Bolívar and his fellow Liberators appeared. Bolívar himself attempted to free Venezuela no fewer than four times before at last succeeding as a result of an epic march from the Orinoco across the flooded llanos of southern Venezuela and over the Andes to surprise the Spanish in Bogotá, and back to Caracas. He then marched south down the dizzying mountain chain to liberate Ecuador, Peru and Bolivia.

His predecessor, Francisco de Miranda, had led an extraordinary career as a libertine, poseur, brilliant general and imprisoned revolutionary. The Liberator of Chile, Bernardo O'Higgins, led the heroic breakout at Rancagua before heading a pitiful refugee exodus across the Andes, then returned with a liberating army commanded by the meticulous Argentinian José de San Martín, taciturn and a natural leader, who marched an army almost without loss across the high Andes to liberate Chile.

San Martín's army was ferried up the Pacific coast of Latin America to capture Lima by the eccentric Scottish admiral, Lord Cochrane, whose feats in subduing the fortress of Valdivia and cutting out the *Esmeralda* had become legendary. Cochrane, after hijacking San Martín's treasure ship, sailed to Brazil to defeat the Portuguese navy in a campaign of dazzling deceptions. He helped consolidate Brazil's independence under the absurdly romantic Emperor Pedro I, who led a nation in revolt against his own father, and whose love affair with the beautiful Domitila helped him to lose his throne, although he fathered two monarchs.

In Mexico the royalist officer Augustín de Itúrbide betrayed his own side to become self-appointed Emperor of a newly independent state, but was deposed and brutally executed on his return from exile. These seven remarkable men liberated their enormous continent from one of the most effective, enduring and militarily repressive empires the world has ever known.

I had succumbed to the lure of South America on my first visit there as a young journalist, in 1975. It is a continent of extremes – desert, jungle and mountains, beauty and ugliness, kindness and cruelty – and in those days of revolutions, civil wars, *coups d'état* and military repression, it was both a tragic and an exciting place. The times and the place bred a remarkable school of talented journalistic specialists, of widely varying political hues: Richard Gott of the *Guardian*, Hugh O'Shaughnessy of the *Financial Times*, Alan Riding of the *New York Times*, my predecessor on the *Economist*, Robert Moss, and, later, Isobel Hilton of the *Independent*. In addition, the two giants of Spanish and Latin American Studies in Britain, Sir Raymond Carr of St Antony's College, Oxford, and Lord Thomas of Swynnerton, with his magisterial study of Cuba, stimulated my interest in that most geographically spectacular and most unpredictable region. A number of able and dedicated locally-based journalists have at one time or another also been of enormous help in furthering my understanding; they include Alberto Tamer, Robert Cox, Jimmy Burns, Sarita Kendall, Paul Ellmann, Sue Branson, Brian Gould, Mary Helen Spooner and Susan Morgan. Guy Elmes's superb screenplay on Bolívar, which he was kind enough to show me, also stimulated my interest.

Since 1975 I have visited Latin America many times, travelling to every country in the continent and making one extended trip, described in my book *Fire Down Below*, which whetted my appetite for further exploration of the region's history. The more I researched Bolívar and the other men who shaped the political history of most of the continent for nearly two hundred years, the more struck I was by the sheer scale of the achievement, and by the extremes of human endurance, heroism, cruelty and folly involved. Almost as remarkable was the dearth of authoritative accounts of the period in English. Salvador de Madariaga's *Bolívar* is of course superbly researched, erudite and well-written, and has been translated, but it is nearly half a century old and was written primarily for a scholarly readership; it also reflects a somewhat Spanish-centred view of the subject. Sergio Corrêa da Costa's *Every Inch a King* is a masterpiece. The very few excellent English-language accounts of individual Liberators are referred to in the Bibliography, particularly Stephen Clissold's superb *O'Higgins*.

In Ciudad Bolívar I resolved to try to tell the epic tale and recount the careers of these particular men, drawing principally on Spanish and Portuguese sources. I am conscious of the limitations that both narrative and the biographical approach impose, but I am sure it is the best way of making this extraordinary story more widely known. To keep the story within bounds, I have limited myself to the seven principal liberators. This has involved rather arbitrarily omitting the Spanish Caribbean and Central America, and will no doubt incense partisans of, for example, Antonio José Sucre (although there is plenty about him in the text). But some limit had to be set.

I am indebted to very many people, in Latin America and elsewhere, for deepening my understanding and, specifically, for encouraging my interest in the continent. In particular, these include: in Brazil, former economy minister Roberto Campos, Sir John Ure, former British Ambassador, and Robert Facey, former British Consul in Rio; in Chile, Pablo Halpern, former foreign minister Hernan Cubillos, Juana Subercaseaux, Paz Prieto, and Sir Reginald and Lady Secondé, former British Ambassador and Ambassadress; in Venezuela, Giles and Alexandra FitzHerbert, former British Ambassador and Ambassadress; in Mexico, Bernard and Mercedes Derbyshire.

I am also deeply in the debt of J.W. Brooks, David Howell, Raymond and Mariabianca Eyre, and others, for their enthusiasm and wisdom about Latin America; and of Andrew Knight, Brian Beedham, Gordon

Lee, Barbara Smith and Trevor Grove as well as the *Economist* and the
Daily Telegraph, for often sending me to the continent. I thank Salvador
de Madariaga, John Edwin Fagg and Timothy Anna for permission to
quote from their works.

Lastly, I am indebted to the ever-penetrating advice and encouragement of Gillon Aitken; to my remarkably meticulous and dedicated
editors, Grant McIntyre, Liz Robinson and Roger Hudson; to Raleigh
Trevelyan for his literary advice; to my indefatigable, tolerant and
efficient assistant Jenny Thomas and her historian husband Geoffrey; to
Gail Pirkis and Caroline Westmore of John Murray; to James Lewis; to
Christine, Richard and Emma and our friends in Meifod; deeply to my
mother and sister for all their encouragement and help; and above all to
my best supporters and critics, Jane and Oliver, who make it all worth-
while.

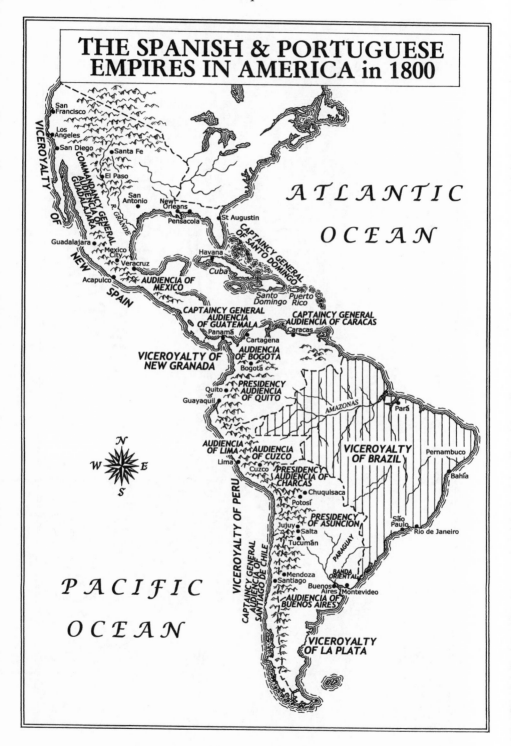

THE SPANISH & PORTUGUESE EMPIRES IN AMERICA in 1800

San Francisco
Los Angeles
San Diego
Santa Fe
El Paso
San Antonio
New Orleans
Pensacola
St Augustin

VICEROYALTY OF NEW SPAIN

COMMANDANCY GENERAL AUDIENCIA OF GUADALAJARA

R. GRANDE

Guadalajara
Mexico City
Veracruz
Acapulco
AUDIENCIA OF MEXICO

Havana
Cuba

CAPTAINCY GENERAL OF SANTO DOMINGO

Santo Domingo
Puerto Rico

ATLANTIC OCEAN

CAPTAINCY GENERAL AUDIENCIA OF GUATEMALA
Panamá

CAPTAINCY GENERAL AUDIENCIA OF CARACAS
Caracas
Cartagena

AUDIENCIA OF BOGOTA
Bogotá

VICEROYALTY OF NEW GRANADA

Quito
Guayaquil
PRESIDENCY AUDIENCIA OF QUITO

AMAZONAS
Pará

AUDIENCIA OF LIMA
Lima
AUDIENCIA OF CUZCO
Cuzco
PRESIDENCY AUDIENCIA OF CHARCAS
Chuquisaca
Potosí

VICEROYALTY OF BRAZIL
Pernambuco
Bahía

São Paulo
Rio de Janeiro

PRESIDENCY OF ASUNCION
Jujuy
Salta
Tucumán

PARAGUAY

VICEROYALTY OF PERU

CAPTAINCY GENERAL AUDIENCIA DE SANTIAGO DE CHILE
Mendoza
Santiago

BANDA ORIENTAL
Buenos Aires
Montevideo
AUDIENCIA OF BUENOS AIRES

N
W E
S

PACIFIC OCEAN

VICEROYALTY OF LA PLATA

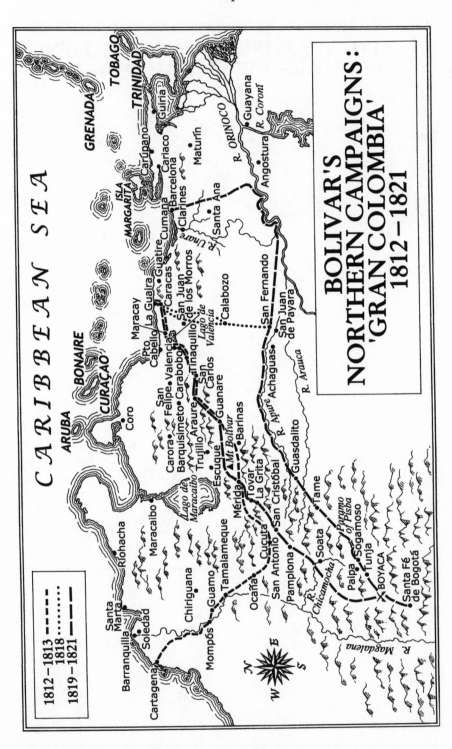

BOLIVAR'S
NORTHERN CAMPAIGNS:
'GRAN COLOMBIA'
1812–1821

1812–1813
1818
1819–1821

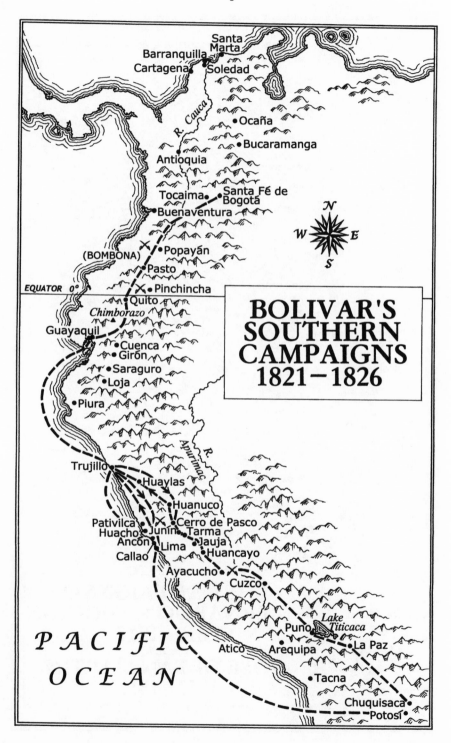

BOLIVAR'S SOUTHERN CAMPAIGNS 1821–1826

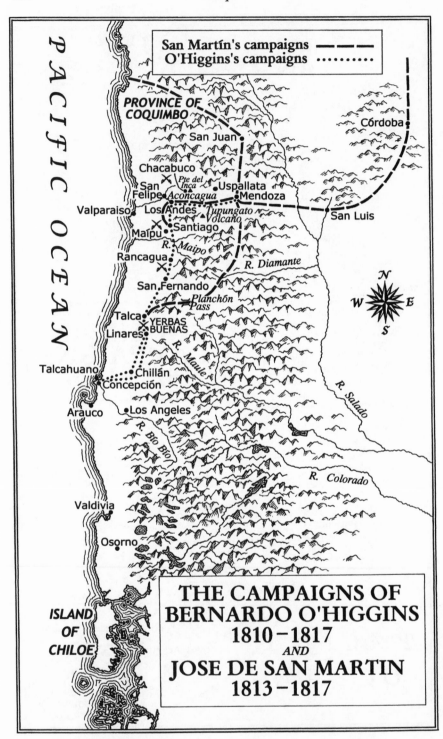

THE CAMPAIGNS OF
BERNARDO O'HIGGINS
1810-1817
AND
JOSE DE SAN MARTIN
1813-1817

COCHRANE'S PACIFIC & ATLANTIC CAMPAIGNS 1819–1825

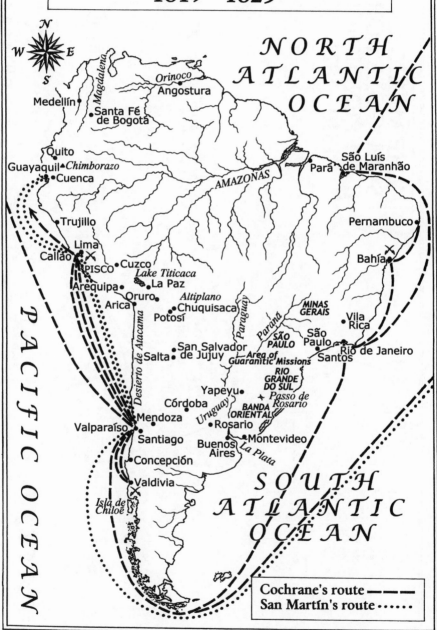

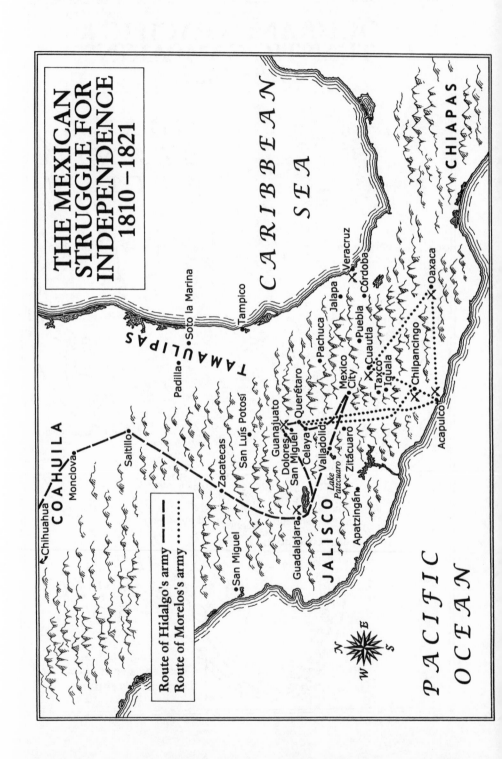

THE MEXICAN
STRUGGLE FOR
INDEPENDENCE
1810–1821

CARIBBEAN SEA

CHIAPAS

PACIFIC OCEAN

COAHUILA

JALISCO

TAMAULIPAS

Route of Hidalgo's army
Route of Morelos's army

Chihuahua
Monclova
Saltillo
San Miguel
Zacatecas
San Luís Potosí
Padilla
Soto la Marina
Tampico
Guanajuato
Dolores
San Miguel
Celaya
Querétaro
Valladolid
Lake Pátzcuaro
Zitácuaro
Apatzingán
Guadalajara
Pachuca
Jalapa
Veracruz
Córdoba
Mexico City
Puebla
Cuautla
Taxco
Iguala
Chilpancingo
Oaxaca
Acapulco

Introduction

It is one of the greatest and most populous continents on earth. It has perhaps the most varied topography and range of climates of any great landmass. With a few significant exceptions—central Argentina, parts of southern Brazil, central Chile, the uplands of Colombia and Venezuela—it is inhospitable and uncultivable. It is the home of the three great civilisations of ancient America—the Maya, the Aztec and the Inca. Its colonisation dates back half a millennium. Its independence has lasted less than two centuries, but its is sequentially second only to the United States in shrugging off the colonial yoke.

At the time of US independence the Spanish Empire was older, richer, and larger than Britain's American colonies and possessed a third of the continental landmass of the modern United States—including most of California, New Mexico, Texas and Florida (on and off). Although subsequently divided into a score of independent countries, these were linked together by their dominant Iberian languages and culture right across the entire continent. Racially it is a mixture of local Indians, white settlers and African-descended blacks, with every conceivable intermixture of the three (mestizos, mulattos, zambos).

It has also been something of a failure. Today its 620 million people provide goods and services worth $1.4 trillion compared to the United States, whose 270 million people yield around six times as much. Every US citizen produces on average some $33,000 compared to $2,300 by each citizen of Latin America. This means that the United States has become a magnet for its southern continental neighbour, with Hispanics becoming the former's largest ethnic minority. The United States looks down upon its much poorer hemispheric neighbour today; but just a couple of centuries ago the opposite was the case

Latin America is 20,570,000 square kilometers in extent, about 14%

of the world's land surface. It contains the fifth largest country in the world, Brazil (after the USSR, Canada, China and the USA), and two very large countries, Argentina and Mexico, as well as three big ones, Peru, Colombia and Venezuela. It stretches over a huge range of latitude, from 30 degrees north of the Equator to 50 degrees south, extending from over 600 kilometers north of the Equator to within 800 kilometers of the nearest tendril of Antarctica. From tip to toe, Tijuana in Mexico to Tierra del Fuego, it is some 11,000 kilometers long, compared with a distance of 7,200 kilometers from Alaska to that of Florida.

Latin America's most significant feature is the world's second highest mountain range, the Andes, stretching for much of that length south of central America, reared up by the movement of the Nazca Plate under the edge of the South American plate, creating a region of intense geological instability with frequent earthquakes and scores of volcanoes. The Andes rise from a narrow series of parallel ranges in the far south, broadening out into the western and eastern cordilleras with great plateaux (altiplanos) averaging 10,000 feet in the middle, and then, further north, dispersing in giant fingers down to the Pacific and the Caribbean through the Magdalena and the Cauca valleys and the Merida spur. Another great upland plateau, albeit much less spectacular than the Andes, dominates central Brazil around the Goias Massif; a much smaller mountain group is the Guiana Highlands to the north.

Latin America is also a continent of great river basins – the giant of them all the Amazon, but also the Orinoco, the Magdalena, the Tocantins, the San Francisco, the Parana, the Colorado and the Negro. Tha Amazon and to a lesser extent the Orinoco drain the world's largest rainforest, covering an area the size of western Europe and containing some 2,500 different species of large trees in a usually three-layered jungle canopy that appears like a green sea to those flying over it.

But desert is also a feature of the continent—the actual one that extends some 2,000 kilometers along the Pacific coast beneath the Andes, the Atacama; and the dry forests, cactus scrub and thorn forests that extend upwards from desolate Patagonia through into the Gran Chaco, as well as the sunbaked slice of north west Brazil known as the sertão and parts of Mexico—inhospitable places providing the poorest of living, or none at all. Finally, large areas of savannah and pampas grasslands cover Venezuelan llanos, and central Brazil and Argentina, where great herds of hardy cattle roam. The proportion of cultivable land on the continent is strikingly small.

Latin America is also surprisingly short of natural resources. There are, or were, large deposits of silver and gold in Peru and Mexico, as well as Minas Gerais in Brazil, celebrated for its gems. But in the more prosaic areas of natural wealth Latin America has so far proved a disappointment. Brazil has significant deposits of iron ore as do Venezuela and Bolivia. Chile and Peru are both significant producers of copper, and Bolivia in tin. But coal deposits are still difficult to extract, while oil and natural gas production are limited to Venezuela, one of the world's great producers (which also has huge coal tar deposits), as well as Mexico and Brazil's offshore fields.

There may be undiscovered mineral wealth, in particular in the mountains of southern Argentina, the Andes and Brazil's vast interior, but both exploration and exploitation are difficult. Indeed, so difficult is the topography that air travel is the main form of intercontinental travel, while road systems are largely limited to domestic travel within each nation, and rail systems are extremely few, if often spectacular, restricted to a few countries like Argentina, Brazil and Peru.

Into this stupendously beautiful but harsh environment, man is believed to have entered from Asia across the Bering Straits and down North America after the last ice age, some 40,000-100,000 years ago, when the water level was lower. The Asiatic, indeed Mongoloid features of America's several Indian nations suggest such an origin, although their blood types are not common to Asia. It is conceivable, although not probable, that some of these people originate from much earlier within America, or even that a few traveled across the Atlantic. The Indians from the Rio Grande down south were more developed than those above. When the Spanish and the Portuguese arrived, they had no horses, no written language (except for the Maya), did not use the wheel for transport, and worked metal only for ornamental purposes. However, they did practice settled agriculture, growing maize, potatoes, cotton and other plants, as well as domesticating livestock in the Andes.

The greatest and earliest civilisation of the pre-Columbian period was that of the Maya in central America, and it remains one of the most mysterious. Unlike the civilisations of the Nile or Mesopotamia, it was not centred around a fertile river valley. Its great flowering was between the fourth and tenth centuries, the Classic Maya period, in densely inhospitable forest with huge rainfalls, the area now occupied by Guatemala and British Honduras. The Maya built elaborate city centres, containing pyramids, amphitheatres, marketplaces, fine paved streets, temples and even observatories. The inhabitants lived in suburbs outside or in nearby villages. Maya architecture was of the highest order, made of brick, mortar and white limestone, with fine ornamentation and proportions, vastly superior to the impressive but martial and obvious buildings of the later Inca and Aztecs.

The Maya were skilled in working jade, wood carvings, painting and pottery, and were particularly adept at shaping animals. Their greatest achievement was a sophisticated concept of mathematics and time, with a calendar more accurate than that being used in Europe at that period. Taking 20 instead of 10 as their base numeral, they elaborated a calendar of 18 months lasting 10 days with five unlucky days at the end, and another every leap year. The Maya were the only one of the America's early civilizations to use symbols in writing rather than the more primitive picture writing (pictographs).

The Maya worshipped several gods, most of them associated with particular periods, although perhaps one more than others. The sun in particular had to be propitiated through occasional human and frequent animal sacrifices. In human sacrifice the victims, many of them voluntary, were, in a slight touch of humanity, drugged before being drowned or having their hearts torn out. The Maya appear to have lived largely peacefully, and been dominated by a priestly upper class rather than an emperor or noblemen.

The great centres of Copán, Uaxactun, Quirigua, Palenque and Tikal were seemingly prosperous and at peace when, between the ninth and tenth centuries, construction suddenly stopped and within a few years the jungle invaded the cultivated and cleared land that sustained them and then the great centres themselves. No one knows for sure what disaster stalked them—epidemic or war (although there is no sign of the latter).

Just as this civilisation was dramatically wiped out, another Maya era—the post-Classic—began in the Yucatan Peninsula in Mexico, probably fuelled by refugees from the disaster further south. The area was almost as inhospitable as the jungles of Guatemala – infertile, hot and dry, with only wells to supply water. Yet the buildings were even more monumental and elaborate in the new centres of Mayapán, Uxmal, and Chichen Itza. They soon adopted Quetzalcoatl as a god. He was possibly an exiled ruler of the Mexican Toltecs who conquered the region in about 1000.

By 200 years later Mayapán had become the capital of the area. Its rule lasted two more centuries, although this dominance seems to have resulted in the corrosion of the civilisation, leading eventually to challenges against the dominant power, civil war and decline, a state in which the Spaniards found them after the conquest of the Aztecs. The latter brought European diseases, and an epidemic wiped out huge numbers of the Maya 1516-7. In 1527 the relatively humane Francisco de Montejo arrived to subdue the Yucatan peninsula, but it took him nearly 20 years, as the remnants of this great civilisation resisted bitterly.

Further north there is fragmentary evidence of major civilisations about which little is known—the Olmecs and the Totonacs along the Gulf of Mexico, and the Mixtecs on the southern Pacific coast, who built the extraordinary city of Mitla, as well as the Zapotecs. The Toltecs were responsible for the biggest of all great pre-Columbian monuments—if hardly the most beautiful—Teotihuacán, with its vast pyramid of the Sun, the largest in the world, as well as several others ranged along huge paved avenues. Quetzalcoatl, their god-ruler, had been driven away, and, according to some legends, had been white and bearded – thus even possibly of European origin; a century later an invasion by the more primitive Chichimecs deposed the Toltecs.

One of these barbarian peoples were the Aztecs, who in the twelfth century moved into the fertile central basin of Mexico, the 7,000-foot high Valley of Mexico, grouped around the great salt lake there. They were driven by enemy tribes onto the islands in the lake in 1325, when, it is said, an eagle, perched on a cactus with a serpent in its mouth greeted them; this is now the symbol of Mexico. Worshipping the hideous, podgy, god of war, Huitzilopochtli, they engaged in attacks on the hostile mainland.

A huge and glittering city, Tenochtitlán, was built up, connected by causeways and extending into raft houses, with temples and palaces connected by streets and canals. Aqueducts brought in fresh water. However the militaristic cult of the Aztecs required prisoners of war to be sacrificed in grisly rituals, with victims' hearts being plucked out, and usually eaten, and victims skinned or even roasted alive on the tops of pyramids. Twenty thousand are said to have died in a single such sacrifice.

The superb military organisation and ruthlessness of the Aztecs, coupled with their strategy of temporary alliances with other tribes, soon permitted the establishment of an empire far beyond the shores of the lake which expanded into most of the south and central Mexico. Customarily, the warriors of the subject states were slaughtered, the women taken, and regular tributes exacted, usually in corn, from these subject states. The economy of the Aztecs was, however, highly sophisticated and they even had the beginnings of a middle class. Like the Maya, the Aztecs believed in five hells and 13 heavens which suggests a common cross-cultural seeding. This was the extraordinary civilisation that Hernan Cortes found when he landed on the east coast of Mexico.

The third great civilisation of what is now Latin America was to be found in the temperate and fertile high plateau and river valleys of the highlands of Peru. This originated from a very ancient culture, the Chavín, dating back to 1200 BC, about which little is known, who were responsible for the creation of the huge city of Pachacamac near modern Lima, and Nazca (with the mysterious giant designs known as the Nazca lines) and Paracas to the south, as well as Tiahuanaco near Lake Titicaca. The Nazca dominated the region, with their superb textiles and pottery between 400 and 1000 AD—roughly the time of the Maya classic period.

In about 1200, however, an inferior tribe, the Inca, led by Manco Capac, who claimed descent from the sun, which had been created by the great god Viracocha, emerged in the spectacular and fertile upland Cuzco valley. Within 300 years the Inca empire, based on military strength and superb organisation, had vastly expanded across Ecuador, and into the Amazon and Chile. Quechua bacame the language of the Andes. Huayna Capac was the last great emperor, reigning until 1526.

The Inca system was supremely authoritarian, ascending in a pyramid of officials governing 10,000 units of 100, 500, 1000 and 5000 males respectively, culminating in the all-powerful emperor. It was based on military might and superb organisation, which created one of the best road networks in the world across the terrifying topography of upper Peru, as well as a remarkable system of terraced irrigation up the steep valleys of the region. The Inca boasted one of the most organised and productive types of cultivation in the world, based on this terracing as well as irrigation and fertilisation. Their buildings were impressive rather than aesthetic structures based on great stones that fitted together without cement; these proved earthquake resistant. The Inca were not particularly cruel, although human sacrifice played a part during the great rituals. The coronation of an emperor was a particularly grisly ceremony in which as many as two hundred children would be killed. Such was the civilization Francisco Pizarro found, and destroyed.

The remaining Indian peoples of Latin America were, like their counterparts north of Mexico, primitive. The Araucanians of southern Chile were remarkably warlike and resisted the attempts of the Inca and the Spaniards to conquer them below the Maipu River. In the far south around Patagonia primitive nomadic tribes like the Puelches and Tehuelches roamed, surviving in skin tents through hunting. Further north were the Charruans, cannibals who inhabited the Buenos Aires and modern Uruguay region, and further north still the peaceful Guaraní (in modern Paraguay) and the stoic dour mountain-born Aymará (occupying modern Bolivia) who were conquered by the Inca.

To the east the Amazon basin was occupied by the most primitive tribes of all, largely belonging to the relatively peaceful and numerous Arawak, who originated in the Caribbean. The more aggressive Caribs (a Spanish term for cannibals), occupied much of central Brazil and the Guianas, as well as the lesser Antilles. In Colombia an agriculturally advanced people dwelt. These were the Chibcha (the origin of the El Dorado legend, based on a man dressed in gilt who dived into a lake in which gold and precious stones were thrown). To the south were the Quito, the Auca and the Jivaro (famous for shrinking heads). The American historian John Edwin Fagg brilliantly sums up the paradox of the native peoples of Latin America as Columbus arrived:

> Religious practices were at their worst grossly barbarous and at their best full of cruelty and superstition, though comparisons on this point might produce parallels unflattering to Old World cults.
>
> No conception of personal liberty seems to have shone through the political system. Everywhere there was despotism, oppression, contempt for human life. The Amerinds abused and exploited one another with little compassion. The masses were passive and given to dissimulation long before the Europeans came, like people who never dreamed of progress . . .
>
> Something else occurs to modern man as he reflects on the ancient cultures of America. These Amerinds seem to have enjoyed a way of life that harmonised with nature instead of seeking to master it. The restless, insatiable citizen of the industrialised world looks with admiration at the orderly life of the Indian, his spirit at peace with the unseen forces that direct the universe and man's place in it. The Indian appears moderate in checking his tendency to greed and self-indulgence, even virtuous in a fashion and austere. His society, whether it be a mere nomadic tribe or a formidable empire, integrated religion, economy, political life, and artistic expression in a way the unsettled, insecure man of Western civilisation has not known for centuries.

Two hours after midnight on the night of October 12, 1492 Christopher Columbus on the Santa Maria, accompanied by two smaller ships, sighted land. On that same day he landed and planted the royal standard of Spain. Columbus was deeply impressed by the warmth of the inhabitants:

> They do not bear arms or know them, for I showed to them swords and they took them by the blade and cut themselves through ignorance. They have no iron. Their spears are certain reeds, without iron, and some of these have a fish tooth at the end, while others are pointed in various ways. They are all generally fairly tall, good looking and well proportioned. I saw some who bore marks of wounds on their bodies, and I made signs to them to ask how this came about, and they indicated to me that people came from other islands, which are near, and wished to capture them, and they defended themselves. And I believe and still believe that they come here from the mainland to take them for slaves. They should be good servants and of quick intelligence, since I see that they very soon say all that is said to them, and I believe that they would easily be made Christians, for it appeared to me that they had no creed . . .
>
> I believe that in the world there is no better race . . . They love their neighbours as themselves, and they have the softest and gentlest voices in the world, and they are always smiling . . .
>
> There are here very extensive lagoons and by them and around them there are wonderful woods, and here and in the whole island all is green and the vegetation is as that of Andalucia in April. The singing of little birds is such that it seems that a man could never wish to leave this place; the flocks of parrots darken the sun, and there are large and small birds of so many different kinds, and so unlike ours, that it is a marvel. There are, moreover, trees of a thousand types, all with their various fruits and all scented, so that it is a wonder.

It was to be the first of many such Spanish explorations. Less than 27 years later, in February, 1519, Hernan Cortes set sail at the head of 700 men, equipped with 17 horses, 10 cannons and 13 muskets for Cuba in defiance of the orders of the Spanish governor in Havana to conquer the mainland of Mexico. Landing near what is now Vera Cruz and scuttling his ships, he decided to march on the rumored Aztec capital in the interior, Tenochtitlán, in August 1519. The Spaniards climbed from the torrid lowlands to the great central plateau of Mexico, making alliances or fighting with the tributary peoples of the Aztrecs as they went, until they were received as gods (Cortes was possibly even mistaken for Quetzoalcatl himself) by Montezuma, the Emperor, in the great city after crossing the five-mile causeway.

Cortes soon took Montezuma into his personal custody, and ruled through him for nearly a year before he had to dash to the coast to counter an expedition sent by the governor of Cuba. When he returned, his lieutenant Pedro de Alvarado had angered the people of the city against both the Spanish and the emperor, and soon afterwards Montezuma was deposed and killed by the council of senior Aztecs; unlike the Inca ruler, the Emperor of the Aztecs was not all-powerful. Cortes and his men had to make their famous escape from the Aztecs along the causeway. A year later he returned to the city, this time with 18 specially constructed boats brought over the mountains to attack from the lake. After a block by block struggle through Tenochtitlán, the decisive battle was won on August 13, 1521. The great colony of New Spain had been founded.

To the south, the vicious Pedro de Alvarado soon led a force through Guatemala. Another even more murderous conquistador, Pedrarias, had acquired Panama. Further south, a former swineherd, Francisco Pizarro, set off by boat from Panama down to the island of Gallo, off Peru, drawing his famous line in the sand to separate those who would fight on with him and those who would not. Twelve did, comprising the Thirteen of Fame. After discerning signs of an advanced civilisation in the interior, he chose to leave to return with greater forces in 1531 with 180 men and 27 horses. He arrived to find Peru in the grip of civil war between Huascar, the legitimate Inca emperor, and Atahualpa, his half brother, who sought the crown for himself; the latter soon prevailed.

Pizarro and his men decided to march up the Peruvian cordillera to seize Atahualpa, pretending that they merely intended to pay their respects to the Emperor. When, on November 16, 1832 Pizarro and Atahualpa met at Cajamarca, the latter was suddenly seized and, leaderless, his huge retinue dispersed. The Emperor was now in the power of Pizarro, much as Montezuma had been in Cortes's grip in Mexico. Pizarro had Atahualpa murdered and installed another puppet, Manco Inca, in his place. The latter staged an uprising two years later which resulted in Cuzco being besieged by 180,000 Inca, but the Spanish prevailed; Pizarro himself was murdered by a follower of his, Diego de Almagro, who had followed him in Peru and was later executed.

Before then Pizarro had authorised the more humane Pedro de Valdivia to capture the lands to the south. After a fierce fight against the tough Araucanian Indians there, a colony of 1000 was established. De Valdivia, however, was captured by a former Araucanian servant of his, Lautaro, who, it is said, had his master's arms and legs amputated with seashells and ate them before the dying man. Another of Pizarro's lieutenants, Sebastián de Belalcázar, rode north to capture the volcano-surrounded city of Quito with 300 men, and then climbed to Colombia, where he met up with the more statesmanlike Gonzalo de Quesada, who had made an epic ascent from the Colombian coast up the mighty Magdalena River. The province of New Granada was born.

In the south, the few Spaniards that landed in the Plate region (called the Silver River because of supposed wealth inland, actually a muddy brown) were driven off or eaten by the ferocious inhabitants, leaving only a stockade called Buenos Aires behind.

The Portuguese have always asserted that Brazil was discovered before 1492 but that the secret was kept so as not to excite Spanish interest. Portugal, impoverished and militarily weak, had nevertheless been an astounding pioneer of sea-exploitation. The Portuguese were much more of a nation of discoverers than the Spanish, having found their own route to Africa andthe Indies. In 1493, a year after Columbus landed, the Portuguese King, João II, insisted that a line dividing Portuguese and Spanish conquests in the New World should be moved much further west. A boundary 100 leagues to the west of the Azores and the Cape Verde islands was established by Pope Alexander VI.

This is always cited as evidence that the Portuguese knew of the existence of Brazil, but whatever documentation there may have been is said to have perished in the fires following the 1755 earthquake in Lisbon. The following year the Spanish rulers Ferdinand and Isabella, under the Treaty of Tordesillas, allowed the line to be moved 370 leagues west of the Cape Verde islands. In 1500 Pedro Alvares Cabral, supposedly negotiating the coast of Africa, landed in Brazil and found the indigenous Indian tribes in the vast but sparsely populated territory there largely welcoming. By the mid-1530s settlements were being founded below modern-day São Paulo and at Rio de Janeiro. Yet by 1550 only 3,000 had settled.

Only with the arrival of a vigorous captain-general, Tomé de Sousa, at Bahia (now Salvador) did the Portuguese consolidate their hold against the challenge of the French. The Church, under Manoel da Nobrega and José de Anchieta, fought vigorously to prevent the Indians being enslaved. But giant sugar estates sprang up in northern Brazil, and thousands of African slaves soon arrived (a total of 18 million over the next three centuries). The slaves not only permitted Brazil's development as largely a plantation society (coffee and cotton were to be the next great boom, then rubber); they radically altered the character of the country, with the black influence far outstripping, racially, those of the whites or Indians.

When the Spanish arrived, it is reckoned that there were at least 13 million Indian inhabitants in Latin America. The number may have fallen to as little as 3 million, prey to white diseases, within a century. By 1800, when the events described in this book took place, the total had recovered to roughly 8 million, compared with nearly 3 million blacks, some 5 million of mixed white and Indian descent, and half a million of mixed white and black descent. Around 4 million whites predominated. The population had more than recovered in size, and had changed dramatically and inalterably in composition after Spanish and Portuguese colonial rule for the best part of three centuries. Meanwhile the American and French revolutions had thrown sparks into the tinder, and Napoleon's invasions of Spain and Portugal had wrought havoc upon the home countries.

It was into this extraordinary geographical, racial, and social mix, set against a roiling European and American background, that the demand for independence erupted after three hundred years of Spanish domination, principally at the instigation of seven remarkable men. This book is their story.

'I am cloaked in the mantle of Iris, from where the majestic Orinoco pays tribute to the God of the waters. I had explored the mysterious sources of the Amazon, and then I sought to ascend to the pinnacle of the Universe. I strove bravely forward in the footsteps of La Condamine and von Humboldt, and nothing could hold me back. I reached the icy region where the thin air made me gasp for breath. No foot of man had yet defiled the glittering crown which the hands of Eternity had placed upon the lofty temples of the Andean peak . . . Seized by an unknown and seemingly divine spirit, I left behind the trail of Humboldt, tarnishing the everlasting crystals which encircle Chimborazo. As if driven on by the spirit which inhabited me, I reached my journey's end and was stunned as my head touched the dome of the firmament, my feet coming to the very abyss.

A feverish delirium seizes my mind; I feel consumed by some strange and overwhelming fire. The God of Colombia possesses me. And suddenly Time appears before me in the venerable shape of a bald old man . . . "I am the Father of the Centuries, the mysterious deposition of fame; and the unknown Eternity was my mother; Infinity marks the borders of my realm; no sepulchre will ever hold me for I am mightier than Death; my vision scans the past and the future, and through my hands the present flows. Why do you take pride in childhood or old age, man or hero? Do you think your Universe is anything, or that to stand atop an atom of creation is a noble act? Do you think that the moments you call centuries can serve to measure my mysteries? Do you imagine that you have witnessed the Holy Truth? Do you foolishly suppose that your deeds have any value to me? They are all but specks of the tiniest matter in the presence of Infinity, who is my brother."

Overcome by holy terror, I reply: "How, O Time, can the wretched mortal who has climbed so high fail to be proud? I have surpassed all honours, for I have raised myself above the heads of all men. I command the land beneath my feet; I stretch out my hands and touch Eternity . . ."

He answers: "Observe, and keep in your mind all that you have seen. Paint for the eyes of your fellow-men the picture of the physical Universe and the moral Universe; do not keep to yourself the secrets which the heavens have revealed to you, but proclaim the truth among men." '

Simón Bolívar, c. 1823

Prologue

In the spring of 1781, on the upland plains outside the Inca capital of Cuzco, a tall man watched as his wife, small children and closest friends were hacked to death. Then it was his turn. His tongue was cut out, and each of his arms and legs was tied to a horse. When the signal was given they were loosed, bolted, and pulled his body apart. Jose Gabriel Condorcanqui was executed by the emissary of the Crown, the *Visitador,* José de Areche, for leading the most dangerous rebellion against the rule of the Spanish Empire in two hundred and thirty years. A devout, educated half-indian, Condorcanqui had been recognised by the Spaniards as Marqués de Oropesa, a title acknowledging descent from the old Inca ruling family of Peru. Suddenly styling himself the second Tupac Amaru – the Gifted One, after the most famous of the last native emperors, also known as Manco Inca, who was himself put to death in 1574 as leader of an uprising – the new rebel had seized a *corregidor* (a Spanish governor) and had him killed.

Dressed in a blue velvet suit bordered with gold, an embroidered surplice, a red velvet cloak and a three-cornered hat, and wearing an image of the sun around his neck, this self-styled reincarnation of the Inca Sun King had led an uprising of several hundred thousand Qechua, Aymara and Araucanian Indians in a lynch war against the whites. He had laid siege to Cuzco, in a restaging of the ten-month investment of that city by 160,000 Indians in 1537. But Spanish cavalry, with the help of 60,000 militia, had eventually crushed the uprising and Condorcanqui had been betrayed. The brutal suppression of the revolt suggested that Spanish rule was as solidly entrenched as ever.

Less than half a century later, Spain's empire had vanished without trace, as had Portugal's dominion over Brazil. In fact, the collapse of Iberian domination of America was astonishingly swift, from its

beginning in 1810 to the last insurrection in 1824. Like its founding by
Cortés, Pizarro and Almagro, the liberation of the Spanish Empire was
primarily the work of a handful of remarkable men, all of them exceptional military commanders. To the observant, the cracks and fissures
running through the monolith were apparent decades before the end. A
unique combination of circumstances was to expose them – the wave of
radicalism that brought about the American and French Revolutions,
the terminal decadence of the Spanish court under Charles IV and
Ferdinand VII, and the destructive havoc wrought by Napoleon upon
the old order across Europe at the beginning of the nineteenth century.
Yet the whole process of disintegration might have been reversed or at
least arrested for decades, had it not been for the leadership displayed by
the seven men who are the subjects of this book.

Latin America, at the time of Tupac Amaru II's uprising, was divided
into five viceroyalties: New Spain, embracing the Audiencia of Mexico
and the Audiencia of Santo Domingo, as well as the Captaincy-General
of Guatemala and Cuba; the Viceroyalty of New Granada, including the
Presidency of Quito (roughly equivalent to modern Ecuador), the
Audiencia of Santa Fé de Bogotá (modern Colombia), and the
Captaincy-General Audiencia of Caracas (modern Venezuela); the
Viceroyalty of Brazil, under the Portuguese crown; the Viceroyalty of La
Plata, which was subdivided into the Audiencia of Buenos Aires
(Argentina), the Presidency of Asunción (Paraguay), the Presidency of
Charcas (Bolivia) and the Banda Oriental (Uruguay); and the most pow-
erful and richest, the Viceroyalty of Peru, embracing the Audiencia of
Cuzco and the Captaincy-General of Santiago de Chile.

Of these subdivisions, Mexico was powerful and productive but its
southern zone was wild and impoverished bandit country and its northern reaches, which extended into modern California, New Mexico,
Texas and Florida, were sparsely populated, much of them desert. The
uplands around Quito and Santa Fé de Bogotá were remote but prosperous, while Caracas was wealthy too, and temperate, in stark contrast
to the torrid wilderness of much of the rest of Venezuela. Colonial Brazil
was in reality just a string of settlements on its long coastline. Buenos
Aires was a commercial centre stimulated by a thriving contraband trade
with Europe which distant Spain had difficulty in policing. In the north
of La Plata, Tucumán and Chuquisaca were prosperous colonial cities,
while Chile was a remote settlement of about half a million people. The

vibrant yet decadent heart of the whole system was the Viceroyalty of Peru where the silver mines had created a glittering city, Lima, of idle rich living alongside a teeming and wretched Indian underclass, and provided the wealth needed to keep the parasitic and crumbling Spanish economy afloat.

So powerful was Peru in this system that it sought to ban Buenos Aires from trading and, ludicrously, all commerce with Spain was required to take place through the ports on the Pacific coast, brought there either by sea and land across the isthmus of Panamá, or by sea alone around Cape Horn in twice-yearly convoys accompanied by Spanish warships; goods for Buenos Aires had to be carried overland from Lima across the Andes and down from Potosí, a journey of three thousand miles which took three months. Only the ports of Cadiz and Seville in Spain were permitted to trade with Spanish America, even by this route. Merchandise sold for five or six times its original cost of production. Trade with other countries was strictly forbidden.

In practice, contraband flourished, in particular in the River Plate estuary and the Orinoco basin. A contemporary British traveller, Captain Basil Hall, summed up the system:

> The sole purpose for which the Americas existed was held to be that of collecting together the precious metals for the Spaniards; and if the wild horses and cattle which overrun the country could have been trained to perform this office the inhabitants might have been altogether dispensed with, and the colonial system would then have been perfect. Unfortunately, however, for that system, the South Americans ... finding that the Spaniards neither could nor would furnish them with an adequate supply of European products, invited the assistance of other nations. To this call the other nations were not slow to listen, and in process of time there was established one of the most extraordinary systems of organized smuggling which the world ever saw ... conducted by the Dutch, Portuguese, French, English, and latterly by the North Americans ... Along with the goods no small portion of knowledge found entrance, in spite of the increased exertions of the Inquisition ... Many foreigners, too, by means of bribes and other arts, succeeded in getting into the country, so that the progress of intelligence was encouraged, to the utter despair of the Spaniards, who knew no other method of governing the colonies but that of brute force.

If the *raison d'être* of the Spanish Empire was to produce silver and provide a dumping-ground for Spanish goods, its structure was one of hierarchy and authoritarianism. The political and military office-holders were peninsular Spaniards, presiding over a class of Spanish-born merchant carpet-baggers, often of lowly origin, who were despised by the wealthy and well-established white aristocracy of criollos or creoles (a corruption of the Spanish word meaning 'to be born', and applied to persons of Spanish blood living outside Spain). This colonial class dominated a growing professional class, and beneath them a strict ranking existed depending precisely upon race, with Indian mestizos set above black mestizos, Indians above blacks, free blacks above slaves.

A third feature of the Spanish Empire was the long-standing rivalry between political and commercial interests on the one hand, and religious ones on the other. It is a measure of the ferocity of Spanish colonial rule that the Inquisition was viewed in Spanish America as an enlightened, liberating force which usually took the side of the underdog. In fact, between 1520 and 1829 the Inquisition in Spanish America judged just six thousand cases – an average of less than twenty a year – and only about a hundred people altogether were burnt at the stake, though others died under torture in prison; most were pardoned and released. This compares favourably with the Inquisition's record in Europe.

The Church pressed in particular for laws to protect the Indians, although in the early years of the Empire it had been blamed for ruthlessly suppressing much of the religious culture, some of it extremely cruel, of the indigenous populations. The laws of Burgos of 1512, for example, provided for Indian self-government in Church lands. In 1537, Pope Paul III declared that the Indians were 'truly men', and should be converted to Christianity. This was a radical idea for the colonisers, who regarded the Indians as subhuman to the extent that, for instance, they believed there was no sin involved in seducing Indian women (even Cortés had an Indian mistress), and the resulting children, the mestizos, were treated as a sub-caste. The friar Bartolomé de Las Casas, the great defender of the Indians, staunchly upheld their cause in Europe. But except in the areas it controlled, the Church failed to make much impression on the Spanish system of punishment, repression, forced labour, extortionate taxation, and virtual slavery.

Under the *mita* system Indians were forced to work in the mines, where they earned but half the meagre wages of agricultural labourers. They were not allowed to wear certain clothes; and those among them who obtained an education found they could study only the humanities, not science. The Spaniards argued that the Indians were better and less cruelly treated than they had been under their ruthless ancient empires, the Maya, Aztec and Inca. This may have been true, but it was an ugly system nevertheless.

For a long time the Church managed to preserve a number of model communities, theocracies, in which the Indians were treated with a measure of human dignity. In Chile the Capuchins established stable settlements even among the primitive, nomadic and often murderous Araucanians. In New Granada and, more successfully, in the Orinoco basin, they set up a series of exemplary mission settlements. The most celebrated of the Church's 'states within a state' was, however, the system of Jesuit 'reductions' in an area sprawling over the borders of present-day Paraguay, Uruguay and Argentina. Some hundred thousand people lived in these forty-eight settlements, which were economically viable and well and humanely run. Soon they attracted the attention of the slave-bosses of Brazil, the *bandeirantes*, who captured more than half the Indians in raids before the Jesuits led them out of reach, below the Iguazu Falls, in a mass migration between 1627 and 1631. The Jesuit reductions continued to attract controversy, both for the way they suborned the colonial caste system and because they represented a challenge to the political power of the state. In 1768, following the expulsion of the Jesuits from Spain, the reductions were also dissolved, and a major experiment in enlightened rule in Spanish America ended.

Classically, the most dangerous moment for an autocratic system is when it tries to reform itself. For all the obloquy heaped upon the Spanish Empire, much of it deserved, it can only be described as spectacularly successful. It was mostly at peace; it provided Spain with vast wealth – nine-tenths of Spanish-American exports to Spain were in silver and gold, accounting for around half of all the bullion circulating in the world at the time; and altogether it survived for three hundred years – longer than any European empire save that of Ancient Rome (the Portuguese and Dutch empires which outlasted it were little more than a string of trading posts). Although administered brutally and exploitatively, it was governed effectively. Uprisings like that of Tupac Amaru II were crushed so easily as to suggest that it would endure indefinitely. Yet the fact that they occurred at all gave a measure of the underlying discontent.

It was the advent to the Spanish throne of an enlightened and able ruler, Charles III, that first undermined the foundations of the Spanish

Empire. The French-aligned Bourbons were established after the War of
the Spanish Succession, and Philip V and Ferdinand VI presided over a
period of long-overdue reforms, such as an end to tax-farming in favour
of centralised collection, the creation of French-style *intendants* to
control the administration of what was little more than an agglomera-
tion of semi-independent republics, a halving of the number of
provincial noblemen, the establishment of a mercantilist system, and a
new flowering of the arts.

Charles III, a plump, homespun personality who succeeded in 1759,
presided over a renaissance of the Spanish crown at the hands of a host
of able men including the Marqués de Sonora, who launched a series of
administrative reforms in Spanish America which radically disrupted the
easy-going autonomy of the colonies. Tobacco taxes were increased and
sales taxes raised. Goods from Spain flooded in, while exports were
stifled. Mexico's textile industry was ruined by imports, and only its
silver mines flourished. Controversially, Sonora initiated the expulsion
of seven hundred Jesuits from Mexico, leaving the many thousands who
attended their missions leaderless and causing an insurrection which he
brutally put down. But he was also responsible for the seizure of New
Orleans from the French, and the colonisation of California as far north
as San Francisco. His successor, Antonio Maria de Bucareli, introduced
popular social reforms. The educated criollos became infected by
modern concepts regarding administration, commerce, agriculture,
industry, science and even political rights. They found it increasingly
difficult to understand why they should be ruled by low-born peninsular officials, why their economies should be so brazenly exploited. By the
late eighteenth century, such seditious ideas, challenging authority, were
commonplace in the schools and universities and in upper-class salons,
but still a long way from active revolt.

What today would be called geopolitics further conspired to undermine the close ties between Spain and its American empire. In 1761 the
Spanish under Charles III joined the French in the Seven Years' War
against the British. This proved disastrous: Spain lost both Manila in the
Philippines, and Havana, while the British occupied the Mosquito
Coast in Honduras, Campeche in the Yucatán peninsula, and Jamaica.
By the Peace of Paris of 1763 Spain regained Manila, but had to accede
to Britain's insistence that she give up Florida to regain Havana. France
ceded half Louisiana to Spain in compensation for her help in the war.
Following the Seven Years' War the global scene was further dramatically

transformed by the uprising of the North American colonies against Britain. To Charles III and the Spanish it seemed a godsend, a significant setback to predatory Britain, although Spain's chief minister, the enlightened and capable Conde de Aranda, a man whom Voltaire described as a close friend, feared that independence in the north would set a dangerous precedent for Spain's own increasingly restless colonists. In the event the intervention of France and Spain behind the North American colonists proved decisive, with the Spanish fleet harassing the British navy and her army conquering Florida.

In 1783, at the Peace of Versailles, Florida, Honduras and Minorca were ceded to Spain, and the threat from Britain seemed over. The cost of the war to France brought on the French Revolution six years later, however; and the example of the independence gained by North America in 1776 was, as Aranda had feared, carefully noted in the south. Moreover Britain, licking her wounds, was determined to wreak revenge on the Spanish Empire, believed in London to be ripe for insurrection.

In 1788 Charles III died and his son, the amiable Charles IV, ascended the Spanish throne. He lacked the political shrewdness of his father and was under the influence of his wife, Maria Luisa of Parma. A strong-willed woman with a notorious temper, now a middle-aged nymphomaniac, her lusts all too often directed Spanish policy. Her favourite lover was a young soldier from Badajoz, promoted to field marshal, Duque de Alcudia and, by 1792, at the age of twenty-five, first minister. Good-looking, shallow, but fairly adroit politically, Manuel Godoy was to dominate a Spanish court now mired in decadence and incompetence.

To this transformation of the global landscape as perceived from South America – the weakening of Britain, the independence of the United States and the sudden decline of the previously enlightened Spanish court – was added the French Revolution of 1789. Initially this further undermined the legitimacy of Spanish absolutism, but as it veered from its early moderate course into revolutionary frenzy, it temporarily boosted Spain's monarchy in her colonies, whose people wanted nothing to do with regicides and *sans-culottes*. They shuddered when civil war broke out between the French-descended upper class and the mulattos of Haiti, soon overtaken by an uprising of the five hundred thousand black slaves in the colony and the massacre of both French and mulattos. Order was restored under the relatively moderate and states-manlike leadership of Toussaint Louverture, a freed slave.

Meanwhile, Charles IV made a botched attempt to rescue Louis XVI and his reward was a declaration of war by France, whose forces crossed into Spain at each end of the Pyrenees and set up revolutionary governments in the towns they took. The war against France was as popular in the Spanish colonies as in Spain, however, and the empire seemed as strong as ever. The British, now allies of the Spanish, no longer intrigued against them or threatened them overseas.

Godoy, however, fearful of French incursions across the frontier and heartened by the re-emergence of moderate elements after the fall of Robespierre, sued for peace in 1795 – a catastrophically inept move which undermined every diplomatic gain of the first four years of his ascendancy. As well as ceding to France Santo Domingo (the western half of the island of Hispaniola, of which Haiti was the eastern half), Godoy sought to appease the French further by introducing some of their reforms into Spain; these included an attack on the Inquisition and on clerical privileges, the threat of land redistribution, and permitting the circulation of revolutionary texts. At a stroke, he alienated Spanish sympathisers and the still dominant Spanish colonial classes, who viewed France's ambitions in the Caribbean with deep suspicion; facilitated the spread of revolutionary ideas; and, not least, reinvigorated the old enmity between Spain and a Britain dismayed by this pro-French tilt.

The British moved to disrupt Spanish trade with the Americas, and the colonists made up their shortfall by trading illicitly with Britain and the United States. British landings were staged in Puerto Rico and Central America, and Trinidad was occupied. A Spanish fleet was mauled off Cape St Vincent in 1797, bringing Horatio Nelson to full prominence for the first time. In the space of just three years, Spanish Americans acquired a withering contempt for the weakness of the mother country to add to the sense of grievance and injustice they had long borne against Spain for her commercial monopoly and the dismal quality of the administrators and traders sent to lord it over them. Meanwhile Godoy, supposedly dismissed in 1800, continued to act as the Court's chief adviser, pursuing his policy of appeasement towards France.

A dramatic new turn ensued with the accession to power in France of Napoleon Bonaparte. His policy towards Spain was to bully her; towards the Americas, to establish a French Empire there. He insisted that Spain and Portugal must close their ports to the British; this the Spanish did promptly, while the Portuguese put up only a show of resistance. The criollo upper class was horrified afresh by these signs of Spanish craven-ness, and by the arrival on their doorstep in 1802 of a French force of twenty thousand under the command of Napoleon's brother-in-law, General Leclerc, Pauline Bonaparte's first husband, despatched to Hispaniola as the vanguard of a new French presence in the Caribbean. Toussaint was seized by the French and sent captive to France, where he died; Leclerc's attempt to reintroduce slavery into Haiti was met by a fresh black revolt, ending with the expulsion of the French into Santo Domingo and in 1804 the assertion of Haitian self-government – the first declaration of independence in Latin America. Leclerc, along with thousands of his men, died of yellow fever.

Napoleon meanwhile treacherously seized the previously ceded half of Louisiana from the Spanish, then forced Spain to declare war on Britain, in order to attach the Spanish navy to his own for his projected invasion across the Channel. The combined fleets were destroyed by Nelson at Trafalgar, and Spain thus lost almost her entire navy at a stroke; this drastically affected her capacity to put down insurrections in her empire – a point which did not go unnoticed there. Resentment against the political and economic impositions of Spain was at its height; Spain was involved in an unpopular alliance with France; and the British were again bent on subverting her empire, desperate for commercial outlets now that Napoleon had closed the Continent to them, and very aware of tempting opportunities. The seriousness of Britain's long-term desire to add the supposedly suppurating Spanish Empire to her domin-ions – thereby making good the losses in North America – should not be underestimated.

On 27 June 1806 the Spanish Viceroy of La Plata, Rafael, Marqués de Sobremonte, was at the theatre in Buenos Aires when he was informed that a British army of 1,600 men had landed outside the city. The first-ever overthrow of a Spanish colonial administration in South America had begun. British soldiers commanded by General William Carr Beresford and naval forces under Commodore Sir Home Popham had sailed from Cape Town, having retaken it in the name of the British Crown following the breakdown of the Peace of Amiens and Nelson's victory at Trafalgar.

Although the British Government almost certainly had no direct hand in the Popham–Beresford expedition, which it was swift to disown, the roots of it ran deep. William Pitt had long coveted South America as a potential market for the products of Britain's growing industrialisation, and other eminent men of the time also interested in its possibilities included Lord Melville, First Lord of the Admiralty between 1802 and 1806; Nicholas Vansittart, a young Tory politician who later became Chancellor of the Exchequer; and the prominent trading house of Turnbull and Sons. As we shall see, the focus of the plotting was Francisco de Miranda, the flamboyant would-be liberator of Venezuela. Popham later recorded that in 1805

> I had a long conversation with [Pitt] on the original project of the expedition to South America; in the course of which Mr Pitt informed me, that from the then state of Europe, and the confederation in part formed, and forming against France, there was a great anxiety to endeavour, by friendly negotiation, to detach Spain from her connection with that power, and, until the result of such an attempt should be known, it was desirable to suspend all hostile operations in South America; but, in case of failure in this object, it was his intention to enter on the original project.

But Pitt died towards the end of January 1806, less than a week after the capitulation of Cape Town; and Popham sailed – without orders – for Buenos Aires. William, Lord Grenville, Pitt's brilliant cousin, formed the 'Ministry of all the Talents', so named for its dazzling array of senior political figures from all parties and its engaging liberalism. It featured such luminaries as Charles James Fox, Foreign Secretary until his death in September 1806, a dissolute figure in his youth who became a politician of notable calibre and Pitt's perennial opponent; Lord Howick, who later as Earl Grey steered Britain to peaceful political reform in 1832; and, as Secretary for War, William Windham, an enthusiast for a British role in South America.

The British forces occupied Buenos Aires with the loss of only a single man and twelve wounded, while Sobremonte fled inland to Córdoba with the treasury. Beresford proclaimed himself Governor on behalf of King George III, but promised that private property and the Catholic faith would be respected by the British Crown, and announced the establishment of free trade – a display of breathtaking arrogance. As Popham later noted, 'The object of this expedition was considered by the natives to apply principally to their independence; by the blacks, to their total liberation; and if General Beresford had felt himself authorized, or justified, in confirming either of these propositions, no exertions whatever would have been made to dispossess him of his conquest.'

But 'exertions' were made: a French-born officer, Santiago de Liniers, assembled a force of irregular soldiers outside Buenos Aires while inside the city Juan Martín de Pueyrredón, an able criollo aristocrat, organised opposition in the form of passive resistance and a general strike. Six weeks later the two forces joined up; the British were surrounded, Popham was taken prisoner, and with impressive magnanimity the whole expedition was placed aboard ship and despatched ignominiously to London. Liniers was treated as a hero while Sobremonte, now regarded as a coward, was informed he would be shot if he returned to Buenos Aires. It was unprecedented for a Spanish viceroy to be so humiliated; he took refuge in Montevideo, capital of the Banda Oriental across the Plate estuary, and Buenos Aires' traditional rival.

When news of Beresford's and Popham's success in Buenos Aires reached London, the City went wild – crowds thronged the streets, singing 'God Save the King' and 'Rule, Britannia!' Britain's trade with South America was already running at £1 million a year, and it seemed as though her next great colonial adventure was beckoning, a sense reinforced by the news of Napoleon's victory at Jena and Davout's at Auerstädt in October 1806, which Grenville thought spelled the end of British influence in Europe. Windham bristled with ideas: Cape Horn would be navigated and the port of Valparaíso in Chile seized, then an expedition eastwards across the Andes would establish a chain of forts before conquering the whole Audiencia of Buenos Aires and thus securing the southern half of the continent. Sir Arthur Wellesley, recently returned from his successes in India, would be appointed to replace Beresford. Grenville himself favoured the seizure of Montevideo, and the despatch of troops from India to take Manila from the Spanish and then sail on across the Pacific to land on the west coast of New Spain (Mexico), while his elder brother the 1st Marquess of Buckingham, twice Lord-Lieutenant of Ireland but now virtually retired from political life, urged attacks on Peru and Panamá.

The news of Beresford's subsequent surrender of Buenos Aires in August 1806 did not reach London until 25 January 1807; when it did, all these dreams crashed to earth with the realisation that here were no ill-used children grateful to exchange the harsh paternalism of the Spanish Crown for the comparative benevolence of the British, but people mature and sophisticated enough to be determined upon securing their independence.

The affront to British arms could not be tolerated; all other plans were to be shelved until Buenos Aires was regained, and an expedition under General Samuel Auchmuty and Lieutenant-General John Whitelocke was despatched to this end. The unfortunate Sobremonte was still in Montevideo when news reached him that twelve thousand British had landed on the east bank of the Plate estuary. The inhabitants of Buenos Aires, across the water, unilaterally deposed him as Viceroy, proclaiming Liniers their chief.

Whitelocke's instructions repeated the error made by Popham: '[you are] not to introduce into the government any other change than that which must necessarily arise from the substitution of His Majesty's authority for that of the King of Spain.' But Whitelocke and Auchmuty soon understood the reality on the ground. Auchmuty announced that the royal court of the Audiencia had been abolished and the Spanish king's authority set aside, and that the Spanish flag should no longer be hoisted; as he wrote later,

> These reports were circulated with avidity, and I soon found that they were acceptable to the principal part of the inhabitants. The persons who before appeared hostile and inveterate, now pressed me to advance a corps to Buenos Aires; and assured me, if I would acknowledge their independence, and promise them the protection of the English government, the place would submit to me ... The party now in power are mostly natives of Spain ... It has been their policy to inflame the minds of the lower orders against the English, by every species of exaggeration and falsehood, and to lead them to such acts of atrocity as may prelude the possibility of any communication with us. The second party consists of natives of the country, with some Spaniards that are settled in it ... They aim at following the steps of the North Americans and erecting an independent state.
>
> If we would promise them independence, they would instantly revolt against the government, and join us with the great mass of the inhabitants. But though nothing less than independence will perfectly satisfy them, they would prefer our government, either to their present anarchy or to the Spanish yoke, provided we would promise not to give up the country to Spain at a peace. But until such a promise is made, we must expect to find them open or secret enemies.

Whitelocke made the same point: 'It has been repeatedly told to me ... that had General Beresford and the Admiral, on their first arrival, and before any blood was shed or property confiscated, declared South

America an independent state, we should now have her as an ally without her witnessing any of the horrors attendant on revolutions.'

But the British government favoured establishing their own foothold on the Plate, and in the summer Whitelocke's forces were ferried across the estuary to march on Buenos Aires. After crossing the swamps of Quilmes, Whitelocke drove back a force of six thousand under Liniers. But as they entered Buenos Aires, calamity ensued: 'The British troops,' as General Mitre wrote later, 'worthy of a better general, marched resolutely to their sacrifice, advancing as fearlessly as on parade along those avenues of death, enfiladed at right angles every 150 yards: Whitelocke remaining with the reserve at the Miserere, entirely cut off from the rest of his army. The result of such tactics could not but prove disastrous.' By nightfall 2,200 Britons had been killed, wounded, or taken prisoner, and Whitelocke had promised to evacuate the Plate region within two months.

Complimented on their good behaviour in defeat, the British sailed away from Montevideo after this latest débâcle. A former protégé of Liniers, Francisco Xavier de Elio, was installed as governor of the city, and Liniers was recognised by the Spanish government itself as acting viceroy. The two immediately quarrelled, however, it being alleged that Liniers was a Bonapartist stooge, and the Spanish took advantage of this to send out their own viceroy, Baltasar Hidalgo de Cisneros. Neither Montevideo nor Buenos Aires was happy with this imposition. In 1808, in the wake of an incendiary pamphlet on the subject of free trade written by Mariano Moreno, a brilliant local economist, Cisneros was obliged to offer to open Buenos Aires as a free port. Twice now the city had cocked a snook at the Spanish government – first in appointing Liniers, now in breaking the Spanish trade monopoly. The British intervention had, unwittingly, sparked off local defiance.

Britain's extraordinary escapade in Buenos Aires was, of course, no more than a side-show for a Spanish government preoccupied with Napoleon. The Court had now divided into two factions: those who supported Charles IV, the Queen and Godoy; and those who looked to Prince Ferdinand, Charles's heir, to rescue them from distasteful appeasement of France.

In 1806, as Napoleon soared to new heights with his victories over the Austrians and Russians at Austerlitz and the Prussians at Jena, Godoy, with consummate ineptness, appeared to switch sides; and the Emperor determined to punish him. An opportunity arose when Godoy too

trustfully invited Napoleon into Spain to enable him to conquer
Portugal, the last piece of Europe outside his control. The plan was that
Charles IV should become Emperor of the Americas and Godoy himself
ruler of a southern portion of Portugal, while the French got the
Portuguese fleet.

In 1807 a substantial French army under General Junot marched into
and across Spain. The mad Queen of Portugal, Maria I, her son João,
the Prince Regent, and the royal court embarked in an armada of
Portuguese ships – the entire Portuguese navy – and were escorted by
the British down the Tagus estuary, bound for Brazil. It was the first link
in the chain of events which was to lead to the independence of that
country in the 1820s (see Part 4). The French may not have got the ships
they wanted, but they occupied Lisbon and then, to the dismay of
Charles IV and Godoy, proceeded to reinforce their army to a hundred
thousand men, annexing a corridor across northern Spain between
France and Portugal. With mounting horror Charles realised that
Napoleon intended to swallow Portugal, and was threatening Spain. The
court moved from Madrid to Aranjuez, to get away from the French and
as a preliminary, perhaps, to escaping to South America like the
Portuguese royal family. But the French intervention on top of decades
of misgovernment now combined to provoke even the sullen, disunited
Spanish to revolt. In March 1808 occurred the Tumult of Aranjuez –
effectively a military coup with mob support – which forced Godoy to
resign at last and then, three days later, Charles IV to abdicate in favour
of his son. The young king, Ferdinand VII, managed to get his parents
to France, for their safety.

Napoleon then ordered both the deposed monarch and his successor
to attend on him at Bayonne, just inside the French border. Ferdinand
agreed, despite the entreaties of his court and of the ordinary people,
who unhitched his horses several times on his journey north. Thus the
fly put himself into the spider's web. At Bayonne, father and son argued
furiously, and Napoleon was able to induce them both to sign abdication instruments. Charles IV, Maria Luisa and Godoy were despatched
to Rome, where they later died, and Ferdinand was immured in a
château on the Loire. Napoleon's older brother, Joseph, was appointed
King of Spain, and a new liberal constitution was introduced.

In Madrid, popular anger against the French exploded, to the astonishment of Napoleon, who had assumed that his new government
would be warmly welcomed. Hundreds of Spaniards were killed by

French troops in the famous massacre of the 'Dos de Mayo' of 1808. Guerrilla bands and civil resistance groups were formed. Local notables led committees against the French. Everywhere French soldiers were ambushed and killed. Joseph, arriving to take his throne, was at first forced out of Madrid but later returned, to be derided as 'Pepe Botellas' (Joe Bottles). In September 1808 the main anti-French resistance organisation was established in Seville in the form of a junta which claimed to rule in the name of Ferdinand VII.

In Spain's colonies these events had the effect, at first, of stimulating patriotic support for the young King Ferdinand. In September 1808 the independent-minded Viceroy of New Spain, José de Iturrigaray, who had begun to take action against the Spanish clergy and merchant houses and was widely supported by the Mexican criollo aristocracy, was arrested and deported to Spain, but it was the following year that the first tremors of real revolt were felt in Spanish America. In May in Upper Peru (modern Bolivia), at Chuquisaca (now Sucre), seat of the Presidency, the students and professors suddenly rose in fury, not against the French but against the authority of the Seville junta; their allegiance, they insisted, was to the Spanish Crown, not to Spain as a nation. The president and the archbishop were deposed. Nearby, in La Paz, another student revolt broke out. In August in Quito a group of liberal criollos headed by the Marqués de Selva Alegre set up an assembly loyal to Ferdinand VII but opposed to the Seville junta – a pretext, in fact, for expelling Spanish officials and governing themselves. In Santa Fé de Bogotá the same thing happened. In Valladolid, near Mexico City, criollos set up an independent junta. The Spanish authorities reacted with speed and firmness. The Viceroy in Lima sent a force to crush the uprising in La Paz. An army from Buenos Aires suppressed the rebellion at Chuquisaca. Another force from Lima restored order in Quito. The Santa Fé de Bogotá and Valladolid rebellions were quickly snuffed out. This left only Venezuela still in the hunt for liberty.

PART ONE: THE NORTH

The Precursor and the Liberator

I

The Turncoat

On 28 March 1750 a boy was born into a peaceful, sleepy, temperate city of red-roofed houses with whitewashed walls. Sebastián Francisco de Miranda was the son of a first-generation immigrant from Spain, of distinguished family but looked upon with scorn by the old Caracas aristocracy; his mother, however, was of good Caracas stock. He had an idyllic childhood, the eldest of two brothers and three sisters, playing with neighbouring children, eating perfumed chocolates and sipping cold drinks in the heat. Instructed first by private tutors, he then attended the Academy of Santa Rosa, followed by the Royal University.

The Captaincy-General Audiencia of Caracas was permeated by a sense of hierarchy and discrimination. There were only about 200,000 whites, outnumbered slightly by the 210,000 Indians and overwhelmingly by the 430,000 free blacks and 60,000 black slaves. The white overclass was uncomfortably aware that it was sitting on a volcano. Yet the whites themselves were sharply divided. The backbone of the country comprised the old settlers, the criollos, the most elevated of whom traced their descent from the conquerors of the continent three hundred years before. They regarded themselves as of (usually exaggerated) noble Spanish descent, but first and foremost as American citizens; and many bore traces of racial intermarriage. They looked with hatred upon the swaggering officials from Spain or the Canary Isles, and with contempt upon Spaniards newly arrived to make their fortunes. In many ways, this colonial aristocracy was not attractive: the contemporary historian Miguel José Sanz describes them as ill-educated (Spain deliberately discouraged education in the colonies), vain, proud, and prone to 'abusing the prerogatives of their birth because they were ignorant of what these were for'.

Francisco was envied for his wealth and snubbed for his Spanish blood. In his teens he was refused entry to the 'White Battalion', the élite junior army cadet corps, and even threatened with prison when he challenged his exclusion. The Spanish government took his side, and he was forcibly admitted – which hardly increased his popularity; the criollo nobility did, however, manage to keep him out of the prestigious senior corps, the Royal Corps of Cadets. Conceited and overbearing, apparently unconcerned about making enemies, he was delighted to be invited subsequently to serve in the army in Spain. In January 1771, not yet twenty-one, he embarked for the two-month journey across the Atlantic to Cadiz. On arrival he set off on a month-long tour of Spain, ending in Madrid. There he found lodgings, studied mathematics, and collected the first volumes of what was to become an impressive library. From the beginning Miranda was a howling snob: from the official college of arms he obtained copies of his family arms and tree, showing his descent from the dukes of Miranda, one of Spain's oldest and most distinguished families.

In December 1772 he finally joined the Spanish army, as an infantry captain. From the first his superiors disapproved of his haughtiness, and of an independence of mind that verged on insubordination. He cut a strong and unusual figure, tall and well-built, always immaculately and expensively dressed, but with a prominent nose which detracted from otherwise refined features, a small, pursed mouth with a disdainful expression and strong, penetrating, determined, intelligent eyes. His chin jutted confidently, and his hair fell forward insouciantly over a large brow. His looks made him irresistible to women, and as vain as a peacock.

He was despatched to serve in Spain's African colonies. In 1775 Abdul Hamid, the Moroccan Pasha, launched a war to expel the Spanish from his country, and Miranda found himself caught up in the siege of the fortress of Melilla. He distinguished himself by leading 230 men in a night attack which succeeded in spiking Hamid's main battery of cannon. The Moroccan way of war – slitting solidiers' throats, executing one of their own generals for failing to break the Spanish resistance – impressed Miranda at an early stage with a horror of unnecessary bloodshed. He himself narrowly avoided death – or worse – when three bullets, passing between his legs, tore his trousers.

In Spain, Miranda's abilities were recognised, but he continued to be prickly, and rude to his superiors, feeling that he was treated as a second-class soldier because of his American origins – which was probably true.

In his mid-twenties he was twice briefly imprisoned in Cadiz for disobedience. Then a new commanding officer accused him of withholding funds he had been given to pay a merchant who supplied his regiment, and of stripping and beating two of his soldiers, wounding one with his sword. Miranda denied the charges, claiming that an adjutant was responsible for the embezzlement and a soldier for the beatings. In truth, such deeds seem out of character: although a strict disciplinarian as a commander, Miranda was neither impetuous nor cruel; nor was he financially dishonest.

But the case was brought to the attention of the inspector-general of the army, the Conde de O'Reilly, who like most of his superiors intensely disliked the bumptious Miranda, and eventually reached the ears of the King himself; Miranda found himself confined to routine duties. He subsequently visited Gibraltar, where he was invited to the governor's New Year Ball: it was the beginning of a lifelong passion for all things British, and it may be that he was even recruited by the British secret service. With his military career in the doldrums, nursing a grudge over his shabby treatment by the Spaniards he had so passionately admired a decade earlier, and alive to the intriguing rife in Cadiz, a hot-bed of Latin American grumbling against Spanish excesses, it was probably about this time that he first began to nurture his revolutionary views.

The American War of Independence broke out in 1775; under the Franco-Spanish alliance of 1779 Spain was obliged to help the fight against the British, and Miranda, appointed aide to General Juan Manuel de Cagigal, the new Spanish commander in Cuba, distinguished himself in the two-month siege of the British stronghold of Pensacola in the spring of 1781. Promoted lieutenant-colonel, he helped a French fleet reach Chesapeake Bay to assist George Washington at the battle of Yorktown in the autumn of that year. At about this time, Miranda's detractors accused him of having permitted a British officer to inspect the defences of Havana – which if true would have amounted to treason. Cagigal, however, demonstrated his confidence in his aide by letting him supervise an exchange of prisoners between Spain and Britain in Jamaica. In 1782 Cagigal and Miranda were sent to the Bahamas to accept the surrender of the capital, New Providence, by the British.

By the age of thirty-two Miranda had the reputation of an able and prominent officer. But if once he had resented the snubs of the criollo aristocracy of Caracas, he now much more deeply disliked the arrogant Spaniards he had served for more than ten years. The American War of Independence led him to conclude that the liberation of the Spanish colonies could not be long delayed; it was unnatural for such vast and far-flung territories to be ruled by a country so many thousands of miles away.

Friends and relations in Venezuela bombarded him with letters complaining of the brutality of Spanish rule under the new Captain-General, Bernardo Galvez – 'a new Nero and Philip II rolled into one!' According to Miranda's correspondents, Galvez had 'just sent an order to all governors that no American gentleman may travel abroad without the King's permission'. They begged Miranda, Venezuela's 'eldest son', to save them: 'The least sign from you will find us ready to follow you as our leader to the end, and to shed the last drop of our blood for causes that are great and honourable . . . in our name and that of our entire province you may make compacts or contracts with our full power and consent. Also, if you judge it convenient, you may negotiate with foreign powers in order to release us from this accursed captivity.'

Returning to Havana Miranda was suddenly arrested, on Galvez's orders, accused of engaging in contraband – clearly a trumped-up charge – and sentenced to ten years in gaol. Cagigal, standing as his guarantor, had him released, and Miranda spent several months under a cloud, sometimes in hiding. He had reached a turning-point: fearful of rearrest, although he was still protected by Cagigal, beset by enemies, suspected of spying and intrigue, he planned, although it was tantamount to desertion, to travel back to Europe, via North America, in order to prove his innocence to the King of Spain in person. In June 1783 he set off, very bitter about the way he had been treated.

He left in style, with a piano, a sofa, and his growing library. He disembarked in North Carolina, where he confided to his diary his astonishment at the sexual liberty afforded single women there, while married ones were forced to live like recluses in their homes. In Philadelphia he was greeted by senior government officials, and in December at last met George Washington. Impressed by the American leader's entry into the city, 'like the redeemer entering Jerusalem', he found him moderate and urbane but curiously lacking in intelligence, and rather taciturn. In New York Miranda met Alexander Hamilton and Thomas Paine, and visited the principal battle sites of the war, Saratoga, Albany, Newhaven and Boston (where he met Lafayette – who impressed him not at all: 'a mediocrity accompanied by activity and perpetual motion').

He was appalled by the low level of debate in Congress, and by the representatives' obsession with trade. 'Why, in a democracy whose basis is Virtue, is there no place assigned to it? On the contrary all the dignity and powers are given to Property, which is the blight of such a democracy. Another point is the contradiction I noticed between admitting as one of the rights of mankind that of worshipping a Supreme Being in the manner and form in which it may please one, yet afterwards excluding a man from office if he did not profess Christianity.' Miranda's visit to America hardened his conviction that his own continent could and must secure its freedom. He became suspicious that the United States' intentions were expansionist when Thomas Jefferson argued that the Confederacy should be thought of as the heart 'from which all America, north and south, should be peopled' and suggested that Spain's colonies could be gained 'piece by piece'.

England, however, held an intellectual fascination for him, and after a year and a half in the United States Miranda arrived in London early in 1785. He lodged at the Royal Hotel and there penned a vigorous defence of his actions to the King of Spain, resigning his commission and seeking a formal exculpation. Even at this stage, it seems, he regarded himself as a loyal Spanish subject bent on having his good name restored. The Spanish Embassy in London received him courteously, but there was no reply from Madrid to his letters.

His extraordinary blend of charm and self-importance proved as seductive in London as it had in the United States. A poseur of a very characteristic Latin American kind, Miranda soon numbered among his friends – although the closeness of the relationship may have been more obvious to him than to them – Jeremy Bentham, Lord Howe, Lord Sydney, Lord Shelburne, Lord Fitzherbert and General Rainsford. Snubbed by Madrid, he decided the time was ripe for public advocacy of independence for Spain's colonies. The *Political Herald & Review* recorded that:

> The jealousy which confined the appointments of government in Spanish America to native Spaniards, and established other distinctions between these and their descendants on the other side of the Atlantic, has been a two-edged sword, and cut two ways. If it has hitherto preserved the sovereignty of Spain in those parts, it has sown the seeds of a deep resentment among the people. Conferences are held, combinations are formed in

secret among a race of men whom we shall distinguish by the appellation of Spanish Provincials. The example of North America is the great subject of discourse, and the grand object of imitation. In London, we are well assured, there is at this moment a Spanish American of great consequence and possessed of the confidence of his fellow-citizens, who aspires to the glory of being the deliverer of his country . . . This gentleman, having visited every province in North America, came to England, which he regards as the mother country of liberty, and the school for political knowledge . . .

He is a man of sublime vision and penetrating genius gifted in modern tongues, learned and worldly-wise. He has spent many years studying politics . . . We admire his talents, we admire his virtues and for the least wish well to the most noble aspiration that can occupy the mind of any mortal, that of giving the benefits of freedom to millions of his fellow citizens.

This glorious tribute signalled to the Spaniards that Miranda was not only beyond redemption, but dangerous as well.

2

The Voluptuary

In the summer of 1785 an American friend, Colonel William Smith, came to England, and he and Miranda decided to tour Europe together. Miranda's motive was to gather diplomatic and financial support for the cause of Latin American independence. Renegade colonel that he was, Miranda particularly wished to observe the military manoeuvres of Frederick the Great of Prussia; Bernardo del Campo, the wily Spanish Ambassador in London, who frequently invited him to dine, obligingly presented Miranda with a letter of introduction to the Spanish Minister in Prussia, but secretly sent word to the Spanish legation in Berlin to watch his movements carefully, with a view to having him extradited once he crossed into Prussia.

In August, with a party which included the Duke of Portland, Miranda and Smith left for Rotterdam, The Hague, Leyden, Haarlem, Amsterdam and Potsdam. Apparently thus protected from, and apparently blissfully unaware of, the Spanish plot to apprehend him, Miranda and his party travelled on to Berlin, where they saw the impressively disciplined ranks of Prussian infantry wheel in formation under the command of General Mollendorf. Treated like an exiled head of state, Miranda was invited to dine by Frederick and grandly toured the libraries and museums of the Prussian capital. His 'royal' progress continued, to Prague, Vienna – where he was lodged in the impressive Schönbrunn – and Hungary. There he met Haydn and visited the famous Esterházy Palace as a guest of the prince, before returning to Vienna in a coach drawn by huge Transylvanian horses.

He turned south now to Venice, then on to Verona, Modena, Florence, Lucca, Pisa and Siena. In Rome he visited the papal apartments, saw every conceivable church and palazzo, visited each of the Seven Hills, the Lateran Palaces, the Terme of Agrippa, Castel

Sant'Angelo, the Sistine Chapel and St Peter's, where he attended a papal Mass.

He was also an indefatigable sexual tourist. Everywhere he went, he gallanted the ladies. Among other amorous escapades, he met an eighteen-year-old girl who punctured his vanity by refusing to sleep with him because she had a son by the King of Sweden, to whom she was devoted. Miranda confided to his diary that it took all his powers of persuasion to get this high-class young courtesan to change her mind. In Viterbo he encountered, so he said, the most beautiful women in the world.

From Italy he travelled to Greece, where in Athens he befriended a French academic, Monsieur Villoison, who had scandalised the city by declaring that 'to put one's hands on the breasts of women [at parties] was not indecent, because that was what was happening in Paris'. When Miranda crossed to Turkey, he complained that the lack of pretty girls there at first caused him severe headaches. From Smyrna to Constantinople he was rowed by thirty-two beautiful negress slaves, and witnessed the conversion of a young Greek man, used by the Turks for sexual purposes, to Islam. He complained of being spat upon in the streets, having been mistaken for a Frenchman. He visited the celebrated cultural salons of Madame Michel and Madame Heidenstan, falling briefly in love with the beautiful Greek Eufrosina Phrossini. He witnessed Turkish orgies, and also managed a trip to the celebrated library of Rahib Pasha. On the way back to Greece he sipped chocolate with Countess Ludolf and, surrounded by beautiful Greek girls, heard the Orthodox Mass sung.

Crossing the Black Sea in a storm, Miranda became one of the first South Americans to visit Russia. As usual he made an impression; he was taken up by the Russian nobility and met Prince Potemkin, chief minister of Catherine the Great, who over tea laced with vodka took an instant liking to him. So began Miranda's extraordinary relationship with the Russian court. He soon became Potemkin's favourite, met his mistress, the Comtesse de Sèvres, went on outings and hunting parties with him, and stayed at his Crimean estate. In front of Potemkin he had a blazing row with the French Prince of Nassau, who had claimed that Spanish women were all dirty whores who smelt of garlic. Miranda retorted sarcastically that the French were of course the best judges of cleanliness.

In February 1787, in Kiev, Miranda was formally presented by Potemkin to the Empress Catherine. So began one of the most curious affairs in history, between a Latin American poseur and Russia's notoriously lascivious but most civilised and intelligent ruler. Her first question was 'How low is the temperature in your country, when it gets cooler?' – a thoughtful enquiry of a man who suffered intensely from the bitter Russian cold, and gloried in the warmth of the palaces. From the head of the table at a banquet, Catherine sent him choice morsels to eat. Afterwards when the Court settled down to cards she asked Miranda if the Inquisition still existed in Spain; he replied that regrettably it did. The Empress said, 'In Russia there are still some Dominican monks that work for the tribunal [of the Inquisition]. But when I see them, I say under my breath, "God help me!"' Discreet laughter coursed around the room, and she left to bows and curtseys. A few days later both attended a party at Prince Vranitsky's house. After a conversation with him, Catherine was heard to remark that Miranda was 'truthful and learned'. At another party they discussed literature. Shortly afterwards Potemkin suggested that unless Miranda left soon, the rivers would be too swollen to navigate. It seems the prince was fuming: not only was Miranda apparently abusing his introduction to the Empress to ingratiate himself in Potemkin's place, but Potemkin missed his protégé's company. Miranda got the message, and prepared to leave. Coldly, Potemkin asked him whether he intended to say goodbye to Catherine before he went. When they next met, Miranda ostentatiously failed to rise as Potemkin entered the room.

The following day, Potemkin told Miranda that the Empress herself insisted he should not travel, because the river crossings had become too dangerous. At a party that evening she chided him: 'Did you want to drown? I would never have permitted it.' At the same party, Potemkin was seen to greet his former friend, now his rival, with all his old warmth. Clearly Catherine had been annoyed by the news of Miranda's imminent departure, and blamed Potemkin, who now had to make amends. From then on, the Empress conversed with Miranda at every reception, while courtiers alternately fawned on and grumbled about the new favourite. Even the Prince of Nassau became deferential, while the Spanish Ambassador seethed. In March, at another party, Miranda was seen to compliment the Empress on her exquisite silk dress, and even to touch it. Catherine smilingly asked what was ailing him. His sexual liaison with her is believed to have begun the same night.

Shortly after this, Potemkin thought he had found another way of ridding the court of Miranda: he ordered him to go to welcome the King of Poland, Stanislaus (like Potemkin, a former lover of the Empress), on Catherine's behalf, at the start of his visit to Russia. Again Miranda's educated, graceful conversation made a favourable impression. He soon returned, not just to the bed of the plump, middle-aged Empress, but also to that of his own court passion, the beautiful Countess Pototka. The Empress was now so infatuated that she pressed a close friend of both Miranda and Potemkin, Marshal Mamonov, to lend him a palace in St Petersburg so he could live there, saying it would be a tragedy if impoverishment consumed such a man. This was a serious proposal and Catherine was intending to establish him as her recognised lover and favourite. Mamonov refused, arguing that Miranda must return to his mission in life, the fight for South America's independence. Almost certainly Potemkin and the other courtiers had now united to oppose Miranda's influence. Faced with this rebuff, Miranda glumly reconsidered his prospects, and wrote to the Empress:

> The only obstacle impeding my accepting the honour of entering in your service, is my endeavour to achieve the freedom of my country . . . Nothing but the great and interesting objective I am now engaged in could prevent me from the agreeable and sweet pleasure of being able, through my services, to satisfy in part all that I owe to your Majesty's generosity, and share with your subjects the precious and invaluable advantages this society enjoys under your illustrious and glorious reign. Nevertheless, as soon as I can fulfil my commitments elsewhere, as I had the honour to inform your Majesty through General Mamonov in Kiev, I would dare to claim your promise, and I hope then your kindness will deign accepting the small services of a sincere man who seeks in all his efforts nothing but the profit and happiness of others.

Catherine replied sadly that she appreciated his way of thinking, 'but I will always give you my imperial protection, wherever you are'. She was as good as her word, and in April 1787 sent the following order to her embassies in Vienna, Paris, London, The Hague, Copenhagen, Stockholm, Berlin and Naples:

> Her Imperial Majesty wishing to give M. de Miranda a clear proof of her esteem and the particular interest She has in him, orders your Excellency, upon receiving this present letter, to reserve for that officer a reception at the level of the appreciation She herself has for his person, and offer him all possible care and attention, giving him help and protection any time it is necessary, and at the very moment he may demand it, and, in an extreme case, offer him your own house as asylum.

It seemed the exotic South American favourite had been successfully ousted. As the day of his departure approached, Miranda bade farewell to his latest, now tearful, conquests, Madame Tarnowska and Princess Lubomircka. On the evening of the celebration of Catherine's saint's day, a spectacular firework display was staged. Miranda appeared with the Empress on the balcony of the imperial palace, where he took his public leave, kissing her hand as the sky blazed with light over the canals and palaces.

In a luxurious coach Miranda travelled across the glistening Russian landscape towards Moscow, where he was put up in the palace of Marshal Roumaintzov. Once again he entered the social whirl, visiting the opera, libraries and museums, and the Russian bath houses, where men and women took the hot waters naked – but, he observed regretfully, none of the women resembled the Venus of the Medici. Then a summons came from the Empress to return to St Petersburg. Prince Orlov invited him to stay at the Hermitage Palace there. A courtier told him how Peter the Great, whose palace it had been, once cut open the stomach of a man who had died in a drunken stupor, in order to observe the condition of the liquid inside him.

Catherine received him once more. The Spanish chargé d'affaires, meanwhile, asked him for proof that he was a count and an officer of the King of Spain – neither of which Miranda could provide. It seemed he was certain to be exposed as a charlatan, until the Empress intervened to say that she supported him as a person, no matter what his official position. She scolded her courtiers for requiring that he kiss her hand on being presented to her, on the grounds that she already knew him, and invited him into her private apartment. He was offered the uniform of a Russian colonel, and Catherine gave him ten thousand roubles and five hundred ducats of gold. But now he refused to stay. He despatched crates of papers and books to London, then embarked himself. It is impossible to say whether his decision to leave was prompted by the certainty that the Empress's infatuation could not last and that his Russian enemies would sooner or later trip him up; whether he felt the tug of destiny and his American ambitions; or whether he simply could not bear the prospect of years of cold Russian winters.

The ship took Miranda across the Baltic to Stockholm, where he was housed in the Russian Embassy. Fearing an attempt to kidnap him to Spain he went incognito at first, meeting only trusted contacts such as the Danish Minister, Rosencrantz, and the Baron Hakelburg. Sweden's celebrated beauties and coal mines were alike objects of his interest: he descended six hundred feet down a mine, meeting the women and children who worked there, and was impressed by their extraordinary cheerfulness in adversity. He also witnessed his first aurora borealis, admired Sweden's canals, and criticised Stockholm's hospitals and prisons.

Soon King Gustav III learnt of his presence, and ordered that all official doors should be opened to him, as a favourite of the Empress of Russia. During his Swedish sojourn Miranda took as his principal lover the passionate Cristina Strandez. After making love with her he would relax with another Swedish friend, Count Rousamousky, who regaled him with court gossip, in particular the story of how the impotent King discovered that his wife was pregnant and behaved as though the prospective infant was his own until its birth, when its colour made it obvious that it was the offspring of a black page. Gustav then arranged for a Swedish page to sleep with the Queen, and the union provided a child which he was able to call his own.

Miranda travelled on to Norway, wondering at the clarity of the night sky as his carriage was pulled across high mountains to the city of Kristiansand; there he was received ceremonially by the authorities, and Count Rantzau placed a seventeen-year-old girl at his disposal to warm his nights, as well as providing a list of available women. After a dangerous journey across broken roads to the town of Uddevalla, during which he fractured his arm, Miranda cuckolded his British host, Mr Holt. Catherine Holt then introduced him to the local bishop, Wingard, who in turn introduced him to his mistress and their children. Miranda and Catherine visited the Holts' country estate, where their love-making urges were frustrated by the presence of another guest. On the way back they copulated passionately in the carriage, but it overturned, and they narrowly avoided being discovered *in flagrante.*

In Denmark, Miranda was unimpressed by Copenhagen and its 'degenerate' royal family, and found the girls unattractive. He did the usual rounds of theatres, art galleries, museums and churches. He considered the Danes a backward, barbarous people; he told the prime minister, Schack-Rathlou, that the law which permitted a father to immure his daughter if she had sex outside marriage must be repealed, and interceded to save the life of a demented girl sentenced to death for infanticide. He also pressed for prison reform – in particular for the separation of the sexes in gaol and of young offenders from hardened criminals, and for one prisoner to a bed in hospital, instead of two sharing.

Back in Germany, in Kiel, he had a fling with one of the three beautiful von Bülow sisters. He was prevented from seducing his pretty fifteen-year-old guide on the top of a church tower, and so fulfilling his fantasy of 'sacrificing to Venus at the highest point in the city', by the attention of other tourists, 'but slept with a beautiful Englishwoman the same night instead'. He also visited 'the Parthenon', a bordello run by Madame Poppe, and boasted of despatching 'two towers and two fine girls' in a single day. In Haarlem Miranda attended musical hideaways 'where staid citizens procure girls cheaply and make love, watched by other equally respectable types smoking pipes, to the sound of a violin'. In Strasbourg he bought a complete edition of the works of Voltaire as well as Virgil's *Georgics*. He was impressed by Holbein, and read the Virgil under a tree by a lake beneath the Black Mountains. In Switzerland he visited the scene of the martyrdom of Jan Hus; observing that Protestant countries were better off than Catholic ones, he wondered whether Catholicism was wholly opposed to material wealth, a theme he discussed with Catholic friends.

He crossed into Italy again before returning to Switzerland and then to France, passing through Lyons and Avignon and down to Toulon, where he inspected French ships. He visited Cannes and Nice, where an actress and a Venetian girl spent successive nights with him. He embarked for Genoa and thence to Turin, where he attended masked balls and slept with ballerinas before returning to Marseilles and then travelling up to the Gironde to taste the region's great wines. From there he went to Brest and on to Paris which, towards the end of May 1789, he found in turmoil, on the brink of revolution – though this failed to distract him from his round of pleasure, before his return to London. There he attended a banquet at which William Pitt was present; and, methodically and admiringly, noted that, in a single day in London, 40,000 lobsters were sold.

Miranda's later apologists argue that the motives behind this fantastic peregrination were always clear and high-minded: the assimilation of culture and information, of political and military ideas, combined with the need to press the cause of Spanish-American independence and to secure allies. Russia and Germany were certainly potential counterweights to France and Spain, often in alliance. Historians of South America view the whole four-year odyssey as the subtle manoeuvrings of a master diplomat, of a New World Talleyrand, Metternich or Lafayette preparing European opinion for the revolutionary idea of Spanish American independence. However, reading his meticulously kept diaries – which have to be considered accurate, even allowing for an element of sexual exaggeration – it is hard to conclude that he was on anything more than a prolonged joy-ride, during which he displayed a truly astonishing variety of sexual and intellectual appetites – in that order. He posed as statesman, aristocrat and military hero, his charm and sheer bravura carrying him from one European court to another, much of the time living lavishly at other people's expense.

Yet Miranda represented nothing. He had resigned his commission under a cloud; he was arguably a traitor and deserter; and he could not establish his credentials as a count. He was a chancer, and he took everyone in, to an awe-inspiring degree. But he was also more interesting than that. In later times he might have made a great journalist. He observed everything, visited everyone who mattered, inspected everything – warships, copper and iron mines, hospitals and prisons, displaying genuinely liberal and enlightened sentiments with indefatigable self-confidence and authority – and always wrote everything down. On top of that his appetite for culture was limitless – music, painting, museums, antiquities, the theatre, local colour, the customs of ordinary people, conversation; and, above all, books, which he vacuumed up as he crossed Europe, despatching them to England to join his ever-swelling collection.

What no one found credible was that Miranda, now nearly forty, was a political figure, or a leader of his people. Hardly anyone in Venezuela, except his family and the most rarefied of intellectual circles, had heard of him. He had been away from his homeland for nearly two decades. His sole political significance was that it suited the British and, to a lesser extent, the Russians (for very different reasons) to take him seriously. To the Germans, Scandinavians, French, Italians, Austrians, Greeks, Turks and Americans he was merely a social phenomenon. Only the Spanish, his old employers, paid him the compliment of regarding him as a potential danger, and shadowing him across the Continent.

3

The Revolutionary

In London, in 1789, Miranda continued to dabble, albeit with a little more method. He found lodgings in Jermyn Street and from there he toured the country, visiting Oxford, Cambridge, Southampton, Winchester and Norwich, shooting hare and pheasant with an English friend. He attended Lady Sheffield's drawing-rooms and fell for the young and beautiful Lady Webster, later to become the formidable Whig hostess, Lady Holland. In 1790 Thomas Pownall, former Governor of Massachusetts, who believed that in exchange for British assistance to the Spanish colonies in shaking off rule from Madrid both Britain and the United States should be given unfettered access to trade with them, succeeded in arranging a discreet meeting between Miranda and Britain's first minister, William Pitt. This was the most important event in Miranda's life to date: Catherine of Russia could merely provide peripheral support to the cause of South American independence, but the helmsman of the world's biggest colonial power apart from Spain was a different matter. The meeting was a sign he was being taken seriously at last.

Miranda prepared himself feverishly, drawing up an ambitious and wholly unrealistic plan for liberation. He gave a careful estimate of the colonies' resources, and of Spanish strength there. There were twenty-one million people, he claimed, in 'the Spanish Indies', half of them Spaniards, criollos, whites and of mixed blood, the rest Indians and blacks. The colonies produced annually about fifty-five million pesos in gold, silver, sugar, cacao, hides, tobacco, indigo and cochineal, and imported roughly twenty-two million pesos' worth of goods from Spain, and a similar amount in contraband. Spain had around 36,000 troops in the colonies, of whom some 20,000 were locally-raised militia, the rest regular soldiers; and a navy of 123 ships and 44,000 sailors. Miranda subtly underlined South America's potential by suggesting – with remarkable foresight – that a canal could be cut through the isthmus of Panamá to facilitate trade to the Far East for Britain and America. He argued that although Spanish America, more populous than Spain, should be able to stage its own revolt, its communities were cut off from one another by distance and poor communications. With control of the seas, the Spanish could send reinforcements wherever they liked: a crucial insight. Britain, he insisted, as a maritime power, could cut the Spanish lines of communication. He argued that Britain was a natural ally for South America, and ended on an elevated and flattering note:

> In view of the similarity that exists in the character of these two nations, and the effects that must naturally flow from liberty and the fact that a good government can instruct the general mass of men, progressively doing away with the religious prejudices that cloud its people's minds . . . these being otherwise honest, hospitable, and generous – we must expect soon to see a respectable and illustrious nation emerging worthy of being the ally of the wisest and most famed power on earth.

His grandiose blueprint was for a kind of united states of Spanish America, stretching from the Pacific to the Atlantic, excluding Brazil and Guiana but including the land east of the Mississippi and south of the source of the river, below Parallel 45. The constitution of this great new state would be an extraordinary hybrid of the monarchical and republican systems: a descendant of the Incas would sit on the throne – this to give the monarchy an authentically pre-Columbus flavour – but he would be accountable, British-style, to a two-chamber congress, with an upper house elected for life and a lower one by regular popular (if restricted) vote. A two-thirds majority would be needed to amend the constitution, as well as a three-quarters majority of a council composed of the Inca emperor sitting with the highest judges of the land. The clergy would retain many of their privileges, but the Inquisition would be done away with. The Spanish monopoly of trade would be ended, and the new state would be open to commercial treaties with Britain and other countries. (On seeing this blueprint later, President Adams of the United States is said to have remarked that he didn't know whether to laugh or cry. The son of the Bostonian James Lloyd, however, wrote to Adams describing Miranda as 'the most extraordinary and marvellously energetic man I have ever met'.)

In May 1790, equipped with his fantastic plan, Miranda met the cold, analytical young man who dominated British politics. He asserted to Pitt that the South American people would rise up in revolt as soon as a British fleet appeared; but he was in no position to give this assurance, having not set foot in South America for twenty years and being in contact only with a handful of wealthy criollo dissidents. He had not the slightest idea of the real opinion of the educated classes there, much less that of the populace. Pitt made it clear that he would help only in the event of a war between Britain and Spain. This in fact looked to be imminent – which was why Pitt's officials had set up the encounter in the first place: Spain was claiming as its own the Nootka Sound, high up on the Pacific coast of North America, then in Britain's possession. Miranda no doubt left the meeting with a spring in his step.

Five months later, however, the Nootka Sound dispute was settled, and the project was off. Miranda, given financial support by the British government as long as his potential nuisance value to the Spaniards was useful, now found this source of funds drying up, and was upset that he had revealed his plan to Pitt. Pownall tried to get them back around the table, unsuccessfully.

Miranda had by now founded the Gran Réunion Americana, a society for Spanish-American dissidents. Its members, now or at a later date, included Bernardo O'Higgins, future liberator of Chile, to whom Miranda taught mathematics; Antonio Nariño, later founder of New Granada's independence movement; Carlos Maria de Alvear, friend and rival of San Martín and, briefly, ruler of Argentina; Francisco Montufar, later aide to General Sucre; and a future Mexican liberator, Vicente Rocafuerte. But Miranda felt harassed by the continuing efforts of the Spanish Ambassador, Bernardo del Campo, to spy on him, and by Spanish attempts to get the British to arrest him for debt. The years of touring the courts of Europe in grand style were past; he was running out of money.

In 1792 Miranda moved to more modest quarters at 33 Great Pulteney Street in Soho. After three years in London, he felt betrayed by the British government, and depressed that all his talk of leading South America to revolution had come to nothing. He switched his attention to the revolutionary ferment in France: a group of monarchists there had tried to get him to join a counter-revolutionary mercenary army of Russians, Swedes, Germans and Frenchmen partly backed by Catherine, who had suggested Miranda's name. But for all his aristocratic pretensions, Miranda's intellectual sympathies lay with the revolutionaries.

He made a good impression on a prominent Girondin who visited London, J. P. Brissot: between them they developed the idea that the revolution in France could be spread both to mainland Spain and to Spanish America. The Girondins were idealistic middle-class revolutionaries, and moderates compared to the Jacobins who replaced them in 1793. Brissot had in fact been lobbying the commander in northern France, General Dumouriez, to appoint Miranda head of an invasion force of 12,000 French infantry and 10,000 mulattos then garrisoned in Santo Domingo who, with the assistance of the French navy, might be expected to topple Spain's hold on her colonies, something France wanted almost as much as Britain.

Crossing to Paris, Miranda found little enthusiasm for the plan there, however, and was considering a return to London when Austrian and Prussian armies invaded France from the east. In August 1792, as the country reeled at the prospect of defeat, Miranda, who had perhaps sold his military credentials a little too successfully, found himself offered the rank of marshal in the French army and the title of baron, as well as a fat stipend, very attractive to a man now hard pressed for the money to live in the grand style to which he had become accustomed. At the age of forty-two he was at last a real nobleman and a real general – both in the service of revolutionary France. His Russian supporters, who loathed the French revolutionaries, were appalled at the transformation, but did not sever their links with him altogether.

To his own surprise, in his first engagement, along the border between Belgium and Holland, his force of 2,000 men succeeded after seven hours of fighting in putting to flight some 6,000 Prussians led by the Graf von Kelkreuth, a capable commander. It was the first French success of the war. With uncharacteristic modesty, Miranda spoke of his 'beginner's luck in the French army'; he was promptly appointed to command a division in the front line, under Dumouriez's overall command. *En route* to Vaux the 10,000-strong division commanded by General Chazot suddenly encountered 1,500 Prussian hussars. The French panicked and fled; a rout seemed imminent, until the retreating forces reached Miranda's position at Wargemoulin. There, sword in hand, he stopped their flight, and reorganised the two forces into three columns to march on Valmy.

Dumouriez boldly attacked, believing that he faced a Prussian army of 50,000 men, and a major battle. Instead he was met only by covering fire; the Prussians had retreated after the French rally. Miranda's reputation soared. The decadent voluptuary was proving himself an outstanding soldier in the field. However, he viewed with distaste the rise of the revolutionary party in France, in particular the Jacobin faction led by Robespierre and Marat; as he wrote to Alexander Hamilton, 'The only danger which I foresee is the introduction of extremist principles which would poison freedom in its cradle and destroy it for us.'

Miranda moved up to join Dumouriez as second in command of the French army in Belgium. He went to the relief of Dumouriez's army at Anderlecht, and was appointed to take over General La Bourdonnais's command of the Northern Army. As the grip of winter intensified Miranda's forces reached the outskirts of Ambères, where he personally supervised the digging of trenches, encouraging his men while maintaining rigid discipline. Ambères was heavily fortified; on 26 November the French guns opened up and were answered from within, but not a single besieger was killed. By five in the afternoon, as plumes of smoke from the burning city curled into the sky, the Austrians were seeking terms. These took four days to negotiate and amounted to unconditional surrender, at the cost of of just thirty casualties to Miranda's army. It was another morale-boosting victory for the hard-pressed French under their inspired new general, who immediately set about reinforcing the city's defences. He arrested some of its leading citizens to exact tribute to pay for provisioning his troops, and dissolved the convents and monasteries, stripping prelates, abbots and monks of their titles. The 22,000 men under his command were soon joined by thousands belonging to the Army of the Ardennes, swelling his command to 70,000 men.

In February 1793, against his own advice, Miranda was ordered to send out 12,000 of his men to besiege Maastricht. As he expected, the 30,000 or so enemy forces proved too well entrenched. They fired some 32,000 cannon-shot in six days, but failed to inflict many casualties upon the smaller French force. Miranda decided to withdraw, lest he lose his guns to an Austrian sortie. He was bitterly criticised for what was clearly a sensible tactical move; he was also hated by many of his own men for his draconian punishments for looting and raping.

Another much more dangerous threat now loomed. Early in March, Miranda's commander-in-chief, Dumouriez, asked his staff officers what they thought of the growing Jacobin outrages against the French army. King Louis XVI had been executed in January, the revolutionary Terror was gathering pace, and the radicals mistrusted nothing so much as the army, even though they depended upon it for the revolution's survival against external enemies. Miranda primly replied that he disapproved of seeking the opinions of soldiers on such issues. Soon afterwards two disgraced generals, La Hove and Stengel, were arrested on grounds of conspiracy. Dumouriez now demanded to know what Miranda would do if the order came to arrest him, Dumouriez. Miranda said that he would have no option but to obey, adding that General Valance, as the senior general in the French army, would however be responsible for executing it. Dumouriez angrily retorted that the army would refuse to carry out any such order. A few days later Dumouriez told Miranda that he intended to march on Paris, to restore freedom; the counter-revolution was under way. To his astonishment Miranda, despite his own disapproval of the increasingly radical turn taken by the revolution, told Dumouriez the soldiers would not obey him and that he, Miranda, might also oppose him. It was a moment of truth: from then on, Dumouriez no longer trusted his subordinate.

Miranda's action is inexplicable, except in terms of self-preservation – he believed Dumouriez could not succeed. Miranda had little romantic commitment to the French Revolution and was privately highly critical of the direction it was taking. His enemies believed his ambition was to replace his superior: already the Girondin leaders had identified him as the best candidate for Dumouriez's post, should anything happen to the commander-in-chief.

Dumouriez then decided on an extraordinarily high-risk tactic, one which Miranda's partisans have always believed was an act of deliberate treachery designed to discredit their hero and lead to his downfall. Holding good defensive positions, though vastly outnumbered and outgunned, Dumouriez determined to risk the whole French flank in an offensive against the Austrian-led forces. His motive may have been to give himself enough prestige, through victory, to march on Paris and take over the reins of power. On 15 March Miranda had successfully repulsed an attack on Tirlemont, but with General Champmorin's forces was then ordered to attack the right flank of the enemy at Neerwinden. It was suicidal, since Miranda's 10,000 men were opposed by Austrian-led forces around 18,000-strong, well entrenched in a defensible position. The French were mown down without pity. Although he was in the thick of the fight, Miranda survived; after nightfall, he had no alternative but to sound the retreat, leaving two thousand of his men dead. The retreat was orderly, and he handled it with great coolness.

It soon emerged that Dumouriez had known the enemy was strongest on their right flank and weakest on their left, where his own forces were superior: the weakest part of the French force, under Miranda, had thus been ordered to attack where the enemy were strongest. From the start Miranda had opposed the plan, which he later described as 'against the rules of the art of warfare. I am astonished that Dumouriez was capable of such an error.' The suspicion must be that Dumouriez wanted Miranda to do badly by comparison with the other commanders, in a bid to discredit and remove him before the coup attempt. But he had miscalculated in believing that the centre would hold, and the whole French army was thrown back as a result of this disastrously conceived attack.

On 21 March the Austrians attacked at Pallemberg. Miranda held his positions for a day, despite severe losses, then staged another orderly night retreat. Four days later Dumouriez and Miranda met, and exchanged furious words. Dumouriez railed against the Jacobins, while Miranda criticised his commander's military ineptness.

The Jacobins at last came to learn of Dumouriez's plotting, and of his criticisms of his second-in-command. Dumouriez was arrested; Miranda was summoned to Paris. Arriving at the end of the month, he was immediately interrogated by Citizen Petiot, a Girondin sympathiser, who arranged for him to appear before the Committee of War and Security. At a hearing on 8 April seventy-three questions were put to him as to the conduct of the war. The questioning was barely polite. Miranda knew that his life was on the line, not just his command. He impressed his interrogators with his calm and eloquent replies, and it appeared that he would be exonerated.

But the Terror was gathering momentum. The radicals alleged that Danton, one of the revolution's most eminent leaders, had been conniving with Dumouriez – a charge which may have been true – and insisted that ordinary soldiers should testify against the actions of their superiors. The ultra radical Montagnards, with Robespierre as their new leader, attempted to incriminate Danton and his Girondin followers, the faction with which Miranda was identified. But Danton dodged the attack by himself joining the Montagnards and denouncing his former Girondin followers, among them Miranda, whose supporters Brissot and Petiot sprang to his defence against Danton and Robespierre.

On 19 April 1793 the much-feared Chief Prosecutor of the Revolution, Fouquier-Tinville, ordered Miranda's arrest, on charges of conspiring with Pitt and the British government as well as with the Russians and the North Americans, and of aiding Dumouriez in his counter-revolutionary attempt to reinstate the monarchy. It seemed all too likely that this dissipated, haughty, good-looking man who had cut a swathe through the beauties and courts of all Europe, who had led his men with brilliance, even perhaps turning the tables in the war, and who had acted with impeccable correctness in spurning Dumouriez's overtures, would be guillotined, a long way from his native Venezuela, on trumped-up charges.

On 20 April he was taken before a Revolutionary Tribunal presided over by Montane, with Fouquier-Tinville prosecuting. Miranda surprised those present by his calm demeanour and his eloquent and natural way of defending himself. He was also vigorously defended by Chaveau-Lagarde (who later attempted unsuccessfully to save Queen Marie Antoinette from the tumbril): 'An irreproachable republican', he argued, 'never fears death but cannot bear the suspicion of crime, and for a month Miranda has been suspected.' Fouquier-Tinville rose, and in the precise, reedy voice which had condemned so many to the blade accused Miranda of negligence in the war, and of being Dumouriez's chief co-conspirator. Meanwhile Marat's rabid newspaper, *L'Ami du peuple*, had charged Miranda with looting Ambères after its capture. A procession of hostile witnesses was led by General La Hove and General Eustace. It was alleged that Miranda had a son and a brother-in-law in Maastricht, hence his discontinuance of the siege. A sergeant testified that the Dutch considered him 'better than a Dutchman'. The national gendarmerie, whose excesses he had tried to contain at Antwerp, accused him of a succession of crimes.

When it was Miranda's turn to speak he calmly recalled that, far from being Dumouriez's accomplice, he had been the general's accuser. He had withdrawn from Maastricht because he was outnumbered, and not on ground of his choosing: 'You cannot win when you don't have the advantage of the ground.' Outraged, General Eustace demanded to speak again, saying that it had been his honour 'to detest Miranda'. Remarkably, the acid, razor-sharp Fouquier-Tinville cut him down, saying he could not call an openly prejudiced witness. The defence witnesses were called. One revealed that at the time the King's head was struck off by the guillotine Miranda had declared to his soldiers, 'This is a great blow for the politics of France.' Thomas Paine himself came from London to argue with passion that Miranda would never have

betrayed France, 'because the cause of the French Revolution is intimately tied to the favourite cause of his heart, the independence of
Spanish America.'

Summing up, Chaveau-Lagarde claimed that no defence was necessary, because Miranda had already defended himself so eloquently; he
should be 'listened to with all the dignity that became true republicans
and with the full confidence the court deserves'. As the judges withdrew
and the prisoners were led away, sobbing could be heard. When the
judges had filed back, generals d'Hangest, Dumouriez and Valance were
pronounced guilty, one by one; Miranda was declared innocent. The
court erupted in applause, in which even Fouquier-Tinville joined.
Miranda rose to declare passionately that 'this brilliant act of justice
must restore the respect of my fellow citizens for me, whose loss would
have been more painful for me even than death.' On 16 May he was
released, and carried through crowds in the streets. He was one of the
very few to stare the Terror in the face, to come under the shadow of the
guillotine, and yet to escape.

Now calm and common sense deserted him. Believing himself
immune from further persecution, he withdrew triumphantly to a luxurious château in Menilmontant to rest, and to defend his reputation
against the unceasing vituperation of Marat's newspaper. The
Montagnards were still raining attacks upon him as 'an intriguer, a
creator of faction' who, it was alleged, had bribed the jurors to let him
go. His wisest course of action would have been to leave at once for
England.

On 2 June the Montagnards overthrew the Girondins. Paché, former
minister of war and an implacable foe, was now appointed Mayor of
Paris. Three days later Miranda's château was surrounded by guards, and
Paché placed him under house arrest. This did not stop him receiving
friends and female company alike. The English poetess Helen Maria
Williams called on him. When a large number of sealed boxes arrived,
the police suspected them to contain arms and ammunition; they were
crammed with books. A servant loyal to his enemies was planted in the
household; Miranda knew this, but pretended otherwise.

On 9 July he was arrested again and conducted to the prison of La
Force, from which very few ever emerged free. Robespierre himself now
demanded the guillotine, for Miranda's alleged connivance in a royalist
plot. On 13 July he was brought before the Convention and again made
a stirring defence, accusing his gaolers of violating the constitution

'because the body politic is oppressed when any citizen is oppressed'. He complained that he had been accused of seeking to flee the country, when he had neither horses nor a carriage and could not move two leagues out of Paris without permission from the government. He accused the dreaded Public Safety Committee of tyranny, in disregarding his previous acquittal.

Miranda had asked his doctor to prepare a dose of poison so that he could cheat the guillotine, undoubtedly a wise precaution: compared to a single major prison in Paris before the revolution, the Bastille, there were now twenty, containing about forty thousand people; seven thousand had already been guillotined; Paris was in the grip of fear.

There was a club-like atmosphere in La Force. Miranda beautifully caught the mood when he wrote that it was as though he were 'making a long journey by boat, during which it was necessary to fill the tiresome emptiness of time with the search for useful knowledge without knowing if the journey would end in death at sea or happy arrival in port'. The Marquis du Châtelet became an inseparable companion; the two men talked at length of art, literature and travel; they played cards with packs from which, to their amusement, the court cards had been removed, and read Tacitus and Cicero. One day du Châtelet decided to swallow poison, leaving his few goods to Miranda and the other prisoners. The weeks passed slowly by.

In August Miranda appeared before the Revolution's Special Criminal Tribunal for Investigation. In September he went before the National Convention again, when he asked to be allowed to go into exile in order to pursue his cause against the Spanish government. The French could not make up their minds what to do about him, but they wanted him out of the way. Miranda's frustration grew more desperate and bitter. He railed against the 'imposter' Saint-Just, and against Danton, who had betrayed him – Danton was executed in April 1794. Robespierre was 'infamous' – he and Saint-Just were guillotined in 'Thermidor', July 1794. The police investigated the source of Miranda's funds, but found no sign that they had been acquired illegally (his money came from his general's pay, and rich patrons). The months continued to drift slowly by, and Miranda made new friends in gaol, including the celebrated antiquarian and savant Antoine-Chrysostome Quatremère de Quincy.

In December 1794 Miranda loosed a formidable broadside against the Convention, denouncing Robespierre's 'execrable maxim that the individual's interest must be sacrificed to the public interest', an 'infernal' idea that had given tyrants from Tiberius to Philip II the justification for their misrule. His letter ended, with courageous dignity, 'I do not ask for mercy from the Convention. I demand the most rigorous justice for myself and for those who have dared . . . to compromise the dignity of the French people and poison the national image.' For a man under the shadow of revolutionary Terror and in gaol for more than a year, Miranda showed an admirably robust and indomitable spirit.

On 26 January 1795 Miranda was finally released from La Force, and promptly installed himself in a splendid *appartement* at rue St-Florentin costing £1,400 a year – a staggering sum for those days. He was determined to make up for the deprivations of the past year and a half, of which sex – although he seems to have had access to some women in prison – was probably the most terrible. Women, the theatre and elegant parties were resumed with renewed vigour. In prison he had met 'Delfina', the beautiful Marquise de Custine, whose husband was also in gaol. Miranda now embarked on a torrid affair with her – until he discovered she had also satisfied the lusts of Chateaubriand, Fouché, Alexandre de Beauharnais, M. de Grouchy, Comte Louis de Ségur, Boissy d'Anglais and Dr Korev. Passionate and intelligent but undoubtedly a nymphomaniac, Delfina failed to win him back to her bed, but they continued to be seen together, and quarrelled with the intensity of lovers. Supposedly an illegitimate daughter of Louis XV, Delfina was the greatest French coquette of her time and, according to a contemporary wit, 'loved everyone, even her husband'. She showered Miranda with letters, saw him frequently, and was his last companion when he left France.

Miranda's sojourn in prison did not deter him from meddling in revolutionary politics. Having twice escaped the guillotine he believed himself a charmed man, and now pursued his own moderate liberal agenda, which was anathema to extremists inside and outside the government. In particular, he showed an exemplary tolerance, in an anti-clerical age, of the more liberal-minded among the clergy; and (in spite of his youthful disdain of the man) he lauded the qualities of George Washington, who 'had obtained the confidence of his fellow countrymen not from his brilliance, which he cloaks, but from the calmness of his spirit and uprightness of his intentions'. Miranda's views on the direction of the French revolution were succinctly expressed: 'I love freedom, but not a freedom based on blood and pitiless towards sex or age, like that which has been the order of the day in this country until recently.' He made no secret of the fact that he wanted to hold office in post-revolutionary France.

Two months after his release Miranda met the young Napoleon Bonaparte for the first time in the salon of Julia de Ségur, then gave him dinner. Napoleon's judgement is worth setting down: 'I dined yesterday in the house of a man who is really extraordinary. I consider him a spy both of the Spanish court and of Britain. He lives on a third floor, and his furniture is that of a satrap. He complains of his misery in the middle of all this luxury . . . I am used to very important people, and he is one of those I most want to see again, a Don Quixote with the difference that he is not mad . . . General Miranda has the sacred fire burning in his soul.' After several further meetings, Napoleon concluded less flatteringly that Miranda was a 'demagogue. He is not a republican.' Miranda himself observed that his guest 'had a surprised air at the luxury which I liked to surround myself with'. Another visitor spoke of Miranda's apartment as 'absolutely beautiful . . . unhappy with the way things are going here [politically], he consoled himself with art and science; he has the most exquisite little library and an apartment with a taste I have never seen bettered. I thought myself in Athens, in the house of Pericles.'

Miranda seems to have been sucked into an alliance between the moderates and the royalists as one of two possible leaders of a military coup. A prominent royalist remarked contemptuously that it would be astonishing if the King of France should be replaced 'by a Spanish Creole, the lieutenant of a provincial regiment of his Catholic Majesty's, and a total stranger in France where he has lived only a few years and where he has only been known since the Revolution.'

As the showdown between royalists and republicans approached, it is unclear whether Miranda sat on the fence or took part. When the government sent 1,500 troops to close down a radical 'electoral body' gathered in a French theatre at two in the morning on 4 October, revolutionary newspapers reported Miranda to have been in charge of the illicit proceedings. Vendimaria and Napoleon fought hard to crush the insurgents. Miranda went underground, was accused of being one of the principal conspirators, and then emerged to declare that he had taken no part in the parliament. Arrested and ordered out of the country, he secured a stay of execution of the order and continued to live in his usual style, but always followed by a gendarme. He managed to give him the slip one night and went into hiding, whence he bombarded the press with letters defending himself and attacking his enemies. He was eventually given official permission to stay, and continued to survive through the after-shocks of revolutionary France, always active in half-plots, always preaching his own brand of liberal anti-monarchism and anti-extremism.

In September 1797 another alleged monarchist conspiracy was suppressed by the government, and again Miranda was named as one of the plotters. Once more he went underground, once more the police were ordered to hold the 'Peruvian' general if he had not, as was widely believed, escaped to Athens. In fact, at last wholly disillusioned with the French revolution, fearing another long spell in prison and especially angry that France had formed an alliance with the Spain he so hated, he had resolved to go to Britain.

Passionately he kissed Delfina goodbye and, wearing a wig and green spectacles and passing as a minor businessman, took coach to Calais, then a Danish boat, arriving in Dover in January 1798. A customs inspection there found that his case had a false bottom, filled with papers. After discussion, documents were furnished for him to travel to London. Flatteringly, he was at once summoned to William Pitt's country home at Holwood in Kent, where he reported on the situation in France and, indefatigably, pressed for support for South American independence. After that first dizzying interview Miranda returned to London, where he set about organising his network of contacts and friends in South America and in Europe.

His experiences in France had changed him: there he had been taken seriously, performed spectacularly as a general, and twice nearly lost his life. The dilettante had become a man of action, of stature, of determination. To his surprise, he was informed that his old mentor Juan Manuel de Cagigal had been acquitted of the charges against him, and that he himself was no longer regarded with suspicion by the Spanish authorities – he could return to his homeland. Miranda immediately assumed this to be a trick to lure him back and arrest him, now that (as he saw it) he had become a tangible threat. He redoubled his efforts to persuade the British to mount an expedition to invade Venezuela, but Pitt continued to prevaricate.

Miranda then made contact with his North American friends in an effort to interest them in his plans. The British authorities refused him a passport to travel to the United States, perhaps fearing the Americans would reap the benefit if he was successful. Miranda, nearly fifty now and more than ever convinced of his ability to raise the standard of revolution in South America, was a middle-aged man in a hurry. He decided to return to France, even though he was under possible sentence of death there, believing Napoleon would prove an ally. He was given a passport at last, in 1800, and set off again across the Channel, hoping both to exact some of the money he insisted the French state owed him, and to persuade Bonaparte to support his project.

Fouché, the Minister of Public Order, a political enemy whose mistress was still Miranda's adored Delfina, heard with horror the news that he had set up in an apartment on the fashionable rue du Faubourg St-Honoré. Two days later the police arrived, but Miranda had already disappeared. He later re-emerged, to dine with Delfina. In March 1801 he was arrested with documents on him which contained prints of Louis XVI and Marie Antoinette – almost certainly planted – accused of being a British spy, gaoled in the Temple prison, and then expelled. By mid April he was back in London.

4

Three Boats and a Man

At fifty Miranda was a figure both sublime and ridiculous. The extraordinarily striking features showed signs of age, the intense and piercing eyes were duller, the curly hair beginning to grey and recede. He was a man without country, job, or title. His Russian partners had cut him off, the French had expelled him, and the Spaniards hoped to lure him into imprisonment. The British were civil, but did nothing to help; his last hope seemed to be the Americans, for whom he had in the past shown such contempt. Yet he was at last a figure of political and military stature.

He made his home now at 27 Grafton Way, a modestly comfortable mid Georgian town house in Bloomsbury which became a Mecca for South American exiles. The young Bernardo O'Higgins from Chile, the most distant part of the Spanish Empire, studied mathematics, politics and the humanities; the brilliant young Venezuelan Andrés Bello studied Greek; and other promising patriots were also taught there, men like Antonio Nariño from Santa Fé de Bogotá. Miranda's views at this time, and his state of mind, were expressed in a letter he wrote to O'Higgins:

> When you leave England do not for a moment forget that outside this country there is in all the world only one other nation where you can breathe a word of politics except to a true friend, and that country is the United States . . .
>
> In my long connection with South America you are the only Chilean I have dealt with, and so I know no more of that country than what its history tells me, which, though so little has been written, presents it in a favourable light. From the facts of that history I hope much from your countrymen, especially in the south where, if I am not mistaken, you intend to live. Their wars and their neighbours should make them skilled in arms, and the proximity of a free country should familiarise their spirits with the idea of liberty and independence.

Returning to the question of your future confidants, trust no man over the age of forty unless you can be sure he is fond of reading. The views of the others are too deep-rooted for any hope of change, and any remedy might be dangerous.

Youth is the age of ardent and generous sentiments. Among your contemporaries you will surely meet many who are eager to listen and are easily persuaded. But youth is also the age of indiscretion and rash actions; you should therefore be as wary of these failings in the young as of timidity and prejudice in the old.

It is also a mistake to think that a man with a tonsure or who has a comfortable canon's living must be an intolerant fanatic and a confirmed enemy of the rights of man. I know from experience that among them are to be found some of the most illustrious and liberal people in South America, but the difficulty is to find them.

The pride and fanaticism of Spaniards is incorrigible. They will despise you because you are American-born and hate you because you were educated in England. Keep away from them always . . .

Love your country! Cherish this feeling always; strengthen it in every possible way, for only if it endures and prospers will you act rightly.

Miranda's obsession now was to launch a formal expedition to Venezuela, which he believed was ripe for revolution. Pitt had been replaced in 1801 by the more modest Addington, whose chief adviser was Nicholas Vansittart, an enthusiast for Miranda's ideas. But in 1802 the Peace of Amiens between Britain, France, Spain and Holland once again dashed any hopes that Britain might help. It lasted only a year, however; now Miranda warned the British that the French might launch their own invasion of Latin America – as they had intended to do, with Miranda as commander, when he was serving France.

To Vansittart, to the first Lord of the Admiralty, Lord St Vincent, and to Admiral Home Popham he proposed a new blueprint for an independent South America: patriotic governments were to be set up, consisting of two executives in charge of justice and the police in each 'liberated' district, advised by eight counsellors. Eventually, when enough territory had been liberated, a federal government would be established headed by two 'Incas' – responsible citizens over forty – one based in the capital, one who would tour the vast outback. They would be responsible to the 'Colombian Council', which would be elected on a franchise without racial bias but with a property qualification. A capital for the new state, to be called Christopher Columbus, would be built on the isthmus of Panamá.

To this pipe-dream constitution was added an even more ambitious plan. An expeditionary force would be assembled on the island of Curaçao off the Venezuelan coast, then landed in Coro: it would march upon San Felipe, Valencia and the Aragua valley. Meanwhile the British fleet based in Grenada and Trinidad would bombard Cumana and La Guaira. After taking Tenerife and Cartagena, further west, an attack would be made on the Viceroyalty of Santa Fé de Bogotá (modern Colombia), while another fleet would sail to Peru and Chile to seize those countries. It was to be an invasion of the whole Spanish Empire, based, with good reason, on sea power, which the British could provide. He brandished long lists of prominent citizens who, he said, would join the 'patriot' forces.

The British said a contingent of their soldiers would be necessary to accompany the insurgents on their march to Caracas, which alarmed Miranda; he had no wish to replace one colonial empire with another. The sizeable sum of £20,000 would have to be spent on the project, and Miranda was to be granted a handsome allowance of £500 a year to maintain himself.

It soon emerged that Addington, ever-cautious, was turning against the project. Desperately Miranda came up with another, much more modest, proposal: in exchange for British military support and the use of six hundred slaves, plus transport ships, arms and ammunition, he promised four thousand head of cattle and a thousand mules in payment – to be obtained after a successful landing. He was working himself into a fever of expectation: reports came daily to the exiles that Venezuela was ripe for insurrection. He believed also that he had the support of some prominent backers in the City of London. The Americans seemed about to go to war with France, and Miranda hoped also for their support.

At the beginning of 1804, however, the British government dropped a bombshell: there would be no strike against Spain's colonies as long as the two countries were at peace, since Britain's interest now lay in securing Spain's support against Napoleonic France. Miranda's rage exploded in a letter he wrote Vansittart in March 1804; he threatened to leave the country – and, by implication, to join forces with Napoleon. By December fortune had begun to favour him once more, however: war was declared between Britain and Spain. He informed Pitt, now restored to office, that he was leaving for Trinidad. Pitt was cordial, but reminded him that he would have to submit himself to the authority of the British governor there, then in January 1805 advised him to be patient, 'because political affairs in Europe are not mature enough to begin the enterprise'. Miranda was incandescent with rage: for three years now his grand design had been forestalled by the British government. Now that the British were at war with Spain, what were they waiting for?

It seems clear that the Foreign Office regarded Miranda as a card with which to threaten the Spanish, but one to be played only *in extremis*. There was no official confidence that Miranda's invasion would succeed, and a botched assault would endanger Britain's colonial possessions in the Caribbean; moreover, Britain's local resources were limited. The priority had to be resisting the Spanish – and possibly the French as well – in European waters.

A new side to Miranda was revealed about this time. He made a trip to Scotland with a pretty English girl, Sarah Andrews; she returned pregnant, and was installed in Grafton Way as his 'housekeeper'. They lived as a couple and many thought them married, but Miranda insisted they were not; two children were born, Leandro and Francisco. The audacious lover had become a family man at last. As he prepared for his great adventure, Miranda drew up a will; his possessions in Venezuela were left to his family by Sarah, his voluminous papers to the city of Caracas, his possessions in London for the upkeep of his children, and his house to Sarah. His executors were a lifelong business friend, John Turnbull, and Nicholas Vansittart.

On 31 August 1805 Miranda set off, determined to secure American support for his expedition in place of Albion's perfidy. His ship, the *Polly*, reached New York in November after a rough voyage of sixty-seven days. Miranda's old friends Rufus King and Colonel Smith were on hand to meet him, and he was introduced to a businessman, Samuel Ogden, who expressed enthusiasm for the venture.

He travelled to Philadelphia and met Vice-President Aaron Burr, whom he considered 'Mephistophelean, detestable and infamous'. Burr's objective was to negotiate Mexico's detachment from the Spanish Empire, and he had no interest at all in the Venezuelan project; he was moreover in constant touch with the Spanish Ambassador, the Marqués de Casa Yrujo, who had Miranda carefully watched. Miranda was received cordially enough by the Secretary of State, James Madison, and on 1 December travelled to Washington to meet the President, Thomas Jefferson. America's policy was laid down at this meeting: he would be given no official help, but private individuals would be permitted to back him. Miranda took this as tacit American approval. He was invited to a lunch in his honour as a guest of the President a week later. Shortly after Christmas he returned to New York, where Ogden had prepared the *Leander* – named after Miranda's son – a brig of 190 tons, along with two smaller ships, the *Ambassador* and the *Hindustan.*

Miranda had received £2,000 from his London friends for the expedition, and had put up his six thousand books as surety. With this money about two hundred young men were recruited from the streets of New York with the offer of good pay and the prospect of making their fortunes in lands abundant with gold and silver. On a bright, breezy day, 2 February 1806, the little expedition set sail on choppy seas. Miranda was vividly described by one of the participants in the expedition:

He is about five feet ten inches high. His limbs are well proportioned; his whole frame is stout and active. His complexion is dark, florid and healthy. His eyes are hazel coloured, but not of the darkest hue. They are piercing, quick and intelligent, expressing more of the severe than the mild feelings. He has good teeth, which he takes much care to keep clean. His nose is large and handsome, rather of the English than Roman cast.

His chest is square and prominent. His hair is grey and he wears it tied long behind with powder. He has strong grey whiskers growing on the outer edges of his ears, as large as most Spaniards have on their cheeks. In the contour of his visage you plainly perceive an expression of pertinaciousness and suspicion. Upon the whole, without saying he is an elegant, we may pronounce him a handsome man.

He has a constant habit of picking his teeth. When sitting he is never perfectly still; his foot or hand must be moving to keep time with his mind which is always in exercise. He always sleeps a few moments after dinner, and then walks till bed time, which with him is about midnight. He is an eminent example of temperance. A scanty or bad meal is never regarded by him as a subject of complaint. He uses no ardent spirits; seldom any wine. Sweetened water is his common beverage.

He is a courtier and gentleman in his manners. Dignity and grace preside in his movements. Unless when angry, he has a great command of his feelings; and can assume what looks and tones he pleases. In general his demeanour is marked by hauteur and distance. When he is angry he loses discretion. He is impatient of contradiction. In discourse he is logical in the management of his thoughts. He appears conversant on all subjects. His iron memory prevents his ever being at a loss for names, dates and authorities . . . He appears the master of languages, of science and literature . . . Modern history and geography afford him abundant topics. He impresses an opinion of his comprehensive views, his inexhaustible fund of learning; his probity, his generosity and patriotism. After all, this man of renown, I fear, must be considered as having more learning than wisdom; more theoretical knowledge than practical talent; too sanguine and too opinionated to distinguish between the vigour of enterprise and the hardiness of infatuation.

It was foolhardy to suppose that one ill-armed brig and two defenceless troop transports carrying two hundred men from the streets of New York would make any impression on the military might of the Spanish Empire when Miranda's own calculations suggested that the Spanish deployed about 35,000 trained and heavily armed men in New Granada alone. Miranda had no grounds for his belief that the Empire was so rotten within that it would need only a small push for it to collapse. He had not set foot in Venezuela for three decades; his hopes were fed only by the feverish stories of exiles – he had no hard, first-hand evidence. Even more culpable were the Americans who gave the enterprise a tacit nod and a wink, and may indeed have subsidised the expedition.

The Spanish Ambassador had precise information about Miranda's exploit, and protested angrily to the American government. The French also complained. Diplomatic relations between the United States and Spain were almost severed. Jefferson denied helping the venture, while the American press, on the whole, supported what they saw as a romantic expedition. James Biggs, a participant, described the scene:

> One side of the quarterdeck is occupied by a printing press, at which several young men of that profession are busy in striking off the general's proclamations to the people of South America and setting the types for printing our commissions. The other side is taken up with two groups of Mars' youngest sons, employed with military books; some studying, some reading, and others looking at the pictures.
>
> His Excellency is at the head of one of these parties, philosophizing on various subjects, and passing from one to another with his peculiar volubility. At this moment he is painting the dangers of a military life . . . I am sorry to find he loves dearly to talk of himself; I believe that vanity and egotism, which are qualities destitute of any recommendation whatever, are generally associated with other traits that have no claim to approbation. I must confess too, that he appears not a little tinctured with pedantry . . .
>
> Next is seen the armourer's bench, with all his apparatus for repairing old muskets, pointless bayonets and rusty swords. This tinker has his

hands full, as our arms are none of the best, and seem to have been already condemned in some other service. Whoever purchased them for the expedition, was either no judge of arms, or he has been kinder to himself than his employer . . . A few feet from the place where I am now writing, is a noisy set of animals called volunteers, going through the manual exercise under the direction of a drill sergeant, who looks as bold as a lion, and roars nearly as loud.

After the cold of New York the Caribbean was blissful – until the little convoy spied a British warship, which called upon it to heave to. Its commander saw that Miranda's papers were in order, however, and he was allowed to continue. The two hundred recruits were divided into engineers, artillerymen, dragoons and infantrymen, given officers and uniforms, and taught, in the close confines of their ships, how to handle weapons. On 12 March Miranda hoisted his flag – white, red and yellow: in fact, an old Russian flag, some of whose white time had soiled to yellow. To the roll of drums the American hands learnt to chant, in Spanish, 'Death to tyranny! Long Live Liberty!' Reaching Jamaica, the ship they were supposed to rendezvous with failed to show up. A row broke out between Miranda and Captain Thomas Lewis. After a month's delay on the island the men re-embarked on the *Bacchus* and the *Bee*, their new transports.

At last the little fleet set sail, and on 27 April the Venezuelan coast came in view. Two Spanish coastguard vessels sighted them off Ocumare, near Puerto Cabello, where Miranda had intended to land. Several shots were fired at the *Leander*, to no effect; Miranda boldly refused to take shelter, but prudently gave the order to disengage. The two poorly-armed transports surrendered, before being sunk. The sixty Americans and Britons aboard were arrested and a few days later ten were hanged, their heads severed and their bodies quartered. The rest were imprisoned and tortured; some died, while others were eventually ransomed and repatriated. Demonstrations of loyalty to the Spanish King took place on the mainland, Miranda was burned in effigy, and a 30,000-peso reward was posted for his capture, dead or alive. The Spanish believed him to command an army of 1,500 men.

In a fit of hysteria immediately after the débâcle Miranda threatened to throw himself off the ship. Captain Lewis had him arrested and taken below for his own safety. The *Leander* spent the next six days dodging Spanish ships, and Miranda's supporters feared Lewis was plotting to hand him over to the Spaniards. But the first ship to encounter this sorry boatload of desperados was English, the *Lily*, and it seems she was just in time to forestall a mutiny by the furious young soldiers and sailors of fortune whose friends had been so cruelly abandoned to their fates. Her captain, Donald Campbell, was able to inform Miranda that William Pitt had died, to be succeeded by his first cousin, Lord Grenville. Miranda's old friend Vansittart had become Chancellor of the Exchequer in Grenville's Ministry of All the Talents.

The *Lily* escorted the *Leander* to Grenada, then to Barbados, where Miranda met Admiral Sir Alexander Cochrane (uncle of the future commander of the Chilean navy). It was a stroke of luck for Miranda, defeated and suicidal as he felt, to encounter a Briton reasonably sympathetic to his cause. The old charmer persuaded Cochrane that he needed help, and that the British would reap huge commercial rewards by overthrowing the Spanish. Cochrane promptly wrote to London demanding five thousand men, while Miranda wrote to Vansittart begging for help. Much heartened, Miranda's flotilla proceeded to Trinidad, escorted by two British vessels, the *Express* and the *Trimmer*, and there he was welcomed warmly by Governor Hislop. He was far from unknown: a disciple of his, Caro, had been sent out in 1797 to scout the island, and the Caribbean. The governor, Thomas Picton (later one of Wellington's most outstanding generals, killed at Waterloo), had immediately put Caro in gaol, although he did occasionally have him to dinner. Caro soon came to understand that Venezuela was far from promising as a breeding-ground for revolt: 'The Venezuelans have no concentrated plan. They do not work with foresight. They are better prepared to change their masters than to become free. They believe that it is the same to acclaim independence as to be independent, and that independence will be accomplished simply by rejecting the yoke of Spain and placing themselves under the protection of some other nation.'

Picton was unimpressed, either by Caro or by what he heard of his master Miranda. Yet Trinidad itself, so close to Venezuela, was under constant threat of attack from Spain, and Picton seems to have thought it useful to keep alive the threat of retaliation. A brutal but able administrator, described by Wellington as 'a rough foul-mouthed fellow as ever lived', he kept a constant watch on events in Venezuela from his offshore base; he had been widely condemned in 1799 for offering to help José de España, a Venezuelan plantation owner who staged an uprising with five thousand men, and then failing to do so. Eventually Picton had Caro expelled from the island. Manuel Gual, an old friend of Miranda's, lingered on there as his agent until he was mysteriously poisoned, possibly by Spanish agents, possibly by Picton himself.

Governor Hislop, a more moderate man who had succeeded the controversial Picton, lodged Miranda in Government House, grandly named but in poor repair. Under Cochrane's prompting Hislop became genuinely intrigued by the extraordinary personality of Miranda, offering him five hundred local recruits to help him in his cause. On 1 August the invasion was set for a second time, far more plausibly, with fifteen small boats and those five hundred volunteers. Colonel de Rouvray and two other British officers, Colonel Downie and Lieutenant Bedingfield, were seconded as Miranda's commanders.

They reached the Venezuelan coast at three in the morning. Pounding surf on the beach delayed the landing but they had the advantage of surprise, and fell upon a contingent of Spanish troops, spiking their guns. Soon they had been forced out of the port of Coro and Miranda's troops were pursuing them up the streets of the main town; by the time he arrived, the Spanish had abandoned it. Miranda proclaimed the territory liberated and had his flag hoisted: he had conquered his first part of Spanish America.

The garrison had fled to the neighbouring hills, but the invaders found few sympathisers in the town and no provisions, and one of Miranda's aides was shot beside him. After a few days he withdrew to the more easily defended port. He issued proclamations and appeals to Venezuelans to join him, set up a provisional government, and declared that all those between the ages of sixteen and forty-four must join up. His 'Colombian' citizens were instructed to wear French revolutionary-style cockades in their hats. But few rallied to his cause: so long away in Europe, he could not have known that Coro was a royalist stronghold. The British sent no more help – Grenville's government in fact disapproved of the pact between Miranda, Cochrane and Hislop. Meanwhile, the Spanish were assembling a formidable force of 1,500 opposite the town. Another four thousand were said to be approaching. Captain Johnson of the *Leander* and six of his sailors were taken prisoner in an ambush. The position began to look desperate.

On 13 August the decision was taken to re-embark, in a raging storm, and the expedition took refuge on the offshore island of Aruba, ready for yet another attempt. There they stayed, until Cochrane told them to return to Trinidad, threatening to withdraw all British aid unless they did so. On 22 September Miranda, perverse and indignant as ever, sailed instead for Grenada, his men hungry and mutinous, then on to Barbados. Only when British support was indeed withdrawn did Miranda finally abandon hope and return as instructed to Trinidad, where he learned of Home Popham's short-lived landing in Buenos Aires. He despatched de Rouvray to London to argue his case for continued aid, but in vain. His only real success was in alarming the Spanish, who denounced him as a thug and a traitor, claiming that he intended to free the slaves in Venezuela, and that he was a foreign agent. This had the reverse effect, immensely boosting the prestige on the mainland of this largely unknown revolutionary. The Spanish authorities in Venezuela sought reinforcements from Spain.

In fading hope Miranda lingered on in Trinidad for a year, hard-pressed by the creditors who had financed his expedition, which appeared to have been a complete failure. His faithful friend Turnbull told him the Grafton Way house might have to be sold, and Sarah and the children turned out. She wrote him pathetic letters:

'My dear Leander has been scribbling this hour to his papa, and telling him he will not tease brother so much, that he will learn his book, but he fonder of his hoop and his top, we have had a fair in the road, he has bought a gun, a sword and drum, so that you can hardly hear one another speak, these are his happiest days my dear Sir.'

Miranda wrote to the British requesting four thousand troops for an invasion; they refused. It was not until November 1807 that he gave in and set sail for Portsmouth, to argue his case personally.

Miranda returned to London in 1808 to a surprisingly warm welcome for a man who had presided over a fiasco and then a failure. The Foreign Secretary, George Canning, received him; Lord Castlereagh met him in Downing Street the following day. His adoring mistress and two small children had to compete for his attention.

Indeed, he was something of a popular hero. *The Times*, while faintly deriding his objectives, suggested that Miranda had won the confidence of the South American people and the British government, and the radical politician Edmund Burke published a pamphlet vigorously arguing that South America should be emancipated. Miranda had, it seems, turned his reverses into what today would be called a public relations triumph. In Venezuela he had been puffed up by the authorities into a far greater danger than he actually represented; in London his Quixotic tilting against the Spanish Empire had captured the popular imagination.

To Miranda's intense excitement, Sir Arthur Wellesley, the general to watch among Britain's senior military establishment, invited him to call. In preparation for this visit, he came up with his most ambitious plan yet for the liberation of Latin America: this time at least ten thousand men would be needed, based on the islands of Grenada and Tortuga, to land at La Guaira itself. The British fleet, meanwhile, would take the fortified harbour of Puerto Cabello. Miranda's fevered calculations called for 6,000 infantry, 2,000 cavalry, 2,000 black soldiers, 300 artillerymen, 30,000 muskets, 2,000 pairs of pistols, 50,000 lances and 4,000 swords. Wellesley was surprisingly sympathetic to these extravagant demands, and to Miranda it seemed that at last the British really had decided to back him. A military expedition began to be assembled at Cork, in southern Ireland. Miranda's only serious fear was that the British might be intending to replace the Spanish Empire with their own: the unauthorised invasion of Buenos Aires by Home Popham and Whitelocke's disastrous expedition suggested this. But the British had dissociated themselves from Popham's actions and court-martialled Whitelocke; now they only wanted access to South American markets, or so they said. At last Miranda's lifelong dream seemed on the verge of being realised. He could not know that Wellesley, having initially fallen in with the idea of a landing in Venezuela, had since concluded that Veracruz in Mexico would provide a better bridgehead for attacking the Spanish Empire – which was his objective.

But then developments in the Peninsula changed everything. The Tumult of Aranjuez and the events of the Dos de Mayo resulted in Wellesley's invasion army being diverted from the Spanish colonies to Portugal, to help the forces resisting Napoleon. The war between Britain and Spain was deemed at an end: now they were allies against the French. Miranda was to be offered a senior post in Wellesley's Peninsular expedition, by way of compensation.

Given the task of informing Miranda of this turn of events, Wellesley decided to take the irascible Venezuelan for a walk. As anticipated, Miranda exploded in fury and stood shouting at him in the street; Sir Arthur chose to distance himself, so as not to draw the attention of passers-by. Once Miranda's fury had subsided a little, he caught up with Wellesley. 'You go to Spain,' he told him. 'You will lose. No one will save

you. That is your problem. What maddens me is that no better opportunity ever presented itself.'

Miranda refused to serve in the expeditionary force; his enmity
towards Spain as regards her colonies was unalterable, and in any case
he did not want to fight his former French comrades-in-arms. That same
month he wrote to his old friend the Marqués del Toro: '. . . civil war
rages in Spain and there is no solution. France and Britain are fighting
over the peninsula which, probably, will be captured by the first. We
must avoid getting involved in this conflict and permitting the
Colombian continent [South America] to be sucked into the calamities
of war. Let us not take part in the quarrel, but take advantage of it to
free ourselves from foreigners.'

Miranda's supporter Edmund Burke fired off an angry broadside:

> . . . The expedition actually preparing to co-operate in the emancipation
> of South America has its destination changed; and is now to be sent with
> all speed to the shores of Old Spain. I should be exceedingly sorry to find
> we thus risked certain and important advantages, for what are extremely
> dubious gains; and that we hazarded by delay the present opportunity –
> rendered so peculiarly favourable, by the events taking place in Spain, for
> successfully offering emancipation to Spanish America – events which, it
> is not improbable, the people of that country will seize for asserting their
> independence themselves.

At first Miranda's and Burke's pessimism seemed justified. Wellesley
arrived in Portugal in July; Napoleon entered Madrid in triumph in
December. At the same time his envoys arrived in Caracas to take formal
control of the colony and supplant the governor, de Las Casas. In a
public café they were insulted openly and aggressively: Las Casas warned
that he could not guarantee their safety. When a mob rioted, the French
envoys slipped away just in time – on a British ship. Englishmen in
Caracas were cheered for opposing Napoleon. All Venezuelans – royalists and independence agitators alike – were united in their hatred of the
French. As Miranda had argued even in his disappointment at the can-
cellation of Wellesley's expedition, events were beginning to play into
the patriots' hands: Venezuelans, in casting off the hand of the French
government in Madrid, established the precedent of self-rule – even
though most remained loyal to the Spanish crown.

Britain's new ally deemed Miranda 'a revolutionary who has become
famous only for betraying his king and country', and demanded that he
be extradited to Spain. A junior Foreign Office official was despatched

to instruct Miranda to stop communicating with sympathisers in Venezuela, on pain of being expelled from Britain. Miranda ignored this and kept up a steady correspondence with his adherents, not just in Venezuela but elsewhere in South America. The visitors to Grafton Way became less frequent, certainly more circumspect. As the Spanish continued to press for his extradition, Castlereagh and Vansittart came to Miranda's defence. Back from Portugal, Wellesley had a long conversation with him and promised that once the war in Spain was over, liberation of the colonies would be next – yet another British promise to be cruelly broken.

Miranda launched *The Colombian*, a newsletter filled with strong attacks on the French, in order to ingratiate himself with the British. Four editions were produced, which circulated from hand to hand in Latin America, before the British judged it expedient to suspend the publication. Hipolito José da Costa, a prominent Brazilian intellectual, arrived in Grafton Way proclaiming Miranda the 'Washington of the Latin American continent'. In mid 1809 he was invited to dine with Lady Hester Stanhope, William Pitt's niece. A highly intelligent lady later notorious for her travels and eccentricities, she enchanted the jaded old womaniser: 'I was highly impressed by her conversation, good judgement, charm and interesting personality. She is one of the most delicious women I have known in my life.' They became close friends.

In Caracas a provisional government had been set up, opposed to the French-backed government in Madrid but swearing allegiance to the Spanish cause. A delegation they despatched to London to seek British support stayed first at a hotel, then spent several weeks on camp beds in a back room at 27 Grafton Way. Andrés Bello was an old habitué, now a poet, who developed into a brilliant negotiator; Luis Lopez Mendes was already a veteran of diplomacy, and became Venezuela's ambassador in London after Miranda's departure. But it was at Martin's Hotel, when they first arrived in July 1810, that the initial meeting took place between Fernando de Miranda, at fifty-nine a statuesque, fastidious, civilised man of the world with a sad smile on his ageing voluptuary's face, and the nominal head of the delegation, a small, callow, twenty-seven-year-old provincial from Caracas – his ardent admirer, Simón Bolívar.

5

Young Bolívar

Simón Bolívar's life to date had not been such as to excite any profound admiration. On the surface he had led the easy, dissolute existence of a rich, spoilt young man; only those who knew him well could perceive the intellect, determination and romantic impulses that lay beneath. The story of his first twenty-seven years seems more like a languid eighteenth-century romantic novel than the stuff of history books.

Simón Bolívar was born in 1783 into a wealthy and distinguished Venezuelan family which traced its roots to the mountainous, windswept region of Vizcaya (Biscay) in northern Spain. An earlier Simón migrated in 1589 to Venezuela, where the family was responsible for fortifying the port of La Guaira, founding several towns and helping to secure the wild interior. A forebear of Bolívar is said to have had a relationship with a black slave, thus accounting for his slightly negroid appearance. Juan Bolívar, Simón's grandfather, had paid the not inconsiderable sum of 22,000 golden dubloons to Philip V to secure the title of Marqués de San Luis; however, the Spanish genealogists sent to ascertain the purity of the Bolívar family line discovered a female antecedent of Indian blood. The title was denied Juan, a snub which incensed a family proud of its Spanish origins. Later, of course, it was remarkably convenient for the Liberator to be able to claim that he was of mixed white, Indian and black extraction – the three racial components of Latin America.

Juan's son, Juan Vicente, was brought up a rich and idle young man leading an agreeable life in the pleasant city of Caracas, set three thousand feet above sea level some forty miles inland from the Caribbean coastline in a deep, fertile valley criss-crossed by rivers, between two mountain ranges. Its forty thousand inhabitants enjoyed a pleasant climate, similar to Lisbon's but more equable, with a short rainy season and cool nights. Juan Vicente lived in a large family mansion in Plaza San Jacinto in the centre of this city of long, narrow streets arranged on a classical grid pattern. The houses were of mud or stone, only one or two storeys high because of the danger of earthquakes in the central highlands. Something of a social lion, Juan was a notorious womaniser, denounced by two sisters, Margarita and Maria Jacinta, as an 'infernal wolf' who had implored them to 'make sin with him', and nearly prosecuted for rape. Not until he was forty-six did Juan Vicente marry the beautiful fifteen-year-old Concepción Palacios y Blanco, daughter of another prominent Caracas family.

Like her famous son, Concepción was dark, vivacious, and passionate, full of energy and ambition. But she could also be moody and dissatisfied. Hard-headed and practical, she would complain: 'It makes one grieve to pay three hundred pesos for slaves which you cannot use for more than eight years, and the black women could barely bring forth many young.' Doña Concepción had four children: a boy, then two girls and, last, Simón. By the time he arrived she was more temperamental than ever and, still very young, bored by her husband's easygoing indolence. She had also begun to suffer from a chest infection – probably tuberculosis – of which she eventually died. Her busy social life (and, it was rumoured, her many lovers of her own age) left her little time for the afterthought in the family. It was in any case common for children of the wealthy to be raised apart from their parents, and the infant Simón was cared for from the beginning by two devoted nurses: Iñes, from a respectable Spanish family, and a black slave, Hipolita. Both, but particularly the latter, were devoted to their lively charge.

Denied his mother's love as a baby, Simón later grew bitterly resentful towards her memory. He loved Iñes, however, and worshipped Hipolita, who sought to meet his every wish. As a slave, she considered it her duty to serve him almost as soon as he could issue commands: Simón grew up spoilt, bossy and capricious. He was also hyper-active, accustomed to getting his own way and – because life was so pleasant – imbued with a dauntless optimism that was to stand him in good stead through the trials and reverses of his later life. After a last stillborn child and the death of her dissipated husband, Doña Concepción could stand no more of what little she saw of her assertive youngest child, and gave him over, aged only three, to the care of the family lawyer, Miguel José Sanz.

This misanthropic pedant determined from the first to improve his charge through a regime of discipline and austerity. It was the young Simón who won, however. At formal luncheons he would interrupt the grownups. On one occasion he was told furiously by Sanz to 'keep quiet and keep your mouth shut'; when the boy was subsequently observed not to be eating, Sanz asked him sharply why. 'Because you told me to keep my mouth shut,' retorted the four-year-old. Within eighteen months Sanz had had enough, and despatched Simón back to the care of his mother. The lovely widow, still only in her twenties but increasingly highly-strung and frail, sent him to be educated by a succession of tough-minded tutors, including the brilliant young Andrés Bello. Each in turn despaired, finding him one of the most unpleasant small boys they had ever dealt with – boastful, imperious, irrepressible, demanding, and fiercely insolent. Simón's mother had by now handed control of the family's affairs to an elderly uncle, Feliciano Palacios, who advised her to give the task of educating the child to a remarkable clerk of his, Simón Rodriguez.

Externally sour and severe, Rodriguez was a most unusual pedagogue for his time, and of an eccentricity bordering on madness. He was a man who had in effect been 'born again'. His bitter and antisocial intellectualism, product of a miserable childhood, had alighted during a trip to France on Rousseau's *Émile*. To Rodriguez the book perfectly explained how upbringing, education and political indoctrination were responsible for all the miseries he had suffered. His emotions thus joyously released, he determined to fight the system that had caused them. Understandably, his views were anathema in stuffy, conventional Caracas. So he accepted with alacrity the task of looking after this troublesome boy. Here was a chance to prove his theories: Simón was to be his Émile.

Formally appointed Simón's tutor on the death of Doña Concepción in 1792, Rodriguez immediately took him to the family's remote and sprawling hacienda at San Mateo – to the relief of his guardian Palacios. There Rodriguez could experiment with his new educational ideas. Following a famous passage of Rousseau's, he believed in giving free vent to the boy's natural inclinations: 'Instead of laying down the law, let him obey the lessons of experience or impotence. Do not give him what he asks, but what he needs. When he commands, don't obey, and when others command him, don't let him obey. Accept his freedom of action as much as your own.' He supplemented this unusually liberal method of raising a child with a regime of intense physical exercise, keeping the boy close to nature. Rodriguez believed, he said, that one should teach one's child 'to protect himself, once a man, to stand the blows of fate, to adapt himself to wealth or poverty, to support life, if necessary, in the bitter cold of Iceland or the burning rock of Malta.' Simón would be woken early and taken for long walks or rides, subsisting on Spartan rations, while Rodriguez taught him how to look after himself in the wild and overcome the dangers he faced there, how to survive and how to keep clean. Simón became an excellent swimmer and horseman. Besides all this, Rodriguez inculcated his own liberal ideas about freedom and the rights of man, and recounted the lives of great men to his eager young listener.

This remarkable mixture of cowboy existence and philosophical indoctrination was a joy to the energetic, rebellious schoolboy, and he delighted in his new life in the wilds as much as he respected his unconventional tutor. Those five years between the ages of nine and fourteen were the formative ones of Bolívar's life.

In 1795 the outside world impinged on this idyllic existence. A revolt against Spanish rule took place in the valley of Curimagua, led by one José Chirinos, who was condemned to be dragged to the gallows and hung, after which his body was beheaded and quartered, and the parts – in iron cages, to keep out the vultures – exhibited at strategic points. Simón, aged twelve, was taken to Caracas to watch the execution. Rodriguez himself was implicated in the rising, and in 1797 he was forced to leave Venezuela. Simón was taken back to Caracas and entrusted again to the care of his uncles. Not conventionally disciplined, intelligent, proud and strong, the boy argued furiously with his guardians, who decided he was quite beyond their powers of control. The solution adopted was to instil some military discipline: he was sent as a cadet to the élite Whites of Aragua corps, which had been founded by his grandfather. There the physical prowess he had acquired in the countryside stood him in good stead, and he quickly shone as a leader of men and a capable and charismatic, if disrespectful and impertinent, young commander. Appointed sub-lieutenant after a year, he returned to Caracas, full of himself and as insufferable as ever, although with a latent charm – his smile was said to light up his face. Whether because of that smile, or his wealthy background, he was warmly received by one of the noted beauties of the capital's *jeunesse dorée*, a girl from the prominent Aristeguieta family. To the surprise of those who considered him all bad, he fell wildly in love. But she quickly tired of his vanity and persistence and, humiliated in his puppy-love, Simón became more disruptive than ever.

His exasperated uncles then hit on the idea of sending him to Madrid, to their cousin, Esteban Palacios – with a warning: 'It is necessary to curtail him . . . firstly because otherwise he will learn to spend money without rules or economy, and second because he is not as clever as he thinks . . . You must talk to him firmly or put him into a college if he does not behave with that judgement and application he should.' His uncles feared he had it in him to lose the substantial fortune he was now heir to.

The first great adventure of Bolívar's life was about to begin. Not sixteen yet, on 18 January 1799 he boarded the *San Ildefonso*, bound for another continent, and relations he had never met. An orphan, the despair of his guardians, adored and spoilt by his surrogate parents – his nurses, one of his sisters, and his now exiled tutor, Simón Rodriguez – even his optimistic spirit may have faltered in face of the heaving emptiness of the sea and the challenge of the wide world before him. Yet he was not entirely alone: the captain of the *San Ildefonso*, José Borja, an old family friend of the Bolívars, dined with him, and talked to him; he formed a favourable opinion of the boy's intelligence and good manners, and became convinced that he had a notable future ahead of him. For his part Simón, on the unfamiliar territory of a ship over which he had no control, for once suppressed his cockiness and behaved himself.

The ship's course was roundabout. For protection against attack from British ships based near Havana it made for Veracruz in what is now Mexico, to join a convoy of Spanish warships. When the ship docked at Veracruz three weeks later, Bolívar obtained permission from Borja to travel to Mexico City, the capital of the Viceroyalty of New Spain. During the long carriage journey from the coast up to the high plateau he was awed by the deserts and the snowcapped volcanoes, so very different from the lush green sierras of his own country. In Mexico City he stayed with another family friend, Don Aguirre, a counsellor to the Viceroy; one account has it that he met the Viceroy, expressed his liberal views, and was listened to indulgently. After a week of sight-seeing he made the long journey back to his ship.

The *San Ildefonso* docked in the Spanish port of Santoña on 5 May, and Simón set off for his family's original domain of Bolívar, near Bilbao, from which his forebears had set forth some two hundred years earlier. There he was dismayed to find, instead of the ruins of the great fortress of family legend, a miserable hamlet of twenty houses and a half-ruined farmhouse beside which, Cervantes-style, a windmill creaked plaintively. As the rain poured down on this desolate scene, the romantic in him felt betrayed. He returned to an uncomfortable inn for the night before setting off for Madrid, which he reached towards the end of June 1799.

Simón's new guardian, Esteban Palacios, occupied a position close to the very heart of the Spanish court. His close friend and protector was Manuel Mallo, the current chief adviser and lover of the Queen, Maria Luisa de Parma, who dominated her ineffectual and capricious husband, King Charles IV. Mallo, himself American-born, was a cheerful, good-looking man who, on his arrival in Madrid, had quickly captivated the ageing Queen, described by the Russian Ambassador in Madrid as 'completely worn out' by illness, excess and hereditary disease. 'The yellow tint of her hair and her loss of teeth were mortal blows for her beauty,' he wrote. She was also growing increasingly fat; but as her attractions diminished, it seemed, her lusts increased, encompassing Mallo, her guardsmen, and the clever and powerful young chief minister, Manuel Godoy. Goya perfectly captured this lascivious woman's fading charms, and the vapidity of her husband.

Godoy owed his present eminence to the Queen's favour but was apparently content, although he distrusted and disliked him, that her desires should be transferred to Mallo. This proved to be a mistake. The Queen developed an insatiable obsession with him, showered him with honours, and gave him a large house close to the royal palace on the edge of the city. Detested by the haughty Spanish courtiers, Mallo surrounded himself with fellow South American *arrivistes*, among them Palacios, whom he put up in his newly-acquired mansion. Palacios was appointed Minister of the Court of the National Treasury, a sinecure which provided him with a comfortable living. Into this privileged household entered Simón Bolívar, aged sixteen. In later life he told a story of how, playing with the heir to the throne, Ferdinand, Prince of the Asturias, he lifted the cap off the boy's head with his lance, to the prince's fury and the Queen's amusement. Daniel O'Leary, usually reliable, claims Bolívar later said: 'How was the prince to know then that I was also to strike from his head the fairest jewel of his crown with my sword?' There is no way of knowing whether this story of a mock duel between the boy who became the worst and most autocratic of Spain's kings and the man who stripped him of an empire is true, or merely a piece of wishful symbolism on Bolívar's part.

Mallo's house was the scene of wild parties, which began with heavy drinking and ended in full-blown sexual orgies, in many of which the Queen participated. It is not known whether Simón was invited to take part, but he would surely have been aware of them. He may have been introduced by Mallo into court circles, but his somewhat priggish moral standards and naïve streak of romanticism where women were concerned – soon to change – combined with his disgust at the spectacle of his often unattractive elders over-indulging themselves to inspire in him a profound contempt for the Empire they represented, that had repeatedly snubbed Spanish Americans generally and his own family in particular.

Always short of money, he fell deep into debt as British harassment of Spanish shipping across the Atlantic reduced the number of yearly convoys to just two. One of his uncles, Pedro, arriving from Caracas, was horrified by the atmosphere of decadence surrounding the boy. Simón was moved out of Mallo's house, and set up in a modest establishment in central Madrid. At seventeen, now living by himself, he came under the influence of a much more respectable figure at court. The Marqués de Ustáriz was a wealthy nobleman from Caracas, at the centre of a literary circle and, above all, a political liberal, at a time when Spain was mired in reactionary decadence and decline. He became a kind of director of studies for Simón, sending him to eminent professors to be tutored in philosophy, history, literature and mathematics, and lending him volumes from his extensive library. Simón was no mere bookworm: he also enjoyed sightseeing around the streets of Madrid, and visiting his friends and relations. But at the Marqués's seminars he heard the French Revolution eagerly defended, and other subversive ideas aired. Slowly his political views began to take shape.

One day Simón was introduced to a tall, palely delicate girl with deep, dark, sad eyes and a complexion of Madonna-like purity. Gentle and almost childishly enthusiastic by nature, she was shy, withdrawn and, to the eager young man two years her junior, irresistibly beautiful. Maria Teresa Rodriguez y Alaiza, whose mother had died in her infancy, had been brought up by her doting father, mostly in a large country villa, in a sheltered, even cloistered existence.

Bolívar fell head over heels in love with her at first sight, and within a few days went to her father, Don Bernardo, to ask her hand in marriage. Bolívar was far too young, and to such a careful parent his impulsiveness and speed were offensive. Within days, ostensibly to flee the heat of a Madrid summer, Don Bernardo and his daughter were on their way to the cooler air of Bilbao in the north.

Distraught, Bolívar abandoned his bachelor apartment for Mallo's house – only to find that the fortunes of its inhabitants had dipped alarmingly. The Queen had tired of her Spanish-American lover and, as his influence waned, Mallo had unwisely sought to retain his hold on her by threatening to publish their love letters. Maria Luisa appealed to Godoy, who promptly ordered the arrest of Mallo and his friends. The former favourite escaped into hiding, but Esteban Palacios was among those seized. Then one morning Bolívar, out riding, was confronted at Madrid's Toledo gate by a company of palace guards, who ordered him to stop. His horse reared up at them, and he drew his sword, shouting that common soldiers had no right to detain him. The officer of the guard informed him he was being arrested for violating a regulation prohibiting the wearing of jewellery in public – there were diamonds in his rings. In reality, it was suspected that he was being used to smuggle out Mallo's love letters from the Queen. Bolívar angrily threatened the soldiers with his sword, they gave way, and he rode off to Ustáriz, who told him he must immediately leave Madrid until the hue and cry against Mallo's friends had died down. Ustáriz further suggested that he should join Maria Teresa and her father in Bilbao – a course of action with such instant appeal that Bolívar fled northwards the next day. Don Bernardo's reaction to Bolívar's arrival is not recorded; but he quickly decided that he and his daughter must return urgently to the capital.

The lovesick young man lingered briefly in Bilbao before suddenly bolting across the border to France, perhaps warned of an intention to arrest him, or perhaps because he hoped to try to strike a deal with the Spanish authorities to secure the release of his cousin Esteban Palacios. Whatever the reason, the next eight months, which Bolívar spent in France, are shrouded in obscurity; but he made his way to Paris, where he fell under Napoleon's spell.

To his astonishment, in April 1802 Bolívar was given permission to return to Spain. With the haste of a man desperately in love he rushed to Madrid, where at last he secured Don Bernardo's consent to his daughter's marriage. On 26 May, in the church of San Sebastián, Bolívar, aged almost nineteen, was married to Maria Teresa, aged twenty-one. The newlyweds left immediately on a necessarily protracted maritime honeymoon, sailing across the Atlantic. The change must have been daunting for Maria Teresa, accustomed as she was to heavy Spanish interiors rather than bracing sea air.

Arriving in Caracas, Bolívar immediately took his beautiful bride off to his hacienda at San Mateo, where Maria Teresa busied herself ordering the household while he supervised the estate. It seemed the young hot-head, only a couple of years from coming of age and inheriting his substantial fortune, was set for a life of idyllic rural tranquillity. It was not to be: two months later, Maria Teresa contracted a fever, weakened rapidly, and on 22 January, just eight months after their marriage, she died. Bolívar, always highly strung, went half-mad with grief: 'I looked upon my wife as an emanation of the Divine Being who gave her life. Heaven believed that she belonged there and tore her from me because she was not created for this earth.'

It was to prove another formative event in his life. For him, Maria Teresa represented an ideal of beauty, perfection and love, which their two years' acquaintance had done nothing to dispel. Most passionate love eventually turns to mere fondness, or to boredom. Bolívar had had no time to grow accustomed to Maria Teresa; for him, the ideal never died. He was to make love to many women, but to none with the romantic intensity he had felt for Maria Teresa. However ardent, his later passions were to him mere affairs by comparison, even if some went deeper than he admitted. Maria Teresa was the love of his life, never dimmed by familiarity.

She had, furthermore, forever transformed him. His cynically insolent, know-all attitude was exposed as a façade: he was an idealist, a romantic, a man bent on achieving the impossible. In place of his search for perfect love – now unachievable, because he had found it, and lost it to Death – came the search for another impossibility: the liberation of a continent, the freeing of a whole people. As Bolívar was later to confide to Peru de Lacroix, 'See how things are: if I hadn't been widowed, perhaps my life would have been different. I would not be General Bolívar, not the Liberator, although I doubt my genius was fitted to be Mayor of San Mateo. The death of my wife placed me on the path of politics very early; it made me follow thereafter the carriage of Mars rather than the arrow of Cupid.'

More immediately, the grief-stricken young widower took ship again for Spain, to return to Don Bernardo some of Maria Teresa's personal belongings. He did not linger long in Madrid, with its painful personal memories. Instead, on the verge of attaining his majority and the enjoyment of a more than comfortable income, he set off for Paris, where he took a house in the rue Vivienne. Surrounded by other exiles from South America, he indulged in a series of frenzied affairs and in reckless gambling at the card tables. His over-assertive but fragile self-confidence had been dealt a piercing blow by Maria Teresa's death, and as he sought to numb the pain in libertine excess, he no longer cared how he behaved. Serviez, one of Bolívar's aides, later recalled that 'With an extreme passion for pleasure, and in particular sensual pleasure, it was truly exciting to hear the Liberator name all the beautiful girls he had known in France, with a precise recollection that does honour to his powers of memory.'

Bolívar spent 150,000 francs in the course of a visit to London, then returned to Paris where he began to frequent the celebrated salon of Fanny de Villars. This passionate, intelligent and attractive woman personified the best reforming spirit of the French Revolution, the belief that in place of the stuffiness of conventional society, people should be free to live and love as they chose. Her salon was the height of fashion among artists, intellectuals and professional people alike, who went there to enjoy affairs with the pretty girls who adorned it. The financial arrangements involved are not clear, but it may have been little more than an upper-class brothel. Fanny was of mixed race, exotic, graceful and stylish. Her husband, in his fifties, was a distinguished botanist who turned a blind eye to her activities.

Bolívar, jaded and sated with ordinary women, was transfixed by this one, older and much more experienced; he lavished money and attention upon her and himself dressed with ludicrous extravagance, behaving almost like a man possessed. He may even have had his only child by her. He once remarked that 'people should not think me sterile, for I have proof to the contrary', and Fanny wrote to him of his 'godson, Simóncito – I hope he is the only one you have in Europe'. Years later one of her other children described how Bolívar, walking in Fanny's garden, would 'destroy everything he found; the branches of trees, vines, flowers, fruits etc. My father, who cultivated his garden with such pride, would enter furiously on seeing him commit such follies. "Pick all the flowers and fruits you wish," he would say, "but by God don't pull out the plants for the sole pleasure of destroying them."'

It was in Fanny's salon that Bolívar encountered Baron von Humboldt, the famous explorer and scientist, recently returned from his travels. Humboldt had visited Venezuela, tracked the Orinoco river to its source, and then travelled across the Andes to Peru. He had voyaged up the Pacific coast in the cold Antarctic current which was later to bear his name, then went to Mexico, where he wrote his *Political Essay on the Kingdom of New Spain*, in which he predicted that Mexico would become a greater power than the United States – and, with rather more insight, that it was ripe for colonial revolt.

Bolívar joined the admiring throng around the baron and, when his conversation touched on the sad fate of Spanish America, condemned to poverty and obscurity under the reactionary rule of Spain, exclaimed that 'the destiny of the New World would be glittering if its people were freed of the yoke that oppresses them'. The baron contemptuously remarked that 'although conditions in South America are favourable to such an enterprise, it lacks men capable of carrying it out' – in the circumstances, one of history's more abject failures of insight. Humboldt, himself brilliant and conceited, disliked the verbose and arrogant young man but was honest enough not to try to adjust the record later, admitting frankly that he had never believed Bolívar 'fitted to be the head of the American crusade', so that '[h]is brilliant career shortly after we met astonished me.'

It seems likely that the young man's sense of destiny and lust for glory were crystallised at just this time by the example of Napoleon, now at the zenith of his power, crowning himself Emperor in Notre Dame amid unparalleled pomp and popular acclaim. Later, however, Bolívar was careful to criticise the Emperor, lest his enemies should wrongly assume that he sought a domination over South America similar to Napoleon's over Europe. He observed, too, that 'the crown that Napoleon put on his head I considered a miserable and gothic affectation. What was great was the universal acclamation and interest that his person aroused.'

According to Peru de Lacroix, Bolívar explained much later that if he had praised Napoleon,

> My enemies . . . would have accused me of wanting to set up a nobility and a military state similar to Napoleon's in power, prerogatives and honours. Do not doubt but that all this would have occurred had I shown myself, as I am, a keen admirer of the French hero; had I been heard praising his policy, speaking enthusiastically of his victories, commending him as the first captain of the world, as a statesman, as a philosopher and as a man of science. These are my opinions on Napoleon, but I have taken the utmost care to hide them. The St Helena Diary, the campaigns of Napoleon and everything connected with him are for me the most agree-

able reading and the most profitable; there it is that the arts of war, of politics and of government should be studied.

In fact, while Bolívar shared the Emperor's vanity and hunger for power, he never abandoned the idealised love of liberty that first fired his ambition. He could be accused of capriciousness and arbitrariness, and of failing in practice to promote liberty; but he was never for long corrupted by power into a megalomaniac or a monster, or into waging unnecessary war, as Napoleon was.

Indolent, spendthrift and sexually exhausted, on the verge of a breakdown after his period of excess, Bolívar, as he approached his twenty-first birthday, was now also a man in search of a cause worthy of what he was convinced was his genius. He needed no prompting, when he heard that his old tutor Simón Rodriguez was in Vienna, to hasten there. He found him far from welcoming. That moody, penetrating intellectual, disappointed in his star pupil, told him that he was wasting his life; now obsessed by Rousseau's *Social Contract*, he at first had no sympathy to spare for the sense of emptiness complained of by Bolívar.

Rodriguez told Bolívar how much he would inherit on his twenty-first birthday – 4,000,000 francs – and then chastised him bitterly, before abruptly suggesting that they set off on a walking tour of Italy to restore the young man's physical and mental stability. Early in 1805 this odd couple set out; it is not recorded for how much of their journey they actually walked.

Bolívar was keen to reach Milan as soon as possible, to witness the coronation of his hero Napoleon as King of Italy. He later told Peru de Lacroix of a great march-past he saw near Castiglione. As de Lacroix recounted it, 'The throne of the Emperor was set on a little hill in the midst of the vast plain; while the army marched in columns past Napoleon, who was seated on his throne, [Bolívar] and a friend [Rodriguez] accompanying him had positioned themselves near the hill, in order to see the Emperor better: he looked at them several times through a small telescope and [Rodriguez] said, "Perhaps Napoleon, who is watching us, is going to suspect we are spies." This observation made them cautious and they decided to withdraw.' Bolívar himself remarked upon

[. . . the] huge and glistening general staff Napoleon had and how simple was his own clothing. All of his officers were covered with gold and rich linings, and he only wore his trousers, a hat with decorations and a tunic without any medals. I like this, and in these countries [America] I assure you I would have adopted this usage myself if I had not been frightened that they would say I had done so to imitate Napoleon, and they would have added that it was my intention to imitate him in all things.

When they got to Rome there was enacted a scene that was surely the height of romantic absurdity – but for the course of Bolívar's later life. As the sun set around the domes of Rome, according to Rodriguez, Bolívar fell to his knees on the Aventine, 'his eyes wet, his breath heaving, his face red, and with an almost fevered manner he told me: "I swear that I will not give rest to my arm nor my sword until the day when we have broken the chains of Spanish power which oppress us."'

After visiting Naples the two returned to Paris, where Bolívar, now convinced of his destiny, rather neglected Fanny, who retaliated by paying more attention to her other lovers. Bolívar seemed unconcerned, and told her of his intention of returning to America. Fanny, now besotted by him, became hysterical at the prospect, but could not persuade him to change his mind.

When Bolívar eventually got back to Venezuela in 1808, he found that his country, like most of Spanish America, was in a state of ferment, and that his own reputation as a headstrong, feckless, irresponsible ladies' man had preceded him. Few there were who took him seriously; fewer still who much liked him; only his wealth and family made him at all impressive, for he had squandered the respect his passion and grief for Maria Teresa had briefly inspired. But this apparently dissipated, debauched loud-mouth nursed within himself a Rousseauesque liberalism, a deep loathing for the corruption and degeneracy he had witnessed in Spain, and a sense of destiny inspired by gazing awestruck at Napoleon. What is more, his return coincided with a series of political earthquakes that were to shatter the stuffy colonial order of Spanish America.

6

The First Republic

The Venezuela Bolívar had been born into was a quintessential plantation society. Rich in natural resources, it sustained three classes of
people: at its pinnacle, a Spanish colonial overclass; beneath them, a
criollo class of wealthy landowners and traders, locally born and often
of mixed blood; and the ordinary people, many of mixed blood, many
of pure Indian descent, but the majority black, some still slaves. The
economy consisted in the growing or mining of primary products for
the Spanish market. It was a recipe for stagnation and exploitation, later
summed up by Bolívar in a powerful passage:

> The Americans, in the Spanish system now in place, perhaps more so than
> ever before, have no other place in society than that of simple consumers;
> even in this they are burdened with shocking restrictions, such as a ban
> on the cultivation of European fruit, with control of these products
> monopolised by the king, a prohibition on factories which not even the
> peninsula possesses, exclusive commercial privileges even over basic
> needs, and customs bans between American provinces so that they cannot
> trade, understand each other or negotiate. In the end, do you know what
> our destiny is? Fields in which to cultivate maize, grain, coffee, cane,
> cocoa and cotton; empty plains to create crops; deserts to capture fierce
> beasts; the depths of the earth to excavate gold which never satisfies this
> greedy nation [Spain]. As I have just explained we were abstracted and,
> let us be honest, absent from the universe as far as the government and
> administration of the state were concerned.

He was not exaggerating. Spain's colonial policy was to suck her
Empire dry and thereby continue to live in the style to which she had
become accustomed. The Spanish prided themselves on being warriors
and administrators; production and commerce were beneath them;
instead, for three centuries they had enjoyed the fruits of the colonies

without the inconvenience of working for them. Moreover, they paid low prices for imperial primary products. As other European nations forged ahead with new agricultural, commercial and industrial developments, Spain merely marked time, corrupted by this cheap inflow, becoming a backward and autarchic parasitic state, acting as a money pump for the rest of Europe, whose own production she stimulated and whose goods she bought. Spain's own agricultural production all but collapsed under the impact of low-priced imports from across the Atlantic. This eventually took its toll: Spain's trade with Europe plunged into the red and she was compelled to exact still more gold and primary produce from her colonies, at still lower prices, to redress the balance. By the late eighteenth century the colonies were groaning under the impact of low prices, high taxation, and the prohibition of trade with countries other than Spain. Four events had the cumulative effect of helping to turn these resentments into open revolt.

The first stimulus was the American Revolution, which gave the criollos and the other more prosperous native-born Americans much food for thought. Thirteen years later, the French Revolution reverberated across the world and it was the turn of the criollo landowners and merchants, like their Spanish overlords, to shudder. Liberty, equality and fraternity could mean but one thing in the colonies: emancipation of the huge Indian, black and mixed-blood underclass. The 'mantuans', or 'veiled ones' – because their women were privileged to wear veils – trembled at the prospect of 'French law', which soon enough provoked a revolution in nearby Haiti, inciting the 'pardo' majority, the 'dumb ones', to revolt. The effect of this should have been to drive the privileged American-born classes to cleave more closely to the traditional Spanish social order. Instead, a third blow was delivered to the colonial hierarchy, by the Spanish Crown itself, when Godoy chose to accommodate the liberalism sweeping Europe in the royal Decree of Aranjuez of 10 February 1794, which gave subordinate races the right to acquire the title 'Don', hitherto a criollo or mantuan privilege. This gesture towards racial equality horrified the criollos. In April 1796 the Caracas city council warned gravely of the threat from the local population, 'in spite of that class being inferior by order of the Author of Nature'. In August 1801 a new royal decree was issued, another slap in the face for the criollos: coloured people were permitted to buy grants of nobility. Small wonder that the mutterings in the coffee houses, tea-parlours, whorehouses and drinking dens of Spanish America were growing ever louder.

All that was needed for this to ignite into open revolt was a final spark, and it was provided by Napoleon's deposition of the Spanish monarchy in 1808. In the blink of an eye, it became patriotic and pro-Spanish to reject the dictates of the new masters in Madrid, a city now under enemy occupation. On 15 January 1809 an emissary from the Spanish Council of the Indies – the body that administered the colonies on Spain's behalf, and now reflected the dictates of the French – arrived in Caracas. This official pompously demanded recognition of Joseph Bonaparte as King of Spain, and of Prince Murat as Lieutenant-General of the kingdom.

The sleepy city in its mountain bowl erupted: mobs swearing allegiance to Ferdinand VII of Spain roamed the streets. Priests denounced Napoleon's 'heretical proclamations'. American-born leaders, seizing the initiative, decided to create a Supreme Council (junta) of Caracas, representing the dominant classes, to replace the French-controlled colonial authority. Juan de Las Casas, the Captain-General and effective ruler of Venezuela, saw that he had no choice but to accede to this. Within a day the news which reached Venezuela that those loyal to Ferdinand had set up a provisional government in the Spanish city of Seville had emboldened de Las Casas to announce the immediate dissolution of the Caracas junta and the setting up of an inquisition against 'traitors to Spain and the monarchy'. He at least understood that the goal of some was nothing less than full independence. In particular, leaflets emanating from Miranda had been distributed to his followers, calling for the formation of 'representative municipal governments which would send envoys to London to establish the security and future of the new world'. De Las Casas knew that the creation of such an assembly would be the forerunner of independence, however much its protagonists protested their loyalty to the King and their opposition to the French.

On 17 April 1810, however, word reached Caracas that the French had occupied most of Andalucia, and overthrown the Seville government. Caracas exploded into mutiny once again: the criollo leaders gathered at the home of one of their number, José Angel Alamo, and planned a mass uprising. The short-lived Seville government had appointed Vincente Emparán to replace de Las Casas as Captain-General, but when he went to meet the Council on the morning of 19 April he encountered angry demonstrations in the streets and the hostility of even the Spanish-appointed councillors. With as much dignity as he could muster, he declared that he was not opposed to the establishment of a native-run council, but that approval should be sought from the Council of

Regency which, set up by the provisional Seville government, had now retreated to Cadiz. He then suspended the sitting and began to make his way to Caracas Cathedral, to take part in the ceremonies for the Thursday before Easter. However, Francisco Salinas, one of the conspirators, seized Emparán by the arm and ordered him back to the council chamber. The chief of his bodyguard, in on the plot, did nothing to stop this outrage to the person of the Crown's representative, and the discomfited Emparán returned to the building, where other prominent citizens had now gathered. They proposed to restore the junta, and invest its titular leadership in Emparán, as Captain-General.

But one of the most radical criollo leaders, Canon José Cortés de Madariaga, a rabid preacher, rose and accused Emparán of perfidy, intrigue and deceit, and pronounced him stripped of all authority. Emparán, reddening angrily, declared that he would resign if he was not welcome, and strode out onto the balcony of the city hall to ask the crowd outside if it would support him. Cortés de Madariaga had his supporters well placed in the throng, however: they orchestrated a cry of 'No! No! No!' Emparán promptly resigned, and Spanish authority in Venezuela was temporarily at an end. The first part of the Spanish Empire had broken away. A revolution had occurred.

The new council went into session at once. It was decided that Emparán should be sent back to Spain. Export tariffs were removed. Non-Spanish goods were no longer to be punitively taxed. Primary produce and food were exempted from taxes altogether. The Indians were absolved from paying tribute, and slavery was prohibited. It was also decided that envoys should be despatched to seek support from Britain and the United States. Simón Bolívar – young, impetuous and disliked for his recklessness, extravagance and womanising, but wealthy – offered to pay the costs of the delegation to London, and was appointed its nominal leader, but Luis Lopez Mendez and Andrés Bello were its real principals.

The Venezuelan mission arrived in Portsmouth on 10 July 1810. Bolívar and his party were met by Foreign Office officials who accompanied them to Martin's Hotel. From the first Bolívar ignored his instructions from the junta in Caracas, of which one was that he should on no account make contact with that dangerously radical and unreliable figure, Francisco de Miranda. Bolívar persuaded his companions that if Miranda first called upon them, this would not violate the letter of their instructions. In fact, he and Lopez Mendez looked forward with eager

anticipation to meeting the famous exile. The small young man introduced to Miranda had a narrow face that broadened out into a
high-domed forehead from which steel-wool-curly dark hair was already
receding. Framed by long sideburns, the lips were pursed and proud, the
nose long, aquiline and distinguished. But it was the eyes that dominated
Bolívar's face. Beneath high dark brows, they examined any interlocutor
with a fiery intensity tempered, in this case, by the hero-worship of a
young man meeting his idol, a seasoned revolutionary, for the first time.

Bolívar's evident admiration, immaturity and nervousness made little
apparent impression on Miranda, who proceeded to lecture the delegation, with his usual eloquence, on the state of opinion in their home
capital, whence they had just arrived but which he had not visited in
decades. The ordinary people of South America, he insisted, were loyal
to Spain and had no wish for independence. Only a small part of the oligarchy was pressing for change. However, in response to Bolívar's
insistence that the continent was ripe for insurrection and looking for a
leader – Miranda himself – the older man advised them to pursue their
cause with the British Foreign Office, and undertook to try to influence
British public opinion through the press, where he had many friends.
With that he departed, as grandly as he had entered. It seemed, at least
on this first meeting, that for him the continued security of his comfortable exile was more important than another attempt to raise the standard
of revolt in South America. But perhaps this green and eager young
admirer could be used to serve his purposes.

A week later the three Venezuelans were offered a meeting with the
Foreign Secretary, the Marquess Wellesley, elder brother of the officer
then making his name in the Peninsular campaigns, Arthur Wellesley,
Viscount Wellington. However, the meeting was not to take place at the
Foreign Office but in Lord Wellesley's private residence, Apsley House,
an elegant mansion on the corner of Hyde Park. Bolívar was furious: he
understood that this was a snub, that the British were hedging their bets.
An invitation to the Foreign Office would have implied recognition of
the new Venezuelan government. The British, while welcoming the
Venezuelan revolution as a setback for the French, were anxious not to
upset their allies in the Spanish government of resistance, and besides
harboured doubts about how long the rebellion could last.

As Bolívar, in his unaccustomed new official role, ascended the steps
of Apsley House to meet one of the most experienced statesmen – a
former Governor-General of India – of one of the world's greatest

powers, he felt nervous and insecure. Invited to state his case, he described what had happened in Caracas and affirmed that he and the government he represented were all still loyal to the Spanish cause. As Bello records, he went on to explain that the circumstances in Caracas were extraordinary and that the uprising there was 'purely provincial and calculated to preserve the province's liberty from any external threat . . . one of the primary aims of the revolution in Caracas was to retain the territorial integrity of Venezuela for the monarch and protect [its citizens] from the intrigues and seductions of the French.' Wellesley put the case strongly that they must display their loyalty to the Spanish Crown through concrete action; Bolívar argued that the Spanish colonies should exercise self-government.

Wellesley dryly observed that Venezuela's declaration of independence was an act without precedent in the annals of Spain and her colonies. Angrily, Bolívar retorted that the American people should not be deprived of the right to defend their essential interests, that a 'new order' was required, and that no one should understand better than Wellesley the vices of Spanish colonial administration. In effect, however, he was conceding Wellesley's point that independence, rather than obedience to Spain, was Venezuela's ultimate aim. The Foreign Secretary smiled, and complimented Bolívar on the passion with which he was defending his country's cause. In return, Bolívar sarcastically congratulated Wellesley for defending Spain's interests so vigorously; whereupon Wellesley asserted that the British had tried to recognise the claims of Spain's colonies to their nationhood. He then ended the interview, agreeing to see the delegation again two days later.

At this second meeting Wellesley greeted the Venezuelans with the demand that in view of the close relations Britain enjoyed with the exiled monarchy, they should end their dispute with the Spanish Crown, in exchange for some military aid against France, and Britain's good offices in urging the Spanish Crown not to take action against Venezuela. But the British would not recognise Venezuela, lest this encourage revolt in Spain's other colonies and cause the diversion to them of resources essential to the continuing struggle against the French. Bolívar emerged from the meeting profoundly cynical about the British position: in January Britain had offered military help to Spain, provided that her colonies be opened up to British commerce; now, the threat that Britain might aid the rebellious Venezuelans would be used to ensure that the Spanish stuck to their agreement.

Nevertheless, Bolívar continued to press his case, with vehemence but also with good humour. And soon Spain overplayed her hand. The Spanish Ambassador in London protested at the British government's cordial reception of the 'Venezuelan separatists', whereupon Wellesley invited the Venezuelans and Spanish to meet, to resolve their differences and unite against Napoleon. The Spanish Ambassador at the last moment refused to attend, and the Venezuelans promptly followed suit.

Having outstayed their official welcome and failed to secure British backing, on 30 August 1810 Bolívar and his companions left London. It was a bitter moment. Bolívar's sole success had been to persuade Miranda to return to Venezuela – but later, on another ship, so as not to associate the celebrated revolutionary too closely with the new Venezuelan government. Yet his conduct of the mission had won him new respect among his countrymen, as he discovered when he arrived in Caracas in November 1810. He set up a 'Patriotic Society of Agriculture and Economy', which he used as a platform for the more radical views espoused by younger criollos. Whipping up popular demand for Miranda's return, Bolívar succeeded in persuading the moderate junta not to refuse him entry on his arrival a month later.

In a land yearning for a truly national leader, the reception of the legendary Miranda on 11 December was tumultuous. He believed he had returned to his homeland to become leader of an independent country. One of his companions on the tortuous journey by carriage up from the coast to Caracas observed that Miranda spoke 'ill of the United States and in the crossing of the Venta river and many other places suggested they needed improvements or repairs and said he would carry them out, as if he had the tiller of the new Republic of Venezuela in his hands'. Miranda's long years in London at the heart of an increasingly out-of-touch Venezuelan community had gone to his head. As it reached Caracas his carriage was surrounded by an enormous crowd and pulled into the city centre. At the banquets which were held for him, he received the toasts in his honour without a word of reply, without raising his glass, simply smiling benevolently, like a king with his subjects. 'He behaved as though all were inferior to his merit. The expressions which usually suggest good education, modesty and decency never came out of his mouth.' But neither he nor his disciple Bolívar was in charge yet.

In February 1811 Miranda was appointed a lieutenant-general by the government of Caracas. The following month the country's new

Congress met, and Miranda was dismayed when it chose as its 'executive power' three worthies; he himself polled insufficient votes, which dented his vanity and caused him to declare, surely with affected modesty, 'I am happy that there are more convenient people than myself to exercise supreme power.' The majority of delegates from the criollo upper classes feared not only Miranda's alleged radicalism, but possible Spanish retaliation if he were chosen. Straight away the assembly found itself divided on the issue of whether to proceed to full independence.

Disquieted, Bolívar, no more than a minor member of Congress, fell back on his power base, the Patriotic Society, which pressed with vigour for outright independence. Angrily, Congress denounced the society for trying to set itself up as an alternative assembly. Bolívar seized the chance to deliver a powerful and extremist speech. 'It is not that there are two congresses . . . They say in Congress that there must be a confederation. As if we were not all confederated against an external tyranny! What does it matter if Spain sells Bonaparte its slaves, or keeps them, if we are resolved to be free? These deals are the sad effects of old chains. It is said that great enterprises must be prepared calmly. Are not three hundred years of calm enough? Do we need another three hundred years?' To shouts of approval, Bolívar went on: 'The Patriotic Society respects, as it must, the nation's Congress; but Congress must listen to the Patriotic Society, centre of light and of all revolutionary interests. Let us lay down the cornerstones of South America's freedom. To vacillate is to yield!' On 5 July 1811, pressured from below by Bolívar's young radicals, Congress passed an act establishing Venezuelan independence.

From the moment it was formed, the new state began to degenerate into chaos and confrontation. A bitter row broke out over whether it should be federal – that is, decentralised, with the scattering of cities and rural communities that made up Venezuela allowed a large measure of autonomy; or unitary – with government from Caracas. Miranda pressed furiously in Congress for a centralised state, and Bolívar advocated it in the Patriotic Society. The two were bitterly attacked, Miranda as a 'foreigner' in the pay of Britain (Britain having supported him in his exile) and Bolívar as a centralist from the capital. In December 1811 the new constitution granted internal self-government to each city, a significant defeat for Miranda and Bolívar.

Much more threateningly, an insurrection against the new government had broken out in the city of Valencia, some eighty miles from Caracas, where local Spaniards allied to 'black followers' declared themselves for Ferdinand VII: the counter-revolution was under way. A force sent out from Caracas was defeated, a setback which threw Congress into a panic. Miranda, as the only competent and experienced general among those favouring independence, was nominated Generalissimo to subdue Venezuela's second city.

Gripped by a strange mixture of pessimism and vainglory, Miranda assembled an army of four thousand peasants, poorly trained, badly armed and all marching out of step. He disdainfully asked his aides where were the armies which a general of his prestige 'could bring to the battle without compromising [his] dignity'. At this stage something extraordinary happened: Bolívar had hoped to serve under Miranda, whom he had persuaded to return and had set up as the revolution's leading figure, but Miranda suddenly turned on his ally, denouncing him as a 'dangerous and uncontrolled young man'. Bolívar was furious, and in his turn denounced his hero as 'a tired-out old soldier who does not know Venezuela, as a nation or as a society. He is a pretentious person, of insatiable vanity. Dangerous youth, indeed! He calls me that because I dare to oppose his erroneous policies!' Miranda's sudden change may have been the result of pressure from congressional conservatives, a price to be paid for being given supreme command of the army. Bolívar instead secured a post in the service of the Marqués del Toro, Miranda's second-in-command and an old aristocratic ally.

When the Venezuelan forces reached the hills of El Morro outside Valencia, they were ambushed: royalist troops opened fire, from behind rocks on one side and from boats hidden in the tall reeds of the vast Lake of Valencia on the other. The leading troops fell back in confusion. Bolívar spurred them forward, yelling and waving his sword in one hand and pistol in the other, displaying both bravery and ferocity in this, his first engagement. After a furious fight the royalists withdrew to the city, and Miranda ordered his troops forward to take it. Once again his forces were ambushed, and he and Bolívar were forced to retreat amid horrendous carnage: 800 government soldiers were killed and 1,500 wounded. Bolívar's friend Fernando del Toro, son of the Marqués, lost a leg in the fighting.

Miranda now brought up cannon to lay siege to the city. In August, outnumbered, outgunned and facing probable starvation, the royalist garrison in Valencia surrendered. The first major campaign of the Latin American wars of independence had been won by the patriots only through superior numbers and cannon. But it was heartening all the same. Another curious episode followed: at a parade after the battle, Miranda publicly berated Bolívar for indiscipline. Again, Miranda may have been trying to reassure his new conservative allies in the Congress; but there can be little doubt that the older man was also intensely jealous of the younger – although their cause was the same. For his part, Bolívar suffered the slights in silence, still believing in the legend of Miranda. He, however, failed to follow up his victory, and returned to Caracas rather than marching to support the embattled patriots in the towns of Coro and Maracaibo to the west. In part because of this failure, he was supplanted as commander-in-chief by the Marqués del Toro.

The new constitution promulgated in December 1811 enshrined federalism, liberty and equality, abolished all distinctions between races, and guaranteed property rights and freedom of the press. It also stripped the clergy of many of their privileges, even though the liberal clergy had been instrumental in bringing about Venezuelan independence. It reflected a compromise between the self-interest of the criollo upper class, which wanted to control the government in its own interests, and the genuine liberals, who sought equality between the races. But Miranda, for one, remarked upon the impracticability of a constitution which dispersed power to the provinces: 'It is not adapted to the population, habits and customs of the states, and may result, not in uniting us in one consolidated group or social body, but in dividing us, jeopardizing our common security and our independence. I enter these observations in fulfillment of my duty.' The new country entered the year 1812 shakily, under blockade from the Spanish, with its economy in ruins, many areas going uncultivated and its trade badly damaged, and a government at odds with itself and no longer in control of a large part of the country.

On 26 March 1812, the Thursday before Easter – and Captain-General Emparán had been deposed on the Thursday before Easter two years earlier – Providence joined forces with the royalists to deliver the cruellest blow of all. At four in the afternoon of a peaceful and pleasant early spring day, a terrifying roar shattered the calm. Houses shook as the ground thundered beneath them: Caracas, Merida, Barquisimeto, Trujillo and San Carlos were left in ruins by the earthquake.

Bolívar was awoken from his siesta. 'I immediately set about trying to save the victims, kneeling and working towards those places where groans and cries of help were coming from. I was engaged upon this task when I saw the pro-Spanish José Domingo Diaz, who looked at me and

1. Idealist, poseur, seducer and tragic founder of Latin America: Francisco de Miranda

2. Miranda's lover: Catherine the Great of Russia

3. Disastrous Spanish sovereigns: Charles IV and Maria Luisa. Painting by Francisco de Goya

4. From playboy to freedom fighter: the young Simón Bolívar

5. Caged at last: the Precursor – Miranda – in prison

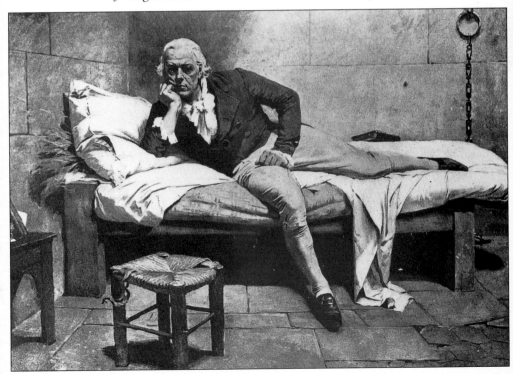

6. William, Lord Grenville: British
Prime Minister and dreamer

7. Humboldt and Bonpland:
naturalists on the Amazon

8. George Canning, who 'called the New World into existence'

9. Bolívar's haven: the Orinoco basin. Painting by A. Göring

10. Despot without pity:
Ferdinand VII of Spain

11. First horseman and *llanero*:
José Antonio Páez

12. Manuela Sáenz: love of Bolívar's life

13. Decisive defeat for Spain: the Battle of Carabobo. Painting by Tovar y Tovar

14. The Liberator: Bolívar in his prime

commented with his usual scorn: "How goes it, Bolívar? It seems that Nature has put itself on the side of the Spaniards." "If Nature is against us, we will fight it and make it obey us," I replied furiously.'

Some ten thousand were killed in Caracas alone, where the mud houses fell in upon themselves. A whole regiment of 1,500 patriots fell into a fissure at Barquisimeto and were killed. San Felipe, along with its 600-strong patriot garrison, was completely wiped out. Superstitious minds noted that royalist strongholds such as Valencia, Coro, Maracaibo and Guayana, as well as all the royalist army, were untouched. On Easter Sunday itself, further violent tremors shook the country. Altogether twenty thousand were killed in the two earthquakes.

Royalist priests preached that this was divine retribution against the deposition of the anointed King's representatives two years before. The Archbishop of Caracas, Coll y Pratt, thundered that the vices of Venezuela were being punished, and invoked the example of Sodom and Gomorrah. The earthquakes shattered the dwindling morale of the patriot forces, and thousands of ordinary Venezuelans now swung over to the royalists.

A new royalist commander now emerged: Domingo Monteverde, a former Spanish naval captain, was energetic, brave and able, besides being abundantly possessed of the cruelty traditionally associated with the Spanish military. Miyares, commander of the Spanish forces in Venezuela, based in Coro, and his superior, General Cortabarria in Puerto Rico, ordered Monteverde to move forward to Carora; the patriots there were butchered, and the town sacked. The rest of the patriots retreated to the garrison town of San Carlos, and most of the country in between was abandoned to the royalists. Valencia now went over to them, after mass desertions from the patriot ranks.

Monteverde ordered his most brutal commander, Captain Eusebio Antoñanzas, forward onto the plains of Calabozo, and on 23 March he took the town of San Juan de los Morros. According to the contemporary historians Baralt and Diaz, 'neither women nor children could find mercy. Captain Antoñanzas enjoyed perpetrating the crimes with his own hands, being the first to set fire to the houses and cutting down the unfortunates who fled the flames.' In Los Guayos, half the garrison defected; the Indian leader of the Sequisiqui also went over to the royalists.

Faced by setbacks on all fronts, Congress discarded the Marqués del Toro as their commander-in-chief and turned again to Miranda, whom they appointed absolute dictator (not, in those days, a pejorative title). The old roué, the powdered, greying dandy of the salons of Europe, at the age of sixty-two found himself at last the leader of his people – in their darkest hour. Although almost certainly no one else could have saved the situation, he was in many ways an inappropriate choice. His prognosis was gloomy: 'They have approached me to preside over Venezuela's funeral, but I cannot deny my services to my country in the calamitous circumstances in which man and nature have placed it.' It was hardly a rallying cry to stir his people. His first act was to try to defend the approach to the capital; he moved his headquarters to Maracay and devised a markedly defensive strategy, when his only hope was to inspire the desperate Venezuelans through bold, even suicidal, leadership. He feared further desertions, and believed the country could survive only if overseas forces came to his help; he despaired of the wretched guerrillas he commanded, contrasting them unfavourably with the comparatively disciplined French ranks he had led in Europe. The prospect of assistance from abroad was remote indeed, however. He despatched emissaries to both the British government and his English acquaintances the Marquess Wellesley, Jeremy Bentham and Lord Castlereagh. But Britain, fearing the worst for the new republic, decided to stay on the sidelines.

Miranda's forces secured a few minor victories against Monteverde, but in La Victoria and Guacara heavy fighting resulted in a stand-off. The Marqués del Toro, piqued by his supercession as commander-in-chief, refused to serve under Miranda. News of a slave uprising in Barcovento further dented morale, then the garrisons of San Juan de los Morros and Guanare passed over to the royalists.

Miranda's only hope seemed to lie in a vigorous offensive, but this he refused to embark upon, for fear of overextending himself, and also of upsetting the British, who were suspicious of his 'revolutionary' intentions. The patriot cause was paralysed by the old man's indecisiveness and his reluctance to shed blood. When the Spanish seized the Heights of Cabrera, overlooking Miranda's forces at Maracay, he retreated to La Victoria, whose garrison was threatened by Monteverde from San Mateo.

Events now moved towards their climax with the intensity of a Greek tragedy, throwing together the two principal protagonists of Latin American independence in a terrible web of deception, disillusion and almost filial betrayal that was to destroy the elder. Having been publicly rebuked by the very hero he had helped to power, Simón Bolívar then enjoyed a partial reinstatement to favour as a result of his undoubted courage and ability (he had also, conveniently, inherited another estate following the death of his brother Juan Vicente in a storm off Bermuda), and was sent as a colonel to command the garrison town of Puerto Cabello which dominated the western approach to La Guaira, strategically crucial gateway to the sea for Caracas.

The garrison at Puerto Cabello was on a small island connected by a bridge to a peninsula jutting out from the mainland. The island was defended by two batteries of cannon and the castle of San Felipe, which overlooked them. This housed the arms and ammunition of the garrison, and was also the local gaol. There were three small warships in port, also under Bolívar's command. The gaol contained a number of royalists taken prisoner at Valencia and the town itself was full of Spanish sympathisers, who managed to smuggle letters to the prisoners.

On 30 June Bolívar was playing cards with his officers when shooting started outside as the prisoners seized control of the castle with the help of a group of a hundred and twenty men led by one Captain Camejo, a patriot who had changed sides; they also seized one of the boats. Bolívar, realising the potential danger of his position, had a few days before asked Miranda to send forces to strengthen his garrison against the royalists at San Mateo. None had come, notwithstanding Miranda's later assertion that Puerto Cabello, like La Guaira, was of the utmost strategic significance. Now the royalists could fire down upon Bolívar's forces at will and controlled most of his arms and munitions. He held on for several days in this desperate situation, first attempting to storm the impregnable fort, then merely exchanging fire, his own side progressively weakened by desertions and lack of supplies.

He had sent a frantic plea to Miranda, but his message went unanswered – possibly because Miranda did not receive it in time. A few days later Bolívar escaped with his officers and a handful of loyal soldiers in the remaining boat. In only his second major military engagement, and his first command, he had failed calamitously.

Landing safely after the short passage to La Guaira, Bolívar travelled up to Caracas, where he locked himself into his house, refusing to see anyone. In his manic and brittle personality, insanity seemed never far beneath the surface. His wretched state of mind is reflected in letters to Miranda. In the first he wrote:

My general: After having exhausted all my material and spiritual resources, only with whatever courage remains could I dare to take up the pen to write to you, having lost Puerto Cabello at my own hands . . . My general, my spirit is so defeated that I do not feel strong enough to command a single soldier. My presumptuousness made me believe that my desire to achieve and my ardent zeal for the fatherland would supply the talents I lacked to command . . .

Thus I ask you to make me obey the lowest official, or give me some days to calm myself and recover the serenity which I lost on losing Puerto Cabello. To this can be added my physical state of health which after three nights of insomnia and grave warnings, finds me in a sort of mortal torpor. I am immediately beginning my report on the operations of the troops that I commanded and the disgraces which ruined the city of Puerto Cabello, to defend in the eyes of public opinion your choice of me as well as my own honour.

I did my duty, my general, and if the soldiers had remained on my side, I would have had strength to fight the enemy. If they abandoned me, it was not my fault. Nothing remained for me to do to contain the enemy and . . . save the fatherland. But, alas! This was lost in my hands.

In such plaintively pathetic rambling self-justification did Bolívar seek approbation and forgiveness from Miranda for a failure which, if only tangentially his fault, nevertheless seemed irrevocably to besmirch his reputation. Whining, hysterical and shrill, the tone accords with Bolívar's persona to the age of twenty-nine: that of a spoilt, highly-strung egocentric show-off, much more concerned with his own reputation than the setback to his cause. He had failed to deal adequately with the danger the prisoners posed: in hindsight, he should have let them go rather than keep them, a pistol pointed at the very heart of his garrison. Now he had run away – although there was nothing else he could have done.

Miranda was disgusted, blind to his own share of the blame for classifying Puerto Cabello as a major strategic objective and then doing nothing to reinforce it. His silence in response to Bolívar's letter was eloquent. The pleas of his young admirer and supporter for his mentor's forgiveness were brushed aside with disdain. Indeed, when news reached Miranda of the defeat, he turned to his soldiers and said: 'Tenez: Venezuela est blessé au coeur – Venezuela is wounded to the heart.' He went on: 'You see, gentlemen, how the affairs of this world are going. A little while ago all was safe; today all is uncertain and ominous. Yesterday Monteverde had no power, lead or muskets; today he can count on

40,000 pounds of powder, lead in abundance and 3,000 muskets [from the arsenal of Puerto Cabello]. Bolívar tells me the royalists are attacking, but on this day they are already in possession of everything.' Bolívar, whom Miranda had begun to find increasingly insupportable, was to be the scapegoat.

A second, shorter, even more imploring letter accompanied Bolívar's official report: 'My general, full of a sort of shame I summon the confidence to send you this enclosure [the account of the battle] which is only a shadow of what really happened. My head, my heart, they are good for nothing. I beg you to permit me an interval of a few days to see if my mind can be returned to its ordinary state. After having lost the best fortress in the land, how can I not be insane, my general? Please do not oblige me to see you face to face. I am not to blame, but I am dispirited and it is enough.'

The great Spanish historian Salvador de Madariaga has a fine passage in which he seeks to unravel the complexity of Bolívar's mind:

Nothing could have saved him from that mental collapse which threatened him at every turn but another natural force in his character strong enough to counteract the dispersive effects of the several planets which pulled his being to and fro in the horizons of his soul. This force was an egotism which made his personal self, his ego, a sun capable of holding together all those planets. Egotism and its chief manifestation, ambition, became thus in Bolívar's life bare necessities without which there could be for him no sanity, perhaps no life at all.

When on the top of the Sacred Mount Simón Bolívar swore to free his country from the tyranny of Spain, he was swearing to rescue Simón Bolívar from insanity and death. For Bolívar, a life of glory was the only alternative to a miserable life as a mental wreck such as his nephew (most like him) lived. But when, at twenty-two, he saw himself ascending the peak of glory, Bolívar did not yet possess the inner force which alone could hold together his many and discordant parts. His youthful petulance and vanity were not of the fibre which his unruly self needed. They had first to be crushed by the hammer of adversity.

Again Miranda did not deign to answer Bolívar's missive. He considered that, with the fall of Puerto Cabello, the game was up. If the royalists seized La Guaira, his own route of escape from Caracas would be cut off. The war was over, and it remained only to come to terms. How justified was Miranda in this decision? The capture of La Guaira would certainly have cut the main supply route to Caracas. The slave uprising in Barcovento, under the cry 'Viva el Rey!', had profoundly alarmed the whites, as householders were massacred and plantations burnt. Meanwhile the treasury was all but exhausted, the currency being issued by the patriots was worthless, and Monteverde's forces were advancing, gathering support, and butchering those who failed to join them as they went.

Miranda was tired, old, luxury-loving, and inclined to pessimism. The two insurrections he had launched had ended in abject failure. As a realist, he was reluctant to sacrifice thousands of lives in a futile cause. A more impassioned, younger man, lacking his fastidiousness and inhibitions, might have waged a more vigorous war from the beginning; but energy and savagery were on the enemy's side, in the person of Monteverde. Miranda had just learnt that his British friends, while disposed to mediate between him and the Spanish Crown, would not intervene on his side. He decided to secure the best terms possible while he still had a few cards left. While his earlier defensiveness cannot be justified, his decision now was probably not at fault.

Certainly the senior members of his government all concurred that Miranda must sue for peace. He asked Monteverde that the persons and property of people in the lands about to be surrendered should be respected, that no one should be imprisoned for their opinions, that passports should be guaranteed to those who wanted to leave the country, and that prisoners should be exchanged. On 25 July these terms were agreed; Miranda accepted the negotiated surrender, but kept the details secret from his people. It is not known whether Bolívar was still in the capital at the time of the capitulation, but he soon joined the throng of refugees making their way down the narrow trail from Caracas to La Guaira, three thousand feet below. By 28 July he was staying in the residence of Manuel de Las Casas, military governor of the port.

In Caracas insurrections broke out in several barracks when news of Miranda's 'betrayal' came through. The cry went up that 'we were sold to Monteverde'. It was rumoured that a secret protocol had been attached to the deal under which the Minister of Finance, the Marqués de Casa Leon, had granted Miranda a thousand ounces of gold and an order for 22,000 pesos, to be transferred to his agent in Curaçao, George Robertson.

There is some evidence for the latter accusation: it would not have been surprising if Miranda had tried to rescue some of the national treasury from the hands of the advancing Spanish in order to finance a future attempt at independence. Vainglorious and full of hauteur as he was, he had sacrificed a life of comfort and pleasure in London to back the revolution under harrowing and unpleasant conditions. He enjoyed the good life, certainly, but it is unlikely that he would now have betrayed the cause he had supported all his life purely out of greed.

Miranda assembled his extensive collection of papers for safe evacuation to a British ship off La Guaira. It was his intention to go west, to the now independent Audiencia of Sante Fé de Bogotá, from where he would seek to continue the revolt. He told his aide, Pedro Gual, that he would join its leader Nariño to launch a new attack on Venezuela, once the defeatism induced by the earthquake and the royalist excesses had passed.

With five thousand or so troops now marching disconsolately back to barracks, complaining that they had been stabbed in the back, Caracas was a hotbed of intrigue, described vividly to Miranda by one of his aides:

> The people are . . . absorbed by intrigue, they know nothing else; they are cowards and at the same time daring. I would not write this to you if I hadn't penetrated their movements, which are to deceive you with words and save themselves. They are trembling with fear . . . They are ignorant men who fear the light; criminal men who flee orders; vile men who prefer their own interests and infamy; men who are robbing and stripping the state and fear being detected and stopped from committing their thefts. Yesterday and the day before various crowds called out, 'Viva Ferdinand VII' . . . You are being conducted towards the precipice . . . You, your friends and your fatherland have never been in such danger as now.

Miranda was denounced from the pulpit by Archbishop Coll y Pratt, denounced too by the commander he had supplanted, the Marqués del Toro – who was Bolívar's patron. It was every man for himself. On 30 July he arrived at eight in the evening at La Guaira, exhausted and despairing of the treachery that surrounded him but greeted by a large crowd, as his baggage was put aboard HMS *Sapphire*. Miranda had been forced to agree, as part of the terms of the surrender, to respect the Spanish blockade of the port, but Captain Haynes of the *Sapphire* urged him to ignore it and come aboard himself, although they would not sail before morning. Tired and in no hurry to reveal to his people that he was fleeing the country, Miranda refused; it was a fatal mistake. He went to de Las Casas's house, where Bolívar had so recently been staying, and went to bed.

De Las Casas disliked Miranda intensely, and had previously criticised him for an order to send 'absolutely naked men, some without even a shirt, their arms in the worst possible state and many without guns or bayonets, to do battle for the port'. He also believed that under the terms of the surrender he would personally be held responsible by the fearsome Monteverde if anyone left the port, and that if Miranda in particular escaped, he, de Las Casas, would be severely punished. The civil governor of the port, Miguel Peña, who disliked de Las Casas, was planning to flee, and had offered to spirit Miranda out for 4,000 pesos; Miranda refused to pay more than 800. But Peña was also treacherously in touch with the Spanish commander, Monteverde.

After Miranda had retired for the night, de Las Casas, Peña, Bolívar and several other officers met. By all accounts Bolívar led the discussion, accusing Miranda of vacillation at Maracay and La Victoria and denouncing his surrender to inferior Spanish forces. Miranda was seeking to escape and leaving them all to their fates – the captain was first to leave the sinking ship; worse, he was fleeing having plundered the treasury. Bolívar's eloquence and ferocity persuaded the others.

The motives of de Las Casas and Peña were less fanatical, more self-interested. They argued that Miranda must be turned over to the Spanish authorities, who would surely exact a terrible vengeance if he were allowed to escape. Already in touch with Monteverde, they hoped to secure safe conducts for themselves or, at the least, favourable treatment. Bolívar argued hotly in favour of executing the 'traitor' by firing squad; in the event, this would have been the more merciful course of action. But de Las Casas and Peña were determined to ingratiate themselves with the Spanish authorities by handing Miranda over to them.

At three in the morning, as rival bands of supporters and opponents of Miranda and the monarchy roamed the streets of the chaotic, refugee-swollen port, Bolívar led two captains and a detachment of soldiers to de Las Casas's residence. Awoken by Soublette, his secretary, in his night-shirt, Miranda believed he was being readied to embark. But then he heard the voices of the conspirators, and knew he was betrayed. Bolívar stepped forward and announced that Miranda was under arrest. The swords of the party he led were drawn, flashing in the light of the lantern carried by Soublette. The weary, haughty old man declared languidly, '*Bochinche, bochinche*, these people are capable of nothing except *bochinche*' – meaning, more and less politely, hubbub or cock-ups. Disdainfully he asked to be allowed to dress. Then he was roughly seized, insulted, and marched off to prison. Peña rode off to Caracas to tell Monteverde what had happened; his reward was to be asked to become the Spanish commander's aide.

One of Monteverde's commanders went down to take control of La Guaira from de Las Casas, who was sent under escort to Caracas but then freed in return for his part in apprehending Miranda. Bolívar and the other young republicans, who had believed they would be allowed to escape but had been prevented from doing so by the treacherous de Las Casas, were arrested by the Spanish.

This was one of history's epic betrayals, a tragedy of Shakespearian dimensions. Two years before, the young playboy had persuaded his hero to return to Venezuela, despite his doubts. At first showing little regard for his disciple, Miranda had at last given him a significant command – in which Bolívar had failed spectacularly, if through little fault of his own. On the edge of a breakdown, apparently spurned and blamed by the figure he had helped bring to power in Venezuela, his hero-worship had undergone a terrible mutation – into pure hatred. His own sense of guilt and culpability was reinforced, refined and metamorphosed into a deadly desire for vengeance. Guilt is perhaps the most powerful human emotion; and Bolívar could save his own reason only by transferring his overwhelming sense of it to the man who had failed to come to his aid – to Miranda, who had fought an unnecessarily defensive war, who had made him the scapegoat for his own surrender, who had planned to flee the country with part of the treasury.

Subconsciously, there may have been a sense of rivalry, a wish to supplant Miranda as the bearer of the standard of independence by killing him off – and throughout Bolívar's career he demonstrated on occasion a streak of psychopathic ruthlessness in removing his rivals, a characteristic which failed him only at the end. To this day Latin American historians, who venerate both men, find it difficult to come to terms with the fact that their greatest hero betrayed their second-greatest into captivity. The two are still portrayed in popular iconography as the closest of friends.

Now the Spanish Empire had at last secured its oldest and most hated enemy. Miranda was taken to the prison of La Guaira; his papers and money escaped aboard HMS *Sapphire* and were handed over to the British authorities in Curaçao, whence they were sent to Lord Bathurst, Secretary of State in Lord Liverpool's government, and eventually placed in storage at Cirencester Park, Lord Bathurst's country seat. In his dark prison, in paranoid terror of being poisoned, Miranda could eat only bread and water. The most mannered and luxurious of bon viveurs was held there for eight months, in complete violation of the armistice agreement, before being transferred to the San Felipe prison in Puerto Cabello where he seems to have been better treated, and was allowed to pen a 'Memorial in Self-Defence'. His powers of advocacy had not deserted him: he portrayed himself as having sought to bring about a reconciliation between Spain and the independent Venezuelan state – which served but to feed the radical view of him as a traitor. Two months later the prospect of another insurgency, aimed at freeing Miranda, caused Monteverde to ship him to Puerto Rico. There he was treated more considerately still, and penned a vigorous attack on the way in which Monteverde had violated the surrender terms, hoping to appeal, as a fellow-reformer, to the liberal faction which had seized power in Madrid in 1812.

His respite was short-lived: in 1814 the return to power of Ferdinand VII, now revealed as a despot, saw Miranda, in chains, taken across the Atlantic to Cadiz, to the fearsome La Carraca prison in the fort of Cuatro Torres, from which few emerged alive. He had first seen it as an eager young man arriving from South America forty-five years before. Another prisoner there heard him declare that his Spanish chains weighed less upon him than the chains of his compatriots. He was allowed to exercise occasionally in the prison yard and was reported as being still dignified, impressive and in good health. His experience of French prisons under the shadow of the guillotine doubtless stood him in good stead.

His hopes were now focused on the influential Englishmen he called his friends, and he believed that Castlereagh, Lord Grenville, Nicholas Vansittart and the Marquess Wellesley were pressing for his release, even if the Foreign Office, anxious to maintain good relations with Spain, was acting with less vigour. In fact, unknown to Miranda, they had decided to betray their old friend, sell out the patriots, and deal directly with Spain. Castlereagh had cynically suggested that if Spain gave Britain freedom to trade with her colonies, Britain would do no more to help the rebel colonists. In 1812, to the commission mediating Spain's dispute with her colonies, he observed:

> The conviction of the British Government is . . . that, if [the Spanish Government] cannot bring themselves to place the inhabitants of America upon a commercial footing of corresponding advantage with the inhabitants of European Spain their separation from the parent state is inevitable and at hand . . .

In pressing this view of the situation upon the Spanish Government it may be desirable to suggest for their consideration the commercial system which we find it not only necessary but advantageous to apply to our East India possessions . . . [which] we govern . . . as far as related to commerce upon a national and not a colonial principle . . . [with] . . . trade . . . open to all neutral nations, and as sovereigns we claim nothing but a commercial preference . . .

. . . You may point out to the Spanish Government . . . that Great Britain has derived more real commercial advantage from North America since the separation than she did when the country was subjected to her dominion and part of her colonial system.

In a letter to Sir Henry, the youngest Wellesley brother, British Ambassador in Madrid, he wrote:

. . . It would be both unwise and unjust to presuppose that the subjects of the Crown of Spain in that quarter of the globe are deliberately prepared to throw off their allegiance. If such should unfortunately prove to be the case in any portion of the great Continent, if they should reject the liberal and benevolent offers of the Parent State, it will be time enough for Spain . . . to consider what ulterior measures are due to herself.

The treaties which unite the two Crowns prescribe to Great Britain, as a fundamental duty, to preserve by all means in her power the integrity of the Spanish monarchy . . . the British Government could not but witness with the deepest regret and displeasure any indications of a purpose so unnatural and unbecoming in any of the Spanish Provinces. It will be their sincere desire to counteract such a disposition by every suitable means.

But [the British government] cannot, for reasons in which Old Spain has a common interest with Great Britain, be bound to make a refusal on [the Provinces'] part the cause of war; because in doing so, the consequence might be, not to replace those Provinces in connexion and under the authority of Spain, but to drive them into a connexion with the common enemy [France].

It was of course impossible for Britain to agree to Spain's request that war against the colonies be declared, should mediation fail. The other question upon which Britain has often been accused of insincerity, this time by Spain, is related to her eagerness to seize every opportunity to trade with the Spanish colonies. As Castlereagh candidly and unfeelingly admitted in the same letter to Sir Henry Wellesley:

. . . Our commercial habits as a nation, and our reluctance to break off intercourse with the Provinces in revolt, have created, not unnaturally, perhaps, doubts of our sincerity, and we may be considered as not unwilling to witness the separation of these Dependencies from the Mother Country. To this view of the question it may fairly be replied that, if the future system of Spain for South America is to be commercial exclusion as heretofore, such might secretly be our wish and our interest, however our conduct as a Government might be regulated by the engagements we have with Spain.

But if Spain can be induced to adopt the only system by which she can save those dominions to herself, what interest can we have in wishing to see them separated from her? Have we not on the contrary the strongest imaginable interest in their continued connexion? The means of carrying on the war in Europe against France depend on their fidelity. If separated, the wealth of America is withdrawn from the cause in Europe; if united and tranquillized, its treasures may again be poured forth in our support.

This was duplicity, fence-sitting and two-facedness of the highest order. British foreign policy has rarely in history stooped so low.

Miranda, dragging out his last days in the wretchedness of his cell at Cadiz, had no way of knowing the depths of cynicism the policy of his 'friends' in Britain, in whom he had placed so much trust, now plumbed. The early enthusiasm, the liberal passions of such men as Burke and Vansittart, the military adventures planned by Grenville, Windham and Wellesley, had long since been dampened down or, more recently, replaced by the cold calculation of Lord Castlereagh. He, like Pitt, saw the commercial possibilities of Latin America but was strongly opposed to any military entanglement there, even more strongly to recognition of the infant republics fighting for their independence. He went so far as to introduce a Bill to prevent the enlistment of Britons in Latin American armies; pressure of public opinion, however, fired perhaps by romantic idealism, rendered this measure unenforceable.

Castlereagh was aristocratic and good-looking, possessed of a brilliant analytical mind but inarticulate, haughty and remote; a contemporary described him as 'a splendid summit of bright and polished frost which, like the travellers in Switzerland, we all admire; but no one can hope, and few would wish, to reach.' His lack of enthusiasm for a Latin America independent of Spain arose from his markedly reactionary foreign policy, based on the attempts of the Congress of Vienna to create, by means of the Grand Alliance, a 'concert of nations in Europe' to balance the yet more reactionary Russian-inspired Holy Alliance. He hoped to establish a treaty mechanism by which future disputes between Russia, the Austro-Hungarian Empire, Prussia and France might be resolved, with Britain holding the ring. As all these Powers were military-backed absolutist monarchies, he saw little profit in upsetting them by any appearance of encouragement for radical republican movements against Spain.

Perhaps the most unsavoury aspect of Castlereagh's attitude to Latin American independence was that for as long as the Peninsular War raged he, as War Minister for most of those years, had effectively held the whip hand: Spanish resistance to the French was wholly dependent on British support, and the Spanish were virtually impotent. Instead of dictating policy, he heeded Spain's threats that she would conclude a separate peace with Napoleon if Britain recognised the colonial insurgents. These threats, and, later, pressure from some of history's most formidably hard-nosed reactionaries – Alexander I of Russia, *soi-disant* mystical instrument of the Apocalypse and vigorous represser of his own people; Prince Metternich, brilliant diplomat and intellectual exponent of a pure monarchical conservatism which served to disguise the relative weakness of the Austrian Empire he served; his timid disciple, Prince Frederick William of Prussia; and Louis XVIII of France, last of the Bourbons – stultified British policy in regard to Latin America for a decade.

Miranda continued gamely to plot his escape. To his delight he found he could smuggle letters out by bribing his gaolers, and in May 1814 sent one to Vansittart: 'All-powerful England in Spain can easily do me the service of asking, via Lord Wellesley to his ambassador in Madrid, that Spain fulfill its armistice terms with respect to me, as it has with others.' Monteverde had, after all, reneged on his promise to give Miranda safe conduct. Miranda also asked for money, complaining that funds he believed were being sent to him via a British merchant, Sir J. Duff, never reached him. He needed (he believed) £1,000 to buy his way out of gaol, but claimed that £5,000 had gone astray: either the money had not been sent, or it had been pocketed by Duff or some other intermediary – 'Adversity seems to pursue me wherever I go, whatever I do.'

He had received some books, however, 'which allow me to pass the time pleasingly and constructively: Horace, Virgil, Cicero, Don Quixote and Ariosto and a New Testament. But I absolutely need some money,' he wrote again to Vansittart. He had now reduced his requirements to only £50. His gaolers also supplied him with another necessity – women;

his ardours had not diminished with age. He plotted his escape to Gibraltar, but fell ill with typhus. Bleeding internally, weak and suffering from stomach disorders, he was transferred to the prison hospital. His plot was discovered, and he was returned to a more secure cell. By March 1816 he had recovered enough to make new plans for escape, but the same month he suffered an apoplectic fit that seemed certain to kill him, and was put in hospital again. He died in the early morning of 14 July 1816, the twenty-seventh anniversary of the fall of the Bastille which had so fired his spirit. He had spent four years in prison and his last words were, 'Let me die in peace.' His cell-mate wrote that no priest was allowed to attend to him: 'He was dragged on the bed he died on using his pillow, sheets and other bedclothes to carry him. Then they came and took all his clothes and goods to burn with him.' Such burning was the standard procedure for any prisoner with a possibly infectious disease, but a pathetic end for a man who is commemorated today by a great empty tomb in the Pantheon in Caracas, held up by the claws of an eagle, and by a statue in London off Fitzroy Square, near his London home.

Miranda's common-law wife continued to live in the house at 27 Grafton Way until her death in 1850. Lady Hester Stanhope, who had become close to Miranda in London, took his children, Leandro and Francisco, under her protection. Leandro, who eventually founded Venezuela's first bank, married a relative of Miranda's old secretary, Soublette, and died in 1886. Francisco, better-looking but more spoilt, became a soldier under Bolívar, killed the Dutch ambassador to Colombia in a duel, and was executed in 1831 for unspecified offences. When Miranda's beloved library was valued it was found to contain six thousand books worth £9,000 – a huge sum for the times.

If Miranda was all he appears or was said to have been – a Don Quixote, lecher, snobbish poseur, sponger, a figure wrapped in his own *folie de grandeur*, an ineffectual leader of Venezuela's revolution and an overly defensive military commander, a failure who spent his last years in the squalor of Cadiz prison – there was yet extraordinary nobility about the exotic old rogue who died, disappointed, at sixty-six. The dreamer had not fulfilled his dreams – but he had lived his life to the full, and he had been the first ruler of an independent Venezuela, if only for a few months. Bolívar's main charge against him, treachery, does not stand up: his faults of leadership notwithstanding, he was no betrayer of his people, or of his cause. Bolívar never expressed remorse for his own betrayal of the man he later labelled 'beginner of the revolution', but seemed by this to recognise his stature. Today Miranda is revered in much of Latin America as 'El Precursor' – John the Baptist – to the Liberator himself.

In revolutionary France Miranda had shown qualities of leadership and bravery in adversity that confounded those who saw him as purely a self-indulgent boaster; those who then and later accused him of cowardice cannot explain away these displays. The symposiums he established at Grafton Way influenced a whole generation of Latin American revolutionaries. Miranda prepared the intellectual case, the overseas climate of sympathy and support among both government leaders and popular opinion that was to smooth the path of Latin American independence. Through sheer force of personality and intellect he pushed this cause to the top of the political agenda. More, although his 'invasions' of South America were accompanied by pathos and disaster, by staging them at all he secured a significant public relations coup which drew attention to the plight of a continent.

That he was a cautious, realistic general, courageous in battle yet disciplined, was, however, his undoing. What the war of Latin American independence required, against one of the largest and most ruthless military machines the world has ever known, was a man of strength, aggression, and no caution at all, a crazed, ruthless criollo without fear or inhibitions. The liberation of Latin America was a task not for a foppish, reasoning, civilised voluptuary, but for a madman. Simón Bolívar, the sorcerer's apprentice who had condemned his master to a slow and terrible death, was just such a one.

7

Reconquest

After his arrest by the Spanish Bolívar was subsequently freed, and rode back to Caracas, to the house of a family friend, Francisco Itúrbide. This worthy was close to the Marqués de Casa Leon, a man of high standing, Minister of Finance in the Venezuelan republic, but allegedly a co-conspirator in Miranda's plot to embezzle its funds. Both now intervened with Domingo Monteverde to secure Bolívar a safe-conduct in gratitude for his role in Miranda's arrest. Having summoned Itúrbide and Bolívar to appear before him, Monteverde chatted amiably with Itúrbide, paying little attention to his sullen young companion. 'I will concede you a passage for your service to the King in surrendering Miranda,' he said to him at length. Rashly outspoken as ever, Bolívar retorted: 'I arrested Miranda because he was a traitor to his country' – which could be taken either way. Monteverde was visibly irritated, Itúrbide apologised, and Bolívar was dismissed. As Monteverde subsequently explained, 'I cannot forget the interesting service of Casas, Bolívar and Peña, owing to which the persons of all three have been respected, and passports for foreign countries given only to the second, since his influence and connections might be dangerous in the circumstances.' He could not know that he had freed the man who was to be not only his destroyer, but the destroyer of Spanish rule in Latin America.

Itúrbide advised Bolívar to leave as soon as possible, before the Spanish changed their minds, and on 12 August he and a few companions sailed from La Guaira for the island of Curaçao. There he learned that he had been stripped of his own and his late brother's estates under a law confiscating the possessions of revolutionaries. Meanwhile, marauding bands of freed slaves and Monteverde's militia alike ignored the terms of the armistice Miranda had agreed. In Guatiré a savage massacre of criollos took place, and altogether some 1,500 patriot leaders were rounded up and tied to the backs of mules to be dragged to prison. Miranda wrote bitterly from his own confinement about Monteverde's violation of the Treaty of San Mateo:

> I have seen old age, youth, rich and poor, the labourer and the priest, in chains, breathing air so foul that it extinguishes a flame, poisons the blood and brings inevitable death. I have seen distinguished citizens, sacrificed to this cruelty, expire in these dungeons, deprived of bodily necessities, of the consolation of their families and of the spiritual rites of our religion – men who would have preferred to die a thousand deaths with the weapons, which they so generously surrendered, in their hands.

He had every reason to be full of remorse. He had justified his surrender as a way to secure reasonable terms and avert unnecessary bloodshed. Instead, his detractors had been proved right: the people of Venezuela might have suffered less if they had fought to the bitter end. There was no compromise to be had with the evil empire.

This was also the conclusion to which Bolívar came during the povery-stricken month he now spent on the sunbaked tropical island of Curaçao, where he was 'detestably received'. As he wrote to a friend, 'hardly had I landed when my baggage was embargoed [by the captain of the brig *Celoso*, in which he had sailed] . . . because my belongings had been in the same house as Miranda's and because the brig . . . had contracted debts in Puerto Cabello which I was now to pay because I was commandant of the harbour when the debts were contracted . . .' He was now a man transformed, displaying traits that those who had previously known him would never have suspected him to possess. One was ruthlessness – the once easygoing dilettante declared passionately that 'by the same methods as the oppressors of Caracas managed to subdue the confederation, with those same methods and with more certainty than them, I will try to redeem my fatherland'. The future was also to reveal his almost superhuman reserves of strength and energy, and a command of language and the written word that inspired a whole continent.

On Curaçao Bolívar and his friends plotted how to strike back at the Spanish Empire. Their goal was Cartagena, the last major city on the northern coast holding out against the Spanish government, a low-lying, torrid natural harbour on the Caribbean dominated by one of the most formidable maritime fortresses in the world. It had many times withstood past British sieges, but had been the first city in the Viceroyalty of

New Granada to rise up, in May 1810, and proclaim its right to free trade. Two weeks later the revolt had spread to Santa Fé de Bogotá, the capital, four hundred miles inland in the mountains, and the Viceroy, the aged and deaf General Antonio Amar y Borbon, was arrested. But large parts of the country declared their continuing allegiance to Spain. Quito, full of royalist soldiers, was followed by Panamá, in the north, in rejecting the uprising. Pasto and Popayán, mountain royalist strongholds, did likewise, as did Cartagena's rival port of Santa Marta. To make matters more complicated still, Cartagena decided she would not submit to Santa Fé de Bogotá, and proclaimed herself an independent city-state. Heated arguments broke out in Bogotá and one faction, the federalists under Camilo Torres, opposed to central rule from the capital, marched to Tunja in the mountains. Antonio Nariño, a longstanding opponent of Spanish rule, often imprisoned, became president of the state of Cundinamarca, based on Bogotá.

When Bolívar and his companions reached Cartagena they offered themselves for military service to the governor, Manuel Rodriguez Torices. Blockaded by the Spanish and running short of supplies, Torices was also desperately short of good fighting men, and had had to resort to employing mercenaries; Bolívar was at once appointed a colonel. One of the mercenaries, a former French pirate, General Labatut, an old friend of Miranda, had become the virtual dictator of Cartagena, and Torices undoubtedly saw in Bolívar a possible means of ridding himself of Labatut's tyranny. Labatut, who knew from Miranda how difficult Bolívar was, now learnt to his horror of his old friend's fate at the latter's hands, and decided to send him as far away as possible, to the small sleepy town of Barrancas on the huge swirling Magdalena river, which drops more than nine thousand feet from its source in the Andes to the sea. There Bolívar settled down to compose his first famous call to arms, the Cartagena Manifesto. In a chillingly authoritarian analysis he lambasted the divisions which had brought down the Venezuelan Republic:

> The most far-reaching error Venezuela committed when it entered politics was without any doubt the disastrous adherence to a system of tolerance: a system proved by the whole thinking world to be weak and ineffective, yet tenaciously adhered to with exceptional blindness to the very end.
>
> The laws were framed by certain well-meaning visionaries who, building republics in the air, have tried to reach political perfection on the assumption that humanity is perfect. So we have had philosophers instead

of leaders, philanthropy instead of legislation, dialectic instead of tactics, and sophists instead of soldiers. [He clearly had Miranda in mind. Now he turned to the federalists.]

Federalism, though it may be the most perfect [system] and the most capable of bringing happiness to human society, is nevertheless the most detrimental to the interests of our infant countries. Generally speaking our citizens are not yet able to exercise their rights fully and for themselves, because they lack the political virtues that characterise true republics . . .

Moreover, what country in the world, however well-behaved and republican it may be, could in the midst of internal strife and foreign wars, be ruled by anything so complex and so weak as a federal government? A government must so to speak identify itself with the kind of circumstances, the times, and the men who surround it. If the latter are prosperous and calm, it should be gentle and protective; but if they are unruly and turbulent, it should be stern and should arm itself with a firmness equal to the dangers, not concerning itself with laws and constitutions until such time as happiness and peace are established . . .

Popular elections by country rustics and intriguing city-dwellers are one more obstacle to the practice of federation among us; because the former are so ignorant that they cast their votes mechanically, and the latter so ambitious that they convert everything into factions; therefore in Venezuela there has never been a free and just vote, and the government has been placed in the hands of men who have either betrayed the cause or were inept or immoral. It is our lack of unity, not Spanish arms, that has returned us to slavery.

He went on to argue that the Viceroyalty of New Granada and the independence of Venezuela were inextricably linked – indeed, that freedom for Venezuela was essential to secure the independence of Santa Fé de Bogotá, for he saw both as parts of a single entity, which he called Gran Colombia.

This justified the plan forming in his mind – that he should use troops from Santa Fé to cross back and liberate Venezuela, a plan which would hardly have been attractive to the people of Bogotá and Cartagena, several hundreds of miles away from and largely indifferent to the fate of Venezuela. He ended with a ringing declaration:

New Granada's glory depends upon her assumption of the task of liberating the cradle of Colombian independence, its martyrs and those meritorious people of Caracas whose outcries can only be directed to their beloved compatriots, the New Granadans, whom they await with mortal impatience as their saviours. Let us hasten to break the chains of those victims who groan in their dungeons, awaiting salvation at your hands! Do not abuse their confidence! Do not turn a deaf ear to the lamentations of your brothers! Let us fly quickly to avenge the dead, to give life to the dying, freedom to the oppressed and liberty to all!

This manifesto was warmly endorsed by Torices, the Governor of Cartagena, and by Camilo Torres, president of the congress in Tunja, to which independent statelet Cartagena had linked herself.

Bolívar did not while away all his time composing manifestos. The soldiers he found at Barrancas were a shambles of ill-trained, ill-dressed, ill-equipped, grumbling, swearing layabouts. With grim determination he set about moulding them into a fighting force; by December 1812 he felt ready to request Torices's permission to move further up-river to deal with Spanish positions there. Without waiting for a reply he set out towards Tenerife, a royalist stronghold. On the way they reached the sleepy hamlet of Salamina, where Bolívar heard of a beautiful blonde girl who spoke a strange language and would talk to no one. Her name was Anita Lénoit, and she was the daughter of a French businessman. He found her, and they spent the rest of the evening reminiscing about Paris. He left her at last, as good manners dictated, and called again the following day, when her father had returned. They spent the rest of the day together, like old and fond lovers, and the night as well.

The following day Bolívar received Torices's authorisation to march on Tenerife, and he set off up the river in a convoy of small rafts which moved slowly along the banks of the Magdalena under the dense jungle canopy, sometimes running aground, seeking to avoid the strong down-stream currents. On 23 December his small force silently surrounded Tenerife, and the Spanish garrison was astonished when a delegation arrived under a white flag, asking them to surrender and offering safe conduct. The local commander refused, and a withering fire broke out from all around the settlement. The Spanish, not knowing the exact strength of the enemy surrounding them and fearing that they were in a trap, hurriedly evacuated the town, leaving behind their artillery and, in the river harbour, their small gunboats.

It is said, but perhaps the story is apocryphal, that Bolívar was resting after the skirmish when Anita Lénoit reappeared, having followed him up-river, and they spent a joyous night together. If so, it was the last time she saw him. But the brief dalliance seems to have made a profound impact on him, for he frequently spoke of her afterwards – the ultimate romantic interlude, a girl loved for only a few days.

Moving upstream, Bolívar's force reached the town of Mompós, which he found the Spanish had abandoned on his approach. He was received enthusiastically, in the first of the triumphal entries that were to mark his career. 'Born in Caracas,' he declared grandly, 'Glory in Mompós.' It was pure bombast, but it didn't matter: it earned him hundreds of recruits. With them he marched on the villages of Guamol and El Banco, where small garrisons were quickly put to flight, then decided to engage the main Spanish force, which had moved north and east, to Chiriguana. His oarsmen pulled the rafts forward vigorously down a tributary of the Magdalena, the Cesar, and fell upon the Spanish in a surprise attack on New Year's Day, 1813. After a few hours the royalists were routed; returning to the main river, Bolívar moved south again and easily took the towns of Tamalameque and, after a bloody skirmish, Puerto Nacional.

A more glittering prize now beckoned: Ocaña, an important city in the mountains to the east of the river. Leaving most of his men on the Magdalena, he set off with a detachment to reconnoitre. No sooner did news of his approach reach the city than the small Spanish garrison there was put to flight by an uprising among the townspeople and Bolívar, without a fight, found himself moving triumphally into the town, in the second of his great entrances.

He was delighted on two accounts: he had freed a large swathe of the royalist-controlled Magdalena and, now, part of the interior of the province; news that Labatut had captured the key port of Santa Marta meant that the whole province of Cartagena was rid of the Spanish. Secondly, Ocaña lay on the way to the Venezuelan border – and Bolívar was far more interested in liberating his homeland and exacting revenge from Monteverde than in ascending further into the interior of New Granada. On 23 January news reached the rebel government in Tunja that a large force of Spaniards under Colonel Ramos Correa was approaching the town of Pamplona, on the New Granadan side of the border with Venezuela. Bolívar's political masters urged him to take action to defend his flank, and he was delighted to comply: it furnished him with the excuse he needed to move towards the Venezuelan border.

Already Bolívar had established a pattern. Rafting their way upstream against the currents of the Magdalena, his forces had proved themselves masters of a new type of warfare: guerrilla attack, the movement of relatively small armies across large distances to inflict surprise attacks on sleepy outposts where they were least expected. In this type of war, as Bolívar well understood, speed, movement, and manoeuvrability were all-important. Most jungle fighting up to then had consisted of desultory exchanges between outposts controlled by one or other side – a small attack, a small victory or small repulse. By using trained irregulars, impervious to the discomfort of covering large distances, he was able to keep the initiative and could secure one surprise victory after another. Moreover, Bolívar's perspective was not merely defensive and regional: it was continental. If necessary, he would march not just across the vast distances of Colombia but across the continent of Latin America itself to secure victory. 'Hit them where they ain't': it might have been his motto, not that of Douglas MacArthur a hundred and thirty years later. It was impossible for the cumbersome royalist armies, however big they might be, to defend all their towns and territory; and by concentrating themselves in one place they left others open to attack, as they had no idea where he would strike next.

That was for the future. For the moment Bolívar was a nuisance on the New Granadan side of the border, and one that the large royalist forces on the Venezuelan side were gathering to deal with. Correa, the royalist commander, had a thousand well-armed men at Cúcuta, while on the New Granadan side the rebel commander Colonel Manuel Castillo had 1,300 at Pamplona, in the foothills to the south.

But between Cúcuta and Bolívar's forces lay the appalling terrain of the Cordillera Oriental, one of the fingers of the Andes which descends nearly to the Caribbean, dense jungle interspersed with soaring, barren plateaux. Correa assumed it to be an impenetrable barrier, which meant that he would be able to destroy Castillo's rebel forces at will. Castillo himself was vain and unimaginative, with no better plan than to entrench himself in a defensive hedgehog position and wait for the attack.

The two men reckoned without Simón Bolívar. Setting off across those uninhabited badlands on 24 January, Bolívar divided his little army into two columns. For the first time the full extent of his extraordinary vigour and energy manifested itself. Tirelessly cajoling, ordering and goading his men on, himself helping to push the animals and pick up exhausted men, he forced his troops through the dense jungle and ferocious thorn-bush lowlands, then up rocky passes where the track clung to ledges which sometimes crumbled away, sending men and animals plunging to their deaths. At night fires kept out the bitter cold of the plateaux, except when freezing rain and sleet paralysed his men in their camps.

Three days later he had at last reached the summit of the pass, the Alto de la Aguada, where a hundred Spaniards waited in the bitter cold: Correa had rushed a small detachment there on learning from his scouts of the rebels' approach by that 'impassable' route. Bolívar, realising that to assault this redoubt from below would be fatal, arranged for a runner to be captured by Correa's men so that he could 'confess' that Castillo's forces were approaching from the rear, to seal the Spanish in a trap; they were taken in by this ruse and started to retreat towards Cúcuta. Bolívar promptly ordered his columns forward, up and across the top of the pass and down, where they fell upon and dispersed Correa's fleeing detachment. Descending rapidly towards Pamplona, he made contact with Castillo's forces, and his own exhausted troops were able to rest. Then he continued along the valley of the Zulia river, encountering minor resistance from Spanish positions. Within days he was on the commanding heights overlooking the great valley of San José de Cúcuta, where Correa was making a stand outside the town.

Bolívar's army was still feeling the effects of their march across that supposedly impassable mountain range, but he recognised that the Spanish must not be given time to dig in. On 28 February he sent forward his advance troops, holding the bulk of his forces in reserve. The Spanish decided that the rebel numbers were small and vulnerable enough to be attacked on the valley floor, and surged out in strength to surround them. Waiting until they had emerged, Bolívar ordered his main force out of the hills nearby. Realising that he was now in danger of being surrounded himself and cut off from the town, in a desperate move Correa ordered his men to seize the rocky hills to the left of the rebels. It proved a brilliant counter-move: Bolívar's men were caught out in the open, and their casualties multiplied. Bolívar ordered his cousin Colonel José Felix Ribas to lead a bayonet charge up the hill – seemingly a suicidal assault. But somehow it succeeded: the royalist lines broke into a panic-stricken retreat through the town and into Venezuela across the Tachira river, where Bolívar, who lacked authorisation to cross the frontier, broke off his pursuit.

He had won his first major, and decisive, victory. Although the battle of Cúcuta had been a close-run thing, it was a remarkable achievement against a superior enemy. His crossing of the cordillera was a deed of astonishing speed and endurance, the first of a series of near-superhuman feats of generalship and leadership carried out over some of the most geographically varied, taxing and savage terrain on earth. He had turned the terrible topography to his advantage.

In the pleasant climate of Cúcuta he prepared his plans for his next offensive: not to liberate more of New Granada, but to march into Venezuela, his homeland, at the head of New Granadan troops. He dared not do so without authorisation, as this would be to risk arrest by his own superiors. Labatut in Cartagena had made his detestation plain; Castillo, the rebel commander in Pamplona, bitterly resented the upstart from across the mountains and opposed any crossing of the border, as did his second-in-command, Major Francisco de Paula Santander, whom Bolívar now met for the first time. As the dispute over Bolívar's plans grew more intense, he threatened to resign; but the Congress in Tunja, refusing to accept his withdrawal, promoted him to brigadier-general and made him a citizen of New Granada.

Bolívar did not propose to waste more time quarrelling with resentful and mediocre local commanders: he would send a mission to Santa Fé de Bogotá to secure backing and reinforcements. Colonel Ribas was therefore despatched up the cordillera to that oldest and most beautiful of the Spanish colonial capitals in the north, in its huge saucer in the mountains. There the Republic of Cundinamarca, confusingly separated from the Congress of Tunja which Bolívar now served, was headed by Antonio Nariño, a brilliant intellectual who had been tutored in London by Miranda and later imprisoned in Cadiz for attempting to circulate a copy of Thomas Paine's *Rights of Man* in Santa Fé de Bogotá. After escaping from Cadiz he had been imprisoned again, in Bogotá itself, but released in the 1810 uprising and set up as president.

Nariño's sole interest was an independent Santa Fé de Bogotá: he had no wider ambitions for Latin America. But he despatched a hundred and fifty soldiers to help Bolívar. Other prominent men, too, now made the difficult journey to Cúcuta: men like Anastasio Girardot, Antonio Ricuarte, Rafael Urdaneta and Pedro Briceño Mendez – young, aristocratic criollos imbued with the same romantic military ardour, some of whom, like Bolívar, had lost all their possessions. The majority of his supporters came from well-to-do families; the Spanish army, by contrast, was almost entirely recruited from among blacks, mestizos and impoverished peasants. Many of them nursed grievances against the landowning aristocracy, but most had joined for the pay and the prospects of plunder. Bolívar recruited vigorously among the inhabitants of the Cúcuta valley and during two months of peace in that tranquil, temperate region drilled his men into a more effective fighting force. His army totalled only about seven hundred, but it was well supplied with guns and ammunition from the captured garrison there, as well as a million pesos from the treasury.

On 7 May Bolívar at last received the order to march on Venezuela – but only to liberate the border provinces of Mérida and Trujillo. It was good enough for him – and it immediately sparked off a furious row with the local commanders, Castillo and Santander. The latter flatly refused to march, whereupon Bolívar threatened to have him shot for disobeying orders. Santander grudgingly gave way, but resented this first slight throughout his life. Bolívar had to pledge solemnly in front of the city council to obey the Congress's orders, such was their fear that he was planning to invade Venezuela as a whole.

Facing the rebel troops were about six thousand of Correa's royalists, dispersed over a fan-shaped spread of towns and villages set back from the border. It was a formidable army, but it was scattered, and Bolívar had already evolved his guerrilla strategy of picking off enemy garrisons one by one, using his speed and manoeuvrability to prevent them joining forces. Advancing on the small town of San Antonio, he ordered Castillo to advance on La Grita. With ill grace Castillo proceeded, and in the steep hills near the town, thanks largely to Santander's brave and skilful leadership, Correa's forward troops were driven back. Castillo reckoned it to be madness to continue the advance into Venezuela, and resigned his command, which fell to Santander. He was just twenty-one, a good-looking New Granadan, highly educated and possessed of a brilliant mind, a devious and formidable tactician – but over-cautious, pedantic, legalistic. He advised Bolívar that it would be folly to proceed, and predicted mass desertions. Contemptuously, Bolívar left him in charge of the frontier garrisons at the rear, and appointed four young lieutenants to command the vanguard. His forces rode out across the endless green foothills under the easternmost spur of the Andes, the mountains of the Cordillera de Mérida towering above them. At first, his judgement seemed amply vindicated: the royalists had apparently melted away. San Cristóbal fell without a fight, and in an easy ride of a fortnight through magnificent rolling country, by 23 May he reached the city of Mérida. He was now a hundred miles into his homeland, Venezuela – a fifth of the way to Caracas, from which he had been so brutally expelled just nine months before, in circumstances of shame and betrayal.

In the mountain air and the steep narrow streets of Mérida, a delightful colonial city beneath nearly seventy peaks with an average height of 13,000 feet, the Liberator's thoughts must have been heady indeed. (The highest mountain of the cordillera, a white-capped giant towering 16,400 feet over the town, was later renamed Mount Bolívar.) There had been no opposition; the whole town had turned out to greet his army, and a volunteer force under a Spaniard, Major Vicente Campo Elias, had joined him. The major pledged to kill every Spaniard he encountered, and then himself and his own family, so that no more of the accursed race should remain alive. With two columns, 560 men in front and 883 in the rear, Bolívar's army was now beginning to attain a respectable size – and its training and discipline were formidable. It seemed that the conquest of Venezuela would be almost too easy.

His run of luck continued to hold. He despatched a force to engage Correa's remaining army at Escuque; defeated in a minor battle, Correa withdrew into the foetid, dismal lowlands around the broad inland sea of Lake Maracaibo, one of the world's hottest and most desolate places. An advance guard was sent forward to the city of Trujillo, and Bolívar himself, after marching along the ancient trail of the Conquistadors with the bulk of his army, arrived there on 14 June. Now half-way to Caracas, he had completed the task set him by the council at Tunja and was at the limits of the territory he was authorised to capture. The only unsettling aspect of the campaign was the way the Spanish had fallen back without a fight, hardly ever stopping to oppose him. It seemed evident to Bolívar that Correa was trying to lure him into overextending his lines of communication – now stretched to two hundred miles – with the intention of encircling him. At the very least, he was refusing to engage in the expectation that the invaders would turn about, leaving the Spanish army intact and in a position to reassert its authority once they had gone.

There were certainly significant Spanish forces north and south of Bolívar, as well as in front of him to the east. If he did not retreat, he appeared to have no choice but to stop, and seek to consolidate the territory gained – or so, evidently, Correa anticipated. Instead, he took everyone – the Spanish and his own side – by surprise: he suddenly flung himself at the enemy in an apparently suicidal and certainly mutinous onslaught that was to deliver his greatest triumph to date – and forever besmirch his reputation as a human being.

The night of 14 June 1813 marked a decisive turning-point for Bolívar. To advance was to use New Granadan troops to promote his own personal cause: the liberation of Venezuela. This he could justify in his own mind: he was a pan-American – he believed in the liberation of all Latin America, not just of New Granada. He had already underlined his belief that as long as Venezuela remained in Spanish hands, the independence of New Granada was under threat (which was undoubtedly true). He could certainly not retreat once he had made the fateful decision to move forward: the penalty for insubordination combined with failure would have been death. Like Hernán Cortés in Mexico in 1519, he was burning his boats.

Unlike the people of Mérida and the mountains, who had welcomed him, the people of Trujillo had fled in the face of the rebel advance. The peasants were in hiding, their animals driven away. The great population of slaves and mestizo labourers around Lake Maracaibo resented the proud criollo landowner class typified by Bolívar, the Spanish having cleverly fostered disaffection between the lower, exploited orders and upper-class Americans. Ordinary people looked to Spain and King to preserve them from the depredations of their local-born masters – ignorant of the fact that the Spanish economic system was of all elements in their lives the most exploitative. Bolívar could hope for little support among such people. Another factor kept them hostile to his cause: fear. Monteverde's legions, recruited from the lowest ranks in society, had violated Miranda's armistice without compunction, and generated a climate of terror across the land: the people were more frightened of Spanish retribution than of Bolívar, who was not exaggerating when he wrote that:

The revolution of blacks, both freemen and slaves, provoked, helped and supported by the agents of Monteverde, these inhuman and atrocious peoples, steeped in the blood and the goods of the patriots . . . marching upon the neighbourhood of Caracas, committed in those villages and in particular in the town of Guatire the most horrible murders, thefts, violence and devastation . . .

Those who had surrendered, peaceful workers, men of the highest esteem, were killed with pistol shots and swords or were barbarically beheaded even after the armistice was published. Blood was everywhere and bodies decorated the squares and streets of Guatire, Calabozo, San Juan de los Morros and other towns occupied by peaceful, hard-working people who, for having taken up arms or on the approach of the troops having fled to the mountains, were dragged, bound, to have their lives taken without further formality, hearing or judgment. Any official was authorised to hand out death sentences to those they considered patriots or whom they wished to rob.

The results of Monteverde's terror had recently been brought home to Bolívar in particularly vivid form when in the course of his advance from the west he heard of an anti-Spanish uprising in the hills led by an old neighbour of his, Antonio Nicolás Briceño, a distinguished and cultivated lawyer of 'gentle and peaceful disposition'. So appalled by Spanish atrocities that his character underwent a complete transformation, Briceño instituted his own local insurrection, in which promotion was based on the number of Spanish heads a soldier took: thirty heads earned him the rank of lieutenant, fifty that of captain. Bolívar, appalled, ordered Briceño's arrest, but received a gift of two heads by way of reply. Before he could act further, the Spanish had captured Briceño and his men, court-martialled them, and shot the avenging lawyer and seven of his followers at Barinas. The Spanish commander, Tizcar, did not however go so far as to massacre all the insurgents.

The death of Briceño, although justified in the circumstances, keenly offended Bolívar, but nothing can excuse what he did next. In Mérida he had already delivered a bitter warning: 'Our vengeance shall rival Spanish ferocity. Our goodwill is at last exhausted; and, since our oppressors compel us to mortal warfare, they shall disappear from America and our land shall be purged of the monsters that infest it. Our hate shall be inexorable and our war shall be to the death.' In Trujillo he now issued a solemn proclamation:

> The Spaniards have served us with rapine and death. They have violated the sacred rights of human beings, violated capitulations and the most solemn treaties; committed, in fact, every crime. They have reduced the Republic of Venezuela to the most frightful desolation. Thus, then, justice demands vengeance and necessity obliges us to take it . . .
>
> Every Spaniard who does not conspire with the most active and effective means possible against the tyranny in favour of our just cause will be held as an enemy and a traitor to the fatherland; and in consequence will be inexorably put to the knife. On the other hand, an absolute and general indulgence will be granted to those who pass to our army with or without their arms . . . Spaniards who render conspicuous service to the State will be treated as Americans . . .

He concluded with this ringingly Solomonic declaration: 'Spaniards and men of the Canary Islands, if you are lukewarm and do not work actively for America's freedom, you may be certain of death. Americans, even if you have done wrong, you may be certain of life.'

There can have been few more terrible pronouncements by a major figure in modern history. While atrocities may be inevitable – even the norm – in warfare, only in the French Revolution were they expressly authorised by the constituted legal authority, and then to a more limited extent. Usually the authorities on either side are at pains to maintain the appearance of legal propriety, whatever the truth on the ground. Monteverde's own agreement to Miranda's armistice of the previous year – which his soldiers promptly flouted – was a typical example. Bolívar's proclamation, in explicitly authorising atrocity and terror, launched what immediately became known as the 'war to the death': Bolívar's secretary subsequently signed his letters 'third [year] of independence and first of war to the death', to underline the point. The purpose was clear – to instil in the populace the same terror of his own forces as Monteverde had through his atrocities: in a land ruled by fear of the Spanish, fear of Bolívar's forces was henceforth to be as potent a weapon. The people of Trujillo would not join him; therefore they must learn to fear him.

Bolívar's South American hagiographers have sprung to the defence of the 'war to the death' proclamation. At first glance this extraordinary document appears crude, yet its most curious feature is that it was in fact very carefully crafted – to be, Bolívar's apologists argue, actually rather merciful. It was nothing less than an amnesty for his American-born opponents – 'even if you have done wrong, you may be certain of life' – because their state of subjugation meant they were not responsible for their actions. The point of this was to secure the allegiance of the ill-educated majority who were serving in the Spanish forces – even though they had been responsible for the worst atrocities; for the Spanish-born, there would be no quarter unless they actively joined Bolívar's ranks – those who were not with him were against him. He hoped to sow among low-caste Americans the same kind of racial and class hatred of the Spanish as the Spanish had so effectively fomented against the criollo rebels; and to secure whatever conversions were possible among the ranks of privileged Spaniards. Uppermost in Bolívar's mind was the confusion of the last days of Miranda's republic, when nominal adherents of the new regime had crossed over without a qualm to Monteverde's side, in the hope of being spared his vengeance.

Now they were to have no such easy option. Unless they openly backed Bolívar, they would be killed – even the peaceful civilians among them. The selectiveness of Bolívar's policy of legitimised slaughter is particularly chilling: this was not a proclamation issued by a young hot-head in the thick of fighting, or the ranting of a murderous local despot. It was the calculated authorisation of racial murder, even of the innocent, to secure the advantage for his own side. Bolívar has been excused, as acting against a truly barbaric enemy. Five years later, Henry Clay thus defended him in a famous speech in the United States Congress:

> The gentleman from Georgia cannot see any parallel between our revolution and that of the South American provinces and contends that their revolution was stained by scenes which had not occurred in ours. If so, it was because execrable outrages had been committed upon them by the troops of the mother country which were not upon us. Can it be believed, if the slaves had been let loose upon us in the South as they have been let loose in Venezuela, if quarter had been refused, capitulations violated, that George Washington would not have resorted to retribution? Retaliation is sometimes mercy, mercy to both parties. The only means by which the coward's soul that indulges in such enormities can be reached is to show him that he will be visited by severe but just retribution.

The Spanish were certainly fiendishly inhuman in their cruelty: they raped women, then tied them in their hammocks and set fires under them, literally roasting them to death. They peeled prisoners' feet and made them walk across hot coals; ears were trophies of war; the catalogue does not stop there. Yet the flaw in Clay's argument is evident. Bolívar was not threatening 'severe but just retribution': he was threatening unjust retribution, indiscriminately targeting Spaniards because of their place of birth, whether they were guilty or innocent. Morever, he was backing his threat with the sanction of law. He was setting himself up as Liberator, a quasi-legal authority, and preaching as part of his new juridical system the savagery of the brute or barbarian.

Bolívar's pretensions to statesmanship were irreparably harmed by this proclamation. Worse, it is possible to trace to it many of the terrible excesses that subsequently befell the continent under a succession of tyrants: the notions that he who is not with us is against us, that atrocity must be met with atrocity, that the many can and should be punished for the acts of the few, that there is no such thing as moderation or a middle way in war – these have reverberated all the way down to the murderous caudillos and military juntas of Latin America of as recently as a couple of decades ago. The bestial cruelties of the Spanish were answered by those of Bolívar, who could instead have broken the vicious circle and kept faith with his political ideals.

It is also true, however, that such vengeful outbursts on his part tended to occur only in times of extreme difficulty. The 'war to the death' proclamation can be seen as a natural response to an apparently desperate situation of encirclement, just as Miranda's arrest may have seemed to Bolívar at the time the only way of salvaging his own reputation. In him, remarkable political acuity could suddenly, under the intolerable pressures his highly-strung mind was subject to, lapse into an almost insane single-mindedness which paid no heed to the consequences of his actions for other people – often including his own men.

While Bolívar's proclamation fatally detracts from his stature, it also reveals more than anything else that within him which was perhaps his most effective weapon as a commander: his near-fanatical, almost-super-human adherence to the cause of victory. He would not retreat in the face of overwhelming odds. He would give no quarter in hostile territory. This demonic ferocity was a significant part of his success, and of the fear he induced in his opponents.

Bolívar now thrust and parried with such speed that his enemies were left dazed and confused. Tizcar commanded an army of 1,500 at Barinas in the foothills of the eastern slopes where the Mérida cordillera meets the Venezuelan plains; to the north and north-east lay some two thousand Spaniards in Coro and Maracaibo. The bulk of Monteverde's army was ahead of Bolívar. The danger was that Tizcar would wheel behind him and cut him off from the frontier. In a master-stroke, Bolívar turned the tables: he led a small force in a rapid march up and over the steep cordillera, tumbling down the other side of the mountains to surprise Guanare, behind Spanish lines, cutting off Tizcar's army from Caracas. Behind him two trusted lieutenants, Girardot and Ribas, marched to protect his flank; some four hundred met a royalist force twice as large at Las Mesitas, where a fierce battle was resolved at last in a successful bayonet charge led by Ribas, a man of engaging simplicity and outstanding bravery who habitually sported the tricolour rosette of Revolutionary France in his hat.

Bolívar meanwhile force-marched on Tizcar at Barinas – to find the

Spanish army had fled on hearing of his approach, leaving behind thirteen cannon and all its stores. He pursued them down into the vast
remoteness of the plains without catching them, then turned about and
swiftly marched his men a hundred miles north and east to Araure, not
far from the town of San Carlos. Ribas, however, failed to prevent the
junction of two Spanish detachments and found himself outnumbered
by three to one – and four cannon. Nevertheless, on 22 July he attacked
the Spanish and was twice repulsed before launching an assault on their
weaker flank and capturing their artillery; this he turned on them, and
they broke into a headlong rout. These brilliant parallel manoeuvres
threw the Spanish so much on the defensive that, having effectively
yielded control of the western third of the country, they were forced to
make a stand in Valencia, Venezuela's second city. It was the Spanish
reoccupation of the year before in reverse, with the latter now defending the central highlands and major cities against the advancing rebels.

Bolívar permitted his united army of 2,500 men only a few days' rest,
then spurred them on to catch up with the Spanish forces retreating
from San Carlos before they could join with Monteverde in Valencia. It
was a race against time, but soon they sighted the Spanish on a mountain spur at Tinaquillo, where marksmen had been left to delay Bolívar's
forces as the main army retreated. The last plain before the mountains
lay ahead. Bolívar improvised desperate, brilliant measures, sending a
hundred cavalrymen forward, an infantryman also mounted on each
horse, to get ahead of the Spanish and cut them off before they could
reach the security of the mountains. These troops scrambled through
scree and bush under heavy fire to burst out onto the plain just ahead of
the retreating royalists, then wheeled about, firing; Bolívar and his main
army, meanwhile, attacked from behind. Caught between two fires, the
Spanish were destroyed. Most were shot or taken prisoner.

In Valencia with his main army, three thousand strong, Domingo
Monteverde was a chastened man. He had already been dealt a bloody
nose in eastern Venezuela by a much smaller insurgency led by Santiago
Mariño, a young landowner of Irish extraction from the island of
Margarita, and José Bermudez. These two had the previous year fled to
Trinidad in company with other young insurgents who included
Manuel Piar, Antonio José de Sucre, and Bermudez's brother. In
Trinidad they were studiously cold-shouldered by the British author-
ities, who were anxious not to antagonise the Spanish. Landing on the
desolate Guiria peninsula (not to be confused with Caracas's main port

of La Guaira) and dashingly commanded by Mariño, some forty-five of these exiles had reached a small army supply point, defeated the local Spanish commander, Antoñanzas of evil repute, seized the provincial capital, Cumana, and the town of Barcelona on the road to Caracas. Monteverde himself had been humiliatingly rebuffed when he attempted to dislodge them from Maturín.

Now, discouraged by stories of Bolívar's successes, Monteverde the Terror of Venezuela decided to avoid open battle and slipped away with his army intact to the royalist stronghold of Puerto Cabello. Manuel del Fierro, acting Captain-General, unprotected in Caracas, had no alternative but to sue for peace. As emissaries he sent the Marqués de Casa León and Francisco Itúrbide, the very men whose intercession before Monteverde had saved the life of Bolívar the year before. Bolívar met them in the town of La Victoria, where he embraced his old friend Itúrbide with warmth and emotion.

8

Horsemen from Hell

On 7 August 1813, just eleven months after the fall of Venezuela's first republic, Bolívar re-entered Caracas in triumph to establish the Second Republic, following one of the most brilliantly executed campaigns in military history. In just three months, a man barely thirty with little previous experience of battle and none at all of generalship had staged a punishing push up-river into enemy-held territory, built up a force of more than two thousand men virtually from scratch and, covering 1,200 kilometres, taken his army across a supposedly impassable mountain barrier, won six battles, and routed five separate armies, to become the liberator of his homeland. He made a formidable impression upon Francisco Itúrbide, who had last seen him in the depths of depression and defeat.

For his first triumphal entry into Caracas, Bolívar's dirty uniform was replaced by a new one of white and blue, with gold buttons, braid and epaulettes. In place of his favourite mule he rode a white Arab stallion at the head of his exhausted army. There followed a display of shameless theatricality, such as Bolívar both enjoyed, and believed to be necessary to enthuse the masses. A French officer, now a mercenary but formerly a member of Napoleon's staff, Ducoudrez-Holstein, takes up the story:

> The women came to crown the Liberator and covered the streets where he would pass with heaps of flowers and branches of laurel and olive. The greetings of thousands of people mixed with the thunder of artillery, the ringing of church bells and the blare of martial music. The prisons were opened and the unfortunate victims there, with their pale and thin faces, looked like ghosts risen from their graves. Before Bolívar's arrival a regal and triumphal cart had been prepared, similar to those which Roman consuls had on their return from a glorious campaign . . . Bolívar went on foot to the cart, his head uncovered, dressed in a general's uniform, carrying a baton as the symbol of command.

The cart, decorated with gilded angels, was drawn by twelve beautiful girls pulling a silken rope. Flowers rained down upon the triumphal procession, and thousands cheered its passage to the city hall. Even Archbishop Coll y Pratt, who had behaved so badly during the revolution, was there to make his peace with the Liberator. Bolívar attended a great ball, and the festivities lasted all night. He returned at length to his old family home in the city, where he was repeatedly called to the window by the crowds. His sisters Maria Antonia and Juana fussed over him; his old black nurse, Hipolita, wept as she embraced him. It was a wonderful homecoming, the apparent dawn of a new era for independent Venezuela. The terms of Bolívar's armistice displayed a magnanimity at odds with his 'war to the death' proclamation. No reprisals were to be taken, and property was to be respected; nevertheless, six thousand refugee royalists, fearing revenge for Monteverde's atrocities, fled down to the port of La Guaira.

Bolívar also had a fresh distraction – Josefina Machado, one of the twelve maidens who had drawn his chariot. Her face was too plump and coarse to be described as pretty, but she made up in allure what she lacked in looks. Not of noble birth, she had been excluded from high society, which left her both resentful and ambitious. Bolívar was a relatively easy prospect for a woman seeking to bed him: the difficulty was to keep him on the hook for any length of time. Josefina, surprisingly, through determination and perseverance, managed to do so. She became his regular mistress and, with her sister and her mother, accompanied him in times both of success and danger. Among his men she came to be known as Señorita Pepa. That acerbic observer Ducoudrez-Holstein commented of her:

> Bolívar paid tribute to the national temperament and, like most of his fellow countrymen, spent much precious time in the boudoirs of his numerous mistresses; he was accused of spending even whole days in his hammock in the midst of a crowd of female admirers. The most important business was in the hands of his admirers, especially Josefina, his known mistress, an intriguing and vengeful woman. I have seen this siren more than a hundred times and I confess that I don't understand the predilection of the dictator for her. His liaison with Josefina lasted, however, until around 1819.

She was reputed to influence affairs of state; she was outspoken, with a sharp tongue; and she was hated by many of Bolívar's intimates and associates for pursuing the interests of her own friends. She was not unusual in that. She was, however, an unusually forceful and homely-looking woman for Bolívar, who generally liked pliable, pretty girls. Her very ambition, and her tenacity in catering to a chronically unfaithful man whose own ambitions for his country and for history were always uppermost, were what enabled her to retain her place beside him for so long.

Bolívar's role and those of the Spanish were now reversed once again. He was left holding the vulnerable centre, while they were still in possession of swathes of the countryside, with their armies intact. Under the authority of the long-suffering Congress of Tunja more than a thousand miles away, in whose name he had marched to Caracas, he now set up a government, and pledged constitutional rule for Venezuela: 'Nothing shall turn me, Venezuelans, from my first and only intentions – your glory and liberty. An assembly of notable, wise and virtuous men must be solemnly convoked to discuss and approve the nature of the government and the functions it shall exercise in the critical and extraordinary circumstances that surround the republic.' Meanwhile, he refused to fall into the federalist trap, and retained supreme executive and legislative powers. He appointed as his two chief ministers his old family lawyer, Miguel José Sanz, and Ustáriz, who had drawn up the declaration of independence the year before. His number two was a civilian governor, Cristóbal Mendoza. Bolívar amicably accepted Mariño's authority in the east of the country (where he had styled himself Supreme Chief and Director), but argued earnestly against dividing the nation: 'Can I answer you with the military frankness which I must use with you? I don't think it's right to delay the establishment of a centre of power for all Venezuela's provinces . . . If we create two independent powers, one in the east, one in the west, we will have two distinct nations, which from their inability to support themselves and to count among others, will look ridiculous. Venezuela even united with New Granada hardly makes a nation which inspires respect among others. Can we divide it into two?'

Bolívar recognised that he still faced immense military challenges: the bulk of the royalist army remained intact in Puerto Cabello, which was strongly fortified; and substantial royalist forces were based at Coro, further up the coast. Unless Spain sent substantial reinforcements, however, he had no reason to believe that the liberation of Venezuela had not been definitively achieved on the second try. He despatched his aides, Rafael Urdaneta and Anastasio Girardot, to the outskirts of Puerto

Cabello. Bolívar had no fleet, so he could not blockade the port. Supplies were ferried in by the Spanish, and 1,200 men under Colonel Salomon were shipped in from Puerto Rico. To intimidate the men holding Puerto Cabello Bolívar had a Spanish war criminal hanged in full view of the garrison – a man who had stitched prisoners together back to back, so that every movement of either was agony, and who had made a collection of rebel ears which he carried on his hat. In a skirmish on the hills of Barbula outside the town young Girardot was killed. In a well-orchestrated propaganda set-piece, the dead hero's heart was placed in a gilded urn and borne before Bolívar amid a large armed guard of honour to the Cathedral in Caracas.

Bolívar was now formally denominated 'Liberator of Venezuela', a title he regarded as 'more glorious and satisfactory than all the empires on earth'. Urdaneta, his most experienced, loyal and cautious commander, was appointed as his chief-of-staff. Meanwhile Monteverde, attempting a sally, had been defeated at Las Trincheras and driven back to Puerto Cabello. Badly wounded in the action, he was replaced as commander by Salomon. Having bottled up Salomon in Puerto Cabello, Bolívar's main concern was to contain the two other armies converging upon the west, about 1,300 loyalists under Ceballos based at Carora and 2,500 under Yañez on the Plains of Apure.

At Barquisimeto, Bolívar unexpectedly suffered his first defeat in this campaign, through a retreat being mistakenly ordered just as victory beckoned. He failed to prevent the armies of Yañez and Ceballos from combining, and on 5 December around 4,800 patriots went into battle against 5,200 royalists, each disposing of infantry, cavalry and artillery, on the Plains of Apure. Bolívar was no more the intrepid guerrilla leader but a general in the field, directing his forces from a low hill, as he had seen Napoleon do on manoeuvres. The set-piece battle lasted all day, until the royalist lines broke, leaving behind a thousand dead, seven hundred prisoners, and all their artillery and supplies. It was by far Bolívar's biggest victory to date. Ceballos's men retreated on Coro licking their wounds, Yañez to the shelter of the cordillera.

Bolívar returned to Caracas and the plaudits of his countrymen, and was appointed 'dictator' by acclamation, in spite of his assertion that supreme authority was painful and depressing for him. Although he had triumphed at Apure, the royalists were far from defeated, and Yañez's forces were regrouping. His army met Urdaneta's at Uspino, where the Spanish were defeated again, and their commander killed, his body dismembered and its parts sent as trophies to nearby villages. But the relatively disciplined royalist forces, against which Bolívar was fighting so energetically and which he might have defeated in due course, were no longer the main danger.

The new threat came from an unexpected quarter. South-east of the great sub-Andean cordillera running south-west to north-east that bisects Venezuela, the mountains descend to forest and then to an immense area that comprises half the land-mass of the country, known as the *llanos*, the plains. The rivers of this region feed the great basin of the Orinoco and its tributaries, the Apure and the Arauca. The llanos are a huge flatland, a kind of green desert of tall, wild grass, resembling the steppes of central Asia though perhaps more hostile to human habitation. In the rainy season, the whole territory floods because its hard, shallow soils fail to absorb the water. In the dry season the water subsides, the grass becomes yellow, and torrid heat is punctuated by swirling storms.

Before the arrival of the Spanish the llanos were almost deserted apart from a handful of fierce tribesmen struggling for existence. With the introduction of horses and cattle by the Spanish, vast herds of both gradually grew up, roaming wild, offering the prospect of a living for poor and desperate men, many of them slaves with absentee owners. The llaneros were extremely tough, as they had to be, and very primitive, South America's equivalent of the Tartars or the Mongols of central Asia. Living in the saddle, they were the cowboys of Venezuela, but there was nothing romantic about them. Largely black, Indian or mestizo, they rode mostly naked except for rough trousers, and broad-brimmed hats to protect them from the sun. Their diet consisted of raw beef, tied to their saddles in strips and salted by the sweat of their horses, washed down by the brackish water of the llanos. They herded their cattle onto dry land in the rainy season, and to oases in time of drought. Theoretically subject to slave overseers – the *hatos*, whom they loathed – their toughness ensured they were in fact subject to no one except their own local leaders. Initially they traded their cattle up the cordillera, across onto the central highlands, and then down to Venezuela's Caribbean ports. But with the opening up of the Orinoco river basin to navigation to the east, a flourishing contraband trade grew up, beyond the control of Caracas. In effect, Venezuela became two separate countries, above and below the cordillera.

A year before Simón Bolívar's birth in 1783, José Tomás Rodríguez Boves was born into a lower middle-class family in the Spanish city of Oviedo. He was sent to the naval academy there and then, at fifteen, to Puerto Cabello in Venezuela, as a pilot. Crafty, rough-hewn, a born leader with a vein of psychopathic cruelty, he became a smuggler but was caught and sentenced to eighteen years in prison. Through the intercession of friends he secured his release at the price of exile, to the town of Calabozo on the llanos. He was soon smuggling again, from the Orinoco region to the town of Barinas on the edge of the llanos, where he established himself as a leader among the local herdsmen, becoming a kind of land pirate. He was small, with a barrel-chested, muscular torso and an unusually large head surmounted by red hair; he had grey eyes, a prominent nose, and a small, cruel mouth in a meagre red beard. When Venezuela's first revolution began in Caracas, Boves immediately perceived that it was doomed by its internal contradictions, and said as much. Arrested as a traitor, he was held in the grim little dungeon at Calabozo, until the notorious Spanish commander Antoñanzas attacked and freed the town, then appointed Boves and other convicts as his officers. He was swiftly promoted, and in August 1814 the new Spanish commander on the llanos, Cagigal, detailed him to raise troops in the Orinoco basin. Inspired leader of men that he was, Boves knew that to secure the allegiance of the savage llaneros he must stimulate their resentment of the white men who were their nominal masters. 'White lands to the blacks' was his rallying cry – notwithstanding the fact that, as a Spaniard, he was white. Blacks were preferred for positions of responsibility in his army, and he was known by his men as *Taita*, Uncle.

He designated the four thousand horsemen he drilled 'the Legion of Hell' (*Legión infernal*); their standard was a black flag he called his 'pennant of death'. For weapons they carried bamboo lances. When he judged his new army sufficiently trained, on his huge black horse Antinoo he led them forward across the llanos to engage the patriot force under Colonel Carlos Padron which had been sent to counter this nuisance. In Santa Catalina canyon, near Calabozo, Padron's troops were speared to the last man. Reaching Calabozo itself, where he had once been imprisoned, Boves gave the order to spare no one, not even women and children. The few prisoners taken were tied to stakes with their heads shaved, to die in the heat of the sun.

When news of the massacres reached Bolívar he despatched his most ruthless general, the Spanish-born Campo Elias, and a thousand men to deal with Boves. At the village of Mosquiteros, near Calabozo, they were attacked by the Legion of Hell. The wild horsemen flung themselves against Campo Elias's left flank, routed it, and massacred the soldiers. But the centre held, and Campo Elias counter-attacked in disciplined ranks, creating havoc among the Legion. He gave the order 'No quarter!' and thousands were butchered, only a few hundred escaping with Boves, who had a lance wound. It seemed that Bolívar had decisively disembarrassed himself of this problem.

Yet when Bolívar returned to Caracas after his triumph in the field of Apure he heard that in the space of a few weeks Boves had assembled a force half as large again which was engaged in an orgy of destruction across the remote settlements of the llanos. On 8 December they fell upon the garrison left at San Marcos by Campo Elias, killing all the soldiers there; the way was now open for this barbarian horde to ascend to the uplands.

Bolivar was to say of Boves that 'He was not nurtured with the delicate milk of a woman but with the blood of tigers and the furies of hell . . . He was the wrath of heaven which hurled its lightning against the *patria* . . . a demon in human flesh which drowned Venezuela in blood.' O'Leary, later Bolívar's closest aide, related the following story about Boves:

> One day an old and emaciated man was brought before him, the only inhabitant of the town from which the rest had fled on learning of his approach. After some questions to which the old man responded gently and truthfully, he was ordered to be decapitated. At that moment a youth of about 15 years came forward and, kneeling in front of the horse of the barbarian, told him, 'I beg you sir, on the blessed Virgin, that you pardon this man who is my father. Save him, and I will be your slave.' 'Good,' said the monster, smiling on hearing the fervent supplication of the young man. 'To save your father's life you will have to allow your nose and ears to be cut off without crying out.' 'Yes, yes,' replied the unhappy boy. 'I give you my life to save my father.' The boy suffered the horrible test with admirable calm. Seeing which, Boves ordered that the boy be killed alongside his father for being too brave and for fear that he too would become an enemy.

Boves's army swelled to about eight thousand strong. To the west Yañez remained a threat and had recaptured Barinas, burning down the town of ten thousand inhabitants and executing the eighty-strong garrison, an atrocity avenged when he was defeated and dismembered at the

Battle of Uspino. To the north Ceballos and Salomon, although beaten back, still had some four thousand men in Coro and Puerto Cabello. To the east Cagigal commanded his own force of three thousand. Nearby a new threat raised its head under the command of another bloodthirsty Spanish general, Rosete, at the head of a thousand men in the valley of the Tuy. He occupied Ocumare, close to Caracas, killing all the inhabitants. Rosete ordered his soldiers to force their way into a church, where they beheaded the entire congregation. A sadist in the Boves mould, he would skin men alive, disembowel women and gouge out the eyes of children, cutting off their heads afterwards.

Bolívar and his army fought magnificently against this sudden surfeit of challenges, tearing up and down the central highlands and valleys of the country, fending off one attack after another. At Carabobo he personally defeated the Spanish and chased them back once again into Puerto Cabello. But from their strongholds in the coastal lowlands, from the baked badlands of the llanos and from the humid lowlands of the east, the provocations proved remorseless. The British, Miranda's great hope, watched cynically, reluctant to antagonise the Spanish Empire. The United States gave nothing. Bolívar, who lacked Miranda's turn for diplomacy and had more or less ignored the need for foreign assistance, was fighting almost entirely from his own resources, against an enemy constantly reinforced and resupplied from the coast by Spanish ships.

In a country where the 200,000 whites were outnumbered by 500,000 blacks and 200,000 Indians, the Spanish could always find recruits motivated by plunder and hatred, while the criollo aristocracy learned that their vision of liberal constitutional rule appealed to few ordinary Venezuelans apart from the resilient mountain people of the west. The Spanish also wholly dominated the war of terror. Although Bolívar preached 'war to the death', only a couple of his commanders actually pursued it with any gusto, unlike Boves, his even more bloodthirsty lieutenant Tomás Morales from the Canary Islands, and Rosete.

The turning-point came when Boves decisively defeated Campo Elias at La Puerta, the strategic gateway to Caracas. The Liberator had three last throws: he ordered Ribas to take the offensive and 'save Caracas at any cost'; he hurried his own forces from Valencia and entrenched himself at his own boyhood family estate at San Mateo; and he continued desperately to beseech Mariño for help, but the strutting supremo of eastern Venezuela had no wish to add to Bolívar's glory.

Ribas rose to the exigencies of the moment. With an army of seven-teen- and eighteen-year-olds recruited from the colleges of the capital he charged the lances of the Legion from Hell time and time again. Unaccustomed to fighting in the highlands or to vigorous resistance, the Legion finally fled when Campo Elias arrived with the remains of his army to reinforce Ribas. The courage of the young was astounding. One dying boy asked to be remembered to Ribas for 'never having taken a backward step'. Three horses were killed under Ribas himself.

The capital had won a respite, and Ribas ignored an order from Bolívar to 'shoot all Europeans and Canarians in the city'. As so often when he was cornered, Bolívar had turned nasty: on 8 February 1814 he ordered the execution of all the 1,300 royalist prisoners held in Caracas and La Guaira. The dreadful head-count began. Palacio, the prison gov-ernor, reported: 'In obedience to the order of the Most Excellent General Liberator for decapitation of all the Spanish and Canary Island prison-ers held in his port, the executions have commenced this night with 100 of them.' [On February 14th:] 'Yesterday afternoon 150 men of the Spanish prisoners were decapitated and between today and tomorrow the rest will be executed.' [On February 15th:] 'Yesterday afternoon 247 Spanish and Canary Island prisoners were decapitated.' [On Feburary 16th:] 'Today all the Spaniards and Canary Islanders who were sick in the hospital were decapitated, constituting the last of all those included in the order of Your Excellency.'

It was one of the most controversial actions of Bolívar's life. He defended himself by pointing out that the governor of Caracas prison had warned him of unrest there; he bitterly remembered the revolt at Puerto Cabello that had so nearly cut short his own career before it began. Had the prisoners succeeded in breaking out, 1,300 would have been returned to the ranks of the royalists. As Bolívar put it, 'One less of such monsters in existence is one less who has slaughtered or would slaughter hundreds of victims.' To many Latin Americans today his act is not only understandable but admirable, evidence that he was a leader capable of the terrible decisions necessary to safeguard the lives of his own men. But nothing, in truth, can excuse it, the worst act of Bolívar's career. Even at that date, as prisoners of war they had a status which their gaolers were bound to respect. They had not as yet committed any act of insurrection. They were helpless and unarmed.

Bolívar was dispirited, suffering from fever and from the piles that resulted from too long spent in the saddle. Yet he believed against all the odds that he could still win, and although his own stature and that of his cause were based on idealism and humanity, he was prepared to resort to the same inhumanity as his opponents to do so. He descended to the level of Boves with his cold-blooded killing of those 1,300 prisoners. In mitigation, it can only be said that he never stooped so low again. He was not of the same order of men as Monteverde and Boves – the very fact which makes this atrocity so shocking.

At San Mateo Bolívar's forces consisted of 1,500 infantry, 600 cavalry and five or six cannon. A witness, Rivas Vicuña, sketches the scene of Bolívar's intended stand: 'The chosen site was a fairly narrow valley crowned on the north side by a chain of mountains whose highest peak was known as Calvary and on another of which was the Liberator's house. To the south were the highest peaks of the range.' There was great skill in Bolívar's choice of the narrow valley – although he may also have been influenced by other considerations: having been stripped of his huge estates once, he seemed here to be fighting as much for his inheritance and fortune as for his country.

When Boves's vanguard attacked the entrenched positions at the head of the valley, they were easily beaten back: Boves, victor of countless engagements in the flatlands below, was out of his element. The following morning he sent his cavalry up the slopes of the southern mountains in an effort to turn the left of the patriot line and reach the heights behind them. As Boves spurred his men on, his beloved black charger Antinoo was shot under him. He fell to the ground and hugged his steed, first sobbing like a baby, then swearing furious vengeance on the horse's killers. But his lancers, although much more numerous than the patriots, were no match for their fire, so he sent a force to seize their armoury, a sugar mill overlooking the valley. It was defended by Antonio Ricuarte, one of Bolívar's aristocratic lieutenants. At the approach of the enemy he saw that his small detachment would be overwhelmed, so he despatched his men to safety and blew up the powder and himself along with it, just as Boves's men reached the door of the depot.

Meanwhile Bolívar's forces continued successfully to hold back wave after wave of attack by the frenzied horsemen, and suddenly it seemed that relief was at hand when it was learned that Mariño had at last decided to come to his fellow liberator's aid. At the head of a force of 3,500 men he had defeated Rosete at Los Pilones and was now on his way to Villa de Cura to combine with Bolívar's forces. Boves reacted quickly, abandoning the siege of San Mateo and hurrying his horsemen to intercept Mariño at Bolachica, where he was beaten off. Meanwhile Bolívar moved back to Valencia, forcing Yañez and Ceballos to raise the siege of the city. He then rode to La Victoria, to meet Mariño. The two egocentrics reached an agreement by which Mariño retained the command of his own forces; Bolívar then departed to help the siege of Puerto Cabello.

It seemed as though the tide was turning. But Mariño, impetuous and over-confident, decided to engage the Spanish forces at Aroa led by Cagigal, and suffered a repulse. Learning nothing from this setback, he then set out on his own against Boves, refusing to wait for reinforcements from Bolívar, and came upon the llanero army near La Puerta. Bolívar hurried his men up from Puerto Cabello, but the enemy had been engaged on his own ground and battle had begun. On 15 June 1814 the second and much more terrible battle of La Puerta took place. Thousands of Boves' horsemen poured out from side valleys to ambush the armies of Mariño and Bolívar. By nightfall a thousand had been killed and a further three hundred captured and put to death. Campo Elias was among the dead, as was Bolívar's chief civilian adviser, Muñoz Tebar. General Freitas killed himself to avoid capture and torture. Bolívar, Mariño and Ribas escaped to Valencia, to arrange the defences of the last major city blocking Boves's road to Caracas. At last Bolívar understood that the Second Republic, like the First, was doomed. His high hopes of the year before, his victorious entry into Caracas, were hollow mockeries beside the reality of thousands slaughtered, and imminent defeat. It was no consolation that Mariño, his rival liberator, had been primarily responsible for the disaster.

The Spanish commander Cagigal's order that Boves should put his troops under his control provoked the insolent retort that Boves had recovered 'the arms, munitions and honour of the flags which Your Excellency lost in Carabobo'. At the head of six thousand horse Boves rode towards Valencia, where for ten days the patriots resisted his siege, as food and ammunition ran low. Then Boves offered terms – surrender, in exchange for sparing both soldiers and civilians. As he rode into the city he was received with rejoicing and a Mass in the Cathedral, at which he swore on the Bible that no blood would be spilt.

By nightfall, the civil governor had been shot. A girl in the household of the former patriot commander of the city was tied in her hammock and raped by several soldiers, after which her tongue was torn out, her breasts cut off, and a fire lit under her so that she was cooked in her bed.

Other women were forced to attend a huge fiesta. 'Meanwhile the men had all been taken into custody, led to the outskirts of the city and put to the lance like bulls, without spiritual consolation . . . The women at the dance swallowed their tears and trembled to hear the hoofbeats of the cavalry outside, fearing what was taking place, while Boves, whip in hand, made them dance the *piquirico* and other [dance] figures of the country, to which he was greatly addicted . . . The killings continued for several nights more.'

Bolívar had ridden back to Caracas, where his request that the churches donate their plate to help his cause provided him with 28,000 ounces of silver. Word soon got about that he and the remnant of his army were to evacuate the capital. Now twenty thousand terrified whites left in a wretched column behind Bolívar and the few who remained loyal to him. He has been criticised for ordering the people out, but their fate at the hands of Boves would have been terrible. It is also suggested that instead of east he should have marched west, to join with the small army of General Urdaneta; but east offered the only chance of reaching the coast, and evacuation.

This miserable exodus consisted largely of the elderly and the gently-born, women and children, and their servants. The privations and miseries of their trek from Caracas down to the coast killed hundreds and drove many insane. After three weeks of picking their way across two hundred miles of swampy lowland the survivors of this wretched column reached the town of Barcelona. Bolívar himself was apparently in a pitiable state, unwilling to assert his authority.

When Boves reached the Plaza de la Trinidad in Caracas he remarked: 'Much blood has been spilled in this square. No matter; for every drop the patriots shed I have spilled a hundred, and that is nothing, until [these] balconies appear one of these morning[s] with dead bodies suspended from them like bunches of grapes.' Even Coll y Pratt, the opportunistic Archbishop of Caracas, who was inclined to support the Spanish, was moved to thunder a fiery denunciation from his pulpit: 'My mind revolts and my soul cannot support the weight of so much evil: theft, rape, pillage, deaths and murders, fires and devastation; the virgin violated, the cry of the widow and the orphan; the father armed against his son and each one looking for his brother to kill him; of those who have migrated; of the thousands who have fled; of the bodies stretched out in the public streets; of the bones which cover the fields, and of so much blood shed on Venezuela's soil.'

Boves sent eight thousand men under Morales in pursuit of the refugees from Caracas. Bolívar's few soldiers linked up with what was left of Mariño's army in the east and with Mariño's fellow-insurgent from Trinidad and Guiria days, Bermudez, and pulled together a force of about three thousand men. Bolívar's plan was to turn and face the approaching enemy along the river Aragua, but Bermudez insisted it would be better to fight in the streets of Barcelona itself. Morales's men crossed the river almost unopposed, and proved Bermudez wrong: the town became a slaughterhouse. 'Everything perished in that day of blood and horror,' writes the Spanish historian Torrente. 'Because they were the battleground, the streets, houses and even churches were all steeped in blood . . .' Some 3,500 civilians took refuge in the Cathedral, where every last one was slain, in the worst massacre of this cruellest of wars.

Bolívar escaped with his depleted refugee column, now only ten thousand strong, to the port of Cumana. Here was the small fleet which had fled the port of La Guaira with the silver and gold of Caracas. It was under the command of Captain Bianchi, an Italian adventurer who had not been paid for his services; on the arrival of Bolívar's bedraggled company, Bianchi raised anchor and left, with the treasure. Bolívar and Mariño commandeered a sailing boat and went in furious pursuit. Catching up with Bianchi on the island of Margarita they negotiated the return of two-thirds of the silver and gold, then set off back to the Venezuelan coast. There, at Carúpano, an angry mob met them on the beach. Ribas, usually so faithful, and Mariño's other fellow-insurgent, Piar, believed they had planned to abscond with the treasure, so the Liberator and the Supremo of the East were seized and flung into prison. Bolívar now stood accused of the very crimes he had charged Miranda with two years before. How contemptuously the Precursor, in his Cadiz gaol, would have laughed if he had known.

Soon after their arrest, Bianchi's little fleet put in from sea; grateful for having been paid at last, he threatened to bombard the port unless Bolívar and Mariño were freed; they were released on condition that they left Venezuela immediately. Ribas appointed himself to the forces of resistance in western Venezuela, Piar those in the east.

Bolívar's career seemed at an end. Stripped of his titles, authority, estates and territory, he prepared to say goodbye to Josefina, who was bound with her family for the small offshore island of Santo Tomás and a new, more peaceful life, then wrote an eloquent testament of the recent terrible events.

If inconstant destiny made victory alternate between ourselves and the enemy, it was only in favour of the American people, who under an inconceivable madness took up arms to destroy their liberties and restore their tyrants. Heaven, for the sake of our humiliation and glory, decided that our conquerors should be our brothers, and that our brothers should triumph over us. The liberating army encountered the enemy arms, defeated them and was careless of them, despising the people we fought in hundreds of engagements . . .

. . . Your own brothers, and *not* the Spaniards, have ripped open your breasts, shed your blood, burnt your homes and condemned you to exile . . . I am very far from having the moral presumption to consider myself blameless for the catastrophe of my fatherland, and indeed suffer from believing myself the unhappy instrument of its frightening miseries, but I am innocent before my conscience because I have never held malice . . .

I promise you, beloved compatriots, that this august title [Liberator] which your gratitude bestowed upon me when I broke your chains will not be vain; I promise you that, as Liberator or in death, I will always deserve the honour that you gave me: no human power on earth will hold me back from the course which I have elected to follow, to return to free you for the second time along the trail of the west, stained by so much blood and adorned by so many heads.

Bolívar went on to excuse those Venezuelans who preferred enslavement to freedom. Then he continued:

Be noble in your grief, as the cause that produces it is noble . . . The destruction of a government . . . the overthrow of established principles, the changing of a way of life, the remoulding of opinion, and, in a word, the establishment of freedom in a land of slaves, is a task beyond all human capacity to carry out quickly. So our excuse for not having achieved what we hoped is inherent in our cause; since even as justice justifies the boldness of having taken it upon us, so does the impossibility of achieving it reflect the inadequacy of the means.

It is praiseworthy, it is noble and sublime, to avenge Nature when it has been outraged by tyranny. Nothing can compare with the greatness of such action, and even if desolation and death are the reward of such a glorious endeavour, there is no reason to condemn it, for it is not the easily attainable that should be undertaken, but that which justice demands that we do . . .

It is fatally stupid to attribute to public men the changes of fortune which the unfolding of events produces in states, for it is not within the sphere of influence of a general or a magistrate, in a moment of unrest, of clashes, and of divergent views, to stem the torrent of human passions.

Agitated by revolutionary movements, these grow in proportion to the force that resists them. And even though serious mistakes or violent passions in the leaders cause frequent harm to the Republic, these very setbacks ought nevertheless to be fairly assessed and their roots sought for in the primary causes of all misfortunes: that is, the frailty of our species and the hazardous nature of all events.

Man is the weak toy of fortune, which he may often predict quite well but can never be sure of; for our situation has no contact with it, it being of a much higher order than ours. To imagine that politics and war will proceed according to our plans, unfolding blindly by the mere strength of our desires and encouraged by the limited means at our disposal, is to wish by human means to emulate divine power.

His testament is lucid and surprisingly reflective for that of a man who had just gone through defeat, victory, and again defeat. It is also vain, self-exculpatory, and imbued with an optimism that seems, in the circumstances, mere hysteria. Bolívar's cause had been crushed, as comprehensively as was imaginable. His dream had ended in the butchery of thousands – at least ten thousand during and after the march from Caracas – yet he finished defiantly, and proudly: 'Do not compare your physical strength with the enemy's, for spirit is not to be compared with matter. You are men, they are beasts, you are free, they are slaves. Fight and you shall win. God grants victory to the steadfast.'

With that, on 7 September 1814 he and his sister Maria Antonia, and Mariño, boarded the appropriately named *El Arrogante*, bound for Curaçao and his second exile in eighteen months. Thousands of other refugees set sail for the Antilles.

As Bolívar set sail, Boves advanced at the head of his horsemen to occupy Cumana, where he had another 'fiesta' and slaughtered a thousand civilians, the men taken off to be executed by night while the women were forced to perform for his men, then raped and killed – as were the musicians. He had a pregnant woman killed and then ripped open, so that he could laugh uproariously at the convulsions of the foetus.

The pitiable but courageous remnant of the patriot army was defeated first at the hamlet of Sabana de El Salado and then at Urica – where a patriot lance, however, cut open Boves's own stomach. He at last perished, but so too did Miguel José Sanz, Bolívar's old family lawyer, and Ustáriz, father of Venezuelan independence and drafter of the first constitution. Piar fled to Jamaica, Bermudez to Margarita. Only Ribas stayed behind on the mainland, and made for the llanos. There he was captured and his head cut off and preserved in oil in a jar sent to Caracas, its jaunty cap with the French revolution tricolour rosette still perched on it, as an example to the people. Morales, crueller even than Boves, killed seven of his brother officers to become the new commander of the Legion of Hell.

On 20 September 1814 Simón Bolívar returned to Cartagena, having without its authority used the troops given him by the government of Tunja for his own purposes. Colonel Castillo, his old enemy, was stirring things up against him, while Brigadier Joaquin Ricuarte sought to have him censured by the Congress: 'The barbaric and unwise project of the War to the Death, which converted whole towns and provinces into enemies, made not only the army but also what it stood for hated, and the very same people who were supposed to receive us with olive and laurel in hand to unite their efforts to ours to throw the Spanish off the territory, seeing our bloody behaviour, became our enemies . . .'

As well as being accused of having waged a campaign of terror, Bolívar was also alleged to be plotting to impose the rule of Venezuela upon New Granada. There, the racial equation that underlay the savagery in Venezuela did not apply. About 900,000 whites easily outnumbered 300,000 Indians, 140,000 free blacks and 70,000 slaves, and never felt threatened by the blacks and the more passive Indians, who could not delude themselves that they would ever hold power.

As Bolívar rode up into the highlands of eastern New Granada, to the capital, Tunja, he must have felt alone and abandoned, but for once luck was with him. On his way, he encountered a division at Ocaña under his most loyal lieutenant, Urdaneta, who had fought furiously and struggled back into New Granada. The exhausted, desperate men fell joyfully upon their leader, breaking ranks to embrace and cheer him. He chided them gently for their indiscipline, but was alive to the fact that he suddenly had a small and effective army at his back, battle-hardened men whom the peaceful people of New Granada were unlikely to want to interfere with. Bolívar and his column were fêted by hundreds as they passed along the mountain trail to Tunja. To the Congress there he delivered a masterly account of his successes and failures:

> The blows upon us have opened our eyes and with the experience and the vision we have acquired, why should we spare ourselves from the perils of

war and politics and from attaining the freedom and the glory which
await us after our sacrifices? These could not have been avoided. It has
always been necessary to pass along the trail of sacrifice to attain triumph.
All of America is steeped in American blood. It was necessary to wash out
so ingrained a stain. It is the first time this unhappy continent, always a
land of desolation but not of freedom, dresses in honour . . . for freedom,
I say the earth has been sown with arms – that earth which only a little
time ago suffered the war of slaves.

Bolívar had by now become a powerful orator, and even his enemies
acknowledged the extraordinary persuasiveness of his arguments face to
face. The president of the assembly, Camilo Torres, invited him to take
a seat on the dais beside him, then turned to him: 'General, while your
sword exists, your country has not died; with it you will return to rescue
it from the realm of its oppressor. The Congress of Granada will give you
this judgement on your rebellion: you have been an unlucky soldier, but
you are a great man.'

There was another reason why Congress speedily embraced Bolívar:
they needed him as a mercenary. Nariño, the intellectual who led
Cundinamarca, the independent province around Santa Fé de Bogotá
which co-existed with the Tunja republic, had been betrayed and captured on an expedition to subdue the royalist stronghold of Pasto in the
towering mountains to the south-west and sent back in chains to
Madrid, to become a companion to the wretched Miranda. One Manuel
Alvarez had since set himself up as dictator of Santa Fé de Bogotá and
declared his opposition to Tunja, if not outright support for the royalists; Bolívar and his desperadoes were the men to bring Bogotá to heel.

Bolívar was unhappy about attacking what he called 'fellow-citizens
of America', but had to fall in with the plan. On 12 December 1814, he
arrived on the outskirts of Bogotá to find that the Spanish had come to
the aid of Alvarez, but nevertheless managed to crush the upstart and his
supporters in three days of hand-to-hand fighting across barricades,
through windows and over roof-tops. It was a much-needed triumph.

Bolívar entered as liberator one of the most beautiful colonial cities
in Latin America – the Athens of America, Humboldt had called it
– nestling in its amphitheatre in the mountains. The Congress of
Tunja moved to Santa Fé de Bogotá as the new capital, and all the
former Viceroyalty of New Granada was now drawn together under a
single government except for the port of Santa Marta, still held by the
royalists.

Bolívar had regained a little of his old confidence and prestige. For a man who had led his country into a disastrous civil war, albeit in a just cause, his powers of recovery and optimism were remarkable, perhaps psychotic and self-delusional – or perhaps he recognised that only by returning directly to the fray could he prevent failure from overwhelming him. Yet his maturity and sense of proportion were what struck the members of the Congress at Tunja most forcibly. He was lucid, calm and rational rather than emotional, a man of destiny not to be distracted from his cause by any setback, however great. His resolve was to prove his greatest strength; his belief that he was the only man capable of doing the job, his worst failing.

Awarded the new title of Pacificador – the Peacekeeper – and nominal command of all New Granada's forces, Bolívar was now despatched to Cartagena to take control of the army there and attack Santa Marta. He was given about two thousand largely unarmed men, who were to receive their weapons in Cartagena.

As his army was transported down the Magdalena river his captains killed first sixteen Spanish prisoners and then a further eleven, among them the Capuchin priest Father Corella. This was grist to the mill of Bolívar's old enemy Castillo, commander in the north; on the Liberator's approach he abandoned his siege of the royalist army in Santa Marta and returned to Cartagena, where he persecuted Bolívar's supporters and effectively placed his sister Maria Antonia under house arrest. Castillo then ordered that Bolívar's forces should come no further than Mompós. Bolívar promptly appealed to Torres, now president of the united republic, who reaffirmed that the Liberator had been appointed to act as commander of the forces in Cartagena. Bolívar was resolved not to fight his own supposed allies – and with too few arms and men was in no position to do so. He promoted Castillo to brigadier-general, as a conciliatory gesture; and even offered his own resignation as commander. But Castillo would not have him in the city. When Bolívar occupied the hills of La Popa above the city, his forces were fired upon and he found that the water supply had been poisoned. The massively built walls and forts which defended Cartagena's beautiful port, originally erected as a defence against English buccaneers, were fifty feet thick and thirty high in places. An attack by Bolívar's forces stood no chance, and both commanders knew it.

His men were now dying from disease. The sympathetic insurrection he had expected would occur in Cartagena when he occupied La Popa never materialised. His only alternative was to move his forces to the front against the Spanish and leave Castillo to his own devices – something he said fourteen years later he wished he had done. But news reached New Granada of a far more terrible threat to her existence than this squabbling between supposed allies: the Spanish Empire was striking back, in force. Following the defeat of the French in Spain, the blatantly reactionary Ferdinand VII – whom Bolívar had allegedly played with in adolescence – had returned to his throne. Fifteen thousand men, many of them veterans of the fighting in Spain, had been despatched in forty-two transport ships escorted by eighteen men-of-war to subdue Spain's rebellious colonies.

Bolívar's reaction was realistic and decisive. Recognising at once that the chances of prevailing against such an army were extremely small, particularly if New Granada's forces were divided, he resigned his command and announced his immediate intention to depart into exile. 'If I remain here, New Granada will divide into parts and domestic war will be eternal. By withdrawing, there will be only the fatherland's party which, being united, will be better.' He had no desire to preside over another catastrophe. He had learned from his mistakes and his decision, if hardly courageous, was entirely sensible. After five months of fruitless stand-off with Castillo, he set sail on 9 March 1815 on an English ship bound for Jamaica.

The cruelties of the Spanish in Venezuela were attested to not only by their patriot enemies – themselves guilty of many atrocities. Llamosa, chaplain of the Spanish forces, sent a memorial of Boves's merciless brutalities to Ferdinand, also highlighting the racial element: 'He [Boves] always repeated that the goods of the whites were for the blacks. In his military calculations and in his type of government this system formed the principal part.' One result of Llamosa's revelations was a change in the tactics to be employed by the formidable army now bound for Venezuela, away from the exacerbation of racially-based resentments.

The commander of these forces was Pablo Morillo, at thirty-seven five years older than Bolívar; of humble birth, from Fuentesecas de León in Spain, he had fought his way up the ranks until, after a particularly distinguished role in the Battle of Vitoria, he had been promoted Field Marshal, and painted alongside Wellington; he had a weakness for high-flown titles. He was strong and toughly-built, of medium height; dark and black-eyed, with prominent black eyebrows and a hard expression;

steely of voice and abrupt of manner. Arriving at Carúpano, he took an instant dislike to the brigand Morales, new commander of the Legion of Hell, five thousand of whose horsemen were drawn up to welcome him. Morillo was a man with a penchant for smart uniforms; most of the Legion, naked to the waist, wore jaguar-skin caps atop their long, straggly hair; and they muttered incomprehensibly among themselves, with savage smiles. Striding up to them, Morillo declared that just one of his companies could wipe them out, then insisted that they be disciplined, or disbanded; Morales warned him that they would prefer to join the insurgents.

Worse was to follow. Their first joint expedition was to the island of Margarita to snuff out a rebellion by Arismendi, once 'a moderate man of peaceful ways', now, after his wife and children had been subjected to reprisals, a patriot guerrilla leader famous for atrocities as appalling as those of the plainsmen, although on a much smaller scale. In the face of overwhelmingly superior forces, he surrendered at once; Morillo was pleased to pardon him in exchange. An English witness described Arismendi:

> . . . his aspect exhibits a peculiar ferocity of expression, which his smile only increases. His laugh never fails to create a momentary shudder, and the dreadful distortion of the muscles of the face which it produces, can only be compared with that of the hyena when under similar excitement. His displeasure is always signified by this demoniacal grin, accompanied by a low lengthened exclamation resembling the suppressed roar of a tiger, his eyes at the same time flashing vengeance; and should the object of his rage be at these moments within its compass, death inevitably ensues. His general appearance might impress a superficial observer with a belief that he is so accustomed to scenes of horror and bloodshed, they afford him gratification rather than uneasiness.

The contemporary Spanish historian Sevilla says that Morales's eyes blazed. He pointed to the kneeling guerrilla leader. 'General, don't do such a thing. This man you see on his knees is not repenting; he is tricking you miserably. This man grovelling before you like a reptile is not a man, but a fierce tiger of the wilds or from hell. The tears are crocodile ones, his protests are bogus and his promises lies. This miserable man sent five hundred peaceful Spanish traders from Caracas to Guaira to be burned alive. Those who escaped the inferno were killed with lances.'

Morillo took no notice, and Morales blackly forecast the destruction of the entire expedition. Morillo dismissed him contemptuously, and

proceeded to Caracas. There he decreed a general amnesty and promised what remained of the criollo upper class that their lands would be
restored and the black uprising reversed. The savage men who had
regained Venezuela for the crown of Spain were thus disowned.

To regain New Granada a two-pronged land offensive was ordered,
one arm advancing through the mountains, the other, commanded by
Morales, along the coast, with Morillo's forces being shipped by sea. The
siege of Cartagena which followed was one of the most heroic and
ghastly in history. It lasted 106 days, during which the Spanish ships'
cannon pounded from the sea and the guns on land thundered from the
hills outside the city. Castillo, inept and cowardly, was replaced by
Bolívar's compatriot Bermudez. Some six thousand died of starvation
before, at length, on 6 December 1815, two thousand survivors embarked
in a small flotilla of fishing boats. Many were capsized by the swell, or
picked up by Spanish ships waiting outside the harbour. The three
hundred that remained inside Cartagena, including Castillo, were executed. Morillo's troops then set off up the Magdalena river towards Santa
Fé de Bogotá, a journey of several months. On the way Morillo, hitherto so self-confidently indulgent, heard that Arismendi had risen in
revolt on Margarita and slaughtered the small Spanish garrison there; he
was incensed that Morales had been proved right, and he himself made
to look a fool.

Although the leaders in Bogotá surrendered the city without a fight,
Morillo set up a 'Pacification Tribunal' to purge the rebel leaders. On 30
May 1816, in desperation, the wives and daughters of the leading citizens
went to him on their knees and begged that mercy be shown to their
menfolk. According to Sevilla, the General pointed out that his pardons
to the rebels on Margarita had been answered by the slaughter of the soldiers he had left there; those soldiers, he said, also had mothers, wives
and daughters: 'If instead of forgiveness I had shot twenty men, I would
not be troubled by remorse for these people today.' Some six hundred
were executed, among them Camilo Torres, president of the new republic and Bolívar's supporter. It seemed that the flames of independence in
Venezuela and New Granada had been extinguished; no one noticed
that the embers were still smouldering.

9

Exile

In Kingston, the capital of Jamaica, the penniless Bolívar found a run-down boarding-house to live in. He also made a friend, Maxwell Hyslop, a successful Scottish merchant who, with his brother, ran a varied import–export trade. Writing to Hyslop, Bolívar remarked perceptively that if Morillo were to act 'with speed and decisiveness, the restoration of Spanish government in South America seems inevitable. The Spanish expedition can increase its support rather than diminish it, through its marches. It is already supposed to have received three thousand recruits in Venezuela . . . let us not delude ourselves. Opinion in America is not well established yet, and while those who think are on the side of independence, the great mass still does not know its views and interests.'

Bolívar's main interest in Hyslop was as a source of financial support, which was doled out in small quantities. He also pleaded desperately with the British for aid. The governor of the island, the Duke of Manchester, not only shunned his company but ignored his letters, as did the Marquess Wellesley. The British government had no wish to antagonise the renascent Spanish Empire for the sake of what seemed a completely lost cause.

Bolívar was depressed, feverish and pathetic. He begged Hyslop for support, and threatened suicide: 'I don't have a penny now. I have sold the little silver I brought. I have no other hope than to seek your favour. Without it, desperation will force me to end my days in a violent manner, in order to avoid the cruel humiliation of begging for help from men harder than their gold. If you don't give me the support I need to sustain my sad life, I am resolved to seek help from nobody else, because it is impossible for me to offer any reward, having lost everything; but my gratitude will be eternal.' Bolívar's days were spent idling in his hammock, playing chess or fencing with his exiled companions. At least three attempts on his life were instigated by the Spanish authorities. A servant of Bolívar's, after several unsuccessful attempts to poison him, repeatedly stabbed what he thought was his master sleeping in his hammock one night; it turned out to be one of the Liberator's body-guards, gone to sleep while Bolívar was out visiting. Consistently threatened with eviction by his hard-nosed landlady, his was a wretched existence.

Relief of a kind came when he met Julia Cobier, a creole lady from Dominica on the rebound from an unsatisfactory love affair. They fell upon each other in mutual need, as sometimes happens between two people who have experienced horrors or personal sadness. She had the added attraction for Bolívar of being wealthy, and beneath her ministra-tions his spirits began to revive. He fell to writing what was to prove his most famous pronouncement, his 'Letter from Jamaica'. Addressed to an anonymous friend (in fact Maxwell Hyslop), it was later published as a pamphlet and attracted world-wide interest. Remarkable for its presci-ence, its idealism and its language, and for the curious mysticism that so often imbued Bolívar's pronouncements, it also revealed the consider-able evolution of his thought since his last exile. He started with a vigorous denunciation of the European allies who had failed to come to his help: 'Is Europe deaf to the clamour of its own interests?' he demanded. It would even be in Spain's interests to lose that empire of hers based on 'precarious trade and tributes extorted from remote, pow-erful and enemy peoples', he argued.

> Europe itself, by policy, should have prepared and carried out plans for South American independence; not only because it is necessary for the proper balance of the world, but because it is a legitimate and safe means for obtaining commercial bases on this side of the ocean . . . [He would] free half the world and place the universe in a state of equilibrium . . . The British can acquire (in return for aid) the provinces of Panamá and Nicaragua, forming with these countries the centre of the world's com-merce by means of canals, which, connecting the two great seas, would shorten the great distances and make England's control over world com-merce permanent.

Although Bolívar at this time paid lip-service to the idea of a single American republic with its capital in Mexico City, he forecast more realistically that the Spanish and Portuguese empires would be divided into fifteen independent republics. In Mexico and Brazil, he believed, monarchies and despotisms would alternate in power – an uncannily accurate prediction. Chile, he said, would have largely stable governments, while Peru would suffer from continuing turbulence because 'she possesses two elements, enemies always of a just and liberal régime – gold and slaves. The first corrupts all; the second is corrupted by itself. The soul of a slave rarely rises to appreciate ordered liberty; it either rises in furious tumult or remains docile in chains.' History has put its stamp of truth upon that.

He anticipated a single republic embracing Venezuela and New Granada, for which he favoured as the form of government an executive elected by men of property, an hereditary senate, and a similarly elected assembly. The views he set out were clearly republican and anti-monarchical; he argued that monarchs were inherently despotic and self-aggrandising. Yet his concept of democracy was clearly limited. Spanish Americans, he argued, were just not ready for it:

> We were in the position of slaves – not in the sense of mistreatment so much as of ignorance. We had no part in our own affairs, no knowledge of the science of government and the administration of state. We were, in effect, slaves, suddenly risen, without knowledge or experience, to play a part in the world as administrators, diplomats, magistrates and legislators. If we had even managed our domestic affairs before, we should have known something about the nature and operation of a state.
>
> Pure representative government is not suitable to our character, customs and present conditions . . . So long as our compatriots do not develop the talents and political virtues which distinguish our brothers of the north [the United States] the entire popular system, far from being suitable to our conditions, may, I fear, be our ruin. Unfortunately, these qualities seemed not to be developed in us to the extent necessary; and, on the contrary, we are dominated by vices which, developed under the guidance of Spain, became weighted with ferocity, ambition, vengeance and cupidity.

He had clearly been influenced by his experience of the horrors of mob and popular rule as represented by the black and llanero uprisings in Venezuela, and this was also crucial in pushing his thinking towards the concept of benevolent autocracy – which was to have a marked effect on Latin American political systems for more than a century to come. For the same reasons, he rejected federalism in favour of centralisation: 'Do not adopt the best system of government, but the one most likely to succeed.'

He touched on the idea of a kind of united nations of Latin America, meeting at a Congress in Panamá: 'How wonderful it would be if the Isthmus of Panamá were for us what the Isthmus of Corinth was to the Greeks! Would to God that some day we may have the good fortune to convene there an august assembly of the representatives of our republics, kingdoms, and empires to deliberate upon the high interests or peace and war with the nations of the other three-quarters of the world.' Then he turned mystical: Quetzalcoatl, the plumed serpent of Mexican fable, 'the Hermes or Buddha of South America', had, he observed, promised to return one day.

> Does not this tradition lead us to suppose that he will shortly reappear? Can you imagine the effect that would be produced if an individual were to turn up among the people having the characteristics of Quetzalcoatl, their Buddha of the forest . . . ? Is it not unity alone that is required to enable us to throw out the Spaniards, their troops, and the supporters of corrupt Spain, in order to establish in these lands a powerful empire with a free government and benevolent laws? . . . Is it not that very prophet or god of Anáhuac, Quetzalcoatl, who will be able to bring about the prodigious changes you suggest? This deity is scarcely known to the Mexican people, and even where he is known he is not greatly honoured: such is the fate of the defeated, even when they are gods.

This obscure disquisition in fact marked another major evolution in his thinking: the concept of the Man of Destiny, the Personality who changes history and leads nations – which eventually evolved into the caudillo system that overshadowed the continent for generations to come.

Bolívar went on to divide the world into a liberal and progressive alliance, represented by Britain and the United States; and a reactionary alliance, of Spain, Austria, Prussia and – now, again – France, the Revolution having run its course. But it was Bolívar's insights into the condition of his own people that provided the key to his next moves. In a separate and much less noticed letter, to the editor of Jamaica's newspaper, he wrote:

> The Spaniards, after having experienced terrible and multiple reverses in Venezuela, succeeded, in the end, in regaining her. The army of General Morillo came to reinforce them, and completed the subjugation of the country. It seemed that the party of independence was desperate, as indeed it was; but, by a single occurrence, those same freed slaves and

slaves who contributed so much, by force, to the triumph of the royalists, have changed to the party of independence which had not offered absolute freedom to the slaves as had the Spaniards. The present protagonists of independence are the partisans of Boves, until now against the white criollos, who never understood our noble cause.

When he wrote it, this was mere wishful thinking, but Bolívar was justified in believing he could convert Boves's half-breed desperadoes and thugs to his own cause: Morillo had brutally destroyed their hopes by reasserting the old social structure and property rights, and retaining slavery. Venezuela's bloody social and racial revolution, masquerading as the restoration of Spanish rule, had now been crushed by the Empire herself. Bolívar proposed nothing less than to take charge of the vicious, uncontrolled forces which had destroyed his independent state, to ride the very whirlwind which had unseated him. It was a brilliant strategy.

Early in December 1815 fate played one of its tricks again: Bolívar received a summons to defend Cartagena from Spanish siege. Delighted, the man of destiny left Julia grieving and embarked once again for the mainland, dodging Spanish warships – only to learn as he was approaching the coast that Cartagena had already fallen, and its refugees were on their way to Haiti. He ordered his small boat to follow them. Arriving on the island of Hispaniola, of which Haiti formed the western half, his luck seemed to take a positive turn. At the port of Aux Cayes he was warmly welcomed by the President of Haiti, Alexandre Pétion, whose liberated slaves had defied Napoleon and established an independent republic; Pétion had admired Bolívar's Letter from Jamaica. He also met a wealthy Jewish merchant from Curaçao, Luis Brion, with whom he had corresponded and who espoused the cause of independence. Brion had a number of ships at his disposal, including a 24-gun corvette and a small frigate. For the first time Bolívar had the prospect of some naval forces and, with them, mobility at sea. A rich Englishman, Robert Southerland, also offered help.

With the refugees from Cartagena had arrived a number of Bolívar's former officers, including Carlos Soublette, once Miranda's aide, with his mother and two sisters; the beautiful Isabel, with her long red hair, became Bolívar's mistress. Old rivals of Bolívar arrived too, among them 'El Supremo' Mariño; Piar, good-looking and smooth-talking; Bermudez – 'an uncouth savage, and unlettered', as O'Leary described him; and Mariano Montilla, a former friend of Bolívar's who had nevertheless backed his enemy Castillo in Cartagena. 'Sir' Gregor MacGregor, a Scottish adventurer replete with kilt and bagpipes, was one of the number; as was Ducoudrez-Holstein, that puffed-up French mercenary and sardonic observer of the Liberator's triumphal entry into Caracas – but he left after two months of petty back-biting against Bolívar and later wrote venomously of their encounters.

When it was proposed that Bolívar become supreme commander of an expedition to reinvade Venezuela, many opposed him – until Brion insisted he would back only Bolívar: without Brion's ships, the planned invasion would get nowhere. Slowly, chaotically, the arrangements were made for three hundred men to sail in seven vessels with quantities of ammunition, several pieces of artillery, and most of the officers' women. Bolívar aroused fury by delaying his departure for several days to wait for the loyal Josefina Machado, Señorita Pepa, and her mother to join him.

At last, in March 1816, the little expedition set out. In full dress uniform Bolívar harangued his troops, comparing them to the three hundred Spartans of Leonidas. His chief opponents, Montilla and Bermudez, stayed behind; Montilla later sailed to the United States. Bolívar's small flotilla soon reached the island of Margarita, controlled by Arismendi for the patriots, and from there declared Venezuela independent once again before setting sail with a few more recruits for the mainland. Landing at Carúpano, in two hours he had seized the port, losing none of his men. Mariño and Piar were sent eastwards to raise support; they soon discovered that the local people were hostile and had withdrawn into the interior, and decided to follow them rather than return under Bolívar's command. Thus abandoned, Bolívar sailed for the little port of Ocumare, beyond La Guaira, hoping to strike behind the Spanish.

He despatched most of his men inland under Soublette and MacGregor, but they were cut off by the main Spanish army, which had reached Valencia. In panic his ships quietly put out to sea, leaving him stranded with a handful of men and all his remaining guns and ammunition; probably an *agent provocateur* named Alzuru had put it about that Bolívar had been defeated. At the last minute he was rescued by a small boat. Sailing eastwards after this series of fiascos, away from Morillo's armies, Bolívar's ship landed him at Guiria, where he intended to combine with Mariño.

Soublette and MacGregor, though cut off by the Spanish, had

managed to avoid being trapped, and had marched hundreds of miles to join Piar, who was recruiting dissident llanero guerrilla leaders in the east. In the course of the march MacGregor won victories against Morales in the Aragua, at Victoria, Sebastián de los Pleyes and Quebrada Henda, before combining with Piar at Barcelona; but they quarrelled after a victory at Juncal, and MacGregor left the country.

Rather than taking them to Guiria, Bolívar, pessimistic about his chances of success, had put Josefina and her mother aboard a ship bound northwards, for their safety. Arriving at Guiria in August and thinking to join forces with Piar, he learned that Bermudez had arrived from Haiti, and had been stirring up Mariño against him. Bermudez put it about that Bolívar was planning to abandon the town of Guiria to the Spanish. A mob gathered, shouting 'Down with the dictator!' and 'Death to Bolívar!' His attempts to defend himself were met with a hail of stones, and he retreated with as much dignity as he could muster to the beach. Bermudez pulled his sword on Bolívar, who fought back, then escaped in a boat. Enraged, Bermudez was restrained from plunging into the water after him by his officers, while stones rained down from the mob.

It was Bolívar's fourth bitter send-off from the mainland, this time at the hands of his brother officers. The invasion had been a shambles from start to finish. 'The band of delinquents', commented Morales with contempt, 'believed themselves to be absolute possessors of Venezuela and, dispersed and disorganised, have disappeared like smoke.' Stoned and humiliated by his own patriot supporters, Bolívar was now but a man of straw, a figure of world vision and grandiose rhetoric who had put his expedition at risk so that his mistress could join him and who could not command respect among his own men, much less make an impression on the enemy. A lesser spirit would have been shattered.

He arrived back in Haiti anticipating the wrath of Pétion, but to his astonishment he was received with honour, and listened to with sympathy. Pétion and Southerland even offered to sponsor a new expedition, but Bolívar was reluctant to risk further humiliation. Brion, who now arrived with his small fleet, urged him to try again; Arismendi from Margarita begged him to do so. Most significantly of all, a group of local resistance leaders, appalled by the rivalry and insubordination of the commanders who had driven Bolívar from the mainland, sent an emissary, Francisco Zea, asking him to return. Zea also saw Pétion, and told him: 'In Venezuela there still survives a remnant of good patriots. The country still lives in hopes; but the one superior man, capable of converting these hopes into reality, is no longer there. With this idea, the army and the cities have turned their eyes upon General Bolívar as the one chief in war.'

10

The Orinoco and the Llanos

On 31 December 1816 Bolívar returned to the port of Barcelona. He could have no way of knowing that he would never leave the mainland again. He proclaimed himself commander-in-chief and, combining with a guerrilla force further inland led by Zaraza, marched along the coast in a bold bid to seize Caracas. He got as far as Clarines before furious cavalry attacks forced him back on Barcelona. He wrote desperately to his old rival, Manuel Piar, that Barcelona was in danger of being lost. But Piar had no intention of coming to his aid: he intended to let Bolívar go down to defeat, and take his place as Liberator. A contemporary account describes Piar as 'young, of medium height and a martial air; brave, impetuous and of lightning speed in action; terse in his views, arrogant and impulsive almost to madness, he had a furious temper to the extent that he sometimes apologised to subordinates he had offended.' Many were convinced that Piar was the illegitimate son of an aristocratic criollo who was also the father of the unfortunate Ribas, decapitated two years before – thus accounting for Piar's bitter resentment against Bolívar, whom he held responsible for the débâcle that had led to his half-brother's death. Others suggested he was the bastard son of Prince Carlos de Braganza of Brazil, or that he was the offspring of a prominent Venezuelan and a black slave.

And so Piar decided to leave Bolívar to his fate: a formidable army under Morillo was approaching Barcelona and a fleet was coming up from Puerto Cabello to cut off his escape by sea. The Spanish attacked as Bolívar and his men retreated into the centre of Barcelona, which hand-to-hand fighting turned once more into a charnel house. All seemed lost when a force under the same Bermudez who had drawn his sword on the Liberator arrived, on Mariño's orders, to help Bolívar; Mariño's fear was that if Barcelona were lost, his own stronghold of

Cumana would be next. The fighting became more bloody and intense, but it was now the Spanish who were being pushed back street by street, until eventually they were compelled to pull out of the city. In a celebrated gesture, Bolívar rode to meet Bermudez and declared, 'I embrace the liberator of the Liberator.' Bermudez, as simple-minded and emotional as he was brutish and uncouth, accepted the hug; but his loyalty was still primarily to Mariño.

Bolivar remained in dire peril, since the Spanish numbers were several times his own, and reinforcements were being brought up; further advance was blocked, and he was cut off from the sea. His only option seemed to be to join Piar in the mountains of Guayana, something he was reluctant to do for fear of playing into his rival's hands. At length, however, he set out due south from Barcelona for the Orinoco river, accompanied by just fifteen officers and leaving his only two assets to follow: his huge arsenal, and Brion's fleet, which would come up the Orinoco. It was a bold move, to escape the Spanish military machine advancing to crush him by disappearing into some of the wildest and remotest territory of Venezuela, in an effort to carry on the struggle rather than be forced back into Caribbean exile.

He left behind four hundred men under General Freite to defend Barcelona. The Spanish advanced on the town and this time Mariño's troops, camped just thirty miles away, refused to come to its help. The Spanish secured an overwhelming victory, killing a thousand people, including women, children, and hospital patients. Morillo, once so lenient, showed no pity. His orders now were to 'burn cities, behead their inhabitants, ravage the country; to respect neither sex nor age, to replace the peaceful farmer with a ferocious warrior, the instrument of the vengeance of an angry king.' So appalled was his lieutenant Bermudez by Mariño's behaviour that he decided to follow Bolívar.

The ground had to some extent been prepared for Bolívar in the east by Piar. Vain, hot-headed and overbearing, Piar was none the less a formidable commander, almost Bolívar's equal. Arriving from the north, he had threatened the city of Angostura, on the Orinoco, with only a handful of troops and recruited in the huge empty outback of Guayana an army of about two thousand, many of them Indians, naked and armed only with bows and arrows. While advancing on the city of Guayana itself, lower down the Orinoco, he had seized the food and supplies of the Capuchin mission on the Caroni river. All twenty-two friars were slaughtered, possibly on Piar's orders; he could be as ruthless as the Spanish themselves.

Just outside Angostura, on the open plain, Piar engaged 1,600 experienced, well-trained Spanish troops under General La Torre; they were outnumbered, but all equipped with muskets. Piar had only five hundred rifles, the rest of his weaponry consisting of bamboo lances and bows and arrows. The battle was ferocious, but Piar's outstanding leadership prevailed, and seven hundred Spanish were killed or taken prisoner; La Torre narrowly escaped to the safety of Angostura. Piar had his three hundred prisoners executed, and laid siege to Guayana and Angostura.

On 4 April 1817, Bolívar caught up with Piar outside Guayana in a primitive hut, there to bargain for the future of the revolution. Piar had just won his greatest victory but Bolívar, not for the first or last time, believed he held the winning hand. He had recently been reinforced by several hundred deserters from Mariño, led by Bermudez, and controlled the main rebel arsenal, as well as the fleet that would be needed to supply the patriots down the Orinoco, while news had just arrived that the Spanish had sent a considerable force of soldiers on transports up the Orinoco to raise the sieges of Angostura and Guayana. Piar's cavalry had proved ineffective against entrenched Spanish positions, and his only hope seemed to be to secure the Liberator's support. The price was to accept Bolívar's leadership. Bolívar, who had long since abandoned the concept of war to the death, scolded Piar for executing his prisoners, then left to join his arsenal, coming up behind.

The Orinoco river is one of the greatest in a continent of great rivers. Not as wide or as long as the Amazon, it is still about four hundred yards across even as far upstream as Angostura, which is named from the narrowing which starts at that point. Huge, brown and sluggish, it wends its way over 1,500 miles from its source in the Serra Parima on Venezuela's border with Brazil – the 'Lost World' table mountain which supposedly inspired Conan Doyle, although it is actually one of many – like a great snake around the country's inland desert, the Grand Savannah, through the llanos to the torrid immensity of its delta. It is navigable for hundreds of miles, with sailing ships benefiting from the easterly winds that blow them upstream, and the currents that speed them down. As already noted, it was an artery for a thriving contraband trade in hides, cattle and horses from the llanos, virtually unpoliceable from Caracas.

Guayana, towards the mouth of the Orinoco, was a run-down, dingy, disease-ridden tropical jungle town filled with smugglers and layabouts. Angostura, 250 miles upriver from the delta, since renamed Ciudad Bolívar, with a just-tolerable climate, was an elegant Spanish city on the edge of the llanos boasting cobbled streets on the familiar colonial grid pattern, one-storey houses with red-tiled roofs, a beautiful cathedral, a spacious city hall, and a plaza. It was the starting-point for what proved to be Bolívar's greatest expedition.

Piar was faithful to his orders once Bolívar had set off up the Orinoco with his precious arsenal. Around San Félix, midway between the two towns under siege, he concentrated his disparate forces: rough-hewn, leather-faced llanero horsemen, half-naked under jaguar-skin caps, served alongside wholly naked Indians, guerrillas from the mountains, and a few regular troops brought by Bermudez. La Torre's Spanish troops, by contrast, were well-disciplined, seasoned veterans, many from the Peninsular War. But La Torre had no cavalry, having come by boat, and he was fighting the irregulars on their own territory.

Bolívar was once again threatened from all sides. Mariño, in the north, had declared a United States of Venezuela, set up an assembly, and pronounced himself commander-in-chief. Piar, his apparent obedience to Bolívar notwithstanding, was conniving against him and still planned to displace him. Mariño proved unlucky. On its return from New Granada the main Spanish army, under Morillo, had decided to proceed down the coast to combine with three thousand troops newly arrived from Spain – initially intended to subjugate a rebellion in Buenos Aires, but diverted on the orders of Morillo. Mariño was forced to evacuate Cumana and then lost battles at Carúpano and Guiria. The whole of Venezuela's coastline, including the far east, was now in the hands of the royalists. Mariño's army disintegrated. Brion's 'navy', which had helped him, was now wholly committed to Bolívar; most of Mariño's supporters, including the young Antonio José de Sucre, moved south to join him; and Mariño himself now begged to be allowed to serve under him. Sorely tried, the Liberator decided to give his old rival one last chance.

Bolívar now ordered Piar to divide his army and himself take one detachment to besiege Guayana, while Bermudez – who hated Piar, blaming him for the death of his brother – besieged Angostura with the other. After a few weeks Piar wrote to Bolívar resigning his command in order (he said) to raise support for the cause in the interior; in fact, he was off to raise the standard against Bolívar, claiming that Bolívar had dismissed him because he was black. One of the officers he tried to suborn reported that Piar had told him, 'I became supreme general through my sword and my luck, but I am a mulatto and I must not govern the republic. However, I have penetrated the great mystery of the present administration and I have sworn my honour to restore freedom to so many innocents who are shedding their blood to shut themselves more and more in disgraceful slavery. I will go to Maturín and to the rest of the world, if necessary, to place myself at the head of those who have no support other than their own efforts.'

This was open insurrection: Bolívar could not continue to act as no more than first among equals in a group of strutting local warlords consumed by personal rivalries who would not obey orders and resigned their commands whenever they felt like it. But it was not simply a matter of who controlled the revolutionary forces. Piar clearly saw himself as another Boves, leader of the blacks, as against the pure-blooded 'mantuan' criollo white, Bolívar. In aspiring to replace his commander on racial grounds, he was threatening to plunge his own side into civil war, to destroy the cause for which so much blood had been shed. Bolívar decided to make an example of him, to exercise a dispassionate ruthlessness, not in the heat of a desperate, hard-pressed campaign but as a result of careful calculation. He sent forces up-country after Piar. Then he issued a thundering denunciation to his troops:

> General Piar, with his insensitive and abominable conspiracy, has alone tried to stir up a war between brothers in which cruel murderers cut the throats of innocent children, of weak women, of tremulous old people, just because they were born of a more or less lighter colour . . . General Piar has infringed the laws, has conspired against the republican system, has disobeyed the government, has resorted to force, has deserted the army and has fled like a coward. He has placed himself outside the law. His destruction is a duty and his destroyer a benefactor.

On 27 July Bolívar's men caught up with their quarry and persuaded Piar's escort not to resist on his behalf. He was bound across the back of a horse, like a common criminal, and transported back to headquarters, where he was sentenced to death by firing squad. Bolívar agreed that he should retain his military honours, but deferred the carrying out of the sentence in the hope that Angostura would soon fall, so that he could make a telling public occasion of it. Meanwhile Bolívar and Bermudez continued the siege of the two river towns.

As a natural leader of the hard men of the llanos Bolívar – small, nervous, intense, intellectual, fastidious, immaculately-uniformed and white – seemed less than their ideal. He set about overcoming his disadvantages in two ways: first, by not abandoning his own aristocratic and reserved personality; and second, by seeking to excel in all that the llaneros prided themselves upon. He shared in the privations of his men, sat with them around the campfire listening and singing to guitars, and slept in his hammock or on the ground; but he also bathed and shaved every day, invariably in water to which eau-de-Cologne had been added, and brushed his teeth. He made a point of feeding and grooming his horse himself, a particular point of honour with the llaneros. According to one description, 'He is in constant agitation. Watching him, you would take him for a crazy man. Walking the forest trails, he goes fast – runs, jumps, tries to leave his companions behind and offers to outjump them. In his hammock he swings violently, singing, talking rapidly, reciting verses in French. He is sometimes loud and sometimes profane. That is when he is among his friends. When a stranger arrives, he shuts up like a clam.'

Two stories recounted by Bolívar himself give a vivid impression of his personality – vain, assertive and slightly ridiculous, and yet aware that only through what we would call public relations, only by impressing people, was he likely to secure the allegiance of the men he needed to carry him to victory.

I remember a singular incident, the act of a madman, although I don't think I am one. One day, bathing in the Orinoco with all my high command, with many generals, one Colonel Martel, who was clerk in my headquarters, claimed to be able to swim better than anyone else. I said something which irritated him, and he replied that he also was a better swimmer than me. About a hundred and fifty yards from where we were, there were two sunken gunboats; and I, also irritated, told Martel that with my hands tied I would be able to reach those boats quicker than he. No one wanted such a test to be made. But, excited, I now shed my clothes and made General Ibarra tie my hands from behind with the braces of my trousers. I threw myself into the water and reached the gunboats with considerable effort. Martel followed me and of course I arrived first. General Ibarra, afraid that I would drown, had ordered two good swimmers into the river to help me. But it was not necessary. This episode proves the tenacity I had then and the willpower which no one could stop. Always forwards, never backwards: that was my maxim, and perhaps to that I owe my successes and anything extraordinary that I did.

Bolívar gave another example:

> I remember that in 1817, when we were in Angostura, I gave one of my horses to my principal aide, General Ibarra, so that he could carry orders to the front at the gallop. The horse was big and very fast, and before saddling her Ibarra was jesting with some of the army commanders that he would tease the horse by mounting from the tail end and vaulting over its head. He did it well, and I arrived at that very moment. I said he had done nothing special, and to prove it to those there, I took the necessary run and jumped, but landed on the neck of the horse, hurting myself where I had rather not talk about.
>
> With my own horse, I did a second jump and fell on the ears, with a worse blow than before. This did not dishearten me. On the contrary I became more determined and on the third attempt vaulted the horse. I confess this was madness, but I didn't want anyone to say they were more agile than me, or to have someone say he could do what I could not. You must not believe that this is of no importance for a man who commands others. In everything, if possible, he must demonstrate his superiority to those who must obey. It's the method of establishing lasting prestige and indispensable for those who occupy the first rank in society and particularly for someone commanding an army.

These were self-inflicted dangers, but life was not without other risks. According to O'Leary:

> During the siege of Angostura and Old Guayana in the year 1817 [Bolívar] established his headquarters at Casacoima, about three leagues from the latter . . . on an inlet of the Orinoco, from which river it is distant about a league. There he had ordered launches to be constructed under the direction of Arismendi. [Bolívar] used to visit the place daily where the workmen were employed.
>
> The Spaniards who were in the fort of Old Guayana were apprised of this by some deserter. A party of infantry and cavalry was ordered to march . . . to surprise him. They effected this so completely that with very little audacity or perseverance they must have made him prisoner. Having alighted from his horse, [Bolívar] was inspecting the gunboats, accompanied by Soublette, Chief of Staff, Arismendi and Torres, a few aides-de-camp and some field officers, when the enemy made their appearance. [Bolívar] and the other chiefs, with the exception of Torres, dashed into the water and made their way to the other bank [not of the Orinoco, but of the inlet]. Torres, with a few soldiers, sword in hand, cut his way through to Casacoima and reported what had taken place. A force immediately marched to the general's aid, but the enemy had retreated with their spoils – the launches and a few horses.

Among those who dashed into the water was Arismendi, who walked on boldly till he got out of depth, when he sank. A servant saved him. On being brought to the side where [Bolívar] was, the latter asked him how he could have got into the water without knowing how to swim. 'If it had been boiling lead, I should have done the same rather than fall into the power of the Spaniards, dead or alive,' was his reply.

Dionisio, his servant, was the last person that arrived at the safe bank. His delay was caused by a large knife which he persisted in bringing across with him, notwithstanding the repeated expostulations of those who witnessed his difficulty in effecting his purpose. On [Bolívar's] enquiring why he took such pains in saving the knife instead of something of more value, he told him that 'he meant to kill His Excellency with it rather than allow him to be taken by the Spaniards'.

After two months of siege Brion appeared at last with his small flotilla, and blockaded the Orinoco, cutting off supplies to the Spanish garrisons at Guayana and Angostura. La Torre made a bolt for it down-river with his troops and hundreds of civilians in flimsy boats, but they were intercepted by Brion's flotilla and about a third of those escaping were captured, along with most of the boats. Only a few reached the mouth of the Orinoco.

Bolívar now established his headquarters in Angostura, and on 11 October in the main square there, under the shadow of the Cathedral, soldiers were lined up. In the words of an eye-witness, 'Arriving at the place of execution, at the foot of the banner of the Battalion of Honour, [Piar] greeted the sentence being read with an air of contempt, keeping his hand in his pocket, moving his right foot and looking in all directions. He didn't want them to blindfold him, and twice pulled off the blindfold they put on him. Blindfolded a third time, he opened his shirt, revealed his chest, and suffered the execution.' Bolívar refused to attend, but must have heard the shots from his residence. For the period and the place, he was a remarkably restrained leader, certainly compared with Piar, a man responsible for executing hundreds of prisoners in cold blood and for wiping out a peaceful Capuchin mission.

The next stages of the operation were then put in train. Bolívar ordered Luis Lopez Mendez, his unofficial ambassador in London at Miranda's old home in Grafton Way, to recruit Britons for the cause. He sent out forces to crush the remaining royalist strongholds along the Orinoco. He issued directives to the five separate rebel forces now operating against the Spanish – Urdaneta along the Orinoco, Bermudez in

Cumana in the centre, Monagas in Maturín in the north, Zaraza on the eastern llanos, and Mariño in Cariaco. And he made contact with the man whose name was beginning to rival his own as the terror of the Spanish forces, now largely confined to the northern highlands of Venezuela: José Antonio Páez, independent commander of the anti-government forces in the western llanos.

The recruitment of the British Legion – or, as it was known in Venezuela, the Albion Legion; its motto was 'Die or Conquer' – was one of the most remarkable elements of the Venezuelan war of independence. Ducoudrez-Holstein, the French mercenary who had known Bolívar in Caracas and Jamaica, was now in London, and helped Lopez Mendez with it. Zea, Bolívar's chief civilian adviser, who had been a distinguished botanist in Madrid, was nominally in charge, and had to find the funds needed to pay the mercenaries. O'Leary takes up the story: 'When Zea reached London he got surrounded by speculators and adventurers who, taking advantage of the rising credit of Colombia, proposed a loan. Zea, having no instructions or credentials for this measure . . . forging full powers for himself, obtained the first loan of 2 millions sterling. . . . Bolívar was indignant when he learned how Zea had abused his trust, protested against the loan and ordered Zea to be recalled.'

The three principal agents in this enterprise were Gregor MacGregor, former hero of Ocumare and Juncal, who had married Bolívar's niece; John d'Evereaux, an Irishman who had been in America; and a Colonel James England. These men knew well that, with the end of the Napoleonic wars, London and Dublin were teeming with penniless, demobbed but battle-hardened soldiers: perfect recruits, easily enticed by promises of generous pay, fine equipment and rapid promotion. Like soldiers, large quantities of military *matériel* were also readily available at low prices. Mendez's press agent, William Walton, told the recruits that the war in Venezuela was all but won, and that it was a rich land where they would be granted extensive properties. Many women and children went as well, to settle the lands their husbands had been promised.

MacGregor was an extraordinary man, only half-sane; besides making a sizeable profit, like the other recruiters, by selling commissions in what was at that stage a phantom army, he also arranged a series of expeditions to America on his own account – including the siege of Fernandina on the coast of Florida, Portobello in Panamá and Riohacha in Colombia – in the course of which he would dump his recruits and sail away with any available booty. Of the 2,200 in total who went with him, including a hundred women and forty children, only two ever returned – apart from MacGregor himself. Yet after a spell in prison in France for fraud, MacGregor went back to Venezuela, by now independent, was appointed a major-general with a generous pension and died, six years later, a prominent citizen.

D'Evereaux, having been paid handsomely for his part in recruiting the Albion Legion, was eventually compelled to sail at the head of an Irish division of a thousand men; they were poorly provisioned and, without food, arrived at Margarita. Arismendi, in control there, was short of food and supplies for his own men, and refused to accept them. The legionnaires landed anyway, and a quarter were dead of typhus within a month. Urdaneta, who hated Arismendi, was sent by Bolívar to take charge of the Battalion. According to a jaundiced British observer,

> Urdaneta . . . was of diminutive stature, pale, effeminate, and a slave to indolence. He was a man so inert, and apparently mindless, that no cause could possibly have been confided to a more incompetent leader. It was vain to look in him for one redeeming characteristic: not the remotest fitness for command could be discerned. A miserable sensualist, he took the field accompanied by two mistresses, and lounged from morning till night in a hammock, the slave to women and cigars.

Brion finally arrived with his flotilla to ship some of them to the Orinoco, while the remainder joined the rebel forces in Colombia and helped free the Magdalena valley from the Spanish – but also burnt down the town of Riohacha in a mutiny.

The main body of British recruits was placed under the command of Lieutenant Gustavus Hippisley – promoted to colonel in consequence – a snobbish but not ineffectual soldier who later complained bitterly of the want of a 'good table', and about other privations of life in Venezuela, not least having to share quarters with ordinary soldiers. They sailed in December 1817 in five ships, one of which, the *India*, immediately foundered in a gale off Ushant with the loss of all aboard. Colonel England's abilities as a commander nearly resulted in a mutiny on his ship. Altogether, about eight thousand left England and Ireland on the expedition, which also included some Italians and Frenchmen, and a disciplined battalion of Hanoverians.

When their ships reached the West Indies – Haiti, Trinidad and

Grenada – they were greeted with indifference or outright hostility, and told that Venezuela, far from being advanced and prosperous, was an untamed outback of jungle, cruelty, wild bears, naked Indians and disease. The Liberator, it was said, was a sadistic madman. On the islands many units broke up through desertion, while scores of recruits died of smallpox, yellow fever, typhus, malaria and dysentery. In Haiti the First Rifle and Artillery Brigades effectively disintegrated, as did the military band. Another group, which included the Hanoverians, reached the mainland of Venezuela and were assigned to Urdaneta's forces. In 1818 they recaptured Barcelona from the Spanish for him, and celebrated with an orgy of drunkenness and looting; the Hanoverians maintained their discipline, but had been reduced from 1,000 to 233 by desertion and sickness. The legionnaires were appalled by the brutality expected of them. According to an anonymous naval officer,

> The Spaniards, who had behaved with great pusillanimity, had no sooner surrendered, than the natives, who had accompanied us, began their murderous work; and it was continued without intermission, until every individual of the entire 1,300 was despatched. Myself and the whole of the British kept aloof from this spectacle as much as possible . . . I received a severe reprimand, as did my brother officers, and the seamen, for not having taken an active part in the slaughter; Admiral Brion, and subsequently General Urdenetta [*sic*], both informed us, that as we had entered the service of Venezuela, we were expected to conform to its usages; and in future they insisted on our personal share of putting the prisoners to death. We made no reply; but I believe that all inwardly resolved never to obey any such order.

Urdaneta decided he would march them to Maturín, which involved crossing a low range of mountains.

> All descriptions of the dreadful sufferings endured must fall far short of the reality. The streams were so swollen and currents rendered so strong and rapid by the falls of rain, that in fording them numbers of men, from their excessive debility, were unable to bear up against the force . . . The rush of waters bears down the body with the rapidity of a shot, dashing it in its course against stumps of trees, jutting rocks, and loose stones, until life is extinct, and the sweeping tide is stained with blood.
> Climbing the mountains their shoes, from being constantly saturated with water, became so enlarged, that they were continually escaping from their feet; and to add to their misery, the surfaces of the mountains were chiefly composed of sharp-pointed stones, resembling in colour broken

Scotch granite, but harder . . . Their feet were attacked by myriads of insects named chegoes . . . These tormenting creatures will penetrate the skin, even when it is unbroken, and breed under it to such an extent that unless they are speedily removed, the swarm becomes incalculable, and sometimes produces mortification. On the plains of Maturín the soldiers drank from puddles until several of them were found dead at the margin of these receptacles for small alligators and snakes of the most poisonous description. Others succumbed to a species of fish, called the raya, which oftentimes seized their thighs and the calves of the legs, and tore large pieces from them, leaving those who survived altogether incapable of further service.

[When they arrived they found] irregular rows of mud-built hovels. The hospital was only two square plots of ground, enclosed with mud walls . . . Dirt, disease, and famine were the reward of the services of men who had left their country to embark in the desperate cause of those who now so ill requited them. Many were lodged in the worst hovels of the town, where they were left to perish . . .

Urdaneta complained bitterly that 'six months with these men is worse than ten campaigns', yet some went on to serve bravely under Mariño. Tiring of the novelty of life in the West Indies, groups of deserters also began to make their way to the Orinoco; when eventually they arrived, it was to play a key role in the campaign that followed. Many of their officers became trusted and disciplined aides to Bolívar. Hope, despair, perseverance and eventual triumph were to be the lot of the survivors of the Albion Legion. Typical among them was Heinrich Meyer, from Hamburg, who ran away from his father's office, was press-ganged aboard a ship bound for Venezuela, then fought for Bolívar; he ended as one of his most famous and distinguished officers, and owner of a sugar-cane estate.

Another was Daniel Florence O'Leary, a name already encountered in connection with Bolívar. Born at Cork, at seventeen he travelled aboard the *Prince* with the newly-formed Red Hussars of Venezuela, and was shocked on first landing.

Hitherto I had seen little to reconcile me to the service I had entered and on our arrival at Achaguas my prospects did not brighten. I was disgusted at the barbarous and unnecessary sacrifice of human lives. Prisoners were frequently brought in, for the most part Americans and that most probably had been compelled to serve with the Spaniards. Groups of ten and twelve were almost daily put to death. Though profuse of blood, the patriots were economic of gunpowder, which was considered a more precious article, and the wretched [prisoners] were doomed to have their sufferings augmented and prolonged by the sword of the executioner. Officers were generally employed in this distinguished service and, to tell the truth, they displayed great dexterity. I have often seen the head severed from the trunk at the first blow. Whenever this occurred a loud laugh from the creole spectators expressed their satisfaction at the ability of the headsman.

O'Leary arrived in Angostura just after Bolívar's defeat at El Semen in March 1818, and was immediately appointed by General Carlos Soublette to the guard of honour of General José Anzoategui; soon promoted to captain, he joined the march across the Andes in July 1819, and on Anzoategui's death was appointed aide-de-camp to Bolívar, at the age of nineteen. He became one of the Liberator's most trusted friends, and married Soublette's sister. On Bolívar's death O'Leary had thoughts of becoming his biographer, but in the event published only his own extensive and fascinating memoirs. These and his jottings are invaluable as lucid and reasonably detached assessments; he was no mere starry-eyed worshipper of the Liberator.

As the legionnaires drifted into Angostura they were welcomed by Bolívar and then sent up to San Fernando, where the local commanders needed reinforcements. Dressed in the finest of discarded uniforms – green, scarlet and gold for the First Venezuelan Hussars, light blue, gold and scarlet for the Second, with Wellington boots and plumed shakos – the British officers and soldiers arrived to find that most remarkable of all the llanero commanders, José Antonio Páez, sleeping under a tree. Hippisley recounts that Páez was exhausted and frothing at the mouth, having lately killed forty Spaniards with his lance in a skirmish at Ortiz. He greeted England, the British commander, warmly. He admired their splendid uniforms, in striking contrast to the half-naked llaneros, and promptly made a guard of honour of them. The British taught him a few words of English, and how to hold a knife and fork.

Páez was, at first glance, no more than another version of Boves. He had been born in 1790 in the town of Curpa near Araure, between the mountains and the llanos, son of a poor white farmer. As a boy he killed one of the hated overseers – apparently in self-defence – and fled to the llanos proper to serve as a cattle rancher under a negro slave, who made the boy wash his feet. But his toughness and skill (he was an excellent vet) soon established him as a farmer, and a leader in his own right. In 1810, aged twenty, he was pressed into service on the Spanish side in the civil war but, unusually for a llanero, deserted and joined the patriot guerrilla bands in the western llanos, leading a squad of his own and staging a raid on Barinas, where he freed a hundred men from the gaol. While Boves led the majority of llaneros against the patriots, Páez formed an independent guerrilla group at Achaguas, which gradually began to acquire a reputation.

He was famous for marching by night, guided by the stars in that vast sea of grass, in order to avoid the heat of the day and to make sure his movements were unobserved: the dust behind the horsemen of the llanos could be seen for miles, as could the buzzards that gathered when cattle were slaughtered for food. He knew the empty, seemingly monotonous terrain intimately, including the location of dry areas during the rainy season and water-holes during the dry. His men averaged sixty miles a day on horseback, and could advance and retreat with astonishing rapidity when necessary.

Usually dressed in a coarse blue cloth shirt, a cloak and a broad-brimmed hat, Páez, like Boves, was a short, tubby man with a barrel chest, enormously powerful shoulders and a thick bull neck. His skin was darkened by the sun, but his blue eyes and light brown hair attested to his white blood. His body was supported by spindly bow legs so adapted to riding that he had an awkward gait, like that of a seaman on land. He was astute and intelligent, but illiterate, and had never been to a city. He exuded natural leadership, shared the lives of his men, and was endowed with two deep-seated Spanish characteristics – *hombria* (manliness), and *simpatía*. He was a demonic fighter who relished the heat of combat, as adept with his machete as his lance. He was subject to epileptic fits at the height of battle, when he would be rescued by his watchful men as he toppled from his horse – usually by a giant of a negro named Canejo, armed with a machete to match, who acted as his valet and chief bodyguard. Picking up his master as he fell, Canejo would sling him across the back of his horse to carry him to safety. The simple cowboys looked upon epilepsy with religious awe. Páez was rough and brutal, without any sentimental respect for human life. He himself used to recount his experience with a Spanish officer he had badly wounded:

> I tried to remove a handsome cartridge belt which he wore about his waist and, as he broke out into a stream of blasphemy and ill-considered words not suited to the situation in which he found himself, I began to exhort him to make a Christian ending and recited the Creed to stimulate him to repeat it after me. Luckily, I looked down and saw that, instead of

accompanying me in my prayers, he had half drawn a dagger from his belt. I confess my charity was completely chilled and, as my indignation did not allow me to waste more time on my adversary's future destiny, by a lance thrust I freed him from the rage that was choking him more than the blood he was losing.

His men, vicious and untamed, regarded plunder and women as theirs by right, and showed no mercy to those who opposed them, although Páez did believe in taking prisoners. However, there was none of the demented cruelty, the sadistic lust for blood and suffering for their own sake that Boves, Morales and his henchmen displayed (possibly under explicit instructions from their Spanish masters, to cow the population). In his patriot ideals, in fact, Páez, although equally rough and humble in origin, was on a far higher level of humanity than Boves. Later he was described as 'an innocent child, a primitive who looked on Bolívar as a god and at other times, when he was afar, as a devil. He was a child even unto his crimes, enamored of anything that shone.'

Later still, this same rough-hewn cowboy became Venezuela's president and dictator intermittently for sixteen years altogether, displaying a mastery of peacetime politics much greater than Bolívar's, ruling with an iron hand but also with shrewdness and without real excess, and becoming something of an international star. He toured Europe, was given an enthusiastic reception in New York and then received by the President, and died in 1873. It was said of him that he was 'a murdering tiger in the hills of Payara and a tame sheep in the salons of adulation.'

All this lay far in the future. As his successes multiplied, so did his army, to become a formidable mobile force. Morales, though even more murderous, lacked Boves's leadership skills, and when Spanish commanders attempted to impose discipline on his ragged army of llaneros they deserted in droves to join Páez, who promised them plunder from the Spanish – the 'haves', once again, to this legion of 'have-nots'.

By 1816 Páez commanded an army of ten thousand men, some of them naked Cunaviche Indians fighting as infantry. This force boasted probably a million head of cattle and half a million horses, perhaps forty thousand of which had been broken. As Páez's reputation grew, the rebel forces over the border in New Granada, under the young Francisco de Paula Santander whom Bolívar had sparred with some four years earlier, determined that he should fight on their side. When Santander and his men rode down to Páez's camp to order him to submit to their authority, they soon became uneasily aware that they were surrounded by thousands of llaneros less than pleased by this display of hauteur towards their leader. Páez replied, politely, that his men would not let him obey Santander's orders; on the contrary, if Santander wanted to get out alive, he must place himself under Páez's command.

Realising his danger, Santander agreed to resign in Páez's favour; but for the llaneros, the command was not Santander's to resign – Páez had always been the legitimate commander. There was a tense stand-off, and for a while it seemed Santander was in danger of being butchered. But Páez himself suddenly relented, leaving Santander humiliated, furious, and not sure whether he had been the victim of an elaborate trick.

Páez had by now also attracted the attention of the Spanish commander, Morillo. Greatly underestimating the strength and organisation of the llanero troops, he despatched three thousand men under La Torre to Maté de Miel, near the Apure river: They were Spanish regulars equipped with artillery and their own cavalry, but there were not enough of them. Páez spotted the Spanish movements by the dust they sent up but they were unaware of his presence, or that of his five-hundred-strong column, moving by night. He attacked at night, too, sending a detachment with fifty horses to stampede the corral holding the Spaniards' horses, then charging in the confusion. The Spanish fled in disarray, leaving their guns, horses and ammunition. Some nine hundred were killed or taken prisoner.

La Torre waited for several months before moving against Páez again; 1,500 Spanish cavalry and 3,000 infantry were camped at Murcuritas, on the edge of the llanos. In another night attack Páez with 1,100 men moved upwind of the enemy so that the dust they raised – it was the height of the dry season – would blow down on the Spanish in a dense cloud. The llaneros were given their usual orders, to attack repeatedly, regroup, and then attack again at will. So well co-ordinated and well-practised were the cowboys and their horses that no further orders were necessary, and they descended in a series of frontal attacks along the entrenched Spanish position, routing the cavalry on their right flank. The initial surprise of a night attack out of a cloud of choking dust passed, and the much larger force of Spanish hussars in the middle held the line, while the infantry retreated to an easily defended wood and water-hole. To dislodge the hussars Páez had the high, dry grass set on fire, and as the wind bore the flames down onto the Spanish, the cowboys rode like demons behind it. At this, even the hussars fled. Morillo wrote to the King of Spain: 'Fourteen consecutive charges on my wearied battalions showed me that those men were not a scanty band of cowards as I had been informed, but organised troops, able to compete with the best in Your Majesty's service.' Bolívar now decided that he must co-ordinate his own actions with the ruler of the western llanos. This would be tricky for, as Páez had shown Santander, he took orders from no one.

The Liberator had been resting and training his men in Angostura. The town was agreeable: the river sliding by, men and women resting half the day in hammocks, the jungle canopy beyond teeming with ring-tail monkeys, snakes, and scarlet flamingos. Tiring of Isabel Soublette, he had her married off to a local merchant, who was delighted with Bolívar's nuptial present of the only four-poster bed in town. Bolívar was addicted to night-time revelry, waltzing in the best houses in town, or by the campfires outside while his men sang and guitars played. Dancing, he claimed, was good for thought. 'There are those', he said, 'who must be alone and away from all confusion in order to think and meditate. I can reflect and meditate in the midst of social gatherings, pleasures or the noise of battle. I am always alone in the midst of many people.'

One observer describes how Bolívar and his staff dressed at this time: 'He wore a hat, a blue jacket with red epaulettes and three sets of gold buttons, blue trousers and, instead of shoes, leather sandals . . . The officers around him were almost all coloured. Few of them had jackets. Their clothing consisted of a shirt made up of different coloured patches, very wide and with huge sleeves; torn white trousers which came down to the knees; and hats of palm with feathers on top. Almost all were barefoot.' O'Leary describes Bolívar himself:

[His] forehead was very high but not unusually broad. It had many wrinkles. His eyebrows were thick, but well shaped; his eyes were dark and keen; his nose rather long and handsome. About the centre it had a small excrescence not perceivable until the year [18]20 when it gave him a little uneasiness, but this passed off as the wart did not grow. His cheek bones were salient, his cheeks sunken ever since I first knew him. His mouth was ugly, his lips being thick, the upper one long. His teeth were regular, white and beautiful. He took particular care of them. His jaw bones and chin were long. His ears were large. His hair, which he wore long, was extremely black and curly. His whiskers and mustachios [were] light coloured. He was of my own height. I don't know what this may be at present, something about 5' 6" or 5' 7", English measure. His chest was narrow and his whole figure thin, his legs particularly so. His skin was dark and rough, his hands and feet remarkably small and pretty.

His countenance at times was pleasing, when in good humour. When irritated, it was ferocious. The change was incredible. [He] was a good eater and though [he] was as well able as anyone I knew or know to live on any sort of diet, he was fond of a good dinner when attainable and did it every justice. He was sober. The wines he liked best were Graves and Champagne. When he drank most, he never took at dinner more than a pint of the former or two glasses of the latter. Whenever he filled his own glass, he helped those who sat on his right and left.

[Bolívar] was always accustomed to take a great deal of exercise and few men were able to endure more fatigue. He generally slept six hours of the four-and-twenty. He was a very bold, though not a graceful, rider.

In the despatch of civil business, which he never neglected, even on campaign, he was quick. Sitting and swinging in his hammock, he listened to his secretary read the thousand memorials which never failed and in an instant dictated his decree, which was generally irrevocable. He asked a question or two when he was not cognisant of the demand or demandant, which very seldom happened, as he knew almost every person in the country and was gifted with a most extraordinary memory. His decrees were sometimes original . . . A curate, who was no great patriot, sought a professional advancement. His decree was laconic, tho' not polite: 'Al culo, mi padre! [Up yours, Father!]'

Even in this comparative paradise, an oasis of peace after the efforts of recent months, life was hard for the ordinary troops and the foreign legionnaires who were trickling to join them. In the hospital, according to Hippisley, men with amputated limbs lay about; many bled to death; others had had half their skulls blown off, exposing their brains. 'Yet hardly a groan escaped from the poor miserable sufferers, some of whom seemed to endure the agony they were undergoing with all the stoical indifference and resolution ascribed to their North American brethren when put to the torture by their conquerors. The only cry I heard was for water.'

When the Spanish army under La Torre descended from the cordillera to the llanos towards the end of 1817 for a major offensive, Bolívar secured Páez's agreement to his command and set out with a thousand men to combine with the llanero general Zaraza in the middle of the country. Zaraza had been ordered to wait until his forces were reinforced by Bolívar, but rashly attacked the Spanish at La Hogaza. La Torre inflicted a terrible defeat on the patriots, killing a thousand, including Bolívar's nephew, and securing all Zaraza's stores and ammunition. Bolívar retreated to Angostura, issued a general call-up and recruited five thousand men, most of them untrained, before setting out with his new force to join Páez. They travelled at astonishing speed in *flechas* – long canoes – covering about two hundred and fifty miles in twenty days to reach Páez's headquarters at San Juan de Payara, near San Fernando de Apure.

On 31 January 1818 Bolívar and a small escort entered Páez's camp, and the two most famous resistance leaders in Venezuela embraced warmly. Bolívar was apprehensive about dealing with the wily little llanero leader seven years his junior. He feared that Páez would not obey him, or that he would prove downright treacherous, as Mariño and Piar had. Páez for his part was surprised to find Bolívar down-to-earth and energetic, much less aristocratic and effete than he had expected. But the tough, well-trained llaneros easily outshone the mixture of trained troops and raw recruits, men and boys, that Bolívar had brought with him.

Bolívar was keen to outflank La Torre by ascending the cordillera and marching straight on Caracas; Páez wanted Bolívar to join him in an assault on the capital of the western plains, San Fernando. As was too often the case, Bolívar was dogged by the problem that his powerful regional commanders were usually more interested in securing their own immediate interests than in prosecuting the wider war: Páez wanted complete control of the western llanos, Zaraza the high plains just under the shadow of the cordillera, and Bermudez the eastern territories and Cumana. Meanwhile Santander, the patriot general in eastern New Granada, had joined them to urge help for his nation.

This particular decision was made for them, however, as the Spanish offensive on the llanos grew too strong to be ignored. The patriots decided to march on Calabozo, the Spanish army base at the foot of the cordillera, and came in sight of it on 10 February. To reach Calabozo they had to cross the fast-flowing Apure river. Pointing to a number of armed Spanish dugouts in midstream Páez proposed to seize them, and Bolívar watched incredulously as he galloped into the water at the head of fifty men riding white horses and armed with lances. The Spanish were so astonished by the sight of the swimming horses and men that they only fired a few desultory shots before fleeing in canoes or plunging into the river. As a later historian, Cunninghame Graham, remarks, this was probably the first time in history that cavalry skirmished against armed boats.

Morillo, taken by surprise, tried to turn the patriots' wings as they reached Calabozo, but his forces were encircled by horsemen who steadily cut them down to the last man, '*culo a culo*', bottom to bottom, as Páez remarked. Morillo was now entirely surrounded, and Bolívar issued a cheeky demand for his surrender, offering those within the camp a pardon. The patriot forces bivouacked for the night in the nearby town of El Rastro, while a detachment remained behind to watch for any sign of Spanish movement. On the night of 14 February, however, which was particularly dark, Morillo and all his forces managed to slip away under the watchers' noses. By morning, when Bolívar was told, the Spanish with several hours' start had escaped to defensive positions in the wooded country on the edge of the cordillera. Bolívar wanted to pursue them, but Páez was most reluctant for his fighters to move out of their natural element on the plains and into the mountains. Instead, he urged again that he should return south to seize San Fernando.

Reluctantly Bolívar agreed, on condition that once the city had surrendered, Páez would rejoin him. By now Morillo had crossed the cordillera to his headquarters at Valencia and called up La Torre, his second-in-command, from Caracas with more troops. Morales and other commanders were also ordered to join him. At last Morillo had realised the extent of the threat posed by the joint armies of Bolívar and Páez. Urgently Bolívar called on Páez and Zaraza to rejoin him: 'The enemy is reinforcing its army by giving the impression that we have been beaten. Our suspension of operations [to allow Páez to settle scores in the south] confirms what they say, and it is not surprising that people have been deceived by appearances. We must not lose a single moment. The speed of our movements and the convergence of our armies is the only hope of winning ... Hesitation will produce ruin and destruction.' Zaraza's forces arrived, but not those of Páez.

In March Bolívar decided to gamble on taking the offensive without Páez's support, in a bid to stop the royalist armies combining. His plan was bold in the extreme: to climb the mountains and block the road between Valencia and Caracas, and then to march on Caracas where the weakest army, that of La Torre, was based. To blockade Morales's forces, he left a detachment behind under Zaraza. It was a daring concept: in one swoop to seize the capital and deal a devastating psychological blow at the royalists. It was also foolhardy to the point of craziness. Even if Bolívar succeeded in taking Caracas, he would be surrounded by hostile armies in the central highlands, as before, where Páez's forces would probably not be able to help him.

On their way up the mountains the patriot army took Maracay, and Bolívar was able briefly to visit his old estate at San Mateo, scene both of childhood joys and of his bitter defeat more than three years before. It was in ruins, but he was recognised with joy by some of his old slaves. The same evening, at Maracay, as Bolívar's officers dined in a comfortable mansion, a message came that Zaraza's forces had been surrounded by those of Morales and that Morillo, heavily reinforced, was riding upon Bolívar. He rushed back into the mess-hall and ordered a retreat down the mountains by the most direct route possible – known as the Road of Death. In a violent electrical storm they rode that night down the rocky, precipitous pass, Bolívar, cloaked, at the head of his troops, while thunder and lightning rolled about them.

At a stream called El Semen he decided to make a stand, to cover the retreat: his rearguard put up a fight for six hours, and Morillo was halted. But when La Torre's armies arrived Bolívar had no choice but to withdraw to La Puerta, already notorious as the place where Boves had destroyed the armies of his Second Republic. There the whole patriot army disintegrated in a headlong retreat amidst appalling bloodshed, leaving a thousand dead, many of them officers. Urdaneta was wounded, and Bolívar himself only narrowly escaped to Calabozo, where the pitiful remnants of his army gathered. It was the most comprehensive military defeat he had yet suffered, and almost entirely self-inflicted: it had been madness, tactically and strategically, to attempt, with an inferior force, to charge straight into the heart of the enemy, on their terrain, where they had vastly superior armies.

Páez, for one, viewed his judgement in not joining Bolívar on his suicidal mission as fully vindicated – although he failed to recognise his contribution to the disaster in not sending reinforcements when these were called for. As Bolívar's pathetic efforts on Venezuela's northern coast in 1816 had also shown, frontal attacks on the Spanish stranglehold on the uplands seemed doomed to failure. To those, like Hippisley, who saw him in Calabozo he appeared exhausted, delirious and wretched: '. . . at the age of 38 he appears 50 . . . dry, thin, restless and feverish. He seems to have borne immense weariness. His dark eyes . . . now are opaque and heavy. He has dark hair tied back by a band, large moustaches, a black handkerchief around his collar, a great blue tunic and trousers of the same colour, boots and epaulettes. In the hammock where he rested wounded, while we talked, he didn't remain in the same position for more than two minutes.'

If not actually broken down or insane, he was a man close to the end of his tether. Over the next few months, with a force of two or three hundred men, he led one small assault after another against the Spanish in the foothills, sometimes losing, sometimes winning. Páez remarked caustically that 'Bolívar was overfond of fighting.' He took foolhardy risks close to enemy lines, as though demonstrations of bravery could purge him of his incompetence as a general. On one occasion a group of enemy soldiers nearly surprised him when he was asleep, and only escaped because the restlessness of his horse woke him. There were rumours that Santander, who hated him, had planned this incident as an assassination attempt. When Bolívar was trying to make his getaway, according to O'Leary,

> A private soldier gave him an unharnessed mule, which had not proceeded far ere it plunged with such violence and constancy that [Bolívar] lost his seat and in the fall sprained his ankle. A sergeant then offered him his horse and mounted himself *en croupe*. This animal became fatigued as a few miles were travelled. [Bolívar would] inevitably have fallen into the power of the enemy had not Colonel Infante overtaken him mounted on a magnificent charger, which he begged the general to accept. This had a few moments previously belonged to Lopez, who commanded the Spanish division and received a mortal wound. This accident saved Bolívar.

On another occasion, he and one of his soldiers narrowly avoided discovery in the bush by a Spanish patrol. The soldier drew his knife, and told Bolívar he intended to kill him before the Spaniards got him. Bolívar gave an odd laugh, and talked of how he intended to create a great union of South America. The guerrilla concluded that his chief really had gone insane. In a third instance,

> . . . he arrived with his staff at a *hato*, where he thought to remain till the next day. A girl, whose pretty figure had smitten him, held forth an inducement by offering to partake of his bed. Whether he suspected that all was not right, or whether it was more convenient for the next day's journey to proceed a little farther, I forget. But he left the house. The girl, who was not a patriot, had despatched a message to a Spanish outpost not far distant and, had he not decamped, he would have fallen into their hands.

It was not only Bolívar's sorties that failed. Patriot commanders everywhere were balked: Páez was forced back from San Carlos and Barinas, Zaraza was pushed out of Calabozo by Morales. Bolívar heard of these reverses while bathed in the sweat of a fever at San Fernando.

The English commander of the foreign legionnaires, Colonel Hippisley, arrived from Angostura with a long list of grievances but missed Bolívar, who had set off downstream in his *flechera* (which had a kind of covered cabin in which he could enjoy his women). Hippisley went after him, all the way back to Angostura, vainly seeking an interview while Bolívar ignored him. In an attempt to put the calamity of La Puerta behind him, his complex mind, as so often before, took refuge in ever more grandiose dreams. The Spanish writer Ciro Bayo said of him: 'His career was a great vanity enlisted in the service of a noble cause.' Under the enforced rest of boat travel and the care of his female companions, Bolívar at last seemed to recover, and evolved a new strategy: he would take advantage of the fact that both Great Britain and President Monroe of the United States had sent emissaries to Angostura to announce the setting-up of a congress to represent the whole of Venezuela, with delegates elected from all provinces by males over twenty-one with a property qualification.

When he reached Angostura Bolívar finally received his insistent pursuer, but refused to promote him to brigadier-general, as he wished, which resulted in Hippisley's furious departure. At that last interview, as a jest, Bolívar offered to buy his fine cocked hat; Hippisley sold it to him, and Bolívar doggedly wore it for a few days. On his return to London Hippisley sued Lopez Mendez for misleading him as to his prospects in Venezuela, and even had him arrested; he later wrote a scathing book about Bolívar; like MacGregor, he was subsequently arrested for his involvement in a bogus scheme for colonising South America. Hippisley was by no means the most rotten apple in the barrel. Once Bolívar had left for Angostura one Colonel Henry Wilson of the Albion Legion began to encourage Páez to challenge the Liberator's authority – which was perhaps not unreasonable, in view of Bolívar's losses and Páez's preservation of his forces. O'Leary, who was there, takes up the story.

The day after General Bolívar had embarked for Angostura [Páez] reviewed our corps. He was dressed in a green ill-cut jacket with red cuffs and collar and small yellow buttons, white jean pantaloons, cotton stockings of the same colour and shoes with silver spurs. On his head he wore a large Spanish cocked hat with silver lace. His horse seemed good and was caparisoned with lots of silver ornaments.

A few days afterwards he dined with Colonel Wilson under a large shed in front of the colonel's house. Wilson flattered him in a most fulsome way. However, the general seemed not to dislike it, or rather accepted it as genuine praise which he was truly entitled to. That afternoon it was agreed that Wilson and the chiefs of Apure were to proclaim Páez Captain-General of the army. Early in the next week a day was named for the purpose. The several chiefs of Apure who were at hand assembled, bringing with them as many llaneros as they could muster.

A motley group it was, to be sure. Some seven or eight hundred men on horseback, all badly clad and some almost in a perfect state of nudity, formed in anything but an orderly style in a plain to the east of the town. Our corps formed to the right of the whole – an honour meant to our splendid uniforms, I suppose. When the farce was ready to commence Páez, accompanied by some thirty or forty field officers and aid[e]s-de-camp, [presented himself]. The general was hailed by loud vivas and, as soon as these had ceased, an *acta* was read naming him Captain-General. Another volley of vivas followed and then some of the most expert horsemen were ordered to show off. The field business over, the chiefs assembled to sign the *acta*. Thus commenced our career in favour of South American independence!!!

Páez, as was natural, was delighted with the new auxiliaries. However, the day had scarcely closed when someone whispered in his ear that he was doing wrong. On consideration, it was determined to send the *acta* to headquarters and require General Bolívar's permission for the acceptance of his new grade. In the meantime Wilson had made him splendid offers. A corps of several thousand Englishmen were to be brought out. Wilson obtained leave to go to Angostura, and recommendations to General Bolívar to have his views attended to.

From Achaguas he set off, but, on his arrival at the capital, the castles he had been building in the air came to the ground. Wilson was arrested, remitted to a fort in Guayana la Vieja until a vessel was ready to sail for Europe, when he was embarked and dismissed the service. Páez received a reprimand, and here ended the business.

Bolívar had no money with which to pay the Albion Legion and claimed – falsely – that they should have been paid by Mendez in London. He did his best, however, to find them food and accommodation, and even considered sending them back to England. Their plight was, in truth, pretty wretched. Led to expect incorporation into a formidable army in a land of wealth, they had braved the miseries of the West Indies to arrive in an even more comfortless tropical settlement on a sluggish river in the middle of a jungle. Dr Robinson, an army surgeon, described how, billeted on his arrival in a large old colonial house in Angostura, he was thrown out by its angry owner in the middle of the night. He found another house, hung his hammock from hooks in the wall, and awoke to find a pile of decomposing bodies outside. The hooks had been used to hang Spaniards. His first encounter with Bolívar's soldiers was scarcely encouraging. They were aged between eighteen and fifty. Many were completely naked, others sported primitive loincloths. General Monagas, their commander, had long, straggly dark hair, the ubiquitous jaguar-skin cap, and a dirty white uniform.

The legionnaires could not stand the dried raw beef *tajajo* eaten by the patriots, and sold their belongings to buy proper food. Gradually the state of their own clothing deteriorated, and they became emaciated by hunger. Robinson wrote that they were 'shrunk and withered to mere walking skeletons . . . struggling patiently with a combination of disappointment and disease . . . unparalleled in the history of the world.' However, it soon became apparent that among their ranks were many stoics and idealists, and these became bulwarks of Bolívar's officer corps and army. The Liberator quickly adopted one as his aide-de-camp: 'Colonel' James Rooke was a big, good-looking former British army major with a beautiful mulatta wife from St Kitts. Others acted as guards of honour. One member of the Albion Legion, Dr J. G. B. Siegert, later evolved the formula for Angostura bitters (essential in a pink gin), concocted (or possibly not) from the bark of a tree, *Galipea officinalis* or *Cusparia febrifuga*, used locally as a tonic and in the treatment of fevers.

Bolívar made a trip up to Maturín, only to discover that the patriot army there had been wiped out. For once, he was openly disheartened: 'In addition to all the other evils that afflict us, we have to deal with incompetence, insubordination and presumption.' He made another visit to San Fernando, this time in much better spirits, even to the point of bombast: 'I am like the sun in the midst of all; my lieutenants have no other brilliance than that which reflects on them from me . . . The intrepid General Páez will lead you to victory and this genius of liberty will inscribe your names in the annals of glory! Llaneros, you are invincible!' The longer Bolívar stayed on in the Orinoco valley, the more fantastic and surreal the whole venture seemed to become. It wasn't just the city of Angostura, 'Queen of the Orinoco', with its picture-book Spanish colonial elegance surrounded by inhospitable jungle; or the bizarre costumes – or lack of costume – of the soldiers and the extraordinary mixture of peoples; or the spectacle of the Liberator waltzing, late into the night, around the campfires of his men. It was, rather, the inherent absurdity of the whole project. Here they were, hundreds of miles from anywhere of the slightest strategic importance, unable to loosen the grip of the Spanish on the prosperous heart of their country, ineffectual and threatened.

And now there met 'an elected congress of the whole nation', in fact attended by only a handful of nominal 'representatives', the rest of the country not being in Bolívar's hands. With just twenty-six delegates present, before Mr Irwin from the United States and Mr Hamilton from England, Bolívar's arrival was marked by a cannonade and a blast of trumpets; then he embarked on the third of his great declarations to the Spanish American people. He began with an unconvincing disclaimer of responsibility for the events which had plunged the patriot nation into its current predicament: 'I have been no more than a plaything in the revolutionary hurricane which blew me about like a feeble straw. I could do neither good nor bad: irresistible forces directed the march of our achievements: to attribute them to me would not be just and would give me an importance I do not deserve.' The tension between Bolívar the constitutional idealist, the protagonist of representative government, and Bolívar the aristocratic autocrat, then quickly emerged.

> Our weak citizens will have to strengthen their spirits greatly before they can take the salutary nourishment of liberty. Their limbs have been numbed by chains, their vision dimmed by the shadows of the dungeons . . . Can they march with firm steps toward that temple [of liberty], sustaining its splendid rays, breathing without oppression its pure air?
>
> . . . It would be better for South America to adopt the Koran than the form of government of the United States, even though it be the best in the world . . . It is a marvel to me . . . that it [the United States] has continued to exist and prosper, that it has not been overthrown at the first sign of danger. In spite of the fact that this people is a singular model of political virtue and moral enlightenment, that liberty has been its cradle, that it has been reared in and fed upon pure liberty, it is a marvel that a system so weak and complicated as the federal has been able to endure . . . It has never even remotely entered my mind to consider a parallel between the positions and natures of two publics as distinct as the Anglo- and Hispano-American . . .
>
> We must face the fact that our race is not European or North American; it is rather a composite of Africa and America than an emanation of Europe, for Spain itself ceased to be European by its African [Moorish] blood, its institutions and character. It is impossible to determine exactly

to what human family we do belong. The greater part of indigenous blood has been wiped out; the European has mixed with the American and African and this has mixed with the Indian and European. Even though all of us were born from the bosom of the same mother, our fathers, differing in origin and blood, are foreigners; and all differ visibly in colouring.

This diversity of origins requires an infinitely firm guide, an infinitely delicate touch to manage this heterogeneous society, whose complex composition becomes destroyed, divided and dissolved with the slightest alteration . . . We must fasten our attention upon these differences, and we will find that the balance of power must be distributed in two ways. In republics the executive must be strongest because everything conspires against it, while in monarchies the legislature must be strongest, because everything conspires in favour of the monarch.

He contended that while the magnificence of the throne protected a king, there was no such protection for a republican leader, who 'must be given more protection than a constitutional prince possesses . . . as no form of government is so weak as democracy, its structures should be of the greatest solidity, and its institutions should be made for stability. If not . . . we will have a society that is loose, tumultuous and anarchic, with no social cohesion and in which happiness, peace and justice do not rule.' He then went on to argue, just as controversially, for the union of Venezuela and New Granada.

It is clear, from a reading of Bolívar's address, that he tipped towards the authoritarian view of government for the best of reasons, and in so doing he was a man of his time. Even in Britain, that beacon of constitutional democracy, the Great Reform Act was not to be passed until 1832 – and that did not provide for anything resembling universal male suffrage. However, his words were fated to outlive their time, to be used for a century and a half by the ruthless, tough-minded autocrats who terrorised the continent after him. Bolívar was wheeled out not merely by the constitutionalists, but by the caudillos as well.

His argument for a republican leader stronger than a monarch tends naturally towards dictatorship. The actual constitution he proposed, however, although impractical, was supposed to provide a check, allowing as it did for civil liberty, freedom of religion and the abolition of slavery, as well as universal male suffrage (with a property and income qualification) – all which concepts of freedom before the law were enlightened for the times. In a reflection of Bolívar's authoritarian bent, the president was to be elected for life. This was an attempt to eliminate the worst aspect of monarchism – the hereditary principle which allowed fools to succeed – while retaining its authority. Bolívar had not completely understood that in England, which he so adored, power had already passed from the monarchy and the nobility. The senate was to be hereditary – another aristocratic concept; the lower house was to be democratic. There was to be a five-man supreme court, an idea borrowed from the United States, and there was to be another chamber, the censors, a kind of supreme constitutional committee, to perform a role which actually belonged in the United States to the Supreme Court.

It was a hodge-podge, unworkable, a kind of authoritarianism-with-checks, in some of its ideas revealing Bolívar to be an out-of-touch aristocrat in his political thinking; and yet its basic ideas were sound – certainly much more so than those of Miranda's projected constitutions – and its intentions were good. The Congress of Angostura, recognising its contradictions, threw out the proposed hereditary senate, the president-for-life (his term was sensibly restricted to four years) and the censors. The British observer, Hamilton, wrote that 'General Bolívar gave so brilliant a proof of moderation and patriotism as is not found in the annals of any country'. In a show for the foreign delegates, Bolívar was chosen as president of the republic, despite the fact that he controlled but a fraction of Venezuela. He presided over a banquet, spoke with charismatic panache and force, then leapt upon the table. 'Thus,' he cried, 'as I cross this table from one end to the other, I shall march from the Atlantic to the Pacific, from Panamá to Cape Horn, until the last Spaniard is expelled!'

II

Across the Andes

On 27 February 1819 Bolívar left on what seemed likely to be yet another doomed assault on the entrenched Spanish positions in the highlands. The plan was that while Morillo was engaged in an intensive campaign against Páez in the west, Bolívar should team up with the forces in the east and some of Páez's men in the centre, to stage an offensive against Caracas. His forces marched along the southern bank of the Orinoco to combine with Páez, travelling 280 miles through jungle and across hills in just eighteen days. The news was all bad. The Spanish had driven Páez from Achaguas, his stronghold; Urdaneta reported that Mariño would not take part in the proposed offensive; nor would Brion; nor would Arismendi, on Margarita.

Bolívar nevertheless attacked the Spanish with vigour, and Páez, taking new heart, descended on Morillo's forces outside Achaguas, killing five hundred and camping there. The rebels now prodded away at Morillo's men, frustrating his attempts to obliterate their strongholds on the llanos, so that just as the patriots could not break through in the highlands, the royalists could not prevail in the lowlands. Morillo withdrew to Calabozo, in the foothills, and the Venezuelan stalemate seemed set to continue.

It was at this point that Bolívar made the most fateful decision of an eventful life – if he had not actually made it already. He resolved to abandon his old goal of liberating Caracas, and to march straight for New Granada and surprise the Spanish there. He later claimed that such had been the object of the expedition all along, since the moment he left Angostura; that he had been planning such a coup for years. The evidence suggests, however, that although he may have toyed with such a strategy, his real obsession was to liberate Caracas – and only as it dawned upon him that to make the attempt would be to lead his troops into yet another débâcle did he change direction. If so, it was a tactical improvisation of pure genius – although at the time it appeared little less than madness.

The first indication of Bolívar's change of mind came in a letter to Santander on 20 May:

> To carry out an operation which I am considering in New Granada, you must group all your forces in the most careful and favourable position for entering the interior as soon as you receive the orders I will communicate when the plan is formed and the movements co-ordinated between this body and the rest who have to take part in this enterprise. I still don't know the day for certain, and have not decided on the method which I will use. I confine myself to indicating to you the direction so that you can prepare yourself, and charge you to the ultimate secrecy, without which nothing may be done. Only you must know it.

This time Bolívar did not propose to cross the spur of the mountains at Ocaña, which had been difficult enough: his intention was to move through the uninhabited south-western llanos into the foothills of the Andes and up over the top of the Cordillera Oriental itself, at one of its highest points – and then descend to battle with the enemy. The only logic for his decision was, first, that he had learnt that the Spanish, believing New Granada to be safe, had left only token garrisons there; and, second, that his former (and future) enemy, but current ally, Santander had put him up to it. But there is no tangible evidence for either view.

On 23 May Bolívar gathered his officers in a hut in the hamlet of Setenta by the Arauca. O'Leary takes up the story:

> There was no table. There were no chairs on which to sit. A party of royalists, who had bivouacked there some time before, had killed several head of cattle. The rain and the sun had bleached the skulls of the bullocks, and they served as seats on which the destiny of a great country was about to be decided. Such perhaps were the chairs on which Romulus and his rude followers sat when they traced the first narrow boundaries of the Eternal City.
>
> The President addressed the assembly [and] spoke of the state of the army – the danger of remaining in the llanos during the winter, which was about commencing, consuming their resources and exposed to the diseases of the climate. He then ordered the Chief of the Staff to read the despatches which had been received from Casanare and finally developed his plan of surprising the enemy in that country. He indicated his inten-

tion of invading the kingdom with the division of Páez and Anzoategui by Cúcuta, while Santander should cause a diversion on the side of Casanare. This was not his idea nor did he execute it. Though he charged the most inviolable secrecy to all present – a confidence which was not betrayed – he did not let his chiefs into his real designs.

His officers were at first astonished, then appalled. This was his craziest scheme yet. But Colonel Rooke of the Albion Legion – he who was by now something of an adopted son to the man with so many lovers but no child – declared he would follow Bolívar all the way to Cape Horn. The others agreed.

So began one of the epic marches of history. There were four battalions of infantry and one rifle battalion, as well as a force of Páez's men and the Albion Legion, making 1,600 infantry and 800 cavalry in all. There were many Indians among them, including some rescued from the Caruni river settlements devastated by Piar, and several hundred women. On 27 May they left on rafts and canoes up the Arauca in rain so dense it was difficult to breathe. Thus they travelled for eight days with relative ease until they reached Guasdualito; many of Páez's men refused to continue from here onto the plains of Casanare, the higher llanos, which lay completely flooded, under torrential rains and dense fog. The penetrating gloom and dampness depressed spirits to the bone. Most still had no idea where they were going. The waist-high floodwater soaked guns and supplies, feet squelched endlessly though mud; they were prey to leeches, and to caribe fish – tiny flesh-eating pests. Their sodden clothes literally rotted away from their bodies. Only at night was there rest, on slight mud-and-grass mounds just above the flood-waters; they could not cook, but ate their beef raw. All the time the rains pounded unceasingly and the mists enshrouded them.

By raft they had to traverse several rivers distinguishable from the floodwaters only by their depth. Bolívar, on his horse, was everywhere during these crossings, splashing and swearing, organising and encouraging his men, helping people and animals with seemingly indefatigable energy. Rooke too urged the men forward, his long red hair and beard dripping with moisture. The Albion Legion suffered most from the climate and the terrain. As the land at last began to rise the oppressive mist thinned and they glimpsed green jungle-covered hills and the humpbacked mountains of the cordillera; the llaneros had never seen mountains before.

Combining with Santander's New Granadan army, 1,200 strong,

consisting of two infantry brigades and one cavalry contingent, they rested for three days at Tame. On dry land the troops began to regain their health, but with horror discovered that they were expected to climb the awesome mountains before them: Bolívar had at first told them he planned only an exploratory mission into the foothills. Páez and Anzoategui, appalled by the deception, plotted to overthrow Bolívar, but no one else supported them. At Páez's instigation, the hussars deserted. His men were finished, desperate; already they had been ordered to eat horses, for fear that they would eat each other. Bolívar himself now appeared quite mad; he wore the helmet of a Russian dragoon, a blue tunic with gold buttons and red epaulettes, and on his bamboo lance carried a banner with a skull and crossbones inscribed in blood red, and the slogan 'Liberty or Death'.

There were three routes into the mountains to choose between. The most important consideration was which pass was least likely to be defended by the Spanish, and for this reason Bolívar chose the Paramo of Pisba, leading to the village of Soata and the valley of the river Chicamocha: it was the highest, at 13,000 feet, and the most difficult. The Spanish would never believe he would attempt to cross it with an army. The troops so recently wading through mud now found themselves clambering up steep hills, and then crags. Bolívar sent forward an advance guard under Santander to attack a garrison of three hundred Spanish troops at the Paya pass, along their way. He destroyed them, and four days after leaving Tame Bolívar's exhausted forces arrived at the pass, following a near-mutiny. From there Bolívar reported back to Angostura: 'The harshness of the mountains is impossible to describe to anyone who doesn't know them. To give an idea of this, it is enough to know that in four marches we lost almost all the horses carrying our arsenal and almost all the cattle we had in reserve. The rigour of the season has helped make the journey more exhausting: there is hardly a day or night when it has not rained.'

The worst still lay ahead: the climb to the Paramo of Pisba. At this stage Bolívar, overwhelmed by the complaints of his officers and men, seriously considered calling off the whole project. Santander seems to have come up with the decisive argument. He said he preferred 'a certain death in the planned operation against the royal enemy of New Granada to retreating to the llanos'. Indeed, the prospect of marching back through the flood-waters was almost worse than that of going on. A contemporary historian sketched the scene:

At this height of the Andes there are no paths. The land is rocky and rough with no sign of vegetation other than obscure lichens. The trail can always be found, because the bones of men and animals who perished crossing the Paramo in bad weather mark it. There are on the rocks a multitude of little memorials left by pious hands in memory of those who fell there and on the ground can be seen fragments of their equipment.

The situation was really frightening: over their heads rose huge blocks of granite, and at their feet were huge abysses. Nothing broke the silence, except the cry of the condor and the murmur of distant streams; the blue sky seemed close . . . and although the sun was not veiled by a cloud, it seemed to have no heat and gave out a pale light, like a full moon.

Men and horses frequently fell from the path, often thousands of feet, noiselessly. When ravines had to be crossed, crude insubstantial bridges were fashioned out of woven vines, and the few remaining cattle and mules were carried across in slings. Streams were forded by the soldiers in twos with their arms around each other's shoulders to keep them steady; a single person falling would be carried away by those violent rushing torrents. They climbed and climbed, men who had never seen hills before; the vegetation grew more sparse, the path more vertiginous, the white, snow-capped peaks ever closer and more terrifying. To this day, the region they crossed is almost empty, the second most impregnable mountain barrier in the world after the Himalayas. Even the best equipped were now in tatters. At these heights Santander's units and the Albion Legion proved the hardiest; the llaneros were entirely out of their element, their horsemen's legs numbed with fatigue by climbing. Many were completely naked, like the large Indian contingent.

Behind came the women – the indomitable wives and loyal girl-friends, most of them half-naked too, who would not abandon their men but nursed the sick and injured on that awesome ascent. The climb was almost silent; only the officers shouted, occasionally, to hearten or cajole their men. In single file they went, along the narrow path that led ever on and up. When they started the climb, the cool of the mountains was a merciful relief from the oppressive, steaming Turkish bath of the sodden llanos below. Now icy rain punished them remorselessly and a terrible new enemy loomed: altitude sickness, *soroche*, the lassitude that overcomes those accustomed to life nearer sea-level.

They began to pant, their hearts to pound; the thinning atmosphere barely sustained their efforts. Their movements slowed, and a metallic taste formed in their mouths; many were constantly sick, not helped by the wretched diet of chopped raw meat. As the wind screamed and the hard rain turned to hail, sleet or snow, more and more fell to the ground. Their comrades beat them mercilessly to induce them to stand up again and continue; but it was easier, with so little to eat, bodies racked by the cold, to succumb to merciful unconsciousness. For six days they climbed, spending the nights huddled together for warmth on the frozen ground. It must have seemed to them that the Liberator had taken them on an insane mass suicide.

The Paramo of Pisba itself was well above the snow-line on a huge rocky plateau, the spectacular peaks towering on one side as beautiful against the blue sky as they were deadly and inhospitable. They spent the night on that terrible plateau, 13,000 feet up. There was no wood for them to make fires with and the lucky ones sheltered in what remained of the carcasses of the few animals killed for food. During that night on the Paramo most were close to death from starvation, exhaustion, or *soroche*; fifty members of the Albion Legion alone died of altitude sickness. The stars seemed to sparkle with unnatural brightness while the cold moon, according to O'Leary, shone with a 'metallic lustre'. At one point, shrieks suddenly pierced the desolation: a woman had given birth. A day later, says O'Leary, 'I saw the mother with her newborn in her arms apparently in the best of health, and in the rear of the column.' They moved forward at first light, leaving behind for the condors the huddled, frozen bodies of those who had died.

At last the journey was downhill; the cold began to ease, the air to improve and the sickness to go. To their bright, fevered eyes the valley of the Chicamocha must have seemed like a vision of paradise. Along with every single horse, mule and cow, two thousand men and women had perished on the journey; only twelve hundred remained. It was the fault of a madman who cared nothing about the lives of his men. When this spectral army of desperate men emerged into the pretty village of Soata, the inhabitants were at first terrified, then tried to accommodate them with food and clothing. His men had travelled 750 miles in four months, but Bolívar knew that he had no time to waste if he was to maintain the element of surprise.

Three thousand Spanish troops under General Barreiro were stationed at Tunja, once seat of the independent republic of Cundinamarca, now defunct, and Tunja was between Bolívar's army and Santa Fé de Bogotá. Bolívar sent out Colonel Lara to forage for horses and recruits: battle was imminent, and he and his men were ill-prepared for it. Lara's return with eight hundred men and a thousand horses proved to Bolívar that he was among friends: 'Hardly had I taken my first steps on this side of the cordillera . . . when I heard resonate in front of me the blessings of men who were awaiting my arms with all the enthusiasm of liberty.' His huge gamble was justified: the people of New Granada, unlike those of his native Venezuela, were ready for freedom. The people of the Venezuelan uplands, so ravaged by civil war, had turned against the patriots; peace under the Spanish was, to them, preferable to more war, more dislocation, more cruelty on both sides. But the people of the New Granadan uplands had experienced little fighting. Tunja had been at the heart of the country's previous experiment in independence and was ripe for insurrection. Bolívar was well known for his leadership in the Magdalena, and as commander of Tunja's armies. Everywhere Bolívar's ragged army went on this side of the cordillera, it was clear that it had popular support.

With the main Spanish forces concentrated in the Venezuelan highlands, several hundred miles away, to fend off attacks from the llanos where the partisan armies were believed to be, Bolívar's aim was to goad Barreiro into battle before he could summon reinforcements. On 5 July he sent his vanguard towards Gameza: Barreiro was compelled to respond, sending forces to the town of Topaga to block them. A sharp defeat the royalists inflicted on the patriots there, who were forced to flee back to Corrales, was offset by a cavalry attack which wiped out a Spanish force of three hundred patrolling the valley below Sogamoso. The problem for the Liberator now was that crossing the rain-swollen river Chicamocha would substantially delay him, giving the Spanish on the other side an opportunity to move up, pounce on him, and make him fight on ground of their choosing. He moved his main force forward, turning the enemy's right flank, but was held up by the river crossing, as he had expected. Barreiro moved fast, securing the rocky hills covering the road at the narrow choke-point of Paso la Balsa. The patriots now had no choice but to advance down the road under the fire of Barreiro's well-armed forces above and in front of them, while on the other side lay a swamp, Pantano de Vargas. It appeared they were walking into a trap.

When Santander attempted to occupy a hill in front of the heights, Barreiro counter-attacked, and forced him back. Bolívar thereupon ordered the crack Albion Legion to storm the heights. This they did in three charges, with magnificent bravery; both Rooke and O'Leary were wounded. But reinforcements had arrived for the Spanish, and Barreiro attacked the patriots on the road from behind while launching another push to regain the heights. Bolívar's army was now completely surrounded. His only chance lay in marching towards the weakest enemy point – the troops holding the road in front of him – before the Albion Legion was forced off the heights. This he did, ordering the llanero cavalry under Colonel Rondon forward, followed by the infantry, up the steep pass where the Spanish were waiting to massacre them. Grim and desperate after their recent ordeal in the mountains, the patriot troops stormed furiously forward: enemy fire was nothing compared to the dreadful experience they had endured. The Spanish, surprised by the recklessness of the patriots, fled before them, and both sides sustained heavy losses. A tropical thunderstorm illuminated the scene as Bolívar's main force arrived. While the patriots scrambled up the rocks, a large part of the Spanish army was able to slip away. Rooke, the giant Englishman so loved by Bolívar, had to have an arm amputated. With his other hand he took the severed limb and cried 'Viva la Patria!' The surgeon asked him which – Ireland, or England? (Rooke, half-Irish, had fought for both.) 'The one which is to give me burial' was the reply – meaning South America. He died a few days later, leaving his beautiful bride a widow. The two armies now withdrew, to watch one another warily. Barreiro's priority was no longer to block Bolívar, but to avoid an open battle until further reinforcements could be brought up by the Spanish Viceroy, Samano. Bolívar's aim, conversely, was to force Barreiro into battle before those reinforcements arrived.

On 4 August he staged a feint, crossing the river Chicamocha, ostensibly to occupy the town of Paipa, then recrossing after dark to gain a back road that took his men behind the royalists, camped on the road between him and Bogotá, and thence to Tunja, where he pulled off a coup in seizing the garrison and arsenal. To escape the trap he thought he detected, Barreiro himself took a circuitous back road which bypassed Tunja and rejoined the main road just behind a hill near a narrow bridge across the Boyaca river ten miles further down. His scouts having spotted the Spanish army, Bolívar climbed the hill separating the two roads, to see Barreiro's forces strung out below, his advance guard about a quarter of a mile in front, the artillery in the rear. Scrambling down, Bolívar ordered his own troops along the much easier main road, in a bid to get to the bridge first. Santander led his advance guard of cavalry at a cracking pace, while the Spanish vanguard, not knowing their secret march had been detected, rested at a farm under some trees on a hill in front of the bridge.

Suddenly, to their astonishment, they spotted the llanero cavalry and, hurriedly remounting, charged them. The llaneros fell back and the Spanish, as intended, imagined them to be a mere scouting party; when they saw the fleeing cavalry regroup with the full support of Santander's advance troops, they realised their mistake and in their turn retreated, scurrying to capture the bridge before Santander got there. This was a fatal mistake, for the bulk of the Spanish army – a full quarter of a mile away – could now be cut off. Meanwhile Bolívar ordered his main body across the rough mile or so that separated the two roads, to fall upon the strung-out Spanish lines. Santander's advance troops reached the river just after the Spanish vanguard had crossed it, and they blazed away from opposite sides, while Santander launched several vigorous charges across the bridge.

Simultaneously the Albion Legion, just behind Santander, pushed forward and captured the road, cut off the Spanish advance guard and began an encircling movement. The heroes of Pantano de Vargas, Colonel Rondon and his llanero horsemen, performed the same manoeuvre to the north of the Spanish army, and then General Anzoategui was ordered by Bolívar to launch a bayonet charge with his infantry at the centre. Soon the Albion Legion and the llanero cavalry had completely encircled the depleted Spanish rump, separated from its vanguard of crack troops – the dragoons and Numancia battalions, pinned down by Santander's forces. It was two battles rather than one. When Bolívar threw his reserves – a battalion of lancers and two of raw recruits – at the trapped Spanish force, Barreiro surrendered his sword to a patriot private. Santander had got across the bridge after fierce fighting, and fifty Spaniards fled south to Santa Fé de Bogotá. It was a brilliantly improvised triumph, with Bolívar taking advantage of his opponent's mistakes and making none himself. The patriots killed about five hundred and captured 1,600 Spanish troops, including the commander, together with their horses, both cavalry and artillery. Two Spanish officers who escaped reported the catastrophe when they reached Bogotá in the middle of the same night, 8 August.

The impact of these reports of events on the Boyaca was dramatic. The Spanish believed Bolívar's old order for 'war to the death' to be still in effect, and had heard of the terrifying army of scarecrows who had climbed up and across the cordillera from the llanos. The Viceroy, Samano, had himself been responsible for terrible cruelties and, fearing vengeance, the Spanish garrison and governing class simply fled in terror into the night. An eye-witness described the scene: 'They . . . abandoned their houses and their shops, which sudden converts to the patriot cause [looters] took over, and they abandoned old people, fathers, wives and children in desolate groups, not daring to look back, so as not to lose a moment, in fear of their lives as refugees . . . Samano . . . fled dressed as a peasant of the savannah, mounted on a fine horse, preceded by a huge escort of cavalry, which pushed aside the wretched refugees, leaving them enveloped in clouds of dust from the galloping horses.'

Among the contingent of prisoners was Francisco Vinoni, whom Bolívar believed to be the traitor responsible for handing over the fort at Puerto Cabello to the Spanish prisoners in 1812. The memory of that terrible failure, which had led to the tragedy with Miranda, continued to haunt the Liberator, and Vinoni was summarily hanged, his body dangling before the crowd in the plaza of the small town of Ventaquemada.

On 10 August 1819 Bolívar arrived in Santa Fé de Bogotá. His reception was emotional, somewhat tentative – that of a people fearful of being put to the sword. A woman ran up to him in the street and grovelled at his right foot. 'God bless you, ghost!' she exclaimed. The experiences of the past few months had clearly taken their toll of him; he grinned, and patted her on the head. He was thin and small and thirty-six, and he wore no shirt under his jacket because he had lost all his linen in the course of the campaign – but to the people of Bogotá Bolívar was superhuman, almost a demi-god. His achievements had indeed been extraordinary, but, as he was at pains to emphasise, the war was just beginning.

Morillo, however, learning of Bolívar's victory, concluded that Spain's hold on Latin America was irredeemably lost. The Marqués de La Puerta, Commander of Spanish forces in Northern Spanish America, wrote to Madrid that

> The seditious Bolívar has occupied Santa Fé, and the fateful result of that battle has placed at his disposition the whole kingdom and the immense resources of a very populated country, rich and abundant, from which he will plunder what he needs to continue the war in these provinces, because the insurgents have no rules or inhibitions, this caudillo least of all.

This disgraceful attack hands to the rebels, in addition to New Granada, many ports on the southern coast, where they will gather their pirates: Popayán, Quito, Pasto and the whole interior of the continent as far as Peru remain at the mercy of whoever governs Santa Fé, to whom, at the same time, are available banks, arsenals, arms factories and everything that the King possesses in the viceroyalty. Bolívar in one day has finished the efforts of five years of campaigning, and in a single battle has reconquered what the King's troops have won in many fights.

He was exaggerating: the patriots had held Bogotá before, as well as much of Venezuela, and still lost all. The considerable Spanish army in Venezuela remained undefeated. But Bolívar's victory provided an immense moral and psychological boost for what had seemed a lost cause.

He wasted no time sitting on his laurels. Soublette and Anzoategui were ordered to mop up Spanish resistance to the north – which was done, with the exception of the coast, but Anzoatagui was soon dead of an infection contracted on the mountain crossing. Samano, the fleeing Viceroy, had descended the Magdalena and embarked for Spain. Bolívar made a triumphal provincial tour, and went to Pamplona to supervise the recruitment and training of the hundreds flocking to join his new army.

Then Bolívar decided to return to Angostura – not in a febrile display of hyperactivity, but to show that the liberation of Venezuela was still high among his priorities, and prompted by disturbing reports of events in his absence. Zea, the well-meaning but weak constitutionalist left behind as President, had been deposed by Arismendi and Mariño, ever disloyal, who had become commander of the army. Bolívar left Santander in charge in New Granada, enjoining him to take no reprisals. Santander immediately had thirty-eight provincial royalists executed, including Barreiro, ostensibly in retaliation for atrocities committed by the Santa Fé garrison commander, Calzada, on his flight from Bogotá to Quito. The real reason was that Santander feared there might be a popular uprising after Bolívar's departure, and wanted to assert his authority. His executions were chillingly cold-blooded:

Shortly before midday, marching in lines of four, they were led to the opposite side of the square. Barreiro, Jiménez and two other officers bound to him by friendship and duty, despite the heavy irons they dragged, had to walk all the way across the square. As he arrived on the spot where his sufferings were to end Barreiro, who was accompanied by a priest, called Colonel Plaza who commanded the troops, spoke a few words to him and, taking from his chest the portrait of the young woman he had meant to marry, begged him to deliver it to her brother, who was serving under Plaza's orders. An instant later he was ordered to kneel and was shot in the back [the thirty-seven others were also shot, as was a protesting spectator]. Santander, preceded by some musicians, rode through the chief streets singing the refrain of a song referring to the event.

Bolívar later fiercely rebuked Santander, but was unable to take action at the time. Galloping like a man possessed, accompanied only by a couple of guards, he made his way along the main roads through New Granada, changing horses as necessary, riding from dawn to dusk. At Barinas he met Páez, and they discussed tactics through the night. Then he was off by fast canoe along the tributaries of the Orinoco to join the main river. On the way he encountered Antonio José de Sucre coming the other way. Born in Cumana and educated in Caracas, at seventeen he had fought under Mariño, and then broken with him to serve Bolívar in Angostura. He was now a remarkably good-looking young man of twenty-five, with an expression of great sincerity, and Zea had made him a general. When Bolívar heard this he was furious, on the grounds that Zea had no right to make such an appointment; but when Sucre at once offered to forgo his promotion, Bolívar forgave him and confirmed it personally. Sucre came, in time, to replace the martyred Rooke in Bolívar's affections, as an adopted son – and became second only to him in the history of the liberation. O'Leary described him thus:

> General Sucre seemed to me the best general of Colombia. He had personal bravery, an excellent *coup-d'oeil*, and was indefatigable. He did everything himself, wrote his own despatches, examined everything, conducted the espionage, reconnoitred, visited by day and night the outposts, saw even the rations delivered. And still he was not much liked in the army. Sucre had read but little and, though he had a brilliant imagination, he wrote badly. Notwithstanding, he was a man of talent and good sense.

Bolívar arrived at Angostura after only five weeks' travelling, surprising Arismendi, who handed over the reins of power. Mariño fêted him at a ball held in his honour. The Liberator now proclaimed a new nation – Gran Colombia, made up of Venezuela and the remainder of New Granada and, significantly, including Quito. He was to be president of the whole and Santander vice-president in New Granada; although

Santander had in fact opposed such a merger, he had no choice but to go along with it.

After just a fortnight in Angostura, Bolívar returned to New Granada – the third time he had made the journey in a year, covering some 2,500 miles altogether. He guessed what was coming, and to consolidate his gains he was ready to travel long and far, to raise and train troops. Morillo had written of him to Ferdinand VII of Spain:

> Nothing can compare with the untiring activity of that leader. His fear-lessness and his talents entitle him to his place at the head of the revolution and of the war; but he possesses as well, from his noble Spanish strain and his education, also Spanish, qualities of elegance and generosity which elevate him far above all who surround him. He is the revolution . . . Bolívar is an indomitable soul whom a single victory of the smallest nature is enough to make master of five hundred leagues of territory.

The king needed little prompting, and a second punitive expeditionary force was assembled: 20,000 infantry, 3,000 cavalry and 100 artillery pieces were to sail on forty-seven warships, many of them supplied by Russia. But they did not. On 1 January 1820 Rafael Riego, commander of one of the supply points for the expedition, mutinied against the government of Madrid and outside Cadiz announced the restoration of the liberal 1812 Constitution which had been discarded by Ferdinand VII after the French were driven from the peninsula. A large part of the army backed him, including most of the expeditionary force, as did the people.

Instead of the expedition, Ferdinand sent a letter: he urged Morillo to negotiate with the rebels, on the basis that they should agree to re-incorporate themselves into the Empire under a liberal constitution. Morillo was appalled. 'They are mad,' he told one of his officers. 'They do not know what they order, they do not know the country, or the enemy, or the developments here. They want me to go through the humiliation of entering into these exchanges. I do so only because my profession is subordination and obedience.' Accordingly Morillo wrote to Bolívar, proposing an armistice and asking the rebels to accept the new Spanish constitution. In Santa Fé, Bolívar heard of the expedition's collapse with a tremendous sense of relief. An armistice would enable him to recruit and train his armies at a time when the Spanish would be receiving no reinforcements – but he contemptuously rejected the idea of submitting to the Crown, as Morillo had predicted, so the fighting went on while the details were negotiated. Bolívar's forces in Venezuela now surged forward in a poorly organised offensive along the cordillera, occupying Merida and Trujillo. It was an area racked by misery, poverty and ancient blood feuds where, seven years earlier, the Spanish had enacted terrible reprisals; what he saw there, it is said, made a strong impression on Bolívar, and engendered in him a conviction that war must no longer be waged in this way. In Trujillo, on 26 November 1820, he sought a treaty with the Spanish to regulate the conduct of the war – an attempt to humanise the conflict, from the very city in which he had pledged 'war to the death'. An armistice was finally signed.

Morillo asked for a meeting with Bolívar, and a parley was fixed at Santa Ana. Morillo appeared in a magnificent uniform, accompanied by a regiment of hussars, and when O'Leary arrived to tell him Bolívar was approaching, asked about the size of his escort.

> I replied: 'Only ten to twelve officers and the Spanish emissaries [sent to organise the ceasefire].' Morillo replied, 'I thought my own escort was small. But my old enemy has trumped my generosity. I will order the hussars to retire.' This he did immediately . . . shortly afterwards the Liberator's party could be seen on the hill dominating the town of Santa Ana. As the riders approached, Morillo wanted to know which was Bolívar. Pointing him out, he exclaimed: 'What, that little man with a blue tunic, a forage cap and mounted on a mule?' He had hardly finished talking when the little man was at his side, and on greeting each other the two generals dismounted and embraced warmly.

By coming so under-dressed to so important a meeting, Bolívar was both expressing contempt for Spanish authority and parading the simplicity of the truly great. They talked, then laid a stone to mark the spot, and the day ended with a banquet. A witness provides an amusing recollection of this:

> Finally, each being completely intoxicated, a toast was given to the healths of both Generals at once, by their order, and according to the custom the glasses were dashed to pieces on the table, which they then severally mounted again to embrace each other. Unfortunately, their motions not being very steady in a sort of *pas de deux* which they were dancing on the table after the embrace was over, it suddenly gave way, and they abruptly descended to the floor, where they rolled for some time, until picked up, still embracing each other with the greatest vehemence. The chiefs being carried to a bed-chamber, they slept in the same room, and all retired till

the next morning, when the second part of this friendly compact was made known.

Two weeks after meeting the Liberator for the first (and last) time, the Pacifier left La Guaira, knowing the royalist cause to be lost after seven years of bitter fighting, and determined not to preside over its funeral. His successor was La Torre – according to Bolívar, 'a man less active, less capable, less a soldier'. Bolívar said of the armistice that

> It was an excuse for time to regulate the war and was adopted exactly as I had written it. It was a sane, humane and politic treaty which put an end to that horrible butchery of slaying the conquered, of giving no quarter to prisoners of war – Spanish barbarism that the patriots were forced to adopt themselves in reprisal, that had pushed back civilization, made the soil of Colombia an abode of cannibals and soaked it with innocent blood until all humanity shuddered. It was an advantage to us, fatal to the Spaniards. Their forces could only diminish, mine augment and organize.

12

Victory

The armistice lasted until 28 April 1821, when Maracaibo rose in revolt against the royalists and Bolívar chose to close the trap he had so meticulously prepared. In the east, Bermudez passed the Unare river and crushed a royalist garrison at El Guapo; in the west, Urdaneta marched from Maracaibo, defeated the royalists at Casiglia and took Coro. Mariño and his ally Cedeño attacked from the south-east. By 15 May Bermudez's forces had reached Caracas and taken most of the city; meanwhile Urdaneta was threatening Puerto Cabello, the main line of evacuation for the Spanish forces.

La Torre now began to panic; he sent part of his large army to San Carlos, to try to block Urdaneta's advance, and deployed another part in the capital, whence the Spanish inhabitants were pouring, in yet another exodus, down the fifty miles to La Guaira. Páez, so long reluctant to send his men up into the Venezuelan highlands, now also despatched his army. As these advanced, La Torre decided to abandon San Carlos and defend instead a line near the Lake of Valencia, with the plains of Carabobo behind him. On 7 June Bolívar and Páez rode up to San Carlos: their combined armies now numbered 6,500, against La Torre's 5,000. They advanced on the Spanish position at the centre of the Carabobo savannah, straddling the main road between Caracas and Valencia.

In an effort to outflank the Spanish and engage them on both sides, Bolívar's forces approached in three columns, one under Páez, another under Cedeño and the third under Colonel Plaza, through narrow ravines that cut northwards across the hills to the south of the plain. La Torre and his army failed to block them, but their path led upwards onto the plain and the Spanish were therefore able to engage them from a superior position. Three charges dispersed the llaneros, but a British battalion – the British Huntsmen – held firm behind them, blasting away with precision in a disciplined line several men deep. One of their officers left a vivid account of the story:

> We halted at dusk on the 23rd at the foot of the ridge. The rain fell in torrents all night and reminded us of the night before Waterloo. Next morning the sky was cloudless when we stood to arms, and presently Bolívar sent us the order to advance. We were moving to get round the enemy's right flank, where his guns and infantry were partly hidden by trees and broken ground. Bolívar, after reconnoitring, ordered us to attack by a deep ravine between the Spanish infantry and artillery. The enemy's guns opened fire and our men began to fall. Meantime the Bravos de Apure had advanced within pistol shot of the Spaniards, and received such a murderous volley from 3,000 muskets that they broke and fled back in disorder upon us.
>
> It was a critical moment, but we managed to keep our ground till the fugitives had got through our ranks back into the ravine, and then our grenadier company . . . formed up and poured in their fire upon the Spaniards, who were only a few paces from them. Checked by this volley, the enemy fell back a little, while our men, pressing eagerly on, formed and delivered their fire, company after company.
>
> Receding before our fire and the long line of British bayonets, the Spaniards fell back to the position from which they had rushed in pursuit of the Apure Bravos. But from thence they kept up a tremendous fire upon us, which we returned as rapidly as we could. As they outnumbered us in the ratio of four to one, and were strongly posted and supported by guns, we waited for reinforcements before storming their position. Not a man, however, came to help us, and after an hour passed in this manner our ammunition failed. It then really seemed to be all over with us. We tried as best we could to make signals of our distress . . .
>
> Our commanding officer apprised General Páez of our situation and called on him to get us a supply of cartridges. It came at last, but by this time many of our officers and men had fallen . . . You may imagine we were not long in breaking open the ammunition boxes; the men numbered off anew, and after delivering a couple of volleys we prepared to charge. At this moment our cavalry, passing as before by our right flank, charged, with General Páez at their head. They went on very gallantly, but soon came galloping back and passed again to our rear without having done any execution on the enemy, while they themselves had suffered considerably.
>
> Why Bolívar at this time, and indeed during the period since our first advance, sent us no support I have never been able to guess. Whatever the

motive, it is certain that the second and third divisions of the army quietly looked on while we were being slaughtered, and made no attempt to help us. The curses of our men were loud and deep, but seeing that they must not expect any help they made up their minds to carry the enemy's position or perish. Out of nine hundred men we had not above six hundred left . . . the colours of the regiment had seven times changed hands and been literally cut to ribands and dyed with the blood of the gallant fellows who carried them.

But in spite of all this the word was passed to charge with the bayonet, and on we went, keeping our line as steadily as on a parade day and with a loud 'hurrah' we were upon them. I must do the Spaniards the justice of saying that they met us gallantly, and the struggle was for a brief time fierce, and the event doubtful. But the bayonet in the hands of British soldiers, more especially such a forlorn hope as we were, is irresistible. The Spaniards, five to one as they were, began to give ground, and at last broke and fled.

Then it was, and not till then, that two companies of the Tiradores came to our help, and our cavalry, hitherto of little use, fiercely pursued the retreating enemy . . . The remains of the corps passed before the Liberator with trailed arms at double quick, and received with a cheer, but without halting, the words '*Salvadores de mi Patria!*'

This assault by the Huntsmen proved decisive to the battle. La Torre sent cavalry to his infantry's aid, but Páez despatched his fast-wheeling llaneros, some to intercept them, others to cut off the retreat of the infantry. In the course of this battle Páez's loyal negro giant, 'El Negro Primero', who had so often scooped up the llanero general from the field, was mortally wounded and galloped up to say goodbye to his master, before falling to the ground.

Along the main road the bulk of the patriot force was now advancing, pressing back the Spanish artillery and the crack Valencey Battalion. Abandoning their cannon and moving in perfect square formation, under impeccable discipline, the Valencey Battalion, under attack from three sides, retreated with great dignity; Cedeño was killed in the fighting. The battalion offered its protection to La Torre and his staff and withdrew with them to Puerto Cabello in a heroic retreat under torrential rain and constant harassment. Nearly half the Spanish army was killed, wounded or taken prisoner in the Battle of Carabobo.

Despatching Páez to follow the retreat to the coast, Bolívar entered Caracas on 28 June seven long years after he had left. He exchanged cordial messages with La Torre, now in Puerto Cabello – a refinement of civilised behaviour hitherto unknown in the course of this war – and then, after granting safe conduct to those who had fled to La Guaira, and forbidding his troops to carry out reprisals, he sought out Francisco Itúrbide, his former protector, now destitute, and restored his properties. Then he withdrew to his estate of San Mateo, where he found just three remaining of more than a thousand slaves, and freed them. In the ruins of his hacienda he contemplated the dangers he saw ahead, arising from the conflicting ambitions of his subordinates. He spoke of 'the terrifying chaos of patriots, profiteers, egotists, whites, blacks, federalists, centralists, republicans, good and bad aristocrats and the whole mass of hierarchies which subdivide into different parts'. Now that the unifying oppressor, Spain, was removed, he feared above all the new state's disintegration into factions, civil war, and anarchy. He tried to divide and rule, giving Páez control of the central region, Bermudez the east and Mariño the west. He wrote despairingly:

> You can have no idea of the spirit which animates our military officers. They are no longer the men you knew. They are men who have fought for years and believe themselves superior; and yet they are humiliated and impoverished, with no hope of enjoying the fruits of the work of their lances. They are often resolute llaneros, ignorant men who think themselves superior to those of greater accomplishments. Even I, who have always been at their head, cannot say of what they might be capable. I treat them with the greatest consideration, but it doesn't seem to inspire them with the spirit which ought to exist among comrades and fellow-citizens. Believe me . . . we are over a volcano about to erupt. I fear peace even more than I fear war.

The Congress of Cúcuta, which Bolívar had summoned to draw up the constitution of the new state of Gran Colombia (New Granada combined with Venezuela), had ignored many of his recommendations. He complained that the constitution they produced was 'very much amended and . . . very bad in some parts'. Worse still, he was beginning to fall out with Santander, his proconsul in Santa Fé de Bogotá. Venezuela, bled dry by a decade of war, was in no position to provide the money for the next stage of his liberating mission: to expel the Spanish from their last and most entrenched stronghold in South America, the Viceroyalty of Peru. Only prosperous, newly peaceful New Granada could do that.

Santander, reflecting the opinion of most of his countrymen, was reluctant to be drawn into the liberation of another country, preferring that his own should safeguard its peace and prosperity. A skilful politician with a legalistic brain, Santander was also a cold fish, calculating and down-to-earth. Bolívar wrote to him wryly: 'There is a good exchange between you and me; you send me specifics and I send you hopes. In ordinary parlance one would say that you were more practical than me, but that would be a mistake. The present has already passed, the future is the property of man, because he lives in the land of illusions, of fictitious appetites and desires.'

It was a shrewd point, but cut little ice with Santander. Bolívar asked him for four or five thousand men; with their help, he said, Peru would give him 'two sisters to Boyaca and Carabobo'. Santander, who considered himself the real ruler of New Granada and Bolívar merely a convenient ally, had to bow to *force majeure*, but privately seethed. Meanwhile Bermudez had driven the last Spaniards in eastern Venezuela from Cumana; and after a fourteen-months' siege, Montilla had taken thick-walled Cartagena.

La Torre sailed to Cadiz, leaving Bolívar's vicious old enemy Morales in control of the last Spanish stronghold, Puerto Cabello. In the city of Panamá a revolution had broken out against the Spanish, and the Panamanians asked to join Colombia. Bolívar now controlled a territory two-thirds the size of western Europe; but more than a quarter of a million had been killed in achieving Gran Colombia's independence.

13

To the Indian Nation

It was time to prepare the campaign to liberate the Presidency of Quito and the Viceroyalty of Peru. Already Bolívar had despatched Sucre and the Albion Legion into the mountains south of New Granada. Brave and brilliantly commanded, they battled their way down the main cordillera, crossing some of the world's most rugged and spectacular country, marked by towering peaks and gorges several thousand feet deep, as far south as the city of Popayán. Sucre was then ordered by Bolívar to go by sea to Guayaquil, two degrees south of the Equator, an historic port of the old Inca Empire and now the port for the Presidency of Quito. Embarking from the port of Buenaventura, Sucre landed at Guayaquil without a fight.

He was soon fending off a series of crises in that yellow-fevered sink of contraband and piracy with its slums built on stilts extending over foetid sea-marshes and its sole export, cacao. He entered into feverish negotiations with the elders of the city, who were likely to join whichever of the patriot commanders – Bolívar from the north or General San Martín from the south – would pay them better. A group of Sucre's own soldiers mutinied and seized six ships, proclaiming their allegiance to the King of Spain. Sucre set off in pursuit with members of the Albion Legion, caught them and brought them back. Having secured the co-operation of the town council, he and his one thousand defenders then found themselves under siege.

Between August and November 1821 he fought a series of indecisive engagements in defence of the city before signing a three-month armistice with the Spanish commander, Aymerich. During the period of the truce he was reinforced by several hundred Peruvians under General Santa Cruz, despatched by San Martín from the south. This gave him sufficient strength to march out of the city and towards Quito, in the mountains. At Pinchincha (now Riobamba) he defeated a small Spanish force, and Aymerich fell back towards Quito. Largely thanks to a vigorous frontal assault by the Albion Legion that divided the royalist forces, three Spanish companies were crushed and the rest fled into Quito, where they surrendered on 24 May 1822. Sucre captured 2,000 men, 1,700 muskets, fourteen cannon and a substantial quantity of ammunition and stores.

On 13 December 1821 Bolívar himself set off from Bogotá at the head of three thousand troops commanded by General Salom, his chief-of-staff, on the fifteen-hundred-mile trek down the spine of the Andes to Peru. Before he left he enjoined Colombians to respect the rule of Santander: 'The law designates the Vice-President as the chief of state while I remain a soldier. He will be a just, beneficent, diligent and altogether worthy leader of Colombia.' Bolívar's restless energies were not satisfied by the business of administration; although he failed to realise it, he had by now become a professional guerrilla, needing always to move on to another objective. Santander, by contrast, was a natural politician, content to rule a country; he was glad to see the back of the Liberator.

Ahead of Bolívar lay another fabulous adventure, another quest for glory – a doubling or trebling of the area he already ruled – and some of the most strongly-held royalist territory on the continent: Pasto, Quito – and Lima. The first phase of his expedition, down the valley of the Cauca, was surprisingly easy. Most of the region had already been cleared of royalists by Sucre, but the presence of a Spanish fleet off the coast made it impossible for Bolívar to take ship for Guayaquil as Sucre had. He had no choice but to travel overland. At Popayán the commander of the Spanish garrison surrendered without a fight. And now the rough country began: negotiating rope bridges across gaping chasms, climbing precipitous mountain trails, scrambling up bare rocky passes, struggling over icy ledges and ridges – it was like that march across the Cordillera Oriental again, if less fearsome, and longer. By the time they neared the royalist stronghold of Pasto, carefully avoiding a fight, they had lost a thousand men. As Bolívar said, 'The enemy can count on forces recruited from Quito to Popayán ... men who have made a tenacious defence of a territory they know and whose natural resources they take advantage of ... The liberating army, from the day it undertook its march, could not count on anything but casualties, loss of men, horses, mules and baggage; and the immobile enemy suffered nothing.' Now that enemy was determined to block Bolívar's path south. Realising that his only alternative was to take a circuitous route of hundreds of miles to avoid them, he decided to confront the Spanish.

In the valley of Bombona, Bolívar and his officers could hardly have had a more hopeless battleground, or one more spectacular. The Spanish were above them, overlooking the gorge which Bolívar was ascending, their left flank on the slopes of the huge Pasto volcano, their centre protected by dense forest, and on the right a rocky precipice along the Guaitara river, a thunderous torrent coursing down the bottom of the ravine. The Spanish had the laugh on the helpless rebels below. They proceeded to raid Bolívar's camp, leaving eight hundred dead and wounded, and destroying five thousand rifles. Bolívar believed he had been beaten. 'The task seems impossible,' he commented. 'But we must conquer, and we will.' He ordered his men forward at three in the afternoon, just three hours before the end of the equatorial day. As they clambered up the slopes to the centre, they were met by paralysing fire. They had no cavalry to charge the entrenched enemy positions, having lost all their horses *en route*. Artillery on the left ripped into them. Suddenly Bolívar noticed that Valdez, one of his commanders, was apparently leading his men directly up one of the cliffs, using bayonets for handholds and footholds. The cliff provided some shelter from enemy fire; Bolívar gave covering fire, and prevented the Spanish positions above being reinforced. Then, for a nail-biting hour, the astonishing spectacle of that almost vertical climb was shrouded in mist.

When it lifted, just as the sun began to fade, the patriots were seen to have reached the unguarded top of the cliff; they were now charging down several hundred feet, bayonets fixed, having reversed the Spanish advantage over the terrain; the enemy beneath, having run out of ammunition, fled before such an unexpected assault. Bolívar ordered all his remaining forces to attack the centre, and the Spanish lines broke. Darkness fell as the patriots climbed over the rough ground to secure the enemy positions, but a full moon allowed them to pursue the Spanish, until eventually they melted away into the mountains. Many escaped: Bolívar had secured a breathing space, but not a decisive victory. While he waited for reinforcements from Santa Fé de Bogotá, he had the satisfaction of knowing that he had pinned down Spanish forces that might otherwise have gone to the relief of Quito, now under siege from Sucre's army.

Once news of the fall of Quito to Sucre reached Garcia, the Spanish commander at Pasto, he surrendered to Bolívar; Aymerich, the Viceroy,

then surrendered the whole territory to the Liberator, and was permitted to leave, with Garcia, for Spain. The country that today is Ecuador
was thus added to Bolívar's trophies – largely through the work of Sucre,
although Bolívar's was the strategy of attacking on two fronts. Santander
had kept Bolívar's army well supplied and reinforced.

On 16 June 1822 Bolívar reached Quito, and one of his biggest triumphal entries yet. This city of half a million was in the heart of Indian
territory, very different from mulatto or black-dominated Venezuela and
white-dominated New Granada. More than half the population were of
pure Indian stock, about a third white, the rest of mixed blood. Bolívar,
although a white man, had freed them from tyranny. The people vener-
ated him almost as a god, and repeatedly broke through the lines of
soldiers to touch him and his great white charger as he rode past. There
was no calculated modesty about his dress on this occasion. He wore his
'green military uniform; a tunic with golden borders, with the epaulettes
and decorations of a general; a magnificent golden sword; very large
trousers, beautifully woven, of fine material; and great riding boots with
spurs. A silk tricolour sash with golden tassels dangling across from his
right shoulder to his left side, was tucked into his belt.'

In front of the bishop's palace twelve beautiful young Quito girls,
dressed as nymphs, crowned Bolívar with laurels. As this was happening, another laurel crown fell upon him, thrown from a balcony. He
looked up and saw a captivatingly beautiful young woman, her black
hair framing a pink and white face with huge dark eyes and full, vivacious lips. The figure-hugging dress worn by colonial women at the time
revealed the sinewy strength, beautifully proportioned curves and trim
waist of her slim, feline figure. Manuela – or Manuelita – Sáenz was the
illegitimate daughter of a Spanish businessman who had moved from
New Granada to Quito in 1790; married, with four children, he kept a
beautiful white woman, Maria Aizpuru, as his mistress in the seaside
apartment in which Manuela was born. In its confines, shared only with
her mother most of the time, Manuela grew into a lively, strong-willed,
cheerful girl.

In 1814 Manuelita, now too much of a handful, was sent to the
convent of Santa Catalina. She already fancied herself in love with a
handsome Spanish hussar officer, Fausto d'Elhuyar, and an illicit
romance was carried on in letters smuggled in and out of the convent;
he ran off with her and then, a few months later, dumped her. In floods
of tears she returned to her mother, now herself an abandoned mistress,

determined not to be made a fool of again, and nursing a burning dislike of Spaniards and a hankering for social standing and propriety, now that she was regarded as dishonoured by her own people. She met a staid, middle-aged English doctor, James Thorne, and in 1817 she married him; newly respectable, she became one of Quito's best-known hostesses. D'Elhuyar reappeared, and attended her parties; when Dr Thorne became aware of Manuelita's renewed intimacy with him, he decided to move to Lima.

Mrs Thorne was delighted to leave stuffy, provincial Quito, although it meant leaving her hussar, too. In Lima her salon became one of the principal centres for political intrigue against the Spanish: as intelligent as she was rebellious, she had developed a passionate interest in politics, and was fascinated by the romantic figure of the patriot leader José de San Martín, who had recently landed further down the Peruvian coast. Disappointment awaited her when she finally met San Martín, aloof, shy and ascetic, who awarded her the Cross of Horsewoman of the Sun for her services to the patriot cause, but she became a close friend of the woman believed to have been his only mistress, Rosita Campuzano.

Doctor Thorne now decided to return to Quito to help Manuelita's father, who was in danger from the patriots there. So it was that the lithely seductive, strong-willed, socially and politically ambitious young woman of twenty-two was in Quito to encounter a hero who more nearly matched her dreams. She made a dead set at Bolívar at the ball given in his honour the evening of his arrival, and he asked her to dance. For four hours they partnered one another, in matched energy and mutual attraction. Like the abandoned Pepa, Manuelita was determined that her future lay in the arms of Simón Bolívar; he found her physically entrancing but also admired her accomplishments and courage – she was a keen horsewoman and fencer – and her political outspokenness. More than any previous woman in Bolívar's life she shared his political interests; and she was prepared to subsume her personality in his, remote and selfish, whose glory, and the cause of independence, always took precedence over mere human relationships. Since the death of his young wife Maria Teresa, no one woman could have been said to be the love of that sexually incontinent man's life; but Manuelita came closer than most.

After the annexation of Quito, Bolívar displayed signs of what looks like megalomania: at a banquet given by his officers, he spoke of liberating

Latin America all the way to Cape Horn. And Chimborazo had him in its spell. This volcano, eighty miles or so south of Quito, stands at just over twenty thousand feet, and the approach to the summit is precipitous. Humboldt had made the ascent in 1802, and Bolívar's own climb inspired him to a remarkable passage of lyrical prose, 'My Dream of Chimborazo': 'I am cloaked in the mantle of Iris, from where the majestic Orinoco pays tribute to the God of the waters. I had explored the mysterious sources of the Amazon, and then I sought to ascend to the pinnacle of the Universe ...' He described how, following in the footsteps of Humboldt but in imagination leaving him far behind, he reached the summit 'as if driven on by the spirit which inhabited me', and there fainted. Time spoke to him, saying: 'I am the father of the Centuries, the mysterious repository of fame; and the unknown Eternity was my mother; Infinity marks the borders of my realm; no sepulchre will ever hold me, for I am mightier than Death; my vision scans the past and the future, and through my hands the presence flows.'

14

The Liberator and the Protector

At a less elevated level, Bolívar was now about to execute the most ruthless coup of his life, displaying the implacable singlemindedness that so often characterised the critical stages of his career and, as much as anything, had been responsible for his success. José de San Martín was a personality in complete contrast to the Liberator. His successes were accompanied by a selflessness and devotion to duty, the counterpart of the frenzied histrionics, the fevered and sometimes murderous determination exhibited by Bolívar. Demonic guerrilla chieftain encountered patriotic pillar of military rectitude and crushed him, not in battle but at a two-day conference. It was Bolívar who emerged the most famous figure in Latin American history, but it was San Martín who, by his dignity and self-abnegation, retained the real affection of much of the continent.

Because so little is known of what was actually said, Latin American historians endlessly debate the significance of the historic meeting between the two men at Guayaquil in July 1822. There are, broadly, three camps: those who sympathise with Bolívar, for whom San Martín is a pompous, priggish reactionary who favoured the reimposition on South America of a string of monarchies; those who side with San Martín, seeing him as a shining example of one who put his duty before his personal interests, the man who surrendered his forces and abandoned his command and his future to Bolívar in the common interest of defeating the Spanish forces; and those concerned to discredit the least idea that the two greatest figures in the wars of liberation detested one another, arguing that reports of division between them are much exaggerated and that the agreement they reached was both logical and cordial. This last view, however convenient to rewriters of history, can be dismissed at once: its tone may be rational, but the bitterness evident in San Martín's letter to Bolívar after the meeting cannot be denied. The evidence points to a modified version of the second view, Bolívar's attempts afterwards to portray himself in the best and San Martín in the worst possible light notwithstanding.

In moving south so speedily after liberating New Granada and Venezuela, Bolívar's prime objective was to get to Peru before San Martín, to steal from him the mantle of principal liberator of the continent, to pre-empt him. Incorporating the Viceroyalty of Peru (which embraced today's Peru and Bolivia) would nearly double the size of his Colombian empire, and dwarf the southern entities of Chile and Argentina. If he could achieve his ambition of annexing these as well, he would rule almost all Spanish America – perhaps the largest dominion under the control of one man in the history of the world, exceeding Napoleon's in extent, if not in population. Only San Martín – and the large Spanish forces still holding out in Peru – stood in his way. The rise from abject failure to dizzying power and success in a mere two years seems to have given Bolívar delusions of grandeur.

In response to a letter of congratulation from San Martín on the creation of Gran Colombia, Bolívar had written to him in glowingly flattering terms. Eighteen months later, after San Martín's entry into Lima, Bolívar was equally fulsome. Referring to San Martín's action in sending the detachment under Santa Cruz which helped turn the tables when Sucre was under siege in Guayaquil and contributed to the victory at Pinchincha that liberated Quito, Bolívar warmly thanked the 'liberators of the south ... who, for so many reasons, we must rate as our best friends and brothers in arms'. In June 1822 Bolívar wrote again to San Martín, offering to allow his men to help him against royalist operations in Peru. By the time the two met, a month later, their fortunes had become startlingly reversed. Bolívar felt a surge of new confidence after capturing Quito; by contrast, San Martín's campaign in Peru (he described it as 'not a war of conquest and glory, but entirely of opinion') was bogged down. Bolívar now sought to make the most of his strong position, and eliminate his rival politically; and he planned his moves as carefully as any military campaign. In his haughty high-mindedness, San Martín believed he was to obtain the services of a slightly inferior but still gentlemanly ally in delivering the *coup de grâce* to the Spanish in Peru; the irony was that Bolívar, more aristocratic by birth than San Martín, proved also far tougher.

Hearing that San Martín was preparing to sail to Guayaquil, Bolívar rushed down the mountain trail from Quito to get there before him.

Guayaquil had in fact secured its 'independence' in 1820 under José Olmedo, supported by both San Martín and Admiral Lord Cochrane. Before Sucre's arrival in 1821, a majority of the population of the port probably favoured a connection with San Martín.

Bolívar reached Guayaquil a fortnight earlier than San Martín, and effectively annexed the port. O'Leary describes how it was done:

> On the third day the partisans of Colombia got together a mob and pulled the flag of Guayaquil from before the residence of General Bolívar – and replaced [it] with the Colombian. The vessels of war in the river immediately saluted the flag ... General Bolívar seemed not to approve of the transaction. He ordered me to remove the Colombian flag and to assure the junta that what had taken place was done without his knowledge and that he highly disapproved of it. However, the flag of Guayaquil had been unfurled for the last time – it was never again hoisted.
>
> In the meantime an assembly, composed of deputies from the different cantons of the province, which had been convoked by the Junta with General Bolívar's consent to decide upon the fate of the province, had now united ...
>
> General Bolívar, who consented to the convocation of this assembly for form['s] sake, became impatient at the length of its session and, when informed of what was going on, made his secretary write to the assembly to say that he understood that points were being discussed which he esteemed as foreign to the question, that he insisted upon an immediate decision. The hint was taken, [and] Guayaquil was declared a province of Colombia ...

His entry was the usual triumph, with arches of flowers, one bearing the words 'To Simón Bolívar – the Lightning of War, the Rainbow of Peace. From the people of Guayaquil.' Bands played and cannon thundered in tribute.

As San Martín, sailing from Lima's port of Callao, picked his way through the estuary of the Guayas river, he received a letter of breathtaking but deceptive unctuousness from Bolívar:

> With the utmost satisfaction, most respected friend, I give you for the first time the title which my heart has granted you. I call you friend, and this is the name we should carry through life, because friendship is the only bond that should unite brothers in arms, in enterprise and in opinion. I would regret as much your not coming to this city as the loss of many battles; but you will not leave unsatisfied the wish I have of embracing on Colombian soil the foremost friend of my heart and my country.

How would it be possible that you should come from so far away without letting us in Guayaquil see the great man that all are anxious to know, and if possible to touch? It is not possible. I am waiting for you and will meet you wherever you indicate; but without desisting from the honour of having you visit this city.

A few hours, as you say, are enough for a discussion between soldiers; but they would not be enough to satisfy the passion for friendship, which is going to begin to enjoy the happiness of knowing the dear object of its affection, which it loved only through opinion, only through fame.

San Martín was, indeed, astonished to be welcomed to 'Colombian soil': one of the main purposes of his trip had been to settle the status of Guayaquil, but he was met with a *fait accompli*. So taken aback was he that, reluctant to signify recognition of Bolívar's coup, he refused to go ashore immediately on his arrival. But he relented the next morning, and was greeted on the quayside by Bolívar. Trumpets sounded out over the port and cannon boomed as this odd couple embraced. They rode into the city, complete opposites: Bolívar, smiling, the consummate showman, nervous, small, and thin, his glittering eyes darting about him; San Martín, tall and dignified, grave, distant and aristocratic in appearance.

A beautiful girl representing the women of Guayaquil placed a crown of laurels on San Martín's head. He was embarrassed; he hated honours, and would have preferred to remove it, as if to emphasise that he had never sought a crown for himself. But he did not want to snub the girl or reject the goodwill of the people of the port, so merely said with his customary diffidence: 'I do not deserve this demonstration. There are others more worthy of it. But I shall keep this souvenir because of the patriotic feeling that inspires it and because of the hands whence it comes, since this is one of the happiest days of my life.'

In the afternoon San Martín went to the city hall to meet Bolívar, and the two men were closeted alone for several hours. The following day they met again in the afternoon, for four hours. Because these meetings were held without a single other witness present, it is impossible to know what was discussed. The only immediate record is a second-hand one, and biased: that of Bolívar's chief adviser, José Gabriel Perez, who, after the event and at the Liberator's dictation, penned a confidential memorandum to the Colombian Foreign Minister:

... The Protector spoke only of what had already been the subject of their conversations, raising vague and unconnected questions on military and political matters without going deeply into any, shifting from one theme to another and mingling the serious with the trivial. If the character of the Protector is not as frivolous as appears in conversation, it must be supposed that he acted thus with a certain purpose. His Excellency is inclined to disbelieve that the Protector's character is what it appeared, but neither does it seem to him that he was calculating his words and behaviour.

Bolívar later claimed to have been more impressed than this seems to indicate: San Martín appeared to be 'very military in character, and ... energetic, quick, and not dull. He has the kind of correct ideas that would please you but he does not seem to be subtle enough for sublimity either in ideas or practice.'

According to Perez's account, San Martín talked vaguely about the issue of Guayaquil – as well he might; he had just been cheated out of the port by Bolívar. Then he declared that he had decided to return to Mendoza (his home in Argentina) once the war against the Spanish had been won; but added that before retiring he would leave the foundations of government well established; and that in Peru this should not be democratic, because it would not suit the country; finally, that a prince from Europe must come and govern Peru.

Bolívar is said to have replied nervously, pacing the room, that the conditions did not exist for the return of monarchy, and that any political system required the participation of the masses, although not a revolution against the existing social order. San Martín is said to have expressed profound concern at the radical turn taken by the revolution in Colombia, and to have predicted that chaos and civil war beckoned; only under a monarchy could social order be restored, he thought. According to Perez, Bolívar's response was to assert that

Democracy, which has flourished even in the polluted soil of Europe, would certainly thrive in the virgin soil of America. Here there is no real element of aristocracy, nothing but a sorry caricature. There are not then, my dear general, elements of monarchy in this land of God. Let a republic be formed here and dignity will grow in men, the necessity and habit for work for social benefits will be created and these will produce territorial wealth and commercial industry which will attract immigration from Europe where the proletariat lack lands and can find them here. It is impossible to hold back the progress of the human race. A monarchy established here would be of short duration, for an idea, once implanted in the people, is impossible to extinguish; and the idea of democracy has been firmly rooted here during twelve years of glorious struggle, full of examples of abnegation and patriotism . . . Neither our generation nor the generation to follow ours will see the brilliance of what we have founded. I see America in chrysalis. There will be a metamorphosis in the existence of its inhabitants, and at last a cast of all the races will produce a homogeneous people. We cannot stay the march of human progress with outmoded constitutions which are foreign to the virgin soil of America.

Thus was the encounter between the two men reduced, according to this account, to a clash between enlightenment, democracy, republicanism (Bolívar) and a stuffy defence of the status quo or, worse, a desire to import a monarchical form of government (San Martín). It is impossible to say how true this is: to support monarchism was essentially equivalent to support for Spanish rule, at the time a treasonable anathema in patriot circles. For Bolívar it made sense thus to taint San Martín. San Martín later vigorously denied the charge, and his supporters alleged that in the whole of the discussions between the two men, the subject of monarchy never once came up. Given Bolívar's penchant for embroidery in his own interests, this is indeed possible. Ironically, he was himself to be suspected of harbouring monarchical ambitions at least twice later in his career. One particular lie put about by San Martín's detractors was that he coveted the throne of Peru for himself; no public word or action of his suggests this; and it seems extremely unlikely in a man of retiring disposition who, as he frequently demonstrated, hated ceremony.

It is now known that prior to his meeting with Bolívar San Martín, with the aim of avoiding further bloodshed, had had discussions with the Spanish Viceroy of Peru, La Serna, in the course of which the possibility of a European monarch taking over was mooted as an idea which might be acceptable to Spain; and he once told Commodore William Bowles that he favoured 'dividing South America amongst principal European powers, and providing a number of kingdoms as might provide for a prince of each royal house'. It may be that San Martín raised some such idea with Bolívar, but he always wholeheartedly rejected any idea of compromise with Spain. Whatever the exact truth, Bolívar's supporters have always held that the conference foundered on San Martín's preference for a monarchy over a republic – thus showing Bolívar in a favourable light.

It seems clear that the discussions were not really about any eventual form of government – or, if they were, only as a side issue. The main question was who would command in the final phase of the struggle against Spanish domination, and thus become the principal Liberator of Spanish America. San Martín had assumed that Bolívar would offer the support of his army in the final battle against the Spanish, just as the Chileans had backed his earlier efforts along the coast; Bolívar was determined that the two armies should not be merged under San Martín's command – he intended to lead the campaign himself, and there was no place in his plans for his rival.

He had decided to play on the Protector's weaknesses, knowing that the Spanish heavily outnumbered San Martín's forces; that the Marqués de Torre Tagle, the former royalist aristocrat whom San Martín had left in charge, was at that moment holding talks with the Spanish behind San Martín's back; and that San Martín was most unpopular in Lima. To deny him military support was to deal a death blow to San Martín's chances of survival.

Feigning helpfulness, Bolívar offered to lend San Martín 1,400 men – quite insufficient to tilt the balance against the Spanish. Now it was San Martín's turn to try to wrong-foot Bolívar: he offered himself and his army to serve under the Liberator in the forthcoming campaign. Bolívar presented lame excuses for not agreeing to this, then delivered the *coup de grâce*, informing San Martín that a conspiracy to oust him was being hatched, as they spoke, among the patriots in Lima; it is possible that Bolívar and his agents were behind it.

It must have appeared to San Martín that Bolívar, so glamorous and popular a contrast to himself, would meet with success if he chose to appeal over his head to his troops and to the supporters of the patriot cause in Lima. Most of the former were Chilean, while San Martín was Argentinian, and the Chileans lacked the stomach to continue the war under his command. He had appealed for help from his native Argentina, but it was denied him by his political opponents there. He was an emperor with no clothes, a general with no troops: only a remarkable combination of hauteur, bluff and luck had got him this far, in charge of an army consisting largely of troops who were not his own in any national sense. He was too proud a man to court open humiliation, and too selfless and public-spirited to force a confrontation. He had been crushed and, good soldier that he was, accepted defeat with notable dignity. At their second meeting he agreed to hand over control of his forces to Bolívar and withdraw from the scene.

Afterwards Bolívar held a glittering banquet and a ball in honour of his rival, the sort of event San Martín most disliked. Egocentrically, Bolívar toasted 'the two greatest men in South America – San Martín and myself'. San Martín drank instead to 'the early end of the war, the organisation of the various republics of the continent, and the health of the Liberator of Colombia'. As Bolívar plunged into the dancing, San Martín watched in distaste, then decided to leave. Seeing this, Bolívar accompanied him into the warm night and, the noise of the festivities fading into the background, bestowed upon him, perhaps predictably, a portrait of himself as a farewell present. San Martín later reciprocated more fittingly, as between general and general. 'The Liberator has won this hand,' he said sadly to his aide as his schooner *Macedonia* slipped away from her moorings. Against the second most powerful man in Latin America Bolívar had given another demonstration of his ruthlessness and inspired more of the fear which assured his survival at the top – until the very end.

San Martín sent a pointedly dignified and hardhitting letter to Bolívar from Peru:

My dear General:

I shall write to you not only with the frankness of my nature, but also with that which is demanded by the high interests of America.

The results of our interview are not those which I foresaw for a quick end of the war. Unfortunately, I am completely convinced that either you have not deemed sincere my offer to serve under your orders with the forces at my command, or that my person is embarrassing for you. The reasons you advanced, that your tact would not allow you ever to give me orders, and that even if that were the case the Colombian Congress would not authorize your separation from the territory of Colombia, have not seemed very plausible to me.

The first one refutes itself. As far as the second one is concerned, I am convinced that if you expressed your wishes you would find unanimous approval, since the object is to end this campaign, which we have started and in which we are engaged, with your co-operation and that of your army, and that the honour of bringing it to an end would fall upon yourself and the Republic over which you preside.

Do not indulge in any illusions, General. The news which you have about the Royalist forces is wrong: they number, in Upper and Lower Peru, more than 19,000 veterans, who may unite within two months. The patriot army, decimated by illness, will not be able to send to the front more than 8,500, and of these a great part are raw recruits. General Santa Cruz's division (the casualties of which, this general writes me, have not been replaced despite his insistence) on its long march overland must experience a considerable loss, and it will not contribute anything to this campaign.

The division of 1,400 Colombians which you are sending will be needed to garrison Callao and keep order in Lima. Consequently, without the backing of the army you command, the operation which is planned by way of the Intermediate Ports [Guayaquil, etc.] will not have the advantages which could be expected unless powerful forces could draw the enemy elsewhere; and in this way the struggle will be indefinitely prolonged. I say indefinitely because I am deeply convinced that, be what may the difficulties of the present war, America's independence is irrevocable; but I am also convinced that the prolongation of the war will be the ruin of its peoples, and it is a sacred duty for the men in whose hands lies [America's] destiny to prevent a continuation of such evils.

Be it as it may, General, my decision has irrevocably been made. I have called the First Congress of Peru for the 20th of next month, and on the day after its installation I shall embark for Chile, satisfied that my presence is the only obstacle which prevents you from coming to Peru with the army at your command. For me it would have been the height of happiness to end the war of independence under the orders of a general to whom America owes its freedom. Destiny orders it otherwise, and one must resign oneself to it.

Having no doubt that after my going the Peruvian Government that may be established will request the active co-operation of Colombia, and that you will not be able to refuse so just a demand, I shall send you a list of all the officers whose conduct, both military and private, may commend themselves to you.

General Arenales will be left in command of the Argentine forces. His honesty, his courage, and knowledge, I am sure, will make him deserving of your every consideration.

I shall say nothing to you about the annexation of Guayaquil to the Republic of Colombia. Allow me, General, to say that I did not believe it behoved us to decide this important matter. At the end of the war the respective governments would have decided it, without the troubles that now may result for the interests of the new states of South America.

I have spoken to you, General, with frankness; but the feelings expressed in this letter will be buried in the deepest silence. If they were known, the enemies of our freedom could take advantage of the fact to our sorrow, and the intriguers and the ambitious would sow discord.

With Major Delgado, the bearer of this letter, I am sending you a shotgun and a pair of pistols, together with my personal horse, which I offered to you in Guayaquil. Accept, General, this souvenir from your foremost admirer.

With these feelings and with the hope that you may have the glory of ending the war of independence of South America, I am,

Your affectionate servant,

José de San Martín.

To O'Higgins in Chile he wrote bitterly: 'I am tired of hearing men call me tyrant, that I wish to make myself King, Emperor, the Devil. On the other hand my health is broken, this climate is killing me. My youth was sacrificed to the service of Spain, my manhood to my own country. I think I have now the right to dispose of my old age.'

In public, to pave the way for Bolívar's campaign against the Spanish, he maintained a brave face: 'I had the satisfaction of embracing the hero of South America. That was one of the happiest days of [my] life. The Liberator of Colombia is helping Peru with three of his brave battalions. Let us all show our eternal gratitude to the immortal Bolívar.'

Having defeated San Martín at the conference table, Bolívar now devoted himself to Manuelita. He arranged to borrow a magnificent hacienda, El Garzal, on the banks of the Guayas river, a slice of paradise with a temperate climate and glorious trees, flowers and birds. General William Miller, San Martín's British aide, who first encountered him at this time, described him thus:

... the expression of [his] countenance is care-worn, lowering, and, some-times, rather fierce. Hs temper, spoiled by adulation, is fiery and capricious. His opinions of men and things are variable. He is rather prone to personal abuse, but makes ample amends to those who will put up with it. Towards such his resentments are not lasting. He is a passion-ate admirer of the fair sex, but jealous to excess. He is fond of waltzing, and is a very quick, but not a very graceful, dancer. His mind is of the most active description ... His voice is loud and harsh but he speaks elo-quently on all subjects ... Although the cigar is almost universally used in South America, Bolívar never smokes, nor does he permit smoking in his presence ... Disinterested in the extreme with regard to pecuniary affairs, he is insatiably covetous of fame.

Bolívar invariably speaks of England, of her institutions and her great men, in terms of admiration. He often dwells with great warmth upon the constancy, fidelity, and sterling merit of the English officers who have served in the cause of independence, under every varying event of the war. As a collateral proof of his predilection towards England, he has always had upon his personal staff a number of British subjects.

Unlike his other loves, who surrendered themselves without a struggle to the great man, Manuelita knew how to play Bolívar like an angler does a fish – how to deny herself to him and excite his jealousy, arousing his passion all the more. Like Fanny de Villiers, his early sexual tutor, and Julia Cobier, his consoler in Jamaica, Manuelita was not afraid of him, or overawed by him. She answered him back, threw tantrums, and treated him as an equal. She would dress in dragoon's uniform, mount a white horse and carry a lance like a man. Bolívar adored it. They enjoyed long weeks of intimacy at the ranch, and when they were apart he wrote to her. His letters bespeak real passion, as distinct from his more empty protestations of ardour to his other women. 'You want to see me with your own eyes,' he wrote on one occasion. 'I want to see you again and again, to touch you and hear you and taste you and unite you to me with every kind of touch. Why do you not love me as I you? For that is the most pure and clear truth. Learn to love and don't even go with God himself.'

Bolívar was in no hurry to enter Peru, partly because he wanted to enjoy his 'honeymoon', partly because he felt he had to consolidate his hold on Quito before the next great challenge – but largely because he wanted the feuding élites of Lima to plead for his entry into the city to save them, after the departure of San Martín. The excuse he gave was that he needed authority from Colombia before proceeding into Peru, but when word reached him that Santander was indeed dragging his feet over providing the necessary authorisation, Bolívar rounded on him: 'The Constitution of Colombia is sacred for ten years. It will not be violated with impunity while blood flows in my veins and the army of Liberators is under my orders.'

When the royalists in the mountain stronghold of Pasto, about a hundred and fifty miles to the north of Quito, suddenly rose again in revolt, Sucre was despatched to quell them and succeeded after two bloody battles, the second of which ended in vicious street-fighting in the city itself. Meanwhile Morales and a detachment of men had managed to slip away from Puerto Cabello, the last royalist stronghold on the Venezuelan coast, and raise the standard of revolt at another point along the coast. Ever-restless, Bolívar was on the point of returning to Venezuela when Páez drove the Spanish forces into the hot-house that was Maracaibo, and locked up their fleet inside its huge inland sea. He had assembled a patriot fleet of 22 ships and 1,300 soldiers, mostly North American volunteers. In July 1823 the fleet's second-in-command, an

Englishman, Captain Walter Chitty, slipped in on the tide at night through the entrance to the lake unnoticed by the local garrison, and appeared in the middle of the Spanish fleet, putting up such a fight that ten Spanish ships were successfully boarded and one sunk. Morales, the longest-surviving fighter for the Spanish cause, at last gave up, and was permitted to sail for Cuba.

Bolívar had not been needed. But now a further general uprising broke out, in Pasto, and its indomitable mountain men moved on Quito and seized the city. By that time Bolívar had sent the bulk of his army to Lima's port, Callao, under Sucre's command, to prepare for his arrival. He had to raise a new army of raw recruits and, in a series of small skirmishes and guerrilla victories, defeated the Pastistas once again, killing eight hundred; his chief-of-staff, Salom, had to fight two more battles before crushing them. Determined to break their spirit for good Bolívar exiled their clergy – who had been instrumental in stirring up the dissent – and marched hundreds of the fighters down to Guayaquil. Many threw themselves off cliffs or into streams on the long march, many others refused food and died of starvation by the roadside, rather than submit. At Guayaquil Bolívar received an embassy from the government of Peru imploring him to fill the power vacuum left by San Martín; it was the message he had been waiting for, and he decided to go.

Manuelita begged to accompany him, but he refused to take her. No love, now, was as dear to him as ambition. Perhaps, too, he felt the need to reassert his freedom, after almost a year of her domination. She was compelled to return to Dr Thorne at Quito, where Bolívar wrote her a hypocritical letter.

> My beautiful and good Manuela, each moment I am thinking of you and the fate which touched you. I see that nothing can unite us under the auspices of innocence and honour. I see well and deplore the horrible situation for you. You must be reconciled with one you do not love and I must be separated from one I adore. Yes, I adore you today more than ever before ... In the future you will be alone, even at the side of your husband; I will be alone in the midst of the world. Only the glory of having conquered ourselves will be our consolation ...

On 1 September 1823 Bolívar landed at last at the port of Callao in Peru, the fiscal heart of the Spanish Empire, source of most of the silver and mineral wealth that had fuelled the motherland for three hundred years. There the greatest Indian nation, the Incas, had been defeated by the

15. The Protector: José de San Martín

16. Peruvian hazard: rope bridge across a canyon

17. President Monroe: he tried to shut out
Britain and France. Painting by Samuel Morse

18. John Quincy Adams: author of American policy to the south

19. Buenos Aires: the first city to shake off Spanish rule

20. Shootout from a corral: before the Battle of Rancagua

21. Angry mountains:
the Chilean flight
across the Andes

22. How San Martín's army crossed: Paso de los Libertadores

23. Irish Viceroy who fathered a changeling: Ambrosio O'Higgins

24. The greatest guerrilla: José Maria Morelos. Painting by unknown artist

25. The Director: Bernardo O'Higgins

most barbarous of the Conquistadors, Francisco Pizarro. There the city of Lima had grown into a byword for opulence, class and race distinction, corruption and immorality. There the greatest Spanish force in America, eighteen thousand well-trained men, had been concentrated in the mountains, their stronghold the ancient Inca capital of Cuzco. They remained undefeated, for San Martín had occupied only the coastal strip between Lima and Trujillo.

The Peruvian criollos, it seemed, were not revolutionary at all. They had never had to turn their hands to work. They simply employed the Indian and mestizo underclass, which outnumbered them by four to one, to dig for minerals and farm their crops; Peru had developed no indigenous industries of her own, really remaining a vast slave labour camp. The whites thus hardly wanted to overthrow the political system; there were, besides, acute fears that any revolution against the status quo might induce rebellion among the Indians and mestizos and result in a blood-bath, of the kind that Tupac Amaru had seemed to foreshadow. An Indian leader who had helped to suppress Tupac Amaru's rebellion, Mateo Pumacahua, led risings in Puno, La Paz and Arequipa before he was captured and executed in 1815. San Martín had understood the danger, and had sought to placate the fears of the privileged classes with his ideas for an independent state – even possibly under a monarchy – which respected social structures.

The Peruvian oligarchy were intensely distrustful of the programmes of social reform and equality for all races which had secured Bolívar the support of Venezuela's llaneros and mestizos. Fearing he would attempt the same in Peru, they were determined to show themselves capable of resisting the Spanish alone. On San Martín's departure a collective leadership of aristocrats set up under the Marqués de Torre Tagle ordered San Martín's recently recruited forces into action against the Spanish. The patriot army of eight thousand was divided: half, under General Arenales, was deemed necessary to maintain order in Lima, while the other half, under General Alvarado, set off to do battle against the royalists entrenched, in far superior numbers, in the mountains.

Even by the standards of the rest of Latin America, the topography of Peru is awesome: out of a narrow strip of coastal desert, a northward extension of Chile's Atacama Desert, in places no more than ten miles wide, sheer, barren, brown and grey mountains rise to passes at twelve or thirteen thousand feet and peaks of fifteen to twenty thousand feet, before falling away to a system of more or less fertile upland river valleys

– of which one of the most spectacular is the valley of the Apurímac, near the head of which is the ancient Inca capital, Cuzco.

The military theory elaborated by the patriot generals in Lima was that, as long as the Viceroy's huge army remained strung out in the interior, it should be relatively easy to concentrate their own forces and pick off outposts singly, before the Spanish were able to bring up reinforcements. The flaw in this theory was that any assault from the coast into the uplands would have to cross appalling country. As a contemporary observer put it, 'To reach [the Spanish lines] you had to cross the coastal desert – thirst, sand in your mouth and in your equipment, lack of provisions; and the mountains – steepness, tiredness and cold.' Such an approach would be slow, of necessity, and easily detectable, permitting its obvious destination to be reinforced at leisure.

Exactly that occurred. The Viceroy, La Serna, ordered his second-in-command, General José de Canterac, to Cuzco and reinforced General Valdez at Arequipa. Alvarado's patriot forces moved to Atico on the coast, from where they went up into the mountains in December: Valdez descended, trapped them, and inflicted a resounding defeat. This resulted in a revolt in Lima and the seizure of power in February 1823 by José de la Riva Agüero, head of Lima's own circle of criollo nationalists, tough-minded, devious, and thoroughly unpleasant.

Riva Agüero at once called on Argentina, Chile and the Colombians for help in staging a final offensive against the Spanish. But the Argentinians had not been prepared to support their own commander, San Martín, in the Peruvian cause, and showed no interest in helping a Peruvian nationalist. The Chileans said they had no troops to spare. Riva Agüero did not want to cede control of the enterprise to Bolívar, and qualified his request for Colombian help with the condition that it should be in a subordinate capacity only. Bolívar was determined to call the upstart's bluff and instructed Sucre, who had arrived in Callao, not to commit his forces 'to any political action with a doubtful outcome. I told the president that you would not come [as Colombia's representative] except with the dignity and character due to the Liberator of Colombia, with the necessary faculties to direct the war and with the full agreement of the provinces in the [Peruvian] assembly.'

Riva Agüero then invited San Martín to return to serve him, and received a witheringly contemptuous reply. So he decided to embark on his own expedition against the Spanish, and set off with most of his troops. On hearing of this de Canterac, the royalist commander, knew that Lima was left virtually undefended, and decided to attack it boldly with nine thousand men. Sucre, appalled by Riva Agüero's stupidity and acting on Bolívar's instructions, ordered the remnants of the patriot forces away from the city, which could not be defended. Meanwhile the city's governing council, under Torre Tagle, deposed Riva Agüero in his absence. De Canterac arrived at the head of his army, seized Lima, imposed a tribute on the city and then, hearing that another of Bolívar's generals, Santa Cruz, was attacking royalist posts in the south, departed to fight him. Sucre was able to ride back into the city with his small band of soldiers.

Riva Agüero had meanwhile fled to Trujillo where, infuriated by his deposition, he initiated contact with the royalists, and ordered Santa Cruz not to obey Sucre. But the order was redundant: Santa Cruz had set off with six thousand men into the impassable sierra and there been driven back by the Spanish; in a terrible retreat across desolate mountains and baking, barren desert his army was reduced to just eight hundred men without another battle being fought. Peru could ill afford to lose any men. The defeated government now begged Bolívar to come; and at last he did. His reception in Lima was tumultuous: fireworks, balls, operas and a bullfight were held in his honour. He was given San Martín's Villa Magdalena, sumptuously fitted out: the dinner service was of solid gold.

Lima was one of the most architecturally distinguished of all Latin American cities, peppered with delightful palaces, such as the Archbishop's, next to the Cathedral, and that of the Torre Tagle. Bolívar rode through the streets beneath the elaborate wooden balconies which protruded from the first floors, covered with lattice-work so that women might watch without being seen. Not that the women of Lima at that time had the reputation of being discreet: they were permitted to gamble, drink and smoke, and were notoriously free with their favours. The fashions of Lima were equally outrageous by European standards: the women wore white trousers with their dresses, and sported men's hats – the little bowlers, cocked to one side, or tall ones like top hats, that to this day the Indian women of Peru wear as the height of chic.

Bolívar's first impression was favourable, in its idiosyncratically self-absorbed way: 'I go down well with everyone: the men admire me and the women love me. The food is excellent, the theatre good, adorned with beautiful objects and a fine carved door. Coaches, horses, walks, bulls, Te Deums – nothing is missing.' Lima, indeed, boasted a staggering eight thousand coaches, and there was a constant competitive social whirl, maintained by the effects of chewing coca leaves, the ubiquitous narcotic of the city. In contrast to the dourly austere San Martín, Bolívar delighted the Limeños. The much-feared wild revolutionary of the north turned out to be as cultivated and aristocratic as they could wish. But he made it clear at once that he was not fighting the Spanish in order to impose a new monarchy. At the official banquet in his honour he gave the toast, that 'the American people should never consent to raise a single throne in all their territory; just as Napoleon was submerged in the immensity of the ocean [in St Helena] and the new Emperor Itúrbide has been deposed from the throne of Mexico, may the usurpers of the rights of the American people fall, so that not a single one remains triumphant in all the huge extension of the New World.' Bolívar later wrote in more sombre and measured terms:

> The country receives us with enthusiasm but gives us nothing. We have need of much tact and great moderation to prevent this nation from becoming entirely reactionary. Money is needed but we ought not and cannot demand it of these unfortunate people, for here the era of home government has been one of crime and pillage. The inhabitants are sound but they are disinclined to military service and it is difficult to organize an army. The natives are what they were at the beginning of the world ... The country is patriotic but unadapted to military service; it is good, but apathetic. There are provisions and transportation but no will to furnish them ... the difficulties are immense, there reigns a disorder that appals the most determined. The theatre of war is equatorial America; our enemies are everywhere, our soldiers are men of all parties and all countries, of different dialects, colour, laws and interests. Only Providence can bring order out of this chaos.

Bernardo O'Higgins met Bolívar for the first time in Lima, and was impressed. Yet it soon became apparent that Bolívar, far from coasting towards a final victory over the Spanish, had placed himself and his men in extreme danger. He wrote to Santander desperately seeking twelve thousand men as reinforcements, but received no answer. The Marqués de Torre Tagle, meanwhile, head of the provisional government in Lima, was secretly negotiating with the royalists to be rid of the 'common enemy', who himself dashed off to Trujillo to put down the 'independent' government set up by Riva Agüero. The commander of the garrison there surrendered, and handed over the inept dictator, whom Bolívar put aboard ship for Europe, to spare him Torre Tagle's order of execution.

Further disaster struck. The garrison of Argentine soldiers at Callao, Lima's port, had been disgruntled ever since the departure of their hero, San Martín; in February 1824 they mutinied, freed the Spanish prisoners in the garrison gaol, and went over to the royalists. Meanwhile Bolívar himself, long accustomed to intermittent bouts of malaria and a variety of other fevers, went down with tabardillo, a rat typhus spread by fleas and lice. He was unable to move from the small village on the coast of Lima where, stricken, he heard of the collapse of his hopes. Torre Tagle and most of the Peruvian forces had followed the Argentinians in defecting to the Spanish; even the Argentine Grenadiers, personally trained by San Martín, went over. The Spanish army entered Lima to a reception greater than that accorded Bolívar the month before. In a proclamation Torre Tagle declared that 'The tyrant Bolívar and his indecent supporters sought to annex Peru, and place this rich country under the control of Colombia, but he has made a mistake. The Spaniards are the only alternative who can avert our ruin.'

With just five thousand Colombian troops at his disposal – he had ordered Sucre to move his forces at once to Trujillo, having first destroyed all guns and equipment he could not carry with him from Lima and Callao – Bolívar now occupied only an enclave along the northern coast of Peru. The Spanish army of the north, under de Canterac in Huancayo, consisted of eight thousand men; about a thousand were based in Cuzco, Valdez had three thousand in Arequipa and Puno, General Olañeta four thousand in Peru's southern highlands (most of modern Bolivia). Another two thousand men made up a mobile force, moving between the various headquarters. For Bolívar, as for Riva Agüero, there was no help to be had from Argentina or from Chile; nor any from Colombia, as Santander hesitated to send in more men to defend what seemed a hopeless position – perhaps he even secretly hoped for Bolívar's defeat, which would leave him in exclusive control, if not of all Gran Colombia, at least of New Granada.

Visiting the sick man, Mosquera, his ambassador to Buenos Aires, was both appalled and impressed:

> I found the Liberator no longer at risk of death from tabardillo, which was past its worst; but so thin and emaciated that his appearance caused me real pain. He was sitting on a ragged cowskin, propped against the wall of a small garden with a white scarf on his head, wearing cut-off riding breeches which allowed me to see his pointed knees and fleshless limbs, his voice hoarse and feeble and his appearance cadaverous.

I had to make an effort to conceal my tears and not let him know my pain and fear for his life. 'What do you think of doing now?' Raising his hollow eyes, with a firm voice he replied, 'Win ...' 'How will you triumph?' In a calm and confident voice he told me: 'I have given orders to raise a force of cavalry in the Trujillo region. I have ordered all the good horses of the country to be requisitioned by my army, and I have requisitioned all the alfalfa grasses to make them fat. When I have recovered my strength I will go to Trujillo. If the Spaniards descend the cordillera to take me, I will inevitably defeat them with my cavalry; if they don't descend within three months I will have a force strong enough to attack them. I will climb the cordillera and defeat the Spaniards at Jauja.'

The message Bolívar wanted so desperately to get across to Santander was that Gran Colombia's security depended on the defeat of the Spanish army in Peru. If it survived, Colombia would be reconquered; Quito and Pasto, for example, were royalist hotbeds yearning to overthrow the patriots. The Spanish had to be defeated everywhere on the continent. He was never more admirable than at this time; when Sucre, and all the commanders of his depleted forces, advised him to conclude an armistice with the Spanish, his contempt was manifest.

He appointed a Peruvian general, José de La Mar, to raise an entirely new local army, in a matter of months.

We need to make ourselves deaf to the clamour of the whole world, because war feeds on despotism and is not fought for love of God. Don't spare yourselves in anything, display a terrible, inexorable character. Discipline the forces at your command, both cavalry and infantry. If there are no guns, there are lances. Moreover, I am expecting 3,000 guns from Colombia any moment; a third or fourth line of lances are not useless in a fight and will replace the casualties which are terrific in a newly recruited army. Raise 5,000 recruits so that 2,000 or 3,000 remain alive. Equip yourselves with many supplies, many fortifications throughout the region. Every tree, every man, serves some purpose. Let us make use of everything to defend Peru to the teeth. Not a straw must go unused in the whole of this free territory.

Bolívar's forces simply press-ganged everyone they could find into the new army. They helped themselves to all the food and supplies they could get their hands on. They destroyed everything they could not bring in, as part of a scorched-earth policy to delay any royalist attack. At last reinforcements arrived from Santander, though much fewer than Bolívar had hoped for: only 2,500 men, under a startlingly young commander – José-Maria Córdoba, aged just twenty-four. It was clear that if Santander could not refuse Bolívar's plea for help point-blank, he was leaving him to wither on the vine. Cold and punctilious, he had disliked Bolívar from the day in 1813 when, as a young captain, he had been threatened with execution by the Liberator, then treated as a coward.

15

The Trail of the Incas

In April 1824 Bolívar heard some surprising news – and embarked on the last great gamble of his career. The army of Upper Peru (today's Bolivia), under the command of General Olañeta, had rebelled on the grounds that they owed their allegiance to Ferdinand VII and not to the liberal constitutionalists now in control in Spain, represented by men like de Canterac and Valdez. In that highest and most remote of all Spanish possessions, the tiny white minority remained imbued with a sense of feudal submission to Spain.

The Viceroy, La Serna, decided that the threat of insubordination from one of his armies in the mountains was more dangerous than that posed by Bolívar's depleted forces far away on the coast, certain as he was that Bolívar was still weak and would not move until significant reinforcements arrived from Colombia. He despatched Valdez with fourteen thousand men to deal with Olañeta. De Canterac, his other general, ignored Valdez's order that he should lead his six-thousand-strong army down from the Jauja valley against Bolívar, and stayed put in the security of the mountains: to the Spanish it seemed inconceivable that they could be threatened there, whereas de Canterac feared Bolívar's ability to defend himself in the lowlands.

Bolívar responded with alacrity, transforming his scorched-earth war in a defensive enclave into an offensive. He proposed to march straight up into that mountain range and attack while the Spanish were divided, before they had a chance to regroup. It was too good a chance to miss. In vain did his officers, including Sucre, entreat him to wait for further Colombian reinforcements; Bolívar shrewdly judged that Santander, who was becoming ever more difficult, would send none. They would march in May, he proposed, and fight in June. If they had not succeeded by July, they would retreat to defend their coastal enclave by Trujillo.

The Liberator was his old self again. It was to be another throw of the dice, another brilliant improvisation to take advantage of a situation that might not recur, another epic march into the mountains. In Huaylas, on the way to the rendezvous point for his different forces at Cerro de Pasco, another pattern repeated itself when a beautiful, dark-skinned girl of eighteen, dressed in white, gave him a crown of flowers. Bolívar had a passionate affair with Manuela Madroño before riding on to Cerro de Pasco. There he saw in the distance the extensive plains onto which he hoped to lure the enemy to do battle; his strategy was to draw the Spanish out of their stronghold and attack them with cavalry. His troops were following a long way behind: there were 3,500 Colombians under Sucre; 3,000 Peruvians under de La Mar; some 1,500 Argentinian cavalrymen under General Necochea accompanied by that capable British commander from Buenos Aires, General William Miller; and 500 artillerymen from Chile under Pedro Juan Luna.

The units converged, like some giant gathering of the clans, their marches remarkable feats of human endurance. Miller's division tramped six hundred miles along the cordillera, leading their horses to ensure that they would be fresh for battle and accompanied by six thousand head of cattle. They wended their way up one craggy mountain pass to the base of a still higher valley, then climbed in turn up the further side of that, in one dizzying ascent after another, the mountain trails often no more than narrow indentations in the rock faces rising forbiddingly above and falling away spectactularly and sickeningly below. Miller set up rudimentary supply depots along the way:

> Some of these depots were established within the line of country nominally possessed by the royalists. That near Pachia, and on the same bank of the Rio Grande, was only eight leagues from Tarma. The entrance of the cave was in the perpendicular side of a cliff fifty or sixty feet from the ground and as many from the top. The only way to get up was by a rope fixed in the cave, and by notches cut in the rock to give foot-holds. Indian corn, salt, charqui (jerked beef), potatoes, and barley, were hoisted up by means of the rope. A few men were sufficient to defend these cavern-depots against any numbers. It often happened that when the *montaneros* [mountain troops] advanced, these depots were left exposed; but the royalists were not always aware of the exact situation, and entertained no suspicion that supplies had been accumulated.

> [He describes the journey:] The shelving ledges, which afforded the only foothold on the rugged sides of the Andes, are so narrow, as to render

the passage indescribably harassing. The troops could advance only one by one. The single file was sometimes lengthened out to an amazing extent by the *mal pasos* formed by deep gullies or breaks in the tracks, by projecting rocks, or by numerous waterfalls; all of which required great caution, and much time to pass in safety.

Each man had, besides the mule on which he rode, a led horse, to be mounted only in sight of the enemy ... The *lasso* was used, as upon every other occasion, with great adroitness. Fastened round the neck of the led horse, it was shortened or lengthened as the tortuous windings of the ascent or descent required ...

It [often] became necessary for every man to dismount, and to lead the two animals in his charge, to avoid going astray, or tumbling down the most frightful precipices. But the utmost precautions did not always prevent the corps from losing their way. Sometimes men, at the head of a battalion, would continue to follow the windings of a deafening torrent, instead of turning abruptly to the right or left, up some rocky acclivity, over which lay their proper course ... One party was frequently heard hallooing from an apparently fathomless ravine, to their comrades passing over some high projecting summit, to know if they were going right. These would answer with their trumpets; but it often occurred that both parties had lost their road. The frequent sound of trumpets along the broken line; the shouting of officers to their men at a distance; the neighing of horses, and the braying of mules, both men and animals being alike anxious to reach a place of rest, produced a strange and fearful concert, echoed, in the darkness of the night, from the horrid solitudes of the Andes.

[Snowblindness was another problem:] A pimple forms in the eyeball, and causes an itching prickling pain, as though needles were continually piercing it. The temporary loss of sight is occasioned by the impossibility of opening the eyelids for a single moment, the smallest ray of light being absolutely insupportable. The only relief is a poultice of snow, but as that melts away the tortures return. Later in the campaign, a whole division was blinded in this way, and the long files of sightless soldiers were led into the nearest village by Indian guides, but not before a hundred stragglers had been lost along the line.

Many suffered from altitude sickness too, as they walked across interminable snowfields. Gonzalo Bulnes described the similar march of the Peruvian army under de La Mar:

A column of Indians carrying supplies on their shoulders preceded the army. The cavalry was mounted on mules, each one leading a horse, shod with makeshift horseshoes ... The trail they covered was, as in all the trails of the cordillera, a narrow path, worn through use, on which one has to trust the animal without driving her. The infantry followed in long and endless lines.

On each pass the contrast appeared between a steep mountain and a deep valley, peaks lost in the clouds and torrents which fell like a thread of water into the vertiginous depths. Often after climbing a dangerous trail, exhausted, without more vegetation than the little mosses which served as food for the llamas, or the lichen from which the Indians made thread, without seeing anything living other than a condor or a flock of vicuña which stopped to look at the travellers, the soldiers found themselves suddenly on the edge of a valley, at the steep bottom of which they would see a small white house with an orchard of the richest fruits. The army would ascend the valley to rise up to a new height, and this continually. When the army stopped the cold froze their weary limbs and in the evening the soldiers had to sleep close to the fires not to freeze.

An immense human line followed the contours of the range, like a huge snake which enveloped, with its coils, in spirals, the indentations in the mountains. In certain places the soldiers had vertigo and needed the help of their companions; in others the thinness of the air prevented them marching, and entire battalions fell to the ground, victims of *soroche* which seems to be the jealous guardian of [the mountains'] eternal solitude. From place to place ... buglers ... illuminated the path with blasts, to avoid the endless column getting lost.

Before reaching the mountains, Sucre's own divisions further south had crossed three hundred miles of the Atacama desert, freezing at night and frying by day; three hundred died of exhaustion.

On 2 August all the divisions were assembled on the great plateau beneath Cerro de Pasco, about twelve thousand feet above the sea. Bolívar reviewed them. 'Soldiers,' he declared, 'you are going to finish the greatest task which heaven can charge to a man: to save a whole world from slavery ... Soldiers, Peru and the whole of America are waiting for you to deliver peace, the child of victory. Even free Europe looks upon you with favour: for the freedom of the New World is the life of the universe.' The combined army set off for the Lake of the Kings (Lago de Junín), at the other end of which lay the valley leading to the plains of Junín.

De Canterac, meanwhile, surprised by the appearance of a large army with horses at the very gates of his supposedly impregnable mountain headquarters, marched down the left side of the lake to intercept them. Too late he discovered that Bolívar's forces were marching up the right side of this immense inland sea in the mountains, towards the head of the now unguarded Jauja valley, and had to order a hurried counter-march, to avoid being cut off from his headquarters. When Bolívar learned of this, he spurred his men frantically forward. The Spanish infantry was now winning the race, however, so Bolívar detached his cavalry to try to prevent them from reaching the neck of the Jauja valley, where they could easily fend off an attack. Only two Argentinian cavalry brigades made it out of the bottleneck – to find themselves facing the whole enemy army. De Canterac, delighted to catch them out in the open with overwhelmingly superior forces behind him, spurred his highly trained hussars forward, himself leading the charge. The only patriot foot soldiers in the vanguard, the Argentinian grenadiers, were quickly overwhelmed. But the half-naked llanero cavalrymen stood their ground, wheeling about to re-form in charge after charge, while Bolívar hurried the rest of his army forward.

The Colombian hussars and the grenadiers now came up in support of the faltering lines of cavalry, whose commander, General Necochea, had been wounded and taken prisoner; with these reinforcements, the patriots surged forward and rescued him. But the royalist army threw in their cavalry reserves, which charged forward at full gallop. Miller, using an old trick he had learnt from the llaneros, ordered their retreat towards the line of patriot infantry, which was waiting in reserve. Defeat seemed certain as the royalist cavalry charged. 'About turn!' yelled Miller, and his cavalry wheeled about and charged straight into the astonished roy-alists, their lances spearing the horses. This charge broke the Spanish lines and they began to fall back, but Bolívar called a halt to the pursuit to allow his rearguard to come up. De Canterac, terrified of being caught out on the plains again, took advantage of nightfall to initiate one of the longest retreats in history: within two days he had covered about seventy miles to his headquarters in Jauja, abandoning that in turn and retreat-ing a further three hundred miles to the Apurimac river.

It had been a spectacular battle in crystal clear light, under blue skies, on a remote mountain plain by a lake. It had lasted barely an hour and not a shot had been fired, the only sounds the drumming of hoofbeats, the clash of opposing lances and the cries of the injured and dying, like some knightly encounter of the Middle Ages. The uniformed and hel-meted Spanish dragoons, glinting in the cold sun, had been routed by long-haired llaneros in jaguar-skin caps, bare torsos and breeches, by dis-ciplined Argentine horsemen, and by Peruvian regiments in ponchos.

The Spanish had lost a thousand, killed or taken prisoner, along with seven hundred muskets and a large quantity of supplies, defeated by miracles of cavalry attack, dispersal and regrouping perfected on the Venezuelan llanos, twelve thousand feet lower and two thousand miles to the north-west.

De Canterac fled all the way to Cuzco, where news of his decisive defeat had reached La Serna at the same time as reports of a brilliant victory gained by General Valdez against Olañeta in Upper Peru. La Serna, horrified by the outcome of Junín, promptly ordered Valdez to return to Cuzco, and there he assembled the full Spanish complement of twelve thousand men. Bolívar, learning this, decided not to fight again until the rainy season which was just beginning should have ended; leaving Sucre in charge of the forces in the mountains, he turned northwards again. Descending to Huaylas in October, he was received by his passionate young girlfriend, Manuela Madroño. In spite of the victory of Junín, Bolívar was pessimistic: he wanted to create a virtually impregnable 'liberated' state in northern Peru, but doubted his chances of prevailing in the mountains against such a large Spanish army.

Santander, the *de facto* president of Colombia, remained a problem. He and the New Granadan leaders, once so grateful to the Liberator, now bitterly resented the union with Venezuela and disliked having a Venezuelan as their titular president. They were not impressed by the argument that a defeat for the patriots in Peru would threaten the very survival of Gran Colombia, and resented having to send expensive Colombian armies south to help Bolívar. They were also suspicious that men like Sucre, having won their spurs as Bolívar's commanders in Peru, might later take over in Gran Colombia when Bolívar returned.

Santander now asked Congress to consider whether the appropriations requested by Bolívar for Peru were legal. As he had anticipated, Congress responded not just by disavowing them but by stripping Bolívar of his title as commander-in-chief of Colombian forces in Peru. The President of Colombia now had no official military status. Informed of this, Bolívar wrote back furiously: 'I ask you to forward my prior resignation to Congress and I shall write to everyone exposing your secret manoeuvres against me.' Sucre and his officers refused to accept his dismissal, and there was nothing Santander could do to enforce it from New Granada.

Bolívar now had to bid goodbye to his mountain love, Manuela, as he set out for the coast. Sucre thought the Spanish armies might be considering a surprise attack down the sierra through Arequipa onto the coastal enclave, but Bolívar considered it unlikely – and indeed, it proved to have been a feint. The royalist armies had instead decided to march from Cuzco across Sucre's rear, cutting him off from retreat to the north. As soon as Sucre grasped their real intention he pulled back, fast enough to escape the flanking movement. Pursued by a much bigger Spanish army trying to force battle upon him in unfavourable mountain territory, he began a cat-and-mouse retreat across the cordillera, on one occasion marching at dead of night to escape ambush.

The Spanish suffered badly from hunger as they trekked across the higher ground. According to Miller, 'The Viceroy was averse to sending detachments in search of cattle, for, on such occasions, a number of men were sure to desert. The consequence of this system was that, during the rapid advance of the royalists, they suffered more than the patriots from want of provisions; so that ... they were reduced to eat the flesh of their horses, mules and asses.'

However hungry, the Spanish troops, accustomed to the altitude, proved too fast for Sucre. He had been instructed by Bolívar to avoid a fight at all costs, but now decided he had had enough of running. On 6 December Sucre's army camped in the village of Quinoa, near the plain of Ayacucho, while the royalists seized the overlooking heights, called Condorcunca – 'worthy of the Condors.' The battle which now seemed inevitable was a relief to Sucre and his officers, even though they were heavily outnumbered and must fight on territory of the royalists' choosing.

Down on the coast, meanwhile, where he had left Urdaneta in charge, Bolívar, finding that Páez had at last despatched men to his aid, some 4,500, had decided to march on Lima. At his approach, the Marqués de Torre Tagle and other treacherous pro-Spanish grandees fled to the safety of the fort at Callao. Reaching Lima on 7 December, Bolívar found the once glittering capital forlorn and its people wretched. It had been presided over since his ouster by Brigadier Ramirez, known as the 'Robespierre of Peru' for his cruelty, who from the elegant surroundings of the Convent of La Merced had amused himself by decapitating young Limeños for wearing 'republican' hats. Grass grew on the deserted streets – the people feared seizure by Ramirez's patrols, or by marauding bands of patriots. Bolívar was greeted with relief by the Limeños, who begged him not to take his army up into the mountains but to stay and restore order.

At 10 a.m. on 9 December 1824 the patriot armies under Sucre and the Spanish armies under the overall control of the Viceroy, La Serna, met for the battle which was to decide the fate of Spanish America. Valdez, the best Spanish general, commanded the right flank; General Monet, positioned on slopes descending to the plain, commanded the centre; on the left were the Spanish reservists under Marshal Gonzalez. Facing them were the Peruvian troops of General de La Mar; the cavalry and infantry divisions of Sucre's youngest general, Córdoba; and the reserves, under the orders of General Lara. The Spanish, in much the stronger position, took the offensive. Reckoning that de La Mar's Peruvians were the weakest, Valdez decided to attack him with his crack troops. Eleven Spanish cannon blazed away against the single Colombian one, and the battle between 9,300 Spaniards and 5,800 patriots was joined.

De La Mar's troops began to panic as cannon and rifle fire played havoc in their ranks, and he tried desperately to calm them, sending for reinforcements from the centre. The Spanish had calculated he would do just this, and intended to launch a frontal attack against the centre once the reinforcements had been despatched, weakening it. However, Monet got carried away and ordered his men down the slopes before the reinforcements left. Sucre ordered them to stay put and told the beleaguered de La Mar to fight to the death with the troops at his disposal. Córdoba, commanding the infantry and cavalry in the centre, theatrically dismounted, and killed his horse, declaring he wanted no means of escape; then he issued his order: 'Soldiers, fire at will! *Paso de Vencedores* – Advance to Victory!'

The charging Spanish cavalry, nearly upon them, was astonished to see the patriots not just standing firm but advancing towards them, many bearing the long lances which had proved so deadly at Junín. Thrusting at the horsemen, these weapons turned the tables in a long half-hour of hand-to-hand fighting. As the confusion began to clear, it became apparent that Córdoba was still advancing, the Spanish retreating. Soon he had gained the crest of the hill, where he seized the Spanish artillery. De La Mar, meanwhile, had somehow managed to hold the right flank, and Sucre now felt able to transfer reserves to him so he could push back Valdez's exhausted soldiers; that general, both proud and courageous, realising the tide of battle was turning, tried to get himself killed in action but was forcibly dragged from the field by one of his colonels.

The Viceroy tried to save the day by sending his reserves up to retake the hill from Córdoba; but they were driven off and their commander, de Canterac, was wounded. Córdoba's cavalry, on the crest of the hill, galloped down from the heights to seize La Serna in his camp at the rear. Monet, however, managed to escape to the mountains with five hundred men. The rest of the Spanish surrendered when Sucre offered them safe passage to Spain. He had captured two lieutenant-generals, La Serna and Canterac; four field marshals, including Valdez; two brigadier-generals, seventeen colonels, seventy eight lieutenant-colonels, 484 majors and junior officers, 2,500 soldiers and a useful quantity of munitions. Some 1,900 Spanish troops lay dead and 700 wounded, compared with 310 patriot dead and more than six hundred wounded. It was a crushing victory won against superior odds, a triumph worthy of the Liberator himself, the last great battle in the liberation of the Americas from Spanish rule. The day after the battle Sucre invited Valdez, whom he admired, to lunch with his senior officers, and toasted him: 'I drink to one who, had he been born in America, would have been the best defender of its independence.' Sucre wrote to Bolívar, presenting him 'with the whole territory of Peru submitted to your authority after five months of campaigning.'

The victory was all the sweeter for being unexpected; Bolívar had doubted that Sucre's inferior forces could win any confrontation with the well-equipped Spanish in the mountains. He is said to have received the news in his luxurious villa of Magdalena outside the capital by throwing his sword and his uniform jacket to the ground and swearing never to use them again. To Sucre he wrote in his usual bombastic style: 'General Sucre is the father of Ayacucho; he is the redeemer of the Children of the Sun; he has broken the chains with which Pizarro bound the Empire of the Incas. Posterity will picture him with one foot on Pichincha and the other on Potosí, bearing in his arms the cradle of Manco Capac and comtemplating the chains broken by his sword.' He appointed Sucre Grand Marshal and Liberator of Peru, then ordered him to proceed to the heights of Upper Peru to put an end to the resistance of General Olañeta, who had refused to obey La Serna's order to surrender. This Sucre did with speed and effeciency; in March 1825 Olañeta was killed after a skirmish, and his army surrendered. Under the Spaniard Rodic the port of Callao held out for a year, the last enclave of Spanish military power on the continent; the garrison suffered appallingly from starvation before its surrender in January

1826. Bolívar was generous with the survivors and allowed them to depart to Spain.

The Peruvians begged Bolívar to stay on as dictator, to which he acceded. He invited Manuelita Sáenz – Mrs Thorne – to abandon her frustratingly staid life in Quito and set up home with him. She became a striking figure in Lima, riding around in tight red trousers, long boots, a black cape, and plumed hat, fencing with Bolívar's officers and presiding as hostess over social events at the Liberator's Residence. Her pet bear cub became famous in the city, as did her negro maid, a fine mimic of the country's top politicians.

Bolívar could now claim to rule one of the greatest empires of any military leader in history, some three million square miles in extent, the size of eastern and western Europe combined. He was on a par with Tamerlane, Genghis Khan, Alexander the Great and Augustus Caesar, far eclipsing Cortés, Pizarro and Clive of India in the scope of his conquests. The investment of personal energy and the distances covered in four army expeditions across well-nigh impassable mountain ranges – west to east across the Andes, back the other way, down the central Andes to Quito, and up again to Cerro de Pasco – were in the heroic mould. In ten years he personally had covered at least twenty thousand miles on horseback – most of it across extremely inhospitable land – and fought in about three hundred battles and skirmishes.

His challenge now was to lay the basis for effective and lasting constitutional government in his beloved South America; he wanted history to remember him as a statesman, as well as a military liberator; but still he entertained the dream of uniting all Spanish America under his rule. Nothing seemed impossible. On 31 December 1824, the British Foreign Secretary, George Canning – in the teeth of opposition from King George IV and the Duke of Wellington – recognised Gran Colombia.

The rebellions in the Spanish colonies had undeniably offered commercial opportunities of which Britain was eager to take advantage. As early as 1805 the trade value of English exports to America outside the United States was nearly £8 million; four years later this had more than doubled, to £18 million; and as late as 1822 Joseph Planta, Castlereagh's Under-Secretary at the Foreign Office, was brazen in his admission to Stratford Canning, British Minister at Madrid, that 'If I were to describe our line, I should say it would be one of as little overt action as possible, but one of securing to our subjects all the commercial advantages enjoyed by any other nation with the South American Provinces. For this object we shall insert a clause in one of our acts of Parliament, I believe the Navigation Act, to permit and protect this trade ... But we shall make as little fuss about it as we can, and reason and defend the matter with Spain as absolutely required from us under the circumstances.'

Castlereagh, so icily smug for so long, was ultimately frustrated in his attempts, at the Congress of Verona that same year, 1822, to keep the quarrelsome European Powers together; in August, in a fit of depression possibly induced by this failure, he cut his own throat, with a penknife. Like most liberals, Byron celebrated his passing:

> Oh Castlereagh! Thou art a patriot now;
> Cato died for his country, so didst thou;
> He perished rather than see Rome enslaved;
> Thou cutt'st thy throat that Britain may be saved!

And, even less reverently:

> Posterity will ne'er survey
> A nobler grave than this;
> Here lie the bones of Castlereagh:
> Stop, traveller, and ——.

The death of Castlereagh heralded a new phase of British policy towards the colonies striving for independence from Spain. As we have seen, the first had been marked by the encouragement given Miranda by a few far-sighted men – Nicholas Vansittart, Lord Melville, the retired Governor Thomas Pownall – and their advocacy of his cause against Pitt's hesitancy. The second phase was the Grenville administration's support for vigorous intervention, albeit of a blatantly imperialistic nature, support which ended all too abruptly with the fall of that ministry. Castlereagh's was the third phase, ultra-cautious and cynically trimmed to the realities of the situation as he saw them: ready to give verbal encouragement and take full commercial advantage of the opportunities offered by the Latin Americans' struggles, even to mediate in their disputes with Spain – but ever reluctant to recognise their independence or take any action likely to have an adverse effect on the chimera of European peace he was pursuing in the Grand Alliance. Despite the contribution to their cause made by British volunteers, particularly after the end of the Napoleonic Wars, patriot leaders like Bolívar became increasingly irritated by the pantomime.

The fourth phase, which opened out after Castlereagh's suicide, not only ensured that Britain was to be the main beneficiary of the collapse of the Spanish Empire – to the extent that, economically at least, she was effectively Spain's replacement in Latin America for several decades – but also displayed her in a new and flattering light. If the first three phases can be summed up as the enlightened caution of Pitt, the liberal imperialism of Grenville and the cynical conservatism of Castlereagh, the fourth featured the idealistic realism of Canning.

George Canning, Castlereagh's successor at the Foreign Office and as leader of the House of Commons, was appointed as the last, reforming hope of Lord Liverpool's stodgily conservative administration, increasingly buffeted by near-revolutionary gales. A Whig, a Jacobin even, in his youth, he entered Parliament in 1793 as a supporter of Pitt, in part through Pitt's personal influence, in part because of his revulsion at the turn taken by the French Revolution – and in part because he did not fit the Whig mould. His father belonged to an originally English family which had been Irish for a hundred and fifty years, was disowned and disinherited at the time of his marriage, and died when Canning was just a year old; his mother, destitute, went on the stage. His father's younger brother, Stratford Canning, took charge of him and sent him to Eton and Oxford, and it was at his house that the young George met such stars in the Whig firmament as Charles James Fox and Richard Sheridan. His background and his change of political allegiance alike engendered suspicion, and his modest means were equally a hindrance to the achievement of high office, but he was a rebel within rather than against the Establishment, and his intellectual abilities and superb oratory, his passion and idealism – even his passing competence as a poet in this Age of Poetry – combined with his position as Pitt's chief confidant to make him more influential than the jobs he held would suggest.

After Grenville's fall he became Foreign Secretary, to the horror of his stuffier detractors. 'We shall see', said Sydney Smith, 'if a nation is to be saved by schoolboy jokes and doggerel rhymes, by affronting petulance and the tones and gestures of Mr Pitt. When [Canning] is jocular he is strong, when he is serious he is like Samson in a wig.' The romantic in Canning was attracted to Miranda's wild schemes; he received him at the Foreign Office in January 1808, and described his ideas as 'certainly very inviting'. As Foreign Secretary he often found himself at odds with Castlereagh, the Secretary of State for War in the Duke of Portland's administration, and the fiasco of the Walcheren Expedition, largely

Castlereagh's brain-child, provoked him to such acerbity – he exclaimed, on being presented with Castlereagh's long justification of the expedition, 'I had rather fight than read it, by God!' – that in September 1810 Castlereagh challenged him to a duel. Canning was wounded in the thigh, and both men were forced from office. Castlereagh soon returned under the conservative Lord Liverpool, but it was many years before Canning again held a post of any significance.

Byron had his fun with Canning, as later with Castlereagh, on the occasion of his falling-out with the radical politician Sir Francis Burdett:

> So Canning and Burdett have been quarrelling: if I mistake not, the last time of their single combats, each was shot in the thigh by his Antagonist; and their correspondence might be headed thus, by any wicked wag:
>
> > BRAVE champions! go on with the farce!
> > Reversing the spot where you bled;
> > Last time both were shot in the —;
> > Now (damn you!) get knock'd on the head!

John Wilson Croker, corrupt Admiralty secretary and persecutor of Admiral Lord Cochrane, wrote of Canning: 'His genius is a bright flame. It is liable to every gust of wind and every change of weather; it flares and it flickers, and it blazes, now climbing the heavens, now stifled in its own smoke, and is of no use but to raise the wonder of distant spectators, and to warm the very narrow circle that immediately surrounds it.'

Canning may have been Castlereagh's successor, but he hated his late opponent's policy involving the Grand Alliance, the endless and seemingly futile mediation between absolutist monarchies, and moved quickly to disown it. His view was that a system of 'periodical meetings of the four great Powers, with a view to the general concerns of Europe [was a] very questionable policy ... it will necessarily involve us deeply in all the politics of the Continent, whereas our true policy has always been not to interfere except in great emergencies, and then with a commanding force.' Uninhibited about provoking the Continental Powers, he had no qualms about altering Britain's stance *vis-à-vis* the new Latin American states, for which (as we have seen) his sympathy was instinctive and of long standing; by November 1822 he had already drawn up a list of consuls to be appointed to them – implicit recognition of their independence.

But this was no mere expression of romantic idealism: the failure of

Castlereagh's policy had by now become only too apparent, as France made preparations to invade Spain with the ostensible aim of rescuing King Ferdinand from the liberals who held him prisoner. It could be argued that action was necessary to prevent France taking over the former Spanish Empire; in fact, however, as Canning was shrewd enough to realise, a far greater threat to British commercial interests in these nascent republics was posed by the United States, manifestly all too ready to take advantage of the vacuum left by Spain's collapse and Britain's vacillations under Castlereagh by seeking to exert her influence and impose her own 'protectorate' south of her borders.

The Atlantic was a four-power lake, the remorseless disintegration of the Spanish Empire during the last quarter of the eighteenth century and the first of the nineteenth having set France, Britain and the United States scrambling to take her place. The French had tried once already, but their main preoccupation was the Continent, where their most recent invasion of Spain had exposed their limitations; their Russian backers offered them worm-infested hulks to carry their forces across the Atlantic. The British under Castlereagh had failed to seize the opportunities which presented themselves. The United States, herself a new nation feeling her way during the first part of this period, was initially reluctant to become involved beyond her borders; towards the end of the period that was no longer the case.

John Quincy Adams, as American Minister in London, had found Castlereagh 'cold, but not absolutely repulsive'. Later, as Secretary of State, he resisted the attempts of his rival Henry Clay to secure recognition for the new Latin American republics, suggesting to Castlereagh merely that Britain and the United States should do so simultaneously. But the American perspective gradually changed, her leaders became increasingly impatient with Castlereagh's procrastination, and early in 1822 she began to recognise the South American republics. Adams wrote advising the American Ambassador in London to soothe nervous British sensibilities: 'We trust it will not be considered, even by the British Cabinet, a rash and hasty measure at this time. Should the subject be mentioned to you ... you will remark that it was not understood or intended as a change of policy on the part of the United States, nor adopted with any desire of turning it to the account of our own interests. Possibly no one of the proposed diplomatic missions may be sent before the next session of Congress.'

The new policy slant arising from Canning's arrival at the Foreign

Office caused a warming of American attitudes to Britain, as reported by Canning's cousin Stratford (son of that benevolent uncle), at the time Britain's Ambassador to the United States: 'The course which you have taken in the great politics of Europe, has had the effect of making the English almost popular ... The improved tone of public feeling is very perceptible, and even Adams has caught something of the soft infection ... On the whole I question whether for a long time there has been so favourable an opportunity – as far as general disposition and good will are concerned – to bring the two countries nearer together.'

In August 1823 Canning had outlined to the Americans, with notable succinctness, Britain's new policy:

1   We conceive the recovery of her colonies by Spain to be hopeless.
2   We conceive the question of the recognition of them as Independent States, to be one of time and circumstance.
3   We are, however, by no means disposed to throw any impediment in the way of an arrangement between them, and the mother country, by amicable negotiation.
4   We aim not at the possession of any portion of them ourselves.
5   We could not see any portion of them transferred to any other power with indifference.

The sting was in the tail: point 5, ostensibly directed towards the French, was also a clear warning to the United States not to rush in. Nevertheless, he was soon dramatically proclaiming that 'The force of blood again prevails, and the daughter and the mother stand together against the world.'

Adams, however, viscerally anti-British and still sceptical about Britain's intentions, had decided that, 'the force of blood' notwithstanding, the daughter would steal a march on the mother: on 23 December 1823 he had promulgated the Monroe Doctrine, which presented Canning with a *fait accompli* that spelled the unravelling of his whole diplomatic strategy. He had alienated the Continental Powers; he had failed to recognise the new South American republics officially; and now the United States had declared South America off-limits to any European Power – including Britain.

Canning's counter-stroke was characteristically vigorous. He withdrew from joint Anglo-American protests against Russia's closure of the Bering Straits and her attempts to colonise the north-western coast of North America. He also broke off boundary negotiations regarding the

North-West Territories. At the same time, he disingenuously informed the European Powers that the Monroe Doctrine was a product of British diplomacy – something they were only to eager to believe as the Continental alliance began to fall apart, the French agreeing not to use force in pursuit of their claims in Latin America, the Austrians retreating into sulks, and the Russians impotently voicing their indignation. Canning also hastily despatched three 'commissions', to Mexico, Colombia and Buenos Aires, with a view to preparing for their imminent official recognition. All three reported favourably to London but it was the outstandingly able Woodbine Parish, leader of the Buenos Aires commission, who decisively disclosed the extent of the continent's commercial potential for Britain. The extensive import-export trade of Buenos Aires was already effectively in British hands; nearly forty British companies were operating there; nearly a quarter of all funds were raised in London, and half the public debt was serviced there. Canning urged the King and Parliament to negotiate a commercial treaty which 'would amount to diplomatic recognition of the state with which it had been concluded', and urged the die-hard cabinet reactionaries, led by the Duke of Wellington, to officially recognise Mexico and Colombia as well:

> The great practical question ... for us seems to be how, in the event of an actual incorporation of the resources of Spain with those of France, such an accession to the power of France can best be counteracted. I have no hesitation in saying this must be by a separation of the resources of Spanish America from those of Spain; and it is (at least in this point of view) a fortunate circumstance that this state of things has already taken place; and that we are in a situation to avail ourselves of it.

As previously noted, in December 1824, to his delight, Canning achieved his objective. 'The deed is done,' he declared, 'the nail is driven, Spanish America is free; and if we do not mismanage our affairs sadly, she is English.'

Princess Lieven, wife of the Russian Ambassador in London, reported the excitement that resulted: 'You cannot imagine how mad everyone here has gone over the companies in South America ... Everybody, from the lady to the footman, is risking pin-money or wages in these enterprises. Huge fortunes have been made in a week. Shares in the gold-mines of Real del Monte, bought at £70, were sold, a week later, for £1350. These sudden fortunes, and the passion for speculation, remind one of the Mississippi Bank in the time of the Regency.' Loans worth about £20 million altogether were extended; mining companies with a total capital of £14 million were set up. Needless to say, the bubble soon collapsed. Yet Canning remained exultant:

> The thing is so done ... The Yankees will shout in triumph; but it is they who lose most by our decision. The great danger of the time – a danger which the policy of the European System would have fostered – was a division of the world into European and American, republican and Monarchical; a league of worn-out governments, on the one hand, and of youthful and stirring nations, with the United States at their head, on the other. We slip in between; and plant ourselves in Mexico. The United States have gotten the start of us in vain; and we link once more America to Europe. Six months more – and the mischief would have been done.

Canning displayed his accustomed brilliance in refraining from active interference in Latin American affairs, on the basis that

> the conservation of monarchy in any portion of South America will tend to break the shock of that inevitable divorce by which the New World is about to be divided from the Old ... But as to putting it forward, as a project or proposition of ours, that is out of the question. Monarchy in Mexico, and monarchy in Brazil, would cure the evils of universal democracy, and prevent the drawing of the line which I almost dread – America versus Europe. The United States, naturally enough, aim at this division and cherish the democracy which leads to it.

After the barren, wasted years of Castlereagh, Canning had formulated a policy of vision which secured the undying gratitude of the Latin American states and, more importantly, frustrated the early stirrings of imperial pretensions on the part of the United States.

16

Potosí

As the year 1825 opened, nothing seemed impossible for Bolívar and his dreams – but there were problems. Sucre heeded the passionate desire of the overwhelmingly Indian population of Upper Peru for independence from the Audiencia of Buenos Aires – now independent Argentina – to which it was nominally subject and on 9 February proclaimed its self-government. Bolívar was initially incensed with his favourite, as this action had the potential to anger both the Argentinians and the Peruvians, of which viceroyalty Upper Peru had formed a part until 1776. But time mellowed him, and in May he was writing paternally to Sucre, who had expressed a desire to relinquish his powers: 'My dear general, fulfil your destiny, yield to the good fortune that courts you ... You are capable of everything and should not hesitate to let yourself be drawn by fortune ... Remember that you have in me a living father who will always rejoice in the glory of his son.'

On 15 April Bolívar had set out from Lima with a large party of his most trusted cronies which included O'Leary and even his old tutor, Simón Rodriguez, on a triumphal progress into the mountains of his new dominion, the ancient empire of the Incas. Manuelita, to her fury, was left behind. The rumours of his mixed blood may have caused the upper classes of Lima to refer to him sneeringly as 'El Sambo', but to the Indians he seemed as white and aristocratic as any Spaniard. Despite this he was their hero, their Liberator, greeted everywhere with delirium. Traditionally this sort of welcome was designed to placate conquerors or figures of authority and stave off punishment and pillage; this time the people were undoubtedly expressing genuine relief, welcoming a conqueror who exacted no vengeance. On 25 June, two months after leaving Lima, Bolívar's procession at last reached Cuzco, at the end of its spectacular valley ten thousand feet up in the cordillera, where another

welcome awaited him. O'Leary describes it: 'From the windows and balconies there fell a rain of flowers and laurel crowns which the delicate
hands of pretty Cuzcan girls threw as the cavalcade passed by, along with
medallions from the people. As in Arequipa, the city fathers presented
him with a horse with a bridle and a saddle of gold and the keys of the
city made from the same metal. After listening to a solemn Te Deum
which was celebrated in the cathedral, he went to the municipal palace,
where the principal ladies of the city presented him with a civic crown
of diamonds and pearls.' Here in Cuzco he issued a decree which pleased
and surprised millions of his subjects, but appalled the old ruling classes
of Lima.

Deep in the valleys and chasms of the Andean cordillera, the tropical
climate renders cultivation impossible; on the uplands the intensity of
the sun, cold nights and the thin atmosphere make life untenable for
farmers and crops alike. The Incas solved the problem by terracing the
steep valley sides and creating a network of water channels and paths;
this system was necessarily a communal effort, founded on strict principles of hierarchy and co-operation. Onto this the Spanish had easily
grafted their own ruthlessly hierarchical colonial controls using Indian
overseers – *caciques* – to impose what amounted to slavery upon the
Indians. Indian forced labour was also used to work the gold, silver and
tin mines. The leaves of the coca plant were habitually chewed in South
America to ease hunger and counter exhaustion; the Spanish encouraged
its use, and its extensive cultivation in the deep tropical valleys by Indian
labourers, who died in their thousands.

Bolívar's decree announced the abolition of the hated overseers, the
caciques; all labourers were to be paid in cash, at fair rates established by
the market, rather than in kind; all forced labour was banned; and all
employment was to be freely and fairly contracted. He announced a programme of land reform, under which Indian farmers were to assume
possession of the land they cultivated and all communal land was to be
divided among landless peasants. Although in practice many of his
reforms were trampled upon in later years, they earned Bolívar the
undying loyalty of most Indians, to whom he became a godlike figure,
an Inca chief reincarnate.

While he was in Cuzco Bolívar indulged in more dalliance – this time
with the most formidable woman in the city: Francisca Zubiaga de
Gamarra, wife of the Prefect of Cuzco (later a President of Peru), was
nicknamed La Mariscala – the Marshaless – for her autocratic and

commanding manner. Deprived of affection in her youth, she had trained as a nun; she had a large nose and wide but expressive eyes set in a broad face beneath long, thick, dark chestnut hair; she was large-boned and masculine, her voice hard and imperious, her tone curt and dry. 'I have to supplement the weakness of my sex by making use of men,' she confided to a friend, and she told a young officer courting her: 'Be gone, with your sighs, your sentimental words and your romances to little girls. I am vulnerable only to the sighs of the cannon, to the words of congress and to the applause and acclamation of the people as I pass through the streets.'

Their shared passion for politics gave Bolívar and La Mariscala much to talk about, but she was not really his type and their liaison was brief, even by his standards. She was so enraged when he terminated the affair that she revealed the details to her husband, who subsequently joined the aristocrats of Lima as a sworn and powerful enemy of Bolívar.

The Liberator of five countries was now offered the chance of even greater glory: in a scene reminiscent of the Temptation he was called up to a high mountain, and a vaster territory still was laid at his feet. He learned that Brazil, at this time under the control of its newly independent emperor Dom Pedro I, had taken advantage of the anarchic conditions prevailing in Argentina to occupy the so-called Banda Oriental, the eastern shore of the Rió de la Plata (the area which today is Uruguay), and was threatening to invade upper Argentina, the region which dominated two rivers which fed into the Plate estuary, the Paraná and the Paraguay. What was left of the government in Buenos Aires sent a mission to seek the Liberator's help in resisting Brazil's ambitions and influence, seen as monarchical, aristocratic, and against the spirit of Bolívar's democratic and reformist aims. He was on the verge, it seemed, of realising his ultimate dream – annexing Argentina to his dominions. More momentous still, the entire continent appeared to be on the brink of war, between Portuguese-speaking Brazil and the rest of (Spanish-speaking) America. Bolívar wrote to Santander seeking authorisation to commit his troops to the Argentinian cause: 'Caesar in Gaul threatened Rome, and I in Upper Peru threaten all the conspirators of America and, consequently, can save all its republics. If I lose my position in the south the conquest of Peru is worthless and the Emperor of Brazil will devour the River Plate and Upper Peru.' Santander must have thought him mad.

With Spain defeated, it seemed Bolívar had found another enemy, in

Brazil's imperial pretensions. But even on the top of the mountain, he was shrewd enough to suggest an alliance of neutrality with the British, whom he rightly suspected of backing Brazilian expansionism.

In February, Bolívar had been annoyed by Sucre's proclamation of independence for Upper Peru; by May he had accepted it; now, on 19 August 1825, on the deserted shore of Lake Titicaca, Bolívar met his brilliant young protégé, and the two rode together into the city of La Paz, dramatically sited in a canyon between the high plateaux and the snowfields of the mountain range. There Bolívar assented to the decision of Upper Peru's congress that the new independent state should be called after himself: Bolivia. Sucre had chosen a shrewd way of reconciling the Liberator to his own insubordinate violation of orders. Bolívar accepted the accolade, but refused the leadership of Bolivia, conferring it instead on Sucre.

After a month in La Paz Bolívar resumed his journey to that most fabulous of cities in all Spanish America after the legendary El Dorado – Potosí, whose silver had provided the wealth which had brought decadence and decline to the Spanish Empire. Here another splendid welcome awaited him, as Indians danced around him and their children were lowered from a giant triumphal arch in a cloud of smoke to rain flowers upon him, and fireworks exploded. Here too he experienced an almost mystical apotheosis, and made one of his most well-known speeches: 'How great must be our joy at seeing so many millions of men regain their rights through perseverance and effort. As for me, with my feet on this mountain of silver called Potosí, whose enormously rich veins were for three hundred years the treasury of Spain, I regard this opulence as nothing when I compare it with the glory of having carried the standard of freedom victoriously from the burning shores of the Orinoco to fix it here, on the peak of this mountain, whose breast is the wonder and the envy of the universe.' It was striking that at this particular moment it was his role as liberator and revolutionary he chose to highlight, rather than that of continental dictator, much less emperor. There can be little doubt that at times he saw himself as the indispensable sole guarantor of Latin America's freedom: 'My destiny decreed that a huge part of the world took advantage of my struggles to break their chains', he wrote. He toyed with the idea of proclaiming himself 'Inca' like the ill-fated Tupac Amaru, and of waging a civil war against privilege across the continent. Although it is marked against him that he did not initiate any genuine social and economic revolution, it is in fact to his credit, since the old 'elites' were still so powerful that the cost in upheaval and bloodshed would have been as great as the likelihood of failure, and he was justified in sparing his people this. Instead he came down off the mountain, proclaiming the ideals of freedom and constitutional rule which he everywhere sought to establish. He had wrestled with the dark side of his own nature, where megalomania and ruthlessness sometimes took control, and the passion for freedom and rationalism had won. Potosí was a defining moment in his greatness.

Bolívar was just forty-two, impelled still by his hunger for glory and political liberty. Now new tasks and lands beckoned. The huge expanse of Argentina lay thousands of feet below him, to the south. At Potosí he received General Alvear, the senior Argentinian leader seeking his intercession against Brazil, who told him that war between Argentina and Brazil was inevitable. Simultaneously, he learned that Brazilian troops had already moved to occupy a province of Bolivia. Outraged, he threatened war, and wrote again to Santander begging for authorisation to go to Argentina's aid, to be told it was not legally possible for Colombian troops to be used for such a purpose. To Bolívar's angry declaration that he would march forward with Peruvian troops instead, Santander's pedantic response was that, as President of Colombia, he would require authorisation from the Colombian Congress to do so.

The Liberator showed no signs of paying any attention, but prepared in high good humour to march down into Argentina. 'His appearance had lost its imposing look of a warrier. He exuded amiability and even in his clothing there were differences. He had changed his military boots for fine shoes and had shaved his moustache.' He was off on another great adventure.

Before leaving he wrote to Manuelita Sáenz, neglected for the best part of a year in Lima, inviting her to join him. Her reply was a series of contradictions: 'I am very good and very ill. Long absences extinguish love and stimulate even greater passions. The little love you extend to me has been killed by long separation. I have conserved my passion for you, to preserve my well-being and my health, and it exists and will exist as long as Manuela lives. I leave on December 1st (and I go because you called me). But don't tell me afterwards to return to Quito, because I had rather die than go there in shame.' To her husband Dr Thorne she wrote brutally:

Leave me, my beloved Englishman. Let us do something else: in heaven let us marry again, but on earth not. Do you think this argument a bad one? Then you must be very discontented. In the celestial kingdom we will spend an angelic life in full spirituality (because as a man you are heavy). There, all will be English-style, because such a monotonous life is perfectly suited to your nation (in love, I say, because as for the rest, who is more able in commerce or shipping?).

[The English] prefer love without pleasure; conversation without grace, and walking slowly; greeting with reverence; getting up and sitting down with care; conversation without laughter. These are divine formalities, but for me, a wretched mortal who laughs even at myself, as well as at you and these English seriousnesses, how badly things would go in heaven!

Manuelita was an irrepressible spirit; she was too much like Bolívar for him to fall out of love with her, or to be able to stand her all the time. 'Do something with her, would you?' he told a subordinate. 'She's such an idiot. You know her as well as I do.'

As he was on his way to La Plata, Bolívar learned that, following Brazil's attempts to annex the Banda Oriental, Argentina had declared war on her; and that Bernardino Rivadavia, the leader of the aristocratic party in Argentina, had been elected head of its government. Rivadavia moved swiftly, summoning the British minister in Buenos Aires, Woodbine Parish, to urge his government to restrain the Brazilians. If that did not happen, Rivadavia warned Parish, Bolívar would widen the war into a general one aimed at spreading republicanism and overthrowing aristocratic and monarchical forms of government, including the British empire. Parish was astute enough to inform the British Foreign Secretary, George Canning, that he considered these arguments purely 'personal resentments' towards Bolívar. The British informed the Argentinians that Brazil would be prepared to withdraw from the Banda Oriental if the region were to be established as an independent buffer state – an idea suggested by the British; Rivadavia grudgingly agreed, provided the new state, Uruguay, was guaranteed by Britain.

17

The Unravelling

War between Argentina and Brazil having been thus averted, Bolívar's mission was left hanging; then came news of tumultuous events in Colombia: the two parts of the country, the former New Granada and Venezuela, were breaking apart, and civil war threatened. Páez, ruling in Venezuela, begged him to return: 'The situation in this country is very similar to that of France when Napoleon was away in Egypt and was recalled by the leaders of the revolution who were convinced that a government which had fallen into the hands of the rabble would not survive; and you are in a position to say what that great man said then, "The conspirators endanger the existence of the nation; let us save it."'

Bolívar wrote haughtily back: 'Colombia is not France, nor I, Napoleon ... The title of Liberator is superior to every other that human pride has conceived; it is unthinkable that I should degrade it.' His beloved sister, Maria Antonia, had already warned him:

I shall rejoice on the day that you come here with troops ... This land has grave need for your presence. There are a thousand abuses and political factions; but the moment you arrive all will disappear. Now they are sending a commission to you to propose a crown. Receive it as the infamous proposition deserves; and try, without resorting to the methods of Europe, to bring an end to this miserable existence at the hands of factions. Say always, as you said in Cumaná in 1814, that you 'will be Liberator or dead.' That is your true title, and one which has elevated you above other great men and which will preserve for you the glories you have attained at the cost of so many sacrifices. Detest all who propose a crown to you, for that will procure your ruin. Remember Bonaparte and Itúrbide and the many others you are not ignorant of. I am well satisfied with your mode of thought and I believe you incapable of such things;

but I can do no less than declare to you the sentiments of my heart out of the interest I have in your happiness ... Will you come quickly? How shall I prepare for you and for the troops you will bring? Here there is nothing, nothing ... shall I prepare a house, and which shall it be – mine, yours or another?'

Bolívar returned swiftly to the Bolivian capital, Chuquisaca (later renamed Sucre), to another tremendous reception, and copious gifts, which included a sword with a scabbard inset with 1,433 diamonds and a hilt of gold. A month later four days' hard riding took him down to Tacna and the coast and he sailed for Lima, arriving there in February 1826. He settled down again in splendour, quarrelling savagely with Manuelita.

Before he returned to Colombia, Bolívar wanted to set the seal on the republics he and Sucre had created in Peru and Bolivia. The constitution he drew up for Bolivia, which was also the model for Peru, represented the last refinement of his political thinking, and he even toyed with the idea of using it for a confederation of all the liberated territories. He outlined his idea to Santander, which was a mistake, for his proposal included himself as president-for-life of any such confederation – with Sucre, not Santander, as his vice-president and anointed successor. Overnight Santander, who had always disliked Bolívar, was turned from political rival into bitter enemy. Bolívar certainly preferred the valiant young Sucre as a man, but reasoned also that, respected as he was in Bolivia, Peru and Ecuador as one of their liberators, he would be the more capable to binding those countries to the confederation.

The constitution prepared for Bolivia and, in slightly modified form, for Peru, contained many of Bolívar's old ideas – which had already been rejected by the congresses of Angostura and Cúcuta. It was based on an elected assembly drawn from men of property, a powerful president-for-life around whom the system would revolve, and a college of 'censors' composed of the great and the good – a kind of supreme court. The idea of a president-for-life, controversial and apparently illiberal, in fact represented a compromise between the radicalism of eighteenth-century liberals who sought to dispense altogether with a powerful executive – with disastrous results wherever the experiment had been tried, as in Venezuela's first republic and in Argentina, leading to anarchy, civil war and, usually, the reimposition of an iron hand – and the old Bourbon concept of absolute monarchy.

As Bolívar put it: 'The President of the Republic in our constitution will be like the sun which, firmly in the centre, gives life to the universe. The supreme authority must be permanent because in non-hereditary systems one needs, more than in others, a fixed point around which circle the magistrates and citizens, men and things. For a people to be free it must have a strong government which possesses sufficient means to free them from popular anarchy and the abuse of the powerful. The savage vastness of this continent by itself rules out monarchy; deserts conduce to independence [of spirit].' It was a formulation of great good sense, around a probably indefensible institution.

Bolívar was not always consistent in his approach to this subject. In a document of March 1825 addressed from Captain Thomas Maling to Viscount Melville, the First Lord of the Admiralty, he is reported thus:

'You may say I have ever been an enemy to monarchies upon general principles; on the contrary, I think it essential to the respectability and well being of new nations, and if any proposal ever comes from the British Cabinet for the establishment of a regular government, that is, of a monarchy or monarchies in the New World, they will find in me a steady and firm promoter of their views, perfectly ready to uphold the sovereign England may propose to place and support upon the throne.

'I know it has been said of me I wish to be a King, but it is not so. I would not accept the Crown for myself, for when I see this country made happy under a good and firm government, I shall again retire into private life ...

'The title of King would perhaps not be popular at first in South America, and therefore it might be as well to meet the prejudice by assuming that of 'Inca' which the Indians are so much attached to. This enslaved and miserable country has hitherto only heard the name of King coupled with its miseries, and Spanish cruelties ... Democracy has its charms for the people, and in theory it appears plausible to have a free government which shall exclude all hereditary distinctions, but England is again our example; how infinitely more respectable your nation is, governed by its King, Lords and Commons, than that which prides itself upon an equality but with little temptation to exertion for the benefit of the state; indeed, I question much whether the present situation will continue very long in the United States ... If we are to have a new government, let it be modelled on yours ...'

This may have been no more than diplomacy intended to ingratiate himself with the British; or it may have represented a genuine hankering after British-style constitutional monarchy, which he clearly understood. In the senate proposed for Bolivia and Peru he sought to enshrine the hereditary principle, nominating a kind of House of Lords, but would not entertain the idea of hereditary monarchy, after the continent's terrible experience of tyranny under the worthless despots of Madrid. He seems not to have foreseen that a presidency-for-life was equally capable to degenerating into tyranny, and that the idea was a recipe for dictatorship of the worst sort, believing rather that it would reassure those who equated republicanism with anarchy. Enshrining the concepts of legislative power and the censors in the constitution would, he thought, ensure sufficient checks to control the presidency.

Where Bolívar was reformist – and indeed almost revolutionary, to the extent of upsetting the very creole aristocracy and ruling class from which he came and which had backed him – was in his concept of equality and rights. As has been seen, he had secured the liberation of Venezuela by harnessing against the creole aristocracy the very forces that had been the bulwark of the monarchy – the dispossessed, the poor, the llaneros, the blacks, the slaves and the freemen, the Indians and the mulattos. In Cuzco again he had sought to emancipate the wretched Indian masses, providing them with elementary rights and property, such as even a president-for-life would, under his proposed constitution, have no power to override.

His belief in the rights of the individual derived in part from his concept of natural rights, originating with Rousseau, as interpreted by his old tutor, Simón Rodriguez (who was appointed minister of education in Bolivia, but proved a disaster, appearing naked in class as an extension of his theories of natural education); in part from his natural affinity with the dispossessed; and in part, too, because across the continent these had been the people who supported him, fought for him, achieved his revolution, and welcomed him.

Bolívar's position on these matters was unequivocal. He wrote: 'I am setting up a constitution ... which revokes the slavery of the masses and all privileges.' And again: 'I have kept intact the law of laws: equality [of rights before the law – not economic equality]. Without it all guarantees perish, as do all rights. We must sacrifice everything for this.' His sometime lieutenant, Peru de Lacroix, explains his thinking in a passage which is worth quoting at length:

> I heard him repeat several times that the state of slavery in which the people find themselves must be done away with; as must the fact that they were beneath the yoke not only of the mayors and the parish priests but

of the two or three magnates in each parish. In the cities it was the same, with the difference that there are many more masters because there are many more clerics and doctors.

Freedom and guarantees were only for these men and for the rich, and not for the people, whose slavery is worse than that even of the Indies; that slaves remained beneath the constitution of Cúcuta and slaves would remain under the most liberal of constitutions; that in Colombia there was an aristocracy of rank, work and riches equivalent, through its pretensions, influence and weight upon the people, to the most despotic aristocracy of titles and birth in Europe. That in that aristocracy there were also clerics, doctors, lawyers, soldiers and demagogues.

Because even if they talk of freedom and guarantees, these apply only to those who want them and not to the people who, they believe, must continue under the oppression. They want equality to raise themselves and become equal to the most powerful but not to level themselves with individuals from the inferior classes of society. These they want always to consider as servants, in spite of their pretensions at demagoguery and liberalism.

In these very radical views – certainly in his scorn for the middle classes – Bolívar can be regarded as the continent's foremost revolutionary. Even today in Latin America, where in all too many countries the masses remain second-class citizens, they align him on the centre-left of the political spectrum. Yet the equality he preached was never of a Marxist, economic kind: he was talking about rights and freedoms, not money or property. It was small wonder that Bolívar became a hero of the great mass of ordinary Latin Americans, worshipped with almost godlike veneration throughout the continent. He was always an élitist, believing the ignorance of the masses made them incapable of governing themselves. But their ignorance did not mean that they lacked personal rights or that they should be condemned to slavery: indeed, one of the prime purposes of government was, or should be, to protect those rights. His was a view at least as enlightened as those of radical English and French social reformers of the time.

The constitution Bolívar drew up for Bolivia – which included civil liberty, freedom of speech, the press, work and movement, and equality before the law, as well as the abolition of slavery and provision for due process of law and trial by jury – was described as the most liberal constitution in the world and 'the most notable philosophic-political speculation of South American history.' From Lima it was carried to Chuquisaca across 1,800 miles of Andean trails in nineteen days by two

Englishmen, Colonel Ferguson and Bedford Wilson. There it was adopted, and Sucre was elected president (although, self-deprecatingly, he insisted on a two-year term only).

Bolívar's second great venture into statecraft was to convene the Congress of Panamá, which met in June 1826. An audacious attempt at continental co-operation intended to include the resolution of disputes and joint declarations of support for independence and democracy by Latin American states – but never, as some alleged, an attempt to unify them into one state, which Bolívar knew to be impossible – it was already failing in its aims by the time it met. Argentina refused to attend, both because of the loss of Bolivia, the former Upper Peru, and because she objected to the proposal to support the Monroe Doctrine promulgated by the United States following the President's declaration of December 1823. Chile also declined. Fatuously, Brazil replied that she would only attend a congress that was neutral as between Latin America and the Spanish Empire. Attendance at the Congress was thus reduced to Colombia, Peru, Central America and (rather doubtfully) Mexico.

Both the United States and Britain were invited to attend. Although Bolívar had received a gold medallion and a lock of Washington's hair from the first president's adopted son, together with a letter from Lafayette, the Americans, for internal reasons, failed to send a delegate. The Congress largely neutralised Bolívar's ambitious plan for joint Latin American armed forces, but it did adopt six basic principles of collaboration – a pledge to neutrality and coexistence among the members; adoption of the Monroe Doctrine; acceptance of international arbitration in disputes between member states; the abolition of slavery; the recognition of the national sovereignty of member states; and guarantees of these principles – which continue to govern relations between Latin American states today, and have proved remarkably effective in the composition of differences arising between them. However, largely owing to Mexican objections, there was no adoption of or commitment to common democratic and republican goals.

The Congress of Panamá was a failure from Bolívar's point of view, since it represented only half the eligible countries, and failed to embrace all his objectives. He defended the attempt, saying it set a marker for the future; but it did more than that. Subtly it exposed the new reality the nascent Latin American countries were about to face: with the failure of Napoleon to establish a foothold on the continent and the defeat of the

Spanish Empire, only two nations were left to contend in the power vacuum – Britain and the United States. Britain had failed to take advantage of the almost universal goodwill prevailing towards her among Latin America's new masters, of the view of most of them that she had the combination of freedoms and stability that they sought to emulate. Until Canning's last period in office British policy towards Latin America had veered ineptly between neglect coupled with opportunism and Beresford's apparent attempt at colonisation. Nevertheless, Bolívar continued to look on Britain as an exemplar; he favoured British subjects in South America enjoying the same rights as its citizens, hoped that Britain would take Spanish America under her wing – rather as independent republics are part of today's British Commonwealth. After an interview with Bolívar, C.M. Ricketts, Britain's representative in Lima, wrote to George Canning that:

> His Excellency ... could not withhold the expression of his anxious hope that Great Britain would not be a silent observer of the discussions which would arise in the Congress, since he was satisfied that they could not terminate in any practical good unless aided by your judicious and impartial counsels. The several states required to be upheld by the power and influence of Great Britain, without which no security could be expected, no consistency preserved, and no social compact maintained. All would be alike subjected to destruction by disputes with each other and by internal anarchy. Different interests were already propelling them; wars which might have been prevented unfortunately raged ... The respective classes of inhabitants began to feel that they had equal rights, and as the coloured population so far exceeded the white, the safety of the latter was threatened.
>
> Under the protection of Great Britain, the South American States would learn the measures most advisable to adopt for the general preservation and tranquility ...

Bolívar's passion for Britain was not merely sentimental. He saw Britain as the hub of the civilised world against the dark forces of the Holy Alliance of reactionary nations in Europe led by Metternich. But he may also have understood the dangers represented by President Monroe's historic speech before the American Congress on 2 December 1823:

> ... the occasion has been judged proper for asserting as a principle in which the rights and interests of the United States are involved, that the American continents, by the free and independent condition which they

have assumed and maintained, are henceforth not to be considered as subject for future colonization by any European powers ... We owe it, therefore, to candour, and the amicable relations existing between the United States and those powers, to declare that we should consider any attempt on their part to extend their system to any portion of this hemisphere as dangerous to our peace and safety. With the existing colonies or dependencies of any European power we have not interfered and shall not interfere ...

Bolívar had opposed inviting the United States to the Panamá congress, but was overriden by Santander. The Monroe Doctrine was ostensibly aimed at Russia's designs in Alaska, but its formulator, John Quincy Adams, was just as determined that Britain should be denied any chance of occupying Cuba and Puerto Rico, a possibility after Spain's cession of Florida to the United States in 1819. By 1823 America had her own ambitions regarding Cuba, which the Spanish continued to occupy and use as a base for raids on their former colonies. Mexico and Colombia both had plans to attack the island; the United States, with her own designs for annexation, cynically preferred that it should remain in Spanish hands, thus providing her with the excuse to 'liberate' it at some future date, and even threatened war with Britain should the latter back Bolívar's designs. Canning was not slow to exploit the irritation this caused in Latin America; as he wrote to the British Ambassador in Washington, 'The avowed pretension of the United States, to put themselves at the head of the confederacy of all the Americas, and to sway that confederacy against Europe (Great Britain included), is not a pretension identified with our interests, or one that we can countenance or tolerate. It is, however, a pretension which there is no use in contesting in the abstract; but we must not say anything, that seems to admit the principle.' In the run-up to the Congress of Panamá, the United States consistently sought to impose her economic hegemony on the hemisphere, arguing that no American nation should grant to any foreign power any favourable commercial or navigational rights that were not extended to all American countries – an effort to attempt to secure a veto over trading relations between Latin America and Europe.

The British, by contrast, sought to retain navigational rights and to support Bolívar's ambitions in Cuba: the British representative, Edward Dawkins, was instructed to inform the Congress that Britain was 'so far from denying the right of the new states of America to make a hostile attack upon Cuba ... that we have uniformly refused to join with the United States in remonstrating with Mexico and Colombia against the supposed intention, or in intimating that we should feel displeasure at the execution of it. We should indeed regret it, but we arrogate to ourselves no right to control the military operations of one belligerent against another.' Briefly it seemed Bolívar would be the spearhead for British ambitions in the Caribbean, leading to war with America. But it was too late: British opportunism and timidity had disappointed her friends, the United States henceforth exerted her political sway over the region (and twenty years later, seized Texas from Mexico). Britain was crowded out (although not economically), even though – ironically enough – it was such humble mercenaries as the British and Irish who made up the Albion Legion and who fought with San Martín who deserved credit as the freedom fighters' only actively participant foreign supporters. As the Pan-American Centennial Congress of 1926 noted, 'it may be asserted that there was no battlefield in the War of Independence on which British blood was not shed.'

On 12 December 1826, pale and ill, Canning had entered the House of Commons and issued his great justification:

> If France occupied Spain, was it necessary, in order to avoid the consequences of that occupation, that we should blockade Cadiz? No; I looked the other way. I sought materials of compensation in another hemisphere. Contemplating Spain, such as our ancestors had known her, I resolved that, if France had Spain, it should not be Spain with the Indies. I called the New World into existence to redress the balance of the Old.

Of course Canning claimed too much. But if this was a gross exaggeration of the part he had played – Britain had played – in the achievement of independence by the countries of Latin America, it was yet a magnificent vindication of his policies. He died in September 1827, having reclaimed for Britain the mantle of Protector of Latin America, even if, as Bolívar and the other founders of Latin American independence well knew, they had delivered themselves. Britain had for long been their only friend, sometimes encouraging, sometimes not, at the last warmly supportive; the United States had been slower to extend the hand of friendship, and sometimes clumsy; both had their political and commercial objectives, and reaped their rewards.

The failure of the Congress of Panamá to be and to achieve what Bolívar had hoped of it was an early indication of the ever-lengthening shadow the United States was to cast over the southern hemisphere. But now Bolívar was needed in Gran Colombia, to shore up his disintegrating achievement there. To Páez in August 1826 he wrote a letter pregnant with foreboding; then he announced he would leave Lima. The carping, sneering aristocracy of the city may have laughed at the Liberator, but he represented, at the very least, stability, and they entreated him to stay. A large demonstration was staged outside his residence at the Villa Magdalena, begging him to reconsider. The women of Lima made their own plea, to which Bolívar replied in his customary florid manner: 'Ladies! Silence is the only answer I ought to give those enchanting expressions ... When beauty speaks, what breast can resist it? I have been the soldier of beauty, because Liberty is bewitchingly beautiful; she diffuses happiness, and decorates the path of life with flowers.' Bolívar delayed his departure only a few days and on 4 September set sail, his parting words being, 'Beware the horses of anarchy.'

The trouble in Gran Colombia arose primarily from the attempted fusion of two inherently different states – New Granada, overwhelmingly white-dominated, with a substantial, prosperous and sophisticated middle class; and Venezuela, tropical, lawless and largely non-white. New Granada was ruled by the fussy, legalistic, scheming Santander; Venezuela was in reality a set of fiefdoms dominated by Bolívar's old commanders, with Páez the first among equals, but including Mariño, Arismendi, Bermudez and Urdaneta. Politics flourished in New Granada under her Congress, languished in Venezuela under the warlords: both groups were tetchy, assertive and difficult. Santander, as Bolívar's vice-president, was nominally in charge of both regions in the President's absence, but his attempts to exert his authority in Venezuela were clumsy. One of his first acts was to have a particularly brutal commander – the black Venezuelan colonel, Leonardo Infante – sentenced to death, as a deterrent. At the head of his troops, Santander attended the execution. This incensed the other Venezuelan leaders. When Santander issued an order that all men between sixteen and fifty be called up for military service, few Venezuelans obeyed. Páez, in an excess of obedience, then forcibly press-ganged thousands, his troops breaking into people's houses – which in turn appalled Santander. Seizing his chance, he ordered Páez to Santa Fé de Bogotá to face charges.

Páez had written to Bolívar imploring him to return to rescue the country from its divisions – and, implicity, from Santander's misrule. Bolívar was now determined to impose his will upon his own creation. As he rode northwards again across the Andean passes, welcomed enthusiastically in such places as Quito and even Pasto, he wrote to Santander, threatening to turn against him unless he agreed to a revision of the Gran Colombian constitution to allow the Bolívarist stamp of firm government to be imposed upon it. Santander, realising he would need Bolívar's support in any confrontation with Páez, was forced to back down. He and the fractious constitutionalists of Santa Fé de Bogotá might resent Bolívar, but they could not resist him. As he approached Bogotá Santander rode out to meet him, at the town of Tocaima. Bolívar's demand for constitutional revision would be met, Santander told him, on condition that he reject Páez's call for him to become dictator, bring the rebellious llanero to heel, and rule out Sucre as vice-president of Gran Colombia. Bolívar agreed to the provisos – unwisely, since it served only to alienate his two principal allies, Páez and Sucre, while failing to appease Santander's rivalry.

Santander returned to Bogotá, where he busily stirred up anti-Bolívar sentiment, putting it about that the Liberator was coming to seize power, with the result that instead of triumphal arches to welcome him, there were slogans declaring 'Viva la Constitución!' News of these events so annoyed Bolívar that he rode at once into the capital, in pouring rain in the middle of the night, his first entry there for five years. Instead of the cheering crowds of old, a small group hastily assembled by Santander was chanting 'Viva la Constitución!' Suppressing his anger, Bolívar stood in his stirrups and yelled back 'Long live the Republic! Long live its distinguished Vice-President [Santander]! Long live the Constitution!' Within a few days Bolívar had begun to win over the leading politicians, and Santander was forced to submit to Bolívar's idea of a confederation between Gran Colombia, Peru and Bolivia.

When news of this reached Páez, who had the backing of the ever-rebellious Mariño, he raised the standard of open rebellion, not just against Santander but against Bolívar as well. In Puerto Cabello, Cumana and Valencia there were revolts, and the old rogue cast off his glorious general's uniform and donned again his llanero garb, riding from Caracas to the llanos, raising once more the spectre of a cowboy war against the privileged whites.

It was Páez who in the first place had suggested Bolívar should emulate Napoleon; now he accused his former chief of seeking a crown for himself. Another civil war loomed over the land which had seen so much bloodshed over the past fifteen years. Bolívar's first declaration to Páez, made as he arrived in Caracas, showed he had lost none of his old belligerence: 'You have conquered with me. You have won glory and fortune with me, and you have been able to hope for everything with me. On the contrary, General Labatut lost against me; General Castillo lost; General Piar lost against me; General Mariño lost against me; General Riva Agüero lost, and General Torre Tagle lost against me. It seems that Providence condemns my enemies to perdition, whether they be Americans or Spaniards. And you see to what Generals Sucre, Santander and Santa Cruz have been elected.'

Bolívar then rode down towards Lake Maracaibo, writing on the way to Santander, 'Everything will be lost for good if we do not act with speed. The war in the west will be very cruel and will last for three or four years. The same will happen as when we fought the Spaniards: today they will be defeated and tomorrow they will return stronger.' He described Páez as 'the most ambitious and vainest man in the world ... the most dangerous man in Colombia'. But he also extended an olive branch: he could take part in the new constitutional assembly. Grasping it, Páez declared that Bolívar, far from coming to wage war against the llaneros, was coming as a simple citizen: 'he comes for our happiness – not to destroy the civil and military authority that I have received from the people, but to aid us with his counsel, with his wisdom and experience; to perfect the work of our reforms ... Venezuelans! Forget your troubles: The Great Bolívar is with us.' Bolívar's response was acid:

> Your proclamation says that I am 'coming as a simple citizen'. And what could I do as a citizen? Who has dissolved the laws of Colombia? ... Who shall tear the reins from my hands? Your friends! The infamy would be a thousand times greater for the ingratitude than for its treason. I cannot believe it. I shall never believe that you carry the ambitions of your friends and the dishonour of your name to this point. It is not possible, General, that you want to see me humiliated for the sake of a handful of deserters whom we have never seen in battle ... What do not all owe me in Venezuela? Do not even you owe me your existence?
>
> ... I have come from Peru to spare you the crime of civil war. I have come that Caracas and Venezuela may not stain themselves with precious

blood. And you want me to come without any legal authority? ... There is no other legitimate authority in Venezuela but mine. I mean supreme authority ... You have your command from municipalities, born from three assassinations. There is nothing glorious in this, my dear general.

... I want to set myself right. I want to know if you obey me or not and if my *patria* recognizes me as its chief. May God forbid that my authority is questioned on my own hearth ... I will yield everything for glory; but I will also combat everything for it ...

Dear General, you will be everything to me, everything, everything. I want nothing for myself. Thus you will be everything, without taking it at the cost of my glory, which has been founded on duty and public good ... Be assured of the affection with which I love you from my heart.

The Liberator now rode on to Puerto Cabello, where on New Year's Day 1827 he announced a pardon for Páez's men and recognised the old warrior as supreme military and civil authority in Venezuela, in exchange for Páez's acceptance of his own authority as President of Gran Colombia. Bolívar then took the road to Valencia, Páez's headquarters, and there in the mountains of Naguanagua, the two old comrades met in a fiercely emotional embrace before heading back to Caracas, where it had all started, in triumph. Bolívar and Páez rode into Caracas together in an open coach deluged with flowers as cannon, bells and bugles sounded. It was a fitting climax to another incredible journey: in four months, since leaving Lima, Bolívar had travelled more than two thousand miles on horseback. Now he had defused a potential civil war. The climax of his reconciliation with Páez was a ceremony in which he gave into Páez's care the jewel-encrusted sword given him at Potosí. Páez wept with gratitude:

He has given me the sword which has liberated a world ... How can I preserve its laurels, its glory, its honour? It demands of me strength which only Bolívar possesses. It bewilders me. The redeeming sword of humanity! ... In my hands this sword shall never be other than Bolívar's. His will shall direct it, my arm shall carry it. I shall perish a hundred times and all my blood shall be spilled before it shall leave my hands or ever attempt to shed the blood it has liberated ... Bolívar's sword is in my hands ... For him I will go with it to eternity.

Bolívar had broken all his pledges to Santander. Having set off to put down Páez's insurrection, he had recognised it. Expected to assert the authority of the government of the two states that comprised Gran Colombia, and of which Santander was vice-president, he had recognised Páez's authority in Venezuela as subordinate only to his own, and virtually acknowledged the independence of Venezuela. Bolívar, who had created Gran Colombia, was now it seemed presiding over its dissolution. He had appeased Páez and recognised the supremacy of force over constitutional law in order to save Venezuela from bloodshed; but for Santander it was the last straw, so he saw no reason to keep his own side of the bargain – to support Bolívar's new constitution. In spite of their deep dislike of one another he had, just, managed to remain on speaking terms with Bolívar: he now became his bitter, implacable enemy.

In hindsight, the episode marked the turning point of Bolívar's fortunes, the moment when he lost his magic touch. The grim determination he had shown in the war against Spain was missing: he should not have sided with Santander in the first place, and he should not have sided with Páez now. For the acrimonious politicians of New Granada and Venezuela he had been the vehicle of their deliverance from Spain, certainly, but now he was just an interfering soldier whose grandiose schemes were at variance with their own comfortable parochial ambitions.

A few days later word reached Santander of a rebellion against the patriot garrison in Lima, led by a New Granadan officer, José Bustamante. Manuelita had dressed as a soldier and infiltrated the garrison in an attempt to avert it, but was seized and put on a ship to Guayaquil, where she tried unsuccessfully to seduce Córdoba, the hero of Ayacucho, before both departed for Quito. Santa Cruz put down the insurrection but Bustamante escaped in his turn to Guayaquil, where he successfully instigated another revolt. Santander may or may not have been behind Bustamante, but he celebrated with parties in Santa Fé de Bogotá. In Lima, the old Peruvian aristocracy used the revolt as a pretext to abandon Bolívar's constitution, only six months after it had been promulgated. Marshal de La Mar was elected President of Peru in place of Bolívar's nominee, Santa Cruz, the radical blocked by the old guard. Santander's support of the revolt incensed Bolívar. 'Santander is perfidious … I have no confidence in either his morality or his heart,' he declared. Bitterly he wrote to tell Santander that he sought no more help from him; and Santander, 'in the serenity inspired by innocence,' promised to send none.

The empire created by Bolívar was now beginning to crumble on all sides. He distracted himself with family affairs, his attention to which was one of his more endearing traits. He had adopted the orphaned children of his dead brother, Juan Vicente. Although he was not particularly close to one of his sisters, Juana, he adored her daughter Benigna, and was very fond of his other sister, Maria Antonia. She managed the family properties in his absence but was plagued by a feckless son, Anacleto, who had abandoned his wife and children, immersed himself in shady political activities, and piled up huge gambling debts. To him, Bolívar played the stern uncle:

> Is this the reward you give to me who sent you to Europe to be educated, to your mother for trying to make you a good man? Doesn't it shame you to see poor, uneducated llaneros who have had no schooling but that of war become gentlemen and good citizens and learn to respect themselves, solely out of respect for me? Doesn't it shame you, considering that you are my nephew, having for a mother a woman of the finest character, to be inferior to so many poor guerrillas who have no other family than the fatherland?

Less admirably, by threatening to disinherit her he forced his niece Felicia, his brother's daughter, into marriage with one of his mulatto officers, General Laurencio Silva. Arranged marriages were common, and it is possible that for political reasons he wanted a public demonstration that race was of no conseqence to him personally; an admirable ideal, but it was brutal to enforce it on her in this way. She regarded the union as shameful, and the marriage proved most unhappy. Her brother, Fernando Bolívar, had been sent to the University of Virginia, and regularly corresponded with his uncle.

Bolívar, who had devoted his personal fortune to the service of his country, was remarkable in being completely uncorrupt. He was addicted to fame, but never used his position to amass wealth. Personally uninterested in money or in business, he demanded of others the utmost scrupulousness in such matters. O'Leary writes:

> An individual once complained that the minister, Unanue, owed him a considerable sum. [Bolívar] immediately ordered [it] to be paid out of his own funds. He disliked having bills of tradesmen questioned except when employed by the state. On such occasions he was not only economic but miserly. The tradesmen employed by the municipality of Lima to fabricate the sword presented to him complained of that body's having deducted 1,000 pesos from their contract; he instantly paid the money himself...

On 5 July 1827 Bolívar left La Guaira aboard the British frigate *Druid* accompanied by Sir Alexander Cockburn, the British minister. It was the anniversary of the first Venezuelan declaration of independence, and he was bound for a final showdown with Santander. He never returned to the city of his birth, to which he had given its freedom. He was not yet forty-four, but looked older, his eyes sunk in his colourless, cadaverous face, his cheeks hollow. He was still capable of sudden bursts of immense energy and irresistible charm, but often fell into lassitude and irritability. His incorrigible optimism was exhausted, yet his style was matchless. From Cartagena he travelled to Santa Fé de Bogotá; Santander, his one-time comrade, then rival, now hated enemy, considered flight, and rebellion. But when Bolívar appeared he embraced Santander, and took charge as President in spite of the hostility of the local political leaders.

He summoned Manuelita from Quito: 'Your goodness and graces reanimate the ice of my years. Your love animates a life which is expiring. I cannot be without you, I cannot deprive myself voluntarily of you, Manuela ... Come, come, come.' And come she did, along the harsh mountain trail to Bogotá. A contemporary describes the woman who had succeeded in taming Bolívar, who had become indispensable to him: 'She was always visible ... her arms were bare; she took no trouble to hide them. She would sew showing the most beautiful fingers in the world. She talked little; she smoked gracefully. She gave and received news. During the day she would appear dressed as an officer. In the evening she was transformed. She certainly wore rouge. Her hair was artistically combed. She was very animated. She was happy, sometimes using quite risqué language. Her graciousness and generosity were limitless.' At Bolívar's country estate outside Bogotá, Quinta de Portocarrero, she entertained the leaders of New Granadan society. The old glamour of Simón and Manuelita that had illuminated Lima shone again, briefly. A reception they gave was recorded by a guest:

> The dining-room, between two gardens, with wide bay windows, was an elegant room in the shape of an ellipse; and had the four seasons painted *al fresco* on its walls. At the head, a portrait of Bolívar crowned by two genii and this inscription: Bolívar is the God of Colombia. The Liberator sat alone, that is with no one right or left, at the head of the table which was set for thirty persons. Some of those present drank toasts to Colombia and to Bolívar without excess flattery but fully expressing their feelings towards their hero.

Bolívar heard them all with his usual indifference but with that mobility of eyes and body which was so typical of his character. And as champagne was served, he raised his glass and answered them all in short sparkling phrases which aroused general enthusiasm. As soon as he sat down, he was surrounded by his guests who, full of admiration, were eager to come close to him and touch his glass; they acclaimed him loudly and embraced him effusively. He, seeing himself mobbed, nearly smothered, stepped on to a chair and then on to a table and with long paces walked from one end to the other breaking plates and cups and upsetting bottles. The tumultuous crowd seized him at the other end and carried him in triumph to the reception hall.

But there were rumbles of distant thunder. As Bolívar left Caracas in July he had had news of an abortive rebellion in Bolivia, stoked by de La Mar in Lima, and General Gamarra – whom he had cuckolded in Cuzco. In October there were reports of fresh fighting in western Venezuela, and Bolívar briefly considered travelling there. In February 1828 a squadron of Spanish warships arrived off the Venezuelan coast from Puerto Rico, and royalist sympathisers rose in the region. Bolívar set off for the Venezuelan border, but the uprising was suppressed before he got there. In Cartagena there was an uprising led by Admiral Padilla. Once again Bolívar set out, once again the revolt was swiftly quelled before his arrival.

Then a greater challenge beckoned. The constitutional convention he had so long sought, to implement his new constitution, was assembling at Ocaña in New Granada, and on his way back from Cartagena Bolívar decided to stay in the town of Bucaramanga, about ninety miles from Ocaña. He was not fighting on ground of his choosing: the battle ahead was a political one, and Santander was a supremely skilful politician. Astute and ceaselessly energetic, he travelled the land securing the election of his own 'federalist' supporters – those who favoured a weak central government and a strong, locally-based congress in Venezuela as well as New Granada. As he said himself, 'In my profession one avoids fighting a powerful and well entrenched enemy in the field when there is hope of destroying him with skirmishes, surprises, ambushes and all kinds of hostilities.'

The convention of Ocaña began its deliberations on 9 April 1828; sixty-eight deputies attended. Its president, beadily aware of Bolívar just a couple of days' ride away, perched in Bucaramanga like some predatory eagle ready to intimidate the delegates, pointedly expressed his hope that 'seduction and terror cannot penetrate these walls.' Bolívar despatched a moderate, reasoned appeal to the delegates: 'Colombians ... [the last congress] busied itself with its rights, not its duties. We have made the legislature alone the sovereign government, when it should be no more than a member of the sovereign government ... We subordinated the executive to it and gave it a much greater part in the general administration than legitimate interests allow.' Agriculture, industry and commerce, he said, were in a deplorable state. 'A firm, powerful and just government is the call of the nation. Put it on its feet over the ruins of the desert which despotism has left pale with fright, fifteen thousand heroes weeping who have died for her, whose blood sown in the fields gave birth to its rights. Give us a government in which the law is obeyed, the magistracy is respected and the people are free.'

He argued passionately that a strong constitutional government was the best guarantee of freedom. It is to his credit that he resisted the temptation to intervene directly to close down the convention; the army was on his side, as were the ordinary people. But the deputies represented the upper and middle classes, and Santander pandered to what they sought: power for themselves as petty local potentates. He rejected any attempt to invite the Liberator to attend the proceedings: 'The man has a blinding and hypnotic presence. I myself have experienced it. Many times, going into his presence, angry and with well-formed and just proposals, I have left disarmed and full of admiration. No man living can oppose Bolívar face to face.' As the convention proceeded to adopt a federalist, Congress-dictated constitution, Bolívar could only wring his hands in frustration. Peru de Lacroix, his military aide at the time, described him as increasingly solitary and irritable, losing his temper when he lost at cards. He remained as driven as ever, rising early, going to bed late, eating little, drinking only two glasses of wine at meals, fastidious as to his personal hygiene, exercising conscientiously.

In a bid to secure the support of New Granada's powerful clergy Bolívar now displayed a pronounced religious streak, attending Mass every morning. O'Leary for one was surprised: 'Bolívar was a complete atheist. Notwithstanding, he thought religion necessary for government. His indiscretion, which was very great at all times, knew no bounds when he spoke of religion, which he used to ridicule in a disgusting manner. At Mass he was sure to have some book or other in his hand and sometimes a gazette.' Playing the civilian, he shed his uniform for white trousers, a blue coat and a broad-brimmed cap, but kept his familiar cavalry boots. He seethed with impatience and resentment towards Santander:

> They are all in my hands. A mere signal from me would exterminate them all. Yet, in my place, they would not only give the signal to kill me but also all my friends, partisans and anyone who doesn't hold their opinions. Such are our so-called liberals – cruel, bloody, frenetic, intolerant and covering their crimes with the word 'liberty'! They believe themselves as justified in their crimes as the Inquisitors and all who have shed human blood in the name of God and religion believed themselves justified in theirs.
>
> Individual interests, ambitions, rivalries, necessity, provincialism, thirst for vengeance and other miserable passions animate our demagogues and unite them now to overthrow existing form; but afterwards they will only separate, and establish their partial sovereignties, and govern the people as slaves and with the old Spanish system.

Like Cromwell, he watched in horror as the elected government in which he believed manifestly failed in its task – knowing that to move against it would be to substitute for constitutional chaos a dictatorship – something almost as abhorrent to him. But he responded at last to the inevitable. Almost certainly on his orders, the delegates faithful to him walked out of the assembly, depriving it of a quorum. The old constitution lay dead, the new one was strangled at birth.

In the resultant vacuum, both the army and the leading citizens called on Bolívar to take power, as he had known they would. He did so as dictator, pending the summoning of a new constitutional convention in two years' time. His reluctance was heartfelt, his fear being that the bearer of freedom would figure in history as a despot. 'Remember what I say. Colombia will be lost because her leader lacks ambition. He has no love for command and little inclination for glory and abhors the imputation of ambition more than he does death and tyranny ... Under a dictatorship, who can talk of freedom? Let us pity both the people who obey and the man who rules alone.'

It was not a stirring call; but it was genuine enough. The man who at Potosí had experienced the glory of having a continent at his feet hardly craved the pleasure of ruling a small part of that continent as dictator. His ambition now was to consolidate what survived of his achievement and endow it with good government. At first, Bolívar ruled with a light hand. Santander was appointed ambassador to Washington (but delayed his departure). There was no censorship of the press, and his opponents were left free to continue their political activities. Old Culo de Hierro – Iron-Bottom – was not, it seemed, made of stern enough stuff to ride roughshod over his fellow countrymen.

18

The Last Campaign

Bolívar's protégé Sucre, President of Bolivia, steely commander in battle, was perhaps too merciful in peace (he had been known to pardon a would-be assassin, and fund his exile); he was also a 'foreigner' to the native leaders, who resented the two thousand Colombian troops he had retained in the country. The reactionary government of General de La Mar in Peru was conspiring with General Gamarra in Cuzco not just to throw off the Gran Colombian yoke, but to assert its own ambition for a greater Peru by occupying Bolivia – the former province of Upper Peru. In the face of this threat Sucre tried to appease his enemies by announcing that Colombian 'occupation' forces would be withdrawn from the country, but at the Peruvians' instigation an insurrection broke out in the barracks of Chuquisaca in April 1828, and as he rode in Sucre was badly injured by a bullet in his right arm, and another which grazed his head. Using this as a pretext, Gamarra sent troops over the border to 'protect the precious life of the Marshal of Ayacucho [Sucre] and free the country from factions and anarchy'. Shortly afterwards Sucre resigned as President, and left Bolivia. Now in his early thirties, this most romantic of Bolívar's lieutenants married a beautiful girl from Quito, Maria Carcelan y Larea, the Marquesa de Solanda, and retired from public life. O'Leary's verdict was that

> Sucre was a very vain man, but he had reason to be so. He was superior to most public men that I have met with in America. In his principles he was liberal, but no republican. The last words he ever said to me were: 'Tell the Liberator to concentrate all the troops he can dispose of and not to allow himself to be dictated to by anyone. Tell him that now is the time to save the country and, if he thinks that the monarchic form is what Colombia wants, let him say it and he shall not want men who will support him.'

Bolivia now saw two presidents murdered and a third installed, in the space of five days – a foretaste of what the future held for a country, as remarkable for its political instability as for its beauty, which has had more presidents than years of independence. Tensions mounted between Peru and Gran Colombia, as Bolívar moved his forces to the frontier and de La Mar assembled his troops. Bolívar was also beset by other minor rebellions, most notably in New Granada. Here in Cartagena, General Padilla's black revolution aimed at installing Santander as President collapsed. More woundingly, in Antioquia General Córdoba, the young hero of Ayacucho, also raised the standard of revolt against Bolívar; he was killed by a British legionnaire – although almost certainly not on Bolívar's orders – and O'Leary crushed the rebels there; of Córdoba he wrote: 'His vanity was unbounded and his knowledge of the world limited ... fighting like a lion, he fell and expired sternly, proud and unrepentant.' Bolívar meanwhile busied himself reluctantly with placing Gran Colombia's finances on a sound footing and doing what he could to revive the economy.

But the minds of others were on matters far removed from the merely fiscal. In Bogotá on 25 September 1828, in the house of one Luis Vargas Tejada, a large number of men gathered, including the commanders of an artillery battalion, the adjutant-general of the armed forces, Lieutenant-Colonel Carujo, and two civilian leaders, Augustín Hermet and Florentino Gonzalez, leading lights of 'committees of public safety' which had been set up in opposition to Bolívar. This gathering had been tacitly approved by the army chief-of-staff, Colonel Guerra, and by Santander himself; he, however, played no active part and wanted the coup it was planning to take place after he had left for the United States. As Gonzalez put it: 'It was necessary that blood should flow, as had occurred in all the great insurrections of people against tyrants. I found myself in a critical position to carry out that hard resolution. Twelve civilians and twenty-five soldiers, under the orders of Commander Carujo, went at midnight to break into the government palace and seize Bolívar dead or alive.' They killed two guard dogs outside, stabbed the sentries, and forced their way upstairs, badly injuring Ibarra, Bolívar's personal bodyguard. A young British legionnaire, William Ferguson, was stabbed to death defending the door to Bolívar's room against the conspirators. Manuelita Sáenz, who was sleeping with the Liberator, takes up the story:

I heard a strange noise which must have been the killing of the sentries. I woke the Liberator, and the first thing he did was to take up his sword and a pistol and try to open the door. I held him back and made him dress, which he did calmly and quickly. He said, 'Good. Now I am dressed. What shall we do? Fight back?' He tried to open the door and I prevented him.

Then something he himself had told me occurred to me. 'Didn't you say to Pepe Paris that this would be a good window to jump from?' (The room was on the first floor.) 'You're right,' he told me, and went to the window. I prevented him from jumping because people were passing, but I gave him the signal when there were no people and because the door was being forced.

I went to intercept them to give him time to flee, but I didn't have time to see him jump, nor to shut the window. When they saw me they seized me. 'Where is Bolívar?' I said he was in the council chamber, which was the first thing that came into my head. They searched the outer room carefully, went into the bedroom, and seeing the open window, exclaimed, 'He has escaped. He has saved himself.'

I told them, 'No, gentlemen, he has not escaped. He is in the council room.' 'And why is this window open?' 'I have just opened it, because I wanted to know what the noise was.' Some believed me, some didn't. They went back into the other room, felt the warm bed, and became more dejected still, although I told them I had been resting there, waiting for him to emerge from the council chamber to give him a bath.'

One rebel wanted to kill her. Instead, they beat her so badly with the flat of a sword that she subsequently spent twelve days in bed. Bolívar, carrying his pistol and his sword, was joined by his loyal chief retainer, José Palacio, and the two made their way through the dark streets, past sounds of fighting and running men, to the Carmen Bridge across the San Agustín River, in which they took refuge, beneath the arches. After two hours Palacio went to reconnoitre, then later returned to accompany Bolívar to the headquarters of the loyal Vargas regiment; order was meanwhile restored.

Commandeering a horse, Bolívar went with his soldiers to the plaza, where Manuelita, still just on her feet, had also gone to find him and bring him home. 'You are the liberator of the Liberator', he told her, as he had once told Bermudez. On the way he prevented the summary beheading of one of his would-be assassins. Told 'These men were going to kill you', he replied, 'It was the power they were going to kill, not the man.' General Rafael Urdaneta, his most loyal commander, was adamant, however, that the ringleaders be executed. For his part, Bolívar insisted on sparing Santander, who had taken refuge in Urdaneta's house during the night to avoid a pro-Bolívar lynch mob. He was sent into exile in France (from which he returned in 1832 to serve a controversial term as Colombia's president). Bolívar was rid of his bane at last.

O'Leary wrote a bitter epitaph on Santander's career:

> Santander was one of those men who, of mediocre talents and much daring, but without any morality, raise themselves in the political tumult to distinguished positions ... False, ungrateful, mean, vengeful, cruel, to the extent of attending executions and delighting himself with seeing the blood shed by his orders. His soul was perverse, without value or merit. As a soldier his career was undistinguished; he was despised by his enemies and sneered at by his comrades. Administratively gifted and very hard-working, he was assiduous at his desk, and with these qualities he could have done good for his country, but his vices weakened his actions and he has not left a single monument of public usefulness behind him.

But Bolívar had been badly shaken by the assassination and coup attempts. He was not only demoralised, but suffering physically as a result of spending four hours in the river, which left his chest and lungs in a poor state. The French minister went to see him shortly afterwards.

> We arrived at his farm and Doña Manuela Sáenz received us. She told us that the hero was very ill, but she would announce our visit. A few moments later there appeared a man with a long and yellow face of gaunt appearance, with a cotton cap, wrapped in his cloak, with his legs protruding from wide canvas trousers. When we addressed our first words to him about his health, he replied, waving his skinny arms, 'Ah, it is not the laws of nature which have put me in this state, but the burdens that weigh upon my heart. My fellow countrymen, who could not kill me with knives, are now trying to assassinate me morally with their ingratitude and calumnies. When I stop existing, the demagogues will devour each other like wolves, and the edifice I built with superhuman effort will sink into the mud of revolution.'

It was a startlingly accurate assessment.

Indeed, in spite of the failure of the insurrection, Bolívar found he was sitting on a tinderbox. The press harried him mercilessly. Although the people remained with him, the New Granadan oligarchy was against him, bitterly resentful of the Venezuelan soldiery that carried out his orders. The fusion of the two countries into one, Gran Colombia, his great dream, was clearly on the brink of failure.

He now resorted to desultory repression, banning public gatherings and curbing the hostile press, but even so his could hardly be called an intolerant regime by any who remembered Spanish rule; rather, his were the actions of a man whose health and power were failing, a stick to prop himself up with. He could not conquer his own mortality, nor control what would come after him. He had no sway over the destiny of the countries he had liberated.

Yet the glory was not quite over yet. His southern dominions had collapsed with breathtaking speed – Bolivia and Peru were now in hostile hands – but New Granada and Venezuela remained united – just.

With the news that the Peruvian leader de La Mar was approaching the frontier with a large force, and that the New Granadan armies there had rebelled against his dictatorship and were backing the Peruvians, Bolívar exerted himself one last time to protect his achievement. Once more he took to the saddle to march southwards, and appointed Sucre, living in retirement in Quito, his commander there. De La Mar had invaded Loja with eight thousand men, and was advancing on Cuenca.

With a force a third the size, Sucre moved to intercept de La Mar, and the Peruvians withdrew to defend positions across the river Saraguro. Sucre and de La Mar initiated negotiations, of which the latter took treacherous advantage, attempting to outflank Sucre's forces by suddenly marching on Girón. Sucre, learning of this in time, moved swiftly towards the same point and despatched two companies to seize the lightly-defended Peruvian positions on the Saraguro, which they achieved without difficulty.

The two armies then shadowed one another, each looking for battle on favourable terrain, as far as Portete de Tarqui, which de La Mar occupied on 26 February. There the following day Sucre's small but well-ordered army advanced on the enemy trenches, and after a brief battle the Peruvians fled. When the weary and ailing Bolívar reached Quito, his adoptive son was able to hand him the enemy lances seized in battle.

The news that de La Mar was raising a new army in Piura proved too much for his colleagues to stomach. Fearful that Bolívar and Sucre would seize upon it as a pretext to reinvade Peru, Gamarra deposed de La Mar and concluded an armistice with the Liberator, over the protests of his scorned, Bolívar-hating wife. More good news reached the Liberator: in Bolivia his other faithful lieutenant, Santa Cruz, had seized power back from the Peruvians and restored the Bolívarist constitution.

Rumours were now buzzing around Gran Colombia that Bolívar, Liberator and dictator, was contemplating a reactionary step: he was said to be considering a European prince as his successor.

The truth was somewhat different, and represented another throw by the great-power rivals for influence in Latin America. With Bolívar's own physical powers visibly waning, Urdaneta, his strongest and most loyal general, had summoned the leaders of the country to consider a proposal by the British ambassador to install a constitutional monarchy in Gran Colombia after Bolívar's demise. Urdaneta and the others believed that no other form of government would ensure legitimacy and continuity once Bolívar had departed the scene. O'Leary tells the story:

> On my arrival at the capital I found that the government was seriously meditating a plan to establish a monarchy. Some of the ministers spoke to me of their projects. It was thought, they said, by all sensible people that republican institutions were in no manner adapted to the country, that the attempt to assassinate General Bolívar had shocked everyone, and that a radical change was indispensable. They told me that there was no idea of consulting General Bolívar until affairs were in a more advanced state, as they dreaded that he would discountenance the plan.
>
> It was intended to solicit the approval of the French and British cabinets. A Bavarian prince was considered the most eligible, as not being closely allied to any of the principal potentates of Europe, though the heir of the House of Orléans would be preferable on account of his wealth. Páez had been consulted and, though he did not openly oppose the project, he recommended its being laid aside for the present. Brizeño and Soublette both opposed it in a very earnest manner, predicting that it would be the cause of a revolution in Venezuela, where General Bolívar's enemies would lay hold of it as a pretext. General Montilla was also of the opinion that it was not the time to execute a project of such magnitude. Some fatality hovered over their counsels. The ministers were deaf to the expostulations of their friends and rashly persisted in the enterprise.
>
> It never was meant that General Bolívar should be crowned, nor were his services to be requited by laying him upon the shelf. It was intended to have him elected chief magistrate *ad vitam* under the popular title of Liberator. After his death the foreign prince was to succeed.

By this plan the British hoped to increase their influence at the expense of the United States, who supported Santander's loose republicanism.

But Urdaneta and his allies believed such a prince should be Latin, Catholic and non-Spanish, which pointed towards France – and this held little appeal for the British.

In distant Guayaquil Bolívar, some of his bounce restored by events in the south, was far from enthusiastic about espousing even in constitutional form the principle against which he had laboured all his life. He replied with a diplomatic 'no' to the British ambassador, Colonel Patrick Campbell:

> I do not know what to say to you about this notion, which is fraught with innumerable difficulties. You must know that there is no objection on my part since I am determined to resign at the next congress. But who is to appease the ambition of our leaders and the fear of inequality among the common people? Do you not think that England would be jealous if a Bourbon prince were chosen? Would not all the new American nations oppose it, and also the United States which seems destined by Providence to plague America with torments in the name of freedom? I already seem to detect a general conspiracy against poor Colombia, which is too much envied by all the American republics.
>
> The whole Press would call for a fresh crusade against those guilty of treachery to freedom, of supporting the Bourbons, and of betraying the American system. In the south the Peruvians, on the Isthmus the Guatemalans and Mexicans, and in the Antilles the Americans and the liberals of all parties would kindle the flame of discord. Santo Domingo would not remain passive but would call upon her brothers to make common cause against a prince of France. Everyone would become our enemy, and Europe would do nothing to help us because it is not worth sacrificing a Holy Alliance for the New World.

To the last he did not betray his republicanism, as some of his enemies were later to allege from this episode. The idea was quietly shelved. William Henry Harrison, the American envoy in Gran Colombia, went so far as to charge that Bolívar himself aspired to the crown, and unwisely lectured him against the dangers of tyranny; he had to leave hurriedly, to avoid expulsion. From Britain, which had done little to help him although her soldiers had done so much, the Liberator's anger had switched to the United States, which had done nothing at all. To his people, Bolívar asserted humorously that no foreign prince would wish to rule so anarchic a land, or one so unable to sustain a lavish court.

Bolívar remained in Guayaquil until the summer of 1829. In August he suffered an attack of 'nervous bile', and for the first time spoke with apparent sincerity of resigning and handing over power. He wrote to O'Leary: 'Considering what I have been all my life, it is incredible how I am; and given that my spiritual strength has suffered much decline and that my constitution has been to a great extent ruined, what cannot be doubted is that I have no strength for anything and that no stimulus can reanimate me. A universal calm, or an absolute indifference has taken hold of me and dominated me completely. I am so convinced of my incapacity to continue my time in public service that I believe myself obliged to reveal to my intimates the wish to hand over my command for good.'

This was no mere gesture. Bolívar wanted to hand over authority while he was still vigorous, and capable of influencing events from behind the scenes. As he wrote, again to O'Leary, 'Would it not be better for Colombia and for me, and still more for public opinion, if a president was nominated and I remained a simple general? I would circle around the government as a bull around a herd of cows. I would defend it with all my forces and those of the republic. This government would be stronger than mine because it would add to my forces those of the government and the strength of the personality it served.'

He had Sucre in mind, but to his astonishment Sucre declined the vice-presidency left vacant by Santander's exile and criticised Bolívar for summoning the Congress as he had promised to do at the end of his two-years' dictatorship – a reply which bitterly disappointed Bolívar, who chided his protégé for failing to understand that the norms of government must be respected. He signed a peace treaty with Peru and, to some extent revived, took to the saddle again for the weary journey from Guayaquil via Pasto to Bogotá. He was comforted by a charming letter from his old comrade-in-arms, Páez, effective dictator of Venezuela, suggesting that the two of them retire to his hacienda in Apure, 'like simple Roman citizens'. Bolívar replied: 'I remain, my beloved general, your grateful friend. The idea has moved me greatly. Would to God I could enjoy the rest of my life in your companionship.'

His beloved general, however, was even then plotting another shock for the ailing Liberator: in November, on the road, he learned of Páez's insistence that, as the New Granadan Santander had held the vice-presidency for so long, it was now the turn of a Venezuelan – Páez himself. Bolívar temporised: Páez threatened that Venezuela would break away from the union with New Granada. He also vigorously denounced Bolívar for seeking to reimpose the rule of 'absolute kings, conniving with the Holy Alliance; planning to re-establish the Inquisition and slavery; and introducing dukes and counts, marquesses and barons, all of them white, destroying the equality of rights conceded to Indians, blacks and mixed races'. As Brutus had Mark Antony, Bolívar's oldest friend betrayed him: Páez was making his bid for the succession. His regime had become ruthless: the vicious Arismendi was chief of the secret police who penetrated the humblest and most obscure peasant huts. It was rumoured that the British were backing Páez, to counter any attempt to impose a French monarch on Gran Colombia.

On 15 January 1830 Bolívar re-entered Santa Fé de Bogotá, to his last triumphal welcome. An eyewitness described the occasion:

> The streets were decorated as never before. All the regiments of militia of cavalry of the savannah ... paraded ... You can be sure that anyone who had a horse or could obtain one came out to meet him. The balconies, windows and towers were full of people.
>
> But in this great multitude sad silence rather than animation reigned. The bursts of artillery, the church bells sounded without producing happiness. The instinct of the masses was that they were witnessing the solemn funeral of the great republic rather than the entry of its glorious founder. Almost certainly even his bitterest enemies were moved ...
>
> When Bolívar appeared, I saw tears being shed. Pale, emaciated, his eyes, shining and expressive in his good days, were now extinguished. His voice was hollow, barely audible. The profile of his face – all, in the end, suggested the imminent collapse of his body and the approaching beginning of eternal life, which excited real sympathy.

The journey had almost wasted him. He told Manuelita, who had ridden out to meet him after yet another long separation, 'I seem an old man of sixty!' On 20 January the new Congress met, as he had promised, and Bolívar resigned his dictatorship.

> Fearing that I am regarded as an obstacle to establishing the Republic on a firm base of happiness, I remove myself from the high office to which you were good enough to elevate me ... Never, never, I swear to you, has the ambition for a monarchy soiled my mind. My enemies have invented that idea to destroy me in your good opinion ... My one desire has been to contribute to your liberty ... The Republic will be happy if, accepting my resignation, you name a president beloved of all the nation ... Hear my prayers. Save the Republic. Save my glory, which is Colombia's.

He had kept his word. He now returned to his hacienda outside Bogotá; and there he learned that his last substantial family property,

some mines at Aroa, had been confiscated by Páez. His sister Maria
Antonia's house had been daubed with doggerel – 'If you want to see
Bolívar, go and walk to the graveyard' – no doubt by Páez's agents. One
of Bolívar's supporters reported that

> He walked slowly and with effort, his voice nearly extinguished, and had
> to make an effort to be intelligible. He walked the banks of the stream ...
> and contemplated it ... 'How long', he said, 'will this water take to flow
> into the immense ocean, as men in the darkness of the grave flow into the
> earth from which they come? A large part will evaporate and disappear,
> like human glory, like fame ...' Suddenly he beat his breast with his hands,
> exclaiming in a tremulous voice, 'My glory! My glory! Why do they take
> it from me? Why do they insult me? Páez! Páez! Bermudez was ...
> offended ... Santander became my rival to replace me, he wanted to kill
> me ...'
>   In this conversation the agonised breathing of Bolívar, the languor of
> his gaze, the deep sighs which emerged from his anguished breast – all
> indicated the weakness of the body and the anguish of the soul, inspiring
> compassion and respect.

As Bolívar had feared, the new Congress adopted the kind of loose
federal constitution he had always resisted. His dictatorship had failed
to influence the parochialism of the New Granadans; worse, as the price
of his reconciliation with New Granada Páez demanded that the
Liberator should quit the country. General Joaquin Mosquera, a supporter of Santander, was elected President by the Congress.

The fight had gone out of him at last: to keep Gran Colombia united,
Bolívar decided to leave it. He told neither Manuelita nor Sucre, the two
closest to him, of his decision, lest they try to dissuade him. He was convinced he would revive, and return; almost certainly he would not have
abandoned Manuelita had he believed himself to be dying. But they
never saw him again.

19

Burnout

On 8 May 1830, in Manuelita's temporary absence up-country, Bolívar left Santa Fé de Bogotá, waved farewell by officials and citizens, many openly weeping. Colonel Campbell, the British minister, remarked: 'He is great – the greatest gentleman of Colombia.' In the outskirts of the city youths jeered at Bolívar and shouted 'Longanizo', 'sausage' – a reference to an idiot well-known in Bogotá who wandered the streets dressed as a soldier. Bad news awaited him at Honda: General Flores, who with Sucre had beaten off the Peruvians, had now proclaimed the independence of Guayaquil, Quito and the southern province of Gran Colombia as the Republic of Ecuador. Sadly Bolívar remarked that 'posterity has not seen a picture more frightening than that offered by [South] America, more for the future than for the present, because who would have imagined that an entire world would collapse in frenzy and devour its own race like cannibals?'

On 16 May Bolívar embarked down the river Magdalena, borne by its strong currents past the scenes of his first triumphs. Arriving in Cartagena on 24 June he suffered the worst blow of his life. He had avoided farewell scenes with Sucre by stealing away from Bogotá. Sucre, disappointed, had decided to return to Quito, to the wife and young son he idolised; before leaving Bogotá he wrote to Bolívar, 'You know it is not your power but your friendship that inspired in me the tenderest affection for your person.'

Now Bolívar learned that on 4 June, not far from Pasto, Sucre had been ambushed and shot dead by hirelings of the local bandit chief, under orders from two anti-Bolívarists in Bogotá, Genaro Santamaria and an old enemy, Obando. There is a possibility that Urdaneta, ever faithful to Bolívar but Sucre's bitter rival for the succession, may have been the instigator. 'God Almighty!' Bolívar exclaimed. 'They have spilt the blood of innocent Abel!' A couple of days later the bitter sorrow of this blow was exacerbated by the arrival of Sucre's letter of farewell:

> My general, when I went to your house to go with you, I found you gone. Perhaps it is well, for it has spared me the sorrow of a last farewell. Right now my heart is empty. I do not know what to say to you.
>
> I have not the words to tell you easily the sentiments of my soul regarding you. You know them well, for you have known me a long time and you know that it has not been your position but only friendship which has inspired in me the deepest affection for your person. I shall conserve it no matter what the fate which befalls us and I beg of you to conserve for me the appreciation you have always bestowed upon me. I shall try in every circumstance to deserve it.
>
> Good-bye, my general. Receive as a token of my friendship the tears which I am shedding at this moment. Be happy, wherever you are going, and be sure always of the devotion and gratitude of your most loyal and passionate friend.

Bolívar was devastated.

Although he was brought low by his protégé's murder, the evidence suggests Bolívar saw himself at this time as staging a strategic retreat, and believed that he would return again to power. In his letters he wrote of returning to public life and he kept in touch with Urdaneta – but he, either because he believed Bolívar was spent, or because he hoped to replace him, became increasingly uncommunicative.

Bolívar was emaciated; his health took a sharp turn for the worse, and he insisted on being carried first to Soledad, then on to Barranquilla, in the quest for a more agreeable climate. His intention had been to take a ship to Trinidad, then on to somewhere in Europe, probably Britain. But he had no strength left. In November 1830 he wrote to Flores, creator of Ecuador, in tragic, acerbic and humorous vein:

> I have arrived at only a few sure conclusions: 1. For us, [South] America is ungovernable. 2. He who serves a revolution ploughs the sea. 3. The only thing we can do in [South] America is emigrate. 4. This country will eventually fall into the hands of the unbridled mob, and will proceed to almost imperceptible petty tyrannies of all complexions and races. 5. Devoured as we are by every kind of crime and annihilated by ferocity, Europeans will not go to the trouble of conquering us. 6. If it were possible for any part of the world to revert to primordial chaos, that would be [South] America's final state.

News reached him: Mosquera, his enemy in Bogotá, had been forced to resign, and faithful Urdaneta was leading a movement to reinstate his former leader; but in Venezuela, his enemies spat upon his name. He was cheered by a letter from his sister Maria Antonia in Caracas which said the people there were clamouring for his return against the tyrants. It was too late, however: he was too ill.

He now sailed up the coast to Santa Marta; he had conceived an idea of gathering and despatching a force to fight Páez, and Santa Marta would be the jumping-off point. He arrived there on 1 December 1830, to take refuge – ironically enough – in the home of the Spanish consul there, Joaquin de Mier, a gracious man with a magnificent *quinta* in the village of San Pedro Alejandrino. He wrote:

> I am about to die, God calls me... I have scarcely strength enough to support the last days that remain of my miserable life... I see no salvation for the country. I believe everything is lost forever. If there were a single sacrifice I could make – my life, my happiness or my honour – believe me, I would not hesitate; but I am convinced the sacrifice would be useless. Since I am unable to secure the happiness of my country, I refuse to rule it. Further, the tyrants have taken my native land from me and therefore I have no longer any country for which to make a sacrifice ...

At de Mier's *quinta* he was attended by a French doctor, Prospero Révérend. Bitterly, only half-deliriously, Bolívar remarked, 'The three great killers of humanity have been Jesus Christ, Don Quixote, and myself' – 'killers' presumably because all were idealists who had deluded their supporters. He was racked by hot flushes and shivering fits, but could still walk about for short periods. He complained bitterly that Urdaneta would not write to him; next door, his officers played cards, and sang. On 9 December, having lost all hope of living, he dictated his last proclamation:

> Colombians! You have witnessed my efforts to plant liberty where tyranny reigned before. I have laboured with disinterestedness, sacrificing my fortune and my own peace. I resigned from command when I saw that you had no faith in my altruism. My enemies took advantage of your credulity and trampled upon what is most sacred to me – my reputation and my love of liberty. I have been the victim of my persecutors, who have led me to the gates of the sepulchre. I forgive them. On disappearing from among you, my affection tells me that I should declare my last wishes. I aspire to no other glory than the consolidation of [Gran] Colombia. All of you must work for the inestimable good of the Union: the people

obeying the government in order to avoid anarchy; the ministers praying to heaven for guidance; and the military using its sword in defence of social guarantees.

Colombians! My last wish is for the happiness of the fatherland. If my death contributes to the end of partisanship and the consolidation of the Union, I shall be lowered in peace into my grave.

This was read out before his nephew and adopted son Fernando, Bedford Wilson, and the faithful José Palacio, and a crowd of weeping villagers. Increasingly now he drifted in and out of delirium. His last words were: 'Let's go, let's go, these people do not want us here.' At around midday on 17 December he died.

It is said that a day later Manuelita Sáenz arrived – too late. She had been cruelly left behind for the last time. As soon as he learned of Bolívar's death, Santander returned to New Granada to seize power, and had Manuelita exiled. When Dr Thorne died she refused his estates, and lived in poverty in Peru, faithful to Bolívar's memory. Garibaldi met her there in 1858 and heard her tales of the Liberator, describing her as the most gracious lady he had ever met. She died of the plague at the age of fifty-nine.

Twelve years to the day after his death, Bolívar's remains were shipped back to Caracas, where they were received by his elderly black nurse, Hipolita; his sister Maria Antonia had recently died. Páez, now president of an independent Venezuela, presided over the return of the hero he had betrayed and wrote of him:

Simon Bolívar belongs to the band of modern men whose equals are to be found only when we reach back to republican times of Greece and Rome ... In the midst of people who had no more tradition than the respect for an authority sanctioned by the acquiescence of three centuries of ignorance, superstition, and fanaticism, nor any political dogma but submission to an order of things supported by might and force, Bolívar succeeded in defying that power ...

Simon Bolívar is a quasi-deity in Latin America today. He is the one non-controversial figure, the one continental leader, the man who freed millions of people from tyranny and did not then enslave them himself. His reputation transcends the bitterness of modern Latin American divisions – between left and right, between militarists and democrats, between oligarchy and revolutionaries. Among the educated and propertied classes, his radicalism has long since been quietly forgotten. To hundreds of millions of ordinary Spanish Americans, many of them illiterate, he was the leader who tried to overcome class and racial divisions, who tried to give rights to that vast swathe of humanity that remains so downtrodden.

In the face of this continent-wide hero-worship, the itch to debunk is strong. There are plenty of charges to answer: his wasted youth; his betrayal of Miranda; his descent into darkness with the War to the Death; the repeated failure of his early attempts at Venezuelan independence, at the cost of horrific suffering for his people; the callousness with which he drove so many of his own men to their deaths; the cold-blooded murder of eight hundred prisoners of war; the madness of trying to stitch together three different nations, against their will, and then add two more; the vainglory, vanity, posturing and preening; his conveyor-belt appetite for women; his whole vast empire, three times bigger than western Europe, crumbling away within five years.

It is not difficult to portray him as a figure of megalomania and evil, one of the great monsters of history. O'Leary mentions one revealing episode: 'Doctor Salazar, having mentioned to Bolívar that his friends complained of his apparent insensitivity, that he saw his partisans and friends fall in battle without eliciting from him the tribute of a tear or a sigh, "Good God," replies Bolívar, "were I to weep for every friend I have lost or am to lose in future I would be called General Jeremiah, not General Bolívar."' His very title, to cynics, rings hollow: he liberated his people from what, for what? What more did he do than 'liberate'? What, even today, does that 'liberation' mean for most of them, steeped in backwardness, poverty and ignorance? How diminutive this small strutting man with his uniform and his grandiose gestures does indeed look beside the simple, towering *gravitas* of a George Washington or a Thomas Jefferson.

Yet men's achievements must be judged within the context of the societies and times they live in, not against some artificial historical absolute, much less by modern standards. Those who see Bolívar as a quasi-mystical figure are almost right, because the life he lived and his achievements were, by any standard, almost superhuman. We can see with hindsight that he had the good fortune to live at a time when the historical tide was turning: the Spanish Empire was buckling under the weight of its own contradictions, but few at first dared challenge its overwhelming military might. Yet he, with a handful of men, overcame a succession of setbacks that would have deterred most other men and tried, and tried, and tried again, until the spark of revolution at last ignited.

His first campaign to reconquer Venezuela was won virtually single-handed. His landings on the Venezuelan coast were triumphs of determination over adversity. His return to the Orinoco was a remark-able leap of the imagination. His march across the Andes was a heroic feat of endurance. His final conquest of Venezuela was a faultless triumph of strategy. He took Quito, Peru and Upper Peru with a string of victories in strange landscapes of almost dreamlike other-worldliness. He crossed and recrossed thousands of miles of some of the most pun-ishing terrain in the world, a feat which continues to astonish anyone who knows that land. In the end, such expenditure of energy may have burnt him out and led him to his tragically early grave – if the cause of his death was not solely the tuberculosis that killed so many in his day, including his mother.

Judged by his military achievements alone, Bolívar deserves a place in the front rank. With ill-trained irregulars he defeated the most feared and formidable army of his day – after those of France and Britain – across the breadth and half the length of a continent. His generalship vies with that of Julius Caesar and Augustus, Alexander the Great, Tamerlane and Genghis Khan: he too was a fighter on the grand scale, his enemies if anything more formidable, his friends fewer and his terrain arguably some of the harshest in the world. When it comes to his role as a statesman, the fact that he was ultimately a failure (or only half a success – he liberated his peoples from Spanish rule, but did not succeed in putting anything permanent in its place) should not obscure the scale or the value of what he was trying to do. If the judgement of this narrative is as much as a quarter right, it is clear that, in spite of occa-sional lapses in times of stress, Bolívar was as close as any actual practitioner of politics can get to being a pure political idealist. He tried to set up representative assemblies in the countries he freed; only in the last resort did he rule by force, then only briefly and reluctantly, and on the whole with a light hand.

He genuinely tried to formulate an enlightened, representative and paternalist rule. Charges that he was a covert monarchist, imperialist or one-man ruler do not stand up to scrutiny. He had an obsessive belief in his own abilities, certainly, but everywhere he sought to leave ordered, constitutional government behind him, and had a clear idea of what that should entail. We may find absurdities in the Bolívarist constitutions, yet they were not illiberal in the context of his time, by comparison with the hereditary absolutisms holding sway over continental Europe.

Bolívar had two great guiding principles. He believed in the need for a strong central state to guarantee the freedom of the weak against the strong, although he always argued that such an executive must be checked by parliament, and have no power to override the inalienable rights of the people. He also argued for a united South America, albeit divided into different countries, undaunted by the knowledge that his dream was almost certainly quixotic. Who, looking at the history of the continent since his death, can say he was wrong? The absence of a tradition of effective democratic government spawned grotesque and fatal alternations between strong dictatorship and weak, populist democratic governments usually undermined by left-wing extremists. The division of Latin America into twenty republics, some in Central America with a population barely the size of a small town in the United States, has made the continent globally irrelevant and fissiparously parochial. The fact that Bolívar was, in his phrase, ploughing the sea – perhaps no one man could have prevailed against the social and political realities of his time – should not detract from the nobility of his vision. He at least set a standard, put down a marker, both for strong representative rule and constitutional government and for pan-Americanism, that to this day is a long way from being met. Bolívar also displayed other, lesser, political skills: as a superb orator; as a crafter of resounding rhetoric; as a formidably devious diplomat; as a brilliant showman.

Why did he so singularly fail, when the North American colonists were able to succeed in creating the United – and constitutional – States? Perhaps because the British Empire in America was primarily an economic construct in a geographical setting without major barriers, overthrown for economic reasons by a trading class, while the Spanish Empire was primarily a military construct, overthrown by military means, leaving a deep divide between landowners and the landless poor; the trading classes played little or no part in its downfall. The North American revolution was a middle-class one, while the revolution of the Spanish colonies was aristocratic and militarist, harnessing undercurrents of class and racial hatred.

Bolívar was one of the few during his period who was a compassionate radical. He genuinely believed in the rights of even the poorest, and in equality of race to the point of brow-beating his niece, his adopted daughter, into marrying a mixed-race officer. He was no egalitarian – he believed in an ordered society, with men of property and education at the top, and despaired of the ignorance of the masses – but he recognised the legal and human rights of even the poorest of the poor, of the most illiterate peasant, the freed slave, the broken-backed Indian *peón* of highland Peru.

It was this that so disturbed most of the Spanish American oligarchies of his time; in this lay his appeal for the masses of Latin America; and it is for this reason that he qualifies as a genuine popular leader – more than Napoleon does, or any twentieth-century demagogue – although his commitment to order and property meant that he was no revolutionary.

As soldier, statesman and man of common humanity, Simón Bolívar stands head and shoulders above any other figure Latin America has produced, and among the greatest men of world history. Small wonder that he remains a symbol of hope for millions of Latin Americans seeking liberation from poverty, ignorance and disease. Does his achievement matter, in view of the suffering the continent has endured since his day? The answer must be an unequivocal yes. It matters that Latin America was freed from a decaying parasitic empire. It is not to the Liberator's account that after its release the continent has taken nearly two centuries to stand on its feet.

PART TWO: THE SOUTH

The Director, the Protector, and the Sea-Devil

20

The Outcast

In about 1775, in a far-away corner of one of the world's remotest and least populated regions – the spectacular mountain-dominated plain near Los Angeles in southern Chile, almost untouched by civilisation and bordered by lands still inhabited by Araucanian Indians – there lived a pretty child of thirteen or fourteen, just making the transition to young womanhood. She was small and slim, with dark hair and unusually large deep-blue eyes, a delicate white complexion, and an expression that was sweet, jolly and sad, all at the same time. Isabel Riquelme came from a respectable local landowning family whose forebears had fought the Moors in Spain, but probably had Araucanian blood in her ancestry. Her mother had died shortly after her birth, and she had been brought up by her father and his second wife. One day she met a distinguished guest of her father's, a lieutenant-colonel of dragoons.

This formidable but unprepossessing man was about fifty-two, stout, severe-looking, with a long pointed nose, a set, determined expression and large, bushy eyebrows. He was so red-faced and short he was nicknamed El Camarón – The Shrimp. A man whose arduous life had prevented him from marrying, he had a stern sense of duty and was not given to humour or laughter, yet something in the pubescent girl captivated him. Within a year, the stern gentleman had asked for her hand and promised to seek permission from the King – as was necessary for any marriage between an official of the Spanish Crown and a colonial. When she was eighteen and he fifty-seven, he persuaded her to his bed. On 20 August 1778 Isabel produced a child, christened Bernardo because he was born on the feast of St Bernard. The monstrous old man, having taken advantage of the girl, now abandoned any pretence of intending marriage and resumed his official duties elsewhere. Her father made no scandal, probably from fear of the powerful seducer.

The unwanted child was given to foster parents, and the affair hushed up. Isabel soon married a respectable neighbour presumably unaware of the love-child, but he died only two years later, in 1782, leaving her a widow with a daughter, Rosita. There, in provincial obscurity, the sad, squalid little tale might have ended. But the chubby, blue-eyed boy, so different from his dark-complexioned companions, was no ordinary child. When he was four, a detachment of dragoons galloped into the town of Chillán and took Bernardo away from the only parents he knew, to an estate near Talca run by an elderly but kind-hearted Portuguese, Dom João Albano. The wrench the boy suffered was in time eased by his friendship with Albano's son, Casimiro.

Occasionally friends of the boy's father would appear to enquire after him. It seemed this gentleman had become very important indeed – governor of the whole province of Concepción. In the autumn of 1788 a small, portly man of great energy but advancing years – he was now sixty-eight – came to visit the Albano household, and was treated with great deference. It was explained to the ten-year-old Bernardo that he was nothing less than the ruler of the whole country – the Captain-General in Chile of the King of Spain. It was the first and last time the awestruck child saw this all-powerful dignitary, whom he did not realise was his father.

Soon afterwards the boy was sent back to Chillán, presumably after pressure from his mother, to an unusual school, founded to educate the children of Araucanian Indian chiefs but also attended by a few white boys. There the young Bernardo played with the lively, hardy sons of the fierce nomads of the virgin forests, lakes and mountains of southern Chile, learning something of their language and culture and taking part in their vigorous games.

After only two years, however, the unseen hand was extended once again and Bernardo was taken by an official to the port of Talcahuano, where he was put on board ship for Peru. It seems his mother had had an affair with a neighbouring landowner: Bernardo was to be removed out of range of this fresh scandal. He was only twelve, and had never lived with his own parents; to be taken fifteen hundred miles away – a fortnight's journey by sea – to a new land, to live among strangers again, must have increased whatever sense of loneliness, deprivation and disorientation he may have felt. But perhaps it was rather exciting, too. In Lima, overseen by Don Ignacio Blake, a friend of his father, the boy who had played with Indian children now attended an altogether different type of school, the Royal College of San Carlos, where the élite youth of the Spanish Empire, children of high officials (a contemporary was a scion of the Torre Tagle family) wore uniforms of black suits and cocked hats. It was an ideal solution for his father – the best possible education, but far away; the scandal that would break if the child's existence became known might have cost the terrifying old man his career. Blake removed Bernardo from the College when he was sixteen, again on his father's instructions, and he was sent to Spain. His father was on the point of elevation to the most powerful position in the Spanish Empire, that of Viceroy of Peru, and such a god-like being could not afford to be tainted.

The lonely adolescent, who had now known four different homes, was received perfunctorily in Cadiz by Nicolás de la Cruz, Albano's wealthy son-in-law, who soon found him a passage to England, again on his father's instructions. Bernardo was sent to Richmond, to the home of a Mr Eeles, who arranged for him to be tutored in a variety of subjects. From there he wrote many times to the remote figure whom he had by now discovered to be his father.

By all accounts affectionate, sensitive, intelligent, and feeling very unloved – although he was well-treated by the Eeles family, and had a juvenile passion for the daughter, Charlotte – the boy enjoyed the life of a middle-class Englishman of the time. He was there for four years, but in spite of the good nature of the Eeleses his circumstances became increasingly difficult, even desperate: his father's agents, a firm of clock-makers, Spencer and Perkins, who administered Bernardo's allowance of £300 a year, were taking much of it for themselves. His father never replied to his many letters, and his feckless guardian in Spain, Nicolás de la Cruz, wrote just once in those four years. Friends raised two or three pounds a month to help him survive financially, and he was offered a passage to Trinidad, or to Philadelphia, so that he could work his way back to Chile.

If he was impecunious and felt unloved, he nevertheless suffered no shortage of companions; in particular, he was now being tutored in maths by a man in his early fifties, brilliant, passionate and overpowering – one Francisco de Miranda. At the centre of a London circle of Latin Americans opposed to the Spanish Crown, he carefully watched the youngster for more than a year, testing his opinions, thinking to use him as a courier to his own native Venezuela. Although Bernardo went by his mother's name of Riquelme, Miranda knew who his father was –

Don Ambrosio O'Higgins, Viceroy of Peru. For Miranda to suborn the boy would be a triumph indeed.

Bernardo wrote with some pathos to his father from London in February 1799:

> My dearest father and benefactor, I pray Your Excellency will excuse my using this term so freely, for I do not rightly know whether I may address you thus or not; but if I must choose between two expressions, I will follow the inclinations of nature (having no other guide), for had I different instructions I would obey them. Although I have written to Your Excellency on several occasions, Fortune has never favoured me with any reply, being seemingly hostile to me in this; but I still trust that she will at length relent and grant my desires.
>
> Your Excellency must not think that I presume to complain, for in the first place this would be taking a liberty to which I have no right. I know that it is to Your Excellency I owe what education I have so far received. I am now twenty-one years old, and I have not yet embarked on any career, nor do I see any likelihood of doing so. I wish to join some naval academy if I can manage it, to learn the career to which I feel myself most attracted, and so hope that, as I have already written in previous letters which I trust Your Excellency received, you will decide about it as seems fit and proper, seeing that I feel myself well suited to it, and that a career of arms can bring advancement and honour with it at present, which is certainly what I would like and feel I have some aptitude for, so that I eagerly await Your Excellency's orders to obey and undertake as you dispose, confident that my duty and intention is only to please you.
>
> I will give Your Excellency a brief account of the moderate progress which I am making here in my studies, which are English, French, geography, history ancient and modern, etc., music, drawing, and the exercise of arms, in the last two of which I can say without boasting that I am tolerably proficient, and I should very much like to send Your Excellency some of my paintings, specially the miniatures, did not present circumstances prevent it.

To his guardian in Spain, Nicolás de la Cruz, he wrote more desperately:

> I am at a loss to account for it. My parent must have disowned me, or something of the like, as otherwise you surely cannot have forgotten and abandoned me in this way. My plight is such that instead of learning and making progress in the various subjects to which I have applied myself I am beginning to forget them for lack of guidance, and seeing myself treated in this way by those I considered my best friends fills me with worry and wretchedness.

Few young men can have had greater reason for turning against a parent. It was no more than poetic justice that Miranda should have become his son's mentor.

Then war broke out between England and Spain, and in April 1799 Don Nicolás did agree to pay for Bernardo's passage back to the peninsula. Miranda entrusted Bernardo with his famous testament (see pages 47–8). The young man copied it on to thin paper and sewed it into the lining of his clothes to preserve it, in spite of Miranda's insistence that he destroy it. Now just short of twenty-one, he was an admirer of the British colonial system, a friend of the Araucanians who had fought against Spanish oppression, and a hater of despotism. He also hated the way his mother had been sacrificed on the altar of his father's career, yet revealed a desperate craving for paternal approval.

21

The Irish Viceroy

Don Ambrosio O'Higgins, notwithstanding his failings as a lover and a father, was almost as remarkable as the son who later eclipsed him. The story of an impoverished Irishman's rise, through his own efforts, to become the most powerful Viceroy in the Spanish Empire is the stuff of romantic epic — were it not for the unromantic nature of the man himself. Ambrosio's passage through life had been hard and, as is often the case, he saw little reason why it should not be the same for the next generation; his son, moreover, was a permanent and politically dangerous reminder of the lapse that once briefly softened his harsh soul.

Ambrose Higgins was born about 1720 in Ireland, at Summerhill in County Meath, where although his parents were minor gentry fallen on hard times he is said to have run errands for the local landowner's wife. But he appears to have been well-educated, and much later told the navigator and explorer George Vancouver that 'at an early period of his life he had entered into the English army; but not obtaining in that service the promotion he had expected, he had embraced more advantageous offers on the continent.'

Some time during his twenties, like many another young Irishman in search of fortune he migrated to Spain, drawn by her Catholicism, a mutual resentment of the English, and the supposedly linked origins of Ireland and Iberia. Spanish law accorded the Irish equal rights with Spanish subjects, and many Irishmen had prospered there. By the age of thirty-two he was a bank clerk in Cadiz, where he worked for five years. Then a younger brother, William, destined for the Church, suddenly left Spain for the Presidency of Asunción (later Paraguay), and Ambrose set off after him. Failing to persuade William to return, Ambrose too decided to stay. He visited Buenos Aires and then travelled the arduous road to Chile and Peru. In Lima he set up modestly in business. When he was forty he returned to Spain in pursuit of a government job in the New World, which he had taken a liking to. The only offer was that of an Irish friend, John Garland, a military engineer who wanted a draughtsman. Ambrose became a lowly and elderly second lieutenant, on 500 pesos a year.

A commercial misjudgement saddled him with a large debt, and altogether the prospects seemed poor indeed for a middle-aged Irishman on the lower rungs of the military ladder. Arriving in Buenos Aires in 1763, he set out on the long trek across the Argentine pampas and arrived at Mendoza in June – when, south of Equator, snow was already blocking the high passes across the Andes to Chile. He later wrote: 'Having set out to cross the Cordillera in the [southern hemisphere] winter of 1763, I very nearly found myself lost, and I managed to escape with my life only through the special mercy of Divine Providence and thanks to [my three] valiant porters, one of whom perished.' Garland caught up with him in Mendoza, where he fell in love with a beautiful Chilean girl. The Captain-General of Santiago de Chile promised to apply for the permission necessary for Garland to marry, and the two friends set off for Valdivia, where they were to reinforce the fortifications. The wait for permission was interminable, the girl found another husband, and Garland was heartbroken.

The port of Valdivia was remote, the last-but-one southward stop for the Spanish before the badlands of lakes, forests and mountains controlled by the dangerous unsubdued Araucanian Indians of southern Chile. Only the island garrison of Chiloé lay beyond, supplied from the sea. Osorno, between the two, had been sacked by the Indians, and Valdivia, containing about a thousand inhabitants and 250 soldiers, was separated by Indian-controlled forests from Concepción, the main Spanish military base, which itself had twice been burnt down. Nevertheless, the Spanish were concerned at the time not so much with Indians as with their European rivals. Garland and Higgins set up brick kilns, and designed a series of forts at the harbour mouth intended to make Valdivia impregnable – the Gibraltar of South America.

Higgins took advantage of a visit by the Captain-General to win his approval of a scheme to build a series of shelters across the Andean passes between Chile and Argentina to save travellers from blizzards and permit passage during most of the winter months. He set up a series of *casuchos* – barrack-like brick structures with sloping roofs so the snow would slide off. Muleteers, who stood to benefit from the scheme, provided the materials free of charge, and the new shelters permitted a postal service to be maintained almost year-round. Higgins was badly affected by the cold and the altitude as he supervised the building of these shelters; in 1766 he retired to Spain but, failing to make much impression there, he returned, with a commission to write a report on Chile.

This remarkably farsighted document urged that emigration from Europe should be encouraged, to exploit Chile's great undeveloped wealth in minerals and agriculture. More cynically, knowing that the Jesuits were being expelled from Paraguay, he drew up a list of the locations of all their settlements in Chile: his aim was to replace the Jesuit missions with new colonies of Irish immigrants, to work the land and defend it against the British, who had aroused Spanish mistrust of their intentions by their occupation of the Falkland Islands; he later claimed that the American War of Independence attracted the Irish who would otherwise have gone to Chile. Higgins also argued – with a degree of radicalism – that free trade would help open up Chile. The final suggestion – and the most important, in Higgins's view – was to put an end to the Indian problem by pushing the Chilean frontier south; the Indians, he argued, should be treated with respect and firmness. He also advised establishing missions as far south as the Magellan Straits and Tierra del Fuego.

Higgins's report was read politely in Madrid and he, still a lowly functionary, returned to Santiago, where he heard of a major Indian uprising. He volunteered for service and, at the advanced age of forty-nine, was appointed a captain of dragoons. The tough-minded Higgins excelled in his unlikely role of warrior, organising a new offensive force – hitherto the Spanish had kept to their stockades – which could act as either cavalry or infantry and was equipped with small four-pounder cannon. His recruits were *huasos*, Chile's equivalent of the Argentine *gauchos* or Venezuelan *llaneros*, and proved themselves a match for the Araucanian lancers.

Higgins held 'parliaments' – the first was a conference between the Captain-General of Santiago de Chile, the Bishop of Concepción, numerous senior officials, and about two hundred Indian chiefs, plus their attendant tribesmen – at which the Indians were, as he had advocated, treated with respect; he encouraged trade with them, and steadfastly resisted calls that they be annihilated or corrupted through liquor: 'Humanity, the right of nations, and the sovereign justice of the King do not permit us to entertain these atrocities, all the more so when they could only result in turning the country into a desert.' Such high-mindedness compared very favourably to Indian policy in the United States, for example. There was a surprisingly strong streak of humanity in this otherwise unbending man.

In 1773 Higgins was invited to Lima to meet the Viceroy, Amat, who ruled a territory three and half thousand miles long by three thousand wide. His celebrated mistress, 'La Perichola', the opera singer immortalised in Thornton Wilder's novel *The Bridge of San Luis Rey*, presided over a splendid house and large estate. Higgins was profoundly impressed by this potentate, who reciprocated the feeling, offering him the rank of lieutenant-colonel on his departure. Soon he was promoted brigadier, then commander-in-chief of the frontier region, and eventually became Governor of Concepción, a city of about seven thousand people, and of its extensive surrounding prairies.

He was now fifty-six, an age at which most men, at a time of short life expectancy, had already retired; but he seemed full of vigour, continued to pacify the southern frontier, and enjoyed a running feud with the other great power in the city, the bishop. This reached its climax when the bishop and his retinue decided on a progress through Araucanian-infested territory; Higgins's offer of an armed escort was brushed aside, and the bishop's party was duly captured. His own loyal Indian retainers offered to play a *chueca* match (a form of hockey) with their attackers: If they won, the bishop and his entourage would be set free. The bishop's Indians were beaten and massacre seemed imminent, until it was decided to play the best of three games. The bishop's retainers won the next two, and freedom. The people of Concepción were indignant, but Higgins refused to take revenge.

In 1787, after just less than ten years as Governor of Concepción, Higgins was appointed Captain-General. His *bando* – a decree issued on entering office – sternly enjoined the 300,000 citizens of Santiago not to let pigs roam the streets, not to do their washing in the water courses, not to throw the clothes of those who had died of infectious disease into the streets. Men were instructed to be faithful to their wives, and to refrain from brawling, carrying arms and swearing in public. Beggars were to join the army or leave the city within three days, and Holy Week penitents were forbidden to indulge in self-flagellation.

An economic crisis had hit Santiago when a modest degree of free trade was introduced and Chile's domestic industries nearly collapsed, although trade multiplied sevenfold. Higgins's response was a vigorous attempt to stimulate domestic industries into competing with overseas ones. Mining, sugar, rice, tobacco and cotton were his priorities, and the north of Chile his target area for development. Travelling there, he found the local landowners resisting his innovations and still practising the *encomienda* system, thinly-disguised slavery; Higgins abolished it and considered prosecuting the worst offenders. He introduced five new taxes, and laid the foundations for a thriving fishing industry. When Charles III of Spain died in 1788, Higgins scandalised conservative opinion by inviting four Araucanian chiefs to celebrate the accession of Charles IV. At about this time he despatched his nephew Demetrio to Ireland, to obtain a spurious genealogy proving his descent from 'Sean Duff O'Higgins, Baron of Ballinary' – no genuine record of any such lineage existed; this, forwarded to the Spanish court, entitled him to become Don Ambrosio O'Higgins, Barón Vallenar. The former bank clerk, minor businessman and middle-aged lieutenant of engineers was now a nobleman with a pedigree (however dubious) showing the requisite quarterings – and felt able to face down the provincial criollo landowners who despised him.

In 1795 George Vancouver, making his way homewards after his renowned surveys of the Pacific coast of North America, was received with great interest and cordiality by O'Higgins who, in his remote fastness, was always keen to converse with civilised Englishmen. Vancouver has left his impressions of the primitive methods used in the construction of the road between Santiago and Chile's principal port, Valparaíso:

> There were about fifty men at work with common pick and shovels, and to supply the place of wheel-barrows for the removal of earth from the higher to the lower side of the road, the hide of an ox was spread on the ground, and when as much earth was thrown on it as would require the strength of two men to remove, the corners of the hide were drawn together by them, and in that state dragged to the depressed side of the road, and emptied where requisite, to preserve a gentle slope in the breadth; or else discharged over the brink and sent down the side of the hill ... The lower side or brink had neither bank nor earth, nor rail of wood, as a fence; nor did we understand that any form of protection was designed to be named, the want of which gave it a very unfinished naked appearance and ... it appeared to be dangerous in a high degree.

Vancouver and his party were favourably impressed by the Captain-General's courtesy – 'His Excellency's character, not only in respect of his great attention and urbanity to strangers, but of his parental care and constant solicitude for the general happiness and comfort of all the people who lived under the government, were the constant topics of our conversation' – but appalled by the housekeeping in his palace. The beds were 'tolerably good, but we could not help being much disgusted at the insufferable uncleanliness of our apartments; the floors of which were covered with filth and dirt. Brooms were not in common use in Santiago; the only alleviation we could obtain was that of water to sprinkle the dust, which was so thick in the officers' apartment that it would rather have required a shovel than a brush for its removal.'

Grubby O'Higgins's palace may have been, and suspect his pedigree, but there was no questioning the authenticity of his appointment by Manuel Godoy in 1795 to the most important job in the Spanish Empire: Viceroy of Peru.

22

Father and Son

The Viceroyalty of Peru was a remarkable achievement for a man whose official career in Spanish service had begun only in his forties. Although neither New Granada, Buenos Aires nor Chile (where he had been succeeded as Captain-General by one of his aristocratic criollo enemies, the Marqués de Avilés) was now controlled from Peru, it remained the jewel in the Spanish Crown and Ambrosio O'Higgins still ruled over a capital of 60,000 people and a population of a million, from a throne-like seat beneath a red velvet canopy in his audience chamber, the Hall of the Viceroys, hung with portraits of his predecessors. He disapproved of much of what he saw in the streets of Lima. It was a sink of idleness and good living, a parasite city fuelled by silver mining from the cordillera, full of gambling and licentiousness, with a huge underclass of impoverished Indians.

Even at seventy-five he had not lost his reforming zeal. He issued a fierce *bando*, a decree of good government, and also proclaimed his intention of building a highroad to link Lima and Cuzco (a project which proved beyond him: even today it is hardly more than a track). The highroad he promised to link Lima and its port of Callao was successfully completed at the beginning of 1799. Unlike the Bishop of Concepción, the Archbishop of Lima was a man after O'Higgins's own heart and shared his stern views, so the city was not riven by antagonism between Church and State (Lima had twenty-two monasteries and fourteen convents as well as scores of churches). He did his duty, but his energies were sapped by worry: Spain and England were again at war, and O'Higgins had but a single frigate and a few warships with which to defend Callao. He prepared his army and militia for the expected British landing on the beaches, urged Godoy to rescind concessions granted to English whalers, and announced that smugglers would be lynched on shore 'without mercy or remission'.

Meanwhile he pined for his beloved Chile, where he had enjoyed his happiest days. He had appointed a young friend, Juan Mackenna, governor of the ravaged colony of Osorno which he himself had refounded. Amid the immorality of Lima, the most powerful man in Latin America dreamed of returning to the clean and bracing air of Osorno, and chose its name for his title when the King elevated him to the rank of marqués.

Then arose an even greater danger than that posed by British fleets – the subversion of the Spanish Crown being preached by revolutionaries nurtured in England by the dangerous Francisco de Miranda. The final blow fell just after the Viceroy's eightieth birthday: details of Miranda's plotting reported in Madrid by a spy revealed that one of the conspirators was Bernardo Riquelme, his own illegitimate son.

Bernardo arrived back in Spain in the summer of 1799. His guardian, Nicolás de la Cruz, now one of the wealthiest merchants in Cadiz, put him in a servant's room and gave him an unpaid job as a clerk – an echo of his father's job in the same city more than fifty years before. Bernardo had hoped to join the navy, but was barred because he was illegitimate: 'My blood boils with envy when I see so many young men setting off for the wars, destined for a rapid career which will bring them either an honourable post in the service of their country or else a glorious death.' He also wrote pathetically to his father that 'To see all my countrymen getting letters from their parents fills me with envy, whilst I, poor wretch, have none', but that stony heart in Lima remained unmoved. Bernardo resolved to break out of his Cinderella existence and return to South America at the earliest opportunity; but Cadiz was being blockaded by the British. At last he joined a merchant ship, part of a convoy; what transpired, he recounted to his father:

At seven in the morning, when I was fast asleep, they roused me with the news that sails had been sighted astern. I had scarcely got half dressed when a cannon ball was fired over the main mast without doing much damage, which made us think that they must be English, so we put on more sail, but this did not help us either, for in less than ten minutes an English frigate and two seventy-four [gun ships] bore down upon us, and in view of the great danger we stood in from being exposed to the continuous fire which they opened upon us from the frigate and the two ships, we made ready to heave to, to find out for sure whether they were English or Spanish.

The forty-six [gun] frigate thereupon came up to windward and the two seventy-fours to starboard, a pistol's shot away, and in the dark we could not make out any flag or show our own. The English frigate hailed us in their language, and I took the megaphone to answer them. They warned us to surrender or else they would sink us, and such-like threats, whilst they kept sending shots over us from time to time. Not a single one of our sailors showed himself on the quarterdeck; they had all taken refuge below. The captain and myself with the megaphone were the only ones to show our faces.

Since we were on the point of being boarded by the frigate and the two other ships, we surrendered. When the English admiral sent a heavily armed boat to take possession of our ship, and convey all the prisoners on board his own, I was kept at his beck and call to act as interpreter. At dawn the following day, the said ships and the English frigate were only a musket's shot from the Spanish frigates *Carmen* and *Florentina,* and opened fire on them and took them after a sharp engagement ... [the rest of the convoy was captured]. After a few days' sail, they took us to Gibraltar. I was stripped of all I had with me. I cannot tell you what I went through; for three days on end I did not have a scrap to eat and I had to sleep on the bare floor for a week, all because I did not have a single *real* with me on board, as I have not received a farthing since leaving London.

From Gibraltar I went on foot to Algeciras, half fainting with hunger, heat and exhaustion, where I had the good fortune to meet with Captain Tomás O'Higgins [a distant cousin], who had also been made a prisoner on board the frigate *Florentina,* where he was a passenger. He was also short of money but gave me a peso. Then, as best I could, I took a passage on board a ship bound for Cadiz, offering to pay on arrival. The next day after setting sail, we were again given chase by the English. A warship bore down upon us in full sail, but we were faster and had the good fortune to reach the protection of the castle of San Pedro, where, at nightfall, we weighed anchor and slipped out under cover of darkness into Cadiz Bay. So I am lodging once again in the house of Don Nicolás de la Cruz, whom I most deeply regret troubling.

The months passed, and again he wrote to the father who never answered: 'It breaks my heart to find myself a prisoner in this unhappy Europe, without any means of escape or any friend to help me. All the time I have been in Spain, I have never known what it was to feel the touch of a *real* in my pocket; but at least I shall have the satisfaction of knowing that I have bothered nobody for as much as a pin, but have rather put up with every conceivable embarrassment, even latterly to the point of not venturing from my room for lack of common necessities...'

In the summer, yellow fever swept Cadiz; Bernardo fell seriously ill, and de la Cruz callously arranged for the last sacraments to be administered and a coffin to be bought for the boy. Fortified by quinine, however, he rallied; by December he had recovered, though he was more miserable than ever.

I am still living in the house of Don Nicolás, in conditions which cannot but drag a man down to the depths of human wretchedness and misery, without a single friend to turn to for help and advice, whilst the very thought of staying on in this house is enough to kill me. During the two years which I have been under his roof, I have not exchanged a single word with its owner, nor have I once unburdened myself of everything which is on my mind or asked or received a single *real* from him, even when I set out for Buenos Aires...

I have been forced to keep to my room as I simply am not fit to appear in company, and with his consent I have sold my piano which I happened to have left in Europe when I embarked, and with some of the proceeds I paid off the debts incurred during my illness. The remainder, which amounted to a hundred pesos, I handed over to Don Nicolás, who wishes to use them to offset past expenses, and thus to deprive me of those few coins and leave me without even an overcoat for these winter months. Lack of resources has forced me to interrupt my studies for fear of public ridicule.

Even if he had been better-clad, Bernardo was not particularly prepossessing. Small and barrel-chested, but thin following his illness, pale and undernourished, he had curly chestnut hair and his mother's blue eyes. The eyes and strong brows replicated his father's determined expression, and his nose was prominent too. His mouth conveyed some of his mother's gentleness and tranquillity. His cheeks were adorned with long, thick sideburns. He was friendly, frank, even naïve by nature, and highly intelligent. He pined to escape his domestic prison and the dreadful Don Nicolás.

The cruellest blow was yet to come. At the beginning of 1801 he was summoned by de la Cruz: he was to be expelled from his guardian's house. He was to be disinherited; his father charged him with ingratitude, and castigated him for his failure to embark upon a career, but did not reveal that this was because he had been informed of his son's involvement in the plotting to overthrow the Spanish Empire. In the utmost consternation, the wretched youth penned yet another desperate letter:

I am my own barber and hairdresser; I do my own sewing and mending, and in fact, for the last year, I have not wasted a single farthing, not for lack of friends willing to lend me money, for there are various Irish houses here who offered me some, but because I did not wish it to be said that I was acting improperly, for I know that the slightest negligence on my part would immediately reach Your Excellency's ears, and for this reason I have suffered, and still suffer, the torments of martyrdom in this house, scorned and treated like the meanest servant, with no more clothes than the modest suit which I have been wearing for the last four years...

Your Excellency will understand that I have had reason enough to try and leave this country, if only to save Your Excellency's own honour, for here you can keep few secrets from anyone, though I have not breathed a word or opened my heart to a living soul apart from my own father; but even one's closest friends abuse friendship. I think I have said enough of that matter; I only trust that [this letter] will reach you in time to cause Your Excellency to form a different judgement as to my conduct, which has always been modest, respectful and full of gratitude for the benefits received at your hands, as also as to the conduct of whoever has persuaded you of the contrary.

When he heard of his son's involvement with Miranda, Don Ambrosio knew his days were numbered: it was bad enough that the Viceroy of Peru should be exposed in Madrid as having an illegitimate son; worse by far that that son should be conspiring with a dangerous enemy of the state. Even as he penned his instructions to Don Nicolás, the order for Don Ambrosio's dismissal was being drawn up, on the grounds of his health and age; his replacement was to be his bitter enemy, the Marqués de Avilés. In January 1801, about the time when Bernardo was learning of his condemnation by his father, Don Ambrosio suffered a cerebral haemorrhage. He knew he was dying. He asked an old friend, Tomás Delfin, to help him make his will, disinheriting Bernardo. Delfin pleaded on behalf of the unfortunate young man, but Don Ambrosio took no notice, and sent Delfin away. On 14 March he at last drew up the will; for the first time he acknowledged Bernardo as his son, and made provision for him. What caused this remarkable last-minute repentance can only be guessed at; four days later, Ambrosio was dead.

The news reached Bernardo weeks later: suddenly, aged twenty-three, he was the owner of a substantial estate in southern Chile, and a famous name. In the spring of the following year he embarked on a frigate and in September 1802 arrived in Valparaíso after a difficult passage around

Cape Horn. It was a sign of Bernardo's generosity of spirit that, in spite of the treatment he had received at his father's hands, he remained devoted to his memory in later life. But his first thoughts were for his adored mother, with whom he had corresponded unceasingly, and for her daughter Rosita, both of whom had been treated just as badly by the old man.

In Valparaíso Bernardo was warmly received by his father's step-nephew, Tomás O'Higgins, whom Don Ambrosio had treated as a son, and who had inherited the bulk of his considerable wealth. To deal with probate, Bernardo had to travel to Lima, where his old schoolfriend the Marqués de Torre Tagle treated him hospitably. But he could not get his legitimacy recognised, so was unable to assume his father's titles of Marqués de Osorno and Barón Vallenar.

Bernardo seemed destined, like Bolívar, for an agreeable life spent overseeing a large country estate; he threw himself into the task with zest, planting 100,000 vines and establishing a herd of 3,000 cattle at Los Canteros. He also dabbled in local politics and was elected to the town council of Concepción, where he occasionally clashed with the governor of the province, Luís de Alava, who watched him carefully for any mani-festation of the subversive contacts he was known to have made in England. O'Higgins was content merely to discuss with his friends the benefits of Britain's liberal system of government; but this was enough to excite Alava's suspicions, as Britain seemed to have ambitions for the country – notably an expeditionary force sent out in 1808 under General Robert Crawford that was intended to land in southern Chile, but which at the last moment was diverted to Buenos Aires following Beresford's and Home Popham's abortive landing there.

O'Higgins fell under the influence of Juan Martínez de Rozas, then in his mid forties, an intelligent and subtle former government official dismissed by Alava for his liberal ideas who succeeded in blocking Alava's elevation to Captain-General of Santiago de Chile on the death of Avilés in February 1808. Rozas's own candidate, an amiable elderly man of no great intellect, was successful and appointed Rozas his adviser. As the real power in the land, Rozas began at once to strengthen the authority of the *cabildo* – the Captain-General's advisory council – and to broaden its representative base by recruiting twelve new members.

Rozas and the young landowners among his supporters, in particular O'Higgins with his earlier exposure to revolutionary ideas, were com-mitted to the cause of independence from Spain at the earliest opportunity. As elsewhere in Spanish America, the criollo aristocracy of Chile resented the superior status accorded the lowly-born officials from the mother country who governed them. They had long had contact with North America though ships putting into Chile's ports, and had admired the success of the American revolution. But the Chileans as a whole were a settled, conservative lot – a half-hearted attempt to establish a republic made by a French adventurer in the 1770s had come to nothing.

23

The Carrera Whirlwind

The fuse was lit, as elsewhere in Latin America, by Napoleon's replacement of Ferdinand VII with his brother Joseph Bonaparte. Rozas
persuaded the Captain-General to pledge his allegiance to Ferdinand,
but Rozas's man was eased out and replaced by an even older figurehead,
the Conde de la Conquista; he floundered about for a year, then a new
and larger *cabildo* voted in a seven-member junta in his stead. This was
on 18 September 1810 – now celebrated as Chile's birthday.

In all this, Bernardo O'Higgins was no more than a bit player, but he
had a sense of duty towards his country in its hour of destiny: 'I might
have become a good farmer and useful citizen, and if it had been my lot
to be born in Great Britain or Ireland, I would have lived and died on
my estates. But fate wished that I should first see the light of day in
Chile, and I cannot forget what I owe to my country.' He believed – cor-
rectly – that Chile's most pressing need was for an effective army to
consolidate her independence and repulse the attempt Spain would
undoubtedly soon make to quash it; Rozas, by contrast, believed in
negotiation. O'Higgins wrote to his father's protégé, the Irishman Juan
Mackenna, former governor of Osorno, proposing to recruit two cavalry
regiments, mostly from among his own tenants, and an infantry militia.
Mackenna told Bernardo that if he was committed to taking up arms,
he must learn from his father – some irony, there, the Viceroy having
been a pillar of Empire.

> If you study the life of your father, you will find in it military lessons
> which are the most useful and relevant to your present situation, and if
> you always keep his brilliant example before your eyes, you will never stray
> from the path of honour, and should you not succeed in winning great
> distinction, at least you will never do anything you need be ashamed of
> ... In my opinion, your venerated father possessed these qualities more

than any other man of the century in which he lived, with the exception of Frederick the Great. He had a clarity of intelligence which simplified the most complicated and difficult problems, and an understanding for whose power of perception nothing was too small.

The life of your father, faithfully related, would present one of the finest moral lessons in the history of humanity. I know of none other better calculated to impress on youthful minds the inestimable value of inflexible honesty, indefatigable work, and immovable firmness...

No one can grasp the miraculous nature of your father's career without knowing by experience the court of Spain, its depravity, its favouritism, and the antipathy of the Spaniards for foreigners. Although your father was Irish – of which I feel proud – he was generally dubbed by the Spaniards 'The English viceroy' – a nickname which more than once brought him to the verge of ruin.

More specifically, Mackenna urged Bernardo to learn the use of carbine, sword and lance from a sergeant of dragoons, to learn to ride to the required military standard, and then to learn how to command, again with the help of such a sergeant. O'Higgins duly set about his crash course in military training; meanwhile, Rozas had assumed effective control of the junta in Santiago. The Spanish economic monopoly was ended. The Church was brought under the control of the new junta, rather than of the Spanish State. A force was sent over the Andes to help Buenos Aires maintain her independence against an expedition expected from Spain. Rozas also summoned a national congress to broaden support for the regime. From Concepción, O'Higgins approved most of this: 'My personal conviction is that the first congress in Chile is bound to display the most puerile ignorance and be guilty of all sorts of stupidity. Such consequences must inevitably follow from our present situation, lacking as we do any sort of knowledge and experience. But we have to begin some time, and the sooner the better.'

Mackenna meanwhile started organising a thousand-strong national army, backed by a militia of 25,000, and put forward proposals for setting up a military training school, fortifying the ports, and building up an arsenal. But opposition to Rozas began to grow; he was accused of corruption, and of staffing the offices of state with his placemen. He was also bitterly criticised for sending help to Argentina when Chile herself was under active threat of a Spanish invasion. An acrimonious dispute erupted between Santiago and Concepción. Rozas resigned in

July 1811, and a junta of 'moderates' – mostly landowners from the Santiago area – took over. A ship arrived with a message seeking financial support for Ferdinand VII against the French; Chile emphasised her increasing independence by refusing to send any.

After Rozas's resignation O'Higgins also withdrew temporarily from the political fray. He and other southerners, like Mackenna and Rozas himself, represented a kind of constitutional opposition, closely tied to the influential Larrain family, known as the '800' for their extensive clan connections based in the south. The stand-off could not last long, and the man who brought matters to a head was José Miguel Carrera, second of three brothers and a sister from a family that considered itself the most aristocratic in Chile, tracing an unbroken line of descent from the conquistadors. A personality with the passion and restlessness of the young Bolívar – although with little of his intelligence, courage, or political judgement – in his teens José Carrera had been savagely outspoken against the government. Before he was twenty he was sent to Peru, then to Spain, where he performed brilliantly as a young officer in the Spanish army. Tall and startlingly good-looking, with dark hair, blazing eyes, a haughty nose, full mouth and broad chin, he had no doubt that he possessed the political and military skills to guide the faltering steps of the new country. He set out from Spain aboard a British ship, landing at Valparaíso, where he called on the governor. This was Juan Mackenna, who guessed that the Larrain clan was planning a coup against the moderate junta in Santiago in alliance with José Miguel and his brothers – the eldest, Juan José, less intelligent and able, and Luís, the youngest, hot-tempered and as impulsive, fiery and aggressive – and his sister, Javiera (by some accounts the most ambitious, fanatical and domineering of them all, she was later said to have goaded José Miguel to some of his wilder antics).

The father of these four siblings, Don Ignacio, was a respected member of the junta they were plotting to overthrow. José Miguel put himself at the head of the plotters and, using Juan José's private force of grenadiers and Luis's private artillery, surrounded the seats of the junta and the congress. When the real power behind the coup – the Larrain clan – took over, the Carreras were offered no more than subordinate posts, which they contemptuously refused. Friar Joaquin Larrain remarked with satisfaction: 'All the presidents are now our own people – the president of congress, the president of the junta, even the president of the high court.' Carrera retorted: 'And who is president of the

bayonets?' The Larrains' protégés Rozas and Mackenna were the governing spirits of the new junta.

Within six weeks José Miguel had reorganised his forces and staged
another coup – this time against the Larrains. As the new boss of
Santiago, he cleverly appointed Rozas the junta member for
Concepción, as a means of defusing opposition in the south to his military dictatorship (the first of countless in the continent). As Rozas was
still in Concepción, José Miguel asked O'Higgins to stand in for him;
O'Higgins reluctantly agreed, only to discover that his mentor
Mackenna had been arrested. He called upon José Miguel to explain
himself to the congress; José, having done so with his customary arrogance, then surrounded the assembly with troops and dissolved it.

Appalled as he was by this high-handed action, O'Higgins was also
gullible enough to let Carrera persuade him to act as peacemaker with
Rozas and the elders of the Larrain clan. He set off for the south, but
learned on his way that José Miguel had raised a thousand men and was
following after him, to put down any dissent in the region. Infuriated,
O'Higgins offered to lead the south in an uprising in support of Rozas;
but the latter preferred to negotiate, and as the months dragged by
Carrera's numbers grew until at length he was strong enough to oust
Rozas from Concepción without a fight and force him into exile in
Argentina, where he died at Mendoza on 3 March 1813.

O'Higgins was now thirty-five; he had seen the overthrow of his two
mentors, Rozas and Mackenna, a near civil war, three military coups,
and the take-over of power by a youthful hothead and his violent and
clannish family. He decided to leave Chile and make himself a new life
as a rancher in Argentina; he was a figure of only marginal importance
in Chilean affairs, and not apparently destined to be otherwise.

On 27 March 1813 O'Higgins, while making preparations to leave
with his mother and sister, learned that a detachment of Spanish troops
had landed in Talcahuano. Accompanied by fifty veterans and a quantity of arms, munitions and uniforms, the commander, Antonio Pareja,
intended to train and supply a royalist army, with the aim of reincorpor-
ating Chile into the Spanish Empire and punishing the rebels. The
provinces of Chiloé and Valdivia at once declared for the King, including the garrison of 1,500 at Chiloé. Concepción went over to the royalist
side, and in Chillán, where O'Higgins had been brought up as a boy, the
Franciscan friars who dominated the city rallied their flocks to the
throne. The royalist forces, now numbering 3,000, picked up a further

2,000 militia on the way north, among them 100 artillerymen, 400 mounted dragoons and 600 infantry. This formidable and united army seemed likely to extinguish without difficulty an independence cause whose patriots were bitterly divided and whose forces consisted of renegade bands in conflict with each other. Moreover, by taking the south so decisively, the Spanish seemed likely to secure the support of the savage Araucanians, who would wish to be on the winning side.

On learning of this formidable royalist advance, O'Higgins did not hesitate; gathering a hundred or so locals armed with lances he rode towards Concepción. Learning that the city was in royalist hands and he himself in danger of capture, he fled northwards with two companies. After two days' hard marching he crossed the river Maule to Talca and joined José Miguel Carrera, who had appointed himself commander-in-chief of the patriots and ridden southwards from Santiago to counter the royalists. O'Higgins proposed a bold plan to slip back across the Maule in the night with a small force and assault the royalist advance guard, already at Linares, calculating that they would not be expecting an attack from their quarry. The operation was a complete success: he surprised the royalists in the main square and sent them back as prisoners to Carrera. Many joined the patriots, as did the local militia, two hundred strong.

Meanwhile the patriot army organised itself with the main body under José Miguel in Talca; an advance guard in front of it under the command of his elder brother, Juan José, between Talca and the Maule river; and a third detachment under the younger brother, Luis, along the Maule itself. José Miguel had ordered the release of Juan Mackenna, the best soldier on the patriot side, who galloped south to help. As an adviser José Miguel took the young United States consul, Joel Poinsett, whose suggestions veered between common sense and idiocy; he thought O'Higgins should take the advance guard across the Maule, which would have exposed it to encirclement and capture.

O'Higgins became ill, and command of his column fell to a militia colonel, Juan de Dios Puga, who instead set out across the hilly countryside with six hundred men to ambush the enemy. At Yerbas Buenas they saw what they took to be the camp fires of the Spanish vanguard; in fact, Puga had stumbled upon the main Spanish army, and his attack caused chaos. The Spanish fired at one another in the darkness, and the patriots captured the artillery and took a large number of prisoners. But triumph turned to disaster: in pulling back with its prizes, the small patriot army found its horses had been scattered, then a contingent of cavalry in reserve was brought up by the Spanish and fell upon Puga's men. They fled in disarray, and as they crossed the Maule the panic spread. Against strong opposition from Mackenna, Luís Carrera decided to abandon his front line on the river and retreated, his officers escaping on horseback in front of their men. The patriot rout would have been complete if Puga's own troops, who had been dispersed by the night attack, had not in turn refused to place themselves in danger by crossing the river. Pareja's forces were now bogged down in the cold of Chile's winter, and he fell seriously ill with pneumonia. The patriots, realising they were not being chased back to Santiago, regrouped and attacked, only to run into stiff resistance backed by artillery. Then the Spanish, demoralised despite this success, withdrew to Chillán. On Poinsett's advice the patriots skirted Chillán and instead attacked Concepción and Talcahuano on the coast, cutting off supply lines to Chillán and capturing a ship carrying reinforcements to Peru. Meanwhile O'Higgins had recovered, and rode down to Los Angeles on the river Bío Bío, where from his estate of Las Canteras and the surrounding countryside he raised about 1,400 men. It seemed the tide was favouring the patriots again.

Carrera laid siege to Chillán, but this proved a disastrous mistake: the town's normal population of 4,000 had been doubled by an influx of refugees and soldiers, and it stood on a slight hill, well defended with earthworks and an extremely solid Franciscan monastery. At the height of winter, the besiegers in their flimsy tents were very exposed. After a month Carrera decided to try to force the issue. Cannon were brought up to attack the city from a nearby hill, and fires were lit at night, on either side of the city, to simulate encampments. O'Higgins commanded the main force. The royalists, lured out to attempt the destruction of the battery, were almost caught in the trap but fought their way back into the city, hotly pursued by the patriots. In vicious hand-to-hand fighting the patriots lost about two hundred killed and another two hundred wounded, and failed to dislodge the royalists from the centre. A lucky royalist shot blew up the patriot arsenal and the royalists counter-attacked, forcing the besiegers back, until the onset of darkness brought a pause and permitted both sides to regroup.

The next day Carrera moved forward again, but instead of attacking the royalists in the city his men indulged in an orgy of rape and looting in the suburbs. When an ammunition train Carrera had been waiting for fell into the hands of the royalists, he had to call his troops off. The disorganisation and barbarity of the patriots in their failure to capture Chillán turned the province against them.

O'Higgins, riding south at the head of three hundred cavalry, was ambushed and nearly captured, then rallied his men and defeated his attackers – but not before they had put his estate of Las Canteras to the torch and taken his mother and sister prisoner. His was an isolated victory. The royalists were now in control of most of the countryside between Chillán and the Bío Bío river, and of all the territory south of it. Worse was to follow. In a minor engagement at El Roble, Carrera and O'Higgins were ambushed; Carrera fled the scene on horseback, leaving O'Higgins wounded in the leg, but still able to direct operations and save his men. This minor incident at last turned the patriots against Carrera's disastrously inept and even cowardly leadership, and the junta decided the steadier and more reliable O'Higgins should replace him. Carrera and his brothers threatened to overthrow the junta. O'Higgins himself, naïve and good-natured as ever, rose to Carrera's defence; he felt it 'essential to make no changes in the present command by the removal of an officer whose services are so very useful and necessary for the expulsion of the enemy.'

The junta insisted upon the change, however. Carrera trampled the order underfoot and imprisoned the messengers who brought it. Mackenna, who was advising the junta, which had moved to Talca to be near the fighting, sternly admonished O'Higgins: 'Courage! Save your country! Should you refuse to accept the command to which you are called by the will of the army and the choice of the government, the whole province will be lost and you will be eternally responsible to God and to your country for its ruin.' Believing that he would be able to control his rival, Carrera eventually gave way to the 'appointment of so worthy a person as Colonel O'Higgins'; he himself was appointed ambassador to Argentina, to get him out of the way, and on receipt of this news he set out from Concepción with his younger brother Luís in the wake of Juan José, who had ridden to Santiago to raise the people against the government.

Few men can have succeeded to leadership of a cause at a less auspicious time than Bernardo O'Higgins, and few can have been less experienced. Appointed commander-in-chief of the patriot forces on 2 February 1814, he looked no more than a stop-gap, put in to preside over inevitable defeat at the hands of the Spanish. He was politically naïve;

of undoubted courage but with no formal training as a soldier; intellectually limited and physically unprepossessing; unmarried, but devoted to his mother and sister (whose freedom he had just gained in exchange for some of his captives); kind and straightforward, to the point of ingenuousness; half-Irish and derided as a bastard; and genuinely wanting only to tend his estate. He was what he seemed, an unambitious anti-hero; and he had drawn the short straw – to him it fell to lead what was left of Chile's army.

Another piece of bad news reached O'Higgins just four days into his new command. On the orders of José Fernando de Abascal y Souza, the energetic Viceroy of Peru, two hundred veterans under the senior Spanish commander, Brigadier Gainza, had landed at Arauco, south of Concepción, to reinforce the royalists; these forces, including more than a thousand crack troops, now numbered several thousand, although many were in poor condition. The patriots, by contrast, had only about 1,800 men altogether, most of them in a deplorable state, ill-fed, ill-clothed, and armed, in some cases, with nothing more effective than clubs. They held only a few outposts south of the Maule, including Concepción and Los Angeles. O'Higgins lamented realistically: 'I dare not call it an army, as I can see nothing, absolutely nothing, in its equipment or morale, which justifies that name.'

Within weeks, the Spanish had crossed the Maule and captured Talca. The Chilean junta had to flee back to Santiago. There was a danger that Juan Mackenna would be cut off at Membrillar, to the south of Talca, and O'Higgins further south, at Concepción. Mackenna's only chance was to move north at speed to overtake the Spanish army and block its advance towards Santiago, just a hundred miles away. Mackenna, desperate to march but reluctant to abandon O'Higgins, pressed his fellow-Irishman: 'Unless you bring up your division at once, everything may be lost… You, my dear friend, are responsible to your country for your present inactivity and for not pressing on with your division … only come, for God's sake, and all will be well.'

O'Higgins did come, but his progress was painfully slow as he had lost all his horses and mules; nevertheless, in a frontal attack he took a supposedly impregnable Spanish position on the heights at El Quilo, while Mackenna succeeded in fending off an attack by the main Spanish force on his position at Membrillar. Equally heartening was the information that on their way north José Miguel Carrera and his brother Luis had been captured by a Spanish patrol. Some of Carrera's partisans suggested that O'Higgins might have tipped off the Spanish; it would have been a welcome sign of toughness on his part – but also completely out of character.

Mackenna now begged O'Higgins to abandon El Quilo and continue northwards to join him; on 23 March the two Irishmen at last came together, and decided to march their combined forces – 1,500 infantry, several hundred militia, and eighteen guns manned by two hundred gunners – further north, in an attempt to overtake Gainza's royalists and block an assault on Santiago. The two sides raced towards the Maule; the royalists got there first, but O'Higgins and Mackenna secured a ford and crossed, then entrenched themselves behind the solid walls of the Quechereguas hacienda; Gainza decided he could not readily dislodge them. With winter again approaching and both sides exhausted, they decided to dig in. A temporary truce was arranged by a British naval captain, James Hillyer. He had been ordered to chase an American ship out of Chilean waters and also to ensure that Spanish resources should not be dissipated in fighting rebels. He met Gainza, O'Higgins and Mackenna at a peasant's house between the two positions.

Gainza's forces were being weakened by desertion and he feared his position at Talca was too exposed, so he agreed to evacuate the town immediately, and the whole province of Concepción within a month, if the patriots would agree to recognise the sovereignty of Ferdinand VII while retaining self-government in Chile. Neither side regarded this truce as more than a device to gain time to re-equip and regroup. The royalists pulled out of Talca, then pleaded the poor condition of the roads as their excuse for not evacuating Chillán and the rest of Concepción province. In Santiago, where a siege had been expected, news of the truce was greeted with widespread astonishment and rejoicing.

The truce had also provided for the release of the two Carrera brothers, who were to be delivered to Hillyer in Valparaíso and taken by him to Brazil, out of harm's way; the junta in Santiago, determined to bring the brothers to account for their attempts to overthrow the government, hoped to intercept and seize them. The royalists, discovering this intention, informed the Carreras that O'Higgins and Mackenna were plotting to take them and send them to the Viceroy in Lima, and arranged for them to escape, covertly providing money, arms, horses, and a bandit guide. The head of the junta, Francisco de la Lastra, appalled by O'Higgins's failure to secure the brothers, thought it must have been deliberate: 'You must learn in future to restrain your natural kindliness and carry through with punctiliousness the resolutions of the government, which are designed to preserve the glories you have won.' He was right to see the Carreras as a continuing danger. The Chileans soon caught Luís, but within two months José Miguel had organised yet another coup, among officers angered by the truce. Once again he seized power in Santiago as dictator, at the head of a three-man junta; la Lastra, Mackenna and dozens of others were arrested; Mackenna was exiled to Argentina. When he saw how the Carreras had taken advantage of the truce, O'Higgins at last understood their true nature: he moved on the capital at the head of a large force. Failing to make much headway in a preliminary skirmish, he reassembled his men for a full-scale assault.

The following day dramatic news arrived: the Viceroy of Peru had repudiated the truce and despatched a further expedition under Colonel Osorio to finish off the job of mopping up rebel resistance in the southern territory begun by Gainza. In light of this O'Higgins immediately proposed that the two rebel factions should sink their differences and combine against the common enemy, but Carrera insisted the rivalry must be resolved. Fearing that this would merely open the door to Spanish reconquest, O'Higgins agreed on 3 September 1814 to join Carrera as a subordinate, on his terms, then set off to command the patriot troops in the south.

There, resistance to the Spanish was fast crumbling. Desertions from the patriot ranks were commonplace – even O'Higgins's own secretary urged him to join the royalists and accept the governorship of Concepción, once held by his father. The Spanish under Osorio, advancing remorselessly, took the whole province of Concepción, crossed the Maule, and occupied Talca again, moving into the south of Santiago province. What had been feared three months earlier, before the truce, now loomed again: the Spanish seemed set to regain Santiago, thanks largely to the internal divisions besetting the patriots.

Carrera floundered, proposing various plans for stopping the Spanish. He had the Viceroy burnt in effigy in the main plaza at Santiago and, in a further futile gesture, placed a reward on the head of the commander of the advancing army. O'Higgins begged him to come to take command of the forces at the front, but Carrera had no more intention of putting himself in O'Higgins's hands than in those of the Spanish. O'Higgins taunted him – 'You should take up the post befitting the

Commander-in-Chief and I will be at your side serving as adjutant or in command of some division or small detachment, or simply with gun in hand' – but Carrera lacked the courage, and preferred to let his brothers represent him. By now the Spanish had reached the Cachapola river, just south of Rancagua, only fifty miles from Santiago itself.

24

¡Rancagua!

On 30 September 1814 Osorio succeeded in crossing the Cachapola river with most of his army and turned right along its bank, towards the town of Rancagua. The detachment that was supposed to be blocking him, under Luís Carrera, had thus been bypassed and was now irrelevant. The next contingent along the river was that commanded by Juan José Carrera; at Osorio's approach he panicked and fled into Rancagua.

O'Higgins, in charge of the third detachment along the river, had hoped to combine with both brothers but now found himself faced with the choice either of joining Luís Carrera's army in a headlong retreat, leaving Juan José cut off in Rancagua and at the mercy of Osorio; or of plunging in to help Juan José. The town, surrounded by much superior Spanish forces, had no natural defences, and O'Higgins's officers told him it would be folly to go in; his response was characteristically brave, generous, humanitarian – but foolhardy, since it put the lives of his soldiers at risk in a doubtful cause:

> It is just because the Carreras are my greatest enemies, that I cannot abandon them now. Honour is more than life. I could retire now, and the real motive for doing so would be the safety of my brave troops. But that is not how men would interpret it, and the thousand tongues of calumny would soon convince the world that I had betrayed and abandoned a comrade-in-arms because I looked on him as a personal enemy.

There followed one of the most futilely courageous epics in military history, akin to the charge of the Light Brigade in the Crimea in its carnage and absurdity. If its cause was as much Bernardo O'Higgins's stubborn pride as the misjudgement of the eldest Carrera brother, it established O'Higgins's greatness and permitted the salvaging of

Chilean national honour, to a degree which rendered inevitable the creation of an independent nation.

On the night of 30 September O'Higgins rode into Rancagua at the head of his column. It was a typical, middle-sized Spanish colonial town, its low buildings in the familiar grid pattern centred around the main square, the four main streets running into the plaza not at each corner but in the middle of each side. In the plaza Juan José, least able of the four Carreras, embraced him with the words, 'Although I am your senior in rank, I place myself under your orders.' O'Higgins replied dryly, 'I accept your command.' He set up barricades across the access streets, placing two cannon to cover each. Snipers were positioned on the roof-tops; the supplies were all gathered in the centre of the square, and the church was used as a look-out. Finally, the Chilean flag was hoisted, draped in black to show that the defenders would fight to the last man. The Spanish had nearly 4,500 well-armed men, about half of them crack troops, including the formidable Talavera Regiment. O'Higgins had fewer than half that number, mostly ill-trained militia who barely knew how to handle a gun – which few possessed.

Next morning, across the plain with its rich green crops beneath the soaring, snow-capped cordillera, the Talaveras charged forward in three columns, to be met with such withering cannon and rifle fire that after only an hour they were forced to retreat. In the afternoon Osorio ordered his men to attack again. Cannon were aimed down the streets where the patriots had mounted their barricades, and Spanish infantrymen were despatched to force the streets and climb along the flat roofs of the houses. As cannon blazed on both sides and muskets crackled, the Spanish advanced inch by inch across the roofs and down the streets, until vicious bayonet charges forced them back again. This brutal street fighting lasted several hours, and the Spanish were close to the plaza when darkness forced the two sides to disengage. Bodies lay heaped in the streets, fires flickered in the two opposing camps, and the groans of the wounded rent the night. O'Higgins reckoned he could hold out only one more day, since he was almost out of water and his ammunition was very low. He had sent a desperate message calling for help from the third column, under Luís Carrera.

On the Spanish side, Osorio was also in a dilemma. He had received instructions from the Viceroy to return to Peru with the Talavera Regiment and other local troops, to deal with the threat of an uprising there; if the war in Chile was not yet over, he was to conclude a truce. Believing victory to be within his grasp, he had ignored these instructions; but he had been twice repulsed, and victory eluded him. He considered calling off the assault, but in the morning gave the order to resume the offensive. His men were slowly closing on the plaza when suddenly there was a cry from the church tower; a patriot lookout, sighting a cloud of dust, signalled the approach of a relief force under Luís Carrera. The Spanish turned and began to change positions to prepare for imminent attack. The tables had been turned and Osorio now faced the grim possibility of being caught between two fires. A ragged cheer broke out from the defenders in the square.

Then the lookout in the tower reported that the relief force was retreating. There was a stunned silence in the square. It was beyond belief. The sudden hush was broken by O'Higgins, who yelled to his men to resume fighting. The Spanish came on with renewed fury, and O'Higgins realised at last that his position was hopeless: the water had run out. In the midday sun the faces of his men were parched and scorched, their lips black. With no water to sponge them out, the cannon got so hot that when charges were put in them, they exploded immediately. As a delaying tactic, O'Higgins ordered that the houses around the square be set on fire; as they blazed, the blackened corpses in front of them also caught. The Spanish fought their way forward to the outskirts of the plaza itself. The patriots' powder store was set alight by a spark and blew up with a roar.

O'Higgins now gave the order for all who could to fight their way out. Like Cortés fighting his way down the causeway at Tenochtitlan, three hundred years before in Mexico, at the head of 500 men O'Higgins on horseback attempted to carve a way down the narrow corpse- and rubble-strewn main street of Rancagua; they drove mules before them to force the attackers back, but O'Higgins was unable even to thrust his own horse over the barricades at the side of square. His adjutant was killed beside him. A Spanish soldier who rode at him narrowly missed him and his horse; another succeeded in killing the horse beneath him but O'Higgins, jumping up on his attacker's, slew him and, slashing about with his sword, led his men out of the square. Of those who attempted to fight their way out of the plaza, fewer than half survived – among them Juan José Carrera, who had kept a good horse ready. The royalists went wild in the square, killing all prisoners, raping the women and slaughtering the children who had taken refuge in the church. The hospital was burnt down, and only those patients who managed to drag themselves out escaped. It took two hours for Osorio and his officers to restore order. Apart from the civilians, about six hundred patriots and a thousand Spanish had been killed.

O'Higgins rode through the night to Santiago, where he burst into José Miguel Carrera's office at the government palace. It seemed that he, not his brother Luís, had given the order that recalled the third division before Rancagua. José Miguel defended himself angrily: O'Higgins should have broken out sooner; Luís Carrera's forces were largely militia, equipped only with lances, and could not have attacked without being destroyed; furthermore, they had heard the noise of fighting die down as they approached, and assumed that O'Higgins had surrendered. The excuses were feeble and unconvincing, and O'Higgins could see but two explanations for the failure to relieve Rancagua: cowardice, or treachery – Carrera wanted to see O'Higgins crushed, and was prepared to risk his elder brother's life in doing so. There was a third, less discreditable motive, that Carrera wanted to preserve the third division as a nucleus for resistance against the Spanish in the north once Santiago had fallen. But O'Higgins also learned something else from his supporters in the capital: had he won the battle of Rancagua, Carrera planned to have him assassinated. With characteristic restraint, O'Higgins announced his intention of escaping across the Andes; Carrera retorted that *he* would fight on, in the north of Chile. Both knew Santiago would have to be abandoned as the Spanish advanced.

O'Higgins sent his beloved mother and sister ahead to the town of Los Andes, beneath the cordillera; a week later he set off himself at the head of a pitiable exodus of refugees, many of them without food or clothes, to cross the awesome mountain range towering above them. On 12 October they reached the summit of the pass at 13,000 feet, where O'Higgins, Isabel Riquelme and Rosita spent the night in one of the very mountain shelters constructed by Ambrosio O'Higgins nearly half a century before. Dragoons and muleteers had to go ahead and beat down the larger snowdrifts to clear a passage. Several days later the column of refugees made its way down into the foothills near Mendoza, where they were comforted by food and wine despatched by Juan Mackenna in his exile, and by the assurances of the local governor, José de San Martín, that he had enough provisions to feed them all. San Martín himself had ridden out towards Uspallata to meet them:

A mob of scattered soldiery, without leaders or officers and thus unre-
strained by any discipline, was struggling for the provisions, cursing and
committing all sorts of excesses and almost making them unusable in
their fury. Some were crying out aloud against the Carreras, whom they
blamed for the loss and destruction of their country. A multitude of old
men, women and children weeping with fatigue and exhaustion, fear and
dismay. A great number of citizens stoutly maintaining that the Carreras
had brought out from Chile more than a million pesos belonging to the
state, hidden in the luggage of their numerous adherents, and beseeching
me not to permit the theft of funds so essential for the task of re-
conquering their country.

In the wake of O'Higgins, Carrera too had fled Santiago, with the aim
of continuing the fighting in the north. He ordered a group of soldiers
to turn refugees away from crossing the Andes, so that they could continue the fight in Chile; the soldiers refused. Carrera decided to make
a stand against the Spanish at Los Andes, then thought better of it and
joined the rearguard of the refugee column across the cordillera. He
despatched his brother Juan José to greet San Martín in the name
of the 'government of Chile'; but San Martín had already met
O'Higgins, and had called on him to assume command of the displaced Chileans.

José Miguel, arriving shortly afterwards, complained angrily about
San Martín's reception of O'Higgins. San Martín smoothly reassured
him that no slight was intended, but when he rode back from Uspallata
the following morning he left instructions that Carrera's baggage was to
be searched; in fact, Carrera was innocent of this particular crime,
Santiago's treasury having been plundered by the Spanish. In reply to
Carrera's indignant note complaining of this insult to the head of the
Chilean government, San Martín pointed out coldly that 'the only
authority in a country is that of its lawful government' – in this instance
himself, as Governor of Mendoza. Carrera seethed. To avoid fighting in
Mendoza between the adherents of Carrera and O'Higgins, towards the
end of October San Martín ordered Carrera down to San Luis, an inhos-
pitable town on the edge of the salt pans in the rain-shadow of the
Argentinian Andes.

Carrera, believing he had support enough, refused. Quietly San
Martín assembled a thousand men and surrounded the Carrera brothers in their billets; the two older brothers and Doña Javiera were sent
under guard to San Luis, their soldiers ordered to Buenos Aires to join

the army there. Mackenna and a young Chilean politician, Antonio José de Irissari, were sent with them to explain the reasons for this drastic action. Luis, the only Carrera still at large, also set out for Buenos Aires, to put the family's side of the case to San Martín's superiors. In that city, in mid November 1815, he challenged Mackenna to a duel. Mackenna, shot in the head, died instantly, and the body of that generous, good-hearted Irishman – Ambrosio O'Higgins's protégé and mentor to his son, Chile's best soldier, almost certainly her first independent president had he not lost the power struggle with the Carreras – was dumped outside the city prison.

O'Higgins's hatred of the Carreras hardened into a blood feud; least vengeful of men, he considered that his guardian had been murdered, and was determined upon revenge. Irissari tried to have Luís arrested and José Miguel, fearing for Luís's safety, rode from San Luis to Buenos Aires, where he was able to induce a young Argentinian friend, Carlos Antonio José de Alvear, from one of the city's oldest families and as head-strong as himself, to prevail upon the head of the Argentinian government to drop the affair. When it began to look as though the Argentinians might recognise José Miguel as head of the Chilean community in exile, San Martín ostentatiously resigned as Governor of Mendoza; he was called back by the acclamations of his officers and his people, however, and resumed his position, virtually independent of the government in Buenos Aires.

In mid 1815 O'Higgins, his mother and his sister, like so many Chilean exiles, had made the dreary journey across the pampas to Buenos Aires. He was thirty-seven now, and almost destitute again, but this time with two dependants to support. They rented a small house where they entertained modestly – Chilean-style *tertulias,* evenings of guitar music and political discussion among family and friends. The women made a little money by selling sweets and rolling cigarettes, and O'Higgins had managed to bring some out of Chile. Like Bolívar in Jamaica, without good reason he continued to hope. By 1816 Buenos Aires was the last area of the continent which had not been recaptured by the Spanish. It seemed the dream of Latin American independence was well and truly crushed, the lives of its leaders squandered in a lost cause.

In the tacky, random settlement that was Buenos Aires, by the great muddy Plate estuary, O'Higgins and his followers were a forlorn sight. Undoubted if reluctant hero of the Chilean resistance, he must have lamented the fate which had taken him from poverty to prosperity, only to strip him of his possessions again, as though in retaliation for his sub-version of his father's glittering achievements within the Spanish Empire. In desultory fashion he plotted his return; he would raise 6,000 men to cross the mountains, and ships would sail around Cape Horn to land more troops on the Chilean coast. Carrera also had plans: to cross into the north of Chile with five hundred men and raise the people there for a triumphal march on Santiago. San Martín dismissed this as ridicu-lous and the former dictator set off instead to the United States, to try to buy ships through the agency of his old friend Poinsett.

After a year of idleness in Buenos Aires, O'Higgins was more than pleased to accept San Martín's invitation to command the patriot con-tingent in his own projected invasion of Chile. Arriving at Mendoza, he found 1,500 men already assembled, trained and organised, and San Martín clearly in the saddle as leader of the expedition. O'Higgins was given the task of preparing the military training camp at Plumerillo – chopping down trees and building houses, something he enjoyed in the way that he had enjoyed running his estate at Las Canteras. He was also modestly paid, and delighted to be active again in the cause of Chilean independence.

In the evenings he pored over military manuals or socialised with Chilean exiles: the appalling cruelties inflicted by the Spanish after Rancagua formed the staple topic of conversation. Osorio, not himself vindictive, had been forced by the Viceroy, Abascal, to apply harsh pun-ishments, and was soon replaced by an effete and incompetent voluptuary, Francisco Marcó del Ponte; he subsequently became an embarrassment even to the Spanish, who mocked his fondness for titles. In his official procedures he was described as:

> Don Francisco Casimiro Marcó del Ponte, Angel, Diaz, and Mendez, Knight of the Order of St James, the Royal Military Order of San Hermenegildo, and the Fleur-de-Lys, Member of the Royal Ronda Equestrian Club, well-deserving of his country to an eminent and heroic degree, Field Marshal of the Royal Armies, Supreme Governor, Captain-General, President of the Royal Audiencia, General Superintendent Sub-delegate of the Royal Exchequer and of Posts, Mails, and Couriers, and Royal Vice Patron of this Kingdom of Chile...

Vicente San Bruno, an officer of the Talavera Regiment, was the real, and detested, power in the land. He became notorious for his wanton butchery in Santiago; sympathisers of the independence movement were dealt with brutally, their lands confiscated, their women violated. Many were exiled to the Juan Fernández islands off the coast. Far from fear of reprisals such as these turning the population against the patriots, however, this policy of brutality turned Chileans originally loyal to the Crown against it.

25

Born a Soldier

In 1820, as part of Brazil's ongoing quarrel with Argentina, a force of Portuguese soldiers under the Marques de Alegre crossed into the beautiful tropical lands between the Uruguay and the Paraná rivers, and in an orgy of destruction, slave-taking and brutality destroyed a series of elegant, symmetrically laid-out towns created by the Jesuits as part of the Guaranitic missions, first established in 1626. Apóstoles, San Carlos, San José, San Javier and Santa Maria La Mayor were razed to the ground, as was the town of Yapeyu, on the right bank of the river Uruguay, where the Guabiradi river flows into it. It was a savage massacre in which three thousand Indians, including children, and their leader, Andres Guacuxrari, a company commander in the Argentine army, were slaughtered. Some 15,000 hostages were taken, churches and houses were pillaged. This atrocity saw the end of an extraordinary experiment in spiritual collectivism – a society run by priests on behalf of the Guarani Indians. Their admirable settlements were left smouldering ruins, never to be rebuilt.

Yapeyu had been the birthplace, more than forty years before, of one José Francisco de San Martín, the fourth and last son of the local governor of this vast, empty and remote outpost, Lieutenant Juan de San Martín. Born in Spain, in León province, like so many he had emigrated to make his career, arriving in the obscure but prosperous backwater of Buenos Aires, in the newly-created Viceroyalty of La Plata. In 1767 the Viceroy of Peru (to which the region at that time belonged), Don Francisco de Paula Bucareli, had at last stamped out the semi-independent theocratic republic which had grown up under the Jesuits in the province of Misiones, and imposed the rule of the Spanish Crown. This annexation, considered a heinous crime by later generations, was carried out without violence, and though the Jesuits themselves were dispersed, much of their economic structure survived. Three years later Lieutenant San Martín was appointed Governor of Yapeyu. Before he left Buenos Aires he asked an army friend, Captain Francisco Somalo, to stand proxy for his marriage to a girl named Gregoria Matorras, from a poor but respectable family of Spanish settlers. The Bishop of Buenos Aires officiated, and Gregoria left shortly afterwards to join her husband in his remote command.

Even as an infant José was distinguished by his exceptionally dark complexion, eyes and hair, so that throughout his life people assumed him to be at least half-Indian, Gregoria's son by a Guarani – a rumour which later did him no harm at all among Latin Americans. The little boy grew up in Yapeyu's school, which doubled as the governor's residence and had been the Jesuits' home. An extensive building with forty-five rooms, it included a large library and a warren of storerooms, as well as the schoolrooms where the Indians had been taught. Remarkably, Yapeyu contained about forty dwellings especially built to house the Indian population, at a time when elsewhere in Latin America they lived in mud huts. The settlement was prosperous, another legacy of the Jesuits, trading hides and meat down the river. There were maté plantations, also oranges, lemons, figs, peaches, apples and pears. About the town grew roses and jasmine, thorn bushes, tala and carob and palm trees, and the countryside was alive with exotic birds, pumas and snakes ('Uruguay' means 'River of the Birds' in Guarani). It was a slice of paradise perched beside a huge, sluggish river.

When José was three his father was recalled to Buenos Aires, where the family spent the next four years and José attended school. Then his father was promoted captain, and posted to Málaga, in peninsular Spain. José was sent to the Madrid Nobles' Seminary, a prestigious school, while his brothers joined the militia and his sister stayed at home with her mother. A dunce at literary pursuits, he shone at maths and geometry. At eleven – remarkably young even for the times, but possibly because of restricted parental funds – he left school and joined the army as a cadet with the Murcia Regiment. At twelve he was sent to Melilla in North Africa, and first saw action by the side of a celebrated Spanish hero, Luis Daoiz. At thirteen, at the siege of Oran, he experienced a thirty-six-hour enemy pounding that left the city devastated. Next he was sent across the Pyrenees, to fight the French, and by the age of seventeen was already a lieutenant. In 1797 he was with the Spanish navy when they were beaten by the British under Jervis and Nelson at Cape

St Vincent. Exactly a year later the British vessel *Lyon* seized the frigate *Santa Dorotea* on which he was serving, but he was subsequently exchanged for a British prisoner. His life could hardly have been more different from that of the pampered young Simón Bolívar.

In 1800 San Martín was back in action, against Portugal, then took part in the blockade of British-held Gibraltar. In 1803, the year he helped deal with a serious epidemic in Cádiz, his father, now commandant of the port of Málaga, died. Little is then known of his life until Napoleon's invasion of Spain. Daoiz, José de San Martín's hero as a young cadet, was executed by the French. On 2 May 1808 San Martín, now thirty, was officer of the watch in Cádiz when an enraged mob urging an attack on the French fleet in the bay besieged the headquarters of General Solano, San Martín's commanding officer and another of his mentors. San Martín ordered the soldiers back into the building, whereupon the mob broke in, chased Solano up onto the roof, and dismembered him. Even for a hardened soldier like San Martín, this was a horribly traumatic event; for the rest of his life he carried everywhere a miniature of Solano, the commander he had failed to protect, and ever afterwards he detested violence indulged in for its own sake and, even more, hated the un-bridled power of the 'mob'.

Appointed adjutant of his regiment, he performed spectacularly at the battle of Arjonilla, charging French positions head on with twenty-one men. He was promoted to captain and then, a few weeks later, when Napoleon's forces were decisively defeated at Bailén, to lieutenant-colonel, having again performed with valour. Two months later he fell seriously ill, and when he had recovered joined the Army of Catalonia, becoming its adjutant-general in 1810. A year later he was given his first really important command, in charge of a regiment of dragoons at Sagunto. He was no disgruntled Miranda, no military amateur like Bolívar, but an outstanding and conscientious career officer clearly des-tined for the highest rank. His brothers were also doing well in the army. Juan Fermín was a commander of hussars in Luzón; Manuel Tadeo was a colonel of infantry; and Justo Rufino, a spendthrift, was colonel of the Almanza Regiment.

26

Defending Argentina

In Cadiz harbour on 14 September 1811 José de San Martín, a distinguished senior officer of apparently no great imagination, from a solid military background, twenty-two years in the Spanish army, slipped aboard a British ship bound for London. He was about to become a traitor and take up arms against the country he had served so loyally, on behalf of a continent he had known only until the age of seven. Our understanding of how this conversion happened is fragmentary. Cadiz, with the largest contingent of Spanish-American exiles in Spain, was a hotbed of plotting. It is known that in 1808 Matias Zapiola, a Spanish naval officer who had been in Buenos Aires, recruited San Martín into a Masonic lodge, the Rational Knights, which had links with Miranda's non-Masonic lodge in London, the Reunion, and contained such prominent pro-independence activists in Buenos Aires as Carlos de Alvear and Juan Martín de Pueyrredón.

The mere fact of his joining this lodge indicates that San Martín must for some time have had doubts about Spanish colonial policy. In 1810, with the Spanish and Portuguese monarchies in exile and in ruins, and uprisings already breaking out in Caracas and Buenos Aires, San Martín must have decided that the future lay with Spain's independent colonies. He was the highest-ranking officer in the Spanish army to make this decision. It seems likely that the accession of such a senior figure was a triumph not just for exiled Argentinians in the network of Masonic lodges, but for the British secret service. In Cadiz Lord Duff (later the fourth Earl Fife) befriended San Martín and made arrangements for his departure through the British diplomat Sir Charles Stuart, who secured him safe passage and a false passport. In December 1811, in civilian clothes, penniless, with just a suitcase, he arrived in London and went into shabby lodgings.

San Martín was immediately taken to Miranda's old home in Grafton Way, now occupied by the Venezuelan poet Andrés Bello and meeting place of the Reunion Lodge which, although not Masonic, drew from Freemasonry its obsession with secrecy and ritual – including oaths and pledges in the Pharaonic and Solomonic traditions. There he met such young recruits as Carlos de Alvear (whom we have recently encountered, five years on, back in Argentina and a friend of the Carrera brothers), aged nineteen, as well as men more his own age, like Manuel Moreno and Tomás Guido. Within a month San Martín had left London aboard a small vessel, the *George Canning*, reaching Buenos Aires in March 1812. Samuel Haigh, writing five years later, remarked of the town: 'There is a wild, unfinished look about it which is anything but pleasing; excepting in a few streets, in the vicinity of the Plaza or Great Square, the houses are low and dirty, and become more so as you approach the environs.'

In Buenos Aires in May 1810 a *cabildo* had been summoned to discuss the fall of the Spanish government. On 25 May the Viceroy appointed after Home Popham's abortive invasion in 1807, Baltasar Cisneros, was deposed and arrested by a junta proclaiming itself to govern on behalf of Ferdinand VII, an action denounced as disloyal by the rival port of Montevideo, across the estuary. Asunción, capital of the province of Paraguay, also resisted the *pronunciamento* from Buenos Aires, proclaiming its own independence in 1811 under the sinister José Gaspar Rodriguez de Francia, a terrifying, morose introvert whom a British captain, Richard Burton, described as 'disinterested and far-seeing, sombre, austere and ascetic, although he would become intolerably fierce when the east wind blew... Evidently the Republic of the Dictator was a reproduction, in somewhat sterner mould, of the Jesuit Reduction System, and it throve because the popular mind was prepared for it.' General Manuel Belgrano, despatched from Buenos Aires to put down this insurrection, failed to do so. Santiago de Liniers, hero of the anti-British resistance, sought to oppose the patriotic movement in Buenos Aires from his stronghold in Córdoba, but he was overwhelmed and shot.

The boldest move determined upon by the Buenos Aires junta – led by Belgrano the soldier, Moreno the radical economist, a leading aristocrat, Bernardino Rivadavia, and a radical lawyer, Juan José Castelli – was that of marching into Upper Peru to seize control of its mineral riches.

And Upper Peru – after 1776 a province of the same Viceroyalty of La Plata to which Buenos Aires had belonged – was the gateway to the Viceroyalty of Peru, seat of Spanish power on the continent and richest of them all. In November 1810 General Balcarce, the new nation's army commander, won the battle of Suipacha, and with his Argentinian forces climbed the awesome rocky passes from the pampas onto the great Andean plateau, the altiplano, 12,000 feet up. One town after another welcomed them – Potosí, Cochabamba, Chuquisaca, La Paz and Oruro, the centres of Spanish mineral wealth. Castelli, now the civil authority in Upper Peru, went about his work with revolutionary zeal, executing Spanish officials and promising radical reform.

Such savage radicalism turned the initial support of the conservative upper classes of the plateau to hostility, however, and in mid 1811 a large Spanish force despatched from Lima to crush the insurgents defeated them convincingly at Huaqui on the Desaguadero river, then again at Sipé-Sipé. An Argentinian force under the able Pueyrredón succeeded in securing an armistice at Potosí and retreating to Jujuy and Tucumán in one piece, but the main retreat of the Argentine survivors across the now freezing plateau was terrible. Only after clambering down thousands of feet to Salta were they able to check the pursuit of the Spanish army. If the Argentinians were crippled on the plateau by altitude and lack of oxygen, the highland Indians in the Spanish army were equally at a disadvantage in the Argentinian lowlands: stalemate.

As a result of these setbacks the junta in Buenos Aires was overthrown and replaced by a more conservative triumvirate. Castelli was arrested, and died disgraced a year later; Moreno died in a shipwreck on his way to Europe; Rivadavia and Belgrano lived to fight another day. Meanwhile a large body of gauchos (the llaneros or cowboys of Argentina) assembled to the east of the River Plate under their colourful leader, José Gervasio Artigas, resisted all attempts at control, either from Buenos Aires or from Montevideo – which itself rejected rule from Buenos Aires. Artigas, essentially an authoritarian bandit, was the epitome of the gaucho commanders who, detesting and mistrusting all things urban, for long ruled the countryside essentially as their personal fiefdoms. Into this unpromising maelstrom of competing cities and warlords, still under threat from the Spanish and struggling in the hands of a succession of transient political leaders, there arrived José de San Martín.

*

San Martín and his party were taken to meet the new triumvirate installed after the downfall of the first junta – Juan Martín de Puerreydón, Bernardino Rivadavia and Feliciano Chiclana. These men viewed San Martín with some suspicion, as a possible Spanish spy, but he persuaded them to recognise his rank as a lieutenant-colonel of cavalry, on the grounds of his service record and obvious knowledge; and to appoint him to set up a new armed force to defend Buenos Aires. The Mounted Grenadiers were to be quartered on marshland by the River Plate improbably named the Field of Glory. Five months later Rivadavia issued an order to bring 'three hundred native young men, tall and strong' to join San Martín and his regiment.

San Martín set about training his men in typically methodical fashion. He instituted severe punishments,

> for cowardice in action, when even lowering the head is to be considered such; for not punishing insults, for not defending the honour of the regiment, for infamous dishonesty, for becoming shamefully familiar with subordinates, for lack of integrity in the handling of funds, for revealing decisions taken at secret meetings, for not helping a comrade in danger, for showing up in public with prostitutes, for gambling with indecent people, for laying hands on a woman, for drunkenness, for speaking ill of a comrade in front of strangers.

Once a month he assembled his officers and soldiers, and any allegations of misconduct were presented; the accused then withdrew, and his fate would be decided upon. The worst transgressions resulted in expulsion from the force – a Masonic form of discipline. He gave each of his cadets a 'war name' – again an echo of Freemasonry. The officer cadets were chosen from among the best families in Buenos Aires, the soldiers were the horsemen of the pampas – the gauchos.

In January 1813, a few months after their formation, the Mounted Grenadiers endured a baptism of fire. A flotilla of eleven Spanish ships was making it way from Montevideo to Rosario, about a hundred and fifty miles up the Paraná river from Buenos Aires. Abandoning his usual blue uniform trimmed in red, his cockaded hat, black leather boots and curved sword, San Martín, dressed like a gaucho in white hat and poncho, took a hundred and twenty men upriver along the bank, travelling at night to avoid detection. Passing Rosario they reached San Lorenzo, where San Martín climbed the tower of the Franciscan monastery and saw the enemy ships which were landing about three hundred infantry. He led his cavalry in an attack, during which his horse was shot under him. As he fell, his leg was trapped; a Spanish soldier slashed his forehead with a bayonet, his companion thrust at him but was killed by one of the grenadiers before he could connect. Another grenadier who ran to San Martín's aid freed him, but was knifed twice and died later.

Within half an hour it was over. The Spanish retreated to their ships leaving forty dead behind them and two cannon, to the grenadiers' fifteen dead and twenty-seven wounded. It was no more than a skirmish, but it caught the imagination of the people of Buenos Aires as the first victory to be secured against the parties of Spanish marauders which periodically raided along the riverside. The Spanish ships now withdrew, and it became easier to supply the patriot army besieging Montevideo, which fell to them soon afterwards.

From the moment of his arrival, San Martín and the zealous young Alvear had begun to organise their own Masonic-style lodge, modelled on those of Cadiz and London; they called it the Lautaro Lodge, after a legendary Araucanian Indian chief at the time of the Spanish conquest three hundred years before. It is not clear whether it was formally associated with international Freemasonry, a powerful force at the time in Spain, France and Britain. Recruits to the Lautaro Lodge were initiated according to the classic rituals and subscribed to the Masonic motto 'Union, Faith and Victory', as well as addressing one another as 'Brother' and their grand master as 'Venerable', but it seems more likely that San Martín simply used Masonic forms and codes of secrecy and conduct as a convenient way of setting up his own secret organisation to propagate the ideal of South American independence. Bernardo O'Higgins was received into the Lodge when he arrived in Buenos Aires in 1816.

The Lautaro Lodge met in a house near the fort in Buenos Aires. In structure it was authoritarian, commanded by a secret council; the compulsory punishment for betrayal of its secrets was death followed by burning, and scattering of the ashes (it is not recorded whether this was ever carried out). Its credo was that: 'Thou shalt never recognize as the legitimate government of the country any other than that which is elected by the free and spontaneous will of the peoples, and the republican system being the most adaptable to the government of the Americas, thou shalt try by all means within thy power to have the peoples adopt it.' Even as an old man San Martín refused to reply to an enquiry about the Lodge from the British general William Miller, a great friend: 'These are entirely private matters, and although they have had and still have great influence upon the events of the revolution in that part of America, they may not be mentioned without my betraying the most sacred promises.'

The Lautaro Lodge formed the nucleus of the more public Patriotic Society, a group of idealistic radicals who played a significant part in the political struggles of Buenos Aires in the succeeding years. It is impossible to know whether San Martín at this stage was motivated more by idealism, or by personal ambition. If the Lodge was a springboard to power in Buenos Aires, it was also a useful means of communication not just with independence sympathisers in Argentina but with similar groups in Chile and Peru, which had to operate underground during the Spanish occupation.

As early as October 1812, a mere two months after receiving their appointment to set up his praetorian guard, San Martín was the prime mover in a coup against the triumvirate; a new liberal constitution was drawn up under the direction of young Alvear, San Martín's right-hand man, who was soon to become critical of him. San Martín now emerged as head of Buenos Aires's armed forces, which put him in a position to seize power; but he took a back seat, preferring to wait until Alvear over-reached himself, and occupying himself meanwhile with finding a bride. Maria de los Remedios was the daughter of Don Antonio José de la Escalada, of one of the principal families of Buenos Aires, by his second wife. Just fifteen, she was extremely beautiful, with an oval face, small sensuous mouth, dreamy eyes and a rosy complexion unusual in Latin America. Her brothers, Mariano and Manuel, had enlisted in San Martín's regiment. San Martín, although aloof and serious, was by no means lacking in charm. Tall and good-looking, with luxuriant sideburns and lively, intelligent eyes, he was described by contemporaries as distinguished and courteous, speaking French well in society, conversant with history, painting and philosophy as well as politics and the army. Maria was not without considerable character of her own: her name was first on the list of Buenos Aires women who supported the independence cause by paying for a musket – 'When public rejoicing carries to their families the news of a victory, they will be able to say with the exultation of their enthusiasm: "I armed the hand of that valiant man who assures his glory and our liberty".' Just six months after his arrival, San Martín was married to his young bride in Buenos Aires Cathedral, with Alvear as a witness.

More pressing matters soon beckoned. The commander of the patriot forces in Argentina, General Manuel Belgrano, a fine administrator but a mediocre soldier, still subscribed, as did most Argentinians, to the view that the power of the Spanish Crown could be broken only by the conquest of Upper Peru – notwithstanding the defeat of Balcarce's army there in 1811. In September 1812 Belgrano, commanding the main Argentinian army, succeeded in routing a large Spanish force at Tucumán, in the north, an elegant Spanish colonial city on a plateau beneath the towering Sierra de Aconquija. A further triumph followed early in 1813 when, moving northwards again, to the hill town of Salta, he completely defeated the royalists. He took three thousand prisoners, then freed them on condition that they remain disarmed – a gentlemanly way of waging war in striking contrast to that practised in Venezuela and, as it turned out, a mistake. Public opinion in the north was on the royalist side; the Spanish regrouped and in October 1813 Belgrano was defeated at Villapugio. A month later his army was completely routed at Ayohuma by a royalist army under Joaquin de la Pezuela. His nerves shattered, Belgrano asked to be relieved of his command.

San Martín was ordered to replace him. He left Buenos Aires in December with the Seventh Infantry, 750 of his grenadiers, and a hundred artillerymen. It was a small army: just 2,000 partially equipped, half-dressed men, supported by the same number of raw recruits from the mountain regions and about three times the number of stragglers. To reach Belgrano's beleaguered forces San Martín had to cross the unpopulated expanses of central Argentina. Belgrano wrote to him: 'I visualise you going through the hardships of your journey, witnessing the misery of our countries and the difficulties which their distances make, together with their lack of population and the consequent lack of resources for operating with the celerity that is necessary.' The journey took more than a month, the grenadiers travelling on horseback, the infantry in wagons. When the two commanders met, between Tucumán and Salta, San Martín was instantly engaged by Belgrano's modesty and humility. He advised the government that the general should be restored to his command of the northern border army: 'He is the most methodical man of all whom I know in America; he is full of integrity and natural talent. He may not have the knowledge of a Moreau or a

Bonaparte as far as the army is concerned, but believe me, he is the best we have in South America.' But Belgrano was later recalled and put on trial for his military failures.

San Martín had no illusions about the difficulty of his task: 'I have found only the sad fragments of a beaten army. A hospital without medicine, without instruments... Naked troops, dressed like beggars.' To pay his own men, he seized a consignment of money waiting to be sent to Buenos Aires.

Arriving in Tucumán, San Martín realised it would be folly to seek out the Spanish in open battle: instead he entrenched himself in a fortified camp just outside the city and concentrated on training his men. His down-to-earth principles were that there cannot be an army without precise planning; and that the soldier is formed in the barracks, not in battle. Subordinates were dressed down for unpunctuality, and for levity. At a staff meeting held before Belgrano's return to Buenos Aires, a Colonel Dorrego mimicked Belgrano's reedy voice. San Martín grabbed a candlestick and smashed it down on the table in front of the insubordinate officer. Dorrego was exiled to another command for his attempt at humour. Training and discipline were San Martín's guiding precepts, and he despaired of the poor quality of the officers under him: 'These misfortunes (I speak of the military) are due to the fact that we do not have a single man able to place himself at the head of an army. Seek six or eight generals in France (who nowadays haven't even got anything to eat), bring them here, and you would see how all operations and events would change. Bear this in mind and you will realise that without this we shall not make any headway. Let us recognise our ignorance and let us not allow our pride to push us into the abyss.'

In this he echoed the exasperation expressed by Miranda, himself a distinguished French general, with regard to the patriot soldiers. San Martín's objective was to introduce European methods of training and discipline – thus turning the lessons learned in two decades of Spanish service to good account against his teachers. But he had no illusions as to what he could achieve. He wrote to Rodriguez Peña, who was his main supporter in Buenos Aires:

> Do not congratulate yourself beforehand, my dear friend, about what I may do here; I won't do anything and I don't like anything here. I do not know the men or the country, and everything is in a condition of anarchy; I know better than anybody else how little I can do. Laugh at gay hopes.

Our country will not make any headway here in the north, outside of a permanent and purely defensive war; for this the brave gauchos of Salta, with two good squadrons of veterans, are enough. To think anything else is to throw men and money down a bottomless pit. Therefore I shall not move or try any expedition.

Belgrano had understood that to win the war he needed the support of the local people:

You will not have to make war there only with arms, but also with public opinion, with the latter being always buttressed by the natural virtues, Christian and religious; but our enemies have made war against us, calling us heretics, and only by this means have they been able to attract the barbarians to arms, telling them that we were attacking religion ... I assure you that you would find yourself in much greater difficulty if they should see in the army under your command that you are opposed to religion and to the excommunications of the Popes...

Remember that you are a Christian, apostolic, Roman general; be careful that in no wise, not even in the most trivial conversations, there be shown a lack of respect to our holy religion; bear in mind not only the generals of the people of Israel, but also those of the pagans and the great Julius Caesar who never neglected to invoke the immortal gods and for whose victories Rome decreed prayers.

However, the atrocities visited by the Spanish on the local people had in any case dramatically reduced local support for the royalist cause: rebel heads impaled on spikes along the highways, towns sacked and prisoners of war sold as slaves to work on plantations and vineyards, soon turned people angrily against the Spanish. Their women acted as spies, their children as messengers, and the Indian horsemen of northern Argentina developed into guerrillas of formidable efficiency. The commander of these gauchos was Martín Guemes, son of a treasury official from Salta, who ranged across these northern frontiers rather as Páez had across the Venezuelan llanos, staging hit-and-run attacks. San Martín relied on these irregulars to deter Spanish attacks from the Bolivian uplands while he was drilling his men in Tucumán.

Guemes's guerrillas penetrated as far as Cuzco, on the other side of the cordillera: he led them for seven years, until he was killed by the Spanish in 1821. His men were concentrated in hidden outposts, and struck at small Spanish units, disrupting lines of communication and robbing depots and munitions dumps. They were sadly ill-equipped; one of his lieutenants wrote after a raid that, armed only with 'clubs, and hand-made spears, they attacked the Spaniards at Sauce Redondo: the tyrants will be amazed, when they see that only thirty men with muskets, helped by unarmed horsemen, attacking against lively fire, will have defeated a force twice as strong; but if they notice that the men who have attacked them want in their hearts to be free, they will have no reason for wonder.' Guemes believed their motivation made up for their lack of weaponry, saying, 'They contribute their own personal efforts, not excepting even the only horse they have.' General Garcia Camba, a Spanish officer, wrote of them: 'They were extraordinary horsemen, skilled in the use of all arms, individually brave, able to disperse and return again to the attack, with a confidence, self-assurance, and cold-bloodedness that roused the admiration of Europeans; as good or better horsemen than the cossacks and the Mamelukes; able to keep, both afoot and mounted, a fire similar to that of a good infantry.'

San Martín did not long retain the command in the north once he had stabilised the line there against the Spanish. Distrustful of the government in Buenos Aires, now increasingly under the sway of the excitable young Alvear, he was also convinced, as his letter to Peña quoted earlier shows, that any northern offensive into Peru was doomed. The land route to the enemy stronghold of Lima was, he increasingly believed, too difficult. In another letter to Peña, he revealed the dramatic conclusion he had reached, that the answer was

> A small and well-disciplined army in Mendoza to go over to Chile and finish the Goths there, giving support to a government of solid friends, in order also to finish the anarchists who are in control; with the allied forces we shall go by sea to take Lima; that is the way and not this one, my friend. Be convinced that the war will not end until we are in Lima. I wish very much that you would appoint someone abler than myself for this post. Do all you can to see that my successor comes soon and tell them that I will accept the governorship of Córdoba. I am ill and broken down; it is better that I withdraw to my corner and dedicate myself to training recruits whom the government may use anywhere else.
>
> What I should like you to give me when I recover is the governorship of Cuyo. There I could organise a small cavalry force to reinforce Balcarce in Chile, which I judge to be greatly necessary if we are to do anything profitable, and I confess to you that I should like to go over as the head of that force.

He was proposing nothing less than a march across the highest Andes to capture Santiago, in Chile, then to embark an army and sail up the

Pacific coast to Lima. Only peasants and their pack mules had hitherto negotiated the southern Andes, the culminating peaks of the range, whose almost impenetrable passes were among the highest in the world; it seemed that Chile was about to revert to Spanish hands; and there was no fleet available – so what San Martín proposed must have seemed complete lunacy on the part of a man previously considered the embodiment of discipline and rationality.

To secure the time to prepare the details of his extraordinary plan, he pleaded illness. He had suffered from asthma and rheumatism in Spain; now he claimed to have severe stomach pains, and to vomit blood; and that he suffered from dyspepsia and insomnia. In June 1814 he set out for Córdoba, about three hundred miles to the south, to recuperate, leaving his command to Rondeau, a lacklustre general. Alvear, whom he had expected would take over from him, was more interested in manoeuvring for political power in Buenos Aires. After defeating the Spanish in Montevideo, that brilliant young man, aged twenty-five, was appointed Supreme Director of the United Provinces of Buenos Aires, in succession to his uncle, Posadas. Three months later San Martín obtained what he had sought, the governorship of Cuyo, one of the remotest of the Andean provinces, with barely 40,000 inhabitants scratching a living on the very slopes of the mountains themselves.

27

Mendoza

It might have seemed to an outsider that the career of San Martín, successful Spanish soldier and patriot, was about to fizzle out in a provincial command in a distant corner of Argentina, a position no more exalted than that held by his father, Governor of Yapeyu. Alvear wrote to him cordially – perhaps ironically: 'Fortune has favoured me admirably in all my undertakings. May she be favourable to you in the same manner.' He was delighted to see San Martín shunted off into such a backwater, unaware of the reason behind it.

The capital of Cuyo province was Mendoza, a pleasant colonial town at about 2,200 feet, with little rainfall but with palm trees and vineyards sustained by irrigation. Above it, from verdant foothills to barren lower slopes, rose the Andes, their white peaks shimmering in the distance. San Martín settled to his duties with relish. First he summoned his young bride from Buenos Aires. With a female relative, a negro slave, Jesúsa, and three attendants, she set out by stagecoach on the seven hundred dusty miles to Mendoza, stopping at rough inns along the way, the journey occasionally enlivened by an encounter with ox-drawn wagon trains, or the sight of ostriches or deer. A lively girl, still only eighteen, Doña Remedios – Remeditos, San Martín called her – settled into the life of the town, doing good works and entertaining local high society. In August 1816 she bore San Martín a daughter, Mercedes Tomása, and the town awarded the baby 200 hectares of land, her father 50; he had grown to love the town and the region, as his graceful letter of thanks makes clear: 'The Province of Cuyo is the one which has finally decided me, because of the good character of its inhabitants, to choose a corner where I could devote myself to breaking the soil, cultivating it and enjoying it.'

San Martín proved a vigorous and patient administrator who looked into issues in minute detail. He placed his province's revenues on a sound footing, levying taxes which were unpopular with the well-to-do – on the Church, on wine and on capital – and confiscating the properties of absentee Spanish landlords. He dispensed justice in Solomonic style. A woman farmer who spoke against her country was ordered to deliver 120 pumpkins to the army kitchens. An army officer who ran up a huge gambling debt confessed this privately to San Martín, 'as a gentleman'. He was given the money to pay, but told: 'Deliver this money to the treasury, but keep the secret; because if General San Martín ever hears that you have revealed what happened, he will have you shot.' A soldier who said he had sworn not to fight the Spanish was informed: 'The governor assumes the responsibility which the supplicant alleges; his hands are now free to attack the enemy, but if a ridiculous worry still binds them, they shall be unbound by the supreme penalty.' San Martín had ordered that no officer should enter the armoury in boots and spurs; a sentry who twice refused to let him in, on these grounds, was rewarded with an ounce of gold.

He would rise at dawn and work until noon, smoking big black cigarettes. He had a curious habit of eating his luncheon standing up, usually stew and cakes washed down by two glasses of wine and a cup of coffee. He would rest in the afternoon, then work in the cool of the evening. After supper he often played chess, before going to bed at ten o'clock. His health continued to trouble him, and he frequently took laudanum – opium – possibly to the point of addiction, to counter rheumatic and stomach pains. He made an imperious figure, with his 'eagle-like look ... as good-looking on horseback [a fine chestnut] as afoot', according to a contemporary officer.

In his peaceful eyrie, San Martín learned of the disasters that befell the cause of Latin American independence hundreds of miles away. When O'Higgins and his rival liberator, Luís Carrera, fled across the Andes with a ragged horde of refugees and camped outside Mendoza, San Martín decided to back O'Higgins, and thus made bitter enemies of the Carrera brothers. To the north the Colombian rebellion was being rolled back; and news reached him that General Morillo was leaving Spain with a large army, bound for the River Plate – which prompted Doña Remedios to embark on another fund-raising venture, urging the ladies of Mendoza to give up their diamonds and pearls for the cause. Worse still, after General Rondeau was defeated at Sipé-Sipé in northern Argentina in November 1815, there were suggestions that the army of Cuyo would be needed to reinforce the north-west frontier. At a banquet San Martín, unenthusiastic about this, proposed a toast 'to the first bullet fired at the oppressors of Chile on the other side of the Andes.'

Alvear attempted to dismiss San Martín, which provoked a revolt among the townspeople and a demand from his officers that he be reinstated; the order was revoked, and Alvear himself was deposed a few months later, San Martín's distinguished father-in-law playing a key role in the coup against him. During the ensuing power vacuum San Martín had considerable influence over the choice of delegates to the Congress of Tucumán which, in the wake of a string of defeats for the Argentine forces in the north, declared formal independence, spurred on no doubt by the Governor's impatient urging:

> How long must we wait to declare our independence? Don't you think it is ridiculous to mint coins, have a flag and coat of arms, and make war against the very government that is supposed to rule over us? What is there to do but to say it? Besides, what international relations can we have when we act as minors under a guardian and the enemy (with perfect reason) calls us insurgents, inasmuch as we still call ourselves vassals? Be sure that nobody will help us under these conditions. Besides, the system would gain fifty per cent with this step. Courage! Great undertakings are for men of courage. Let us see clearly, my friend: if this is not done, the Congress will be invalid in all it does, inasmuch as if it assumes sovereignty, this would be an usurpation against him who believes himself the true sovereign, that is, little Ferdinand [the King of Spain].

But San Martín was bitterly opposed by many of the factions at the congress. As he wrote to his faithful supporter, Tomás Guido:

> When the expedition to Chile is undertaken, it will be too late. I was convinced that it would not be done, only because I was at the head of it. A curse be on my star, which only awakens suspicions! That is why I have never expressed an opinion about it. Oh, my friend, what miserable creatures are we, bipeds without feathers!
>
> I knew well that as long as I was at the head of these troops not only would there be no expedition to Chile, but I would not be helped. My resignations have been repeated not so much because of my ill health but because of those reasons. San Martín will always be a suspected man in his country.

San Martín was one of three candidates put forward for the post of Supreme Director of the United Provinces, in succession to Alvear:

together with Belgrano, another candidate, he succeeded in installing a compromise figure, Juan Martín de Pueyrredón, a close ally of both. In July 1816 Pueyrredón met San Martín at Córdoba, on his way to take up his post at Buenos Aires, and formally confirmed his decision to give his official backing to the proposed expedition across the Andes. In a sense he had no option: the defeat at Sipé-Sipé had demonstrated the futility of attempting to advance northwards again.

As a beginning, Pueyrredón despatched 180 raw recruits of the Eleventh Battalion to Mendoza; then the Seventh Battalion was sent from Buenos Aires – 450 men and 220 mounted grenadiers. San Martín also ceaselessly recruited from among the inhabitants of Cuyo. By the end of the year he had assembled an army about five thousand strong, consisting of some 700 mounted grenadiers as cavalry, 3,000 infantry, 250 artillerymen, 120 engineers and 1,200 horsemen for transport and other jobs. He appointed young men from good local families as his officers. Gauchos, usually of mixed race, formed his cavalry. Freed slaves made up the bulk of his infantry; most were black, recruited by telling them that the Spanish planned to reintroduce slavery. He organised the Chilean refugees into two corps of infantry, a battalion of artillery, and a detachment of dragoons, the 'Patriotic League of the State'. To the Chileans he issued a proclamation:

> Chile, enriched with the treasures of nature, arbiter of the Pacific Ocean because of its location, well peopled and endowed with industries and easy means of communication with the bordering provinces, is almost the centre of this region of America, and its restoration is going to establish the bases of our political being. Peru will fall under its influence and the continent will become unified… Nothing must occupy our minds but the larger objective of universal freedom… The foundation of the Chilean army will carry this task to completion.

San Martín also set up a company of British chasseurs, allowing them to choose their own officers – John Young was captain, James Lindsay second-in-command. Pueyrredón, making brave efforts to provide the supplies demanded by San Martín, chided him good-naturedly:

> Besides the 4,000 blankets sent from Córdoba I have only been able to find 500 ponchos … the order has been given to send you the 1,000 *arrobas* [30,000 lbs] of jerked beef which you request for the middle of December: it will be done. Notes of thanks are being sent to the town council and the other cities of Cuyo. Here go the clothes ordered, and

many shirts. If by chance there should be a shortage of blankets in Córdoba, ask for donations of blankets, ponchos or old blankets from the citizens of your city or San Juan; there is not a house that cannot spare an old blanket: it is better to beg when there is no other choice.

Here are 40 saddle blankets. By separate post go, in a small box, the only two bugles I have been able to find. In January of this year you shall be sent 1,387 *arrobas* of jerked beef ... Here are the 2,000 spare sabres you request. Here are 200 tents, and there are no more. Here is the World. Here is the Devil. Here is the Flesh.

I don't know how I shall ever extricate myself from the debts I have incurred for this. One of these days I shall just go bankrupt, thus cancelling everybody's bills, and go over to you, so you can feed me the jerked beef I am sending you. H——! Don't ask me for anything else, if you don't want to hear that I have been found hanging from a rafter in the fort.

Having made his astonishing leap of imagination, San Martín applied himself with his usual energy, meticulousness and attention to detail to an expedition without parallel in history, across passes three times the height of those crossed by Hannibal in the Alps. 'It is not the strength of the enemy that spoils my sleep but how to cross these huge mountains,' he wrote. As he saw it, the challenge could be overcome only by thorough and scientific preparation of his army for the march, two years later.

He entrusted Major José Antonio Alvarez Condarco, an engineer from Tucumán, with the task of making gunpowder from the region's nitrates, and Condarco set up a manufactory for saltpetre. Two Chileans, Major Plaza and Captain Picarte, became the expedition's armourers. A Mendozan miller, Tejeda, was instructed to set up a water-powered textile mill, using yarn from San Luis to make cloth; this was dyed blue, and the women of Mendoza offered to sew it into uniforms. The medical corps was placed under the command of an efficient Englishman with the improbable name of Dr Diego Parossien, and a Peruvian, Dr Zapata. Dr Veray Puntado was in charge of military discipline and justice. José Gregorio Lemos became the army's accountant.

Most intriguing of all was Padre Luís Beltrán, a chaplain from a poor background, born in Mendoza, who became a kind of magical military inventor for the Army of the Andes. Beltran had taught himself maths, physics and chemistry. He could make watches and fireworks; he was a skilled carpenter, cobbler, blacksmith, doctor, draughtsman and architect. His inventiveness and improvisation seemed to know no limits. Church bells were melted to make guns and bullets. The horns of cows were turned into water-carriers. He and his workers made knapsacks, skis, saddles, horseshoes, bayonets and swords. He despatched wagons to pre-position supplies up the steep passes; above all, he perfected the equipment to take San Martín's artillery across rivers and ravines, having his men build portable suspension bridges and make blocks-and-tackles to swing the guns and heavy equipment in slings across chasms. 'He wants wings for the cannon,' he said of San Martín. 'And he shall have them.'

San Martín himself was everywhere, inspecting, urging, encouraging, fussing. The incredible detail that his mind had to encompass is illustrated in his meticulously kept notebooks. The entries for just half a day will suffice to illustrate this:

Call a meeting of blacksmiths and have the best horses shod. Have Saro come here, sending a message through Major Lemos. Send the town council six bags with pins and rings for padlocks for the army hospital. Have a list made of all the Europeans living in Corocanto and their jurisdictions, in order to get information and act. Tell Plaza to deliver an accounting of the ponchos given to Lemos, in order to send it to the Customs. Alvarez C.'s commission to see the cloth factory.

Order 8 sprinklers for the camp. Write the town council asking for a list of existing blocks-and-tackles, showing their owners, to be sent within four days. Tell the commanders of all the units to send a list of the mules needed for carrying ammunition, 3 boxes with wine bottles and 2 with eau-de-vie. Tell the commander of the cavalry to add 40 single men to his troops within 8 days. Ditto, ditto.

To the commander of coloured, 15 men. Tell San Luis to send 60 recruits. Tell S.J. to increase the number of artillerymen to 30, besides increasing the effectives of the Eleventh. Tell San Luis there is one Gregorio Blanco at Rio Quinto who is useful to catch deserters and vagrants. Commission him if useful. Tell Vera to send the papers on the four bolts of cloth. Tell Captain Vicente to come. Write to the town council about saddle mules. Call the Negro cook of Don Juan González tomorrow. Ask the town council to give 20 pesos to the police. Also tell the council that everything gathered by the Supply Commission must be taken to the Custom House.

Send 400 goatskins to San Luis. Ask the commercial judge to gather packing boxes from the business firms. Tell Videla that he should deliver the saddle cloths to Plaza, 400 goatskins to San Luis, 200 white and 200 black. Three kegs of eau-de-vie and one of wine to the commander at Chacayes. Ask the Customs to look at the cloth in the stores and attach it, giving notice.

The gaol guard to be decreased: 12 privates, 1 sergeant, 1 corporal. The hospital guard to be one corporal and four men. Eliminate the appropriations for Villota. The San Juan mules to be branded if they have not been returned to their owners, and the branding irons to be returned. Tell Sosa to offer the Indians anything he thinks suitable in exchange for producing *huici*.

In all this detail, San Martín did not forget the importance of deception, and of what we would call psychological warfare. A side of his nature was secretive, as illustrated perhaps by his ready adoption of Masonic mores; certainly he seemed to relish softening-up operations, and spying. He knew that these were practised by the Spanish across the Andes, where he himself was vilified from the pulpit as a heretic who should not use the name San Martín, after a saint, but Martín, after Luther; the patriots were labelled 'detestable heretics, abortions of hell, envoys of Satan, fellows thirsty for blood and for robbery'. San Martín's response was to insist that his own clergy promulgate the patriots' message: the priests were told to justify the liberal cause from the pulpit, and those who did not 'carry out so sacred a duty' would be punished. He ordered the Father Superior of the Church of San Francisco in Mendoza to confine to the cloisters four friars who were 'opposed to the sacred cause of our political regeneration' and forbid them to hear confessions or preach. The Father Superior was blandly threatened with the assurance that the Governor, 'convinced of your immense patriotism, does not doubt that this order will be faithfully complied with.' San Martín sent agents into Chile to spread false reports about his state of preparation and the likely direction of his attack. The royalists somewhat naïvely recruited these men to infiltrate his own camp, so they were able to report which of the Chilean refugees at Mendoza were acting as spies for the royalists. These were arrested and then themselves 'turned', made to send letters dictated by San Martín suggesting that he was planning an attack into Chile through the lower passes of the southern Andes.

In September 1816, on the Chilean side of the border, Manuel Rodriguez, a patriot guerrilla leader associated with the Carreras, launched an insurrection in the south, and the Captain-General of Santiago de Chile, the buffoonish Marcó del Ponte, despatched troops to quell it. San Martín arranged for a letter of congratulation to Rodriguez, giving the impression that this was part of his plan for the invasion of the south, to fall into the hands of the royalists. He also made full use of the Indians of the region in his intelligence offensive. As Bolívar had in the north, so the Argentinian revolution always sought to enlist the country's Indians. In 1810 Castelli had proclaimed the freedom of the indigenous population in the Inca ruins at Tiahuanaco in Upper Peru. Argentine proclamations had been translated into Quechua and Aymara, and Belgrano himself had used Guarani when addressing the population of the huge area between the Paraguay, Uruguay and Paraná rivers.

San Martín now sought an alliance with the Araucanian Indians of the southern Andes. Already one of his emissaries had promised them that: 'Your happy posterity will not see arbitrariness and despotism reigning in our America. We and you, who have been born upon this soil where the blood of our forefathers has so many times been shed, let us be the rulers. Let us re-establish the mercy and the justice which distinguished the throne of the Incas.' In September 1816 San Martín paid a visit to Fort San Carlos, an outpost on Indian land beyond the Diamante river: some fifty chiefs, lords of the southern Andes valleys, attended. Their spokesman was Necuñan, representing men with such evocative names as Huanguenecul, Neyancari, Calimilla, Millatur, Manqueri, Antepan, Peñalef, Ancai, Jamin, Goyco, Marilinco and Epiman. Their chaplain, Father Ynalican, acted as interpreter, although San Martín had taken the trouble to learn some Araucanian, in the same way that he had earlier addressed the Indian tribes of the pampas, the Pehuenches and the Mapuches, in their own language.

He presented them with quantities of *aguardiente* – Argentinian brandy – wine, cloth, saddles, glass beads and sweets, brought by mule from Mendoza, and asked them to watch over the southern passes where, he hinted, he intended to cross. After six days of singing and dancing he secured his treaty of alliance, each of the chiefs embracing him. The chiefs returned the visit three months later, providing him with information about Spanish movements. They met at Plumerillo, just outside Mendoza, where San Martín impressed them by staging a display of military manoeuvres and a long cannonade. When he remarked, 'I myself am also an Indian' – not implausibly, in view of his dark skin – the well-built, naked men before him shouted with enthusiasm and, 'smelling like horses', embraced him and vowed to die for him. As he had expected, news of his proposed invasion across the southern passes leaked from the Indians to the Spanish.

San Martín's last great espionage coup was to send Alvarez Condarco, his armourer, to deliver a copy of the Argentine declaration of independence personally to Marcó del Ponte in Chile. He calculated that if his envoy was not treated with respect, he would at least be sent back unharmed. His intention was that Alvarez Condarco should travel via the pass of Los Patos – the longest route to the north; then, on being expelled, he would probably be sent back by the shortest route, via Uspallata further south: he was to scout and comprehensively map the routes as he went. As expected, Marcó del Ponte reacted strongly on receiving the declaration of independence – he had it publicly burnt. The contemptuous reply he sent to San Martín ended, characteristically, 'I sign as a white man, not like San Martín whose hand is black.'

At the height of summer, in January 1817, when snow no longer blocked the Andean passes, the finishing touches were put to San Martín's meticulous preparations: *charquican* was prepared – dried beef, ground to a powder and mixed with fat and chillies to provide maximum nourishment for minimum weight, an early kind of processed instant food; saddles were made from the hides of the cattle killed to make the *charquican*. Apart from the beef, there were huge quantities of toasted corn flour, biscuits, cheese, wine and aqua vitae, as well as corn and oats for the animals and wood for fires, there being no vegetation in the high Andes. Medical supplies, which included onions and garlic to ward off the cold and altitude sickness, were also carried. Some 30,000 shoes were provided for the animals.

When assembled, the Army of the Andes included 5,200 men altogether, along with 10,600 saddle and pack mules, 1,600 cavalry horses and 700 cattle to be killed and used for food along the way. They carried 9,000 rounds of musket and carbine shot, 2,000 cannon balls, 2,000 rounds of shrapnel and 600 shells.

28

The Army of the Andes

San Martín assembled the bulk of his army at Plumerillo on 12 January 1817 and then marched through Mendoza, which was adorned with flowers, flags and bunting. The Virgin was proclaimed Patroness of the army, and the 'Flag of the Andes' was raised – white and light blue, with a coat of arms between a branch of laurel and a branch of olive, and two hands lifting the Phrygian Cap of Liberty above the Andes, with the rising sun above the cap. 'Soldiers,' declared San Martín, 'this is the first independence flag to be blessed in America.' He then called for an oath of allegiance 'to die in defence of the flag'. Bells pealed, cannon belched, and the populace cheered. A bullfight followed: Indians, gauchos and blacks paraded on horseback, colourfully arrayed and wildly exuberant. San Martín remarked, 'Our country needs these madmen.' When a bull was killed, a young officer who acted as matador castrated it and offered the genitals to Doña Remedios. She blushed – she was only twenty – but San Martín insisted she accept them. Usually so undemonstrative, for once he appreciated, like Bolívar, the need for show and spectacle to rally his men, many of whom might be marching to their death.

At about the same time an itinerant vendor arriving at the home of Soler, San Martín's principal spy in Chile, announced: 'I have fat chicks, landlord.' The vendor, a messenger from San Martín, handed Soler a note: 'January 15. Brother 5. I am sending through Los Patos 4,000 pesos. Within one month Brother José will be with you.' It was a signal that the army, four thousand strong, would start on its way on 15 January.

That day, his vanguard having already departed, San Martín left Mendoza in his blue grenadier uniform and bicorn hat with the Argentine rosette, black boots and gold spurs. He had a cloak against the mountain cold, and a tunic of beaver skin. Like his men, he rode a mule with wooden stirrups; sure-footed mules were better than horses, travelling in single file through the narrow passes. He was preceded by Estay, a faithful servant, and followed by an attendant carrying food and medicines.

It was vital that the enemy should remain confused about the direction of the invasion, and San Martín's disinformation techniques had been masterly. Marcó del Ponte had despatched a contingent to the south, where the invasion was anticipated, another to the ports in case of incursions from the sea, a third to the west of the Uspallata pass. San Martín too had divided his army. One column had marched out of San Juan on 12 January, aiming for the northern passes. On 8 February it secured the Chilean province of Coquimbo unopposed, welcomed with open arms: all sparsely-populated northern Chile was thus liberated without a fight. Another detachment which left to cross the much lower Planchon pass in the south unexpectedly entered and occupied Talca, cutting off the Spanish forces sent south from Santiago and securing the support of Manuel Rodriguez's guerrillas. In the centre San Martín had concentrated his main army with mathematical precision: the two main passes were Los Patos, by the great mountain of Aconcagua; and Uspallata, in the valley of the Aconcagua, which also forked into the valley of Portillo, a beautiful, snow-covered expanse by the Lake of the Inca (so-called because an Inca princess was said to have drowned herself in it for love). Juan Gregorio de La Heras led a smaller force across this more direct route.

San Martín ascended with the vanguard of his army through Los Patos, his commander Miguel Soler, while Bernardo O'Higgins brought up the rearguard. San Martín later gave a characteristically low-key description of the mountain crossing:

> The chief difficulties were the lack of population and roads, the lack of game, and especially of pasture. The army had 10,600 saddle and pack mules, 1,600 horses, and 700 head of cattle, and despite the most scrupulous care there arrived in Chile only 4,300 mules and 511 horses in very bad condition. The rest either died or were rendered useless during the crossing of the mountains.
>
> Two six-inch howitzers and ten four-inch field pieces, which went through Uspallata, were transported by 500 wheeled carriages, although a great part of the way they had to be carried by hand, with the help of block and tackle, when reaching the higher peaks. Food supplies for the twenty days the march was to last were taken on muleback, inasmuch as

there was no house or town between Mendoza and Chile by way of Uspallata, and five mountain ranges had to be crossed.

The greater part of the army suffered from lack of oxygen, as a result of which several soldiers died, besides others who succumbed to the intense cold. Everyone was convinced that the obstacles which had been overcome did not leave the slightest hope for a retreat; but, on the other hand, there reigned a great confidence among the ranks, who carried out their tasks heroically, in the midst of keen rivalry among the different units.

Across vineyards and alfalfa fields they went, climbing steadily to the small town of Uspallata. From there the Camino de los Andes rises to the great brown and grey broken rocks, shale and volcanic ash of the range. A vast undulating plain beneath those rocks, covered in uninviting thorn and yellow brush, took the army a couple of days to cross. As the endless, winding mule train climbed higher the air became thinner and the brightness of the clear blue sky rendered the scenery clearer still. The altitude was beginning to have its effect: men were falling ill, and the cold numbed their bones even as they huddled around camp fires at night.

To the north, on San Martín's right, there rose a magnificent view of snow-covered mountains and glaciers. His column reached the head of the desolate plain, where it narrowed into the Rio Blanco, a raging mountain torrent into which white waterfalls tumbled from the heights above. Up the Tupungato valley on the left was the huge snow-capped cone of the great volcano of that name, looming over them; about thirty-five miles away could be seen a great collection of rock spikes, known as Los Penitentes because the higher ones look like a great cathedral, the lower like monks worshipping. And dominating all was the most majestic peak of all – Aconcagua, another extinct volcano, a pure white thumb soaring into the sky.

The effort of crossing the mountain torrents and canyons added to the difficulties of the ascent. Beltrán's improvised bridges and ropes and tackle swung supplies, ammunition and cannon across, while the animals and men wound their way tortuously down narrow tracks one side and up the other. Crossing the Los Patos river they passed the hamlets of Carrizal and Manantiales near a lesser peak, La Ramada, the path winding along the Volcan river. Two weeks into the journey and more than a hundred miles from Mendoza, a few of the sick were dying, as were increasing numbers of animals.

They reached a spectacular natural rock bridge, the Puente del Inca, spanning the river Mendoza – about ninety feet wide and sixty feet long, sixty feet above the river. The army had by now reached about 8,000 feet, and the high peaks were still ahead; the trail seemed endless, and rose ever more steeply. San Martín was exhausted, and full of laudanum. The night before he had sat by one of the small camp fires – they were conserving wood by now – trying to keep the aggressive cold at bay. As the embers glowed in the desolate, engulfing darkness, he had come close to despair. Now, as the line of mules trudged ever more slowly and disconsolately onwards and the path wound still further upwards, the skies darkened to unleash a furious hailstorm, accompanied by a spec-tacular rainbow. San Martín took refuge in a cave and slept. Waking several hours later to a temperature of six degrees below freezing, he sent his servant for a bottle of *aguardente* and smoked a cigar. Then he ordered his band to strike up, and the national anthem of independent Argentina resounded through the rocky crags surrounding them.

A few days later they had climbed to 12,000 feet. The animals died by the score and the weaker men fell by the wayside, all left to the elements and the ever-circling condors. But they were now only six hundred feet from the summit of the pass, and it was with a feeling of spiritual elation that the grim figure in the cape at last saw the track fall steeply away down the Chilean side of the border. It had taken more than three weeks to get there and the going was still difficult, down the shale-strewn slopes, but as oxygen filled the lungs of his exhausted men, so they began to recover and their spirits to soar.

San Martín's march inevitably invites comparison with Bolívar's crossing of the Andes two and a half years later. Bolívar's feat was the greater in that in the course of four months he traversed 750 miles of swamp and mountains, including a pass at 15,000 feet; San Martín took a month to cover 150 miles at a maximum height three-quarters that of Bolívar's route. Yet Bolívar's achievement was secured at the appalling cost of two-thirds of his men and all his horses and mules; San Martín, with twice the number of men, lost fewer than a hundred, and retained a third or more of his mules and horses. It was the difference between an unprepared, demonically-driven throw of the dice, and a triumph of meticulous planning which enabled San Martín to arrive in a condition to do battle with the Spanish forces camped on the Chilean plains below.

29

Chacabuco

Las Heras's detachment, marching over the shorter Uspallata pass, crossed before San Martín; two days after traversing the highest point, on 2 February, he attacked and dislodged a royalist outpost, then feigned a retreat into the mountains to deceive the Spanish. A few days later Las Heras descended upon and captured the small town of Santa Rosa in the hills below. Soler, commanding the main contingent travelling with San Martín, after skirmishing with the Spanish outside San Felipe on 7 February, also staged a retreat, then regrouped and attacked again, driving them south of the town, which they destroyed as they left. But within days his offensive was halted.

By then San Martín and the bulk of the army had crossed the pass and were looking down upon the broken plain that lay before the Chacabuco spur of the Andes, a finger which stretched out from the cordillera to the sea at a height of a few hundred feet. Beneath these hills lay the Chacabuco ranch, the Spanish headquarters. San Martín, surveying his men on the evening of 11 February, decided to attack down the road leading to the ranch, his right flank under the command of Soler, the left under O'Higgins, whose forces had by now descended from the Portillo pass. Soler was also to try to outflank the Spanish to the rear of the Chacabuco hills, and cut off their retreat to Santiago to the south.

During the night of 11 February San Martín sent an advance force of 2,000 down into the broken terrain of hillocks criss-crossed by streams and dotted with clumps of *quillai*, soapbark trees, which provided ideal cover under the light of the moon. By dawn they were close to the enemy camp. The Spanish were rather fewer in number than their attackers: General Rafael Maroto commanded the élite Talavera Regiment, accompanied by the Abascal Carabineros, the Penco Dragoons and a cavalry brigade under Colonel Altero, as well as the Chiloé Volunteers.

Maroto's two field commanders were the able Elerreaga and San Bruno, the power behind the Viceroy, notorious for his cruelty, mutilator of prisoners after the battle of Rancagua.

With San Martín watching from above, battle began at dawn on 12 February. For the Spanish it was to prove one of the bloodiest in the wars of independence. San Martín had taken a risk in ordering the attack so soon: many of his men had not yet descended from the pass, only a few of the cannon were in place, and the troops were far from rested after the mountain crossing. But he was anxious lest the Spanish should summon reinforcements. The patriot troops, much closer to the Spanish position than they anticipated, and seeking to attack the bridge across the Chacabuco, found themselves hard-pressed, but fought with fury and determination.

Suddenly, to San Martín's horror, he saw a large detachment of his own cavalry charging forward, in violation of the agreed plan, in an attack on the left flank and the centre – straight into the enemy guns: it appeared that O'Higgins, overcome by the emotion of seeing his native land, had rashly and impulsively decided to challenge the enemy head on. The truth behind this incident remains to this day an issue of furious controversy between Chileans who support O'Higgins and Argentinians favouring San Martín.

O'Higgins had been ordered to check the royalists on their right (the east) flank, while Soler, commanding the Argentinian forces facing the Spanish left flank, took a longer trail a few miles west. His advance over the foothills of the Andes had been slow and difficult, sometimes under Spanish fire, and he had lost his two guns over a cliff on the way. San Martín, in great pain and plentifully sedated with opium, had ridden to join him on the ridge above Chacabuco, where they agreed that O'Higgins should pursue the retreating enemy down a steep, rough track in the small valley to the east of the position – but San Martín was adamant that no general attack should take place until Soler's forces joined him. It was this order that O'Higgins was said to have defied, in a rash attempt to reconquer his own country by himself.

According to O'Higgins, the truth was very different: as his men made their way down the narrow track in single file, he observed that the Spanish had halted their retreat and were moving forward again. Drawing up his men in a defensive line at the bottom of the ravine they had descended, he realised there was no going back up that path – his men would be picked off one by one. There was nothing for it but to make a stand. After heavy exchanges of fire, his position became untenable and he sent desperately for reinforcements from Soler; but none came. His 1,500 men were being increasingly hard-pressed, and his second-in-command, Colonel Cramer, insisted their only chance of survival was to attack. Moreover, he argued, if they waited for Soler's assistance, the enemy would be able to retreat intact towards Santiago, thus frustrating the whole objective of the patriots' offensive. 'General, let us attack with the bayonets,' urged Cramer. After a moment's reflection, 'The Devil take me if we won't!' O'Higgins cried. Forming his men into two columns, he marched forward against the Talaveras, on the Spanish right.

San Martín, watching from above and unaware of O'Higgins's predicament, ordered the cavalry under Soler to charge on the left flank, just as the Spanish concentrated their forces against O'Higgins. Hastily the Spanish wheeled about to meet this new threat and O'Higgins, although checked in his advance, was not pushed back. Fighting continued all morning, and into the afternoon. Elerreaga, the best Spanish commander, was killed early on. Eventually the Spanish launched a cavalry charge in an attempt to break the impasse, but this was easily repulsed by San Martín's brother-in-law Escalada.

Soler's cavalry now launched a further attack which, by capturing several cannon and killing many of the artillerymen, neutralised the Spaniards' main advantage. The patriot infantry took new heart and O'Higgins led a frontal assault which overwhelmed the enemy's forward positions. The Spanish formed a square, but they were beginning to be beaten back. Soler's cavalry, meanwhile, had succeeded in getting behind them, as originally planned, and when the Spanish at last decided to retreat, they found they were surrounded. San Martín, scenting the kill, could not now resist charging into the thick of the fighting himself, sword in hand, on his fine horse. The remaining Spanish defenders took refuge in the ranch house, fighting hand-to-hand in the vineyards and olive groves. But the victory was won, and soon became a massacre. In the end some 500 Spanish were killed and 600 taken prisoner; fewer than a quarter escaped. San Martín lost but twelve dead in battle, although many of his 120 wounded did not survive.

When it was all over, Soler rode up and furiously berated O'Higgins for nearly throwing away the battle. Turning on his heel, the Chilean leader demanded that San Martín give him men to chase the fleeing

Spanish and cut them off, urging him to march at once on Santiago. San Martín refused, fearing lest his men should be attacked by superior Spanish forces further on. It was another example of the methodical caution that on occasion so infuriated the other commanders – and he was to be criticised bitterly for it: the Spanish who escaped to fight another day nearly won. O'Higgins's view was that had he not made his 'rash' advance, his own detachment would have been overwhelmed and the Spanish opposing him would have been able to withdraw almost intact from the battle. In any event, a great victory had been won: San Martín had been vindicated in his decision to give battle at once. Weary, he slept in the ranch house, and the following day the bodies were gathered and burnt in a great funeral pyre.

Hearing of the Spanish defeat the Captain-General, Marcó del Ponte, who had taken no part in the battle, tried to flee to the port of Valparaíso, but was caught. The day after Chacabuco San Martín, arriving unrecognised in Santiago, received Marcó del Ponte in his own palace with the words, 'Señor General, let me shake that white hand' – a reference to that earlier racist taunt. When Marcó del Ponte symbolically offered him his sword, San Martín remarked icily: 'Let that foil remain on the belt of Your Excellency, Señor General, because that is the place where it can least hurt me.' He had little regard for a general who chose not to fight with his men. Marcó del Ponte was taken under escort first to Mendoza and then to San Luis, where in 1819 he was killed trying to escape.

The bloodthirsty San Bruno was bound backwards on a mule for the journey from Chacabuco to Santiago, where the people threw stones, mud and filth at him. Sentenced to death for murder, he was taken to the gallows in a large basket tied on the back of a horse, such as was used for the transportation of goods like coal. On the way the mob overpowered his guard, so that at his execution 'his face was a horrible mask because the populace had gouged one of his eyes out, and it was blood-covered … When the executioner tore off his bandage he let out a cry of agony, which only awakened the contempt of the multitude.'

San Martín despatched his brother-in-law Escalada back across the Andes; it took him just two weeks to reach Buenos Aires, where news of the victory was received with joyous relief by the beleaguered government, which had just heard of a fresh Spanish offensive in the north. Wild celebrations in the streets of Buenos Aires acclaimed the 'hero of the Andes', whose picture, crowned by winged Victory, was put on display in the central plaza. The grateful council of Santiago wanted to make San Martín their ruler, and offered him a considerable sum of money. He declined both, saying he had come to liberate Chile, not to rule it. O'Higgins was installed as Supreme Director, and proclaimed: 'Chile announces a new refuge in these countries for the industry, the friendship, and all the citizens of the globe ... The wisdom and the resources of the neighbouring Argentine nation, which has decided our emancipation, warrant the hope of a prosperous and happy future for these regions.'

Celebrations were staged in honour of San Martín. In the home of a prominent Chilean nobleman, Don Enrique Rosales, the General was offered 'roast turkeys with gilded heads and with flags in their beaks, suckling pigs, stuffed, with oranges in their snouts, hams from Chiloé, almonds prepared by the nuns, custards and other sweets. Sliced cold roast pork, pickled onions, and olives stuffed with red peppers stimulated the thirst for Santiago's *chacoli*, Concepción's *asoleado*, and some Spanish wines.' He toasted the freedom of America, then smashed his glass, so no one could sully it in toasting any other cause.

The next few days were busy ones: San Martín organised an arsenal, ordered that a training camp be set up for new recruits, and drew up a blueprint for a navy; he also set up a Chilean Lautaro Lodge, both to carry on the underground war and to provide a means of covert control of the country. Las Heras was despatched to mop up the remains of the royalist forces in southern Chile. A week later San Martín told his aide, O'Brien, that they would leave for Buenos Aires the following morning, accompanied only by his servant and guide Estay. The crossing of the Andes and the victory at Chacabuco represented, it will be remembered, only the first stage of San Martín's strategy; the second was to sail up the Pacific coast to the very heart of Spanish power, Lima. To secure the necessary resources from quarrelsome, cash-strapped Buenos Aires, he needed to follow up Chacabuco with a personal intervention; to waste time would be disastrous, for his victory would be soon forgotten.

His decision to leave Chile proved a disastrous miscalculation. The back of Spanish domination in Chile had not, as he believed, been broken. The Spanish Viceroy in Lima had recognised the danger inherent in San Martín's victory, and the empire was not about to roll over. Las Heras, in charge of the mopping-up operation, not only failed to take Talcahuano, the port where the royalists were concentrated, but was badly beaten at Talca. A further attack by Las Heras directly against the Spanish fortress there was repulsed – something San Martín blamed on

General Brayer, French veteran of Hohlinden, Austerlitz and Waterloo, brought in to help the patriots.

San Martín arrived without notice in Buenos Aires, where the government appointed him a brigadier-general. But he declined the honour: 'Long ago I gave my word solemnly that I would not accept any rank or military or political position; for this reason I hope that Your Excellency will not compromise my honour before the people, and that you will not attribute my returning this appointment to excessive pride.' He refused all gifts of money, and the government had to make do with giving his daughter a pension of 600 pesos a year, which he could not refuse on her behalf (and which later was used for her education). A huge triumphal parade was staged for this reluctant hero, who could not avoid the seemingly inevitable 'four girls dressed as Fame [who] placed upon his head a crown of flowers, as a symbol of the homage with which he was being received; [but] San Martín instantly removed it from his head and kept on going.'

He lobbied unceasingly for support in setting up the navy for his expedition to Peru. As he wrote to O'Higgins, 'The first thing to do is to move the army with safety, and this cannot be done without a naval force of five corvettes, no less, well equipped and armed; but money is needed for this. See whether 300,000 pesos can be obtained in Chile. We have estimated that this will be sufficient for the armament and crews.' Pueyrredón suggested that top priority should rather be given to the continuing war with royalist forces in Uruguay, and to ending the chaos in rural Argentina; but for San Martín these were mere sideshows. The overwhelming force of his personality combined with his extraordinary triumph secured the promises of support that he needed. After a brief reunion he left behind his young wife, who had fallen ill, and once again set off from Buenos Aires across the deserted pampas of central Argentina, then over the mountains to Santiago where, after yet another triumphal welcome, he installed himself on a farm outside the city.

30

Triumph and Disaster

The disdain displayed by San Martín for the trappings of success – later cited by admirers and biographers as evidence of his 'saintliness' – began to manifest itself as an almost pathological hatred of any show of public affection, display of pomp and glory, reward, or accolade. Bolívar was like San Martín in never availing himself of the opportunities at every turn to accumulate a fortune, but he loved to bask in the acclaim of his admirers, and always understood the utility of morale-boosting fiestas and military celebrations. Almost certainly San Martín's attitude was affected by illness; he was by now addicted to the opiates he had been prescribed for arthritis attacks and, in constant pain and fever, felt that he was nearing the end of his days. For most of the time he also lacked a private life, faithful to a young wife he seldom saw. He seemed unable to understand that his refusal to accept expressions of gratitude or appreciation in any form caused nearly as much offence to his admirers as if he had actively sought acclaim and money. He rejected a 10,000-peso pension offered by the Chilean government; he rejected a set of silver tableware and a salary of 6,000 pesos a year from the same source. In answer to a 'supreme order' to him to accept the gifts, because of his personal needs and to maintain the dignity of his position – 'his frugality will appear to foreigners not as Spartan virtue but as censurable poverty' – San Martín replied that 'these are not the times for such luxuries', and asked for the exchange of letters not to be made public.

He moved into the Bishop's Palace in Santiago, where he lived in sparsely furnished rooms, and got his tailor to reline his tunic and his campaign cloak. When a sycophant gave the tailor cloth for a new tunic, San Martín was so furious that he ordered the tailor to make eight frock-coats for his benefactor, whom he ordered 'to put on a new coat every day and show up in front of the palace and bow deeply at his window'.

His old habits of early rising, eating a simple lunch standing up, and going to bed at ten persisted. His chaplain reported:

> At four o'clock in the morning he used to rise from his portable campaign bed, and he himself prepared his morning coffee. His breakfast was very light. At one o'clock in the afternoon he had his only heavy meal, in the kitchen, in soldierly conversation with his negro cook, choosing two dishes which he washed down with a couple of glasses of the wine of his beloved Mendoza. His favourite dish was roast beef ...
>
> At four in the afternoon the state dinner was served, at his expense, on which he spent ten pesos a day and at which Don Tomás Guido, his intimate friend ... presided. He used to appear at the end of the meal to have his coffee, and on these occasions he behaved in a comradely manner, telling jokes and anecdotes, which he seasoned with the Andalusian spice of his days spent at Cádiz.

He noted that San Martín 'liked to see other people enjoy themselves, and understood that gaiety, and the social cordiality of banquets and dances, are simple means for ruling men.' An English traveller, Samuel Haigh, saw the 'Hannibal of the Andes' at a party:

> The gathering was most brilliant, composed of all the first-rank people in Santiago, as well as of all the higher officers of the Army; hundreds gave themselves to the pleasure of the waltz, and general contentment was visible on all the faces. To be so suddenly removed from the lonesome mountain that I had just crossed in a horrible voyage to this gathering of gentlemen and beauties of the capital, in the midst of civilisation and elegance, seemed to me a thing of magic.
>
> Frank, easy-mannered, and charming, San Martín, in the flower of his years, reigned in the salons and was the most notable figure, present everywhere ...

Attractive as he was, nearly all-powerful, and separated by hundreds of miles from his wife, no stories from this time link San Martín's name with that of any Chilean woman, even in mild flirtation. His officers and associates womanised or married – but in the absence of his beloved Remeditos, San Martín remained the austere military celibate he had always been.

Until 1817 the Chileans had no navy at all, although a British sailor, Admiral William Brown, had been commissioned by the government of Buenos Aires to harass the Spanish along the Pacific coast, which he did with gusto and some success. San Martín and Pueyrredón now managed to scrape together a motley flotilla under an Argentinian naval officer, Blanco Encalada: this embryonic navy consisted of a frigate, the *Lautaro*, formerly the *Wyndham*; two brigantines, the *Pueyrredón*, formerly the *Aguila*, and the *Auracano*, formerly the *Columbus*; and the corvette *Chacabuco*, formerly the *Coquinho*. A training school for midshipmen was set up in Valparaíso: sailors were hard to come by because the pirate ships in the Pacific paid better, and offered the prospect of prizes. Blanco Encalada got the little flotilla off to a flying start by sailing 1,200 men down the coast to the Spanish enclave of Talcahuano, where he bombarded and captured the frigate *Maria Isabel*, and also seized two transport ships at Valdivia. The frigate, renamed *O'Hggins*, joined the Chilean fleet as its flagship.

Shortly afterwards Alvarez Condarco, despatched to buy ships in England, secured the *Cumberland*, renamed *San Martín*. Condarco claimed to have 100,000 pesos to spend on ships – in fact he had less than a third of that, enough to buy only one. Later it was said San Martín had embezzled the rest: in truth, Alvarez Condarco had been putting on an impressive front to interest sellers. A corvette, the *Curatius*, to be renamed the *Independencia*, was bought from the United States by another emissary. There was also an English ship, the *Grafton*, which had been bought by José Miguel Carrera, O'Higgins's old rival, also in the United States, under false pretences; when he failed to pay for it, the government of Buenos Aires had to make good the shortfall. Thus San Martín secured the rudiments of the navy he sought.

Espionage also played its part in San Martín's campaign against the Spanish in Peru. Commodore Bowles, the British Commander in the Pacific, had been despatched with Major Domingo Torres to talk to the Viceroy, Pezuela, and to offer an exchange of prisoners. His real mission was to make contact with the pro-independence forces in Peru which had staged an abortive attempt against the Spanish Crown at Cuzco in 1814. Prominent among these was José de Riva Agüero, who became as much a thorn in San Martín's flesh as in Bólivar's. A schooner moored off the coast of Peru commanded by Alvarez Jonte was the centre for San Martín's intelligence operation.

Obsessed by his determination to strike directly into Peru, San Martín took no part in the difficult campaign to dislodge the troublesome Spanish enclave at Talcahuano in the south, leaving it to O'Higgins and Las Heras, who were also beset by the continued plotting of the Carrera brothers and their unreliable ally, the guerrilla leader

Manuel Rodriguez. San Martín's poor health and reliance on opium may have contributed to his decision to stay in Santiago. Tomás Guido, his faithful acolyte, remarked that 'this drug having become in the judgement of the patient, indispensable for his life, he closed his ears to the urgings of friends, who endeavored to make him abandon this narcotic (many times I myself took away the little tubes containing it) and he did not pay any heed to the noxious effect of the drug, which slowly but steadily undermined his physique and threatened his morale.' Pueyrredón's son, Manuel, who lived with San Martín for a time, woke him each morning: 'As soon as I had complied with this duty, he would give me the key of a chest which he had in the room and ask me to fetch him a small glass containing medicine, which was thick and greenish and which he drank in one gulp.' Pueyrredón himself had already tried in vain to get San Martín to give up opium. There is no evidence to support his enemies' allegations that he was also an alcoholic; reliable accounts suggest a man who habitually drank no more than four glasses of wine a day, though probably more when in company. He was however afflicted by bouts of depression, possibly induced by the opium: 'I force myself to continue living in this country. In the midst of its beauties, everything in it is repulsive to me. The men, especially, are of a nature which does not agree with my principles, and here I live in a continuous ill-humour, which corrodes my sad existence.'

For whatever reason, the man looked up to as a leader by Spanish American patriots failed to anticipate what happened next. In January 1818 five thousand well-equipped Spanish troops arrived in Talcahuano, despatched by the Viceroy of Peru, Don Joaquin de la Pezuela, and under the command of General Manuel Osorio. It seemed that the early history of independent Chile, ending with O'Higgins's defeat, was about to be repeated, thanks to San Martín's complacency and negligence.

Always at his best under pressure, however, San Martín responded with alacrity and defiance. To rally the country he formally proclaimed Chile independent of Spain: O'Higgins did the same in the south, on 12 February, the anniversary of Chacabuco. San Martín ordered O'Higgins to curb his usual impulsiveness and retreat before the Spanish army across the Maule river in the direction of Talca, where reinforcements could be brought up to catch them in a trap; as he explained, 'We do not mind losing a few leagues of land, as long as we feel certain of reoccupying them solidly later. Let us concentrate our forces and we shall be invincible.' San Martín himself, meanwhile, organised the raising of reserves around the country, equipped the Santiago arsenal with 14,000 lances for distribution to civilians, and then departed southwards at the head of his own contingent. By mid March he had combined with O'Higgins to make a joint force of six thousand, divided into three corps, outnumbering the Spanish but less well-equipped.

An advance force of 1,700 cavalry he sent to attack the Spanish soon came up against a natural obstacle, a great swathe of ditches at Cancha Rayada ('furrowed fields' – but they were not man-made). The patriot army camped where they were, and during the night of 19 March the three royalist generals – Osorio, Ordoñez and Primo de Rivera – made a brilliantly successful surprise attack: the patriots' huge herd of pack mules stampeded, causing utter confusion. O'Higgins, stumbling about in the dark, was badly wounded by a musket ball. In the chaos the patriot army broke ranks and fled. The royalists seemed set to march on Santiago to deal the death-blow to the second Chilean republic.

In the capital, news of the débâcle was greeted with blind fear. Houses and shops were abandoned, and looted by the mob. To resist this anarchy the large English community in the city formed a group they called the 'Death's Hussars'. The Chilean government attempted to stop the exodus by closing the Andean passes. Five days later O'Higgins returned to Santiago, his arm in a sling, and announced the formation of a committee of public safety to restore order. He and San Martín had been trying to regroup the remains of their defeated army at San Fernando, where the right wing, under Las Heras, remained united and intact with around 3,500 men. San Martín arrived in Santiago the day after O'Higgins, appeared on the balcony of the palace, and then rode among the large crowd on horseback, before addressing them:

> Chileans! One of those hazards that man does not know how to avoid made our army suffer a defeat. It was natural that this unexpected blow and the consequent uncertainty should make you hesitate. But it is now time to take stock of yourselves and to realise that our country's army is holding with glory in the face of the enemy; that your companions at arms are gathering fast and that the resources of patriotism are inexhaustible. The tyrants have not advanced a single step in their entrenchment. I have put in motion a force of over four thousand men, without counting the militia. The Fatherland exists and shall triumph, and I give my word of honour that I shall shortly give a day of glory to South America.

It turned out that the scale of the patriot defeat was somewhat smaller than first reports suggested: 120 killed and about the same number wounded and taken prisoner; the royalist soldiers had also attacked each other in the darkness. Instead of pursuing the patriots they had then sacked Talca, leaving Las Heras's force to escape.

But the position was still critical. San Martín insisted on securing all available resources: 'I would rather that we use spoons made of bone and wear crude sandals than that the enemy should hang us.' His orders reeked of last-stand desperation:

> Each soldier will have for this battle one hundred cartridges and ten stones, half of which he will carry with him, the other half being kept behind with his respective unit. Before the beginning of the battle he will be given a ration of wine or *aguardiente*, the former to be preferred. Commanders will address words of encouragement to the troops before joining battle, and shall impose the penalty of death on anyone who deserts his position, either when advancing or when withdrawing ...
>
> If any unit of infantry or cavalry is attacked with sidearms, it shall not wait standing still for the attack, but instead it shall advance fifty paces to meet the attack, with bayonet or sword. The wounded who cannot walk unaided shall not be saved while the battle lasts, because four men are needed for every one wounded, and this would weaken the line in a moment. In the place where the commander-in-chief will be a tricolour flag will fly, and a red flag will show the location of the reserve ammunition.
>
> When at the place where the commander-in-chief finds himself three flags are raised at the same time, that is, the tricolour of Chile, the bicolour of Buenos Aires, and a red one, all the troops will shout, 'Long Live Our Country!' and forthwith each unit shall charge with bayonet or sword on the enemy facing it. As soon as the enemy line is broken he shall be pursued hotly, and at the bugle call of assembly everyone shall be in line. The chiefs of staff must be persuaded this battle is going to decide the fate of all America and that it is preferable to die on the field of honour than at the hands of our executioners.
>
> I am sure of victory with the help of the army chiefs, to whom I recommend to keep these remarks in mind. I advise the cavalry chiefs to keep behind a squad of twenty-five to thirty men, to strike with their swords the soldiers who turn their backs to the enemy, as well as to pursue the enemy while the rest of the squadron is gathered. Inasmuch as the nature of our soldiers lends itself better to offence than to defence, the chiefs shall not forget that in case of emergency they should take the offensive.

Within a week he had assembled four thousand men, although they were hardly well-equipped or confident enough to do battle. On 3 April he left Santiago, to lead his troops. It was not a moment too soon. Believing the patriots to be shattered, the royalist army had travelled northwards at great speed. When Osorio realised that remnants of the patriot forces were still blocking the way, he turned towards the coast to cover his back and approached the Maipo river, just two miles from Santiago, from the south-west.

31

Maipú

Beyond the river was the plain of Maipú, along the east of which ran another river, the Mapocho, which formed a natural boundary of Santiago itself; on the north side was a low line of mountains. Like some great football field, the plain had its 'goals': on the north side Loma Blanca ('small white hill'), beneath which the patriot army was assembled; and on the south side Espejo ('mirror'), another hill, with a ranch which became the royalist command point.

San Martín's staff officers favoured sending a few units to defend the fords across the Mapocho river while keeping the bulk of the army under the protection of the Santiago suburbs. San Martín disagreed. He feared that the forward positions would be at once overrun, giving the enemy heart and demoralising the patriots, and that fighting on the very outskirts of the city itself would cause a rapid collapse of morale in Santiago. Instead he favoured the apparently suicidal tactic of engaging the enemy on the open plain of Maipú – his four thousand nervous, ill-equipped men against six thousand confident, well-armed Spanish troops. Brayer, the French general San Martín blamed for the patriots' failure to capture Talcahuano after Chacabuco, considered his superior quite mad, and advised O'Higgins to save himself.

The following day the two armies came within sight of each other; San Martín allowed the royalists to cross the river Maipú unmolested, then draw up at the southern end of the plain. He went to bed exhausted, wrapped in his cape, in a mill beneath Loma Blanca. Awoken before dawn with the news that the enemy had begun to move, he donned a Chilean poncho and peasant hat and rode out with two aides towards the south. On the way he met Brayer who, pleading a rheumatic leg, asked leave to attend the baths at nearby Colna. San Martín responded acidly: 'With the same permission with which you withdrew from Talca, you may go to the baths. Within a half-hour we are going to decide the fate of Chile. You could remain, if your illness allows you to.' Brayer repeated his request. According to Haigh, who was present, San Martín replied, 'You, General, are a c——' – but the official version records: 'The least drummer in the army has more honour than Your Lordship, General.' San Martín later confirmed that he had wanted to have Brayer shot. The general left in disgrace the same day; he later joined forces with Carrera and wrote pamphlets against San Martín, becoming a lifelong enemy.

San Martín, continuing his ride towards the south, saw that the Spanish were moving westward towards the road between Santiago and the sea, with the obvious intention of marching along the road and cutting the patriots off from the city. 'How stupid are these Spaniards!' he exulted, looking through his field glasses. 'Osorio is a bigger fool than I thought. Victory is ours today. The sun is my witness.' He ordered his forces to move rapidly north towards the passes at the eastern end of the road. Frustrated, the Spanish moved along the Espejo hill, where they took up defensive positions. The sun had by this time risen on the shimmering white wall of the mountains in the distance: so vertical is the drop of the Andes towards the almost flat plain of Chile that it is one of the most striking sights in the world. A participant described the scene:

> In the morning of Sunday, April 5, the most delicious time of the year in Chile, not a single cloud darkened the brilliant and eternal blue of the firmament; birds sang and orange blossoms gave off a delicious perfume, which was carried away by the breeze. There was a balmlike softness in the air, characteristic of that climate. Church bells were summoning the faithful, and a religious feeling permeated the senses with the sanctity of the day. It seemed sacrilegious that such a holy quiet should be interrupted by the noise of battle.

The crack Burgos Regiment, much feared, was on the Spanish right under General Moria, along with several cannon; the infantry from Peru were concentrated in the centre, and the Infante Don Carlos Regiment under Ordoñez was on the left. Primo de Rivera had the four heaviest Spanish guns on a hillock to the east. San Martín had Las Heras's regiment drawn up on his right, and on his left Alvarado's. Just behind he had the reserves, the infantry under Balcarce, and the cavalry under Quintana. O'Higgins, wounded, had been placed in charge of Santiago's defence, and his men had been frantically digging trenches in the streets for the expected hand-to-hand fighting. The Spanish infantry were in grey uniforms with white belts, their cavalry in blue and dragoons in red. The patriots wore blue with white belting; many of the patriot regiments were made up entirely of blacks, freed slaves who fought and died heroically in defence of their recently acquired status. San Martín gave the order to advance with a cannonade, to which the Spanish responded in kind: the fate of the *Cono Sur* – the Southern Cone, the lower third of South America – was to be decided.

San Martín ordered his left flank under Alvarado forward, and in response the royalist left moved forward to attack his right. Alvarado's men, though extremely brave black fighters, were his least effective soldiers, and the crack Burgos Regiment opposing them soon began to gain the upper hand there. On San Martín's right, by contrast, the attack of the Infante Dan Carlos Regiment was met squarely by Las Heras's still-fresh troops, and by heavy artillery fire. A group of cavalry led by San Martín's brother-in-law, Colonel Manuel Escalada, stormed the hillock and captured Primo de Rivera's four heavy guns.

The Spanish line thus became skewed around in an anti-clockwise direction as the Burgos Regiment found that resistance collapsed before it, while the Infante Don Carlos made no headway on its left – just as San Martín had foreseen. He now ordered Quintana's cavalry, kept in reserve, to circle around to their left and attack the overextended flank of the Burgos Regiment. 'The battle of Maipú was won by his courage,' San Martín later said of Quintana; but it was his own classic strategy of oblique attack that broke the Spaniards. Haigh describes the scene in detail, from the moment when

> ... the reserves commanded by Quintana were ordered to attack. The Burgos Regiment advanced so rapidly that it became partly disorganised, and it had withdrawn somewhat in order to re-form its ranks when the patriot reserves threw themselves upon it, suffering a deadly fire aimed with admirable precision and effect and with such regularity as if this were only a manoeuvre. This was, without doubt, the most doubtful moment of the action; and so it was considered by Quintana, who, having been reinforced by a squadron of mounted grenadiers, gave the order to charge ...
>
> The clash was tremendous. The fire ceased suddenly and both sides crossed bayonets. The repeated cries of 'Long Live the King!' and 'Long Live Our Country!' were proof that every inch of terrain was being desperately fought for; but, because of the dust and smoke, we could hardly

tell which side was being favoured by victory. Finally, the Royalist cry was muted, and the patriots, advancing at the cry of 'Long Live Liberty!', proclaimed that victory was theirs.

When the Burgos Regiment realised that its ranks were broken it abandoned all idea of further resistance and fled in all directions, although chiefly toward Espejo's mill. They were pursued by the cavalry and pitilessly cut to pieces. The virtue of pity had disappeared from both sides. The butchery was very great, and some officers who had served in Europe told me that they had never seen anything bloodier than what happened on this part of the battlefield.

By placing his weakest infantry against the enemy's strongest and thus enticing the latter forward to be attacked on its flank, San Martín had brilliantly led the Spanish into a trap. By early afternoon on the field of Maipú (which in Araucanian means, appropriately, 'native soil') the battle had effectively been won. It was San Martín's finest hour: he had outmanoeuvred the Spanish in a set-piece field engagement of the kind he had been trained for – by them – all his life.

He rode back to the mill, converted into a field hospital under the English doctor Diego Parossien. As the doctor amputated a leg, San Martín picked up a bloodstained piece of paper from the floor and wrote to O'Higgins: 'We have just obtained a complete victory. Our cavalry pursues them to finish them. The country is free.' There were many who later alleged that San Martín was drunk when he wrote this despatch; no doubt, in view of the high stakes involved, and the nervous energy expended, he drank to celebrate his victory; but he was probably drunk on relief.

Haigh took the note to Santiago, which soon reverberated with shouts of 'Viva San Martín! Viva Libertad! Viva La Patria!' But he missed O'Higgins, who in a state of high excitement had already ridden out to the battlefield where, in a celebrated scene, he embraced San Martín with the words 'Glory to the Saviour of Chile!' San Martín is said to have replied, 'General, Chile will not forget your sacrifice in presenting yourself on the battlefield with your glorious wound still open.'

The bloodletting was not at an end. Many of the royalists had fled across the fields to the south, but a considerable number had barricaded themselves in the farmhouse at Espejo, which was surrounded by three enclosed corrals. The patriots broke into the corrals; the royalists hoisted a white flag in surrender but the patriots took no notice and brought up a cannon to blast their way in. The royalists opened fire again and the attackers, further enraged, broke in; those inside were massacred on the spot, or chased into the nearby vineyard and butchered there. About five hundred were slaughtered before the arrival of General Las Heras restored order. The farm had become a charnel house, bodies littering the courtyards and vineyard, blood spattering the walls and floors. Here Captain-General Ordoñez was brought to San Martín, and they embraced: in their twenties, in Cádiz, they had been friends, and dancing companions. The Spanish commander was later taken to San Luis gaol, where he was killed in an abortive uprising a few years later. Osorio and about two hundred cavalry had managed to escape back to Talcahuano.

The official figures for the cost to the Spanish of San Martín's victory are sobering: 2,000 royalists killed and 2,200 taken prisoner, including the Captain-General of Chile, Ordoñez, 4 colonels, 7 lieutenant-colonels and 150 lesser officers; 12 cannon captured, nearly 4,000 muskets, 1,200 blunderbusses and all the Spanish stores and ammunition. The patriots lost about a thousand killed or seriously injured. At the end of the nineteenth century the historian Bartolomé Mitre, sometime President of Argentina, wrote the epitaph for Maipú:

> Maipú is noteworthy because it was the first great American battle, from a historic and scientific viewpoint, because of the accurate strategic marches that preceded it and because of the able tactical manoeuvres upon the field, as well as the able co-ordination and timely use of the [various military] arms.
>
> Militarily it is a notable model, almost perfect, of a parallel attack which becomes an oblique attack; it is outstanding for the skilful use of the reserves upon the weakest flank of the enemy, an inspiration which decided the victory. It is to be noted that San Martín, like Epaminondas, won only two great battles, and both by the use of the same oblique attack invented by the immortal Greek genius. The battle of Maipú is matched only by those of Boyacá, which was its immediate consequence, and of Ayacucho, which was its final consequence; but without Maipú, there would not have been either a Boyacá or an Ayacucho.

San Martín had decisively thrown the Spanish out of the lower half of South America, and never again did they attempt a major attack there. Argentina and Chile were truly free, while for the first time the Spanish were on the defensive throughout the entire continent. It seemed possible, after all, that the nascent independent countries of South America would be able to consolidate their achievement, rather than suffer overthrow by a reinvigorated Spanish Empire. Bolívar in Angostura, still labouring against the odds in his occupied homeland, understood the significance of the victory. 'The day of America has arrived,' he pronounced definitively.

San Martín set out once again on the long journey to Buenos Aires, this time at Pueyrredón's urgent request that he should satisfy the people's craving to celebrate their hero and his victory. 'It is ... absolutely necessary that you measure your daily travelling so that you enter the city in the daytime; and that from your last stop you let me know one hour beforehand the time of your arrival, so that the General Staff, etc., may go to meet you at San José de Flores.' Typically San Martín, expected on 12 May, arrived at dawn on the 11th, and rode unheralded to his parents-in-law's house to embrace the wife and daughter he was so devoted to. The government of Buenos Aires gave a house in the central square over to his use, awarding it to his daughter so that he could not refuse it; and he was forced to attend a solemn celebration in the plaza, with parades and speeches, followed at night by a performance of the Death of Caesar, and a lengthy procession with more than 3,500 candles.

But San Martín had come principally to argue his case for a sea-borne attack on Lima; and this he did in heated discussions with Pueyrredón and the leading citizens of Buenos Aires, who wanted him to return with his army to crush the remaining Spanish resistance along the River Plate, and to oppose the 20,000-strong Spanish invasion supposedly being planned in Madrid. San Martín scoffed that the trouble along the River Plate could be sorted out by the Argentinians themselves, and that the impending invasion was merely a Spanish scare-story. Sensing, however, that the argument was going against him, he suddenly threatened to resign. Alarmed, Pueyrredón agreed to finance an expedition to capture the ports south of Lima and to instigate an insurrection among the Peruvians – a much more limited objective than San Martín's plan to seize the capital of the Spanish Empire itself, which was seen as too costly and too difficult. But he accepted the half-loaf proffered.

The Argentines agreed to provide 500,000 pesos, and in mid June San Martín departed with his wife and daughter to spend a happy month in his beloved Mendoza. Then Pueyrredón wrote to tell him that it had proved impossible to raise the promised money. Furiously, San Martín despatched his resignation; driven to distraction, Pueyrredón responded: 'I don't know why I haven't gone crazy. Let us forget now about resignations; if circumstances made yours excusable it is not so now, and I swear to you on my life that if you persist in it I will forthwith resign myself. We have to come out of this honourably, helping each other'. San Martín withdrew his resignation; to raise the money, he confiscated the funds of businessmen travelling through his province between Chile and Buenos Aires, issuing promissory notes on the government which Pueyrredón had to honour. He did also receive about 200,000 pesos despatched from Buenos Aires. Then he left his adored family in Mendoza, and crossed the Andes again to Santiago.

The year 1819 was to prove a nerve-racking and decisive one for San Martín. Threats loomed in Argentina: quite apart from the rumoured Spanish expedition, civil war, always in the offing, broke out between the provinces and the capital; Pueyrredón ordered San Martín to return from Santiago to Buenos Aires with his Army of the Andes. In fact, the army said to be destined for the Americas mutinied in Cadiz before its departure; but Buenos Aires still had to fight the rebellious provinces. San Martín obediently sent about 2,000 men to Mendoza, leaving him with 2,800 Argentinian soldiers in Chile, plus 4,400 Chileans. His dismay at seeing his dream of an attack on Peru evaporating yet again brought on another bout of nervous illness, however, and he sent in his resignation. At the same time he travelled back to Mendoza with half his remaining men, all the while seeking to buy time. With utter despair he heard that Argentina's Army of the North had mutinied, taking Belgrano prisoner. Haigh, who visited him in Mendoza, found 'the hero of Maipú sick in bed, looking so pale and thin that if it had not been for the brilliance of his eyes I would hardly have recognised him. He received me with a languid smile and put out his hand to welcome me.'

San Martín then had himself carried back again across the Andes, to Valparaíso, where others were engaged in preparations for the invasion, and there calamitous news followed him: the government of his friend Pueyrredón had fallen. San Martín declared that as the government which had appointed him no longer existed, he would call upon his officers to choose their own commander; when they chose him, he concluded that as his authority now derived from them, not from Buenos Aires, he was free to disregard the fallen government's order to return with his army to the capital. Thus, on specious grounds, he carried more than half his army into open mutiny. Predictably, a torrent of abuse was directed against him from Buenos Aires. For the second time in his life – the first being when he deserted from Spain – he was denounced as a rebel and a traitor. He was accused of stealing an Argentinian army and neglecting the troubles of his homeland. He was charged with seeking to go to Lima to seize power for himself. He was said to have stolen 500,000 pesos from the Argentinian treasury – when he had in fact received no more than 200,000, and that for an approved project. But in his heart San Martín knew that to eliminate Spanish power from its very stronghold was more important than the local squabbles of Argentina. Now it fell to the impecunious Chileans to support him in this endeavour.

Usually a man of few words, in July 1820 he issued to the people of the former Viceroyalty of La Plata a defiant proclamation and self-justification. He warned prophetically that

> If, obeying the experience of ten years of conflicts, you do not give your wishes a more prudent direction, I fear that, tired of anarchy, you may hope at the end for a return of oppression and that you may welcome the yoke of the first fortunate adventurer who shows up, who, far from consolidating your destiny, will only prolong your servitude.
>
> Fellow countrymen: I leave you with a deep regret that I experience at the prospect of your misfortunes; you have accused me of not having contributed to increase them, for such would have been the result if I had taken an active part in the [civil wars]: my army was the only one that kept its morale, and I would have exposed it to the danger of losing it if I had become involved in a campaign in which licentiousness would assuredly have infected my troops. In such a case it would have been necessary to renounce the undertaking of liberating Peru, and supposing that fate had favoured my arms in the civil war, I would have had to deplore the victory along with the beaten themselves. No, General San Martín will never shed the blood of his compatriots, and he will unsheath his sword only against the enemies of the independence of South America.

With half the 2,000 soldiers he had despatched to Mendoza now returned to support him, he had about 4,700 troops for his invasion of Lima, compared with the 6,000 he believed to be necessary. The expedition set sail in August 1820, from the beautiful bay of Valparaíso. It was equipped with 25 cannon, 15,000 muskets, 2,000 swords, food for 5,000 men, including biscuits, flour, beans and dried beef; ammunition and saddles; 800 horses; and a printing press.

32

Supreme Director

About a tenth of the Army of the Andes first assembled by San Martín in January 1817 had consisted of Chilean exiles. Of these, three men were prominent: Bernardo O'Higgins; Ramón Freire, a young captain; and San Martín's secretary, José Ignacio Zenteño, a meticulous, austere man, with a talent for organisation. On 12 January the expedition set off, and on 2 February O'Higgins was able to gaze down upon his beloved Chile again. His heroic but controversial performance at Chacabuco has been described in Chapter 29, followed by his appointment as 'Supreme Director' of Chile by San Martín.

It was a heady moment, but the new leader was not permitted to rest on his laurels. The remains of the royalist army were regrouping at Talcahuano and, as we have seen, San Martín had chosen not to run them to ground. The strong Argentinian presence in Chile soon became unpopular: San Martín's Lautaro Lodge was seen as being the power behind the scenes and certainly O'Higgins, as a member, was bound to consult it in all appointments and matters of state. Moreover, the aims of the Lodge were pan-American. Its statutes stated that

> This Society has been established for the purpose of grouping together American gentlemen who, distinguished by the liberality of their ideas and the fervour of their patriotic zeal, shall work together systematically and methodically for the independence and well-being of America, devoting to this most noble end all their strength, their influence, their faculties and talents, loyally sustaining one another, labouring honourably and proceeding with justice ...

In practice, this meant that San Martín effectively controlled the Chilean government. It was said that from being a Spanish colony, Chile had become an Argentine one. When news came that the Spanish were mounting a new expedition to Chile to regain the country, O'Higgins delegated his political powers to Colonel Quintana, an Argentinian not popular in Santiago, and hurried south to take charge of the Chilean army there.

Meanwhile José Miguel Carrera arrived in Buenos Aires aboard the *Grafton*, the 400-tonne corvette he had acquired in the United States, together with a score of volunteers he had recruited. His North American trip had largely been a failure, because his friend Poinsett lacked the connections to secure influential backers. Poinsett disapproved of O'Higgins, believing him to be too pro-British, and favoured Carrera as the vehicle for US interests in Chile; but few others were impressed by him – a good-looking but volubly self-important former dictator – or by his mad schemes for landing on the Chilean coast. In Buenos Aires Carrera disposed of his ship and, learning of the liberation of Chile, wrote ingratiatingly to O'Higgins asking to be allowed to return.

The Argentine leader Pueyrredón, mindful of their aristocratic connections, recommended that the Carreras be treated with consideration, but O'Higgins was so embittered by their involvement in the death of his mentor Mackenna that he was adamant in his refusal to readmit them to Chile. His obduracy was vindicated by Pueyrredón's discovery that José Miguel was plotting a landing on the Chilean coast. Pueyrredón had him arrested for deportation to the United States, but Carrera managed to escape across the River Plate to Montevideo.

From her home in Buenos Aires the next most powerful member of the family, Doña Javiera, now took a hand: her plan was that Juan José and Luís should return incognito, organise sympathisers in the armed forces to seize San Martín and O'Higgins, and force them to resign. If this failed, they could initiate a guerrilla war. The unpopular Argentine army would be sent home, and the conquest of Peru would be accomplished by 10,000 Chileans instead. José Miguel in Uruguay disapproved of this harebrained plan, which he presciently forecast would be 'the ruin of my brothers'. It was uncovered by the authorities as the two were making their way to Chile in disguise; they were arrested, and imprisoned at Mendoza. O'Higgins displayed implacable ruthlessness in writing to San Martín –

> Nothing which you tell me about the Carreras surprises me in the least. They have always been the same, and only death will change them. So long as they are alive, the country will be torn wih incessant convulsions … If fortune has favoured us now with revealing their dark designs and

disposing their capture, it may not be so propitious next time. A swift and exemplary punishment is the only cure for this grave evil. Let the three iniquitous Carreras disappear from our midst. Let them be brought to judgment and die, for this they deserve more than the greatest enemies of America. Let their followers be expelled to countries which are less worthy than ours to be free.

– but soon relented: the two brothers remained in Mendoza, where Luis plotted to assassinate the new governor there, and invade Chile from the east over the Andes all over again.

This latest Carrera plot was uncovered just as the alarming news of the defeat at Cancha Rayada came in, suggesting that Chile was about to be recovered by the royalists. Refugees began streaming once again across the Andean passes, and one of the earliest was San Martín's chief adviser, Bernardo Monteagudo, a sadistic, sensual and unprincipled Argentine mulatto who, believing everything to be lost, fled to save his own skin. He advised the authorities in Mendoza that, at this critical time for the survival of the Chilean state, San Martín and O'Higgins wanted the Carrera brothers to be put to death; in fact, they had granted a petition by Juan José's wife for the brothers' release, and instructions were on their way to the governor of Mendoza. Too late: astonished and enraged by the information that he was to be shot, Luís eventually controlled himself, made his confession, and persuaded his brother to cease his hysteria. They faced the firing squad calmly. Just after the executions, news arrived of the Chilean victory at Maipú, together with the instructions from O'Higgins to take no action against the Carreras.

There was a violent reaction in Santiago to the execution of two members of the country's most prominent family. It was widely assumed that the Argentinian San Martín, the plebeian anti-aristocratic half-Irishman O'Higgins and their sinister Lautaro Lodge were responsible. A mob broke into the courtyard of the government palace, and its leaders were taken before O'Higgins, still in bed recovering from his wound at Cancha Rayada. Coldly he informed them that he had no wish to remain Supreme Director, but had to do his duty. Monteagudo arranged for one of the brothers' most ardent and enduring supporters, Manuel Rodriguez, who with his 'Death's Head Hussars' had tried to overthrow the O'Higgins government after the defeat at Cancha Rayada, to be shot while attempting to escape; this was contrary to the Director's instructions, but he was widely believed to have been responsible.

José Miguel is said to have foamed at the mouth with fury on learning of the execution of his brothers. His missives bombarded Chile: 'The blood of the Carreras cries for vengeance. Vengeance, fellow countrymen! Hatred eternal for the despots of South America ... Chile is to be a mere colony of Buenos Aires, as she once was a colony of Spain ... From the Argentine they send governors for your provinces, magistrates for your towns, generals and armies for your frontiers.' At Doña Javiera's house an assassination squad was prepared, to go into Chile and kill O'Higgins and San Martín, but the plot was uncovered and the hellcat sister was thrown into prison.

After the fall of Pueyrredón in 1820, San Martín was not the only figure to ignore the government in Buenos Aires: Argentina disintegrated into provincial warlordism. José Miguel Carrera returned to the capital and set up the Chilean Legion, six hundred strong, which became the most feared of several armed bands laying waste to the great central pampas of Argentina. It recruited a large number of Indians attracted by the prospect of plunder, became a byword for brutality, and made ready to cross the mountains into Chile. Salta was sacked, the men massacred, the woman raped and the children borne off as slaves. In the end the Governor of Cuyo succeeded in defeating José Miguel. The last and most terrible of the Carrera brothers was taken captive to Mendoza, where he was sentenced to die in the same square as his siblings. 'I die for the liberty of America,' he proclaimed as he was shot: his body was quartered and put on show in iron cages, quite in the old Spanish colonial manner. He at least fully deserved his fate in the Argentina he had plundered. In Chile, where he was still a romantic hero to some, a few tears were shed for him. O'Higgins pronounced a grim epitaph on Carrera and his Chilean Legion in a letter to the Governor of Cuyo: 'These men dared to rend their country limb from limb, and in just retribution fell victim to their own fierce and wanton audacity. Such monsters must be crushed beneath the full weight of rightful authority, justice and the execration of the whole world.'

By 1822 O'Higgins's government, which had been in power nearly five years, was growing increasingly unpopular. Creating a navy and equipping the expedition it was to carry to Peru had proved expensive undertakings for a country of Chile's meagre resources, and San Martín was always making more demands, to sustain his efforts. Meanwhile the south of Chile was in turmoil as the brigand chief Vicente Benavides led a large armed force of royalist irregulars and Indians in plundering the country.

Concepción had become a nightmare province of banditry and of wandering groups of starving women, children and elderly trying to survive. The national treasury was virtually bankrupt. O'Higgins complained that 'there is no one here who has money to lend, even at 40 per cent interest. There is no money to pay our army in the south; since the expedition left, public servants, including myself, have had no salary paid to them. Things have got to such a pitch that I even have the humiliation of having to find someone to lend me 500 pesos every month for my own needs.'

O'Higgins's reforms had soon set important vested interests against him. He took on the powerful families who had supported the Spanish: 'Aristocracy is naturally abhorrent to me,' he declared, 'and adored equality is my idol.' Titles were abolished and coats-of-arms removed from houses – Chilean noblemen sneered that this was the vengeance of the bastard son of a 'new' family. O'Higgins also declared war on the clerical hierarchy, supporters of the royalists. The Bishop of Santiago was exiled to Mendoza, and the most superstitious practices of the Church were suppressed. O'Higgins resurrected an old reform his father had introduced: the burial of the dead in graveyards rather than in churches, which he considered an unhygienic practice. Such changes aroused resistance in conservative-minded churchgoers, and his attempts to modernise the country clergy also provoked intense opposition. He toyed with plans to outlaw confession and the celibacy of the clergy, and was narrowly dissuaded from airing them in public. More popular were his construction projects – the Avenida O'Higgins (now called the Alameda) in central Santiago, a three-kilometre-long, hundred-metre-wide boulevard, and the Maipú Canal, which irrigated the approaches to Santiago. His desire to encourage elementary education foundered against intense opposition from entrenched interests, combined with shortage of funds in a country at war.

Although to some extent he shared his father's keen interest in modernising reforms, O'Higgins was at heart a political autocrat. He controlled the press. He told a visiting American that 'in times of revolution, it is dangerous to carry through fundamental changes suddenly, however reasonable and desirable they may be in themselves. This is to risk losing everything.' It was with some reluctance that he set up a government of ministers and an advisory five-man senate. When finally he permitted elections to a constituent assembly, he made himself still more unpopular by instructing provincial governors to ensure that his supporters were elected.

26. The Sea-Devil: Thomas, Lord Cochrane

27. Maria Graham: she followed Cochrane from
Chile to Brazil. Painting by Thomas Lawrence

28. Cutting out the *Esmeralda*

29. Mexico's godfather: Antonio López de Santa Anna

30. A city fit for a Viceroy: Mexico City

31. Tragic peacemaker: Agustín de Itúrbide

32. Cynical observer: Lord Castlereagh. Painting by Thomas Lawrence

33. Old man in a hurry: Padre Hidalgo

34. Shy King: Dom João VI of Portugal

35. Destination for a court: Rio de Janeiro

36. Count Metternich: Pedro's bane, and enemy of liberation. Sketch by Anton Graff

37. Beauty that tamed the beast in Pedro: Empress Amelia of Brazil

38. Emperor and freedom fighter: Dom Pedro I

His biggest drawback was his chief adviser, José Antonio Rodriguez Aldea, a wily lawyer born, like himself, in Chillán, and once chief adviser to the royalist commander Gainza. Aldea was quick-witted, hard-working and unscrupulous, and charmed the two women in O'Higgins's life, his mother and his sister. He was also markedly corrupt, and implicated Rosita in his scandals, although not seriously. O'Higgins was warned of the damage being done to his reputation by his shady minister, but it was not until January 1823 that Aldea was at last forced to resign.

O'Higgins remained an endearingly straightforward character. He lived with his mother Isabel and sister Rosita in the government palace in Santiago. His mother was a benign figurehead and it was Rosita, short, well-built and direct in manner – her detractors nicknamed her 'the general in petticoats' – who looked after the household arrangements. Although O'Higgins was the only one of the Liberators who never married, there was not the least suggestion of homosexuality (which would have damned him in the macho culture of Latin America). Indeed, while staying in Concepción in 1817, he had enjoyed a steamy affair with a vibrant, fair-haired young woman, Rosaria Puga y Vibuarre, daughter of an officer, who had left her husband. She was considered hard – she was known as *la punta de diamante*, the diamond point – and the affair soon ended. Its legacy to O'Higgins was an uncanny repetition of his own history: an illegimate son, Pedro Demetrio, whom he neglected. But Isabel brought her grandson into the household, which already included two adopted Araucanian girls O'Higgins had rescued during the fighting in the south. O'Higgins would seem to have been too damaged by his father's neglect to want (or need, or be able) to sustain any closer emotional ties than those involved in serving his mother and sister, equally neglected.

By all accounts, as a man O'Higgins was remarkably nice and simple. Admiral Lord Cochrane described him as 'above meanness'; San Martín said 'there was more wax than steel in his heart'; José Maria de la Cruz, a close friend, wrote:

In private intercourse he was affable, unassuming and cautious. He liked better to listen than to speak, and he had a peculiar talent for summing up in a few words the ideas or points under discussion; and another peculiarity, that is to say, his ability to present to the world a countenance reflecting nothing of the amusement or gaiety customary among intimates, which resulted in his being classed as reserved ... In his home life he was invariably the same. I never knew him to speak sharply to his servants, and some of them he treated as if they had been relatives of the family. He idolised his mother, treating her with a consideration and respect such as I have never known in anyone of his age. When he came in from the office he would walk up and down in the inner courtyard, where he would find his mother's parrot and parakeet and, taking one in his hand and the other on his shoulder, he would begin to talk to them, the conversation usually consisting of chidings on account of the disputes in which they had been involved. The two pets were his table companions practically every day; he would place one on either side of him and feed them himself.

The palace was reasonably opulent; Maria Graham, lively widow of a naval officer, who lived in Chile and Brazil after 1822 and moved in government circles, described it: 'The rooms are handsome but plainly furnished; English cast-iron grates; Scotch carpets; some French china and time-pieces, little or nothing that looked Spanish, still less Chileno.' O'Higgins worked there with a somewhat driven devotion to duty. 'I am kept busy with papers and business the whole day long,' he wrote to Irisarri, his London envoy, in March 1822, 'from six in the morning to eleven at night, with only a break for lunch and a rest. It has been such a strain that I feel I cannot keep it up much longer.' His sole relaxations were music – he habitually carried an accordion with him on campaign, and enjoyed musical *tertulias* – and his estate outside Santiago. In that simple farmhouse, according to Maria Graham again, 'The Director ... sleeps on a little portable camp-bed, and to judge by his room, is not very studious of personal accommodation.' She described O'Higgins pithily as 'short and fat, yet very active; his blue eyes, light hair, and ruddy and rather coarse complexion do not belie his Irish extraction; whilst his small and short hands and feet belong to his Araucanian pedigree.' She was not an entirely unbiased observer, however, as she was besotted with José Miguel Carrera's good looks, and was one of those who deplored what his partisans regarded as his ill-treatment by O'Higgins.

Meanwhile the Supreme Director set up a network of police in an attempt to counter the crime wave sweeping the countryside, abolished bullfights, and initiated campaigns against gambling and alcoholism – all measures calculated to heighten the popular perception of him as a priggish mother's boy. He apparently never understood why his perfectly well-intentioned reforms did not win him friends, and his ineptitude in achieving popularity is somehow more endearing than San Martín's emphatic aversion to it. He succeeded at various times in disappointing the landed aristocracy, the Church, the business class and the ordinary people: although none particularly hated him, nor had he many enthusiastic adherents. Under him, nevertheless, Chile probably enjoyed as good, benevolent and uncorrupt a government as was possible during those early years of independence.

33

'Always go at them'

One night in about 1773, on the northern shore of Scotland's Firth of Forth, in the grounds of Culross Abbey, a man was conducting a scientific experiment. Like some crazed laird in one of Robert Louis Stevenson's later romances, he was fixing a gun-barrel to a kiln's outlet pipe in order to carry upwards the poisonous and maybe explosive vapours given off in the process of distilling coal tar. He lit the fumes at the barrel end, which gave a light so bright that it could be seen across the Forth, burning unstoppably. He had created the gas lighting which the inventor James Watt, whom he had recently met, had speculated would be necessary to illuminate the towns mushrooming across the Britain of the industrial revolution. But the night-worker of Culross failed to appreciate the possibilities: the process was patented by another man twenty years later.

This amateur inventor was the young Archibald Cochrane, later ninth Earl of Dundonald. The Cochranes were ennobled by Charles I and advanced to the earldom by Charles II, and the succession of soldiers who held the titles included one who served under General Wolfe and died at the siege of Louisberg. Archibald's grandfather had married the Bruce heiress who brought Culross into the family, but by Archibald's time money was short. A brilliantly inventive man, he sought to develop an important industrial process, as the only way to restore the family fortunes. His idea was to use the coal so freely available on his estate to produce coal tar with which to treat the hulls of ships, frequently riddled with worm holes even before they left the shipyards. He raised money towards its manufacture and initial tests on a buoy were strikingly successful, but the Admiralty was completely uninterested: many of its senior officials were in the pay of the shipbuilders whose bread-and-butter was the replacement of rotting ships. Not until

1822, when Cochrane's patent was long expired, did the Admiralty 'discover' this use of coal tar.

The noble inventor then turned his attention to the artificial manufacture of salt, and in the course of his work discovered another by-product, soda, suitable for the manufacture of soap and glass. Again, this was developed by others at a later date. He also dabbled in producing salammoniac, white lead, and alumina for silk and calico printing; he even tried to produce bread from potatoes, as a staple for the poor. In his treatise 'showing the intimate connection that subsists between agriculture and chemistry', he anticipated Sir Humphry Davy's revolutionary methods of intensive farming two decades later. His inventive genius never translated into profits, however; he succeeded his father as Earl of Dundonald in 1778, and bankruptcy forced him to sell his estate in 1788. His beautiful first wife Anne had died in 1784, leaving him four sons. He married again, a widow, Isabella Mayne (née Raymond), who died in 1808, then went to live with a mistress in Paris.

The eldest of his sons, Thomas, Lord Cochrane by courtesy after 1778, was brought up by a succession of suitably eccentric tutors, but when idyllic Culross was sold off he was enrolled, aged thirteen, in an army academy in London, destined for a military career. Thomas hated the life, and told his father he wished to join the navy. Clad in a vivid yellow waistcoat and trousers, his head shaved and plastered down 'in a vile composition of candlegrease and flour', he was instead despatched to join the 14th Foot. His appearance attracted derision from London street urchins and his army contemporaries alike. Humiliated and furious, he made his way back home, where his incensed father boxed his ears but eventually gave way to his demand.

At seventeen, Midshipman Lord Cochrane boarded the frigate *Hind*, off Sheerness, to experience all the joys of ship-board life at the end of the eighteenth century – the bullying of his fellow midshipmen, including 'cobbing', being beaten with a bag filled with water; the appalling food – weevilly biscuits that tasted like blancmange, brown water with plenty of animal life in it, wine that tasted like sawdust and bulls' blood, the occasional treat of potatoes and bread brought around at first light by vendors from the shore; leaky decks, which often meant wet bedding; the stifling conditions below-deck in summer. But Cochrane was a natural seaman and a good learner, and in 1796 he was promoted to lieutenant, achieving a measure of comfort with his own tiny cabin; two years later, engaged in the frustrating duty of blockading the French fleet at Cádiz, he fell foul of a petty-minded superior officer.

In 1799, while his ship was off Palermo, Cochrane became acquainted with Nelson, who advised him 'Never mind manoeuvres, always go at them'. In May 1800, at the age of twenty-four, he was appointed to command his own small ship, the brig *Speedy*. A year later, off the Spanish coast, he began to display the skill in deception that was to become his trademark. Having repainted his ship to resemble a Dutch neutral, he hoisted the yellow quarantine flag – causing the Spanish frigate about to board him to pull hastily away. On another occasion he hoaxed a Spanish pursuer by dropping a wooden barrel with a candle burning in it into the water at night, extinguishing his own lights, and then slipping away in the darkness while the Spanish went after the barrel.

In May 1801 Cochrane pulled off his first real coup. Having chased some Spanish gunboats into Barcelona, his little ship found herself face to face with a 32-gun Spanish frigate. Instead of fleeing, Cochrane hoisted an American flag to confuse the Spanish and made straight for the frigate, bringing the *Speedy* almost alongside where, as he wrote, 'From the height of the frigate out of the water, the whole of her shot must necessarily go over our heads, whilst our guns, being elevated, would blow up the main-deck ... The great disparity of force rendering it necessary to adopt some measure that might prove decisive, I resolved to board.' With blackened faces, half his men climbed aboard the prow of the frigate, surprising the Spanish into doubtful immobility long enough for him to lead the rest aboard into a surprise attack. After furious fighting, Cochrane yelled orders to his ship for another wave of attackers to come over: in fact, he had none. The Spanish then saw their flag being struck, signalling surrender, and they duly did so – not knowing it had been lowered by Cochrane's men. Forty-eight of them had captured 263 Spanish, who were crowded into the hold, with two cannon pointing at them through the hatch to deter them from any attempted counter-trickery. The frigate was taken prize to Minorca, and the engagement caught British public imagination. The promotions Cochrane had expected for himself and requested for his first lieutenant were not forthcoming, however, and *Speedy* was assigned to humdrum escort duties between Minorca and Gibraltar.

Cochrane's calculated dash and brio were accompanied by a good measure of arrogance. As a young lieutenant he had found himself in trouble over a minor insubordination; returning home on shore leave in late summer 1801, he proceeded to make an enemy of Earl St Vincent, the First Lord of the Admiralty, over the matter of Admiralty peculation regarding prize-money, and of his first lieutenant's promotion. His badgering provoked St Vincent to assert somewhat absurdly that 'the small number of men killed on board the *Speedy* did not warrant the application [for promotion]', prompting the unwise observation from Cochrane that only one man had been killed aboard the First Lord's own flagship at Cape St Vincent – unwise, because St Vincent was sensitive on this point, it having been often suggested that he had kept well away from the fighting that day.

The extension to his leave provided by the Peace of Amiens of March 1802 enabled Cochrane to repair some of the gaps in his education. Always aware of these, he was often to be found reading when not annoying his superiors or being tricky at sea; now he took himself off to Edinburgh and enrolled at the university to study under the celebrated Professor of Moral Philosophy, Dugald Stewart.

In May 1803, when war was resumed between Britain and France, St Vincent relented, to the extent of giving Cochrane command of a former collier, HMS *Arab*: when Cochrane first saw her, in Plymouth, he remarked that 'she will sail like a haystack'. In her he spent more than a year protecting fishing vessels in the Orkneys. St Vincent described him as 'not to be trusted out of sight ... mad, romantic, money-getting and not truth telling'. But by 1804 St Vincent had been replaced, and Cochrane was appointed captain of the 38-gun frigate *Pallas*. As obsessed (in view of his family's ruin) with financial gain as with his career, he luckily proved immensely skilful at capturing prizes, and in a matter of weeks his share of those taken amounted to £75,000.

On her way home from the Azores in March 1805 *Pallas* was surprised by three large enemy ships. In a strengthening wind and heavy seas Cochrane piled on sail and zig-zagged before them; but they gradually caught up to within half a mile on either side, the third farther off, and were preparing to fire. Suddenly an order was given. Every sail on the *Pallas* was hauled down at the same moment and, simultaneously, her helm was swung round to take her across the path of the storm. The enemy ships shot past her, her sails went up again, and off she sped in the opposite direction, making 13 knots. It took the enemy sail several miles to alter course and resume their pursuit, and at nightfall Cochrane successfully resorted once more to his barrel-and-lantern ruse.

Safely home and with money to spend, Cochrane now determined to enter politics, standing for election as MP to the rotten borough of Honiton, near Plymouth. His refusal to buy votes cost him the seat, but he afterwards rewarded his supporters with the sum of 10 guineas a head – twice what his victorious opponent had given for their votes – 'as a reward for having withstood the influence of bribery'.

After a spell on convoy duty between Plymouth and Quebec, early in 1806 he and the *Pallas* were assigned to the Channel Fleet operating off the French coast. Here in April 1806, learning that some French corvettes were sheltering in the Garonne, he sent off his ships' boats – leaving a skeleton crew aboard the *Pallas* – in a night attack upon the guardship *Tapageuse*; they succeeded, but three more enemy ships now appeared in the river. Again Cochrane resorted to ingenious trickery: by means of a complex system of ropes he caused all *Pallas*'s sails to be unfurled simultaneously, giving the illusion that she was both powerfully and efficiently manned. The French ships, altering course in some alarm, ran themselves aground, enabling Cochrane to get the *Tapageuse* and his seamen away. When Napoleon heard of the incident he dubbed Cochrane 'le Loup de Mer' – the Sea-Wolf.

In August 1806 Cochrane was given command of the frigate *Impérieuse*, a 38-gun, 1046-tonner which had been captured from the Spanish and was the fastest ship of her class in the navy. Among the midshipmen was the young Frederick Marryat (later the novelist Captain Marryat), who years afterward wrote:

> I never knew anyone so careful of the lives of his ship's company as Lord Cochrane, or any who calculated so closely the risks attending any expedition. Many of the most brilliant achievements were performed without the loss of a single life, so well did he calculate the chances; and one half the merit he deserves for what he did accomplish has never been awarded him, merely because, in the official despatches, there has not been a long list of killed and wounded to please the appetite of the English public.

Early in 1807 a convoy of French merchantmen in the Bay of Biscay took shelter in the Arcachon basin, where the troops from the fort there moved down to guard the ships at night. Seizing the fort when it was virtually unmanned, Cochrane then attacked the troops from behind; they fled, leaving the convoy unprotected, and seven enemy ships were destroyed. In the middle of February the *Impérieuse* returned to Plymouth.

In 1806 Cochrane had been elected MP for Honiton in Devon at the second attempt; in the General Election of spring 1807 he was returned for the City of Westminster, Charles James Fox's old seat, defeating the playwright-politician Richard Brinsley Sheridan. He immediately launched into a series of attacks on naval abuses and Admiralty corruption, and should not have been surprised to find himself hastily ordered to the Mediterranean, where he raided French shore positions with all his accustomed inventiveness, and mercilessly harried shipping supplying the French troops in the Peninsula.

One of his more spectacular exploits took place at Mongat, just outside Barcelona. The bulk of its French garrison was absent, engaged in besieging the Spanish at Gerona, and Cochrane was persuaded by local guerrillas to attack. At night he blocked the two roads into the fort, then bombarded it from the sea. The French soon surrendered, but the local Spanish were intent on revenge and Cochrane had to fight to get his 95 French captives down to the ships without losing them to the mob. On another occasion he sent ship's boys dressed as marines off in small boats, to feign a landing to one side of Port Vendre, with the aim of luring the defending French cavalry out to attack them. Then he bombarded the town, blew up the shore batteries, and wiped out a detachment of returning cavalry with well-aimed grapeshot from the sea.

In November 1808, with about eighty men from the *Impérieuse*, Cochrane occupied Fort Trinidad, overlooking the town of Rosas through which reinforcements for the French army in the Peninsula were due to pass once the French had taken the fort from the Spanish. A French battery bombarding the fort from the hills above had breached the tower about fifty feet above its base, and Cochrane's first move was to booby-trap the breach against incursion, with greased planks to send any intruders hurtling to the bottom of the tower and a barricade of ships' chains hung with fish hooks on which they might impale themselves. The tower was mined with explosives. Cochrane showed himself mockingly on the parapets, but was hit in the nose and mouth – not too seriously – by flying fragments of stone. On 30 November the anticipated reinforcements arrived, and an advance guard of 1200 began to scale the walls of the tower, only to fall foul of the booby traps and the defenders' fire. Cochrane's men then withdrew, luring the French on before the explosive was detonated. Dozens were killed and wounded, but still they came on. Bombarded with hand grenades, the French at last faltered, and fell back to a safe distance. On 5 December circumstances obliged Cochrane to evacuate the garrison and his men from Fort Trinidad; in a final act of defiance, he blew up its main tower. He had managed to delay an army of 6,000 for nearly two weeks, at a cost of no more than three of his own men.

He became even more of a popular hero at home, and the *Naval Chronicle* observed:

> Seeing what Lord Cochrane has done with his single ship upon the French shores, we may easily conceive, what he would have achieved if he had been entrusted with a sufficient squadron of ships, and a few thousand military, hovering along the whole extent of the French coast, which it would take a considerable portion of the army of France to defend.

This view echoed his own conviction that to tie up French troops in this way and disrupt Napoleon's supply lines would be more effectual than Wellington's Peninsular expedition. It was not a view that found favour at the Admiralty – but an officer of just his daring and cunning was desperately needed, for a French fleet under Admiral Willaumez had slipped through the Royal Navy's blockade of Brest in a gale and was now free to attack British shipping.

34

The Sea-Wolf

In March 1809, barely a week after returning from the Mediterranean, Cochrane was summoned by the First Lord of the Admiralty, Lord Mulgrave. The escaped French fleet of eleven battleships and several frigates had at last been sighted in the Basque Roads, off the port of Rochefort in the Bay of Biscay. Only fireships could destroy shipping in that well-protected anchorage but Admiral Lord Gambier, commander of the British fleet in the Bay, was reluctant to use them. Cochrane suggested that a successful attack might be possible if preceded by 'explosion vessels' of his own design. He was thereupon placed on special assignment, over the heads of many senior commanders. He tried to decline, but was ordered to his post, and arrived at the end of March to find the French fleet anchored close to shore in the Aix Roads, between the tiny Ile d'Aix and the much larger Ile d'Oléron. Cochrane's first thought was that the islands could be occupied, thus disrupting communications between France and Spain.

Meanwhile, however, with his usual vigour he set about making ready for his attack. The fireships were prepared by laying down lengths of gunpowder in a criss-cross formation across the decks, and piling up wood and canvas between them. Tarred canvas was hung from above and the rigging was hung with tarred ropes. The decks were doused in resin and turpentine, and four big holes were cut in either side of each ship to provide air to feed the flames. Finally, grappling chains were attached to the fireships. They would become floating infernos, burning slowly and steadily and destroying anything they came into contact with.

Cochrane's own practical flair suggested to him that the French would have erected a boom across the entrance; unless this could be destroyed, the fireships could not be got close to the French fleet, and this was where his 'explosion vessels' came in. The sides of three ships were strengthened, to concentrate the force of the blasts from the 1,500 barrels of gunpowder, 1,500 ten-inch shells and 3,000 grenades which he caused to be bound together into what he described as 'gigantic mortar[s]' and placed in their holds – with a slow-burning fuse to give the crews a chance of escape. In the end, Cochrane had twenty-two fireships as well as his three explosion vessels.

A popular verse by Thomas Hood mocked Admiral Lord Gambier:

> 'Oh Admiral Gam – I dare not mention *bier*,
> In such a temperate ear;
> Oh! Admiral Gam – an Admiral of the Blue,
> Of course, to read the Navy List aright,
> For strictly shunning wine of either hue,
> You can't be Admiral of the Red or White.'

He was quite unsuited to his command, a religious fanatic, a tractarian, detested by his subordinates and cautious to the point of cowardice, haughtily advising Cochrane to wait, for fear the fireships might be bombarded and the crews murdered by the French: 'If you choose to rush on to self-destruction that is your own affair, but it is my duty to take care of the lives of others, and I will not place the crews of the fire-ships in palpable danger.' The lack of chemistry between the two men, the one so impulsive, the other so cautious, can well be imagined, and in addition Gambier resented the slight implied in sending Cochrane out on special assignment to assist him. Gambier told Cochrane he considered the passage between the Ile d'Aix and the Boyart shoal to be highly dangerous and exposed, but although Aix had a garrison of 2,000 Cochrane's reconnaissance had persuaded him that the fortress there was 'quite open'.

When the wind and sea rose on 11 April, Cochrane saw his opportunity. Conditions were right for the fireships, properly positioned, to be blown into the anchorage; the more difficult problem would be for those positioning them to get away against the wind and the tide. While Gambier hovered prudently eight miles off the coast, on the evening of the 11th Cochrane sailed in the first of the three explosion ships towards the giant two-mile-long wooden boom, anchored with heavy chains to the sea floor, that protected the French fleet. He lit the fuse of his ship about ten minutes, as he judged it, away from the boom, jumped aboard a gig alongside and, a hundred yards from the explosion ship, realised he had left the ship's mascot, a dog, on board. They rowed back, and Cochrane clambered aboard to grab the dog, as the seconds ticked away. Then he and his men rowed for all they were worth, against the tide. A few minutes later a mighty explosion rent the sky, and débris and shrapnel shot over their heads to land in a circle just beyond them; had they not delayed to rescue the dog, they would have been hit by it.

An observer with Gambier's ships reported a large flash followed by a sky 'red with the lurid glare arising from the simultaneous ignition' of all that gunpowder; Cochrane and his companions in the little boat were suddenly hit by the aftershock: 'The sea was convulsed as if by an earthquake' and they were lifted 'like a cork and dropped into the trough of a gigantic wave', certain they would be killed. Somehow they stayed upright, after which 'nothing but a heavy rolling sea had to be encountered, all having again become silent and darkness'. Moments later a second fireball sundered the night air as the next explosion ship struck what was left of the boom. The third ship failed to ignite.

Sinister, darkened shapes were now driven by wind and tide towards the breach; in fact, only four of the fireships – fewer than a fifth of the total – got through and into the anchorage, one after another exploding into flame. The captains of Gambier's fleet had cut loose the fireships fully a mile and a half out to sea, so that most of them missed the channel they were supposed to enter. But the four that did get through caused havoc among the ships packed tightly at anchorage. Thinking they were explosion ships of the kind they had just seen dazzle the night skies, the terrified French crews panicked; their ships collided, and many were deliberately run aground so that the men could escape. As the tide ebbed, these were left beached on their sides. Cochrane was exultant: now was the time to move in for the kill, and riddle their exposed hulls.

At 5.48 on the morning of that long night he signalled Gambier's flagship, the *Caledonian*: 'Half the fleet can destroy the enemy. Seven [ships] on shore.' The reply was a pennant signifying 'Very good'. An hour later Cochrane, exasperated, signalled again: 'Eleven on shore.' The same pennant was flown in reply. An hour later he signalled again, 'Only two afloat', and was told a third time, 'Very good'.

The outgoing tide had left the French fleet stranded and helpless. Now was the ideal moment to ride the inflowing tide and attack. But Gambier would do nothing, even though the entire French fleet was at his mercy. Cochrane signalled that he wanted to go in: 'The frigates alone can destroy the enemy.' This was ignored: he later heard that the

signal was considered impertinent. Nearly two hours later, as the tide
came in, he signalled that the enemy was 'preparing to haul off'. 'Very
good' came the reply. Not until 11 a.m. did the British fleet move – and
then only to drop anchor three and a half miles out. Gambier had
decreed the attack to have been successful, and considered there was no
further need 'to risk any part of the fleet'. Cochrane fumed as the French
ships gradually refloated on the incoming tide, and then decided to defy
his chief. Raising his own anchor, he allowed his ship to float unobtru-
sively backwards into the Aix–Boyart channel, under desultory fire from
those guns on Aix that Gambier was apparently so frightened of. The
Impérieuse then opened fire on three stranded French ships, meanwhile
signalling to Gambier that she was 'in distress'. At last, two hours later,
two battleships and five frigates from the British fleet arrived to reinforce
Cochrane's lone effort. A fourth French ship was easily destroyed, but
the bulk of the fleet escaped. Cochrane hoped to destroy the French
flagship before she reached the safety of the Charente estuary with the
others, but was ordered back by Gambier: 'You have done your part so
admirably', wrote Gambier, 'that I will not suffer you to tarnish it by
attempting impossibilities', and he subsequently ordered Cochrane to
carry his despatches concerning the action to London. Cochrane was
there made a Knight Commander of the Bath, but learned that Gambier
had given the credit for the initial attack to Captain Woolridge of the
Mediator fireship, and that he himself was to be congratulated only for
his part in the final encounter; Gambier was to receive a vote of thanks
in the House of Commons for what was described as a contribution as
great as Nelson's at the Nile and Copenhagen. This was too much for
Cochrane, who told Mulgrave: 'In my capacity as one of the Members
for Westminster, I will oppose the motion, on the ground that the commander-in-chief has not only done nothing to merit a vote of thanks,
but has neglected to destroy the French fleet in Aix Roads, when it was
clearly in his power to do so.'

Cochrane declined Mulgrave's offer of a prestigious command, recognising it as the bribe it doubtless was, and when details of the affair were
made public the press took his side. 'It very forcibly struck us,' observed
the *Naval Chronicle*, 'that an extraordinary time *did* elapse from the
appearance of Lord Cochrane's telegraphic communication "that seven
of the enemy's ships were on shore, and might be destroyed", till the
period when the requisite assistance was afforded.' Gambier insisted on
a court martial to vindicate himself. The court was packed with senior

officers, many of them Gambier's friends. Cochrane's manner was characteristically aggressive, and he shocked the court by effectively accusing its members of ignorance. The testimony of Gambier's companions at sea as to the reasonableness of his conduct was backed by charts showing submerged rocks just twelve feet down in the Aix–Boyart channel which, it was attested, it would have been madness for his flagship to attempt to cross. An English captain had encountered no such rocks, however, and Cochrane had drifted across them with impunity, as had the French fleet; French charts showed the rocks to be thirty feet down. The English charts were demonstrably and deliberately false, drawn up by men who had never been in the Basque Roads.

Gambier was acquitted 'most honourably'. Cochrane, once acclaimed the hero of the Basque Roads, was disgraced, his reputation tainted and traduced; Lord St Vincent declared he was not to be trusted. The man who had remained eight miles from the battle was given the honours, and the man in the thick of the fighting was stripped of them. Napoleon himself later commented: 'The French admiral was an *imbécile*, but yours was just as bad. I assure you that, if Cochrane had been supported, he would have taken every one of the ships. They ought not to have been alarmed by your *brûlots* [fireships], but fear deprived them of their senses, and they no longer knew how to act in their own defence.'

Cochrane was stripped of his command of the *Impérieuse*, and therefore took no part in the farce of the Walcheren Expedition. In his enforced idleness, he busied himself with further inventions. He refined the design of his explosion ships – now dubbed 'Temporary Mortars'; he devised 'sulphur ships', 'stink vessels' carrying a cargo of burning charcoal and sulphur whose poisonous gas emissions he thought would kill men by the hundreds. He also carried on with his campaign to root out naval corruption, in furtherance of which he travelled to Malta to expose the practices of the 'prize court' there. This body, which dealt with the awarding of prize money, was theoretically presided over by two officials, the Marshal and the Proctor, who were entitled to charge one another for their services. But as Donald Thomas, one of Cochrane's biographers, writes:

> The great discovery of Cochrane's visit to Malta was that one man, Mr Jackson, held both posts and both salaries of marshal and proctor. He was busily and legally amassing a fortune by fees for visiting himself to ask himself to sign monitions and other legal documents, and for agreeing with himself to do it. He was also paying himself for negotiating fees with

himself, and indeed for administering the oath to himself. Still more extraordinary was the fact that the monitions which he asked himself to draw up were also addressed to himself. As Cochrane pointed out, Jackson was entitled to consult with himself as often as he felt necessary and to charge the victims of the court several pounds for doing so.

Cochrane demanded to see the table of fees, and found it pinned to the back of the judges' lavatory door. He took it, and was arrested. Refusing bail, he was imprisoned in the town gaol, where he entertained his friends and at length escaped, using a file to cut the bars and a rope to lower himself out of the window. His gaoler, 'purposely made very tipsy', was delighted to see the back of him, as were the authorities in Malta. In England he regaled the House of Commons with the story. A bill of Mr Jackson's charges for a single case, unrolled, reached from the Speaker's table to the bar of the House of Commons. His performance had the House convulsed.

Then his fellow Westminster MP Sir Francis Burdett was sentenced by the House of Commons to imprisonment in the Tower of London, for having accused his fellow members of exercising arbitrary government. In support of Burdett the houses of various ministers were attacked by the mob, which had to be dispersed by a charge of the Life Guards in Piccadilly. Cochrane brought a large barrel of gunpowder to blow up the front of Burdett's house when the authorities came for him, at which his fellow rebels protested, asking him to take it away. The same night Burdett was arrested by soldiers who crept into his house the back way.

Cochrane had by now established himself as a persistent thorn in the side of the conservative elements in Parliament. He was usually a poor speaker, but nevertheless made a celebrated denunciation of the Wellesley family, then the most powerful in the government, on the issue of pensions and sinecures. He pointed out the anomalies between the pensions paid to those worn out or injured in the service and to the civilians who administered it. An officer who had lost a leg received £40, the Secretary to the Admiralty £1,500 a year. William Wellesley-Pole, himself a former Secretary to the Admiralty, defended his family and went on to deliver a prescient warning against the blind alley down which the behaviour of this once distinguished national hero was leading him: 'Let me advise him that adherence to the pursuits of his profession, of which he is so great an ornament, will tend more to his honour and to the advantage of his country than a perseverance in the conduct which he has of late adopted, conduct which can only lead him into error, and make him the dupe of those who use the authority of his name to advance their own mischievous purposes.'

The one bright light on Cochrane's darkening horizon was meeting and marrying a beautiful sixteen-year-old schoolgirl, Kitty Barnes, orphaned daughter of a Spanish dancer and an Englishman. Kitty had neither birth, wealth nor connections to recommend her to Cochrane's relations, so the oddly-assorted couple (Cochrane was twenty-one years Kitty's senior, and beginning to grow portly) eloped to Scotland, where they married in a civil ceremony at Arran on 8 August 1812. His uncle Basil disinherited him, but Cochrane later gallantly recorded that, for his sacrifice, he 'had a rich equivalent in the acquisition of a wife whom no amount of wealth could have purchased'. He remained on good terms with his uncle, nevertheless, and he and Kitty lived in Basil's house in Portman Square for the first eighteen months of their marriage. Cochrane found nuptial bliss some compensation for his status as a half-pay officer; but in 1812 war had broken out between Britain and the United States, and early in 1814 he was appointed Flag Captain to his uncle Admiral Sir Alexander Cochrane, newly in command of the North American station. After five years' absence from the sea, Cochrane had the pleasure of involving himself in the refitting of his flagship, HMS *Tonnant*.

35

Disgrace

On 21 February 1814 Cochrane breakfasted with a disreputable uncle from the West Indies, Andrew Cochrane-Johnstone, and a business partner, Richard Butt, then went to a factory where he was developing a new oil-lamp. An urgent message to the factory summoned him home again, where a man was waiting to see him. Random de Berenger, a mercenary who had run into debt, was now seeking to join the crew of the *Tonnant*. De Berenger was dressed in the green uniform of a sharp-shooter, and asked Cochrane for a change of clothes, expressing a fear that his leave of absence from debtors' prison would be cancelled if his uniform led to suspicion that he was breaking bounds and planning to abscond. Such a request, while curious, appealed to Cochrane's generous and impulsive streak.

What Cochrane did not know – or so he later claimed – was that in the middle of the previous night a 'Lieutenant-Colonel du Bourg, aide-de-camp to the British ambassador in Russia', had arrived in Dover, announcing the Allies' complete victory over Napoleon in eastern France; the Emperor, he asserted, had been slain and dismembered by Russian Cossacks. Du Bourg set out by post-chaise for London, where a few hours later another post-chaise, this time carrying three French officers wearing the white cockade of the Bourbons, went through the City of London, its occupants tossing out papers bearing the words 'Vive le Roi', 'Vivent les Bourbons!'

The stock exchange went wild. Omnium, the principal government stock involved in the comparatively new practice of margin trading, soared from 26½ points to 32 in a few hours. Fortunes were made. Yet by the end of the day it was clear that the City had been hoaxed: Napoleon, undefeated, was alive and well (although he had indeed narrowly escaped death at the hands of a Cossack patrol a few days before).

The stock exchange set up an immediate enquiry, and one fact that emerged was that Cochrane-Johnstone and Butt had been large profit-takers that day. Butt, as Lord Cochrane's stock-broker, had also sold Cochrane's holding of Omnium, but – following a prior instruction – had done so as soon as the market had risen by a mere one per cent, so that Cochrane's gains were a fraction of those made by others that day.

A connection was discovered between Cochrane's uncle and his partner and the three men later identified as those purporting to be French officers. Most damningly of all, it transpired that de Berenger was none other than the bogus Colonel du Bourg. De Berenger was found in possession of money given him by Cochrane and papers connecting him with Cochrane-Johnstone and Butt. On 27 April Cochrane, his uncle and Butt were indicted as principals in the stock exchange fraud, and Cochrane was stripped of his captaincy of the *Tonnant*: he had met the main perpetrator of the fraud, and had (apparently) helped him with money and a change of disguise on the very day it was carried out.

Certainly Cochrane had gained from the fraud – not very much, as a result of that prior instruction; yet, it was argued, this might have been designed to deflect suspicion, with an arrangement to share afterwards in his partners' greater profits. The money traceable to Cochrane in de Berenger's hands had in fact passed through Butt's, in payment of a loan, but this might have been nothing less than what would today be described as prudent money-laundering. There was little doubt of the complicity of Cochrane-Johnstone and Butt, and they had met Cochrane on the very morning of the fraud.

In addition, the public perception of Cochrane's position was as unhelpful as it was in some respects inaccurate: he was under financial pressure, lately married, disinherited by his wealthy uncle and thrown out of his house; his work on new inventions was reminiscent of his father's efforts to raise money; and his future in the navy uncertain, at the least. Finally, most convincingly, the whole extraordinary hoax, with its cheeky exploitation of greedy City gullibility and its colourful masquerade, fairly reeked of the sort of deception he was famous for.

The only defence possible was that he had been duped by his uncle and his partners. Certainly Cochrane-Johnstone was unscrupulous enough to have done so. But why? What was the point of implicating Cochrane? Did they think, mistakenly, that his reputation was such as to protect them from criminal charges? It must have seemed just as likely that the idea was Cochrane's, using his uncle and Butt as his front-men to escape incrimination. Cochrane did not attend the hearing – on the advice of his lawyers, he later maintained, but it bore an appearance of arrogance which did not help his cause.

Scenting blood, his many enemies crowded in for the kill. The judge, Lord Chief Justice Ellenborough, was a sworn enemy of the radical party Cochrane supported in Parliament. The prosecuting counsel was his own former lawyer, Richard Gurney. The solicitor for the prosecution was the Admiralty Solicitor and had worked against Cochrane in the Gambier court martial. On a superficial examination of the evidence Cochrane looked to be guilty, and the Establishment was determined to ensure that he was so found.

The trial lasted two days. Cochrane's defence easily refuted the charge that he had made any substantial profit from the fraud, and the accusation that he had paid de Berenger directly. But de Berenger himself could not be shrugged off so easily. Sworn testimony varied as to whether he had been wearing a green sharpshooter's uniform or the scarlet and medals of the self-styled Colonel du Bourg on his arrival at Cochrane's house. Whatever he was wearing, the fact remained that he, the chief perpetrator, had arrived there on the morning of the fraud, and had been given a change of clothing. It did not look well.

As the time for the verdict approached, Cochrane-Johnstone absconded. On 20 June Cochrane, Butt and de Berenger and the other principal defendants were each sentenced to twelve months in prison; Cochrane, additionally, was fined £1,000. He, Butt and de Berenger were also condemned to stand for an hour in the pillory opposite the Royal Exchange. Napoleon, aghast at the way the British were treating one of their most daring heroes, wrote from exile on Elba, 'Such a man should not be made to suffer so degrading a punishment.' Fearing a riot, the government subsequently remitted the pillorying.

Cochrane's name was struck off the Navy List, he was expelled from Parliament, and the Prince Regent declared: 'I will never permit a service, hitherto of unblemished honour, to be disgraced by the continuance of Lord Cochrane as a member of it. I shall also strip him of the Order of the Bath.'

In the King's Bench State House, the prison for financial miscreants, the discomfort was not too great for a man accustomed to the rigours of naval life. Cochrane had two rooms – for which he had to pay, as well as for his food – and was offered the privilege of walking outside the buildings. This he refused, but he made use of the writing materials he was permitted, and continued to work on his oil-lamp. In March 1815, at dead of night, he climbed out of the high, unbarred window of his cell onto the roof of the building. He threw a coiled rope (which had been smuggled in to him) across to the spikes of the wall surrounding the gaol, and, hand-over-hand, pulled himself across it, over the spikes and down another rope, which snapped when he was still twenty feet above the ground. Badly bruised, he crawled to the house of a friend and disappeared, the only news of him being a letter to the Speaker of the House of Commons declaring his intention to take the seat to which he had been re-elected while in prison, by voters still convinced of his innocence. A fortnight later Cochrane appeared in the chamber of the House. Bow Street Runners were sent in to arrest him, but he refused to go quietly and was carried out struggling. He was held for three weeks in solitary confinement in the strong room of the King's Bench Prison, a damp, underground, unheated chamber, until he contracted chest pains, diagnosed as a sign of approaching typhus. Two months later, as news of the great victory at Waterloo reached England, his sentence was served. For a fortnight he refused to pay his fine, and did so at last by a note-of-hand with a message written on the back of it: 'My health having suffered by long and close confinement, and my oppressors being resolved to deprive me of property or life, I submit to robbery to protect myself from murder, in the hope that I shall live to bring the delinquents to justice.'

In July 1815 he took his seat once again in the House of Commons, where he cast the deciding vote against the government's proposal to increase the allowance to the Prince Regent's brother, the Duke of Cumberland – a man who was said to have murdered his valet, indecently assaulted the wife of the Lord Chancellor, and fathered a child on his sister, Princess Sophie.

Next Cochrane attempted to impeach the Lord Chief Justice, Ellenborough, who he alleged had sent him to prison on grounds of 'partiality, misrepresentation, injustice and oppression'; but he was supported only by Burdett. Cochrane's imprisonment had transformed him into a popular radical hero, and he became a champion of universal suffrage, demand for which was fuelled by the economic discontent which followed the end of the Napoleonic wars, and by the contempt in which the monarchy was increasingly held. Cochrane addressed a packed meeting of 20,000 people in Bristol, another in Yorkshire and a

third, of some 24,000, in London. The government response was to suppress opposition newspapers and suspend the Act of Habeas Corpus.
Britain appeared to be hovering on the brink of revolution. Cochrane,
despite his fiery reputation, favoured reform rather than revolution, but
warned in June 1818 that if the House did not reform itself, it would be
reformed from outside 'with a vengeance'.

In the same speech he astonished his hearers with the information
that this was 'probably the last time I shall ever have the honour of
addressing the House of Commons on any subject'. The truth was that
Cochrane, as ever, needed money: a few weeks earlier his house at Holly
Hill in Hampshire had been placed under siege by the sheriff of the
county and twenty-five constables to recover a debt of £1,200 incurred
as long ago as 1806, for a dinner for the electors of Honiton. Cochrane
had written defiantly: 'I still hold out ... Explosion-bags are set in the
lower embrasures, and all the garrison is under arms.' He was bluffing,
and was eventually taken, as he sat at breakfast, and forced to settle. It
was unlikely that he would again be given command of a ship in the
British navy. But he had been approached by Don José Alvarez, Chile's
ambassador to London, with an intriguing offer – to take command of
the naval force which was to ferry San Martín's expedition from Chile
to Peru.

36

Scottish Liberator

San Martín's projected expedition appealed to Cochrane's quixotic sense of adventure; furthermore, he was promised the rich rewards he had coveted all his life (he was still in conflict with Gambier over his fair share of the prize money for the Battle of the Basque Roads). In August 1818 Cochrane and Kitty reached Boulogne. He had planned to take one of the new steamships, the *Rising Star*, to spread terror among the Spanish, but the ship was not yet ready so they embarked instead aboard a sailing ship, the *Rose*. Cochrane had meanwhile conceived a plan, fantastic even by his exacting standards, which he was concealing from the Chileans who had hired him. His intention was to land at St Helena, where Napoleon was in exile. 'Determined at all hazards to outwit the English Government, whose ministers were full of suspicion against him, believing that he had a plot in view for the rescue of the Royal Exile', he was 'making for St Helena, begging for an interview, and ascertaining His Majesty's wishes as regarded placing him on the throne of South America'. It is not known whether Napoleon had any knowledge of this remarkable plan. Cochrane's aim was to become chief lieutenant of a vast new empire under the man he had once fought against so valiantly, but greatly admired – a possibility Napoleon himself had discussed with his commanders before Waterloo.

The Chileans raised no objection to Cochrane's plan to stop at St Helena, but before he could do so news reached his party that royalist forces had regrouped at Valdivia, south of Santiago. Matters were clearly urgent, and he hurried southwards around Cape Horn, arriving at Valparaíso in Chile at the end of November.

Valparaíso proved a surprisingly congenial landfall for him and for Kitty and his sons, four-year-old Thomas and eight-month-old William. The Spanish threat had receded and he was welcomed by Bernardo

O'Higgins and his Argentinian ally San Martín – to whom Cochrane took an instant dislike. Several English vessels were stationed there – the *Andromache* and the *Blossom* had set up rival cricket teams; there were many English volunteers in the Chilean forces; and Kitty Cochrane soon became one of the belles of Valparaíso society, presiding over dinners and receptions at which young British officers were overwhelmed by the beauty of Chilean girls, their hair wreathed in jasmine buds 'which in the course of an hour will open and present the appearance of a bushy powdered wig'. Dressed as a Scottish clan chief, Cochrane gave a St Andrew's Day banquet. In his memoirs William Miller, a young major of marines who became as much an admirer of Cochrane as Marryat, recalled that 'Extraordinary good cheer was followed by toasts drunk with uncommon enthusiasm in extraordinary good wine. No one escaped its enlivening influence. St Andrew was voted the patron saint of champagne, and many curious adventures of that night have furnished the subject of some still remembered anecdotes.' Cochrane was invited by O'Higgins to a lavish banquet in the government palace in Santiago, a round of picnics, and a performance of *Othello*.

This cheerful atmosphere was disrupted only by the grumbles of Blanco Encalada, the young Chilean admiral who was forced to make way for Cochrane, by Cochrane's own indignation at being accorded subordinate status to General San Martín, and by the sniping of two British mercenary sailors, Captain Guise and Captain Spry, who detested Cochrane's flamboyance. In addition, San Martín's banefully pervasive Lautaro Lodge was suspicious of Cochrane's commitment to the Latin American cause, and appointed one of their number, Alvarez Jonte, as his secretary, to keep an eye on him.

After nine years' absence from naval command, Cochrane was in a state of high excitement: for the first time in his life he had a significant squadron under his command. He found that O'Higgins's rudimentary navy had already fought a major battle. Valparaíso had been blockaded by the royalist flagship *Esmeralda* and the brigantine *Pezuela*. Under a former Royal Navy officer, William O'Brien, and the dashing but inexperienced young Blanco Encalada, the Chilean's *Lautaro*, 800 tonnes and 34 guns (the former East Indiaman *Wyndham*), had attacked and briefly boarded the much bigger *Esmeralda*. O'Brien was killed as *Esmeralda's* crew beat off the boarders, but both Spanish ships then ended the blockade by fleeing to Talcahuano. Now the Chilean navy had seven ships, largely officered by Englishmen and manned by Chilean,

English and American sailors, to pit against fourteen Spanish ships and twenty-eight gunboats.

Cochrane at once set about introducing into the fleet his own standards of discipline and organisation, and new equipment, a process which took him a year. His first project was to sail northwards up the coast, into the heart of enemy territory – to Lima's port of Callao, strongly fortified – with his four biggest ships, *O'Higgins*, *San Martín*, *Lautaro* and *Chacabuco*.

As Kitty waved her farewells on 16 January 1819, to her horror she saw Thomas being carried down the beach by the last crewmen: he was aboard the rowing-boat before she could reach him. Cochrane could not delay his departure, so took his son with him: the sailors aboard *O'Higgins* rigged him out as a miniature midshipman. Then there was a mutiny aboard the *Lautaro*, and a group of seamen on the *Chacabuco* attempted to turn pirate, but Cochrane cowed them all without difficulty.

As Cochrane approached Callao he captured a Spanish gunboat with ease, then found himself sailing into thick fog. His flagship *O'Higgins*, with the *Lautaro*, drifted in and became becalmed. The *Lautaro* had drifted away again by the time the fog eventually lifted and, alone and unable to escape, *O'Higgins* found herself at the mercy of the 110-gun shore battery and the 350 guns of the entire Spanish fleet, just a few hundred yards off. A cannonade opened up and, to his horror, Cochrane found that Tom had got out of the cabin he had been locked in, by climbing through the window. He was splattered with the brains of a man killed near him, but was otherwise unhurt. As the wind picked up, Cochrane retreated to the island of San Lorenzo off the coast; he freed a handful of emaciated Chilean prisoners he found there, then proceeded to blockade Callao. According to a contemporary Spanish account, 'A laboratory was formed upon San Lorenzo, under the superintendence of Major Miller [for the construction of another of Cochrane's explosion vessels]. On the 19th of March, an accidental explosion took place, which scorched the major and ten men in a dreadful manner. The former lost the nails from both hands, and the injury was so severe that his face was swelled to twice its natural dimensions . . . He was blind and delirious for some days, and was confined to his cabin for six weeks.' The explosion vessel was launched against the Spanish fleet but sunk by gunfire, and Cochrane had no materials to build another.

In reply to a suggestion from Cochrane for a general exchange of prisoners, the Spanish Viceroy in Lima criticised him for having joined the rebels; Cochrane replied that 'A British nobleman is a free man, and therefore has a right to adopt any country which is endeavouring to re-establish the rights of aggrieved humanity.'

Cochrane left Blanco Encalada to blockade Callao and contented himself with six months' cruising along the coast, raiding Spanish shipping and supply depots ashore. He captured 70,000 dollars at Pativilca, north of Callao, and almost as much again on taking the *Gazelle*. He became known as El Diablo to the Spanish, and most of them fled at his approach. It was easy pickings: but the Spanish fleet remained largely untouched. Encalada, meanwhile, claiming to be short of supplies, returned unexpectedly to Valparaíso. O'Higgins, incensed, had him court-martialled. Three weeks later, at the end of June 1819, Cochrane himself returned, having arrested his secretary Jonge, the Lautaro Lodge's spy, for prying into his personal papers.

Here Cochrane heard of the rumoured Spanish invasion force of 20,000 men, said to be destined first for the Plate region, then for Chile. San Martín argued that the Chilean fleet should sail round Cape Horn to intercept the Spanish. Cochrane refused, partly because his men were ill-equipped to face the rigours of such a voyage, partly because it would leave Chile at the mercy of the Spanish Pacific squadron. O'Higgins agreed. The debate was anyway resolved when it emerged that the Spanish invasion force would not materialise. Cochrane resolved to sail back to Callao. Despite the insistence of José Zenteño, the Chilean navy minister, that he pledge not to take the precious Chilean fleet within range of the shore guns, 'Cochrane', San Martín observed, 'assures me that on the twenty-fourth of [September] shortly after eight in the evening, the shipping in Callao will all be ablaze and that by the 15th October I shall have received his despatch. I am sure that Cochrane will be as good as his word.'

This seemingly impossible feat was to be achieved by the use of Congreve's rockets, fired from rafts; a supply had been assembled locally but, according to a British observer,

> Not more than one rocket in six went off properly. Some burst from the
> badness of the cylinders; some took a wrong direction, in consequence of
> the sticks being made of knotty wood; and most of them fell short. The
> [mortar] shells sunk a gun-boat, and did some execution in the forts and
> amongst the shipping; but the lashings of the mortar-bed gave way, and

it was with difficulty that the logs of which the raft was composed were kept together. A great deal of time was lost in repairing the defective state of the fastenings. Daylight began to appear, and the rockets having completely failed, the rafts were ordered to retire, and were towed off ...

Spanish prisoners ... as was found on examination, had embraced every opportunity of inserting handfuls of sand, sawdust, and even manure, at intervals in the tubes, thus impeding the process of combustion, whilst in the majority of instances they had so thoroughly mixed the neutralizing matter with the ingredients supplied, that the charge would not ignite at all, the result being complete failure in the object of the expedition ...

Cochrane tried to goad the Spanish fleet out to do battle, but to no avail. Forbidden to enter Callao, he decided to seek another target; his thoughts turned to the port of Valdivia in southern Chile, still in Spanish hands. Known as Chile's Gibraltar for its impregnability, the fortifications had been constructed, ironically enough, by O'Higgins's father. The harbour at Valdivia consisted of a finger of sea ending in a single narrow 1,200-yard channel leading to the river Valdes. The anchorage, almost landlocked, was covered on one side by no fewer than four forts, and by one significant fort and four smaller ones on the other side. In the middle of the channel was the fortified island of Manzanera. It would be suicide for any ship to attack under all these guns.

Arriving off the coast, Cochrane made a reconnaissance. Hearing that three Spanish ships were expected in Valdivia, and knowing one to have been delayed, another sunk off Cape Horn, and a third in hiding, he hoisted a Spanish flag, coolly dropped anchor off the port, and requested a pilot. As soon as the pilot's party arrived they were seized, and the pilot was compelled to take Cochrane into the entrance of the channel, where he was able to ascertain the positions and strengths of the forts before sailing out again, to the astonishment of the Spanish on shore. From the pilot Cochrane also learned that another ship was approaching the estuary; this he captured, together with the 20,000 dollars aboard.

Cochrane then sailed north to Concepción, where General Freire, a protégé of O'Higgins, was governor, borrowed 250 soldiers from him, and returned to Valdivia at the end of January 1820. Off Valdivia, on the night of 29 January while Cochrane slept and only a midshipman was left in charge, *O'Higgins* ran onto a reef. The damage was serious, the water level rose in the hold, and the ship's pumps packed up. She appeared to be in danger of foundering. Since his Chilean crew were ignorant of the workings of the pumps, Cochrane himself repaired them. He then put out an anchor and his men worked the ship off the reef. She was severely crippled, but out of danger. Cochrane made a decision: 'Cool calculation would make it appear that the attempt to take Valdivia is madness. This is one reason why the Spaniards will hardly believe us in earnest, even when we commence. And you will see that a bold onset, and a little perseverance afterwards, will give a complete triumph.'

Cochrane determined to attack not from the sea but from the land, immobilising the forts that covered the entrance. Transferring his men from the crippled flagship, which he feared would be recognised in Valdivia, to two small companion ships, the brig *Intrepido* and the schooner *Montezuma*, he determined to land on a surf-strewn beach just outside the entrance to the harbour, the Aguada del Ingles, behind Fort Ingles. But to reach it his ships would have to come within range of Fort Ingles itself. Once again he made use of Spanish flags to approach close enough for a Spanish-born officer to inform the commander of the fort that they were escorts for a Spanish convoy which had been detached from the main fleet, but had lost their boats and so could not land. The boats were in fact concealed on the seaward side of the ships, but one drifted free, and the lie was detected.

The alarm was given, and Fort Ingles opened fire at point-blank range. Cochrane immediately sent in Miller, in command of 44 marines. The boats' oars snagged in seaweed, and they were peppered with musket-shot from a detachment of 75 Spaniards on the beach, which Miller's ordered bayonet charge soon dispersed; the 250 Chilean troops behind this advance guard were landed safely and dug themselves in.

When darkness fell, Cochrane divided his men into two groups, one to go in front and one creeping around the back of the fort. Those in front were to attack, creating the maximum disturbance to concentrate the garrison's attention, while the second party, under Ensign Vidal, silently climbed the ramparts behind the Spanish troops. This party then launched into action to the furious cries of the Araucanian Indians of southern Chile. The garrison fled, and in so doing panicked the three hundred troops sent to reinforce the fort when news of the Chilean landing reached the other Spanish positions. With frenzied bayonet charges the Chileans turned a retreat into a rout, pursuing the Spanish to Fort Carlos, where the defenders were unable to close the gates before their Chilean assailants broke in. The disorderly retreat, now swollen by the occupants of Fort Carlos, continued to Fort Amargos, and once again the Chileans broke into the garrison hard on the Spaniards' heels. The ever-growing horde fled onwards to Corral Castle, where they at last succeeded in keeping out the Chileans. The castle was much better defended than the other forts, capable of withstanding a prolonged siege.

Exhausted but elated, Cochrane surveyed his night's work: he had succeeded in taking three of the four forts commanding the western approaches to the channel. But the Spanish fleet was still protected by Corral Castle and Fort Niebla on the eastern shore and Manzanera Island in the middle, which could catch in their crossfire any ship attempting to run the passage. He had the satisfaction, however, of having captured part of the Spanish artillery in Fort Chorocomayo, overlooking Corral Castle: at daylight, he could bombard the castle.

The Spanish had lost a hundred killed and a hundred prisoners taken, and there were only about three hundred left, facing about the same number of Chileans. Colonel Hayas, commander of Corral Castle, considered his position to be hopeless and was sinking into an alcoholic stupor; before daylight he ordered half his men into the boats below the castle, to cross the harbour, and himself surrendered with the rest to Miller. Cochrane had secured the whole western bank of the 'impregnable' harbour at Valdivia through the simple expedient of attacking from the land rather than the sea. The following morning his two small ships, *Intrepido* and *Montezuma*, sailed into the channel under the fire of the remaining forts, and anchored off Corral Castle to ferry Chilean troops across for an attack on the other side of the harbour. A moment later, on Cochrane's orders, *O'Higgins* appeared. The Spanish assumed she was bringing another wave of troops, and their morale finally collapsed. Fort Niebla and the other eastern defences were abandoned as the Spanish troops evacuated upriver to Valdivia. In fact *O'Higgins* had no troops aboard, only a skeleton crew – not even enough to man the guns – and was steadily sinking; she only just made it to the beach. But Cochrane's calculation that she would complete the demoralisation of the Spanish proved accurate.

Two days later Cochrane sent *Intrepido* and *Montezuma* upriver towards Valdivia. *Intrepido* ran around, but in any case he found the Spanish garrison and the army fled, and the local notables ready to sue for peace. Cochrane had captured Ambrosio O'Higgins's 'Gibraltar', plus 10,000 cannon balls, 170,000 cartridges, 128 pieces of artillery, 50 tons of gunpowder and a ship – at a cost of seven dead.

Three weeks later, Cochrane returned to Valparaíso in triumph. But his determination to mend his fortunes, combined with the way he had in past campaigns been cheated (he considered) of his due prize money, prompted him to refuse to hand over the booty he had seized at Valdivia. Chilean gratitude turned to anger, and prosecution was considered. Cochrane at once threatened to resign, taking twenty-three of his officers with him, and had his chief rival, Captain Guise, arrested for insubordination. The Chilean navy minister Zenteño begged him to stay, as did O'Higgins and San Martín. Cochrane, mollified, reinstated Guise; he also felt emboldened to pursue his private designs: he despatched an officer on the long journey around Cape Horn to St Helena. But he arrived to find Napoleon's health so badly deteriorated that he was in no condition to leave the island. Cochrane's most lunatic dream was over.

37

The Taking of the Esmeralda

'Four small ships once gave Spain the dominion of America; these will wrest if from her.' The ships to which O'Higgins was referring in this declaration, the ships that were to liberate Peru, numbered twenty-four in all: eight warships – a man-of-war, three frigates, three brigantines and one schooner – and sixteen troop transports. On 21 August 1820 Cochrane led the way out of Valparaíso in *O'Higgins*, San Martín brought up the rear in the ship named after him. They were headed for Pisco, about 150 miles south of Lima.

San Martín's plan was two-pronged: first, to liberate slaves in the area and recruit them into his army; second, to send an expeditionary force into the interior to stir up insurrection and then combine with another detachment he proposed to land north of Lima, thus encircling the capital. Blockaded from the sea as well, it would be starved into capitulating without a fight.

The fleet reached Pisco after two weeks' sailing, and landed 3,000 troops under the command of Las Heras. Alas for the first part of San Martín's plan: he found most of the slaves had been moved inland by their owners, and managed to liberate only about six hundred. General Arenales was despatched to lead the force into the interior.

Belligerent as ever, Cochrane fumed with impatience at these cautious tactics, and was insistent that an attack be made immediately on Lima. Six weeks after landing at Pisco San Martín re-embarked his army and sailed past Lima to land at Ancón. Cochrane had now decided that whatever San Martín's plans were – and he regarded them as cowardly and dilatory – he would launch his own attack. On 3 November he sailed *O'Higgins* down to Callao on a reconnaissance mission. Two of the biggest Spanish warships, *Prueba* and *Venganza*, were absent; but the 44-gun frigate *Esmeralda*, flagship of the Spanish fleet, was at anchor among

27 gunboats and several blockships. The shore battery had three hundred guns, and the harbour was protected by an anchored boom.

Commanding just 160 seamen and 80 marines, Cochrane now aimed to cut out the *Esmeralda* from the rest of the fleet. He equipped each of his men with a pistol and a cutlass, and had them wear blue bands on their left arms for identification. At 10 p.m. on 5 November 1820 the little force set out from *O'Higgins*, anchored just out of sight of the harbour, rowing in fourteen small boats through a gap in the boom which Cochrane had noticed on his reconnaissance. Just past the boom, the silent armada was challenged by a guard-boat. Cochrane, coming up alongside, offered to surrender – but the Spanish commander suddenly realised he was confronted by a boatload of armed men and surrounded by others, so he yielded quietly.

They now rowed past the bulk of a United States warship, the *Macedonian*. As one of Cochrane's officers noted, 'many of her officers hung over the bulwarks, cheered us in whispers, wishing us success, and wishing also that they themselves could join us.' The sentries aboard a British ship, *Hyperion*, then challenged Cochrane's boats so loudly that he feared the Spanish would be alerted. Yet all remained silent elsewhere. Soon Cochrane's boats were alongside the *Esmeralda*, and he and his men were climbing the main chains. The hyperbole of the Colombian writer Simón Camacho seems justified:

> It was like a march of ghosts through the night shadows ... Had it not been for the terrible and bloody image presented it would have had a poetic beauty.
>
> The Spanish ... awoke startled and with the innate bravery of their race, which had made them so successful in the New World, hurried to defend their vessel. The patriots' daring, which for a moment paralysed the royalists, was comparable to the bravery of those splendid leaders born to fight and knowing no fear. The deck was too narrow for so many heroes. The night needed the midday sun to light up such prowess. Yet for those brave ones who fell shouting 'Long Live Spain', and hurling abuse at the 'pirates', it was in vain. The main tops were full of the Admiral's sailors who, from their height, were able to shoot straight at their victims while their swords destroyed the brave Spaniards.

Cochrane himself was one of the first to reach the deck. But the sentries had heard the rattle of the chains. A blow from a musket butt sent him crashing back into his boat and he injured his back severely on a thole-pin, which penetrated near his spine. In agony, he climbed up again to shoot the sentry. Another sentry fired at him, and was himself shot. Cochrane's men streamed aboard, but they had lost the element of surprise. The Spanish captain gathered his crew on the forecastle, from which they rained down a fusillade of shots on the deck. Cochrane and Captain Guise led an attack, but Cochrane was shot in the leg; forced to pull back, he sat on a gun to direct the assault. The tide turned against the Spanish and many dived into the sea. Captain Coig surrendered to Cochrane, but was injured by a stray shot shortly afterwards. With the loss of eleven dead and thirty wounded, in just seventeen minutes of intense fighting Cochrane had seized the Spanish flagship.

Now the difficult part began: getting *Esmeralda* out of the harbour. As soon as he got aboard Cochrane had ordered men up the rigging to prepare for sailing; but first he wanted to capture the brig *Maipú*, nearby, and set other ships adrift. This seemed a foolhardy desire, when about three hundred yards away the main shore batteries and gunboats were blazing blindly away in the dark. It was surely only a matter of time before the ship was hit – meanwhile the Chileans were plundering her and the English crewmen were getting drunk, having broken into the spirit room. Cochrane, noting the distinctive identification lights being shown by the nearby British and American ships as they made their way out of the harbour to get away from the fighting, ordered the same lights to be hoisted aboard *Esmeralda*, judging that the Spanish would be chary of sinking a neutral ship. He was right: the guns suddenly fell silent.

Having in the meantime been rowed back to *O'Higgins* to have his wounds attended to, Cochrane was enraged to discover that in his absence Guise had given the order for *Esmeralda* to sail at full speed out of the harbour, before every vessel there had been 'either captured or burned', as Cochrane wanted. Discretion may in this case have been the better part of valour: it was surely more important to carry off the pride of the Spanish navy and absorb her into the rebel fleet than to risk her in attempting to inflict further damage. When the Spanish guns opened up again, *Esmeralda* was safely away, along with two captured gunboats. A boat from the American ship *Macedonian*, which had cheered Cochrane in, went ashore as usual at Callao the following day for provisions, whereupon its crew were lynched for suspected collaboration. It was certainly one of the most daring raids in naval history, and the single most noteworthy feat in Cochrane's extraordinary career.

The significance of *Esmeralda's* capture, following the loss of the stronghold of Valdivia, was incalculable. Just as San Martín's crossing of the

Andes was the key to the consolidation of Argentinian and Chilean independence, and Bolívar's crossing of the northern Andes at last led to the Spanish being outflanked in the north, so Cochrane's mastery of the Pacific Coast was the turning-point in the destruction of Peru, the last great redoubt of Spanish power on the continent. Lima, surrounded by inhospitable desert, was supplied from the sea; without Cochrane's feats, the safe transport and supply of San Martín's expeditionary force would have been impossible. As Francisco Encina, Chile's greatest historian, said:

> This attack had not the slightest possibility of success in rational terms, but what filled the most courageous sailor with dread was a stimulant to Cochrane. We often said that the impossible attracted him with a certain fascination ... His career would certainly have lasted only a short time without the trait that constituted the essence of his genius: his incredible resourcefulness in the face of the unexpected and the catastrophic. Most of his attacks were doomed to failure before they began, but in the uproar of the fight, while others become blinded or confused, his eagle eye discovers the enemy's weakness or vacillation.

Cochrane was generous with his praise for the crew of the *O'Higgins*: 'I had never seen a greater display of bravery than that of my comrades. The best crew of a British boat would not have improved the perfect way in which orders were carried out.'

Cochrane was in undisputed control of the coast, and the remainder of the Spanish fleet was blockaded in Callao: food became increasingly scarce in Lima. About 650 of the crack Numancia Battalion deserted to the Chileans in the aftermath of *Esmeralda*'s capture, and news also came through that the 1,500-strong garrison at the port of Guayaquil further up the coast had revolted against the Spanish. Meanwhile Arenales, in the mountains, won the battle of Cerro de Pasco, in which the Spanish lost 58 dead and 300 taken prisoner. Cochrane again urged San Martín to go in for the kill, but he refused, well satisfied with his policy of blockade and slow strangulation. Cochrane suspected a sinister motive: 'It now became evident to me that the army had been kept inert for the purpose of preserving it entire to further the ambitious views of the General, and that, with the whole force now at Lima, the inhabitants were completely at the mercy of their pretended liberator, but in reality their conqueror.'

Cochrane's brilliance as a captain, his skilful and shameless use of deception and deployment of calculated boldness to wrong-foot his enemies were one thing; but when called on to exercise strategic command of several ships, or to employ political skills, he was not at his best. He was a loner, and cussedly awkward. He soon became involved in a row with his own crew, who objected to the renaming of *Esmeralda* – *Valdivia* may have been one of Cochrane's triumphs, but it also recalled the hated Pedro de Valdivia, conquistador of Chile. Instead of bowing to the justifiable reluctance of his men, Cochrane court-martialled the rebellious officers. Captain Guise thereupon resigned his own command in sympathy, followed by Captain Spry, captain of the *Galvarino*, whom Cochrane later had court-martialled in retaliation. The two captains went to join San Martín's staff on shore. Cochrane had by now developed an obsessive hatred of the 'cowardly' commander-in-chief.

In November 1820 San Martín, who considered his work around the capital completed, re-embarked and sailed his army north of Lima to stir up the people in the region of Huaylas. The fleet anchored at Huacho, where fever began to break out among the troops and the sailors to complain about the back pay owing to them. Bad news had also come from Upper Peru, where Guemes, the Argentine guerrilla leader, had been defeated. Yet San Martín's patient campaign of subversion among the black, Indian and mestizo population around Lima was beginning to bear fruit. With Lima cut off by Arenales's flanking movement and Callao blockaded by the fleet, food ran short, and the Spanish soldiers in the city fostered resentment by helping themselves to most of the stores. Propaganda generated by San Martín's printing press was every-where. The council of Lima complained to the authorities: 'If this town continues like this, what will be our fate within a short time? Peace is the general vote of the people. The public is gathering perfidiously under the banner of San Martín. The public has forcefully increased our silence and already has begun to fear evils worse than the war itself.' In February 1821 the Viceroy, the Marqués de la Pezuela, was overthrown by a liberal commander, General José de La Serna; the French general de Canterac took control of the army.

The war of attrition and of nerves he had instigated was far from easy for San Martín; he wrote to O'Higgins:

> I am going mad. Believe me truly when I say that at times I find myself desperate and I have been on the point of attacking the enemy and trying my luck in a decisive action in order to leave this hell as soon as I can and to rest for once; but the thought that on the success of this campaign rests the good of so many generations makes me go on suffering . . . I have

Lima half blockaded; I am proceeding to inundate it with patriot followers who are harassing it so that they have arrived to within one league of
the Peruvian capital. Each soldier, in order to eat, and badly, too, costs the
viceroy four *reales* daily. From this you can ascertain whether the city can
hold out much longer, especially with all the northern provinces in a state
of insurrection, with no entry and Callao in a rigorous blockade ... You
cannot imagine how well I could use even a thousand carbines, muskets,
old shotguns, indeed, any firearms at all which you are not using, in order
to arm the guerrilla factions.

Alvarado wrote later: 'Never had San Martín shown himself to be more
of a genius than at that time: now undermining Lima and its outskirts
with warriors; now hiding our definite weakness from the enemy; now
undertaking a campaign against the mountains, with skeletons instead
of men; now making an expedition against the coast; now, finally, negotiating and intriguing to gain sufficient time to overcome that fearful
condition. Never, on any occasion, did I find him greater.'

San Martín's worst enemy was fever: on a single day, a hundred of his
men died; altogether, some 2,500 fell ill, including himself, and many
died. But through recruitment he was still able to increase the size of his
army from 4,900 to 6,700 – almost the level of the royalist garrison of
7,000 men in Lima. In a masterful propaganda coup San Martín proposed letting food into Lima to ease the people's suffering and to feed
sick soldiers – 'for the soldiers are my enemies only on the battlefield'.
The people of the countryside were now beginning to come his way.

The arrival of Kitty Cochrane with her children on board the British
ship *Andromaque* in January 1821 provided a welcome distraction for
Cochrane from his irritation with San Martín's 'cowardly policy'. At
twenty-five Kitty was now established as a forceful figure in her own
right. She had endured the difficulties of a 'secret' marriage and the
humiliation of her husband's imprisonment; in Chile, she had been
threatened at knife-point by a man who broke into her country home
at Quilleta; he was condemned to death, but Kitty successfully urged the
commutation of the sentence to exile. She had crossed the Andes to San
Martín's Mendoza, sleeping on a dead bullock's hide at the Puente del
Inca. On the way down, a stray Spanish soldier had attacked her and
very nearly pushed her into an abyss before being driven off by Chileans
accompanying her. Now, arriving off Callao, Kitty arranged for the wife
of the deposed Viceroy, Doña Angela Pezuela, to be given safe passage
to Europe. Doña Angela met Cochrane, and pronounced him 'a polite

rational being, and not the ferocious brute she had been taught to consider me' – the admiral was amused. Miller described the effect of Lady
Cochrane, vivacious and spirited, on his troops in Huacho, some time
after her arrival:

> The sudden appearance of youth and beauty on a fiery horse, managed
> with skill and elegance, absolutely electrified the men, who had never
> before seen an English lady. *Que hermosa! Que graciosa! Que linda! Que
> guapa! Que airosa! Es un ángel del cielo!* were exclamations that escaped
> from one end of the line to the other … Her ladyship turned her spark-
> ling eyes towards the line, and bowed graciously. The troops could no
> longer confine their expressions of admiration to half-suppressed interjec-
> tions; loud *vivas* burst from officers as well as men. Lady Cochrane smiled
> her acknowledgements and cantered off the ground with the grace of a
> fairy.

On a visit to the interior, word reached Kitty that some Spanish soldiers
were plotting to seize her and her baby daughter as hostages. With the
Spaniards in hot pursuit, her party fled. At one point she had to cross a
primitive rope bridge on hands and knees, as it swayed alarmingly and
threatened to break. On yet another occasion, she was aboard the
O'Higgins when her husband attacked a Spanish ship laden with treasure, escaping from Callao. She intrepidly lit the fuse of a cannon, and
fainted when it went off.

Events elsewhere were now beginning to shape themselves to San
Martín's ends. In Spain the year before – in March 1820 – Ferdinand,
forced to bow to pressure from the army, had restored the liberal constitution of 1812, and the new moderation gradually made itself felt in the
colonies. Towards the end of May 1821 the acting Viceroy, La Serna,
signed an armistice with San Martín. The two men met, and in a warm
and friendly manner San Martín sought acknowledgement of Peru's
independence.

> I consider this one of the happiest days of my life. I have come to Peru
> from the shores of the River Plate, not to shed blood but to establish the
> freedom and the rights which the motherland herself established when
> she proclaimed the constitution of 1812, which Your Excellency and your
> generals defended. The liberals of the world are brothers everywhere …
> Let there be appointed a regency, designated by the Viceroy, which would
> rule an independent Peru, until an agreement is reached in Spain about a
> prince of the reigning house who would take the throne of the new
> nation.

This was more than the Spanish, on the verge of surrender, had any right to expect. They favoured the idea, although it was subsequently overruled from Madrid. But San Martín was now irrevocably tarnished as a monarchist, particularly among Bolívar's followers – a woundingly unfair charge against a man who had spent the last decade fighting the Spanish crown, and whose views on social and political reform were almost identical with Bolívar's. Almost certainly the motive for his proposal was that with his men decimated by disease and himself weak and tired he was afraid that his siege would not prevail. So he was seeking a compromise – the introduction of a constitutional monarchy – to make surrender more palatable to the Spanish. Later San Martín, stung by accusations that he had sold out to the monarchy – and writing in the third person, as he so often did – justified himself: 'General San Martín, who had a deep knowledge of the policies of the Madrid cabinet, was well persuaded that the cabinet would never approve this treaty; but inasmuch as its main object was that of compromising the Spanish chiefs, as in fact they were compromised if they recognised the independence, they had no other way to choose than that of joining their own destiny to the American cause.'

In June 1821 Captain Basil Hall, of the Royal Navy's fleet off the coast of South America, took San Martín a letter from his wife; he left this picture:

At first sight there was little that was striking about his appearance; but when he stood up and began to speak, his superiority was evident. He received us on deck very simply, dressed in a loose coat and a large fur cap. He was seated close to a table made from several board planks and placed over some empty barrels. He is a handsome man, tall, erect, well proportioned, with a large aquiline nose, abundant black hair, and long black whiskers which extend from one ear to the other and below his chin; his eyes are large and penetrating, as black as ebony, and his whole appearance is completely military.

He is highly courteous and simple, unaffected in his mannerisms, excessively cordial and unassuming, and possessed of a kindly nature; in short, I have never seen a person whose enchanting manner was more irresistible. In a conversation touching important topics, he disliked wasting time with details; he listened attentively and answered with clarity and brilliance of language, showing admirable resources of argumentation and a ready abundance of knowledge, the effect of which was to make those people with whom he talked feel that they were understood as they desired to be.

Hall described a mummy which San Martín kept as a trophy:

> The figure was a man seated on the ground with his knees almost touching his chin, his elbows pressed against his sides, and his hands pressed to his cheek-bones. The half-open mouth showed two rows of beautiful teeth. The body, although shrunken to an extraordinary degree, had all the appearance of being human, with skin intact everywhere except on the shoulder. The face carried an acute expression of agony. Tradition concerning this and other similar bodies has it that in the time of the conquest many Incas and their families suffered such persecution that they actually allowed themselves to be buried alive rather than submit to the fate the Spaniards had in store for them.

San Martín told Hall that his chief weapon was public opinion: 'The Spaniards, incapable of directing it, have prohibited its use; but now they are experiencing its force and importance.' He went on:

> The people are asking why I do not march on Lima immediately. I could do it and I would do it right now if it were convenient to my plans; but it is not convenient. I do not seek military glory, nor am I ambitious for the title of conqueror of Peru: I only wish to free it from oppression. What good would Lima do me if its inhabitants were hostile politically? How could I further the cause of independence if I were to take Lima by military force, or even the entire country? My views are very different. I want all people to think as I do and not to take one single step ahead of the progressive march of public opinion; since the capital is ready now to show its feelings, I shall give it the opportunity without danger.

38

The City of the Kings

At the beginning of July 1821 La Serna, the acting Viceroy, announced that his army was abandoning Lima for the fortress of Callao. This caused panic among the royalists of Lima, stoked by rumours that slaves and Indians were about to sack the city, and by the portrayal of San Martín as a monster. The city council, fearing the slaves and Indians more than the monster, begged him to enter Lima and protect it. He replied: 'I do not wish to enter as conqueror. I will not go unless the people invite me to.' But he let it be known that he would leave his army outside. On 9 July, the anniversary of Argentine independence, when he finally marched into Lima, an earthquake greeted his arrival – a sign of divine anger, said the royalists; the welcome of the Incas in their tombs, said the patriots. San Martín had won a remarkable victory – through patience, subtlety and strategic brilliance, and with little bloodshed: he had captured the citadel of Spanish power in the Americas by bombarding it with propaganda, and by starving it out. In the main plaza he was met with fawning obeisance, and it seemed that all the prettiest girls in Lima were there to pay their respects. One embraced his legs, two more his head, another fell on his chest. He succumbed, and kissed her tenderly.

Although San Martín was in Lima, the Spanish fleet in the Pacific still posed a threat, and on 14 July 1821 Cochrane instigated another remarkable raid. He ordered Commander Crosbie from his flagship *O'Higgins* to break through a gap in the boom defending Callao with eight boats: as firing erupted from the batteries in the fortress, Crosbie and his men boarded three enemy craft, *Resolución*, *San Fernando* and *Mingo*, with 34 guns between them, and cut out all three, a valuable addition to the Chilean fleet. This triumph was followed by depressing news for Cochrane personally: on 5 May 1821 Napoleon, whom he had intended to place on the 'throne' of South America, had died at St Helena.

On 18 July San Martín proclaimed Peru independent. During his delirious reception by the populace, Hall records, 'a fleeting expression of impatience or disgust of himself could be seen in his face, for lending himself to this masquerade, but if it were so, he soon recovered his customary aspect of attention and goodwill toward those who surrounded him.' San Martín had defined the limits of his ambition to Hall: 'My whole desire is that this country should be ruled by itself, and only by itself. As to the manner in which it governs itself, it does not concern me in the least. I propose only to give to the people the means of declaring themselves independent, establishing an adequate form of government. And when this is done, I shall consider my task done and I shall withdraw.'

He assumed the title Protector of Peru; much derided as cloaking his ambitions, in fact it concealed his lack of them. He went through the pain – for him – of celebrations and balls, and gave one himself, at the palace of the viceroys, with *tapadas* – the famously voluptuous dancers of Peru. He attended the bullfight, where he was embarrassed by a poem the crowd sang for him:

> Thou who art the object
> Of such solemn pomp,
> San Martín, who art the delight
> Of all America,
> Accept the grateful worship
> Which Lima, faithful and heroic,
> Joyfully tenders thee
> And earnestly offers thee.

Cochrane had entered Lima on 17 July, and he too received a hero's welcome. His men had been promised their pay when victory was achieved; his main concern now was to ensure that they got it, and that he was awarded his own share of the prize money. San Martín prevaricated, under the influence of his sinister aide Bernardo Monteagudo, who detested Cochrane, and planned that the Chilean fleet should become Peru's. Increasingly befuddled by opium and drink, San Martín acquiesced, to Cochrane's fury. On 4 August the two men had a blazing row in the presidential palace. San Martín distrusted Cochrane as a hothead, and Cochrane considered San Martín a coward, a drunken addict, and a potential despot. He was not, but he was short of money, and acutely aware that his political power depended on the troops he had borrowed from Chile. When he offered to 'buy' Chile's fleet for Peru in exchange for the arrears of pay owing, Cochrane greeted this idea with such scorn that San Martín stood huffily on his dignity, advising him to remember he was addressing the 'Protector of Peru'. Cochrane replied, 'It now becomes me, as the senior officer of Chile and consequently the representative of the nation, to request the fulfilment of all the promises made to Chile and the squadron; but first and principally the squadron.' San Martín retorted angrily: 'Chile! Chile! I will never pay a single *real* to Chile! As to the squadron, you may take it where you please, and go where you choose. A couple of schooners are quite enough for me.' Then, recovering himself, he asked Cochrane to 'Forget, my Lord, what is past.' 'I will when I can,' replied Cochrane, turning on his heel. San Martín followed, offering him command of the new Peruvian fleet – which Cochrane described as a 'dishonourable proposition'. San Martín, angered afresh, reiterated his refusal to pay the sailors.

Cochrane had his own methods. San Martín's treasure ship, the *Sacramento*, had just departed from Callao for Ancón, further up the coast. Discovering that 'my own view coincided with' that of his crews, Cochrane set off in pursuit, boarded the *Sacramento* and helped himself to a 'yacht-load' of silver and seven sacks of gold. In fact he took 285,000 dollars' worth to pay his men, and gave 40,000 dollars to the army – to his credit, he took nothing for himself. Furious, San Martín ordered Cochrane to return to Lima, but instead he set off in pursuit of the two Spanish frigates that had so far eluded him, the *Venganza* and the *Prueba*. By January 1822 he had reached Acapulco in Mexico without sighting them. He learned that they had taken refuge in Guayaquil, and before he could reach them they had surrendered to representatives of San Martín. Angry at being balked of his prey, and possibly in danger of arrest and execution, Cochrane wisely avoided Lima and sailed further south, to Valparaíso, where he was received splendidly. He issued dire warnings about San Martín's treachery, and his attempt to cheat Chile by seizing her navy; later, as San Martín made his sad way into exile, he did what he could to get him arrested. O'Higgins, meanwhile, sup-ported both sides. To Cochrane he wrote:

> I give you and the worthy officers under your orders my warmest thanks for your loyalty and heroism in the cause of Chile ... You have no reason to receive orders from Lima, either direct or indirect, since from the moment of the declaration of the independence of that country under the protectorship of San Martín, the provisional power entrusted to him over

the fleet ceased ... We must by no means declare him a pirate, as he might then turn the blockade against us or make common cause with some other country.

Cochrane saw that O'Higgins was increasingly under the influence of his corrupt and manipulative adviser, Rodriguez Aldea. Cochrane admired O'Higgins but, as he put it:

Being himself above meanness, he was led to rely on the honesty of others from the uprightness of his own motives. Though in every way disposed to believe, with Burke, that 'what is morally wrong can never be politically right', he was led to believe that a crooked policy was a necessary evil of government; and as such a policy was adverse to his own nature, he was the more easily induced to surrender the administration to others who were free from his conscientious principles.

He tried to warn O'Higgins explicitly: 'I wish to give Your Excellency one more proof of my attachment by imploring you to open your eyes to the general discontent prevailing amongst all classes regarding both the declared and the secret measures of Minister Rodriguez.'

Cochrane remained in Valparaíso, trying to extract the payment of the further prize money he felt he was owed. Then came the prospect of a new adventure: he was approached to help secure the independence of Brazil. On 18 January 1823, shortly after the arrival in Chile of the *Rising Star*, the steamship he had commissioned before leaving for South America, he set off again on the perilous journey around Cape Horn, leaving behind a brief statement: 'You know that independence is purchased at the point of the bayonet. Know also that liberty is founded on good faith, and on the laws of honour, and that those who infringe upon these, are your only enemies, amongst whom you will never find Lord Cochrane.' It was an oddly wise and moving pronouncement from a man usually considered to lack any political sense.

39

Decline of the Protector

While San Martín was at the theatre in Lima in September 1821 news arrived that the Viceroy of Peru's main army was on its way from the mountains, led by General de Canterac, to the relief of Callao. San Martín rose in his box to calm the people, then ordered barricades to be erected, and went off to take command of his own forces outside Lima. His troops numbered 7,000 compared to de Canterac's army of around 12,000, but as he watched the royalists approaching across the dust-bowl he seemed curiously optimistic. 'They are lost,' he declared. 'Callao is ours. They haven't got food for fifteen days.' He rejected his commanders' advice to attack de Canterac, because he knew he might easily lose such a fight; and besides, it was unnecessary. He had secured Lima in the first place in part as a consequence of one inescapable geographical fact: the city lies at the centre of the narrow, two-thousand-mile-long coastal strip which stretches from Guayaquil in modern Ecuador to the Atacama Desert, an area where the average annual rainfall is a mere two inches. Towns and cities along the coast could only be supplied by sea, or from the fertile plateaux thirty miles or so inland. But San Martín had blockaded the sea access, and the routes from the mountains traversed empty, hostile territory which even a small force could control.

Now de Canterac's army was in the desert, with insufficient food. He might lay siege to Lima – but Lima in San Martín's hands was again open to the sea, and the Spaniards' own precarious lines of supply lay across that wasteland, so that the besiegers were more likely to suffer shortages, and sooner, than the besieged. For San Martín it was just a matter of waiting, out of de Canterac's reach, until he and his army ran out of food. It was not a bold policy, but it was right. Cochrane, excitably Latin in temperament as compared with the calculating, phlegmatic San

Martín, had urged him to fight; to which the general's laconic reply was, 'My decisions have been taken.' De Canterac, realising his predicament, withdrew within a matter of days.

San Martín had ordered Arenales to bring his forces down from the mountains, and Las Heras was sent in pursuit of the retreating royalists to trap them in a pincer movement. Both moves were frustrated: Arenales, receiving an erroneous order, withdrew to the other side of the mountains, and his men were too exhausted to return; and Las Heras was dogged by the same problem as de Canterac, lacking sufficient food to pursue the royalists across the desert to the mountains. He thus got away.

San Martín was later vilified for what was seen as his cowardice, in failing to trap, fight and overcome the enemy. But Lima remained free; and a patriot defeat in open battle – which was likely, given the size of the Spanish army – would surely have been disastrous for the cause of independence. The Spanish stronghold of Callao, desperately short of food and expecting relief from de Canterac's army, was completely demoralised by his withdrawal. General de La Mar, in charge of the Spanish forces there, surrendered, and the wraiths in Callao's grim dungeons were liberated. San Martín had won another victory through calculation, rather than bloodshed. His reputation for humanity was besmirched, however, in the aftermath of the surrender, by the butchery of about six hundred of the Callao garrison. It is the first atrocity known under his command, and may not have been his fault; it was seized upon by his enemies as evidence of a deterioration in his character.

As self-styled Protector of Peru San Martín now settled down to vigorous political and administrative activity. He created the nucleus of a Peruvian army, the Peruvian Legion, under Miller. He placed Lima on a sound financial basis. He freed slaves, and ended the second-class status of the Peruvian Indians – the overwhelming majority of the people – 'because it is against nature and the principles of liberty.' In this he anticipated Bolívar, who was committed to these ideals, but had yet to act on them. Punishment, torture, censorship and the Inquisition were done away with. Habeas corpus, individual freedoms and the independence of the judiciary were recognised. The terrible massacre at Callao was the only shadow on the magnanimity he displayed towards his defeated foes. On the face of it, San Martín had reached the pinnacle of his career: he had brought a large army almost unscathed across some of the world's highest mountains, then sailed a thousand miles to capture the citadel of Spanish power on the continent, the very heart of one of the longest-lived, most powerful and most militaristic empires the world had seen, and done so largely by peaceful means and through the exercise of tactical cunning. He had consolidated the freedom of Argentina, delivered liberty to Chile, and now presided over Peru as its Protector.

San Martín's was the most famous name in Latin America. In the north, Bolívar had lately liberated Venezuela and New Granada from the Spanish yoke; but San Martín was the giant. Yet his protectorate immediately encountered opposition. First there was the Peruvian aristocracy, led by his nominal second-in-command, the Marqués de Torre Tagle. Their dislike of the ideals San Martín stood for was visceral, and they were in constant contact with the Spanish forces outside Lima. Another source of enmity was the Peruvian José de la Riva Agüero, who sorely resented the fact that the Peruvian independence he had long advocated had been secured by an outsider. There was also a plot against San Martín among his own army officers, on the grounds of his failure to pursue de Canterac after the fall of Lima, and they dubbed him 'King José', for his remote and haughty ways. Finally, as we have seen, San Martín fell out fatally with Admiral Cochrane over money.

The surprise of this period of his life was that San Martín took a Peruvian mistress, Rosita Campuzano, soon popularly labelled 'The Protectress'. Small and delicate, with the white complexion so admired by the Peruvian aristocracy, she took an intelligent interest in politics and was able to influence San Martín, but she was no favourite with the Peruvian intelligentsia. San Martín used to walk anonymously around the streets of Lima to learn what people thought, and soon discovered that his early popularity had been dissipated.

In fact, his position was impossible. As long as the royalist army lurked in the mountains, his enemies in the capital would conspire with them. His small Argentinian force owed its loyalty to its own country, which had disowned him, and his larger Chilean contingent was only there at the pleasure of Santiago, and might be withdrawn at any moment. He had failed to acquire the Chilean navy from Cochrane, who had also hijacked part of his treasury. Many of the Argentinian and Chilean soldiers did not recognise his title of Protector of Peru – he was not a Peruvian, and had merely appointed himself to the post. Increasingly he was seen as a conqueror rather than a liberator. With his power-base melting away, his only hope seemed to lie in uniting with his fellow liberator Simón Bolívar, now approaching from the north, in a concerted offensive against the Spanish forces in the mountains.

The details of San Martín's meeting with Bolívar at Guayaquil in July 1822 have been recounted in Chapter 14. When San Martín returned from Guayaquil, almost exactly a year after he had first occupied Lima, it was to preside over the country's first representative Congress, at which he astonished his detractors – those who had alleged that he wanted to establish himself as King of Peru – by resigning: 'When I return the insignia of the Supreme Ruler of Peru, I only carry out my duty and the dictates of my heart … Today, on resigning, I pray to the Supreme Being for the wisdom, the enlightenment, and the prudence which are needed for the happiness of the governed. From this moment the Sovereign Congress is installed and the people reassume the power in all its manifestations.'

The news was greeted with disbelief, and the assumption that he was merely staging a tactical withdrawal. Congress tried to dissuade him, then to bestow upon him the position of colonel-in-chief of Peru's armed forces, an annual pension of 12,000 pesos, and honours such as the title Father of Peruvian Liberty. San Martín declined them all, and returned to his villa outside Lima, La Magdalena. In a letter to Congress he clarified his position:

> I was present at the declaration [of independence] of the states of Chile and Peru; I have in my possession the standard which Pizarro brought with him to enslave the Empire of the Incas; therewith I am more than repaid for ten years of revolution and war. My promises to the peoples in whose lands I have conducted warfare have been fulfilled: to obtain their independence and to leave the election of their governments to their own will. The presence of a fortunate soldier, be he as selfless as may be, is to be feared by states which are newly formed.
>
> Besides, I am bored with hearing that I am trying to enthrone myself. I shall always be ready to make the last sacrifice for the freedom of the country, but only as a private individual, and nothing else. So far as my public conduct is concerned, my compatriots (as generally happens) will be of divided opinions; their sons will reach a true verdict.

To his chief aide, Colonel Guido, he gave the real reason for his withdrawal:

> There is a greater difficulty, a difficulty which I could meet only at the cost of the fate of the country and my own reputation: Bolívar and myself cannot be in Peru at the same time. I have penetrated his thoughts; I have

understood his annoyance at the glory that could be mine for ending the war. He would use any means to enter Peru and perhaps I could not avoid a conflict, giving a scandal to the world, and the only ones who would profit by it would be the enemy. That, never! Let Bolívar come into Peru, and if he makes safe what we have gained, I will be happy because America will win in any event. It will not be San Martín who will give a day of joy to the Spaniards.

On the night of 20 September 1822, wearing black civilian dress, San Martín boarded the brigantine *Belgrano* in the port of Callao.

The voyage down the Pacific coast took a month. He was welcomed in Valparaíso by General Prieto, O'Higgins's aide. But already his enemies were circling like birds of prey around a dead body: it was said in Chile that he had left Peru because he had been frustrated in his ambition to become emperor; or because he was too cowardly to take on the Spanish in the mountains; or because his officers had rebelled; or with the bulk of the Peruvian treasury.

Cochrane had by this time returned to Chile, and became a close friend of Maria Graham, the lively naval widow who arrived at Valparaíso in the spring of 1822. Biased as she was in the admiral's favour, her description of San Martín on his return is not unsympathetic: she met 'a very tall, fine-looking man, dressed in plain black clothes. [His] eyes possess a peculiarity which I have only once before seen ... [they] are black and handsome, but restless; they look fixedly only an instant, but in that instant they tell you everything ... He was extremely courteous; his words, as much as his manners, seemed to me full of gracefulness, and now I believe what I have so many times heard about him: that few can best him at a dance.' San Martín stayed two months in Chile, ill for much of the time, before for the sixth and last time crossing the Andes, by mule. In January 1823 he reached his modest farm outside Mendoza, to which years before he had written wistfully of retiring. Letters reached him there from Peru, begging him to return. Riva Agüero, who had done so much to undermine his rule and helped bring about the fall of Monteagudo, insisted that it was his duty to do so – in view of Riva Agüero's treachery, this message left San Martín trembling with anger.

More urgently, his beloved wife had fallen seriously ill. He had sent her from Mendoza to Buenos Aires in 1819 because 'the opinion of the doctors is that if she stays in Mendoza, her life will be very short'. He longed to travel to Buenos Aires to see her – to say goodbye, she told him – but the journey was too dangerous: he was still a controversial figure in Argentina, if not actually an outlaw, having effectively hijacked its army for his own purposes. He was warned that 'there were guerrillas on the road to seize me like a villain'. She died, aged only twenty-six, on 12 August 1823.

In October the Governor of Santa Fé in Argentina, unaware of how broken he was, wrote to San Martín urging that he was the man to restore order in the country. The following month he made the journey across the barren pampas of central Argentina, and was not attacked or arrested. He stayed a few months in Buenos Aires, erected a headstone to his young wife – 'Here lies Remedios, adored wife and friend of General San Martín' – and quarrelled with his widowed mother-in-law, who in his estimation had been pampering his daughter Mercedes since his wife's death.

With the excuse that he wanted to give the girl a good education in Europe, he left with her for France, but the authorities considered him an enemy of Spain and he was prevented from landing; he went instead to England, where he stayed a few months, and finally settled in Belgium, which he found 'cheap and free'. Inflation in Argentina had reduced the value of his assets there, and his income from Peru was only intermittent: he had barely enough to live on. He doted on his daughter. In his systematic way he drew up eleven rules for her, and they are revealing of the man:

1. Humanise her character, making it sensitive, even towards harmless insects. Sterne said to a fly, opening the window for it: 'Go, poor animal: the world is large enough for both of us.'
2. Instil in her a love of truth and hatred of lies.
3. Inspire in her confidence and friendliness, but always with respect.
4. Encourage in her charity towards the poor.
5. Respect for other people's property.
6. Get her used to keeping secrets.
7. Inspire in her a feeling of respect towards all religions.
8. Gentleness with servants, the poor and the old.
9. Let her talk little and say only what is necessary.
10. Get her used to being quiet and serious at table.
11. Teach her to love cleanliness and to have contempt for luxury.

For several years he sheltered his younger brother, Justo Rufino, a Spanish colonel fallen on hard times (three of his other brothers were now dead; a fifth lived until 1851). But he was often lonely and unhappy, and often there is a despondent note in his letters to friends:

> Since I last wrote you, I have only experienced ills and misfortunes: the carriage in which I was going to visit an acquaintance in the country having overturned, my right arm was dislocated, and on top of that I developed an attack of erysipelas from which I have not yet entirely recovered. My brother Justo unwisely guaranteed a loan for the Marquis of Vignola in Paris, in the amount of 68,000 francs, to complete his bail and release him. My sister recently lost her husband, whose property was confiscated by the ruthless Spanish Government because he emigrated, being a Constitutionalist, and finds herself now in the uttermost poverty. In short, I assure you that were it not for the consolation I derive from Mercedita's company, my life would be unbearable.

And he complained of the cold:

> What can I tell you about the horrible winter we are having? In human memory there hasn't been another like it. For three months I haven't stirred from my house, thanks to my wound, and in such circumstances I have come to appreciate the worth of my daughter's tender consolation. She is enjoying the best of health, and the wonderful personality she displays gives me reason to hope that she will become a loyal wife and loving mother.

He lived a very simple life with his brother and his daughter. Still old comrades wrote, urging him to return and restore order to Argentina, to Peru. His former aide Colonel Guido tempted him: 'I see the war with Brazil as a new theatre opening to the glories of General San Martín.' At first he resisted; but with the fall of his enemy Rivadavia, he felt the tug of destiny again. He was still only fifty. At the end of 1828, accompanied by a servant, he embarked from Falmouth, using the name José Matorras (his mother's maiden name), to aid his homeland in her war with Brazil over the lands north of the Plate estuary, the Banda Oriental. The voyage took 75 days, and the ship nearly foundered, just at the end, in an appalling storm in the Plate.

San Martín reached Buenos Aires on 6 February 1829, to the news that the Banda Oriental had recently become an independent country, Uruguay, under British protection, although its leader, the gaucho warrior Artigas, had been overthrown. It was too late for him to lead his country against the Brazilians, as he had hoped. Nevertheless, when his ship anchored he was bombarded with pleas from old friends that he should rescue Argentina from the endemic chaos and civil war in which she was now languishing. But the government did not invite him ashore, or give him a passport. After a week spent kicking his heels on board, he announced his intention of departing. Two former subordinates went to see him – Alvarez Condarca, the engineer who had built mills to make gunpowder for his invasion across the Andes; and Colonel Olazabal, who described him thus: 'San Martín was in slippers and was dressed in a frock coat of cheap cloth which reached his ankles. He had become greyer and fatter, but he still retained a magnetic sparkle in his eyes and that martial posture from the days when he led his legions to victory.' The government denied it was preventing him from landing. But in view of his frosty official reception, San Martín's famous caution, or realism, prevailed.

On 13 February, boarding another ship, he departed for Montevideo in Uruguay, where he lingered in considerable luxury for the best part of two months, awaiting a summons from his partisans across the estuary. When it came, it was from the brutal young leader who had temporarily seized power, Juan Lavalle. San Martín was offered command of the army, but disdained to be used to lend legitimacy to an usurper, or to accept a command in a civil war in which thousands of Argentinians would be killed. On 23 April he left for Europe, having refused the last role he was ever to be offered in Latin America:

What is needed is a saviour who will combine the prestige of victory with respect for all the provinces, and who, with above all a strong arm, will rescue the nation from the evils which menace it. There is a consensus that presents San Martín as a candidate for this, and I base this observation on innumerable letters and conversations I have had with respect to this particular matter. I also find myself in accord somewhat, in view of the circumstances of the day.

Very well. Granted that it is absolutely necessary that one of the contending factions disappear from the scene, since the presence of both is incompatible with the public peace, would it be possible for me to make myself the one chosen to be an assassin of my countrymen and, like another Sulla, burden my country with proscriptions?

No, never! I would a thousand times rather perish in the turmoil that threatens her than be the instrument of such horror. It is a foregone conclusion that I would never be allowed to exercise the clemency which the situation would demand; judging from the sanguinary vows of the factions, at the moment when one of them becomes victorious I would be obliged to be the agent of unbridled passions which know no other principle but vengeance.

The present national situation is such that the man who becomes its
leader has no alternative to a complete dependence on one single faction,
save the complete renunciation of authority. This last is what I choose ...

If, once again, his decision was less than assertive, it was almost certainly the right one. But it meant that the whole journey had been an
anticlimax, a pathetic waste of time. And he continued to suffer misfortune on the roads: once back in Brussels he wrote mournfully to
O'Higgins: 'As the old maxim has it, "When it rains, it pours". On my
trip back from America, between Falmouth and London, my coach
overturned and broken glass from one of the windows cut my left arm
deeply. But not wanting to be dragged into the public eye by the papers,
I carefully remained incognito.'

In 1831, the year his great rival Bolívar died so wretchedly near Santa
Marta, San Martín moved to a three-bedroomed house on the outskirts
of Paris. There he ran into an old friend, Alejandro Aguado, who had
served with him in the Murcia Regiment and had since become
immensely wealthy. Aguado bought a two-storey house with a large
garden, the Grand Bourg, as a retirement home for San Martín – a
godsend to the exile, who like his daughter was recovering from a bout
of cholera.

It was at this time that San Martín was visited by the son of a prominent Argentinian, General Balcarce. Mariano Balcarce fell in love with
Mercedes; they were married in 1832, and left for Buenos Aires. San
Martín was delighted, as he was with his new life; Mariano's brother left
this description, some years after Mercedes's marriage, of the tenor of his
days: 'The general enjoys to the utmost this solitary and peaceful life he
so desires. One day I find him serving as armourer, cleaning his pistols
and shotguns. Another day he is a carpenter, and so he spends every
minute in some occupation that distracts him from other thoughts and
gives him good health ... Mercedes spends her days battling with her
little ones, more and more mischievous all the time.' Aguado died on a
visit to Spain in 1843, but San Martín was nominated his executor and
guardian to his children, and Aguado had arranged that he should continue to enjoy the use of the Paris house. After a decade of penury, San
Martín was now quite comfortably circumstanced. He made a rare trip
abroad, to Rome and Naples, which helped to stimulate a new passion
for painting. Seeing him at about this time, when he was in his mid
sixties, a visitor 'was surprised to find him looking younger and more

agile than any of the war-for-independence generals' he had known. It was also during this period that San Martín offered his services to the first and also one of the nastiest of Argentina's great dictators, Juan Manuel de Rosas, to fight English and French aggression; the offer was politely declined.

In these years San Martín reflected upon his fellow liberator Bolívar, 'a man of extreme fickleness of principle and full of childish vanity' (Bolívar had been more generous: '[San Martín] laid the foundation stones of liberty and independence, although he has been ill-rewarded. He went away and left the work unfinished.'):

> General Bolívar seemed to have excessive pride, which would be in contradiction to his habit of not looking squarely in the face of the person with whom he was talking, unless it were someone greatly inferior to him. I was convinced of his lack of frankness during the conferences I had with him in Guayaquil, since he did not respond in a decisive manner to my propositions, but always evasively. The tone he used with his generals was extremely haughty and hardly of the kind to win affection ...
>
> His speech was at times vulgar, but this defect was not natural, only affected to give himself a more military air. Public opinion accused him of excessive ambition and a burning thirst for power, which he later proceeded to justify. They [the people] likewise attributed a great disinterestedness to him, which is just, since he has died in indigence ...
>
> As for this general's military deeds, one can say that they have earned him, justly, the fame of being considered as the most astonishing man South America has known. What characterises him best, and is in a certain sense his special property, is his perfect steadiness which fortified him in his difficulties and refused to allow him to be overcome by them, no matter how great these dangers were which his flaming spirit brought on him.

By 1845, in his late sixties, San Martín had developed cataracts, and Mercedes had to read to him. Nor was he granted a peaceful end in his beloved home of the past seventeen years. In 1848 revolution broke out in Paris, as over much of Europe. He decided to remove himself and his family to safety, and took a flat at Boulogne. But he was failing. His blindness depressed his spirits and he suffered from asthma, rheumatism, pain from old wounds on both his arms, and stomach cramps, as well as from the effects of drugs. His final message to the countries he had done so much for – 'I cherish a profound faith in the future of these nations' – was a contrast to Bolívar's death-bed pessimism. On 17 August

1850, after twenty-five years in exile, San Martín died following a violent attack of stomach cramps, and was buried in the church of Notre Dame in Boulogne. He had willed that his heart should be buried in Buenos Aires: the city that once rejected him honoured him with a magnificent equestrian statue in 1862, and in 1878 his remains were transported to the cathedral there. His beloved daughter Mercedes died in 1875, her husband ten years later. One of their daughters died young and unmarried; the other married and settled in France, where she died, childless, in her eighties. So ended the line of South America's second greatest liberator.

It would be hard to imagine two more different personalities than José de San Martín and Simón Bolívar. It is not hard to see why they should have disliked each other. San Martín, the lower middle-class professional soldier, was the more aristocratic and reserved in his habits; Bolívar, the aristocrat of immense wealth, the more vulgar, ostentatious and inconsiderate. Yet these two quite different men achieved remarkably similar things. Bolívar, for all the surface glitter, was at heart a serious man with a carefully thought-out vision for South America whose strategy, adapted and readapted, proved brilliantly successful following a string of failures – and, in the march over the Andes, was probably copied from San Martín. He, the dour, square-bashing general, displayed an ambition and imagination that if anything exceeded Bolívar's. It took genius to understand the inherent futility of those endless overland campaigns to dislodge the Spanish from Peru, and to conceive instead of crossing the Andes in the south and launching a sea-borne invasion.

Bolívar, constantly dicing with death, galloping from one country to another, launching his own sea-borne invasions, exhorting his men across jungle, swamp, desert and mountain, is the stuff of romantic legend; but prosaic, taciturn, disciplined San Martín was no less essentially romantic and courageous in the four great risks he took in his life: deserting Spain; hijacking Argentina's army in order to launch his attack on Chile; gaining command of the sea in order to starve Lima; and surrendering his power without a fight after his meeting with Bolívar. The spiritual strength these required was the equal of Bolívar's restless physical courage.

Bolívar may be deemed the greater of the two for expending so much energy in an attempt to establish lasting institutions; that he failed to create them was not for want of trying. San Martín, by contrast, three times delivered independence, then left this task to others. Perhaps he was simply more realistic. His defenders say that unlike Bolívar he was no *caudillo*, no military chief bent upon imposing his will, but preferred to let Argentines, Chileans and Peruvians sort out their own destinies; yet there is an intellectual laziness implicit in defeating the enemy, and then moving on. He refused to be a part of civil wars in which he would have to kill his fellow Americans: the Spanish were the enemy. Bolívar by contrast attempted to confront the continent's warlords after the Spanish had left, and it was his failure to assert his authority over Páez that led to the disintegration of Gran Colombia and, ultimately, his downfall.

In the final analysis Bolívar's sense of political duty – of responsibility towards those millions he freed – and his attempts to exercise it undoubtedly make him the greater man of the two, and he would surely have been the more intriguing to meet. But San Martín's was undoubtedly the more humane and upright, the nobler character, and for these virtues he has been characterised as the George Washington of Latin America, dubbed 'the saint with a sword'.

It was Providence that delivered the *coup de grâce* to O'Higgins the unloved liberator. On 19 November 1822, after a still, sunny day with an exceptionally high tide, a small earth tremor in Valparaíso brought many people out of their houses at half past ten at night; it was followed by a devastating earthquake that brought down all the churches and many of the houses. Fires ignited in the rubble, there was a three-minute-long succession of serious tremors, and huge tidal waves came crashing onto the shore. In the course of that night a further thirty-six big tremors were felt. O'Higgins was in the governor's palace and ran out at the first shock, to be pulled clear as the big one started and the building collapsed. The earthquake was followed by widespread looting and by rioting against 'gringos' who had come to Chile, disturbances which O'Higgins put down with his customary firmness. Although seven hundred buildings had been destroyed, because of the warning tremor only a hundred people in the port were killed. Nevertheless, to a spiritual people inclined to be superstitious, it seemed that the Almighty was wreaking His vengeance both upon the foreigners who lived in Valparaíso and upon the ungodly, anti-Church, half-gringo leader who accommodated them.

Further south, in the province of Concepción, Ramón Freire, a protégé of O'Higgins as well as one of his oldest friends, was faced with near-starvation, lawlessness, and a severe shortage of government funds. He began to agitate against the Director's 'usurpation of power which you exercise against the will of the people'. Freire won support from Valparaíso and Coquimbo but in Santiago the aristocracy, while opposed to O'Higgins, did not want Freire or another subordinate in his place. O'Higgins's response was to mobilise the southern garrisons and, at last following Cochrane's advice, to fire the widely-hated Rodriguez Aldea. But it made little difference, and Freire attacked him again. O'Higgins countered wearily: 'Could you really imagine that threats, and the steps you have already taken, could intimidate me? You and everyone know whether I can look death in the face. But an act of ingratitude has more power to move me than a gun levelled at my breast. Now I have drained the cup of bitterness to its dregs.' In fact he wanted nothing more than to follow the example of San Martín and retire gracefully from the scene, to farm in peace.

At the end of January 1823 the leading citizens of Santiago gathered in a kind of improvised parliament to discuss the Director's removal, and the head of his guard of honour was unable to close down the assembly. They sent a delegate to O'Higgins asking him to attend, but he refused to recognise 'a handful of demagogues and café-waiters'. He rode to the city barracks, where the soldiers were rumoured to be on the verge of mutiny, ordered all the officers involved to be put under arrest, and received pledges of support from the rest. Displaying similar courage, he then went to confront the impromptu assembly, walking through the ranks of his enemies and asking what they wanted. Their spokesman replied: 'The people, sir, fully esteem your important services and look on Your Excellency as the father of the country. But mindful of the difficult situation through which it is passing, and the civil war and destructive anarchy which threaten it, they respectfully request you to put an end to these ills by resigning the high office which you hold.' O'Higgins answered: 'I refuse to take part in public arguments like this. If you seriously wish to discuss the situation of the country and find a remedy for its ills, elect some responsible spokesman who can discuss serious matters seriously.'

Shortly afterwards he received reports relating to the unrest elsewhere in the country, and decided to resign. He addressed the crowd which had gathered:

If it has not been granted me to consolidate the new institutions of the Republic, I have at least the satisfaction of leaving it free and independent, respected abroad, and covered with the glory won by its victorious arms. I thank heaven for the favours it has granted my government and I pray that it may protect those who are to follow me ...

Now I am a private citizen. During the time of my government I have wielded almost absolute powers. I ask you to believe me that whatever wrongs I may have done have been the result of the difficult conditions in which it was my lot to govern, and not the fruit of evil passions. I am ready to answer any accusations you wish to make against me. And if the wrongs I have done can be purged by my blood, then take of me the vengeance you will. Here is my breast!

Once again O'Higgins behaved with honour in adversity. He withdrew to Valparaíso, leaving a junta in his place; but Freire arrived by sea and had the former Supreme Director arrested. O'Higgins's health collapsed, and he replied bitterly to San Martín's letter congratulating him on his resignation: 'The humiliations and loss of liberty which I have suffered since giving up office have shown me what I may expect in future from my country, though I would not exchange these last thirteen years of sacrifice and unheard-of effort for anything in the world.' As the months passed, he became more reflective:

I have felt more at home on the field of battle, I know nothing of these tortuous arts by which a man may aspire to govern a state torn by envy, parties, and factions. This evil is almost always unavoidable in newly-fledged governments, which must look to themselves for sustenance and growth; men are always reluctant to recognise one of themselves as a superior, even when they have elected him themselves. It is useless to grant institutions and guarantees, for these they despise and condemn. My experience and what scant understanding of politics I possess have convinced me that our peoples will only find well-being under compulsion; but my repugnance for compulsion is so great that I am loath to employ it even to achieve their well-being.

On 17 July Freire permitted O'Higgins and his family to go into exile in Peru. He arrived to a friendly reception from his old schoolfriend, the Marqués de Torre Tagle, and was housed grandly in San Martín's former residence; but the estate he had been granted lay ravaged in enemy hands.

O'Higgins offered to serve under Bolívar, Peru's new ruler, in his final campaigns against the royalist armies in the mountains. Bolívar was gracious, although he regarded the Chilean as little more than a stooge of San Martín. O'Higgins set out on a month-long journey to join Bolívar in the mountains and reached the battlefield of Junín just after the royalist defeat there. He caught up with Bolívar at Huancayo where, Miller recalled, he revealed himself as 'just the same honest, kind-hearted, straightforward, unsuspecting character we always found him to be'. But both Bolívar and O'Higgins had departed before the final defeat of the royalists at Ayacucho by the patriots under Sucre's command.

O'Higgins was now able to return to his large, run-down estate forty miles to the south of Lima, Montalvan, where he dressed and lived simply, indulging in tea, tobacco and music, but little alcohol. Remarkably, while he could scarcely have been kinder to the Araucanian girls he had adopted, he treated his illegitimate son Pedro as a servant, a continuing reflection of his own usage at his father's hands and probably a result of the bitterness he felt towards the boy's mother, whom he regarded as having seduced and used him.

Chile drifted into chaos following his departure and an effort was made to bring him back; he planned to return, until Freire himself fell, when the country disintegrated into warring factions, and O'Higgins knew his opportunity was past: 'I have solemnly renounced all political power. I shall never reassume it – never – even should the votes of the nation seek to restore me to it. This I have publicly declared, and I do not go back on my word.' Later he wrote: 'For the independence of Chile and America I sacrificed my youth, my health, and my fortune; I wish for nothing further than the satisfaction of recalling services which were not wholly in vain.' In 1830, when his old friend General Prieto came to power, O'Higgins briefly hoped he might be recalled to his homeland; but Prieto's deputy was Diego Portales, a tough-minded man who soon restored the kind of benevolent authoritarianism O'Higgins had practised, and which had aroused so little enthusiasm; Portales was opposed to the return of a 'caudillo', as he characterised O'Higgins.

The duplicitous Freire, also now exiled, sought to reinvade Chile with Peruvian backing, but was caught and exiled to Australia. Conflict broke out between Chile and Peru and Lima was occupied by the Chileans, who went on to win a crushing victory at Yungay in 1839. O'Higgins, now past sixty, was moved to see his country's troops once more, but in April 1840 he suffered a severe blow with the death of his beloved mother, Doña Isabel; she was buried with full honours.

O'Higgins maintained an almost obsessive regard for the father who had so ill-treated him – he wrote of 'my native land … which he so greatly benefited' and considered it his duty 'to emulate his illustrious example' – yet Bernardo was by far the greater man of the two. His remaining years of exile were devoted to farming, and he continued to recommend the colonisation of the southern part of Chile and to promote the political values of Britain, which he always admired. He urged an alliance between Britain and Chile, and advocated substantial English and Irish immigration. He was sent a portrait of Charlotte Eeles – 'your old sweetheart' – who had died; she had never married, never forgotten the young man she had known at Richmond.

At last O'Higgins was invited to return to his homeland – but the day he was due to embark, he had a heart attack. He died in October 1842, aged sixty-four. He left his estate to his sister Rosita – and, on her death, to his illegitimate son, Pedro, a provision he made on his death-bed, just like Ambrosio.

Bernardo O'Higgins was in many ways the most likeable and straight-forward of the Liberators. He was more direct than San Martín, a devious man with much of the secret agent about him. O'Higgins was a reluctant warrior and a reluctant leader of his people, things he did out of duty. If his military skills were limited, he nevertheless displayed exemplary valour at Rancagua and at Chacabuco.

O'Higgins survived in power longer than Bolívar or San Martín, and his rule was enlightened, energetic and modernising. If he was auto-cratic, that was the spirit of the times – and the years of chaos that succeeded him suggest a firm hand was needed in the aftermath of the Spanish Empire. He was intellectually limited, and sometimes led astray by his advisers. He was never repressive or cruel: the killing of the Carreras cannot be laid at his door.

Essentially a gentleman, he was unkind to his illegitimate son, but recognised his claims at the end, and his somewhat barren private life is readily explicable as a result of his treatment at the hands of the father he met only once, but to whose memory he remained inexplicably devoted.

PART THREE: NEW SPAIN

The Pacifier

40

Turbulent Priests

In 1783 – the same year as Bolívar – Agustín de Itúrbide was born in Valladolid (now Morelia), west of Mexico City, into a moderately wealthy Mexican family. He probably enjoyed the pleasant, undemanding society of the local landowners, and played with their children. He had a sister, Nicolasa, and his parents lived well into his adult life, so it may be supposed that he experienced little of the early emotional turmoil that afflicted the other liberators. And of them all, only San Martín had an earlier experience of military life: it was an obsession with Itúrbide, and at fourteen he joined the local militia as an ensign. Unlike San Martín, however, Itúrbide saw little active service in his youth. He grew up to be tall and fairly good-looking, apart from slightly pinched eyes, chubby cheeks, and a protruding chin. From an early age he stood out as a leader of men, natural officer material – decisive, dominant, athletic, respected by his peers.

Agustín de Itúrbide is the non-liberator, an embarrassment, the man whom to this day Mexicans prefer not to regard as the founder of their nation. Unquestionably he did create the Mexican nation – and remarkably, in a country with such a sanguinary history, he did so largely without shedding blood. But the title of Liberator is commonly awarded to two priests, Hidalgo and Morelos, who tried and lamentably failed to do the same thing, amidst unspeakable carnage.

In 1809, when he was twenty-six, an age at which the other liberators had already made their mark, Itúrbide sprang to modest prominence for the first time, as a zealous royalist officer denouncing a pro-independence conspiracy in his native Valladolid. The following year, when the first significant pro-independence insurrection in the Viceroyalty of New Spain broke out, the young captain condemned it in ringing terms as dragging the nation towards 'disorder, massacre and devastation'. Like

St Paul's before the road to Damascus, Itúrbide's career now prospered – as one of the most promising persecutors of the independence movement. In 1813 he was promoted colonel by the Spanish Viceroy, Felix Maria Calleja, and soon to command of the crack Celaya Regiment. In 1815, after defeating Morelos, he was appointed commander of the intendancy of Guanajuato, then Commander of the North. His prospects were dizzying, the Viceroyalty of New Spain not out of reach. He was a keen and rigorous prosecutor of the war against the rebels, setting up local militias and ensuring that towns and farms were loyal, fortified and organised for defence. To deter others from joining the rebellion, he had the mothers and children of patriots imprisoned.

The war of independence in New Spain followed a bizarre course almost completely different from the experience elsewhere in Spanish America: it was not a rebellion by the local criollo oligarchy against exploitation by peninsular Spaniards, but from the first a war of class against class. Only in Venezuela and, to a lesser extent, Peru was class a feature of the independence movement, and in both instances at a much later and more subordinate stage. The Viceroyalty of New Spain also differed from the others in being by far the largest of the Spanish dominions. Peru with its fabulous mineral wealth was of course the richest, exploiting a slave population in a very poor hinterland. New Spain stretched as far north as San Francisco and included the territory that now forms the states of Arizona, New Mexico, Texas and Florida, as well as southern California; southwards it embraced all of modern Central America as far as Panamá: about twice the extent of modern Mexico.

By 1810 the population was made up of about four million Indians, an increase from the million or so of a century and a half earlier, but nowhere near the level of about fifteen million when Hernan Cortés arrived in 1519. There were slightly more than a million whites, about two million of mixed race and hardly any blacks, except on the Caribbean coast. The whites were thus not only dominant, but numerous, and the caste structure was as usual: the darker the skin, the greater the inferiority. Another feature of New Spain was the size of Mexico City, at the centre of this vast land of scattered settlements separated by deserts and mountains. With 170,000 inhabitants, it was the largest city in the western hemisphere (as it still is – indeed, possibly the largest in the world); it possessed the oldest university in the Americas, north or south – the Royal and Pontifical University of Mexico, founded in 1553

– as well as its oldest opera, newspapers and publishing house, and even a renowned college of mining and geology.

Occupying a much bigger land area, possessed of long-established settlement as well as the memory of the awesomely sophisticated (albeit annihilated) native culture of the Mayas and the Aztecs, the Viceroyalty of New Spain had every reason to look down with disdain upon the much newer United States and Upper and Lower Canada to the north, and the Spanish and Portuguese colonies to the south. It considered itself to be the venerable trunk of the Spanish Empire, its most powerful and virile expression. New Spain was not only powerful, and large; it had enjoyed perhaps the most impressive succession of viceroys of all the colonies, throughout the centuries of Spanish domination. The Marqués de Gelves, the Duque d'Escalona, the Marqués de La Laguna, the Conde de Monclova, the Conde de Galve, the Conde de Montezuma, the Duque d'Albuquerque, the Duque de Linares, the Marqués de Valero, the Marqués de Casafuerte and the Marqués de Sonora were some of the illustrious figures to have graced the viceregal palace in Mexico City prior to the corrupt appointees of the later Bourbons. The country over which they presided had a flourishing agriculture, the potential of which had scarcely been exploited; silver, mostly from Guanajuato, Zacatecas, Guadalajara, San Luis Potosí, Pachuca and Taxco, formed nine-tenths of New Spain's exports. The Indians were third-class citizens, obliged to work for the state under the *cuatequil* system for eight weeks a year, later bonded to landowners through debt peonage; but both systems were at least superior to slavery.

The Viceroyalty of New Spain was different from other Spanish American colonies in at least one other respect too: the pre-eminence there of the Church. More than anywhere else, in New Spain the power of the Church balanced, and even sometimes exceeded, that of the state, exercised through the monastic orders to be found throughout the impoverished countryside, which regarded themselves as the heirs of the great friars of the seventeenth century (including such reformers as Bartolomé de las Casas), and through the secular priests. This pre-eminence was to prove significant in Mexico's struggle for independence.

For all her differences, New Spain also had many features in common with other Spanish American colonies. The peninsular Spanish – derided as *gachupinos* by the locals – dominated all the senior administrative posts, and the criollos intensely resented their arrogance. Spanish taxes upon cochineal, indigo, sugar, cacao, cotton, tobacco and vanilla were bitterly resented, as was the dumping at grossly inflated prices of fabrics, clothing, shoes, wine, candles, paper and steel from the mother country. The reforms of the enlightened earlier Bourbons eased these impositions a little, but local resentment was thereby all the greater under the corrupt later Bourbons. Increasingly the criollo aristocracy took on its own independent identity. As Humbolt wrote in his *Political Essay on the Kingdom of New Spain*: 'The natives [meaning the criollos] prefer the denomination of Americans to that of Creoles. Since the peace of Versailles [1783], and, in particular, since the year 1789, we frequently hear proudly declared: "I am not a Spaniard, I am an American!", words that betray the workings of a long resentment.'

It was a *gachupino* – the Viceroy himself, José de Iturrigaray – who first began to side with the growing criollo discontent: observing the course of events as France crushed the monarchy in Spain, he harboured an ambition to lead New Spain to independence and become her first king. This provoked such alarm among his fellow Spaniards that in 1808 he was arrested and sent back to prison in Spain. The real ferment in New Spain was not among the aristocracy, however, but among the people, given focus and articulation by the rural priests across the country.

In 1753, just three years after the birth of Miranda, Miguel Hidalgo y Costilla was born into a comfortably-off middle-class family in Guanajuato Province, north-east of Mexico City. He attended college at San Nicolas in Valladolid, before going on to the Royal and Pontifical University in 1773. He was exceedingly bright and clearly destined for a notable career; after teaching at Valladolid, he entered the priesthood in 1778 and became rector of the college there in 1790. But Hidalgo soon fell from grace: he was accused of trying to alter the curriculum by introducing liberal ideas, and of mishandling college funds – a common complaint against those with suspect views. The charges were sufficiently serious for him to be dismissed, and his promising career seemed at an end.

Transferred to the position of a lowly parish priest outside the city, he behaved with extraordinary abandon. He preached that hell did not exist, and that sex outside marriage was not a sin: he himself had at least one mistress who bore him several illegitimate daughters, and was rumoured to have several more. He was also said to have espoused the cause of independence from Spain, and of revolution. Investigated by the Inquisition in 1800, Hidalgo denied the charges, recanted, and was assigned to a sleepy provincial town, Dolores in Guanajuato. There his behaviour was just as scandalous: not only did he consort with women but he gambled, hunted, partied, circulated forbidden books, and employed the locals in such industries as beekeeping and silkmaking. He also encouraged them to grow vines and olive trees – which was forbidden, in order to preserve the Spanish monopoly in wine and olive oil. His house became known as Little France, on account of the liberal gatherings held there. In 1808 the Inquisition again summoned him for interrogation; he was not charged, however, but permitted to continue as parish priest in Dolores.

Hidalgo became friendly with Ignacio Allende, garrison commander of the nearby small town, Querétaro, with his colleague Juan Aldama, and with a local manufacturer, Miguel Dominguez, and his fiery wife, later dubbed La Corregidora – all covert revolutionaries. La Corregidora had been in touch with him as early as 1807, through La Sociedad de los Guadalupes, an organisation of middle-class criollos, and through the network of Mexican 'safety juntas', ostensibly formed to prevent French control of Mexico but essentially secret recruiting societies for opponents of the government. As Allende explained in a letter to Hidalgo,

> We decided to act carefully, concealing our aims, because if the movement were frankly revolutionary it would not be supported by the general mass of people ... Since the natives are indifferent to the word liberty it is necessary to make them believe that the rising is undertaken simply to favour King Ferdinand.

The group began to plot an insurrection, to take place in December 1810, to proclaim independence from Spain and a better deal for the poor. The well-to-do criollos who backed Padre Hidalgo believed they were promoting nothing more than long overdue political and social reforms, as did the rebellious priest himself. Word of the conspiracy was leaked, however, and several minor members were arrested in September. Hidalgo, Allende and Aldama fled from Querétaro; and on 16 September met together at the priest's church in Dolores. Fearing execution if they surrendered, Hidalgo had the church bells rung to summon the workers from the fields. Hundreds gathered, to whom Hidalgo – a poor parish priest in his late fifties with a cadaverous face, blazing, intelligent eyes with thick dark eyebrows, his head with a large, domed, bald forehead and long white hair at the sides – made the impassioned speech that has become known as the *Grito de Dolores*, the Cry of Dolores; there is no verbatim record of his words, but he called for liberty, land redistribution, and the support of the Virgin of Guadalupe, the patron saint of the Indians. 'Viva la Libertad!' he declaimed, 'Viva la Virgen de Guadalupe!' The crowd responded, 'Muerte a los gachupines!' He had sparked a popular uprising far beyond both his expectation and his ability to control. This day – 16 September – is regarded as the first day of Mexican independence, although it was nothing of the kind.

Bearing a banner of the Virgin of Guadalupe Hidalgo led his farm workers and his handful of middle-class co-conspirators towards the town of San Miguel. Hundreds joined from nearby farms and mines. The militia in San Miguel, under the influence of Allende, joined the uprising. But as the rabble, now swollen to several thousand, entered the town, they began to sack shops and loot houses belonging to whites. The same happened in the town of Celaya and in Querétaro itself. In the countryside, houses were pillaged and crops destroyed. Allende urged Hidalgo to put him in charge of the revolutionaries, to impose discipline. But Hidalgo refused, and the looting and plundering went on; dozens of whites were killed.

By 28 September the mob had reached the provincial capital, Guanajuato. The commander there assembled the white population in the town granary, a well-stocked warehouse, and his militia opened fire on the insurgents. About two thousand were massacred and the crowd, inflamed to madness, battered down the door, broke in, and slaughtered the five hundred inside. Lucás Alamán, one of Mexico's finest historians, who as an eighteen-year-old survived the massacre, described it: 'When the insurgents had taken the Alhondiga [the granary] they gave rein to their vengeance. In vain those who had surrendered begged on their knees for mercy ... The building presented a most horrible spectacle. The food that had been stored there was strewn about everywhere; naked bodies lay half-buried in maize, or in money, and everything was spotted with blood.'

The rebel army, growing all the time, moved on Valladolid, whose capture must have been sweet to the man driven out of the college there twenty years before. One town after another fell before him. The insurgents now numbered 50,000, a huge, uncontrollable human hurricane destroying all in its path. Hidalgo, despite his upbringing and his civilised ideals, was either unable or unwilling to control the excesses;

perhaps he regarded them as the necessary price of revolution. He now believed his force to be so big as to be unstoppable, and directed it towards Mexico City. The rebels were met by General Trujillo at the head of 7,000 soldiers on the hills to the west of the city, at Monte de las Cruces, where bandits were crucified. After a fierce fight Trujillo and his men, heavily outnumbered as they were, retreated. Matters were suddenly at a turning-point.

Almost certainly the elderly, fiery priest could have taken the capital, but he paused: he had been bloodied in the battle; his army of beggars had lost many of their weapons; it may be that he was sick of the killing, sickened by the thought of what the mob might do in the capital. He ordered his men north-west to the provincial city of Guadalajara, three hundred miles away across spectacular mountain country. Allende and Aldama, the professional soldiers, were appalled. They argued that the uprising would lose its impetus, and with it a momentous opportunity. Indeed, large numbers of Hidalgo's Indian supporters now began to drift back to their towns and farms. Another royalist general, Felix Calleja, began an attack, then veered away, and desertions increased. But once they were in Guadalajara the rebels' fortunes seemed to improve. Allende energetically trained new recruits, and the army swelled to 80,000. Yet the initiative had passed from Hidalgo: from being a struggle for independence, his rebellion had turned into a ferocious class and racial war that alienated the criollo aristocracy and the middle classes.

Calleja, moving north-west with a small army of 6,000 well-trained troops, regained Guanajuato, and on January 1811 he reached Calderón, near Guadalajara. There, against Allende's advice, Hidalgo decided to fight a pitched battle. His rebels, who outnumbered the royalists thirteen to one, held their ground for six hours, until a lucky shot blew up their ammunition dump, which set fire to the long grass of the plain. 'Deer, wolves, and coyotes emerged terrified from their caves and became entangled with the men ... as if by their astonishment they wished to show that the cruelty of wars was even greater among men than among beasts.' The rebels panicked and fled, despite Allende's best efforts. Allende and Hidalgo retreated with about a thousand men north-east to Saltillo, intending to ignite revolution among the northern provinces. Their hopes were soon dashed, however, and they became desperate and bitter. Allende and the others, blaming Hidalgo for the shambles, deposed him as their leader.

A group under Ignacio Elizonde deserted the rebel remnant in

Saltillo, and when they reached the huge empty desert badlands of Coahuila state Elizonde joined the pursuing royalists and set up an ambush. On 21 February, near Monclova, the straggling rebel column was attacked and Allende and Hidalgo were taken prisoner. Many insurgents were shot out-of-hand. Hidalgo issued a rambling proclamation against the treachery of his fellow Americans:

> Do you not realise that this war is waged against them [European tyrants] alone, and that it would therefore be a war without enemies, and would be all over in a day, if you did not help them to fight?
>
> Do not let yourselves be deceived, Americans, or allow them ... to make you believe that we are God's enemies and want to overthrow His holy religion ... Open your eyes; remember that the Europeans are trying to set Creole against Creole while they themselves look on from a safe distance. If things turn out favourably they will take the credit for having conquered us, and will mock and despise whatever is Creole ...

In the windblown desert capital of Coahuila Allende was shot in the back, as a traitor; Hidalgo, as a priest, was subjected to the tortures of the Inquisition. After pathetically recanting under pressure, he was executed by firing squad on 30 July. According to his executioner, Hidalgo sat on a stool, a crucifix in his hands. Three bullets hit him in the stomach, one in the arm, but he did not die. Instead he fixed 'those beautiful eyes' of his on the executioners. A second volley struck him again in the stomach, but still he did not die. The soldiers trembled 'like quicksilver' at the third try, and missed him again. For ten years the heads of Hidalgo, Allende and Aldama were exhibited on the Alhondiga, the scene of their most notorious massacre.

This disastrous old man is today celebrated as the architect of Mexico's independence, the day of the *Grito de Dolores* as Mexico's independence day. Even allowing for modern Mexico's obsession with her 'revolutionary' credentials – which refer specifically to the Mexican Revolution of 1917 – Hidalgo's canonisation as Mexico's founding father remains extraordinary.

His uprising badly scared the criollo classes and almost certainly, therefore, delayed the dawn of independence by several years. It was characterised by appalling suffering, carnage and disorganisation – hardly the building-blocks of national self-respect. It failed to a great extent because of Hidalgo's inadequacies as a leader, and because of his tactical ineptitude in not attacking Mexico City while the tide was running in his favour. His political principles remain obscure and ill-defined: they were not set out in anything resembling a manifesto, and seemed largely driven by his downfall after early years of promise. His commitment to Indian ownership of land, to the breaking-up of the big estates and to ending slavery were admirable, and sufficiently account for his devoted following among Mexico's poor majority. None of this, however, added up to a coherent political programme, and his support for the cause of independence seems to have been secondary to his desire for social revolution.

The second 'father' of Mexican independence is a much more plausible figure than Hidalgo. José Maria Morelos y Pavon came from impoverished lower middle-class stock. Less than five feet tall, he was plump and thickset with an ugly scarred face which usually wore an expression of grim determination. His nose had been broken when, as a young man, he crashed into a tree while escaping from a bull. He lacked Hidalgo's quick tongue and intellectual charm as well as his physical presence. A native of Valladolid, he was, as a mestizo, automatically condemned to second-class status. In his youth he had been taught by Hidalgo, but then led a harsh life as a farmer, a mule-driver, and a teacher. In 1797 he became a priest, of an impoverished parish near Lake Pátzcuaro, west of Mexico City. Like Hidalgo he showed little respect for his vocation but fathered several children, and read revolutionary works. When Hidalgo's rebellion broke out in 1810 he hurried to offer his services as chaplain to the rebels; instead, he was assigned to lead the revolt in southern Mexico. Sent with a thousand men to attack Acapulco, he was beaten back.

He then recruited and trained a thousand infantry and two thousand cavalry, creating a force much more effective than Hidalgo's with which he staged guerrilla attacks in and out of the mountains, surprising royalist convoys and disrupting their lines of communication. Three able men supported him: Vicente Guerrero, Manuel Felix Fernandez (soon to become famous as Guadalupe Victoria – in honour of the Virgin of Guadalupe) and Father Mariano Matamoros, a superb commander in battle.

In May 1811, as Hidalgo's uprising came to its sorry end, Morelos succeeded in capturing the town of Chilpancingo to the north of Acapulco. He then raided spectacularly north, seizing the town of Cuautla, barely forty miles south of Mexico City. Calleja, fresh from his defeat of Hidalgo but himself ill, decided to wipe out this last remnant of resistance, and with ten thousand men laid siege to Cuautla. But the town lies in an open depression south of Mexico City: the climate and the lower altitude favoured Morelos's men, mostly recruited from the jungles to the south, and set the government forces, more accustomed to the 9,000-foot-high plateau, at a disadvantage. The siege became an epic. Morelos's men ran short of water and grain and dozens died of starvation, but they organised fiestas and dances along the walls to taunt the enemy. Tubby little Morelos, who suffered from malaria and migraine, strode about the battlements, easily distinguishable by the white scarf soaked in vinegar he wore wrapped around his head.

Calleja, watching in wonderment as the rebels apparently buried their dead with rites of joyous celebration, called Morelos 'a second Mohammed'. Attempts were made on his life, one by 'a pot-bellied man'. Asked about this, Morelos replied, 'Though my illnesses have wasted me, I'm the only pot-belly around here.'

From 19 February until the end of April the siege went on, and only when an expedition by Matamoros in search of food was driven back did Morelos decide to abandon the town. Offered a pardon by Calleja, he laconically replied, 'I concede the same indulgence to Calleja and his troops.'

On the night of 2 May Morelos's men slipped out of the town in silence. When a royalist patrol chanced upon them they were forced to fire, but even as Calleja realised what was happening and hurriedly attacked, they disappeared into the hills, to regroup hundreds of miles further south. Although technically defeated, by holding out for 72 days just south of Mexico City, against the might of the viceroyalty, the rebels had secured a decided propaganda victory. Calleja inflicted reprisals on the civilian population of Cuautla, thus sending Morelos another eight hundred recruits, peasants thirsting for revenge. He now veered southeast and captured the city of Oaxaca, then marched due west to Acapulco and captured it at last, after a long siege.

The government appointed Calleja Viceroy, to crush the rebellion, but Morelos now moved again towards Mexico City, and reoccupied Chilpancingo. Here he convoked a congress to proclaim Mexico's independence and establish a coherent political programme. Matamoros presided over it, and Morelos allowed himself to be proclaimed the supreme chief or 'servant of the nation'. According to one rebel leader present, this was a mistake: 'The bandage of error covered Morelos's eyes, and his scant experience of the world made him the victim of a plot concocted by the ambition of certain people who, flattering him and persuading him to serve as an instrument for their own ends, were so able to confuse him that he endorsed a project which only a short while before he had himself disapproved.'

In his inaugural address Morelos proclaimed that the basis of the new republic 'should be such as to moderate both opulence and indigence by raising the wages of the poor, improving their habits, and lifting them above ignorance, plunder, and theft'. In November 1814 a Solemn Declaration of Independence was promulgated for what was described therein as the pre-Hispanic Kingdom of Anáhuac. The constitution was remarkably sophisticated and well-intentioned. Subscribing to the Catholic faith, it established a system based upon a separation of powers between legislature, executive and judiciary; an elected assembly; the outlawing of slavery; and equality before the law for all races. More muddle-headed was the proposal that the position of head of state should alternate among a committee of three, each acting as president for four months – presumably an arrangement devised to accommodate the three principal guerrilla leaders.

This was the first coherent statement of aims by the Mexican patriots, and clearly attempted to reconcile the aspirations of both the dispossessed masses and the white middle classes, unlike Hidalgo's movement which had been a purely popular one. But for all its pretensions, Morelos's congress was no more than an assembly of guerrilla leaders; and they were now thrown on the defensive. Obliged to flee Chilpancingo and then Apatzingán before superior royalist forces, they then headed north-east towards Valladolid, Morelos's birthplace and the cradle of Hidalgo's revolution.

There in December 1814 a tough young officer, Agustín de Itúrbide, attacked Morelos, routed the twenty thousand men of the rebel army and captured Matamoros. Morelos desperately sought an exchange of prisoners for his fellow warrior-priest, but Matamoros was executed in Valladolid early in 1815. Morelos's columns then trekked southwards several hundred exhausting miles towards Puebla, to escape a trap, but on 5 November they encountered six hundred royalist troops.

Morelos led a rearguard action so that the bulk of his men could escape; he himself was captured and taken in chains to Mexico City. He was tortured by the Inquisition, and it was said that he informed on his colleagues; but unlike Hidalgo he did not recant. He behaved with great dignity at his military trial, and refused his gaoler's offer to help him escape – if the attempt failed, he said, he might be forced to betray him.

On 22 December, he asked for a crucifix and declared, 'Lord, if I have done well, Thou knowest; and if ill, I abandon myself to Thine infinite mercy'. He was shot, twice, in the back.

In almost every respect the stocky little half-caste Morelos was a far more impressive leader, and a more authentic figure as architect of Mexico's independence, than the posturing Hidalgo. Modest and intelligent, he had enunciated a political programme and issued a formal declaration of independence; he had secured significant victories with inferior forces; and his achievements were not marred by acts of senseless cruelty. He even succeeded in rallying part of the white middle class to his banner. What is more, he maintained the struggle for independence for much longer than Hidalgo.

Two thousand rebels escaped with Guadalupe Victoria and holed up in Puebla, where they were considered to pose no threat to the capital. There were also about a thousand in Oaxaca under Vicente Guerrero. The flame of independence smouldered on in distant provinces, but by 1816 it seemed the insurrection was at an end. The cost was between 200,000 and 500,000 dead, out of a population of six million – one of the highest tolls, not excepting the carnage in Venezuela. The following year a Spanish officer, Francisco Mina, thinking to emulate Bolívar, landed on a lonely spot north of Tampico on the Gulf of Mexico, with a band of Britons, North Americans and Europeans. He won a few skirmishes, but neither the criollos nor the local rebel leaders rallied to him; he was captured and executed in November 1817. Truly, the soil of New Spain seemed too stony for independence.

41

Emperor of the Flies

As we have seen, the seizure of power in Spain by the liberals in 1820 which forced Ferdinand VII to reinstate the constitution of 1812, and the consequent reversal of colonial policy, had its effect on independence movements throughout Spanish America. In New Spain the conservative ruling class and the Spanish government officials were alike horrified, among them Agustín de Itúrbide, commander of the intendancy of Guanajuato, and of the Army of the North. He was tough with the rebels, but also high-handed in his dealings with local landowners, from whom he was accused of extorting money. By 1816 the volume of complaints against him could no longer be ignored. Accused of the creation of trade monopolies, of plundering private property, and of misappropriation, he was recalled from his appointments. It is impossible to say whether the charges were based on the authorities' early perception of his radical beliefs, or whether he became embittered and therefore rebellious as a result of these accusations.

Exonerated in 1817, but not restored to his command, Itúrbide festered in Mexico City, nursing his grievances against the Viceroy, Felix Calleja. Calleja's successor, Juan Ruiz de Apodaca, Conde de Venadito, was a more enlightened man whose decency in his dealings with the insurgents won many over. He did, however, appoint Itúrbide, at the head of two thousand men, to extinguish what was left of Guerrero's sputtering rebellion in southern Mexico. Itúrbide offered the veteran guerrilla chief a parley; the assumption was that he would also offer a pardon. Guerrero may have been tired, and his forces depleted, but it seemed unlikely that he would surrender; indeed, in his initial conversation with Itúrbide he proclaimed 'Independence or death!'

What Itúrbide actually did, in the village of Iguala, about seventy miles south-west of Mexico City, on 24 February 1821, was issue a 'plan'.

The 'Plan de Iguala' contained twenty-three articles; its 'Three Guarantees' covered Religion, Independence, and the Constitution. Article One provided that the religion of Mexico should be Catholic, although other faiths would be tolerated, thus pleasing both conservative and liberal clergy; Article Two called for independence; Article Three suggested the establishment of a monarchy accountable to a constitution. The King of Spain or a member of his family was to be invited to Mexico as emperor, but a regency and a junta would govern in the interregnum; Spain was flatteringly described as 'the most Catholic, pious, heroic and magnanimous nation on earth'. Other articles promised to respect private property, the privileges of the clergy, and all existing Mexican institutions. An army was to be established which integrated rebel and loyalist forces.

One prominent opposition cleric described the Plan de Iguala as a masterpiece: 'the object ... is independence, the rest is calculated to avoid the scoffing of rebels'. It was not negotiated with the rebels but submitted as an ultimatum; nevertheless, a fortnight later they accepted it, and both Guadalupe Victoria and the opposition leader acceded to it. The steps by which one of the most conservative and ruthless officers of the Spanish army in the Viceroyalty of New Spain came to execute such a complete volte-face remain a matter of conjecture; Guerrero called Itúrbide 'a magnanimous leader' and 'the father of the nation'.

What was more extraordinary was that the army pronounced itself in favour of the Plan almost *en masse*, and almost at once: Antonio López de Santa Anna, then a young lieutenant-colonel of twenty-six in control of Veracruz, also came over, and the military governors of Zitácuaro, Nueva Galicia, Zacatecas, and San Luis Potosí soon followed suit. Bloodstained Valladolid declared in May, Guadalajara and Querétaro in June, Puebla in July; only Mexico City and Acapulco held firm to the royalist cause. In July Apodaca resigned, to be replaced as Viceroy – the last, as it transpired – by Juan O'Donojú.

It is hard to believe that all this was uncoordinated, that it had not been carefully prepared. The Plan of Iguala was not negotiated, but issued to the rebels as an ultimatum – rebels who were at their last gasp, and had little choice but to accept. While conceding that Mexico should be independent, it conceded none of the other rebel demands. It was an almost entirely conservative settlement, acceptable to the criollo oligarchy, to the army, and to the conservative clergy. It was in effect the imposition on the Mexican nation of a conservative solution, one which even acknowledged the King of Spain as Mexico's potential ruler. Independence was the only radical element it contained.

The speed with which the Plan was accepted by military garrisons across Mexico suggests at the very least that a number of commanders were in on the scheme. Although Itúrbide had had plenty of time in Mexico City to draft such a plan and co-ordinate his views with those of senior officers, clergy and criollos, it seems unlikely that he was the creator – or the sole creator – of such a cunningly crafted document. There is no evidence to support it, but a theory that the liberal Viceroy Apodaca had a hand in the matter is not entirely untenable. If it is unclear whether Itúrbide was the creator of the Plan or merely its executor, there is no doubt that he saw himself in the former role.

Events continued to move with remarkable speed and a notable lack of bloodshed. O'Donojú, arriving to take up his post, found that 'virtually the whole country was against the crown'. On 5 August in Puebla, at Itúrbide's instigation, the provincial adherents of the Plan swore a formal Oath of Independence. There he received letters from O'Donojú addressed to him as 'Commander-in-Chief of the Imperial force of the Three Guarantees', and as a friend. O'Donojú, himself a liberal, asked to meet Itúrbide, and a parley was held in the village of Córdoba. There the new Spanish Viceroy was effectively taken prisoner; he wrote back to the government in Spain that since Itúrbide commanded 30,000 trained men as against the 4,500 or so royalist troops in Mexico City, to resist was a 'vain hope'. The Treaty of Córdoba was concluded, by the terms of which the Plan of Iguala was implemented and O'Donojú was appointed a member of the council of regency; in exchange he agreed to order the remaining Spanish garrisons to join Itúrbide's army. Francisco Novella, commander of the royalist forces in Mexico City, renounced O'Donojú as his superior officer and accepted his instructions to obey Itúrbide.

On 27 September, Itúrbide's thirty-eighth birthday, he entered Mexico City in triumph; the following day he assumed the viceregal seat in the cathedral to sign the formal 'Act of Independence of the Mexican Empire'. Insurrections costing many hundreds of thousands of lives had failed: he had secured Mexico's independence at a cost of fewer than a hundred and fifty. Formally he was no more than president of a five-man Council of Regency, a generalissimo; in reality, he wielded absolute military authority. As president of the council he was granted the title Serene Highness, and pamphleteers vied with one another to flatter 'the

Second Constantine ... Unconquered General of the Nation ...
Frightener of the impious, valiant Hero, Great defender of our religion.'

Some even argued that he, not Ferdinand VII, should be supreme
ruler of the new empire: 'We should think of a monarch who unites in
himself the circumstances of being from this country, Catholic, prudent,
known, valiant, a lover of the Fatherland and loved by its people. And
who more fits this case than the Hero of our days?' Itúrbide later asserted
that 'at my entry in Mexico [City] on the 27th of September ... they
wanted me even then to be emperor; I was not proclaimed only because
I would not be, and I had great difficulty to make those who had raised
their voices desist from the project.' He noted how Hidalgo and his followers had 'desolated the country' and 'increased the obstacles that
opposed' independence; he, by contrast, had 'sallied out ... to be useful
to the Mexicans, to the King of Spain, and to the Spaniards.' A month
after the declaration of independence O'Donojú, whose conduct
throughout had been marked by practicality and impeccable correctness, died of pleurisy contracted at Veracruz.

Itúrbide, now overwhelmingly the most powerful figure in the
country, frequently quarrelled with the Council of Regency. Only one
member of the council, a priest, Manuel de la Barcena, was at all radical:
power in the new Mexico was divided between the criollo oligarchy, the
army as represented by Itúrbide, and what was left of the original pro-
independence opposition. The criollos, repressed by their own congress,
became determined to seek a reduction in their tax burden. The army,
starved of funds, increasingly made common cause with the old radicals,
and Itúrbide found himself becoming the champion not just of the soldiers but also of the dispossessed, against conservative interests: an odd
development on the face of it, but one that later came to characterise
many Latin American countries, whose military leaders often regarded
themselves as representing the impoverished among their fellow-coun-
trymen.

In March 1822 army salaries were cut by a fifth: Itúrbide wrote angrily
to the congress that soldiers were dying of hunger, and that 'to die of
hunger is not a death for the brave'; purely for effect, he demanded a
proportionate cut in his own salary. That same month news arrived that
in February the Spanish Cortes had rejected the Treaty of Córdoba:
neither Ferdinand nor any scion of his family would assume the throne
of Mexico. It is impossible to establish whether Itúrbide had anticipated
this. He was intelligent, an able military leader and a considerable dip-

lomat, and he did not lack vision: it seems unlikely that he can genuinely have expected the Spanish King to accept the throne of one of his own former colonies, even in the case of the Spanish government permitting it.

Itúrbide's populist stance during the months of the regency suggests that his purpose was to establish himself as the obvious choice for the proposed new monarch. It would be fair to say that any constitutional settlement which did not involve a monarchy would have antagonised Mexican conservatives, and almost certainly he came to believe, as the months of Mexico's early independence passed, that only he could rescue the country from the threat of civil war between the 'haves' and the 'have nots'. The Plan de Iguala had cleverly papered over the tensions between these two elements, and just as he had kept the peace at the time of its introduction, so he was determined to do the same in the future.

On the night of 18 May 1822 Sergeant Pio Marcha, of Itúrbide's own Celeya Regiment, led an ever-swelling demonstration through the streets of Mexico City. The congress had just been browbeaten by the military into accepting Itúrbide's demand that a national army of 35,000 regular soldiers and a 30,000-strong militia be set up. He had angrily declared that the country was 'without an army ... without a navy, with all her flanks exposed, with her inhabitants distracted ... Is this country properly designated a nation?' he demanded. Almost certainly Itúrbide and his supporters in the armed forces were behind the demonstration; in any case, it appeared to be in tune with popular feeling, and in danger of running out of control. On the 19th, the congress proclaimed him Emperor, as Agustín I.

As a contemporary noted, his supporters were 'the clergy, the miserable nobility of the country, the army in its greater part, and the common people who saw in that chief nothing more than the liberator of their country'. Itúrbide later declared ('with my heart on my lips') that he had had no wish to become Emperor, but that

> I was the depository of the will of the Mexicans; in the first place because what I signed in their name is what they ought to have wished for; in the second place because they had already given me many strong proofs of their real approbation to it, joining to me those amongst them capable of bearing arms, others assisting me by all the means that were in their power, and receiving me in all the towns through which I passed with

acclamations and praise ... As no one was compelled by force to make these demonstrations, it is evident that they approved my design, and that their will was similar to mine.

My first impulse was to go forth and make known to the people my reluctance to accept a crown whose weight already oppressed me excessively. If I restrained myself from appearing before them for that purpose, it was a compliance with the advice of a friend who happened at that moment to be at my side. 'They will consider it to be an insult,' he scarcely had time to say, 'and, believing themselves treated with contempt, an irritated people can become a monster. You must make this fresh sacrifice for the public good. The country is in danger; remain a moment longer undecided, and you will hear the death shouts.' I felt it necessary to submit to this misfortune, which was the greatest I had yet suffered ...

It is to Itúrbide's credit that he genuinely believed in sharing power. As he later remarked, 'When I entered Mexico [City] my own will was the law; I commanded the public force ... and who compelled me to divide the powers? Myself, and myself alone, because I thought it was right. If I did not choose to be absolute then, why should I have wished to be so afterwards?' Certainly he had established a congress, and had always supported the principle of a constitutional rather than an absolute monarchy. Moreover, perceived (as he was) as representing the military interest and the dispossessed against the powerful oligarchy that controlled Congress, he was at first genuinely popular, in a real sense the heir of Hidalgo and Morelos.

Yet he appears to have become rather swiftly afflicted by the *folie de grandeur* which seems to be the lot of many who rise swiftly and unexpectedly to supreme power and such as had threatened to overcome Bolívar and San Martín. His wife Ana was named Empress; his eldest son was declared Prince of the Empire, and his seven other children were all accorded royal status. His sister became Princess Itúrbide. His birthday and those of his children were proclaimed national holidays. His coronation was set for 21 July, and he sent to France for the designers of Napoleon's uniforms: bowing and curtseying were carefully rehearsed by his courtiers and their ladies. On the day, the president of Congress placed the crown on Itúrbide's head, and he himself crowned his Empress. The whole ceremony lasted five hours and the United States consul, William Taylor, the only foreign diplomat present, described it as a tiresome, tinselled pantomine.

Writing to Bolívar, the new Emperor defended himself: 'I am far from considering as a benefit an act which lays upon my shoulders a burden that oppresses me! I lack the strength needed to sustain the sceptre. I abhorred it, but in the end I agreed to accept it in order to prevent evils to the country which was about to succumb anew, if not to the former slavery, at least to the horrors of anarchy.'

The Emperor's household of a hundred and thirty-four included sixteen gentlemen pages, three confessors and six chaplains, and had a budget of a million and a half pesos – almost half the entire government payroll, and four times that of the last Viceroy's household. As one critical supporter noted: 'Those who a few months before had Itúrbide as their companion or their subordinate, the upper class and the middle class of society who had seen his family as inferior or equal, did not consider his rapid elevation as anything but a theatrical coup, and they could not accustom themselves to pronounce without a smile the titles of princes and princesses.' Did Mexico really need such an imperial poseur? Itúrbide had one compelling argument on his side: a monarchy was the only possible restraint on an assembly which represented the oligarchy and, increasingly, respected no rules. The Plan of Iguala had specified a monarchical form of government: in the absence of Ferdinand VII or a scion of his house, who else should occupy the throne but Mexico's military strong-man?

If Agustín's social pretensions made him bitter enemies at home, they also failed to win friends abroad. Miguel Santa Maria, ambassador of Bolívar's Gran Colombia, an ardent republican, was not impressed; nor was the new American ambassador, Joel Poinsett:

> He is accused of having been the most cruel and blood-thirsty persecutor of the patriots [the followers of Hidalgo and Morelos], and never to have spared a prisoner ... In the interval between the defeat of the patriot cause and the last revolution, he resided in the capital, and in a society not remarkable for strict morals, he was distinguished for his immorality ... To judge from [his] public papers, I do not think him a man of talents. He is prompt, bold and decisive, and not scrupulous about the means he employs to obtain his ends.

Poinsett was both anti-monarchical and, specifically, anti-Itúrbide; but his views, however hostile, are at least partly believable.

Problems quickly piled up for the new Emperor, as he financed his spending through borrowing. Food prices rose sharply, disappointing the expectations of those millions of Mexicans who had been led to believe that prosperity would come with independence. Both agriculture and mining production stagnated, and he showed no magic ability to revive them. He quarrelled increasingly bitterly with Congress, which voted to strip him of his power of veto and tried to award itself the right to appoint the senior members of the judiciary: he sought to impose military tribunals throughout the country. By the summer a conspiracy was being organised among leading members of Congress to stage an uprising in Mexico City, seize Agustín, strip him of his office, and proclaim a republic. The chief plotters were three leading congressmen, Servando Teresa de Mier, Juan Pablo Anaya and Carlos Maria Bustamante. Another intriguer was the Colombian ambassador Santa Maria; behind him stood Simón Bolívar himself.

The Emperor learned of the plot, however, and sixty-six people were arrested. Agustín personally supervised the seizure of Bustamante. Santa Maria was ordered out of the country but travelled only as far as Veracruz, where he continued his agitation against the Emperor. Most of those arrested had been freed by December – at this stage, at least, Agustín showed himself to be neither cruel nor vindictive. He continued to defend himself vigorously: 'I have sworn to the nation to govern it under a constitutional system; I will be loyal to my word respecting [the system] that actually exists as far as the good of the empire permits me. But if, through the vices of its organisation or the passions of its agents, it wants to convert itself into an instrument of anarchy, the nation itself in use of its sovereign rights will give a new representation, and I will be the first to invoke it.' It seemed that most of the nation sided with him against the self-interested representatives of the landed class. There were strong arguments on Agustín's side: Congress, supposed to be drafting a constitution, had spent months debating procedural matters, and the Emperor could not secure passage of essential legislation. It can be argued that at this stage Agustín was too soft on his opponents.

Eventually he lost patience, and on 31 October ordered his army to dissolve the assembly; the deputies went meekly home, to be replaced by a national junta from which Agustín's opponents were ruthlessly excluded. But the new body proved no more able to raise money than the old Congress. The government was virtually bankrupt, paralysed by lack of revenue: in November Agustín resorted to forced loans and the seizure of funds held on deposit for Spaniards who had left Mexico. Furiously condemned, still he defended himself: 'Who is culpable in this state of things? I, who to find a remedy to an extreme necessity conformed myself to the natural and public right, making use of the funds of the country, or the Congress which in eight months' time had neither formed a plan of finance nor given a system to the public revenues?' The government then resorted to printing money, and imposed a 40 per cent tax on property. By now Agustín had won himself the hatred of the professional classes, and even his poorer followers were beginning to grow restless. So far, the army remained on his side.

Then a new threat loomed: a brilliant and ambitious young officer in his late twenties, Antonio Lopez de Santa Anna. Promoted to command the Mexican forces near Veracruz, where the fortress of Ulua was still held by six hundred Spanish troops, he conspired to make himself captain-general of the province of Veracruz; Agustín decided to dismiss him from his command, and to do so in person. He travelled at the head of a large party to Jalapa, and ordered Santa Anna to return to the capital with him. Santa Anna declined to do so immediately, requesting time to sort out his personal affairs. In fact, he was incensed: 'So rude a blow wounded my military pride and tore the bandage from my eyes. I beheld absolutism in all its power; and I felt encouraged to enter into a struggle against Agustín I.' He rode back to Veracruz, and in December 1822 raised the standard of revolt.

The uprising, if localised, was potentially serious, from the possibility that Santa Anna's men might join forces with the Spanish garrison under General Lemaur. However, it had a faltering start: Santa Anna attacked Jalapa but failed ignominiously to take it, almost all his men being killed or captured. He had formed an alliance with Guadalupe Victoria, one of the original guerrilla leaders, and now proposed they should flee to the United States; but Victoria refused, and the insurgents were joined by another veteran, Vicente Guerrero.

José Antonio Echevarrí was sent by Agustín to command the government forces against the rebels. The Emperor, meanwhile, apparently drinking heavily, moved into and treated as his own a country house in San Cosmé, to the disgust of its aristocratic owners. He maintained a show of lofty confidence, as here, writing to Echevarrí: 'From all the Empire where news of the action of Santa Anna has arrived they write full of indignation against this wretch and the public tranquillity has not altered in any way despite the efforts that those few who expect early promotions and improvement of their fortunes have made, so that I believe today that the project of Santa Anna ... is going to produce much more good than evil for us; we can clean the land of many weeds and leave it prepared to bring forth good fruit.'

Guerrero's small army in the south was attacked in late January 1823 by loyalist forces under Brigadier José Gabriel de Armijo; the guerrilla chieftain, badly wounded, managed to escape by hiding in a ravine and was nursed back to health by an Indian peasant. The government believed him to be dead. With Santa Anna confined to Veracruz, Agustín was confident that the unrest was being easily contained, and Empire Day was celebrated in Mexico City with fiestas and bullfights.

Echevarrí had been ordered to continue the siege of Veracruz, but here Santa Anna was well placed: the Spanish had promised their help in his insurrection, and kept him supplied by sea. Despairing of ever taking Veracruz, on 1 February 1823 Echevarrí and his commanders reached an agreement with Santa Anna for an armistice. This was called the 'Plan de Casa Mata', and under it a new congress was to be elected (Santa Anna had previously demanded the re-convocation of the original Congress), while in exchange the army was to reaffirm its loyalty to the Emperor: 'It being incontrovertible that sovereignty resides essentially in the nation, the Congress will be installed with all possible speed … The army will never make any attempt against the person of the Emperor.' It was a bizarre compromise. As the Emperor was quick to point out, he had himself called for the installation of a new congress. But it was also in effect an act of rebellion on the part of the Emperor's own commander, since Echevarrí had not been authorised to treat with Santa Anna or to conclude any agreement; in fact, it represented a rebuff to Agustín's objective of crushing Santa Anna.

Because the Plan proclaimed the army's loyalty to the Emperor, it quickly gained adherents in the isolated garrisons that made up the Mexican military establishment; its provisions for the decentralisation of military and political power, which would ensure provincial centres a strong element of self-government, had their appeal for both military commanders and those wielding local power. The garrisons at Oaxaca and Puebla quickly came out in support of the document, but even so its declared adherents numbered only about a thousand soldiers, compared with the 30,000 or so nominally loyal to Agustín. Once again his instinct was to compromise and negotiate, rather than to make a stand. He declared, 'I have force and judgement to make myself respected and obeyed, but it would cost blood, and by me not a drop will ever be shed' – an admirably humanitarian approach, but not the right one, in that place at that time, for a man who wanted to preserve his throne. His opponents continued to profess their loyalty to him, all the time alert for any opportunity to seize the initiative.

By late February the pamphleteers had spread details of the Plan's provisions throughout the provinces; decentralisation of power held such appeal that cities and their garrisons declared their support for the Plan at a steadily accelerating rate – and since in it the Emperor's position was formally upheld, many believed they were manifesting no disloyalty. Then General Pedro Negrete, Agustín's most trusted aide, sent to negotiate with the rebels, announced that he had gone over to them.

42

The Return

In Mexico City key army units defected and such political prisoners as Bustamante and Padre Mier were set free. The Emperor now controlled only a part of the capital, and the province of Chiapas in the south-east. He had no choice but to offer the rebels what they sought – restoration of the old Congress – in the hope that they would hold to their protestations of loyalty to him as constitutional monarch. The Congress met early in March 1823 and was opened by Agustín – a stinging humiliation for him – calling for national reconciliation. Agustín now moved his headquarters to his residence outside the city at Tacubaya. Then he marched into Mexico City with the crack First Infantry Battalion. He was fêted by a large crowd of supporters, and when he attempted to leave people unharnessed the horses of his coach and pulled it back to his palace in the city. He lost his watch in the triumphal mêlée. From the balcony of the palace he addressed the crowds, urging them to remain peaceful. There was no food in the palace, so he borrowed some chocolate from Bishop Perez of Puebla, who lived across the street. Some of Agustín's detractors suggested he had orchestrated the demonstrations, but they were far too large for that, and were rather evidence of the support he still enjoyed among ordinary people. Rumours spread of an impending uprising against the landed classes.

Certainly the gulf between rich and poor was awesome. Fanny Calderón de la Barca, an Englishwoman married to a Spanish diplomat, describes the women of the criollo upper class: 'One, for example, would have a scarlet satin petticoat, and over it a pink satin robe, trimmed with scarlet ribbons to match. Another, a short rich blue satin dress, beneath which appeared a purple satin petticoat … All had diamonds and pearls … I did not see one without earrings, necklace, and brooch.' Poinsett, the American envoy, provides a striking contrast with his picture of the 'lepers', the beggars of Mexico City:

> In front of the churches and in the neighbourhood of them we saw an unusual number of beggars, and they openly exposed their disgusting sores and deformities to excite our compassion. I observed one among them wrapped in a large white sheet, who as soon as he perceived that he had attracted my attention, advanced towards me, and unfolding his covering, disclosed his person perfectly naked and covered from head to heel with ulcers ... No city in Italy contains so many miserable beggars, and no town in the world so many blind.

Congress, thrown into a panic by these rumblings of discontent, decreed that the government must take steps to maintain order, but Agustín kept his soldiers outside the city. On 17 March fighting broke out here and there, and it began to seem that Mexico, spared a war of independence, was now headed for a civil war between the urban masses, supporting the Emperor, and the aristocracy, middle classes and provincial élites, supporting those opposed to him.

After days of inaction, on 19 March 1823 Agustín stunned the whole country by proclaiming his abdication. He declared that he had always occupied the throne with reluctance, and that he was now vacating it in order to avoid civil war. He volunteered to go into exile and asked for a fortnight to settle his affairs. Within days the 'liberating army' of the rebels had moved into Mexico City, where it was met by the population with sullenness and hostility. Seven people were killed and fifty arrested in violent clashes. Agustín's decision had come as a bolt from the blue: it had not been among the rebels' demands, although no doubt many welcomed it.

There seem to be three discernible motives for his abdication. He was genuinely reluctant to plunge the country into civil war, and it had become evident that while he enjoyed the support of the masses, his followers in the army were very much in a minority. Nor did he see any future in attempting to rule when he was opposed by an independent Congress and virtually autonomous regional governments; his efforts to raise taxes had already been frustrated for months. And he may have believed that such anarchy would follow his departure that the Empire he had founded would recall him.

The circumstances of Agustín's abdication found an echo a decade later when Emperor Pedro I of Brazil, frustrated by a recalcitrant congress which made the country all but ungovernable, found himself unwilling to shed blood in what was likely to be a losing cause. There were similarities, too, with Bolívar's decision to leave Santa Fé de Bogotá for the last time, and even with San Martín's abdication. Latin American history repeatedly illustrates the fact that to create an independent country is not enough: again and again the politically simple-minded attempts of 'liberators' to govern have foundered on the rock of parliaments which believe themselves to be all-powerful, in a conflict between despotism and the self-interest of the ruling classes.

Agustín's last address to the congress was full of pathos and dignity: 'I love the land where I was born and I believe that I will leave to my children a more solidly glorious name in sacrificing myself for it than in governing the people from the dangerous height of the throne.' In spite of his early fearsome reputation, Agustín's period as Emperor suggests a man who preferred conciliation to confrontation, a skilled negotiator who showed little stomach for repression.

The Plan of Iguala and the Plan of Casa Mata were subsequently erased from the Mexican record, and Itúrbide became an object of scorn and derision. Bustamante, his most venomous enemy, denounced the former Emperor as a stooge for a Bourbon restoration in Mexico who had been frustrated by the refusal of Congress to be manipulated. This was transparent nonsense: he had displaced the Bourbons, and Congress, out of self-interest, had frustrated his attempts to govern.

The province of Jalisco on the west coast issued a proclamation typical of the vituperation now launched against him: 'Itúrbide was not our liberator, he was a hypocrite who tricked us as his partisans today want to do. He did not break our chains ... he renewed them ... Yes, citizens, Itúrbide was a traitor, a hypocrite and an impious man who destroyed the assembly in which the people had deposited their sovereignty in order to appropriate it all to himself.' In his place, Hidalgo and Morelos were undeservedly elevated to the status of founders of the Mexican state.

Itúrbide was accompanied to the coast by one of his chief opponents, General Nicolás Bravo. Bravo considered him a mere prisoner, while Itúrbide regarded himself as a former ruler who was leaving the country of his own free will. He and his retinue were greeted with fervent demonstrations of loyalty in the many villages they passed through in the course of the long descent from the plateau. Each man was accompanied by an escort of loyal troops, and inevitably there were clashes between them *en route*. Eventually the new government recalled Itúrbide's supporters, and ordered the arrest of his secretary Francisco de Paula Alvarez, together with several officers and clergy. Ill-health forced his sister Nicolasa and his elderly father to return to Mexico City, but his wife and eight children were among the party of twenty-eight who were to accompany him.

At Veracruz Itúrbide asked that his baggage be inspected, in order to refute the allegations that he was smuggling money out of the country, but the customs officials respectfully refused. He took with him 340 cases of claret, twelve barrels of Spanish wine, and personal effects which included silver, jewels, and works by Rubens and Velázquez. He sailed from Veracruz on 11 May 1823, and reached Livorno in Italy three months later. But he felt himself to be in danger from Spanish royalists in Italy, and in any case wanted an English education for his children, so in December 1823 he set off through Switzerland, Germany and the Netherlands, and reached London on 1 January 1824. He then moved to a large house in Bath, and sent his eldest son to Ampleforth.

There can be little doubt that he maintained contacts with his supporters at home, and his removal to England caused grave unease in Mexico, where the government feared, rightly, that he was planning a comeback, even that he was intending to restore Spanish rule. In April 1824 a motion was passed in Congress that Itúrbide was to be treated as an outlaw should he ever again set foot in Mexico – that is to say, he could be executed immediately, without trial. Meanwhile Itúrbide had approached Britain's Foreign Secretary, George Canning, for help in creating a British-style constitutional monarchy in Mexico, but Canning refused to meet him, and the Foreign Office offered no help at a lower level. During his absence Mexico had effectively disintegrated into separate states, and he believed his countrymen would rally behind him: 'In truth, I do not have such a high opinion of myself; but as I am assured that it is in my power to contribute to reuniting a great number of interests of those provinces and to calm the exalted passions that would produce disastrous anarchy, I leave with this intention.' Captain Basil Hall, who knew him, recorded: 'That it is a patriotic and disinterested decision I have not the smallest doubt; and there does not appear the least reason for apprehending that his views have any other direction than the service of Mexico.'

On 11 May 1824 Itúrbide left aboard a British ship with his wife and two younger children, and a printing press, bound for Mexico. Details of the order outlawing him arrived too late: he sailed in ignorance of it, and probably crossed the ship bearing the news somewhere in the mid Atlantic. In mid July Itúrbide landed near the remote town of Soto la Marina in the state of Tamaulipas. He was immediately arrested by the local commander, Felipé de La Garza, and taken inland to the town of Padilla, where the state legislature decreed that the law passed in April must at once be implemented.

Having expected his landing to trigger an uprising, Itúrbide was taken completely by surprise. On 19 July, two days after his arrest, he began a letter to Congress in which he asked what crime he had committeed; before he had finished it, he was told he was to be executed at six o'clock that evening (presumably before the authorities in Mexico City could be notified). He was allowed to write one further letter, to his wife Ana, 'blessed woman of my heart'. He asked for his watch and rosary to be sent to her as 'the only inheritance that constitutes this bloody memento of your unfortunate Agustín'. The man who had expected to be welcomed as a redeemer was to be shot without trial, like a dog, in an obscure provincial town. With great dignity he ordered gold coins to be distributed to the members of the firing squad – to ensure that they did their job efficiently. He was confessed, blindfolded and bound. He declared: 'Mexicans, I die with honour, and not as a traitor. That stain I will not bequeath to my children and their posterity; I am not a traitor, no.' One bullet hit him beside the nose, another lodged in his throat, a third, which killed him, in his forehead. His body was then taken to the local parliament building, which doubled as the chapel. Clothed in a Franciscan habit, the former Emperor Agustín was buried the following day in the ruins of the local parish church. In the view of the great late nineteenth-century Mexican historian and novelist, Justo Sierra, 'It was a political act, not a just one. Itúrbide had done his country a supreme service which cannot be belittled by calling it an act of treason against Spain. He did not rise to the heights his work demanded, but neither did he deserve the scaffold for reward. If the nation could have spoken, it would have absolved him.'

The trajectory of Itúrbide's career was the briefest and most rocket-like of that of any of the Liberators. A mere army officer in 1821, seven months later he was Liberator of New Spain, a land more extensive than the United States today, and only eight months later its Emperor. Ten months after that he was forced to abdicate, and fifteen months later he was ignominiously executed. The pathos of his death held a fascination for two men. Manuel Mier y Teran, the general who unsuccessfully defended Texas against the United States in 1836, subsequently went to Padillo and lived for a while in the rooms in which Itúrbide had been held. One day, having inspected the former Emperor's grave, he went to the spot where he had been executed, and fell on his sword; he was buried in the same tomb. In 1838 General Anastacio Bustamante, one of Itúrbide's chief supporters, had his remains brought to Mexico City. He did not dare to have them interred alongside the 'heroes' of Mexican independence, Hidalgo and Morelos, but an inscription in the Cathedral commemorated him thus:

> Agustín de Itúrbide,
> Author of Mexican Independence.
> Compatriot, weep for him.
> Passer-by, admire him.
> This monument guards the ashes of a hero.
> His soul rests in the bosom of God.

Bustamante arranged that he himself should be buried beside Itúrbide.

The former Empress, Ana Maria, who was carrying Itúrbide's ninth child at the time of his execution, had been allowed to sail to New Orleans. From there she travelled to Philadelphia, where she remained for the rest of her life, a wealthy widow, holding court for itinerant Mexicans, including General Echevarrí, who had been instrumental in her husband's downfall and subsequently himself became a political exile. In 1864, under the brief and tragic second Mexican Empire of Archduke Maximilian of Hapsburg, Itúrbide's family were restored to princely status and Itúrbide's son Agustín was even considered as a possible heir to the throne. But when after Maximilian's execution, with only his loyal friend the Italian Ambassador Curtopassi to lend him a shirt, the country lurched into nationalism and revolution, Itúrbide again became a non-person in Mexico. His body was not removed to the great Independence Monument erected in 1925 with those of Hidalgo, Morelos, Matamoros and Guerrero – all of whom had so signally failed to secure Mexico's independence. The man who actually gave Mexico nationhood remains despised and obscure.

Meanwhile, the populist government which succeeded Itúrbide proved to be disastrously chaotic. The veteran rebel leader Guadalupe Victoria – Manuel Felix Fernandez – became the republic's first president and ruled for five years over conflict between the government and the provinces in conditions of virtual bankruptcy, as the army swelled to 50,000 men. Vicente Guerrero, the other senior surviving guerrilla chief, succeeded Guadalupe Victoria in 1829 but was overthrown a year later – after Santa Anna had defeated an attempted Spanish reinvasion – by General Bustamante. In 1833 Santa Anna, the military strong man who had brought about Itúrbide's overthrow, himself became president.

This martinet, as strange and contradictory a personality as Itúrbide, remained a presence in the political arena for the next two decades, but seemed to dislike the visible exercise of power; pleading ill-health, he resigned after only a few months in the presidency, and alternated in the office with various substitutes. In 1836 he was defeated and captured by the Texans, but returned to Mexico in 1837 and was called out of retirement in 1838 when the French blockaded Veracruz; he lost a leg in this action. Between 1833 and 1855 the presidency changed hands thirty-six times; Santa Anna held the office eleven times. From being a comparatively liberal federalist he rapidly became a fiercely conservative centralist, to the extent of hand-picking town mayors, state governors, and congressmen. The man who destroyed Itúrbide proved a far more ruthlessly efficient despot.

The recent perceptive and well-researched study of Itúrbide by Timothy Anna concludes that

> The manner in which the Plan of Iguala swept all elements before it profoundly convinced Itúrbide that he was, as he put it, the single voice of the will of the people. At worst, that is egocentrism, not tyranny. He was catapulted without prior preparation to national leadership. He then struggled to create a unified state and the apparatus of functioning government. His willingness to restore the dissolved Constituent Congress suggests that he was beginning to learn the need to accommodate, though his dedication to order remained paramount and imposed severe limits on how lenient he could be. It was, after all, his fear that the provinces would fly away in all directions, leading to the atomization of Mexico, that brought him home in 1824.

A tough, scheming and seemingly unprincipled soldier, Itúrbide is the most unattractive of the liberators, possessing none of the picaresque idealism of Miranda, the brilliance of Bolívar, the meticulous industry of San Martín, the doggedness of O'Higgins, the flair of Cochrane, nor the romanticism of Pedro of Brazil. He was vain, overweening and *arriviste*, his imperial displays grotesque, even – in an all but bankrupt country – criminal. He was a complete failure as a ruler.

There is almost nothing to be said for him as a person. But the fact remains that, virtually without bloodshed, Itúrbide led Spain's largest overseas province, New Spain, to independence after a decade of war under more exalted and attractive personalities that cost at least half a million lives.

Itúrbide failed in part because he was a conciliator rather than a dictator – a man who, in the end, was not prepared to shed blood to defend his own power. His attempt to reconcile effective government with representative rule was far from contemptible. Had he been tougher and more ruthless, he might have survived longer.

Itúrbide's impact on his own country was great, and largely beneficial, in spite of his personal failings. Yet it is easy to see why, given that his 'revolution' was essentially a coup led by conservatives against radicals, subsequent 'revolutionary' governments in Mexico came to detest the very idea that Itúrbide should have been the father of their nation. Despite their failure and the suffering they caused, the two revolutionary priests made better icons than a cynical, opportunistic military leader – who, however, deserves better from the huge and ungrateful nation he created.

PART FOUR: THE EAST

The Emperor

43

Prince of Freedom

Lisbon boasts a variety of royal palaces along the Tagus, and it was in the magnificent one closest to the huge square pedestrianly entitled the Praça do Comércio that the most improbable, and only royal, Latin American liberator was born, in 1798. Pedro de Braganza was a minor scion of one of the most ancient royal families in Europe, a younger son of the second in line to the Portuguese throne. An ancestor, the Infante Dom Pedro, later King Pedro I, was notorious for a passionate affair with Inêz de Castro, his wife's cousin, and famously beautiful. In 1355 Inêz was murdered at the instigation of those jealous of her family's influence, and when he became King, Pedro took his revenge. It is said that he tore out the hearts of her assassins with his own hands and drank their blood, then exhumed Inêz's body and had it crowned and enthroned beside him. His assembled nobles swore fealty on her withered hand.

Pedro de Braganza's great-grandfather, José I, was an epileptic who could barely walk, from gout and ulcerated legs. His daughter, Queen Maria, a depressive who inherited a religious obsession from her mother, was forced for dynastic reasons to marry her uncle, twenty years her senior. Of their two sons and a daughter the eldest son, another José, was good-looking, healthy, full of charm and vigour. In his teens he studied Voltaire, and showed early signs of independence from the stultifying conformity of the Portuguese court. The daughter was likewise refreshingly normal, and married a Spanish prince. Only the second son, João – Pedro's father – was a disappointment: fat, quiet, gentle and idle, he shared his mother's obsession with religion, preferred the company of monks, and spent his time chanting plainsong in the monastery of Mafra. João was married at eighteen to a Spanish princess, Carlota Joaquina. She was thirteen, small, skinny and hideous, with a moustache, and a pointed nose and chin. Her angry black eyes expressed her implacably fierce and bitter temperament. On their first meeting she is said to have bitten her easy-going husband on the ear when he tried to kiss her, then to have struck him across the forehead with a candlestick. The ill-assorted couple nevertheless produced ten children, but after 1806, when Carlota was discovered to be plotting a coup against João, they ceased to live together as man and wife.

By comparison with her Spanish American neighbours and the British colonies of North America, Brazil was slow to feel the stirrings of any profound yearning for independence. Almost certainly this was a result of the light hand – an indolence amounting to invisibility – with which Portugal's colonial overseers had exercised their rule since her official 'discovery' in 1500 by Pedro Alvarez Cabral. In 1798 an uprising in Bahia (now Salvador) of mulattos and blacks espousing the ideals of the French Revolution had been easily suppressed, but the shudder which ran through most of the white ruling class at the prospect of *Haitianismo* – black revolt – caused them to cleave closer to Portugal, and it was events there and in Europe, rather than in South America, which formed the background to Brazilian independence.

Dynastic accident set in train the events which were to transform both Portugal and Brazil, beginning with the death from smallpox in 1788 of Queen Maria's attractive elder son José. The Queen had opposed inoculation on religious grounds: her daughter, her son-in-law and their small child also perished. Queen Maria's always delicate mental balance was upset, and she came to view these deaths as divine punishment for the crimes of her father's dynamic and despotic chief minister, the Marques de Pombal, who had brought the Enlightenment to Portugal and expelled the Jesuits from the kingdom. Devoting herself to extreme religious observance, she soon began to hear voices and to see demons, devils with tridents, Satan himself. She screamed and sobbed that she was already in Hell. George III's doctor was sent for from England, to no avail.

In 1792 the Queen's surviving child, João, was made Regent. Amiable, idle and reclusive, still addicted to Gregorian chant, João was only a marginal improvement on his mother; he left his ministers to govern the country while the shrewish Carlota pursued her amours and her plots. In a further twist, in 1802 his eldest son Antonio died at the age of seven, leaving four-year-old Pedro as João's heir.

The Napoleonic hurricane sweeping across Europe now bore down upon Portugal, tucked away in the south-western corner of the Iberian Peninsula. After his hopes of invasion were ended at the Battle of Trafalgar in 1805, Napoleon was determined to blockade Britain from the Continent. His subsequent victories in Austria, Prussia and Russia meant that by 1807 only Portugal and Sweden were still beyond his control. Portugal – a traditional ally of Britain – was to be threatened with invasion across a compliant Spain. João's ministers advised that resistance was useless. At the same time, they feared that if Napoleon took Portugal he would also seize Brazil and the Azores, much bigger prizes. In October 1807 an army of 20,000 French veterans under General Junot crossed the Pyrenees, headed for Portugal.

There followed a remarkable exodus. On 27 November 1807 the nine-year-old Pedro de Braganza was taken in a royal carriage through the crowded, muddy streets of Lisbon to the docks. His grandmother, the mad Queen Maria, made an appalling scene on the quayside, refusing to embark because she believed she was being taken to die on the guillotine, like Louis XVI. She had to be forced aboard gently. Almost the entire court and nobility of Portugal were leaving Lisbon. With them the royal family took the crown jewels, the royal library, the royal silver, the royal carriages, a multitude of other belongings, and a huge personal retinue. About ten thousand Portuguese retainers and officials boarded some forty ships to make the long journey across the Atlantic to Brazil, escorted by British warships.

All were aboard, but there was no wind. On the 28th Junot reached Santarém, his progress held up by an incessant downpour and the resultant mud. The following day he had reached Cartaxo, but a slight breeze had by then enabled the ships to slip down the Tagus as far as the mouth of the estuary. The speed with which the Portuguese court moved took Junot by surprise; on the night he heard of it he leapt from his bed at Cartaxo and ordered a thousand of his grenadiers down the rain-sodden road to Lisbon. The following day they reached the Bay of Bom Suceso at the tip of the Tagus estuary in time to open fire on the sails disappearing over the horizon. When news of the Portuguese court's escape reached Napoleon he exploded in one of his most spectacular rages, and in exile on St Helena years later he described João as 'the only one who ever tricked me'.

The Atlantic crossing took just over four months. Conditions on board were cramped, and chaotic thanks to the last-minute nature of the evacuation. The genteel ladies of the court were compelled to shave their hair to deal with lice and other infestations. After the initial excitement had worn off, the voyage must have seemed long and tedious to a boy accustomed to a pampered life at court and in the Regent's country residence at Queluz. The Queen was hysterical and subject to occasional bouts of epilepsy. Pedro's mother Carlota, depressed and angry at the prospect of life in remote Brazil, so far from her beloved Madrid, railed against the 'land of negroes and lice'. Her lovers – from a coachman, Santos, to the Marques de Marialva – had been the talk of Lisbon; but in the close confines of a ship such scandalous conduct was impossible.

A few days before they reached Bahia, the closest Brazilian port to Europe and former capital of the colony, the royal party were informed, to their astonishment, that the gaol in Rio de Janeiro was being made ready to receive them. It had to be hastily explained that the prison was the building next to the Viceroy's Palace, the Bobadela, which was being enlarged to accommodate them; it was being stripped and decorated, and was to be connected to the palace by means of a glass-covered passage. News of the impending influx of high-ranking exiles and their retinues had thrown the sleepy colony into a frenzy. In a city of only about 50,000, space had to be found for 10,000 more. The houses of the well-to-do were requisitioned by having the letters PR painted on them, standing for Prince Regent – or, said the locals with somewhat bleak humour, *ponha-se na rua*, 'put out into the street'.

When the bulk of the royal party landed at Rio on 7 March 1808 they were escorted by crowds through flower-strewn streets into the cathedral for a Te Deum. João, usually so bored and apathetic, seemed invigorated despite the torrid climate by the simplicity and spontaneity of the welcome the people accorded their hitherto remote royal masters. Three days later Queen Maria disembarked, pale and dishevelled; no salutes were fired, for fear they would frighten her, and she was taken to the Carmelite monastery amid wondering stares.

The natural beauty of Rio de Janeiro, with its harbour enclosed by two long mountainous promontories and the sharp rocky peak of the Corcovado (Hunchback) towering over the stubbier Pão de Açucar – the Sugar Loaf – struck the Portuguese with just as much wonder as it does new arrivals today. In the unblinking sun it looked even more fabulous than they had been led to believe. The steep hills were covered with pretty white houses, and all around the great amphitheatre of mountains and sea the lush forests, a hundred shades of green, beckoned the onlooker into the mysterious interior of the vast continent.

They would have remarked upon the large number of blacks on the streets, most of them slaves, and the far fewer number of Indians. The rich travelled in coaches, or in litters carried by animals or sedan chairs carried by blacks. Black servants in fine livery but barefoot – they refused to wear shoes – added another exotic touch. The wealthy young men and women of Rio wore Paris fashions twenty years out of date, most notably the tall wigs supported by frames weighing sometimes as much as fifteen pounds, from which dangled scissors, knives, ribbons, even vegetables. In the intense heat the glue needed to keep such wigs together often ran down their faces. But most women were firmly confined at home, except for an occasional outing.

Pedro's official duty was to attend his father at luncheon, when he held a basin for his father to wash his hands before eating pudding. He and his younger brother Miguel, and a first cousin, were at first inseparable companions. Carlota lived apart from the Prince Regent in her own house on the sea at Botafogo, with their numerous daughters. Miguel, much closer to her than Pedro, frequently visited her there. Under the benevolent and indulgent eye of his now jovial father, who seemed to discover in Rio that life could be enjoyable, Pedro grew into his teens. His schooling was extremely lax; João having instructed his tutors not to bother the child unduly, only one, João Rademaker, a diplomat, scholar and linguist, captured his imagination; but he died two or three years later.

Otherwise the young princes ran wild. They played with stable boys and street children. Pedro's best friend was a raffish groom, Chalaca – the Jester; he rose to become a highly-placed courtier in later life, Francisco Gomez da Silva. Pedro happily indulged in street fights with his friends, and disdained his noble contemporaries. He was notorious for slapping the cheeks of boys of good family who came to pay their respects by kissing his hand, and laughing at their reaction. He enjoyed the outdoor life, in particular riding, usually barefoot and in rough trousers, and he became skilled at shoeing horses. He had his own gang of black boy-slaves and these, armed with clubs and wooden muskets, fought Miguel's rival gang. The results of his skimped education, later all too obvious, were Pedro's appalling spelling and poor writing, his crude French (still the *lingua franca* of a civilised man), and his limited knowledge of the humanities. But he had two keen interests: he was a meticulous and skilful carpenter and wood carver, turning out fine models of ships, and even billiard tables; and a more than competent musician who played the flute, bassoon, trombone and violin, composed music, and enjoyed conducting.

In Pedro's early teens another characteristic became apparent, probably inherited from his lascivious mother – an insatiable appetite for sex. Foreign diplomats noticed it: one wrote that he was 'very frisky with the ladies' while another commented that 'the objects of his gallantry, a new one each week, are chosen from among Brazilian, Italian, French and even Spanish-American ladies, but none seems able to hold his affections.' From the time he was about fifteen he would go out at night on horseback in search of beautiful women, accosting coaches and peering into them. It was difficult to refuse the son of the Prince Regent, already a very good-looking youth, tall and strong, with curly red hair and fashionably long sideburns, a broad forehead, a direct and honest if sometimes arrogant gaze, a long, aquiline nose, small mouth and firm chin. His vitality and energy were irresistible – if his position were not commendation enough. João may have been sometimes embarrassed by his son's adventures and the need to pay off his paramours, but Rio de Janeiro was a city notoriously relaxed in its attitude to love.

A more serious matter than Pedro's wild oats was Prince João's desire to achieve a diplomatic alliance by means of his marriage. As early as 1807, before Napoleon's base designs on Portugal became obvious, he had tried for the hand of the Emperor's niece, daughter of his brother-in-law Murat, ruler of Naples; then for the sister of Tsar Alexander of Russia. Meanwhile, the heir to the Kingdom of the Two Sicilies was in his turn courting Pedro as a match for his daughter. These projects all came to nothing, but a still more spectacular match was in prospect: one of the younger daughters of the Emperor of Austria, whose eldest girl Marie Louise had been married to Napoleon. The Marques de Montealva, Portugal's ambassador in Paris, sent to open the negotiations, arrived in style in Vienna with a retinue of eight princes and nine counts in carriages drawn by six horses each, accompanied by a small army of servants. The gifts lavishly distributed, not least to the all-important Count Metternich, included 'various jewels and rich medals of honour for him to distribute, valued at £5,800, together with 167 diamonds to be set in those medals that were to be struck off in Europe, and seventeen bars of gold destined for certain persons who would be much more pleased to receive such a gift as this than other presents that were purely ornamental.'

The Austrian Emperor promised his youngest daughter, Leopoldina, and the marriage was performed by proxy in Vienna on 13 May 1817. Pedro was represented by the bride's uncle, the Archduke Charles; a magnificent ball followed. The total cost of this to the Portuguese was about £15 million at today's values; in exchange the dashing eighteen-year-old rake of Rio, bane of the city's beautiful young women, elder surviving son of the King of Portugal (poor mad Maria had died in 1816), became the brother-in-law of the former Empress of France and son-in-law to the Habsburg Emperor.

Leopoldina, as carefully educated as Pedro was unlettered and whose passion was science, departed in an ecstasy of excitement: 'Don't worry about the long voyage; for me there could be no greater pleasure in this world than that of going to America ... The voyage has no terrors for me. Indeed, I think it is a matter of fate, seeing that America has always had a singular attraction for me, and even as a child I used to say that I wanted to visit it some time.' She was accompanied by six noblemen, a chaplain, a librarian, a botanist, a mineralogist, a zoologist, an entymologist and several artists, as well as a large personal household, in a ship considerably more comfortable and less crowded than the one in which Pedro had travelled to Brazil nine years before. Arriving at that most beautiful of the world's ports to salutes, fireworks and balls, she was bowled over by the handsome young prince wearing a general's uniform with a tall collar and a chestful of gleaming decorations. He, too, was agog – at his bride's plainness. Leopoldina was small and plump, blue-eyed and pink-cheeked, with a small nose – and the prognathous jaw and slack mouth of the Habsburgs. She was not ugly, but she was not pretty, either; and she barely bothered with cosmetics – as a child of the Enlightenment, she was more interested in minerals and butterflies than in making herself attractive.

A sweet and naïve soul, Leopoldina delighted in the flora and fauna of her new world, as much as in Pedro's gallant attempts to please her. They shared a love of music, and she accompanied him on the piano. After the birth of their first child, a girl, in April 1819, she threw herself into the role of mother with cheerful devotion. Fortunately, Pedro himself was partial to children, as Leopoldina attested: 'He is the best of fathers; always playing with her, he carries her in his arms all the time we are out walking and is never tired of caressing her.' But he could no more abandon his pursuit of beautiful women for his sweet but dumpy Austrian princess than he could change his appearance. He was fond of her, but unfaithful to her from the beginning.

In Pernambuco, three months after Leopoldina's arrival, the ballerina Noemi Valençay gave birth to a child by Pedro, and the list of his conquests during the early years of his marriage was awesome. They included Anna Steinhausen, the wife of Leopoldina's librarian; the wife of the famous French naturalist Aimé Bonpland (later a friend of Admiral Lord Cochrane); Senhora de Avilez, wife of the commander of the Portuguese garrison at Rio; Madame de Saturville, married to a rich jewel merchant; the Baroness de Sorocaba; a mulatto woman, Joana Mosqueira; a beauty from the Banda Oriental, Carmen Garcia; and Clémence Saisset, French wife of a dress designer, whom he visited quite openly until someone, possibly a rival lover, fired a bullet through the window of Saisset's shop and he and Clémence were packed off to Europe with the illegitimate son she had borne. Like Simón Bolívar, Pedro simply regarded pretty girls and other people's wives as there for the taking, regardless of the offence and scandal he caused, the enemies he made, and the fact that he was taking advantage of his position as his father's heir. As he saw it, for him to take a woman to bed was little more than a compliment to her beauty.

If he expressed himself rather primly, the British minister resident in Rio de Janeiro at about this time revealed his acuity, as well as some appreciation of the difficulties of Pedro's position, in thus summing up his character: 'He is young, utterly non-instructed and inexperienced in business, impetuous and warm in his character, seeking ardently for employment more from curiosity than knowledge and occupying the vacancy, to which he is condemned, in the most violent and boisterous amusements.'

44

The Cry of Ypiranga

Dom João's introduction of free trade did much to dispel any resentment arising from the Portuguese court's sudden arrival in Brazil. José da Silva Lisboa, an economist of the Adam Smith school, had persuaded João that Brazil's ports should be opened up to friendly nations, and also that a charter of 1785 prohibiting manufacturing in Brazil should be revoked. Brazilians and foreigners were placed on an equal footing, and immigration from Europe was encouraged.

What had been a backwater was soon thriving. Rio was visited by only ninety ships in 1807, but by 400 the following year, while some 2,000 ships called at Bahia. As trade began to flourish and the colony grew more prosperous, its people took to the royal family with real affection. João adored his adopted homeland, and after Queen Maria's death in March 1816 settled comfortably into his full kingly status. But after the defeat of Napoleon in 1815 unrest under the regency which had been established to govern Portugal in the royal family's absence began to suggest that a return to Lisbon was imperative. The vacant throne was an open invitation to revolution, something neither Metternich's Holy Alliance nor the British wished to see. Additionally, the Lisbon regency increasingly resented having to support the royal family in Brazil, support which included such items as the provision of nearly nine thousand men for an invasion in 1814 of the Banda Oriental, the east bank of the River Plate, supposedly to consolidate Brazil's southern frontiers. Great Britain's Prince Regent placed a fleet at João's disposal, and George Canning was appointed ambassador to Portugal to supervise arrangements for João's return.

Pressure was also exerted upon João by his estranged wife Carlota. Following Napoleon's imprisonment of her father and her brother Ferdinand VII, she whiled away some of the years in the Brazil she hated with a fantastic scheme to secure the Spanish throne for herself, ruling from Buenos Aires. This dream evaporated with Ferdinand's return to Spain in 1814, and from that date she begged to go back to Europe. Carlota, four foot ten tall, with a skewed shoulder, was hated by most Brazilians. When she travelled the streets her armed attendants compelled all she passed to make grovelling obeisance, not excluding the ambassadors of foreign countries. The British ambassador, Lord Strangford, was beaten up for failing to observe this protocol, as was Commodore Bowles of the British naval contingent. Only the American envoy Sumner escaped, by threatening her attendants with pistols.

The King resolutely refused to leave until, in 1820, the worst fears of the Holy Alliance and the British were confirmed. A revolution broke out in Spain, and General Lord Beresford (he who had seized Buenos Aires with Popham in 1806; he later commanded the Portuguese forces in the Peninsular War, and remained afterwards as Commander-in-Chief of the Portuguese Army) feared the uprising would spread to leaderless Portugal. He travelled to Brazil to persuade the King to return, but João simply assigned him the task of reviewing the army in Brazil and inspecting its hospitals and depots. Frustrated, Beresford found on his return to Portugal that revolution had indeed broken out, in Oporto: the Regency had been swept aside, and the côrtes, which had not met for more than a century, had been summoned to draw up a constitution.

João's response was toleration, following the advice of his foreign minister, Count Palmela, and an offer to send his son Pedro to Portugal as a constitutional monarch. Meanwhile, revolutionary ferment was spreading to Brazil. In Pará (now Belém) and elsewhere in the north-east, people took to the streets demanding freedom; in February 1821 an assembly was set up in Bahia. The King's response was to set up a côrtes in Rio with limited powers, which only inflamed opinion further. On 26 February a crowd of mutinous soldiers and a mob of agitators assembled in the main square of Rio to demand the adoption of the new constitution promulgated by the côrtes in Portugal. Pedro, twenty-three now, was sent to calm the demonstrators by announcing that João accepted the constitution: 'Why all this commotion when everything has already been attended to?' he asked them. 'The troops may now retire to their barracks and the officers may go and kiss the hand of my august father.' The crowd, however, demanded the right to sack the government and appoint a new one. Pedro agreed. Later the same day João himself came to the square, to a tumultuous reception. But he regarded his concessions with cynicism: as he asked a diplomat the following day, 'Doesn't it strike you as humorous, forcing someone to swear to a thing [the constitution] that does not exist and may never come into existence?'

The revolutionary impulse seemed to be growing more dangerous, and the terminology of the French Revolution lived on. A 'National Convention' was set up in Rio, two months later, and Luiz Duprat, twenty-year-old son of a French tailor, together with a priest, a merchant and a surgeon, calling themselves a revolutionary committee, demanded the introduction of a more radical constitution to resemble the liberal Spanish Constitution of 1812, recently restored. A delegation was sent to the King, who agreed to this latest demand. The cry then went up that he was preparing to flee abroad with the country's gold. Summoning the military governor of Rio to the convention, Duprat screamed that the port must be closed. Pedro was made of sterner stuff than his father, however. He assembled a battalion of chasseurs, a detachment of artillery and a battalion of infantry, then ordered its commander, Major Peixoto, to surround the convention building and set up two cannon aimed at the entrance. At four in the morning, using bayonets and rifle butts, they chased the revolutionaries out. A bullet narrowly missed Peixoto, several convention members were killed jumping from the windows, and Duprat was arrested and taken to Snake Island, the prison off Rio.

The revolution had been crushed, but the King had fatally damaged his authority by his vacillation and wavering in the face of anarchy. João had earlier tried to despatch his son to Lisbon as his proconsul; now it was Pedro who effectively despatched his father to Portugal, to restore the authority of the monarchy there while he remained in Brazil and sought to control the revolutionary turbulence threatening to grip the country. On 22 April 1821 the amiable, indolent monk-King appointed his son Regent, and two days later, to his deep chagrin, left for Lisbon, never to return to his beloved Brazil. His estranged wife Carlota went with him, delighted to escape. Pedro was left behind with his plain, bookish Austrian wife and his bevy of mistresses.

From the first, Pedro displayed energy and verve. Rising at four in the morning, he visited barracks and inspected troops and equipment. After a quick breakfast at nine, he saw his ministers and discussed state business for five hours before a snack and a siesta. At four he usually rode out on horseback, and at six he and Leopoldina played music together.

Formal evening parties and state occasions permitting, he went to bed
at nine – but often slipped out later to visit a mistress.

If João had not exactly fled with all the country's gold, he had taken
with him from the Brazilian treasury about £750 million at today's
values. Pedro moved quickly to deal with the critical financial situation,
abolishing the tax on salt to stimulate the cattle and fishing industries,
slashing the salaries and pensions of civil servants, and reducing his own
allowance by half. Although his assumption of power displayed a certain
authoritarian toughness, he was in many respects liberal and enlightened. Censorship was done away with, and he proclaimed his support
for the freedom of the individual. Dungeons, forced labour, arm-irons
and the flogging of prisoners were abolished; prison, he said, was for 'the
detention of persons and not for flagellating them or undermining their
health'.

Keenly resentful of his own lack of education, he set up a series of new
schools and other educational establishments and an observatory,
encouraged the dissemination of scientific works – probably at the
behest of his wife – and set historians the task of writing the history of
the Portuguese empire. But rebelliousness continued to simmer in the
radical towns of northern Brazil.

Meanwhile, in Portugal King João was little more than a puppet,
incapable of acting against the new liberal majority in the côrtes, which
appointed the ministers in Lisbon. They decided that the quasi independence Brazil had enjoyed since the arrival of the court in 1807 must be
brought to an end, and a series of decrees revoked Brazil's trading privileges. The Portuguese commander of the Rio de Janeiro garrison –
known as the Legion – was instructed to act as the guarantor of
Portugal's authority in the colony.

These displays of arrogance in Lisbon began to unite Brazilians
around the energetic figure of the young Regent. Already a secret pro-
independence movement of separatists had begun to form, based upon
a network of Masonic lodges around the country, and the Conde do
Arcos, Pedro's first minister, was known to be sympathetic to Brazilian
self-government.

The truth was that Brazil had been effectively independent for fourteen years – indeed, had become the dominant partner in the Portuguese
Empire – and was not prepared to be reabsorbed without a struggle. On
leaving Rio the King had advised his son, 'If Brazil should decide on separation, let it be under your leadership, since you are bound to respect

me, rather than under one of these adventurers.' In secret communications from Lisbon João now urged Pedro to resist reassimilation into Portugal, foreseeing that it would lead inevitably to such radical revolution as was being experienced throughout Spanish America.

On 5 June 1821 the Legion seized power in Rio de Janeiro and in an ultimatum to Pedro demanded that Arcos be dismissed and an anti-independence junta be set up as the new *de facto* government. Pedro's first impulse was to raise Brazilian forces to fight the Legion, but the Portuguese forces were superior in numbers and equipment. Surrendering to the Legion's demands, Pedro faced a storm of opprobrium from his own supporters, disillusioned by his betrayal of Brazil's interests. Two months later, the côrtes in Lisbon commanded his return to Europe for a grand tour 'to complete his political education'. Obviously, they feared he would become the figurehead of the independence movement. Pedro's response was to seek the advice of the people, sending emissaries to all the main towns in Brazil. The results were overwhelming: he should stay. In January 1822 a huge crowd converged on the Regent's palace in Rio, and the political leaders of the city, fearful that anarchy would ensue if he were to leave the country, requested him to stay. He agreed to do so: 'As it is for the good of all and the general well-being of the nation, I hereby consent; you may say to the people that I will remain.' '*Fico!*' – 'I will remain' – became one of the rallying cries of Brazilian independence.

Pedro's defiance of the Portuguese government electrified the crowd, but the Legion's response was swift: he was to be arrested and taken to Lisbon by force. On 11 January General de Avilez, commander of the Legion, assembled his troops on the strategic heights in the centre of the city overlooking the Campo de Sant'ana, where Pedro was organising a numerous but motley force which included both loyal military units and popular militia armed with blunderbusses, pistols, cudgels and knives. A tense stand-off ensued, with the Portuguese cavalry in position to slaughter the rebels and take control. But de Avilez hesitated to take such a step against the heir to his country's throne. The ill-organised army below was now moving to surround the troops on the heights, and de Avilez ordered his men back to Praia Grande across the Bay.

Through de Avilez's hesitation, the Portuguese lost the initiative. Pedro placed his men on the landward side of the Portuguese garrison, ordered troop ships to stand ready in the Bay, and informed de Avilez that he and the Legion must embark for Portugal. De Avilez determined to stay put in his secure position and wait for reinforcements from across the sea. Pedro summoned further forces from the provinces of Minas Gerais and São Paulo in the hinterland of Rio, brought up cannon to the scene, and occupied the forts of Santa Cruz and Pico to threaten the Portuguese. Even then, the Portuguese could almost certainly have held out: they occupied a strong position and were disciplined and well-trained in comparison with Pedro's numerically superior but largely amateur and haphazard forces. Nevertheless, Pedro issued an ultimatum: either the Portuguese soldiers embarked, or they would be put to the sword. It may have been a bluff – he was hardly unaware of the shortcomings of his own 'army' as against the trained soldiers of the Legion; yet on 15 February the Portuguese agreed to board the troop transports Pedro had placed at their disposal. He had won the first round.

The rupture was not yet formal, however, and the Portuguese government now tried to entice Pedro back by other means. Then in April the Greek independence movement asked King João for Pedro as their king. Pedro's refusal was immediate, and instead he vigorously set about paving the way for independence.

Following his announcement that he would remain in Brazil, Pedro had formed a ministry under the leadership of José Bonifácio de Andrada e Silva, an energetic and wily scholar, formerly Professor of Metallurgy at the University of Coimbra. A French diplomat described him as possessing 'a volcanic head with white hair'. Former counsellor to King João, poet and philosopher as well as metallurgist, he was a fervent conservative whose aim was to persuade Pedro to support the landed interests against liberal influences – in particular, those emanating from Portugal at this time. He was also instrumental in spreading the Freemasonry which had incubated so many of the pro-independence movements in South America. He nominally headed the Grand Orient Lodge which was set up in Rio in May 1822, but it was effectively hijacked by the senior warder, Gonçalves Ledo, a much less conservative figure who favoured a monarchy with very limited powers and soon engineered Bonifácio's replacement as Grand Master by Dom Pedro, under the Masonic name Guatimozin.

In June 1822, calling himself the Perpetual Defender of Brazil, Pedro set up a council of state to administer the country and summon a constituent assembly. Still professing loyalty to his father, he wrote with contempt of the côrtes that actually governed Portugal:

I say to that bloodthirsty mob that I, as Prince Regent of Brazil and its Perpetual Defender, mean to declare null and void all the decrees of those stinking and pestiferous Machiavellian troublemakers, and that those decrees will not be carried out ... If this frank declaration should irritate those Lusitanian-Spaniards, let them send an army against us, and we will show them what Brazilian valour is.

As part of the ritual of the Grand Orient Lodge, Ledo made Dom Pedro swear to abide by the decisions of the proposed constituent assembly, and Pedro raised no objection to this until Bonifácio (who had meanwhile established another Lodge, The Apostolate of the Noble Order of the Knights of the Holy Cross) persuaded him that he had been tricked, insisting – he was a brilliant constitutionalist – that his authority derived from the people as a whole, not just from the constituent assembly. Angrily, Pedro dissolved the Grand Orient and arrested Ledo, who had tried to escape to Buenos Aires dressed as a black woman. It seemed Bonifácio had scattered his enemies; he proceeded to sustain Pedro's imperial authority with a rule of iron, tracking down and arresting more liberal-minded constitutionalists. He also set up close contacts with Metternich and the Holy Alliance.

Meanwhile, Pedro set about winning over the rest of the country, shifting his attention to Minas Gerais, the mineral-rich state to the north, which refused to recognise his authority. Setting out for Vila Rica, the state capital, some two hundred miles away, he was joined by a growing army of pro-independence militia. He entered Vila Rica with only a few civilian escorts, however, a display of courage which so delighted the people that he was fulsomely welcomed by a large crowd. His opponents surrendered, there was no bloodshed, and he was able to ride straight back to Rio – displaying the same kind of speed and stamina over long distances that characterised his fellow liberators Bolívar and San Martín. In August he was off again, to São Paulo, to suppress another revolt. With a retinue of just five men he entered the country's second city, to be received with the same uproarious welcome – bells, salvos of artillery, fireworks, crowds, girls throwing flowers – as at Vila Rica. Mounted on his huge horse with silver trappings, he was the romantic hero–leader personified.

Resting briefly in São Paulo, he was riding one day outside the city with his aide, Lieutenant Canto e Melo, when he spotted a group of black slaves bearing a heavy litter trying to ford a stream. Pedro rode down to help them, and a face peered out of the litter to thank him: it was Canto e Melo's sister, Domitila de Castro, and the encounter was almost certainly arranged by her brother. By a curious twist of fate, the Canto e Melo family was descended from the mistress whose murder was so terribly avenged by Pedro's own ancestor Pedro I. According to contemporary reports, Domitila was strikingly beautiful, tall, green-eyed and graceful, highly intelligent, with a gentle, languorous voice. She instantly captivated the conqueror of so many women, and he fell head-over-heels in love with her. A year older than the Prince, Domitila was no innocent. At fourteen she had been married to a cavalry lieuten-ant; after bearing him two children she had had an affair with another officer, which incited her jealous husband to stab her in the thigh and abdomen, and they were now separated.

On his way back to São Paulo shortly afterwards from a visit to its port of Santos, Pedro was met by a court messenger. The letter he bore was from Bonifácio, with the information that General Madeira, Governor of Bahia, had proclaimed his refusal to submit to Pedro's regency, and that an expedition was being prepared in Portugal to come to his aid: the Portuguese côrtes was opposed to any form of self-gov-ernment for Brazil. On a green plain outside São Paulo a guard of honour had been drawn up to await Pedro's return. Riding up to his sol-diers, he began to tear the Portuguse insignia off his own blue uniform. 'Off with these emblems, soldiers,' he ordered, and they followed suit. Drawing his sword and raising it in the air he proclaimed: 'By the blood that flows in my veins and upon my honour, I swear to God to free Brazil!' The soldiers unsheathed their swords and swore the same oath. 'Independence or death!' he cried. The date was 7 September 1822, and this was the famous 'grito' – cry – of Ypiranga. That evening he com-posed the nation's first hymn of freedom: 'Arise, ye noble citizens, cast out all fear for good or ill, / for our brave breasts and our arms, shall be the walls that guard Brazil.' An even more poetic anthem was composed by the people of the city: '*Saracura, sabia, Bem-te-vi* and *beija-flor* (these are the names of four tropical birds, the last the humming-bird), / Let all sing, let all shout: / Long life to our Emperor.'

Some three months later, on 1 December 1822, the Archbishop of Rio de Janeiro crowned Pedro Emperor in a ceremony of gaudy pomp lasting several hours and deliberately modelled on that used in the cor-onation of the Holy Roman Emperors.

45

The Emperor's Burdens

European monarchs, even when absolute, tended to be bound by the conventions of tradition. Pedro, by contrast, was not only the natural hereditary monarch of Brazil but, as he saw it, empowered by a direct mandate from the people – a view which caused him to disregard other centres of power and led him into other similarly serious errors. The saving grace was that, despite his impulsiveness and occasional arbitrariness, Pedro was a man of civilised principles and genuine good intent, who mostly resisted tyrannical impulses.

The country he now ruled was by far the largest of the new nations of South America, and its population of four million was four times that of King João's Portugal. More than a quarter were black slaves; about 800,000 were pure-blooded Indians largely untouched by civilisation and living in the interior. There were 400,000 free blacks and about 300,000 'civilised' – that is, urban – Indians. About 700,000 were of mixed white, black and Indian blood. Only about 500,000 – an eighth – were pure white, the upper swathe of society. Of these, the most powerful were the bureaucracy, the mine-owners and ranchers in the south, the planters of the north, and the merchants and middle classes in the coastal towns. In addition to those from these privileged groups who resisted Brazil's declaration of independence, Pedro faced opposition from radicals and republicans who were suspicious of a monarch leading an independence movement, distrusting his commitment to real reform. There were others, too, who simply disapproved of his loose living and impulsive nature. Almost as soon as he became Emperor, the war for his ear began, between the conservatives and the radicals; victory went first one way, then the other. It was a sign of unexpected skill in so headstrong and untutored a young man that he should have survived longer than any other Liberator by playing off one faction against another.

His first task was to consolidate the independence he had proclaimed. The northern provinces of Bahia, Maranhão and Pará were still firmly in the hands of Portuguese troops and landowners loyal to Portugal's sovereignty and opposed to Pedro, but the distances involved meant that expeditions against them by land were impracticable. Fortuitously, there arrived in Rio de Janeiro in the middle of March 1823 the renowned Admiral Lord Cochrane, he who had so recently performed the miracles of subduing Spanish seapower in the Pacific and escorting San Martín's mission from Chile to Peru.

Cochrane had already been approached on the subject of entering Brazilian service in November 1822, by Antonio Correa, Brazil's consul in Buenos Aires, when his immediate response was cool: 'The war in the Pacific having been happily terminated by the total destruction of the Spanish naval force, I am, of course, free for the crusade of liberty in any other quarter of the globe ... I confess, however, that I had not hitherto directed my attention to the Brazils; considering that the struggle for the liberties of Greece – the most oppressed of modern states – afforded the fairest opportunity for enterprise and exertion.' But Rio de Janeiro was on his way back to Europe; on arriving there, he was escorted at once to the Emperor. Unusually, the two men took an immediate liking to one another. Pedro genuinely admired the crusty and sometimes difficult man nearly twice his age, and there was something about Pedro that appealed to Cochrane's paternal instincts. Impetuosity was certainly a characteristic they shared.

For 8,000 dollars a year, a handsome salary for the times, Cochrane agreed to enter the Emperor's service. Together they inspected the fleet. Compared even with his flotilla in Chile, it was a sorry spectacle – just eight ships, two of them unseaworthy and two of use only as fireships; a fifth, the *Maria de Gloria*, was 'little calculated to do substantial service'. Only his flagship, the 74-gun *Pedro Primeiro*, and the frigate *Piranga* were impressive; the *Liberal* was just adequate. The Portuguese fleet, by contrast, was known to consist of thirteen good ships – a battleship, five frigates, five corvettes, a schooner and a brig – and Cochrane's first encounter with them suggested that at last he had taken on too much. The *Pedro Primeiro*, under his command, led the three other seaworthy ships proudly into battle, sailing through a gap in the Portuguese lines and cutting four ships off from the main fleet. When Cochrane then ordered his ships to engage the enemy, the three others kept their distance, and the *Pedro Primeiro* found herself on her own.

Cochrane soon noticed that only a few of his guns were firing, and spo-
radically at that: the two sailors directing the gunnery were, he
discovered, trying to save on powder. Humiliated, the *Pedro Primeiro*
had to disengage. Her 160-strong crew consisted of some English and
American sailors, freed slaves, and the 'vagabondage' of Rio de Janeiro;
in a fury Cochrane, on returning to port, stripped the other three ships
of their British and American seamen and took them all aboard the
Pedro Primeiro to replace the most unsatisfactory of his existing crew. As
so often in his naval career, he was happiest commanding a single ship
against far greater odds.

His next target, in June 1823, was the Portuguese-held port of Bahia,
eight hundred miles or more up the coast towards the Equator. He
reconnoitred in typically bold fashion, sailing at night into the huge bay
there to map the anchorage where the Portuguese fleet lay. When hailed
by a nearby warship, he claimed to be a British merchant vessel. It was
a moonless night, and the wind suddenly dropped, becalming him right
under the guns of the Portuguese fleet and the shore batteries. Keeping
his nerve, he allowed his ship to drift downriver on the ebb tide, using
anchors when necessary to stop her foundering on rocks. Cochrane's
reputation earned in France and Chile had preceded him, and when
General Madeira at Bahia learned that the mysterious interloper had
been Cochrane's flagship, he remembered the Basque Roads and was
gripped with terror lest the fleet, trapped in its anchorage, should fall
easy prey to fireships and explosion ships.

Cochrane resorted to psychological warfare instead, urging Madeira
to surrender to avoid civilians being killed. Meanwhile the garrison at
Bahia was running short of supplies, as Cochrane's ships blockaded the
port. It seems remarkable that the Portuguese fleet should have been so
paralysed by what was, in effect, a one-ship flotilla. On 2 July Madeira
decided to evacuate the entire garrison and most of the civilian population, in some seventy transports, accompanied by the thirteen
Portuguese warships, to the safer anchorage of São Luis de Maranhão,
more than a thousand miles away on the northern coast. Cochrane's four
ships, working like jackals round a herd on the savannahs, began to pick
off the transports one by one. The Portuguese warships preferred to keep
their distance, while even the armed troop-ships put up little resistance.
Cochrane's men simply boarded one ship after another and, as he had
not sailors to spare to man them, dismasted them so that they could
travel no further but were blown back into the Bay of Bahia.

Several thousand soldiers were thus immobilised. Cochrane hoped to lure the Portuguese warships into attacking him, so that he could detach them from the rest of the convoy in a futile chase into mid ocean, but they steered clear. Next, on 16 July, he attempted to launch a night attack on the warships themselves. The *Pedro Primeiro* was crippled when her mainsail split into two, but because of the dark the Portuguese did not realise what had happened and Cochrane was able to break off the engagement safely. Having disabled half the Portuguese garrison at Bahia, he was frustrated by the sight of the other half, and the warships, sailing off into the equatorial haze.

But if he had lost the Portuguese fleet, he at least knew – from captured despatches – where it was headed, and also that once her mainsail had been repaired the greater speed of the *Pedro Primeiro* would enable him to overtake it. Leaving his three lesser ships behind he sped northwards as soon as he could towards São Luís de Maranhão, where he arrived on 26 July, well ahead of the sluggish Portuguese fleet. He hoisted Portuguese colours, and awaited a brig sent out from shore by the Governor, Dom Agostinho Antonio de Fama, who believed him to be the advance guard of the Portuguese evacuation fleet from Bahia.

As they boarded the *Pedro Primeiro* the members of the welcoming party were immediately seized; the captain was then despatched ashore with a message from Cochrane to the Governor, asserting that the Portuguese fleet had been completely destroyed, and that the *Pedro Primeiro* was the advance guard of an awesome Brazilian convoy. Cochrane's message declared: 'I am anxious not to let loose the Imperial troops of Bahia upon Maranhão, exasperated as they are at the injuries and cruelties exercised towards themselves and their countrymen, as well as by the plunder of the people and churches of Bahia.' It was suggested that his own ship was filled with just such bloodthirsty men. However, he went on to offer generous terms, which included the repatriation to Portugal aboard merchant ships of the Portuguese troops in Maranhão. In fact, of course, Cochrane was most anxious to get them away before the genuine Portuguese fleet arrived to expose his bluff. He had only his ship's crew to pit against the several thousand men stationed at Maranhão, the well-defended shore batteries, and the reduced but still formidable force being brought in by Madeira.

To Cochrane's gratified astonishment, Dom Agostinho at once agreed to his terms. Cochrane's meagre force occupied the defences while the

Portuguese garrison was evacuated; as they headed for Portugal, oblivious to the last, they must have crossed on the open seas with the Portuguese fleet bound for Maranhão.

Finding Maranhão under Cochrane's control, Madeira and the fleet turned northwards towards the last remaining Portuguese stronghold, Pará. But Cochrane had already despatched Captain Grenfell, in a captured ship, to repeat the trick there, and although Pará's authorities were not deceived they knew that they could not hold out long without assistance; but one of the two royalist armies was on its way to Portugal and the other, Madeira's, had not arrived from Maranhão. On 12 August they surrendered. After just six months under the Portuguese flag, and as a result of perhaps the greatest hoax in naval history, Cochrane had delivered to Pedro the whole of northern Brazil. Of all his escapades this was the most audacious, if not the most dangerous.

Under the influence of Bonifácio, Pedro as Emperor had begun increasingly to resemble an old-style Portuguese colonial monarch, and Latin America's other newly independent republics saw his empire as a reactionary Trojan horse in their midst. Bonifácio's policies did however have the merit of inducing the European Powers to refrain from conspiring to overthrow Pedro, who was seen as the puppet of a powerful conservative minister in league (through Metternich) with Europe's absolute monarchies.

Both Emperor and minister had to work within the constraints of the radicals' proposal for a constituent assembly as a means of uniting the country's separate provinces at the centre, and this assembly became a focus of opposition to Bonifácio. Too often high-handed in his dealings with others, he was increasingly resented by Pedro, too, as an overbearing father-figure. On 15 July 1823 the Emperor, reasserting his independence, suddenly forced his chief minister out of office. Learning, at a time when he was swathed in bandages following a riding accident, of a plot by Bonifácio's 'Apostles' to assassinate him, he rose unhesitatingly from his sick-bed, made for the Masonic meeting hall with a group of soldiers, and exposed the traitors. Metternich, when he heard of Bonifácio's fall, observed with cold fury that Pedro 'had given fresh proof of his weakness of character and a weak-mindedness that borders on dementia'.

Bonifácio, in spite of his conservatism, now joined the opposition in the constituent assembly led by Antonio Carlos, head of the 'Brazilian' faction, who held that Pedro was too closely associated with Brazil's wealthy Portuguese merchants and landowners. The Emperor was in considerable danger, now that his ultra-conservative former supporters had allied themselves against him with his radical opponents. The press, in particular the radical newspaper *Tamoyo*, called for the government's overthrow. The assembly began to threaten the Emperor's prerogatives, in particular when it voted itself the power to override the imperial veto. *Tamoyo*, none too subtly recalling the fates of Charles I and Louis XVI, argued that 'a government which goes counter to the will of the nation must be overthrown at once ... It is dangerous to drive the people to despair and force them to demand by violence that which they as yet seek only by constitutional means.'

Such was the state of affairs when Cochrane returned triumphantly to Rio in November 1823. A mere two days later – 11 November – the Emperor, resentful of his treatment at the hands of the assembly, sent an armed detachment to close it down, and arrested its principal leaders. Bonifácio was exiled (an exile which was to last seven years), and a Council of State, its members nominated by the Emperor, was set the task of drawing up a new constitution. Cochrane made himself no friends by warning Pedro against 'individuals who will wickedly take advantage [of the dissolution of the assembly] to kindle the flames of discord', and suggesting that the Emperor should adopt the British constitution 'in its most perfect practical form': the British constitution was considered far too liberal by many of Pedro's supporters, while its limitations on the powers of the monarch were not to his own taste.

Nevertheless, Pedro's regard for the admiral and his romantic exploits remained unshaken, even when the usual argument broke out over Cochrane's share of the prize money, which he calculated should be £122,000, since £1 million had been seized in Maranhão. However, the Emperor was in an awkward position, since the 'prize' money was largely the property of his own subjects, who now professed their loyalty to him. He did not interfere when the prize tribunal awarded Cochrane only about an eighth of what he sought, some £14,000. Again the admiral was left furious at being cheated of what he considered were his just deserts. Kitty and his baby daughter, finding the Rio summer unhealthy, sailed back to England in February 1824, and the following month Cochrane tendered his resignation.

The new constitution which came into effect in March 1824 gave the Emperor wide-ranging powers – as 'moderator' – to bypass the legislature, the judiciary, and local authorities. He appointed provincial presidents and he appointed senators – for life. He could dissolve parliament, and he could veto legislation. The Church was placed under his control. Only a chamber of deputies and local councils elected on a tightly restricted suffrage retained some power.

As the months passed, it became apparent that Cochrane's outspoken views and litigious behaviour were making the new authorities in Rio suspicious of the British officers in the Brazilian Navy. In May the heroic Captain Grenfell – who later became Admiral of Brazil, but had been denied any share of the prize money from the northern provinces – was arrested and his possessions and papers seized from his ship. In June Cochrane was warned by Madame Bonpland (the botanist's wife) of a sinister plot against himself. His house had been surrounded by troops, but Cochrane climbed out of a window and rode straight to the Emperor. Pedro had gone to bed, but Cochrane insisted on seeing him. He was assured that the Emperor knew nothing of the plot; he then suggested that the naval review scheduled for the next day, during which the proposed seizures were to be carried out, should be cancelled on the grounds of Pedro's indisposition. The ministers who had planned the coup would thus be obliged to attend upon the Emperor, while Cochrane and his men could slip aboard his ship to resist any attempt on the part of the 'anti-Brazilian administration' to board it; any who did so 'would certainly be regarded as pirates and treated as such'. Pedro agreed, the plan worked perfectly, and Cochrane naturally called on the Emperor the following day to pay his respects at the 'sickbed'.

Within weeks, Brazil's government again had need of the man it had attempted to destroy. Civil war was raging between rival factions in Maranhão. In Pernambuco (now Recife) an insurrection of republicans and radicals led by a Carmelite named Caneca had broken out. But Cochrane's sailors had not been paid, and the admiral was more than reluctant to become involved. Pedro then himself guaranteed Cochrane his salary as First Admiral of Brazil for as long as he wished, and half-pay for the rest of his life following his retirement; in addition, the sum of £100,000 was to be awarded to the crews. This proved acceptable, and in August 1824 1,200 troops aboard transports were convoyed north by Cochrane's fleet to control the rebellion, reaching Pernambuco in mid August. Cochrane was still infuriated by the behaviour of the Brazilian government, and his attitude to the rebels was ambivalent. Fearing that the Emperor would take Brazil back under Portuguese domination, they argued the case for a 'Confederation of the Equator, a kind of republican United States of Northern South America'. Cochrane got on well with the President of Pernambuco, Manuel de Carvalho, but refused to join him, and Carvalho refused Cochrane's offer of mediation.

Somewhat reluctantly, Cochrane sent the schooner *Leopoldina*, his smallest available ship, to negotiate the shallow waters of the bay and bombard the town, but she had to withdraw because of the damage the rebel guns were inflicting on her. The governor of Pernambuco was sufficiently demoralised to surrender in September to the troops Cochrane put ashore; Carvalho escaped on a raft, and was later picked up by a British ship. Caneca, chief ideologist of the rebellion, was captured, and executed early in 1825 – an uncharacteristic act of ruthlessness on the Emperor's part.

Cochrane went on to Maranhão, where Miguel Bruce, 'president' of the local junta, accompanied by an army of bloodthirsty freed slaves, was the chief instigator among many sources of trouble. For this reason, rather than because he favoured any of the others, he had Bruce's men rounded up and confined to ships in the harbour, then took upon himself the office of president. Fighting continued to break out intermittently between the rival factions, and Cochrane went ashore every so often to restore order.

As the months dragged on, Cochrane and many of his men began to fall ill in the foetid equatorial climate. Despairing of the politics of Brazil and certain he would get no further money from the government in Rio, he made the decision to sail in search of 'cooler climates' – had he had it in mind since leaving Rio? He transferred to a smaller ship, the *Piranga*, sent the *Pedro Primeiro* back to Rio, and set off in the middle of May. By early June he had 'drifted' as far as the Azores. Cochrane later insisted that he had planned to return to Rio, once he and his men had recovered from the heat – but odd problems arose: the timbers of the *Piranga* were found to be rotten, the masts and the rigging badly affected by gales. Cochrane found he could not make it back to Rio, but must sail for England: the *Piranga* arrived at Spithead on 26 June 1825, where his salute was returned as he sailed in. It was the first recognition accorded the Brazilian flag by any European power.

How crucial a role did Cochrane play in Brazil's independence struggle? Some Brazilian historians (for example, Sergio Correa da Costa, author of an excellent biography of Dom Pedro) fail to mention him at all. Their reluctance is understandable. Through trickery, allied to apparently effortless seamanship and a complete disregard for danger which contrasted sharply with the ineptitude and cowardice of local commanders, Cochrane made victory appear almost ridiculously simple. Brazilians could hardly boast of having hired this foreign admiral to show how easily their opponents could be routed. In any case, there was much less satisfaction in overthrowing the relatively benevolent Portuguese rule than other South Americans derived from overthrowing Spanish oppression. But without Cochrane's intervention, it is probable that the revolt against Portugal would have been confined to the south: he was responsible for sending the Portuguese forces in Bahia and Maranhão packing, and for securing the northern strongholds for the Emperor with remarkably little bloodshed.

In Portugal the Vilafrancada uprising of 1823 swept away the liberal côrtes and Pedro's ageing father, João VI, regained control. He despatched an emissary to reincorporate Brazil under the Portuguese Crown – but the envoy was not permitted to land. Privately João told Pedro that he could not recognise Brazil for fear of arousing opposition in Portugal – but that he would not actually send troops to crush independence there: he 'would only send Portuguese troops in order to aid the Crown Prince in putting down an insurrection'. Following the promulgation of the new constitution in March 1824 Brazil was irreversibly independent, under an Emperor with virtually absolute powers who could boast that he had liberated Brazil from colonial rule largely without resort to the bloodshed, strife and dislocation that had characterised the wars of independence of Spanish America.

His crowning moment came in August 1825 when the negotiations of Great Britain's Foreign Secretary, George Canning, and the British ambassador in Rio, Sir Charles Stuart, to mediate a settlement with Portugal which permitted international recognition of the new state reached a successful conclusion. Under the terms of the agreement Pedro was to pay £2m in respect of Portuguese debts to Britain and João's personal property in Brazil; João VI assumed the title of Emperor of Brazil *pro forma*, but resigned it in favour of Pedro; and Brazil, under pressure from the British, agreed to stop importing slaves by 1830.

This marked a turning-point in Pedro's popularity. The agreement with respect to slavery incensed the planters of the north, and there was considerable resentment about the transfer of funds in favour of the former colonial leech, Portugal, and especially of João, who had sailed away with the national treasury in 1821. Worse was to follow: in 1826 King João died, and it seemed to Brazilians that their country had been reunited with Portugal at a stroke as a Court official arrived in Rio to render the Brazilian Emperor homage as Pedro IV, King of Portugal. Pedro accepted the tribute, appointed seventy-seven peers and introduced a new constitution – then conditionally abdicated in favour of his daughter, Maria da Glória, aged seven. He understood that only by renouncing the Portuguese throne could he save his Brazilian empire – Brazilians would not accept a unification of the two crowns – but his actions precipitated a crisis.

The constitutional Charter he had promulgated for Portugal was viewed throughout most of continental Europe as ultra-liberal: Spain recoiled at the idea of having such a regime on her doorstep; the Russian Foreign Minister, Nesselrode, declared that Brazil had cast a firebrand into Europe; Metternich thundered that it was 'in the highest degree improper that a New World potentate should introduce a constitution into the Old World and turn a strict monarchy into a limited one.' Only Canning applauded.

In Portugal herself the clergy, the judiciary, the nobility and the gentry all turned against the new constitution. It was argued that the monarch could not live outside Portugal; moreover, that Pedro was no longer Portuguese, Portugal having formally recognised Brazil as an independent nation. This was the cue for Pedro's venomous mother, Queen Carlota, to step onto the stage again. Already in 1824 she had tried to instigate the overthrow by absolutists, under the leadership of her favourite son Miguel, of the constitutionalists supporting her estranged husband King João. João, narrowly escaping aboard a British ship, had rallied his forces and despatched Miguel into exile in Vienna. Carlota now argued that, as Pedro had no rights to it, the throne should therefore pass not to Maria da Glória but to Miguel, and poured her vast inherited wealth into the hands of the absolutists who supported him. Pedro had in fact made it a condition of his abdication in his daughter's favour that Miguel should take his oath to the Charter and marry Maria, acting as Regent during her minority. Adhesion to the Charter formed no part of the plans of Carlota, the absolutists or Miguel, but early in

October 1827, prompted by Metternich, Miguel swore to uphold it, and at the end of the month was formally betrothed to Maria. He returned to Portugal in February 1828 to wild demonstrations of enthusiasm; in June he was offered the Crown 'by acclamation', and in July he took the oath as King before the côrtes. The absolutists, now confident in their power, decreed the extirpation of liberalism and Freemasonry, and executions and imprisonments ran rife. 'Cut off heads for me! Cut off heads for me!' demanded the terrible Dowager Queen Carlota. 'The French Revolution cut off forty thousand, and for all that the population did not diminish!'

Further crisis marked the fateful year 1826: war on Brazil's southern frontier. In 1817 King João had invaded the Banda Oriental del Uruguay, the 'Eastern Shore' of the river Uruguay, on the pretext of restoring order following Artigas's declaration of independence and the subsequent hostilities with Argentina; four years later it had been absorbed formally into Brazil. In April 1825 a group of Uruguayan nationalists – the Immortal Thirty-Three, as they dubbed themselves – crossed the Paraná river to wage guerrilla war against Brazil. Supported by Buenos Aires, they secured popular backing for a reincorporation of the Banda into Argentina. An army under General Lecor and a small fleet under Admiral Rodrigo Lobo despatched by the Emperor made no headway: both were incompetent, their men ill-equipped and underfed. At this stage, when he badly needed friends, Pedro fell out with the imperious Sir Charles Stuart, the British ambassador, who had always opposed Brazil's expansionist pretensions and now warned of Simón Bolívar's disapproval. When Stuart had the temerity to complain of an occasion on which the Emperor left Rio without informing him, Pedro's reply was scorching:

> Upon leaving, I had the ship's gun fired for the precise purpose of letting you know that I was going and did not care to wait. And do not come around to me again with any revelations as to how Bolívar with twelve thousand men is marching on our frontiers. I am not afraid of the King of France, nor the King of England, nor anyone else. I am a man who knows how to die sword in hand. As for you, sir, if you have any business to transact with me, go back to Rio and wait.

Canning also declined to support Brazil in this matter, happy enough to see the establishment under British auspices of an independent state on the east bank of the Plate which could serve as a British naval base in the South Atlantic. Pedro despatched a new commander, the Marques de Barbacena, in an attempt to stem the tide of failure in the south. Then, as Argentinian and Uruguayan forces threatened to invade the Brazilian state of Rio Grande do Sul, he prepared to take command himself. In November he sailed from Rio with ten ships.

46

Leopoldina, Domitila and Amelia

An ever-present complication for Pedro during these years was his continuing infatuation with Domitila de Castro. Ever since first setting eyes on her outside São Paulo in 1821, he had been obsessed with her, and his cavalcade of lovers was forgotten in his indiscreet devotion to her. He rained preferment upon her, and upon her family. He rode through a storm one night to beat up her former husband for making insulting remarks about her. When Domitila was refused admission to the Rio theatre, Pedro closed it down at once. The court ladies snubbed her, but the unsuspecting Empress appointed her First Lady-in-Waiting.

In May 1824 Domitila bore Pedro a daughter. In October 1825 he created his mistress a viscountess, and early in December she had a second child by him, a boy – just days after Leopoldina bore him his legitimate heir, Pedro. The Emperor and his mistress carefully concealed their liaison from Leopoldina; she was too other-worldly, too engrossed in her scientific studies to suspect, and no one at court dared enlighten her. The Austrian ambassador Mareschal, who acted as her adviser and kept an eye on her interests, noted carefully: 'Notwithstanding the fact that he has a favourite mistress, he has never ceased for an instant to show himself a good husband, and takes advantage of every opportunity to praise the virtues of his consort.' Pedro wrote to Domitila that the Empress had been

> near catching me in the act, but your prayers saved me ... It is better when I go out in the daytime that I should not come past for a word with you, in order that she may not suspect our – our holy love – and this, even if I have to go out of my way; and it is also best for me not to speak of you at home but rather of any other woman whatsoever, in order that she may suspect another and we may go on living in peace and enjoying this wonderful love of ours.

It was in the course of a sea voyage to Bahia province, when Pedro would steal away to meet his beloved elsewhere in the ship, that the Empress became fully aware of the liaison and its intensity. When they returned to Rio, Pedro had Domitila installed in a luxurious house near the royal palace. From its windows he could exchange signals with her: 'Let me know who is there; I can see from here two chaises standing in front of the house ... You were seated at the window but did not answer my signal, although I was looking through my glass for a sight of you ... I was about to have supper; it was around twenty minutes past nine, and I saw that you were very prudently accompanied by a taper.' During the following months he appeared to lose all sense of shame and discretion. In May 1826 he officially recognised Domitila's illegitimate daughter as his own, and in July made her a duchess; she was to be addressed as 'Your Highness'. He openly looked after the child himself, and wrote to her mother with the solicitude of a nanny:

> Maria Isabel was inoculated by me today ... There is nothing the matter with the child; she slept well, but the only thing is she had difficulty in moving her bowels; I am going to give her some Viennese Water, which ought to help her ... Mariquita has taken an ounce of water and still no action; I gave her another and she vomited; and if she does not have an action within the next three hours, I shall give her some more ... The Duchess has a high colour and there are dried sores on her skin.

In full dress uniform he attended a splendid banquet at Domitila's house; in October 1826 he raised her to the rank of marchioness, created her father a viscount, and gave five other relatives senior positions about the court. Always an outgoing, spontaneous person, prepared to wrestle with his own bodyguards or to tackle major confrontations himself, the Emperor was a slave to Domitila's moods, and a prey to childish jealousy. Sometimes he wrote to her angrily: 'I do not care to take second place to anyone, not even to God, if that were possible ... I may tell you that your habit of looking up at the ceiling when I catch you gazing at others is not very clever ... How can you expect me not to have doubts when they are born of love?' On other occasions he begged her for forgiveness, as a slave to love: 'My girl, if I am sometimes a bit rude with you, this is due to my despair at not being able to enjoy your company as much as I should like. This it is that makes me do such things. They do not come from the heart, for my heart adores you, and always feels for you something that I cannot express ... My girl, do not hold it against me; for I love you with all my heart ...'

Their passion had its moments of comedy. Meeting a young officer leaving her house late one night as he was going in, Pedro attacked him with his riding whip. The young man fired his pistol – but the bullet struck a painting. It seems he was not punished. Domitila suspected her own sister, recently created a baroness, of intending to deceive her with Pedro. On another occasion, following a quarrel, she noticed that the Emperor was watching her window through his spyglass; she had the shutters firmly closed, and he promptly sent her a note: 'Much obliged for shutting the windows just when I was trying to get a sight of you ... forgive me if I use strong language, but it is my heart, which belongs to you, that is speaking.'

Domitila was portrayed by the Emperor's enemies as a possessive schemer who had Pedro in the palm of her hand, and was likened to his shrewish, interfering mother. The truth was different. She was extremely beautiful, and deeply in love with him. She certainly liked to spend money on clothes and jewels, and loyally and assiduously promoted her family and friends; but there is no evidence that she used her power for political purposes, or indeed was even much interested in affairs of state. She seems to have been strong-willed, and inspired respect in those who met her, but was a good deal less impulsive, more restrained and discreet than her royal lover.

The Empress Leopoldina, plain and plump, science-obsessed and motherly, was widely popular. A close friend admitted that, 'not to exaggerate in the least, she was dressed like a true gypsy, down to the slippers even; no necklace, no earrings, not a ring on her fingers.' Her very scattiness, and her lack of pomposity – in pleasing contrast to the dragon Carlota, suffered by Brazilians for most of a decade – won her the admiration of court and country alike. When she discovered Pedro's affair with Domitila, and its intensity, she maintained a stiff upper lip. Mareschal was exasperated: 'It appears to me impossible that Madame the Archduchess does not see what is going on under her very eyes.' The French ambassador wrote to his government: 'The Empress's self-restraint is sometimes carried to the point of insouciance as regards the liaison of her august Consort with Madame de Santós [Domitila].'

The truth was that, despite his philandering, she was desperately in love with Pedro, who remained her romantic ideal of a prince, and afraid of losing him if she confronted him. Only twice is she known to have done so, when he spent two days by the bedside of Domitila's dying father, and when he created his mistress a marchioness. On the second occasion she asked Mareschal to alert her father, the Emperor of Austria, to the scandal. The sadness and rage she suppressed within herself sometimes slipped out in letters to a European friend: 'I could bear anything, as I have in the past, except seeing the little one treated as my children's equal; I tremble with rage when I look at her, and it is the greatest sacrifice on my part to receive her.' She compared Domitila to 'infamous women like Pompadour and Maintenon, especially when they are possessed of no education whatsoever'.

What really affected her was the mounting evidence that Pedro was besottedly in love with Domitila, as he had never been with his other mistresses, nor with her. In the summer of that fateful year, 1826, it seemed that tension and misery, caused by the flaunting of her husband's relationship, finally began to destroy Leopoldina: she fell into deep depression and melancholy. When Pedro left on his expedition to Rio Grande do Sul, she was pregnant again. She gave him a ring set with two diamonds, on the inside their names, intertwined with two hearts. A week later she miscarried, and started to run a high fever. After a few days she briefly improved, then began to hallucinate: she was sure she was being poisoned, and that Domitila and her infant daughter were using black magic against her. She died on 11 December; the actual cause was probably an infection following her miscarriage, but almost certainly Leopoldina herself would have said that she died of a broken heart.

A senior minister, the Marques de Paranagua, warned Pedro: 'I ought not to conceal from Your Imperial Majesty the fact that the people are murmuring, and greatly, regarding the origin of the affliction, choosing to attribute it to moral rather than to physical causes.' The rumour mill in Rio in fact ran wild. It was suggested, with some plausibility, that during a row about Domitila Pedro had kicked Leopoldina, causing her miscarriage. More luridly, it was said she had been poisoned by Domitila, who had also swapped her own son Pedro for the Infante Pedro. What had been merely a subject of amusement and gossip in Court circles now assumed tragic, even dangerous, proportions: the people's Emperor was seen as responsible for his wife's death – whether this was the result of neglect, humiliation and callousness, or of connivance with the hated Domitila.

As soon as the news reached Pedro in the south he commandeered a ship, refusing to wait for it to be provisioned, so that the crew had to survive on a diet of rice and salt beef. When the ship was becalmed, he tried to get himself rowed the last thirty miles. In a paroxysm of grief he carved a wooden crown for his wife's bier, shaped her rosewood coffin with his own hands, mourned her in verse. With her death, he discovered the depth of his feelings for her, deeper perhaps than for the beautiful, passionate Domitila. For six months, bad-tempered and remorseful, he was often to be found inconsolably embracing Leopoldina's portrait. He shunned Domitila – whether for political reasons, because of her unpopularity, or because he blamed her for the tragedy, is not known. Then he began to weaken: he went to see Domitila's latest child by him, another girl. By September 1827 he was writing to her: 'Goodbye, my dear girl, until eleven o'clock, when I shall be there without fail to enjoy the greatest pleasure that I know, that of embracing you.'

Pedro's abrupt departure from Rio Grande do Sul in December 1826 had left Barbacena as commander there. In February 1827 he confronted an Argentine–Uruguayan thrust near Passo do Rosário on the Brazilian side of the border. The 7,000 Brazilian defenders fought vigorously against 12,000 opponents, but their cavalry were savaged. After eleven hours' vicious fighting, which left 500 Argentinians dead to the Brazilians' 120, the Brazilians retreated; but the Argentinians, having run out of money and ammunition with which to fight the campaign, had also had enough, and withdrew across the border.

Six months later, under determined pressure from the British and the French, whose commerce had been disrupted by the war, both Brazil and Argentina gave up their claims to the Banda Oriental. On 27 April 1827 Uruguay was born – the República Oriental del Uruguay, the latest independent Spanish American republic. The war had been unpopular in Brazil, because it was expensive, and because it was seen as an unwise extension of João's imperialistic follies. Pedro's employment of Irish and German mercenaries also contributed to its unpopularity. Perhaps unfairly, he was blamed for it, as he had been criticised for the Brazilian–Portuguese treaty of 1825.

The new national assembly met in May 1826, and its first sessions reflected the growing resentment against the Emperor. A deputy, Pedro de Araujo Lima, was appointed prime minister as a conciliatory gesture towards parliamentary institutions, although he was not firm enough for Pedro, and was considered too moderate by other members of the assembly. Tensions continued to mount in Rio. On one celebrated occasion, Pedro hurled a stream of abuse from a palace window as the deputies entered the assembly building. There were rumours that the assembly would depose him, counter-rumours that he was preparing a military coup against it – something the senators and deputies sought to avert by denying the army funds.

After Leopoldina's death, Pedro's ministers had insisted that if he were not to lose his throne he must find a new Empress, one to restore to it respect, and popularity – which ruled out the scandalous and unpopular Domitila. Reluctantly he agreed that a European princess be sought; meanwhile, the death of their third child from meningitis effected a reconciliation between the Emperor and his mistress, and by April 1828 she was back in Rio. The Russian Ambassador reported her as 'aiming at marrying, and at the throne'. In a note to her in May Pedro signed himself her 'friend and lover until death'. The Swedish ambassador noted at this time that her influence was 'greater than it ever was before'.

The two emissaries despatched to secure a new Empress – the Marques de Rezende and the Marques de Barbacena (Pedro's chief minister) – had meanwhile, with astonishing naïvety, first approached Leopoldina's father, the Emperor of Austria. His minister Metternich, brilliantly astute architect of the reactionary Holy Alliance and supporter of Pedro's mother and brother, considered the Emperor of Brazil a dangerous subversive and therefore settled down gleefully to a relentless and devious campaign to discredit him. European newspapers depicted Pedro as a serial adulterer, and his court as little better than a brothel, dominated by Domitila. By February 1828, several princesses had refused the honour of becoming Empress of Brazil, but Barbacena thought he knew why: 'Secret. Suspect treachery to keep you from having more children. Do not give the least indication of this as I expect to get at the truth of the matter within a week.'

This was not soon enough to avert a further humiliation. At Metternich's prompting, Rezende had asked the Prince of Sweden, in exile at the Austrian Court, for the hand of his sister Cecilia. Barbacena reported the outcome: 'The prince pretended to accept the offer and let it become known to the Emperor of Austria, whereupon the entire diplomatic corps became aware of it; and there was poor Rezende betaking himself to Karlsruhe on the day specified and at the appointed hour to make the formal request of the princess herself, only to receive from her a round No, a fact which Metternich took care to have published in all the gazettes.' Convinced that the affair was enough 'to convince the most incredulous of Metternich's perfidy', he set about the task of finding 'some princess who is not under (Austrian) domination' – one who also met Pedro's desire for 'a princess who by reason of her birth, beauty, virtue, and education shall bring happiness to me and to the empire ... if any of [these four qualities] are to be dispensed with, let it be the first and the last ...' It was not easy. Barbacena called next on Princess Louisa of Denmark – but returned 'with a face that would scare a child from the breast', and explained why:

> I now know that the princess is, true enough, an elegant young lady; but her eyes, eyelids, and eyebrows are those of an albino, as is the case with all the princesses of that country, which is enough to render even the greatest beauty in the world repulsive-looking. Albinos are what we in Brazil call 'high yellows', or octoroons, and would Your Imperial Majesty care for such a bride as that? Certainly not. I therefore shall let matters drop in this quarter and carry on elsewhere.

Rezende at last discovered a suitable girl: the Princess Amelia Napoleon of Leuchtenberg, both chaste and beautiful, was a granddaughter of Napoleon's first Empress, Joséphine, and belonged to a minor German princely family hostile to Metternich. According to Rezende, she had 'an airy body such as that which the painter Correggio in his pictures bestows upon the Queen of Sheba, and an affability that melts the hearts of all who know her; upon returning home I had to exclaim, "By the five wounds of Our Lord, Jesus Christ, sinner that I am, why am not I the Emperor of Brazil?"' Metternich continued her subversion by mischievously leaking the allegation that Pedro had already secretly wed Domitila, but to no avail: in Munich, on 2 August 1829, Pedro was married by proxy for the second time.

The acquisition of a new Empress went some way towards bolstering the Emperor's position. He had already regained a measure of respect by disentangling himself from Domitila, whose banishment from court was a precondition of the marriage negotiations. She resigned herself to the situation with remarkably good grace, became the mistress of a general in São Paulo, Rafael Tobias, by whom she had six children, and eventually married him in 1842. She was widowed before her sixtieth birthday, having become noted for her charitable work, and also a vigorous political figure in her own right.

The Emperor, it seemed, was a reformed man as he rapturously greeted his seventeen-year-old bride, recognising her from the picture he had been sent. It showed Amelia to have inherited the stunning looks of her Beauharnais grandmother, and Chalaca, Pedro's former groom of the wardrobe and childhood crony, noted how 'our master, ever since that picture came, has been another person; he no longer sleeps away from home but always pays his calls accompanied by chamberlains, and there is nothing new to report [on the sexual front].' At first the young Empress was understandably shy, but the ice was broken when Pedro welcomed her in his execrable French and she burst out laughing. Barbacena wrote: 'Ever since that moment the bridal couple have been as wrapped up in each other as if they had been in love for many years, and the enthusiasm on each side is so great that at this moment I look upon them as the two happiest beings in all the world.' Little more than half Pedro's age, Amelia proved quite unlike the blue-stocking Leopoldina: beautiful, stylishly dressed and self-assured, she reorganised the royal household 'even to the expenses of the pantry', and played a politely benevolent role in supporting Barbacena.

But the tug-of-war between the Emperor and the assembly continued, until Barbacena was appointed chief minister in December 1829. Able and courageous, he began to restore firm government while at the same time reining back the assembly by constitutional means. But hardline conservative elements who blamed the parliamentary style of government for Brazil's constitutional paralysis were increasingly in the ascendant, advising Pedro that he must take firm action, and that Barbacena was too liberal.

Events now moved to a head. In July 1830 the absolutist Charles X of France was overthrown, and the contagion of revolution spread again to Brazil. Pedro was assaulted in the press, most famously perhaps by Evaristo de Veiga: 'Charles X has ceased to reign, and may the same thing happen to any monarch who, betraying his vows, shall undertake to destroy the free institutions of his country.' An Italian journalist was murdered, apparently by government officials, after writing in support of the 1830 revolution. In this incendiary climate, Pedro was persuaded to dismiss Barbacena, with the result that, travelling in Minas Gerais, he was greeted with outright hostility by the same people who years before had welcomed him so joyously. On his return the Rio crowds, more loyal, called out 'Long live the Emperor, so long as he abides by the constitution'. He was accused of having set up a secret cabinet headed by Chalaca. As the confrontation worsened, he was advised to appoint a liberal chief minister, in order to defuse his critics. But Pedro, however progressive his instincts, would not be dictated to.

The old autocrat José Bonifácio de Andrada was invited back from exile – perhaps with a view to making him chief minister; but with his ultra-conservative antecedents he was hardly the man to placate the opposition. Pedro then appointed a group of men who had supported him in the earliest days of independence; now all gloriously ennobled, they included the marquesses of Paranagua, Baependi, Inhambupe and Aracati. The 'ministry of the marquesses' proved the last straw for both his detractors in the assembly and the growing swell of popular opinion. On the morning of 6 April 1831 a huge crowd gathered in Rio's extensive Sant'Ana park, demanding that the old government be reinstated. Pedro sent them a dismissive message:

> You may say to the people, that I have received their petition. You may further tell them that the late ministry did not merit my confidence, and that I shall do what I think best. You may remind them, also, that I am acting in accordance with the constitution. It is necessary for me to defend those rights of mine that are guaranteed by that constitution, even at the sacrifice of everything that I possess, and of my own person. I am ready to do everything for the people, but nothing under compulsion by the people.

Worryingly, many soldiers began to join the demonstrators; but Pedro refused to back down. His principal military commander, Major Luiz Alves de Lima (later, as Duque de Caxias, Brazil's most famous soldier), begged him in the small hours of the same morning for permission to disperse the demonstrators by force: 'If Your Majesty wishes to put down the movement, nothing could be easier. All you will have to do is to go this very night to your Santa Cruz plantation and there assemble the militia. I myself am prepared to lead them.' Pedro replied, 'The plan is one worthy of the loyal Major Lima; but I cannot accept it, for I would not have a single drop of Brazilian blood spilled for my sake. And so, let the major and his battalion also proceed at once to the Campo de Sant'Ana.' He strode up and down his study, exhausted and pale. By his refusal to use force that fateful morning it seemed that he had abandoned any choice: there was nothing for it but to surrender to the demonstrators, and install the government they wanted.

Or was there? Perhaps he had one last surprise in store. He dashed off a note and said, as he handed it to the rebels' emissary: 'There they have my abdication; I hope that they will be happy. I am going to Europe, leaving behind me a country that I have always loved and still love deeply.' Then he explained his decision to the British and French ambassadors, who were present:

> I prefer to descend from the throne with honour rather than to go on reigning as a sovereign who has been dishonoured and degraded. Those born in Brazil no longer want me, for the reason that I am Portuguese. I have been expecting this for a long time, have seen it coming ever since I visited Minas. My son has the advantage over me in that he is a Brazilian by birth. The Brazilians respect him. He will have no difficulty in governing, and the constitution will guarantee him his rights. I renounce the crown with the glory of ending as I began – constitutionally.

With this he embraced Amelia, weeping. The French ambassador commented that 'he knows better how to abdicate than to reign. In the course of that unforgettable night, in the eyes of all who beheld him, the sovereign rose above himself.' Pedro then went to the apartments of his five-year-old son by sad Leopoldina, and kissed goodbye forever the new Emperor of Brazil, Pedro II. Later the same morning, to the lamentations of their servants, the Duke and Duchess of Braganza, as Pedro and Amelia were to be known, boarded the British ship *Warspite* in Guanabara Bay bound for Europe. The aged Bonifácio, until a few months before Pedro's exiled enemy, was appointed his son's guardian and custodian of the nation he had created.

In that simple act of abdication, Pedro regained the popularity and admiration he had squandered during eleven years as Regent and Emperor, and by choosing not to inflict bloodshed in order to retain personal power, he set an example to his people. Brazil's subsequent history has to this day been remarkably bloodless, by contrast to the savageries of Spanish America. Pedro had responded to the wise advice of those who believed that his authoritarian instincts and 'Portugueseness' would destroy the new nation's established order; even so, it was several difficult years before this was fully restored. His brilliant and statesmanslike son was then to rule with enlightened sagacity from his teens until 1889, when he was deposed by a republican military coup.

47

The Last Battle

Pedro de Braganza's abdication at the age of thirty-three was not the end of his story: further challenges awaited him.

In July 1828, when Miguel and the absolutists seized power in Lisbon, the young Queen Maria's supporters fled to London, and she joined them there. Canning had died in 1827, and the policy of Wellington and Aberdeen, who succeeded him, was officially one of non-intervention. British troops had been withdrawn from Portugal in April 1828, and the young Queen and her party were received with the bare minimum of courtesy. Wellington told Barbacena that 'even supposing the Queen had right on her side, the Portuguese do not want any ruler other than Dom Miguel'. Before he could go so far as to order the exiles out of the country, the Queen returned to Brazil in August 1829. Earlier that year a Regency in her name had been established by Palmella at Angra on the island of Terceira in the Azores. Then in January 1830 Queen Carlota died; an abortive liberal rebellion in Lisbon was cruelly repressed, and the reign of terror in Portugal rose to its frenzied height.

This was against the tendency elsewhere in Europe, where revolution in France in July and August placed the citizen-King Louis-Philippe on the throne, and in November Wellington's government was replaced by that of the Liberal Earl Grey. Both France and Britain now found themselves opposed to the activities of the absolutist Miguelistas in Portugal, and so it was that Pedro, Duke of Braganza, arriving in Europe in the early summer of 1831, received a warm reception. At once he was able to set about organising an expedition to reconquer Portugal on behalf of his daughter. Louis-Philippe lent him three ports in which to assemble his expedition, and installed him in the Château de Meudon; Lord Grey's government allowed him to recruit three hundred mercenaries under the command of a Colonel Hodges.

Pedro lingered in France to await the birth of Amelia's first child, a daughter, who was also given the name Amelia. 'She is Brazilian', he declared, 'in that she was conceived before my departure.' In January 1832 he kissed the head of his daughter the Queen and, bidding her farewell with the words 'My lady, here stands a Portuguese general who goes to defend your rights and restore you your crown', set off on his next great adventure. He reached the Azores at the end of February, and spent the next few months in a whirlwind of organisation and preparation. Of the seven thousand or so men he assembled, however, only Colonel Hodges's troops and a battalion of five hundred French mercenaries were of any quality.

Nevertheless, on 27 June the expedition set sail for the Peninsula in two frigates, the *Rainha* and the *Dona Maria II*, the brigs *Vila-Flôr* and *Liberal*, eight schooners, a corvette, a barge and eighteen smaller ships, accompanying about thirty troop transports. News of Pedro's arrival in the Azores and of his intended expedition had inflamed Portugal in support of Miguel, and tens of thousands flocked to volunteer. But the Miguelistas, expecting an initial attack on Lisbon, had concentrated their forces there, and Pedro was able to land unopposed north of Oporto. General Santa Marta, the Miguelist commander guarding the northern coast, had a division of 12,000 men, of whom four thousand garrisoned Oporto. Nevertheless, he evacuated Oporto, and Pedro took possession of it on 9 July. Santa Marta explained the strategy – 'They are certainly going to die by cannonball or hunger or be burned alive, and the worthy city of Oporto with them' – and a Portuguese official noted that the only reason why Pedro's expedition had not been attacked at sea was from a desire that 'the troops [should] be freely permitted to land in order that they might be encircled and cut to pieces as soon as they had left the sea-coast and had proceeded a certain distance inland'.

Pedro entrenched himself in Oporto, then on 23 July marched with the bulk of his army against Santa Marta's position at Ponte Ferreira. The battle swung first one way and then the other until Colonel Hodges, attacking on the left, and troops under Pedro on the right forced Santa Marta up the hills behind him and some way along the road towards Lisbon. But the necessity of countering false rumours circulating in Oporto that the Miguelistas had won meant that Pedro felt he had no choice but to return to reassure his supporters.

The Miguelist forces were gathering, and Pedro and his army now settled down in earnest to the defence of Oporto. Batteries of guns were set up, deep trenches were built containing 'compression globes' – an early version of the landmine – and barricades were built across the streets. The Miguelist bombardment which began early in September included one of the first recorded uses of gas, bombs containing 'blankets saturated with sulphur and soaked in a solution that gave off dense fumes and suffocating vapours that were unendurable'. However, an assault against the city on 29 September was repulsed at a cost of four thousand killed, and another attack a fortnight later left 1,500 dead. Pedro was victorious in Oporto, but the country was not rallying to the banner of Queen Maria as he had expected.

The Miguelistas now tried to blockade the Douro river and starve the city out. Oporto was supplied from Foz do Douro, on the coast, and the Miguelistas managed to bring guns to bear on the beachhead. Under fierce fire a former Brazilian soldier, General Saldanha, managed to set up his own batteries on the north side of the river, building ramparts from the empty hogsheads which proliferated in Oporto. A thousand Miguelistas were killed trying to dislodge him. The city's lifeline was preserved, but gales in February 1833 prevented food being landed at Foz for a month; starvation rations prevailed, dogs and cats were eaten, typhus and cholera raged, and the supply of munitions dwindled.

The weather improved, Saldanha maintained his possession of Foz do Douro, and a plan began to take shape in London, where Pedro's loyal supporter the Duke of Palmella raised £80,000 from a British public horrified by the suffering and heroism in Oporto. Captain Charles Napier used the money to organise a 'steamboat expedition' for the relief of the city. On 1 June 1833 Napier and Palmella landed at Foz with five steamers, two hundred mercenaries, and a considerable sum of money. On 21 June Napier took a contingent under the command of Vila-Flôr, now Ducque de Terceira, to the Algarve, virtually undefended as Miguel concentrated his forces in and around Lisbon and Oporto. The people of the Algarve were no less Miguelistas than those elsewhere, but by the end of the month Terceira had taken the capital, Faro, where Palmella established a provisional government.

Napier then went in search of the Miguelist fleet, which made the cardinal error of emerging from the security of the Tagus estuary to meet him. Compared with Napier's five transport steamers, three frigates, a corvette and a brig, mounting 176 guns in all, the Portuguese armada was formidable – two battleships, two frigates, two corvettes, three brigs and a schooner, with 354 guns between them. Napier was eminently in the tradition of the eccentric British naval commander, described by the Portuguese historian Soriano as 'a man of ordinary stature, somewhat corpulent, with a round face and with a black silk handkerchief under his beard and attached to his head as if he had the toothache; a large, round, broad-brimmed hat of the kind the Quakers wear; wide blue trousers, white shoes and stockings, and a navy officer's greatcoat.' As aware of the poor quality of the Portuguese crews compared with his own British seamen as he was of their superior fire power, Napier determined to avoid an artillery battle; on 5 July, off Cape St Vincent, approaching from windward, he bore down upon the Portuguese fleet, ordering his captains to go straight for the enemy, grapple, and board. In two hours it was over. The men-of-war, the frigates and a corvette hauled down their flags. Only two small ships escaped to Lisbon. Thanks to Napier, Pedro had gained control of the sea.

The Duke of Terceira was emboldened to march north from the Algarve. The Miguelist forces, believing his objective to be the city of Beja, which had declared for Queen Maria, moved towards it, leaving open the road to Lisbon. Terceira bypassed them, and headed for the capital. The Miguelistas set out in pursuit, but by 22 July Terceira had reached Setúbal, across the Tagus from Lisbon. There he attacked and routed Miguel's forces, who fled with the news of his approach to Lisbon. Terceira's unexpected arrival, coupled with the defeat of the Portuguese fleet, broke the nerve of Dom Miguel's ministers, and early on 24 July they took the decision to abandon Lisbon. Some 12,000 troops departed in orderly fashion for Coimbra, along with the Court, the nobility and the clergy. When the soldiers had left, a man on the wharf at Sodre uttered the celebrated cry, 'Viva dona Maria! Long live the Constitutional Charter!' A popular revolt against the Miguelistas spread across the capital, and Pedro was warmly welcomed when he arrived there on 28 July.

In the middle of July King Miguel had appointed a veteran of the Napoleonic wars, Louis de Ghaisne, Comte de Bourmont and Marshal of France, who had gone into exile with Charles X, to command his troops, but the Marshal's attack on Oporto on 25 July was pushed back with the loss of four thousand men. The next day, the siege was at an end: on learning of the fall of Lisbon, the King and de Bourmont moved the bulk of the army south to combine with the Miguelistas at Coimbra and prepare for an attack on Lisbon. But they moved far too slowly. Pedro had ample time to organise the defence of Lisbon, and used it tirelessly: 'There were days when dawn found him among the fortifications and when he did not return to the palace until sundown.' Pedro recruited a new cavalry regiment, three infantry corps and twenty militia battalions, and reinforcements were ferried from Oporto by sea. The Miguelistas had regarded Lisbon as indefensible, but now 'the fortifications, distributed in a semicircle, crowned the heights from Xabregas to Alcantara, with 184 cannon. In this manner both the banks of the Tagus were protected; and on the river were the warships, lined up from Junqueira to Belém and from Beato to Vila-Franca.' Many of his 19,000 men were raw recruits and poorly armed, but their enthusiasm counted for much, the public mood was on Pedro's side, and morale was high. An assault on 5 September was beaten back; Terceira was wounded in the action, and in the redoubt he was defending Pedro himself only narrowly survived sniper fire. A night attack by de Bourmont on 14 September also failed, and General MacDonnell, a Scot, replaced him.

Towards the end of October a successful sortie by Saldanha forced the Miguelistas to retreat to Santarém. In January 1834 Saldanha took Leiria, cutting the Miguelistas off from Coimbra, then Pernes and, in February, Almoster. At Asseirceira in May the Miguelistas lost nearly two and a half thousand men and officers killed or captured.

The King and the rump of his forces were surrounded at Santarém; Miguel ordered a retreat across the Tagus and south-east to Evora-Monte where, on 26 May 1834, he at last surrendered. He was sentenced to perpetual exile from Portugal, his men were pardoned. Pedro's troops were obliged to protect him from attack by angry mobs as he made his way south to Sines and the frigate *Stag*, which was to take him to Italy.

Fate had one final, bitter twist in store for Pedro. On the day the terms of his agreement with Miguel became known, he attended the theatre. His carriage was pelted with mud and stones, and in the theatre he was booed and hissed: he had underestimated the depth of the people's hatred of Miguel. In the theatre he coughed, put a handkerchief to his mouth, and the hubbub died away as the audience saw there was blood in it. Pedro motioned to the conductor to begin. Like Bolívar he had fallen prey to tuberculosis, brought on by the past two years' exertion and hardship in Oporto and Lisbon. He was a dying man. He visited

Oporto once more, where he was rapturously received by the people whose sufferings he had shared throughout the siege. At the end of August he took the oath as Regent on behalf of his daughter during her minority. On 18 September he relinquished the Regency: 'The state of my health ... prohibits me from taking cognisance of public affairs, and in these circumstances I request you to provide the proper remedy. My most ardent prayers go up to Heaven for the public welfare.' At the age of fifteen, his daughter Queen Maria II assumed her duties, and in his room awarded him the Grand Cross of the Most Noble Order of the Tower and the Sword.

For six days he hovered between life and death, attended always by the young Queen and his former Empress, Amelia. To her he declared: 'Darling Amelia, when my heart is taken from my bosom, send it to the city of Oporto. I bequeath it as an eternal symbol of my gratitude to that city's loyal sons.' He died in the palace on the afternoon of 24 September 1834 in the Don Quixote Chamber, the same room in which he had been born thirty-six years before.

Impetuous, handsome ladies' man, vibrant with energy, strength and courage, well-intentioned; but fated to die before the promise of his more mature years could be fulfilled – Pedro of Braganza seems almost a cardboard cut-out of a mythical prince from a vanished age. It would be easy to dismiss him as a lightweight, a man of little intellect and less learning who was manipulated by his ministers into declaring Brazil independent, then floundered hopelessly out of his depth as her ruler before his abdication condemned her to years of chaos during his son's minority; a king who abandoned his Portuguese throne to a child and then waged war on his usurping brother to regain it for her; a rash commander who won largely through luck rather than by good generalship.

Easy, but wrong. Pedro of Braganza was in every sense the father of Brazilian independence. His decision to throw off the Portuguese yoke in 1822 not only preserved his throne but averted for Brazil the social chaos and civil war that marked the achievement of independence in so much of Spanish America. It demonstrated remarkably mature judgement for a young man of just twenty-four, brought up in the monarchical obscurantism of the Portuguese royal family. Because the principal royalist had defected to the patriots, the Portuguese forces in Brazil were leaderless from the start, and bitter and bloody conflict between royalists and patriots was avoided.

When it came to a crisis, Pedro usually acted with firmness and decision – in propping up his father's throne, in facing down the Portuguese government in 1822, in repeatedly rejecting the attempts of rival factions in government to assert their authority. His decision to abdicate in 1831, not that of the arbitrary despot his enemies portrayed, spared his people carnage and absolutism. In returning to Portugal to fight on the side of liberalism, he appended the seal of enlightened monarchy to the forces resisting the vindictive tide of reaction that swept Europe in the aftermath of Napoleon's defeat.

Mistakes were made during the Portuguese campaign, but it is hard to fault Pedro's fundamental judgements. It was surely right to make a stand in Oporto, rather than expose his forces in a futile assault on Lisbon, then to strike northwards through the comparatively undefended Algarve; to stake everything on such enthusiasm and audacity that a small, ill-trained force possessed of them was able to surprise into demoralised defeat the much more numerous Portuguese army.

Certainly Pedro had personal flaws, and they were his unmaking in Brazil. His ego and vanity blinded him to the destructive effect his flaunting of his mistress Domitila had on his own popularity. His instincts, though liberal, were also arbitrary, and his reluctance to share power with parliament created an inherently unstable government. Nevertheless, his period as Emperor was marked by sensible decision-making on the whole, and by the consolidation of Brazil's independence. The very decisions that were so unpopular – the settlement with Portugal, the abandonment of Brazil's disastrous imperial ambitions in Uruguay, economic liberalisation – were probably the right ones.

Of all the liberators, Pedro of Brazil survived in power much the longest – eleven years; only O'Higgins's six years, presiding over a much smaller country, could compete. All the liberators were great warriors, but only Pedro – and again, to a lesser extent, O'Higgins – could call himself a statesman. To have brought his country to independence without bloodshed or civil war and to have provided stable government for a decade were no mean achievements: he was surely the greatest administrator among the liberators.

Elements of Pedro's life may be the stuff of melodrama – a passionate affair that broke a young empress's heart and drove her to her grave; war with his own brother, usurper of a child's throne, backed by an evil mother; death tragically young, on the morrow of a victory – but for all that it is a moving story, one of the great royal epics, and certainly one of the least known. Pedro merits the attention not just of Brazilians, for whom he is a hero, but of anyone who believes in independence, enlightenment, liberalism, benevolent rule, humanitarianism, or pure lust for life. He was the last and best advertisement for the romance of royalty.

48

Cochrane in Greece

What of Admiral Lord Cochrane, whom we last saw being saluted at Spithead in June 1825? From the moment of his arrival he was again the popular hero, the man who had helped deliver independence to Peru and Brazil, a figure of romance. At the theatre in Edinburgh he was greeted with a standing ovation, and Kitty burst into tears. Sir Walter Scott recorded the occasion in verse:

> Even now, as through the air the plaudits rung,
>   I marked the smiles that in her features came;
> She caught the word that fell from every tongue,
>   And her eye brightened at her Cochrane's name;
> And brighter yet became her bright eyes' blaze;
> It was his country, and she felt the praise.

Greek independence was the current great enthusiasm sweeping Britain, and it is clear that by the end of 1825 Cochrane had accepted the invitation of Prince Alexander Mavrocordatos, secretary of the Greek National Assembly, to involve himself in Greek affairs. Although theirs was a just cause, the Greeks were bitterly divided among themselves, as untrustworthy and almost as bloodthirsty as the Turks from whose oppressive rule they sought to free themselves. Eight thousand Turks were slaughtered by the Greeks at Tripolitza. The Turks retaliated with the most notorious atrocity of the war, butchering 25,000 men and boys on the island of Chios and carrying off the female population as slaves. The Greeks were left in control of the Peloponnese, while the Turks retained the north, the Greek navy having prevented the Turks from re-capturing most of the islands and coastal towns.

The part played by Cochrane in the Greek wars was inglorious. The language barrier between him and his men was almost complete, and the

Greeks made indifferent soldiers and sailors, while the Greek commanders behaved more like rival gangsters than leaders of a cause. He failed
in his attempt to relieve the Acropolis, Athens' citadel, when it was
under siege by the Turks; his attack on Turkish ships in the harbour at
Alexandria was unsuccessful; and it was Admiral Codrington, not he,
who in command of a combined French, Russian and British fleet
destroyed the Turkish navy at Navarino. However, for the first time
Cochrane emerged from an adventure pleased with his financial position. He had invested – in Greek Loan stock – the £37,000 given him
by the Greeks at the outset, and once the Turks had been defeated, the
stock rose dramatically. When he returned to England in 1829 he was
fifty-four, and £100,000 the richer.

Undoubtedly there was a streak of the romantic adventurer about
Cochrane; equally undoubtedly, any struggle for independence had its
appeal for the anti-authoritarian in him, although he often ended by
despising the leaders beside whom he fought. He was a radical thirty
years before radicalism became fashionable; but when it did, he reaped
a rich harvest.

   As well as the fall of the absolutist Charles X of France, 1830 saw the
death of King George IV, and the formation of a liberal ministry under
Lord Grey, following the resignation of Wellington. In 1831 Cochrane's
spendthrift old father died, and Cochrane succeeded to the earldom as
tenth Earl of Dundonald. His next move was to seek an audience of the
new king, William IV (himself a sailor, and an admirer of Cochrane). At
the Royal Pavilion in Brighton William promised to see that the old stock
exchange scandal was fairly looked into. Grey was sympathetic, but two
members of his cabinet continued to object. At last, rather than seeking
to get the conviction overturned, Dundonald gave in to Kitty's pleas that
he should seek a Royal Pardon – which he had hitherto resisted, rightly
considering that to do so would imply an admission that he had committed an offence. A pardon was granted in May 1832, and Dundonald
was restored at last to the navy, as a Rear Admiral of the Fleet. The following day he was summoned to a royal Levee. It was his hour of greatest
triumph – and, coincidentally, the morning of the passage of the Great
Reform Bill. He who had previously been regarded as a half-mad,
money-obsessed criminal and crank, downright dangerous as a commander, was now, with equal exaggeration, seen as the personification of
naval valour, the single-handed liberator of foreign lands.

Having been responsible for the retractable paddles with which the *Rising Star*, the first steamship to cross the Atlantic for Chile, had been equipped, in the late 1830s Dundonald set himself to design a rotary engine to turn a ship's paddle or propeller. Always ultra-conservative, the Admiralty viewed his ideas sympathetically, but refrained from adopting them. In the 1840s a new First Lord of the Admiralty, the Earl of Haddington, gave Dundonald a small steamship, the *Firefly*, to experiment upon, and in 1845 ordered a new steam frigate, HMS *Janus*, for which Dundonald designed the propeller, one of the earliest, and an improved boiler. Six years later, a secret committee under another sympathetic First Sea Lord considered three of Cochrane's proposals: camouflage, saturation bombardment and gas attack. They recommended that the first be adopted, but that the other two did not 'accord with the feelings and principles of civilised warfare'.

The Earl failed in his efforts to secure reinstatement as a Knight Companion of the Order of the Bath – of which honour he had been so humiliatingly stripped in his darkest hour – but Queen Victoria (another admirer) promised instead that he should have the next vacancy in the Order. At his installation, fittingly enough, the son of his old enemy Lord Ellenborough was called upon by Prince Albert to sponsor him, and the now aged Duke of Wellington congratulated him. What was perhaps more remarkable was his appointment as Commander-in-Chief of the North American and West Indian Station. There was no prospect of exciting conflict here, the Atlantic Fleet's duties being confined to fishery protection, suppression of the slave trade and patrolling the Gulf of Mexico during the wars between the United States and Mexico, but Cochrane threw himself into his command with his usual vigour. He visited Nova Scotia and Trinidad, where he was captivated by the 'Pitch Lake', a mile-wide expanse of bitumen, which he tried, unsuccessfully, to promote for development as fuel and as a material for constructing sewers, tunnels, and embankments to the Thames and improve its flow. He also recommended help for the freed slaves of Jamaica, now unemployed and impoverished.

Admiral Lord Cochrane, tenth Earl of Dundonald, died in 1856, just before his eighty-fifth birthday, a very British – perhaps a very Scottish – hero. He was a mass of contradictions. For a romantic hero he was in many respects a most unlikeable, even an unpleasant man. Although he was highly intelligent, could be kind, and was apparently agreeable to meet socially, he was also notably unforgiving towards his enemies; possessed of an egotism which led him to champion any cause of his own to the point of obsession; chronically sensitive to slight or insult, real or imagined; and driven by insecurity to a desperate desire for financial reward, and to believe – sometimes with justification – that he was being cheated of it. If he was not actually a common criminal, he certainly associated unwisely and closely with men who were in the process of carrying out a crime, and thus was guilty of an unfortunate lack of judgement for so public a figure.

As a naval commander, Cochrane's skill combined with his outrageous daring and effrontery to capture the imagination – now, as they did in his own day. If Nelson was unquestionably Britain's greatest admiral since Drake, Cochrane was her greatest single-ship captain; indeed, he was the last of his kind, as the grey age of steam he so forcefully championed came to replace the far more romantic age of sail. As a master of naval deception and trickery, he was in a class of his own.

Cochrane qualifies to be regarded as an Immortal on the basis of his imaginative fighting exploits alone. But, although destined to play no decisive part in his own country's history, he altered its course in another theatre: of the seven extraordinary characters most responsible for the destruction of Iberia's empire in Latin America, Cochrane was the most improbable of all. It is too much to assert that without Cochrane's intervention the Spanish Empire would have survived: it was under pressure from all sides, and must have disintegrated sooner or later. But it is certainly probable that without the command of Pacific coastal waters which was his legacy to Chile and Peru, the Spanish would have tried again, from the south, to overturn Chile's revolution; that San Martín's expedition, had it been able to sail at all, would have been defeated at sea; and that Lima would have been able to hold out almost indefinitely as the centre of an embattled but still determined Spanish imperial effort. In Brazil, his masterly seizure of the northern provinces ensured that independence was not confined to the south. The struggle for independence in all these countries might have lasted decades longer; for averting this, Cochrane deserves a place in the front rank of the Liberators. Cussed, bloody-minded and egotistical, his relentless pursuit of his own self-interest and liberties led him to fight for the self-interest and liberties of others.

49

The Legacy

With Cochrane died the last of the seven Liberators. Their achievement was magnificent – the freeing of a continent from centuries-old empires founded on repression and military force. Each one was possessed of exceptional qualities: Francisco de Miranda's erudition, and determination in the face of ridicule and adversity; Simón Bolívar's energy, political brilliance and military daring; José de San Martín's precision, strategic skill and intelligence; Bernardo O'Higgins's stubborn honesty and courage; Admiral Lord Cochrane's daring, deceit and boldness; Agustín de Itúrbide's political skill – initially, at least; and Pedro de Braganza's dash, bravery and leadership. Each in his own way was also possessed of formidable charisma and ability. And each man was genuinely motivated by idealism and a desire to do his best for his own people. Itúrbide, perhaps, sought power as a means of personal enrichment – but, curiously, under him Mexico, for all her violent history, was spared the bloodshed that occurred elsewhere during the wars of liberation. Of the others Miranda, although he loved luxury, sacrificed the good life for his cause; Cochrane, although always eager to repair his ruined fortunes, was largely unsuccessful financially; and Bolívar, San Martín, O'Higgins and Pedro were remarkable for their comparative lack of interest in money.

Judged by results, the Liberators seem to merit the sneers of their worst critics. Their own fates seemed to foreshadow the terrible sufferings to come: Miranda, betrayed by his followers, was left to rot to death in a Spanish gaol; Bolívar died of tuberculosis and disappointment in an obscure village near the Colombian coast; San Martín died, a broken man, after more than two decades in exile; O'Higgins, ousted and exiled, expired on the very eve of his return to his homeland; Itúrbide was seized and executed in a remote provincial town; Pedro died, tragically young, on the morrow of his greatest triumph. Only Cochrane endured into splendid old age.

The men who came after were not of the same stamp. Their kind was foreshadowed by José Gaspar Rodriguez de Francia, the sinister figure who came to power in the secretive and backward nation of Paraguay as the wars of independence raged. 'El Supremo', as he styled himself, was a mestizo of both Portuguese and Spanish blood, with a hawk nose, piercing eyes, a tight little mouth and protruding chin. Professing a knowledge of Rousseau and warped by a pathological hatred of the outside world and of women, he waged war on his country's white over-class and virtually eliminated them, with the compliance of the Guarani Indian population. He created an extensive spy network. He was a thoroughgoing dictator – there was no government or congress, just a few cronies through whom the administration was carried on. Newspapers, books, even schools were banned. Hardly any trade was permitted with the outside world (Buenos Aires, in any case, consistently blockaded Paraguay down-river), and the few foreigners who penetrated the country were soon glad enough to leave it. He died, aged seventy-four, in 1840, and his successors were in the same mould: Carlos Antonio Lopez, while more humane, generous and gregarious, was monstrously corrupt; about half the cultivated farmland of Paraguay found its way into his possession. His son Francisco Solano Lopez, a megalomaniac, in declaring war on Brazil, Argentina and Uruguay almost simultaneously, caused a reduction in the population of his country of more than half: four-fifths of adult males died.

The American historian John Edwin Fagg has summed up the fate of the continent:

> Men of violence often seized control of the republics and held it by force until they were betrayed by caudillos as primitive as themselves. That they were sometimes colourful and attractive as personalities does not diminish the harm they did. The riotous character of public life discouraged the penetration of Latin America by educators, immigrants, investors, traders and experts. If they came at all, it was usually for brief periods of exploitation, not for patient, constructive labours. Europe, the United States, and other happier areas regarded Latin America with pity and scorn. And while many individuals of the region shared the artistic, literary, and scientific interests of the outside world, the general cultural level in most of these countries rose little, if at all, above that of colonial times. Social change was seldom in the direction of humanitarianism. Economic con-

ditions remained bad almost everywhere, in contrast to the striking advances in other parts of the world.

Venezuela, at least, came under the sway of one of the more benevolent 'great dictators': that same José Antonio Paéz who proved so unreliable as Bolívar's ally. Paéz exercised his despotism with some skill, contriving to placate both the conservative upper class and his llanero supporters, and on the whole without great excess. He dominated Venezuela's politics, off and on, between 1819 and 1863, and set the pattern for a succession of dictatorships, some better than others.

Santander, Bolívar's nemesis, ruled Colombia, more aristocratic, more civic-minded, by more or less constitutional means. After him, weak congress-led governments alternated through most of the nineteenth century with such strongmen as General Tomás de Mosquera and Rafael Nuñez. In Ecuador, the third of Bolívar's creations, his old henchman General Flores held sway until 1845, and disorder followed him before another benevolent despot, Gabriel Garcia Moreno, assumed power in 1860. Peru, with its sophisticated political class, was fortunate enough to come under the control of two moderate rulers: General Agustín Gamarra, the husband of the formidable lady seduced by Bolívar in Cuzco, and Ramón Castilla, a genuinely popular politician.

Bolivia was well administered by Bolívar's able lieutenant Andrés Santa Cruz, until he decided to annex Peru. Early success was followed by invasion by Chile from the south, whereupon Bolivia descended into chaos. Of those who competed for power the most notorious were the mob leader Manuel Belzu and Manuel Melgarejo, a psychopath who shot Belzu, and indulged in orgies of rape and murder both inside the presidential palace and out of it.

San Martín's native Argentina was one of the worst sufferers. The sophisticated Buenos Aires élite proved incapable of dominating the vast, largely primitive hinterland, where gaucho warlords held sway until one, Juan Manuel de Rosas, took power. After a spell of enlightened rule Rosas governed through street thugs, the *mazoracas*, and imposed Francia-like policies of economic isolation. A tenth of the population preferred exile to his tyranny. Rosas's xenophobic nationalism involved Argentina in conflict with Brazil, Uruguay, Bolivia, Chile, Britain and France, and it was only in 1852 that he was finally ousted by another gaucho thug, Justo José Urquiza. Not until Bartolomé Mitre, a statesmanlike and cultivated man, came to power a decade later did the country begin to settle down and realise its enormous potential.

After a short interlude, O'Higgins's heir in Chile was Diego Portales, able and autocratic, who cut back the professional army and created a militia system. He was ousted and murdered by the army in 1837, but not before he had laid the foundations for economic growth, constitutional rule and relative political freedom, under such men as General Manuel Bulnes and Manuel Montt.

Itúrbide's legacy was less promising. His destroyer, Santa Anna, was utterly unprincipled, worthless and crooked. During his domination of Mexican politics between 1832 and 1855 he undermined any attempt to create stable constitutional government, lost Texas to the United States through his own crass negligence, and even permitted Mexico City itself to fall into American hands in 1847, during the war with the United States.

The prospect for Brazil following Pedro's departure seemed unpromising. The five-year-old Pedro II had to be spirited out of Rio as the country descended into political factionalism between liberals and conservatives, and secessionism erupted in Pará, Maranhão, Minas Gerais and Rio Grande do Sul. In 1840 Pedro, not yet fifteen, was declared of age by the dominant liberal faction, and crowned Emperor the next year. The liberals were soon ousted in favour of the conservatives, and with the support of the brilliant soldier Luis Alves de Lima, an old loyalist of his father, Pedro II subdued the country, which then enjoyed forty years of comparative peace and progress under this most enlightened and gentle of monarchs. He is often compared with his contemporary Queen Victoria, but enjoyed far more real power. After the abolition of slavery in 1888, however, conservative slave interests made common cause with republicans clamouring for real democracy, and the army ousted Pedro in a coup the following year. The country lurched for a while into a struggle between soldiers and constitutionalists.

With the exceptions of Peru and Chile, the fates of the former territories of the Spanish Empire were dismal indeed, and the Liberators have been heaped with blame for the ruin they left behind. Those strutting, heroic figures who destroyed Spanish rule were, it seemed, unable themselves to rule for any significant period of time, or to build lasting institutions. Worse, the cult of personality that grew up around them served as a precedent for the two most serious evils that were to afflict Latin America until well into the late twentieth century – populist dictatorship and *caudillismo*, military rule – which alternated in many countries, and even sometimes merged, with doubly tragic results. Latin America's underdevelopment since independence, particularly as compared with the United States, has been largely ascribed to such misgovernment.

While Latin America's political leadership undoubtedly played its part in the region's post-independence difficulties, it is of course a facile over-simplification to blame either the Liberators or their successors for all Latin America's troubles. The Liberators did not create the twin curses of charismatic leadership and military rule; rather, these were the natural successors of Spanish domination combined with a centuries'-old tradition of hierarchical indigenous rule.

British rule in North America permitted a large measure of self-government, was only very rarely enforced by military means (which inevitably provoked rebellion), and was exercised through a governing class of common national origin and political and economic values; Spanish rule, by contrast, although more enlightened than is commonly believed, was imposed by local proconsuls and enforced through military repression. The push for independence in the United States arose from a mixture of economic self-interest and political idealism, and only when war loomed did it transform itself into military resistance. In Latin America, while both these motives were certainly in evidence, the overpowering military presence made it inevitable that the leaders of the independence movement should be military men. George Washington was an exception among civilians like Samuel and John Adams, Patrick Henry, John Hancock, Thomas Jefferson, James Madison and Alexander Hamilton. In North America, lawyers blasted the British government with wordy broadsides, and resorted to military action only with reluctance, and as a reaction to Britain's response.

Since in Latin America military force underpinned Spanish rule, military leaders – some trained, like Miranda, San Martín, Cochrane and Itúrbide; some self-taught, like Bolívar, O'Higgins and Pedro – were inevitably required to destroy it. Moreover, many of the Liberators aspired to non-military leadership, once independence was won, and formulated complicated political philosophies and structures for their countries. This was particularly true of Miranda and Bolívar, but also, to a lesser extent, of the less politically sophisticated Itúrbide, O'Higgins and Pedro. Inadequate to the task they may have been, but they were not entirely lacking in political sensitivities.

They were, however, faced with problems and circumstances very different from those the Founding Fathers to the north had to contend with. The thirteen colonies of the United States were compactly situated along the eastern seaboard of America – continental expansion was only just beginning in 1776 – and communications were good, particularly by sea. They enjoyed a common Anglo-Saxon heritage – albeit one spiced by immigration – and the Indian under-class and, in the south, the numerous black slave population were without rights or a political voice.

In South America, only Brazil had many of these characteristics. Spanish America was a continent-wide empire of long standing at the time of independence, one in which each province had over three hundred years developed its own separate identity. Moreover, the character of each was profoundly affected by considerable indigenous populations which, neither exterminated nor marginalised, as happened later in the United States, had been dominated or integrated.

Mexico, with its large and partly sophisticated Indian and mixed-blood population, was quite different from predominantly white and prosperous Colombia, from Venezuela, with its large black and mestizo population, from the Portuguese-black-Indian mélange in Brazil, from Argentina's mix of outback Indians and buccaneering port-dwellers, from Chile's stable European farmer class, from the white élite and numerous Indian population in bondage in Peru, from Bolivia's almost entirely Indian population. These regions, moreover, were separated from one another by all but insuperable natural obstacles – mountain, jungle or desert – and distance. Although it did not stop him striving for a degree of co-operation, with patent lack of success, Bolívar had the insight to appreciate that unity on the United States model was unachievable in Latin America precisely because of the long history of settlement and the consequent strongly established ethnic and cultural differences that had grown up between the colonies.

Unity was the real key to the success of the United States. The constitution of 1787 was in many respects the imposition of a central national government upon the quarrelsome states and, in addition, of a conservative, middle-class settlement upon more radical men and ideas. From then on it was clear that any disorder threatening the unity or viability of the nation would be stamped upon – and America's rulers pursued a vigorous policy of expanding westwards and southwards into largely empty lands. In a country so constituted, the weaknesses of one state were compensated for by the strengths of another.

Latin America, by contrast, inevitably split into its component states once the sole unifying force – imperial rule – was removed. Each pursued jealously nationalist policies that not only retarded development but made difficult if not impossible the movement of capital, commerce and peoples that would encourage it. The agricultural plenty of the Argentine and southern Brazil was not used to feed the peoples of Bolivia or Peru; the mineral wealth of Peru was not used to provide the capital to develop the industries of Brazil or Venezuela, and so on. Instead, most of the new nations made themselves into jealously tariff-protected enclaves, forswearing even such co-operation as had existed in the days of Empire. The worst aspect of this was that the divided continent proved easy prey for overseas commercial interests (primarily at first the British, followed by the Americans) which were able to penetrate deep into Argentina, Chile, Brazil, Peru and Mexico. They at least left behind the rudiments of an infrastructure, most notably exemplified by the continent's network of railways. And when it came to external political and commercial policy the United States – half a continent, speaking with a united voice – was soon able to join the ranks of the major powers, while the divided chorus of the Latin American nations counted for almost nothing in the world, leaving them all the more vulnerable to exploitation.

All these factors, scarcely the fault of the Liberators and their political successors, contributed decisively to Latin America's post-independence stagnation. The social makeup of the newly independent republics was another significant element. Although this varied between countries, as we have seen, in general it was characterised by a dominant aristocratic upper class of white landowners; a much smaller and largely white middle class of professionals and traders in the cities; and a majority under-class of mixed-race people, Indians and blacks. By contrast, although it included followers from both the landowning and the 'mechanical' classes, the spearhead of the revolution in the United States was the dominant middle class. It was clearly easier for this middle class to make common cause with those above and below them in the social divide than it was for the aristocratic landowners who largely instigated the revolutions in the south. These had to rely either on armies which provided the brute force necessary for them to survive, or on populist dictators capable of appealing to the masses while constituting no threat to the established social order. In a further twist, it was that very division which blighted the emergence of a powerful middle class in these countries – a situation which in many endured until the last third or so of the twentieth century, effectively frustrating their political evolution.

In the United States it was from the outset the middle classes who seized power and vigorously pursued their agenda of economic development and commercial expansion. The American Revolution was truly a revolutionary movement, while the Latin American wars of independence were largely aristocratic assertions of self-interest against the mother country. The *caudillos* and the demagogues pursued their own interests, sometimes brutally, sometimes in an enlightened way, power alternating between the two all too often, and both based on the cult of personality. As economic growth and the expansion of the middle class have at last occurred in the course of the last third of the twentieth century, it has become possible to suggest that the era of extremes has passed. How quickly economic and political co-operation between the Latin American nations will follow remains to be seen.

The Liberators threw off the Spanish yoke – one of the greatest military achievements in human history. In their inability to establish viable or stable political structures, although most wanted to do so, they were the victims of their time and place; and they were aware of their failure. The tragedy was that this failure, exacerbated by a vicious circle of political and economic underdevelopment, was to last the best part of a century and a half. The cycle may now have been broken; if so, the independence and self-respect for which the Liberators fought so hard may at last be in prospect for the millions of Latin America.

Chronology

1750	Birth of Francisco de Miranda in Caracas
1759	Accession of Charles III of Spain
1763	Ambrose Higgins arrives in Buenos Aires
1775	Outbreak of American War of Independence
	Birth of Thomas, later Lord Cochrane, near Edinburgh
1777	Ambrosio O'Higgins becomes Captain-General of Santiago de Chile
1778	Birth of Bernardo O'Higgins in Concepción, southern Chile
	Birth of José de San Martín in Yapeyú, north of Buenos Aires
1781	Execution of Tupac Amarú II in Cuzco
1783	Birth of Simón Bolívar in Caracas
	Desertion of Miranda from the Spanish army to the United States
	Birth of Agustín de Itúrbide in Valladolid, New Spain
	End of the American War of Independence
1785–89	Miranda's grand tour of Europe
1788	Accession of Charles IV of Spain
1789	Start of French Revolution
1792	Miranda joins French revolutionary army
1793	Miranda arrested
1795	Miranda released; meets Napoleon
	Bernardo O'Higgins arrives in London
	Ambrosio O'Higgins becomes Viceroy of Peru
1797	Miranda flees France
1798	Birth of Pedro de Braganza in Lisbon
1799	Bolívar arrives in Spain
1801	Death of Ambrosio O'Higgins
1804	Napoleon's coronation in Paris
1805	In Rome, Bolívar swears to liberate South America
1806	Miranda's *Leander* expedition leaves New York for Venezuela
	Defeat of Popham and Beresford's expedition to Buenos Aires
1807	Napoleon invades Spain and Portugal; Portuguese court flees Lisbon for Rio de Janeiro
1808	Miranda returns to London
	Whitelocke's expedition defeated in Buenos Aires
	Tumult of Aranjuez forces abdication of Charles IV and succession of Ferdinand VII
	Napoleon deposes Ferdinand VII and instals Joseph Bonaparte
	Venezuela swears loyalty to anti-French junta formed in Seville
1810	Seville junta overthrown
	Captain-General of Venezuela overthrown

Bolívar travels to London as Venezuela's emissary, meets Miranda
Chile declares independence
Hidalgo and Allende's uprising in New Spain
Buenos Aires declares independence and invades Spanish Upper Peru
Bolívar and Miranda return to Venezuela

1811   Defeat of the Argentinians by Spain in Upper Peru
Venezuela declares independence
Miranda appointed commander-in-chief in Venezuela
Defection of San Martín from Spanish army
Hidalgo loses the Battle of Calderón and is executed

1812   Venezuelan earthquake kills 20,000
Miranda appointed dictator of Venezuela
Siege of Morelos's forces at Cuautla, south of Mexico City
Bolívar routed at Puerto Cabello
Miranda sues for peace with Spain
Miranda betrayed into captivity by Bolívar
Carrera seizes power in Chile
Liberals seize power in Cadiz and promulgate new constitution
Bolívar flees to Cartagena and composes Cartagena Manifesto
Bolívar embarks on River Magdalena expedition
Morelos proclaims constitution of Chilpancingo in New Spain

1813   Bolívar crosses the Cordillera Oriental and wins Battle of Cucutá
Bolívar marches on Venezuela and captures Merida
The Spanish reinvade Chile
Bolívar proclaims the War to the Death
Bolívar recaptures Caracas

1814   Bolívar defeated at the Battle of La Puerta
Evacuation of Caracas
Bolívar flees Venezuela for Cartagena
San Martín becomes Governor of Cuyo in western Argentina
O'Higgins loses Battle of Rancagua in Chile
Chilean exodus across the Andes
Capture and execution of Morelos in New Spain
Bolívar captures Santa Fé de Bogotá
Defeat of Napoleon in Spain
Return of Ferdinand VII
Restoration of absolutism in Spain

1815   Battle of Waterloo marks final defeat of Napoleon
Bolívar sails from Cartagena to Jamaica
Morillo's army sails from Spain
Spanish capture Cartagena
Bolívar writes Jamaica Letter
Bolívar travels to Haiti

1816   Bolívar lands again in Venezuela
Bolívar escapes back to Haiti
Bolívar returns to Venezuela
Death of Miranda in gaol in Cadiz
San Martín's army crosses the Andes
San Martín and O'Higgins win the Battle of Chacabuco
San Martín and O'Higgins take Santiago

1817   Bolívar establishes his base on the Orinoco
Bolívar executes his rival Manuel Piar
Brazil invades the Banda Oriental

Bolívar captures Guayana and Angostura

1818 Bolívar meets José Antonio Páez, leader of the llaneros
Bolívar defeated at El Semen
Spanish reinvasion of Chile
Spanish defeat of O'Higgins at Cancha Rayada
San Martín wins Battle of Maipú

1819 Bolívar holds Congress of Angostura
Bolívar crosses the plains of Casanaré and the Andes
Bolívar wins the Battle of Boyaca and retakes Santa Fé de Bogotá

1820 Admiral Lord Cochrane takes Valdivia
Mutiny in Cadiz restores the 1812 constitution
Bolívar invades Venezuela
Bolívar concludes an armistice with the Spanish commander Morillo
Execution of José Miguel Carrera in Argentina
San Martín's and Cochrane's expeditionary force leaves Chile for Peru by sea
Cochrane's capture of the *Esmeralda*

1821 End of armistice in Venezuela
Bolívar wins decisive Battle of Carabobo and declares independence of Gran Colombia
Attempted revolution in Rio de Janeiro crushed
Plan of Iguala issued by Itúrbide in New Spain; Mexico becomes independent
San Martín occupies Lima
Cochrane hijacks San Martín's treasure ship

1822 Bolívar wins Battle of Bombona in southern Colombia
Bolívar enters Quito; meets Manuela Sáenz
Bolívar's soliloquy on Chimborazo
Cochrane returns to Chile
Pedro declares Brazil independent and becomes Emperor
Bolívar meets San Martín in Guayaquil
San Martín abdicates power and returns to Chile
Itúrbide becomes Emperor of Mexico
Canning promulgates his Latin American doctrine
Earthquake in Valparaíso

1823 Bolívar takes control of Lima
O'Higgins deposed in Chile
Bolívar forced out of Lima
Cochrane captures Bahia and Maranhão
Following French intervention, absolutism reimposed in Spain under Ferdinand VII
Itúrbide abdicates as Emperor of Mexico and leaves for Europe
Monroe Doctrine promulgated by United States

1824 Bolívar wins Battle of Junín
Sucre wins Battle of Ayacucho: final defeat for Spanish forces in Latin America
San Martín departs for exile in Europe
Cochrane subdues Pernambuco
Itúrbide returns to Mexico, where he is executed

1825 Bolívar travels to Cuzco and Potosí
Cochrane returns to Britain

1826 Bolívar draws up constitution for Bolivia, installing Sucre as president
Bolívar draws up constitution for Peru
Congress of Panamá
Death of the Empress Leopoldina of Brazil
Bolívar leaves Peru

1827   Bolívar's reconciliation with Páez
        Brazil gives up the Banda Oriental, which becomes Uruguay
        Death of Canning
1828   Sucre is overthrown in Bolivia
        Convention of Ocaña dissolved; Bolívia becomes dictator of Gran Colombia
        Coup and assassination attempt against Bolívar in Santa Fé de Bogotá
        Sucre defeats invading Peruvians at Portete de Tarqui
1829   Bolívar travels to Quito and Guayaquil
        San Martín returns to Buenos Aires, thence to Europe again
1830   Bolívar returns to Santa Fé de Bogotá
        Bolívar departs for the coast
        Sucre assassinated
        Death of Bolívar at San Pedro Alejandrino
1831   Abdication of Emperor Pedro I
1832   Pedro arrives in Oporto; siege of the city begins
1833   End of the siege of Oporto
1834   Pedro captures Lisbon
        Death of Pedro
1842   Death of O'Higgins in Peru
1850   Death of San Martín in Boulogne
1856   Death of Cochrane (now Earl of Dondonald) in London

Dramatis Personae

Francisco de Miranda, the Precursor (1750–1816)

His friends
Juan Manuel de Cagigal, Spanish general
George Washington, US President
Prince Potemkin, Russian chief minister
Catherine the Great, Empress of Russia
Thomas Paine, American revolutionary
J. P. Brissot, French revolutionary
General Dumouriez, French army commander
Marquise de Custine, French courtesan
William Pitt, British Prime Minister
Lord Grenville, British Prime Minister
Nicholas Vansittart, British politician
Thomas Jefferson, US President
James Madison, US Secretary of State
Admiral Sir Alexander Cochrane, British naval commander
Lord Castlereagh, British Foreign Secretary
George Canning, British Foreign Secretary
Arthur Wellesley (later Duke of Wellington), British army commander
Sarah Andrews, his mistress
Lady Hester Stanhope, friend in London
Marquess Wellesley, British Foreign Secretary

His followers
Antonio Nariño, New Granadan independence leader
Carlos Maria de Alvear, Argentinian independence leader
Bernardo O'Higgins, Chilean independence leader
Andrés Bello, Venezuelan poet and statesman
Luís Lopez Mendez, Venezuelan diplomat

His enemies
Bernardo del Campo, Spanish ambassador to Court of St James
King Charles IV of Spain
Manuel Godoy, Spanish chief minister
King Ferdinand VII of Spain
Fouquier-Tinville, Chief French revolutionary prosecutor
Robespierre, leader of French radicals

Simón Bolívar, the Liberator (1783–1830)

His women
Concepción Palacios y Blanco, his mother
Iñes, his nurse
Hipólita, a slave
Maria Antonia, his sister
Maria Teresa Rodriguez y Alaiza, his wife
Fanny de Villars, his French mistress
Anita Lénoit, his mistress on the Magdalena
Josefina Machado, his mistress in Caracas
Julia Cobier, his mistress in Jamaica
Isabel Soublette, his mistress on the Orinoco
Manuelita Sáenz, his principal mistress
Manuela Madroño, his mistress in Huaylas, Peru
Francisca Zubiaga de Gamarra, his mistress in Cuzco, Peru

His supporters
Miguel José Sanz, early guardian and family lawyer
Simón Rodriguez, eccentric tutor
José Felix Ribas, cousin and romantic revolutionary, executed in 1815
Rafael Urdaneta, aristocratic general and longest-lasting supporter
Anastasio Girardot, aristocratic general, killed in 1813
Santiago Mariño, rival liberator of eastern Venezuela
José Bermudez, simple-minded sometime critic and supporter
Manuel Piar, his most dangerous rival, executed by him in 1817
Antonio José de Sucre, his protégé and heir-apparent until assassinated in 1830
Ducoudrez-Holstein, French mercenary who became one of Bolívar's bitterest critics
Campo Elias, vicious Spanish supporter
General Arismendi, cruellest lieutenant
Carlos Soublette, a principal aide
Gregor MacGregor, Scottish mercenary and adventurer
Gustavus Hippisley, commander of the Albion Legion
Daniel Florence O'Leary, Irish adventurer and closest aide
José Antonio Páez, leader of the llaneros, later President of Venezuela
General Zaraza, llanero guerrilla leader
Colonel Henry Wilson, Albion Legion officer who tried to lead a revolt against Bolívar
Colonel James Rooke, Albion Legion officer, regarded as a son until his death in 1819
Francisco de Paula Santander, later his most formidable political enemy, and President of
    Colombia
Francisco Zea, civilian supporter
José de la Mar, principal Peruvian general, who later turned against Colombia
José-Maria Córdoba, youngest of Bolívar's generals in Peru and hero of Ayacucho
Colonel William Ferguson, British aide, killed in Bogotá coup
Bedford Wilson, Albion Legion officer who carried Bolivia's constitution to Peru with
    Ferguson
Colonel Patrick Campbell, British minister in Santa Fé de Bogotá
General Juan de Flores, founder of Ecuador

His enemies
Domingo Monteverde, Spanish commander in Venezuela
José Tomás Rodriguez Boves, leader of the 'Legion from Hell'
Tomás Morales, successor to Boves as leader of the 'Legion from Hell'
Pablo Morillo, Spanish commander in Venezuela and Colombia

General La Torre, Morillo's successor
General José de Canterac, principal Spanish commander in Peru

José de San Martín, the Protector (1778–1850)

His supporters
General Solano, military mentor, killed in Cadiz in 1808
Maria de los Remedios, his wife
General Manuel Belgrano, admirer and commander of Argentinian forces
Martín Guemes, Argentine guerrilla leader
Colonel Tomás Guido, most loyal lieutenant
Juan Martín de Pueyrredón, ruler of Argentina
José Antonio Alvarez Condarco, San Martín's chief spy and armourer
Diego Parossien, surgeon to the Army of the Andes
Padre Luís Beltrán, chief engineer to the Army of the Andes
Juan Gregorio de Las Heras, one of his chief commanders
Miguel Soler, another of his chief commanders
General William Miller, commander of San Martín's foreign auxiliaries and the Peruvian
    Legion
Captain Basil Hall, commander of the sympathetic British flotilla in the Pacific
Bernardo Monteagudo, sinister political aide
Rosita Campuzano, his mistress
Mercedes, his daughter
Mariano Balcarce, his son-in-law
Alejandro Aguado, financial patron

His enemies
Don Francisco Marcó del Ponte, Spanish captain-general of Santiago de Chile
Colonel Vicente San Bruno, commander of Spanish forces in Chile
Marqués de la Pezuela, Viceroy of Peru
General José de La Serna, Viceroy of Peru
Marqués de Torre Tagle, principal Peruvian nobleman
José de la Riva Agüero, Peruvian independence leader

Bernardo O'Higgins, the Director (1778–1842)

His supporters
Ambrosio O'Higgins, his father
Isabel Riquende, his mother
Rosita Riquende, his sister
Charlotte Eeles, girlfriend of his teenage years
Juan Martínez de Rozas, Chilean independence leader
Juan Mackenna, military mentor
Rosaria Puga y Vibuarre, his mistress
Ramón Freire, Governor of Concepción, who eventually turned against him
Rodriguez Aldea, chief minister
General Prieto, aristocratic friend

His enemies
Nicolás de la Cruz, guardian in Spain
José Miguel Carrera, dictator of Chile
Juan José Carrera, José Miguel's brother
Luís Carrera, José Miguel's brother
Javiera Carrera, José Miguel's sister

Joel Poinsett, US consul in Chile
General Manuel Osorio, commander of Spanish forces in Chile

Thomas, Lord Cochrane (later tenth Earl of Dundonald), the Sea-Devil (1775–1856)

His supporters
Frederick Marryat, midshipman aboard the *Impérieuse*, later celebrated author
Sir Francis Burdett, radical MP
Kitty Barnes, his wife
Basil Cochrane, his uncle
Admiral Sir Alexander Cochrane, his uncle
Maria Graham, British observer in Chile and Brazil
King William IV

His enemies
Napoleon's commanders
Earl St Vincent, First Lord of the Admiralty
Admiral Lord Gambier, commander of the British fleet in the Bay of Biscay
Andrew Cochrane-Johnstone, his uncle
Random de Berenger, adventurer
Lord Ellenborough, Lord Chief Justice
The Wellesley family
Blanco Encalada, commander of the Chilean navy
John Wilson Croker, Secretary to the Admiralty
King George IV

Agustín de Itúrbide, the Pacifier (1783–1824)

His supporters
Juan O'Donojú, Viceroy of New Spain
Ana de Itúrbide, his wife
Sergeant Pio Marcha, his aide
General Anastasio Bustamante, chief military commander

His enemies
Padre Miguel Hidalgo, leader of 1810 insurrection
Padre José Maria Morelos, leader of 1811 insurrection defeated by Itúrbide
Felix Calleja, Viceroy of New Spain
Carlos Maria Bustamante, Mexican politician
Vicente Guerrero, Mexican guerrilla leader
Guadalupe Victoria, Mexican guerrilla leader
Antonio López de Santa Anna, commander of Veracruz garrison
José Antonio Echevarrí, Mexican army commander
General Nicolás Bravo, Mexican politician

Pedro de Braganza, the Emperor (1798–1834)

His supporters
King João IV, his father
Chalaca, his groom and counsellor
Leopoldina von Habsburg, his first wife and Empress
José Bonifácio de Andrada e Silva, his chief minister
Domitila de Castro, his mistress
Sir Charles Stuart, British envoy in Rio de Janeiro
Marques de Barbacena, his second chief minister

Marques de Rezende, his chief aide
General Luis Alves de Lima, his principal military commander
Amelia of Leuchtenberg, his second wife and Empress
Maria da Glória of Portugal, his daughter
Pedro II of Brazil, his son
General Saldanha, his principal commander in Portugal
Captain Charles Napier, commander of his fleet off Portugal

His enemies
Queen Carlota of Portugal, his mother
Prince Miguel de Braganza, his brother
General de Avilez, commander of Portuguese forces in Brazil
Luiz Duprat, Brazilian revolutionary leader
Count Metternich, chief minister to the Habsburg Emperor

Bibliography

Miranda

Atkinson, William Christopher, *Miranda: his life and times* (Canning House Lecture, 1950)

Becerra, Ricardo, *Vida de Don Francisco de Miranda* (Madrid, 1927)

Carr, Raymond, *Spain 1838–1939* (CUP, 1966)

Carrasco, Ricardo, *Francisco de Miranda, Precursor de la Independencia Hispano-Americana 1750–1792* (Editorial Bell, S.A., Buenos Aires, 1951)

Garcia, Lautico, *Francisco de Miranda y el antiguo régimen espãnol* (XXX)

Grases, Pedro, *El regreso de Miranda a Caracas en 1810* (1957)

——*La biblioteca de Francisco de Miranda* (1966)

Jane, Cecil, *Liberty and despotism in Spanish America* (CUP, 1929)

Miranda, Francisco de, *Archivo del General Miranda* (Caracas, 1930)

Pueyrredón, Carlos Alberto, *En tiempo de los virreyes* (1932)

Nucete-Sardi, José, *Adventura y tragedia de don Francisco de Miranda* (1956)

Parra-Perez, Carraciolo, Lectures at the Spanish Institute of the University of Paris, 1947

——*Páginas de historia y de polémica* (1943)

——*Miranda et Madame de Custine* (1950)

——*Historia de la primera republic de Venezuela* (1959)

Parry, J. H., *The Spanish seaborne empire* (Hutchinson, 1966)

Pendle, George, *A history of Latin America* (Pelican, 1963)

Rippy, J. Fred, *Latin America: a modern history* (University of Michigan Press, 1959)

Rojas, A., *Miranda dans la révolution française* (Caracas, 1889)

Rumazo González, Alfonso, *Miranda, protolíder de la independencia americana* (1985)

Rydjord, John, *Foreign interest in the independence of New Spain* (Duke University, NC, 1935)

Verjerano, Jorge Ricardo, *La vida fabulosa de Miranda* (1945)

Villoro, Luís, *El proceso ideológico de la revolución de independencia* (Universidad Nacional Autónomo de Mexico, Mexico City, 1967)

Webster, C. K. (Ed.), *Britain and the independence of Latin America, 1812–1830* (selected documents from the Foreign Office archives, OUP, 1938)

——*Foreign policy of Castlereagh, 1812–1822* (Bell and Sons, 1934)

Bolívar

Abreu y Lima, José Ignacio de, *Resumen historico de la uliima dictadura del Libertador Simón Bolívar* (Rio de Janeiro, 1922)

Academia Nacional de la Historia, *Archivo Santander* (Bogotá, 1932)

Acosta Saignes, Miguel, *Acción y útopia del hombre de las dificultades* (1977)

André, Marius, *Bolívar y la democracia* (Barcelona, 1924)

Angell, Hildegarde, *Simón Bolívar, South American Liberator* (New York, 1930)

Arias, Harmodo, *The international policy of Bolívar* (New York, 1918)

Arocha Moreno, Jesús, *Bolívar juzgado por el General San Martín* (Caracas, 1930)
Barbagelata, Hugo, *Bolívar y San Martín* (Paris, 1911)
Barnola, *Porqué Bolívar* (1960)
Bayo, Ciro, *Bolívar y sus tenientes* (Madrid, 1929)
Bazán, Armando, *San Martín y Bolívar: paralelo de sus vidas* (1949)
Beltrán Avila, Marcos, *El tabú Bolívarista, 1825–1828* (1960)
Bolívar, Simón, *Cartas, 1799–1830* (4 vols, notas de R. Blanco-Fombona, Madrid and Paris, 1912–22)
——*Papeles publicados por Vicente Lecuna* (2 vols, Madrid, 1920)
——*Decretos del Libertador* (3 vols, Imprenta Nacional, Caracas, 1961)
Brading, D. A., *Classical republicanism and creole patriotism: Simón Bolívar* (1983)
Brice, Angél Francisco, *El Bolívar de Marx ampliado por Madariaga* (1952)
Bulnes, Gonzalo, *Bolívar en el Peru* (2 vols, Madrid, 1919)
——*Historia de la expedición libertadora del Peru* (2 vols, Santiago, 1888)
Carrillo Moreno, José, *Bolívar, maestro del pueblo* (1971)
Cova Maza, J. M., *Mocedades de Simón Bolívar* (Barcelona, 1924)
Cuervo, Luis Augusto, *La monarquía en Colombia* (Bogota, 1916)
Dalencour, François, *Alexandre Pétion devant l'Humanité; Alexandre Pétion et Simón Bolívar; Haiti et l'Amérique Latine; Et l'expédition de Bolívar par Marion Ainé* (Port-au-Prince, 1928)
Ducoudray-Holstein, H. L. V., *Memoirs of Simón Bolívar*, (2 vols, Henry Colbur and Richard Bentley, 1830)
Elliott, J. H., *Imperial Spain, 1496–1716* (Edward Arnold, 1963)
Garcia Marquez, Gabriel, *The General in His Labyrinth*, trans. (Jonathan Cape, London, 1991)
Gil Fortoul, José, *Historia constitucional de Venezuela* (Caracas, 1930)
Goenaga, José Manuel, *La Entrevista de Guayaquil* (Bogotá, 1911)
Gómez Picón, Alirio, *Bolívar y Santander: Historia de una amistad* (1971)
González, Juan Vicente, *Biografía del General José Felix Ribas* (Madrid, 1918)
Graham, Robert Cunninghame, *José Antonio Páez* (1929)
Grisanti, Angel, *Bolívar, su idilio y matrimonio en Madrid* (1959)
Guevara, Arturo, *Historia clínica del Libertador* (1948)
Hasbrouck, Alfred, *Foreign legionaries in the Liberation of Spanish America* (Columbia UP, New York, 1928)
Herder, *Genio y apoteósis de Bolívar en la campaña del Perú*
Herring, Hubert, *A history of Latin America* (Knopf, New York, 1961)
Hildebrandt, Martha, *Los peruanismos en el léxico de Bolívar* (1960)
Hippisley, G., *A narrative of the expedition to the Rivers Orinoco and Apuré . . .* (John Murray, 1819)
Humphreys, R. A., 'British merchants and South American Independence', in *Proceedings of the British Academy* (Vol. 51, 1965)
Izquierdo, José, *Simón Bolívar: reseña histórica* (1967)
Jane, Cecil, *Liberty and despotism in Spanish America* (OUP, 1929)
Jaramillo, Juan Diego, *Bolívar y Canning, 1822–7: desde el congreso de Verona* (1983)
Lafond, Georges et Tersane, Gabriel, *Bolívar et la libération de l'Amérique du Sud* (Paris, 1931)
Larrazabal, Felipe, *La vida y correspondencia general del Libertador Simón Bolívar* (New York, 1878)
Lecuña, Vicente (Ed.), *Cartas del Libertador* (10 vols, Caracas, 1939)
——*Proclamas y discursos del Libertador* (Caracas, 1939)
——*Simón Bolívar, obras completas* (3 vols, Havana, 1950)
——*Simón Bolívar, selected writings* (2 vols, New York, 1951)
——*Crónica razónada de las guerras de Bolívar* (1950)
——*Historia de la casa de Bolívar* (1924)
——*La casa natal del Libertador* (1954)

Lemboke, Jorge Bailey, *La verdadera Manuelita Sáenz* (Caracas, 1927)
Lemly, Henry, *Bolívar, Liberator of Venezuela, Colombia, Peru and Bolívia* (Boston, 1928)
Llevano Aguirre, Indalecio, *Simón Bolívar* (Caracas, n.d.)
López, Ismael, *Las amadas de Bolívar* (Lima, 1924)
Lynch, John, *Simón Bolívar and the age of revolution* (1983)
Madariaga, Salvador de, *Bolívar* (Madrid, 1951)
Marschall, Phyllis, *Bolívar* (1949)
Masur, Gerhard, *Simón Bolívar* (1948)
Mijares, Augusto, *El Libertador* (1983)
Miller, John, *Memoirs of General Miller . . .* (2 vols, Longman, 1828)
Moses, Bernard, *The intellectual background of the revolution in South America, 1810–24* (New York, 1926)
Mosquera, Tomás Cipriano de, *Memorias sobre la vida del Libertador Simón Bolívar* (New York, 1853)
Navarro, Nicolás, *La Cristiana muerte del Libertador* (1930)
O'Leary, Daniel Florencio, *Memorias del General O'Leary* (6 vols, Caracas, 1952)
Olmedo, José de, *La victoria de Junín* (1974)
Páez, José Antonio, *Autobiografía* (2 vols, New York, 1867)
Palma, Ricardo, *Bolívar en las tradiciones* (Peruanas, Madrid, 1930)
Parra Perez, Caracciolo, *Páginas de historia y polémica* (1943)
——*La Monarquía en la Gran Colombia* (1957)
——*Miranda–Bolívar: Lectures* (University of Paris, 1947)
Perez, Diaz, *Estudio medico-psicológico de Bolívar* (Caracas, 1915)
Perez y Soto, Juan Bautista (Comp.), *Defensa de Bolívar* (Lima, 1878)
Perez Vila, Manuel, *La biblioteca del Libertador*
——*Documentos apócrifos atribuidos al Libertador* (1968)
——*Simón Bolívar, el Libertador: Sintesis biografica* (1972)
——*Bolívar y su época: cartas y testimonios de extranjeros* (1953)
——*Simón Bolívar, his basic thoughts* (1980)
Perú de Lacroix, Louis, *Bolívar jugé par un officier de Napoléon* (1913)
——*Diario de Bucaramanga* (Caracas, 1935)
Petre, Francis Loraine, *Simón Bolívar 'El Libertador'* (New York, 1910)
Pike, Frederick, *The modern history of Peru* (Weidenfeld & Nicolson, 1967)
Piñeda, C., Manuel Antonio, *Bolívar ante la historia* (Cartagena, 1930)
Piñeyro, Enrique, *Biografías americanas: Simón Bolívar* (1906)
Pinilla, Sabino, *La creación de Bolivia* (Madrid, 1917)
Pividal, Francisco, *Bolívar, pensamiento precursor del antimperialismo* (1977)
Polanco Cántara, Tomás, *Simón Bolívar: ensayo de interpretación* (1994)
Ponte, Andrés, *Bolívar y otros ensayos* (Caracas, 1919)
——*La puebla de Bolívar* (1946)
Porras Troconis, Gabriel, *Campañas bolivarianas de la libertad* (1953)
Pradt, Dominique de Fourt de, Archbishop of Mechlin, *Congrès de Panamá* (Paris 1825)
Révérend, Alejandro Próspero, *Diario sobre la enfermadad que padece S.E. El Libertador* (Caracas, 1930)
Rio, Daniel A. del, *Simón Bolíver* (1965)
Rippy, J. Fredo, *Latin America, a modern history* (University of Michigan Press, 1959)
Rivas-Vicuña, Francisco, *Las guerras de Bolívar* (Caracas, 1921–2)
Robertson, William Spence, *France and Latin American Independence* (Johns Hopkins Press, Baltimore, 1939)
——*History of Latin American nations* (Appleton, New York, 1925)
——*Rise of the Spanish American republics* (New York, 1918)
Rodriguez, Simón, *Defensa de Bolívar* (Caracas, 1916)
Roig, Arturo, *Bolívarismo y filosofía latinoamericana* (1984)
Rojas, Ricardo, *La entrevista de Guayaquil* (1950)

Rojas, José María, *Simón Bolívar* (Paris, 1883)
Rourke, Thomas, *Simón Bolívar* (1940)
Sáenz, Vincente, *Morelos y Bolívar* (1956)
Salcedo-Bastardo, J. L., *Bolívar, un continente ye un destino* (1972)
——— *Visión y revisión de Bolívar* (1977)
——— *Un hombre diáfano: vida de Simón Bolívar para los nuevos* (1976)
Saurat, Gilette, *Bolívar le Libertador* (1979)
Santana, Arturo, *La campana de Carabobo* (Caracas, 1921)
Sherwell, Guillermo Antonio, *Simón Bolívar (El Libertador)* (Washington, 1921)
Sociedad Bolívariano del Perú, *Testimonios peruanos sobre El Libertador* (1964)
Soler, Ricuarte, *Cuatros ensayos de historia* (1985)
Sucre, Antonio José de, *Cartas de Sucre el Libertador* (2 vols, Madrid, 1919)
Tejera, Humberto, *Bolívar, guía democrático de America* (1944)
Trend, J. B., *Bolívar and the independence of Spanish America* (1946)
Trompiz, G., *Bolívar, auténtico y actual: ensayos sobre la armonía*
Urdaneta, Rafael, *Memorias* (Madrid, 1916)
Uribe White, Enrique, *Iconografía del Libertador*
——— *El Libertador: campaña de 1819, episodios en su vida* (1969)
Urueta Insignares, Raúl, *Bolívar: estudio y antología*
Urrutia, Francisco José, *El ideal internacional de Bolívar* (Quito, 1911)
Vallejo, Carlos María de, *Romancero del libertador Simón Bolívar* (1942)
Vascoñez Hurtado, Gustavo, *Cartas de Bolívar al general Juan José Flores* (1976)
Vaucaire, Michel, *Bolívar, the Liberator* (Boston, 1929)
Verna, Paul, *Robert Sutherland: un amigo de Bolívar en Haiti* (1966)
——— *Pétion y Bolívar: una etapa decisiva en la emancipación*
Ybarra, T. R., *Bolívar, the passionate warrior* (New York, 1929)

San Martín

Academia Nacional de la Historia (Argentina), *La autenticidad de la carta de San Martín a Bolívar*
Aguirre Molina, Rául, *San Martín, amigo de libros*
Barcía, Trelles, *José de San Martín en España* (1941)
——— *San Martín en America* (3 vols, Buenos Aires, 1943)
Bazán, Armando, *San Martín y Bolívar, paralelo de sus vidas*
Capdevila, Arturo, *El pensamiento vivo el General San Martín* (1945)
——— *El hombre de Guayaquil* (1950)
Draghi Lucero, Juan, *San Martín* (1944)
Estrella Gutiérrez, Fermín, *San Martín* (1950)
Humphreys, R. A., *The career of James Paroissien* (Athlone Press, 1952)
Medrano, Samuel, *San Martín* (1945)
——— *El Libertador José de San Martín* (1950)
Miller, John, *Memoirs of General Miller in the Service of the Republic of Peru* (2 vols, Longman, 1828)
Mitre, Bartolomé, *The History of San Martín*
Napolitano, Leonardo, *Aportes a la historia patria* (Buenos Aires, 1940)
Obligado, Pastor Servando, *El General San Martín en las tradiciónes de Pastor s. Obligado* (1950)
Onsari, Fabian, *San Martín, la Logia Lautaro y la franco-masoneria*
Pilling, William, *The emancipation of South America* (taken from *The History of San Martín* by Mitre) (Chapman and Hall, 1893)
Piñeyro, Enrique, *Biografías Americanas: El General San Martín* (1906)
Ramos Perez, Demetrio, *San Martín: el libertador del sur* (1988)
Raufet, Roberto, *Sanmartíniana* (1950)
Rojas, Ricardo, *La entrevista de Guayaquil* (1950)

Sarmiento, Domingo Faustino, *El General San Martín* (1950)
Valcarcel, Carlos Daniel, *San Martín* (1972)
Vicuña Mackenna, Benjamin, *El General San Martín in Europa* (1942)

O'Higgins
Clissold, Stephen, *Bernardo O'Higgins and the independence of Chile* (1968)
Collier, Simon, *Ideas and politics of Chilean independence* (Cambridge UP, 1967)
Eyzaguirre, Jaime, *O'Higgins* (1946)
Galdames, Luís, *A history of Chile* (North Carolina UP, 1941)
Graham, Maria, *Journal of a residence in Chile during the year 1822 and a voyage from Chile to Brazil in 1823* (Praeger, New York, 1969)
Hall, Basil, *Extracts from a journal written on the coasts of Chile, Peru, and Mexico in the years 1820, 1821, 1822* (2 vols, 1824)
Mitchell, David, *Bernardo O'Higgins* (1975)
Razuvaev, Vladimir, *Bernardo O'Higgins: conspirador, general, estadista*

Cochrane
Allen, Joseph, *Life of the Earl of Dundonald* (1861)
Atlay, James B., *The trial of Lord Cochrane before Lord Ellenborough* (1897)
Berenger, Charles Random de, *The noble stock-jobber* (1816)
Brenton, Edward, *Life and correspondence of John, Earl of St Vincent* (2 vols, 1838)
Bunster, Enrique, *Lord Cochrane* (Santiago, 1966)
Cecil, Henry, *A matter of speculation: the case of Lord Cochrane* (1965)
Chatterton, Georgiana, Lady, *Memorials personal and historical of Admiral Lord Gambier* (2 vols, 1861)
Cochrane, Archibald, *Account of the qualities and uses of coal tar* (1785)
Cochrane, Thomas, Lord, *The trial of Lord Cochrane for conspiracy* (1814)
——*A letter to Lord Ellenborough* (1815)
——*Lord Cochrane's reasons for escaping* (1816)
——*Narrative of services in the liberation of Chile, Peru and Brazil* (2 vols, 1858)
——*The autobiography of a seaman* (2 vols, 1860)
Cochrane, Thomas, 11th Earl of Dundonald, *The life of Thomas Cochrane, 10th Earl of Dundonald* (1869)
Cochrane-Johnstone, Andrew, *Defence of the Honourable Andrew Cochrane-Johnstone* (Edinburgh)
Cruz, Ernesto de la, *Epistolario de D. Bernardo O'Higgins* (2 vols, Santiago, 1916)
Ellenborough, Lord, *The guilt of Lord Cochrane in 1814* (1914)
Finlay, George, *History of the Greek Revolution* (2 vols, 1861)
Gambier, Lord, *Minutes of a court martial* (1809)
Giffard, Edward, *Deeds of naval daring* (1852)
Grimble, Ian, *The Sea Wolf* (Blond and Briggs, London, 1978)
Gurney, W. B., *The trial of Lord Gambier* (1809)
Hodgkin, Thomas, *An Essay on naval discipline* (1813)
Jervis, John, Earl of St Vincent, *Letters* (Naval Records Society, 1955)
Lloyd, Christopher, *Lord Cochrane* (1947)
Mallalieu, J. P. W., *Extraordinary seaman* (1957)
Marryat, Florence (ed.), *Life and letters of Captain Marryat* (2 vols, 1872)
Martel, Alamiro de Avila, *Cochrane y la independencia del Pacífico* (Santiago, 1976)
McRae, Alexander, *A disclosure of the hoax practiced upon the stock exchange* (1815)
Tute, Warren, *Cochrane* (1965)
Thomas, Donald, *Cochrane* (André Deutsch, London, 1978)
Twitchett, E. G., *Life of a seaman* (1951)
Zenteno, J. L., *Documentos justificativos sobre la expedición libertadora del Perú* (Santiago, 1861)

Itúrbide

Anna, Timothy E., *The fall of the royal government in Mexico City* (Nebraska UP, 1978)
—— *The independence of Mexico and central America* (in the Cambridge History of Latin America: Cambridge UP, 1985)
—— *Itúrbide*
Archivo histórico militar de Mexico, *La correspondencia de Agustín de Itúrbide después de la proclamación del Plan de Iguala* (Mexico City, 1945)
Benson, Nettie Lee, 'The plan of Casa Mata', in *Hispanic American Historical Review* (1945)
—— *Mexico and the Spanish Cortes, 1810–22* (Texas UP, 1966)
Bulnes, Francisco, *La guerra de independencia: Hidalgo–Itúrbide* (Mexico City, 1910)
Bustamante, Carlos María, *Continuación del cuadro histórico: Historia del Emperador D. Agustín de Itúrbide hasta su muerte* (Mexico, 1846)
—— *Resumen histórico de la revolución* (1828)
Castellanos, Francisco, *El triunfo, gloria y martírio de Augustín de Itúrbide* (Mexico, 1982)
Chavez, Ezequiel, *Agustín de Itúrbide: Libertador de Mexico* (Mexico City, 1957)
Flores Caballero, Romeo, *La contra-revolución e la independencia* (Mexico City, 1969)
Fuentes Mares, José, *Santa Anna, El Hombre* (Mexico City, 1982)
Green, Stanley, *The Mexican Republic: the first decade, 1823–32* (Pittsburgh UP, 1987)
Harrison, Horace, *The Republican conspiracy against Agustín de Itúrbide* (Institute of Latin American Studies, Austin, 1958)
Junco, Alonso, *Insurgentes y liberales ante Itúrbide* (Mexico City, 1971)
Ladd, Dories, *The Mexican nobility at independence, 1780–1826* (Texas UP, 1976)
Lombardi, John, *The political ideology of Fray Servando Teresa de Mier* (Cuernavaca, 1968)
Mancisidor, José, *Hidalgo, Morelos, Guerrero* (Mexico City, 1966)
McEllhannon, Joseph Carl, *Relations between imperial Mexico and the United States* (Institute of Latin American Studies, Austin)
Navarro y Rodrigo, Carlos, *Vida de Agustín de Itúrbide* (Madrid, 1919)
Parkes, Henry, *A history of Mexico* (Houghton Mifflin, Boston, 1960)
Parton, Dorothy, *The diplomatic career of Joel Roberts Poinsett* (Catholic University of America, 1934)
Poinsett, Joel, *Notes on Mexico made in the autumn of 1822* (Praeger, New York, 1969)
—— *The present political state of Mexico* (Salisbury, NC, 1976)
Rivera Cambas, Manuel, *Agustín de Itúrbide* (Mexico City, 1972)
Robertson, William Spence, *Itúrbide of Mexico* (Duke UP, NC, 1952)
Romero de Terreros, Manuel, *La Corte de Agustín I, Emperador de Mexico* (Mexico City, 1922)
Santa Anna, Antonio López de, *The Eagle: the Autobiography of Santa Anna* (Pemberton Press, 1967)
Suarez y Navarro, Juan, *Historia de Mexico y del General Antónío Lopez de Santa Anna* (2 vols, Mexico City, 1850–1)
Trens, Manuel, *Historia de Veracruz* (6 vols, Jalapa, 1948)
Trueba, Alfonso, *Nicolás Bravo: El Mexicano que perdonó* (Mexico City, 1976)
USA archives, *Mexico and Mr Poinsett* (Philadelphia, 1829)
Valle, Rafael, *Como era Itúrbide*, (Mexico City, 1922)
—— *Itúrbide, Varón de Dios* (Mexico City, 1944)
Van Young, Eric, *Millenium on the northern marches* (Comparative Studies in Society and History, 1986)
—— *Quetzalcoatl, King Ferdinand and Ignácio Allende go to the seashore* (California UP, 1987)
Villoro, Luis, *El Proceso ideológico de la revolución de independencia* (Mexico City, 1967)
Ward, H. G., *Mexico* (Praeger, New York, 1968)
Zamacois, Niceto de, *Historia de Mexico* (18 vols, Barcelona, 1876–88)
Zerecero, Anastasío, *Memorias para la historia de las revoluciones de Mexico* (Mexico City, 1869)

Pedro

Aguiar, Antonio Augusto de, *Vida do Marques de Barbacena* (Rio, 1896)

Anna, Timothy, 'The Buenos Aires Expedition and Spain's secret plan to conquer Portugal, 1814–20', in *Americas* (1978)

Armitage, John, *A history of Brazil from the period of the arrival of the Braganza family to the abdication of Dom Pedro I* (2 vols, 1836)

Arnade, Charles, *The emergence of the republic of Bolivia* (New York, 1970)

Beraza, Augustín, *Los corsarios de Artigas* (Montevideo, 1949)

Bethell, Leslie, *The Independence of Brazil* (Cambridge History of Latin America, Cambridge UP, 1985)

Brandão, Ulysses de Carvalho Soares, *Pernambuco d'outr' ora: A confederação do Equador* (Recife, 1924)

Calmon, Pedro, *O Rei Cavaleiro* (São Paulo, 1933)

——*O Rei do Brasil* (Rio, 1935)

——*Brasil e America* (Rio, 1943)

Camara Cascudo, Luiz da, *O Marques de Olinda e seu tempo* (São Paulo, 1938)

Cartas Andradinas (Rio, 1886)

Cartas ineditas de la Imperatriz D. Maria Leopoldina (Rio, 1821–26)

Cartas a D. João VI pelo principe real o Senhor D. Pedro de Alcantara (Lisbon, 1822)

Corrêa da Costa, Sérgio, *As quatro corôas de Pedro I* (Rio, 1941)

——*D. Pedro I e Metternich* (Rio, 1942)

——*Every Inch a King*, trans.

Diario da assamblea geral costitituente e legislativo do imperio do Brasil (2 vols, Rio, 1923)

Fernandes Tomás, Manuel, *A revolução de 1820* (Lisbon, 1974)

Freyre, Gilberto, *Masters and slaves* (Putnam, New York, 1946)

Glover, Michael, 'Beresford and his fighting cocks', in *History Today* (1976)

Herrick, Jane, 'Hípolito da Costa, the Reluctant Revolutionist', in *Americas* (1950)

Hilton, Stanley E., *The United States and Brazilian independence* (Baltimore, 1975)

Historia da revolução do Brasil no dia 7 d'abril de 1831 (Rio, 1831)

Hoornaert, Eduardo, *The Catholic Church in Colonial Brazil* (Cambridge History of Latin America, CUP, 1974)

Karasch, Mary, *Rio de Janeiro: from colonial town to imperial capital, 1808–1850* (Dordrecht, Holland, 1985)

Lavradio, Marques do, *D. João VI e a Independencia do Brasil* (Lisbon, 1937)

Lima, Oliveira, *O reconhecimento do império* (Rio, 1901)

——*Dom Pedro a Dom Miguel* (São Paulo, 1907)

——*Dom João VI no Brasil* (Rio, 1909)

Lindley, Thomas, *Narrative of a voyage to Brazil . . .* (1805)

Livermore, Harold, *A history of Portugal* (Cambridge UP, 1947)

Lyra, Heitor, 'Trabalha da diplomacia brasileira para casar D. Pedro I', in *Americana* (1919)

Manchester, Alan K., *British preeminence in Brazil: its rise and decline* (Durham, NC, 1933)

——'The rise of the Brazilian aristocracy', in *Hispanic American Historical Review* (May, 1931)

——*The transfer of the Portuguese court to Rio de Janeiro: Conflict and continuity in Brazilian society* (Columbia, SC, 1969)

Mansuy-Diniz Silva, Andrée, *Portugal and Brazil: Imperial Reorganisation 1750–1808* (Cambridge History of Latin America, CUP, 1984)

McBeth, Michael, *The politicians v. the generals: the decline of the Brazilian army during the first empire, 1822–31* (University of Washington, 1972)

——*Brazilian army during the first empire, 1822–31* (University of Washington, 1972)

Monteiro, D. J. L de Souza, *Vida de Dom Pedro IV* (Lisbon, 1836)

Monteiro, Tobias, *História do império* (Rio, 1927)

Nogueira, Octaviano (Ed.), *Obras politica de José Bonifácio* (2 vols, Brasilia, 1973)

Novais, Fernando, *Brasil e Portugal no crise do antigo sistema colonial* (São Paulo, 1979)

Oliveira Lima, Manoel de, *Dom João VI no Brasil, 1808–20* (3 vols, Rio, 1945)
——*Dom Pedro e Dom Miguel, a querela da successão, 1828–8* (São Paulo)
Oliveira Torres, João Camilo de, *A democracia coroada* (Rio, 1964)
Owen, Hugh, *The civil war in Portugal* (1836)
Pace, Carlo, *Resume Histórico de la maçónaria no Brasil* (Rio, 1896)
Passos, Carlos de, *D. Pedro IV a D. Miguel I* (Porto, 1936)
Pereira da Silva, João Manuel, *História da fundação do império brasileiro* (7 vols, Rio, 1864–68)
Pinto de Campos, Joaquim, *Vida do Luís Alves de Lima e Silva* (Rio, 1958)
Piteira Santos, Fernando, *Geografia e economia da revolução de 1820* (Lisbon, 1962)
Platt, Desmond, *Latin America and British trade, 1806–1914* (1972)
Ramos, Donald, 'Social revolution frustrated: the conspiracy of the tailors in Bahia', in *Luso-Brazilian Review* (Summer, 1976)
Rangel, Alberto, *D. Pedro I e a Marquesa de Santos* (Rio, 1968)
——*Marginados: anotacões ás cartas de D. Pedro I a D. Domitila* (Rio, 1974)
Resende, Marques de, *Elogio historico do senhor Rei Dom Pedro IV* (Lisbon, 1867)
——*Correspondencia . . .* (Rio, 1916)
Rizzini, Carlos, *Hipólito da Costa e o correio Brasiliense* (São Paulo, 1957)
Rodrigues, José Honorio, *A assembleia constituente do 1823* (Petropolis, Rio, 1974)
——*Brazil and Africa* (Berkeley, California, 1965)
——*Independencia: revolução e contra-revolução* (5 vols, Rio, 1975)
Russell-Wood, A. J. R. (Ed.), *From colony to nation: essays on the independence of Brazil* (Baltimore, Maryland, 1975)
Seckinger, Ron, *The Brazilian monarchy and the South American republics, 1822–31* (Baton Rouge, La., 1984)
Sousa, Octavio Tarquinio de, *História dos fundadores do império do Brasil* (10 vols, Rio, 1957)
Street, John, *Artigas and the emancipation of Uruguay* (Cambridge UP, 1959)
Varnhagen, Francisco Adolfo, *História da independencia do Brasil* (São Paulo)
——*História geral do Brasil* (5 vols, São Paulo)
Vianna, Helio, *D. Pedro I e D. Pedro II* (São Paulo, 1966)
——*D. Pedro I, jornalista* (São Paulo, 1967)
——*Estudos de história impérial* (São Paulo, 1950)
Webster, Charles K. (Ed.), *Britain and the independence of Latin America, 1812–1830* (2 vols, 1938)

Index